Believers Church
Bible Commentary

Douglas B. Miller and Loren L. Johns, Editors

BELIEVERS CHURCH BIBLE COMMENTARY

Old Testament
Genesis, by Eugene F. Roop, 1987
Exodus, by Waldemar Janzen, 2000
Deuteronomy, by Gerald E. Gerbrandt, 2015
Joshua, by Gordon H. Matties, 2012
Judges, by Terry L. Brensinger, 1999
Ruth, Jonah, Esther, by Eugene F. Roop, 2002
Psalms, by James H. Waltner, 2006
Proverbs, by John W. Miller, 2004
Ecclesiastes, by Douglas B. Miller, 2010
Isaiah, by Ivan D. Friesen, 2009
Jeremiah, by Elmer A. Martens, 1986
Lamentations, Song of Songs, by Wilma Ann Bailey, Christina Bucher, 2015
Ezekiel, by Millard C. Lind, 1996
Daniel, by Paul M. Lederach, 1994
Hosea, Amos, by Allen R. Guenther, 1998

New Testament
Matthew, by Richard B. Gardner, 1991
Mark, by Timothy J. Geddert, 2001
John by Willard M. Swartley, 2013
Acts, by Chalmer E. Faw, 1993
Romans, by John E. Toews, 2004
2 Corinthians, by V. George Shillington, 1998
Galatians, by George R. Brunk III, 2015
Ephesians, by Thomas R. Yoder Neufeld, 2002
Colossians, Philemon, by Ernest D. Martin, 1993
1-2 Thessalonians, by Jacob W. Elias, 1995
1-2 Timothy, Titus, by Paul M. Zehr, 2010
1-2 Peter, Jude, by Erland Waltner, J. Daryl Charles, 1999
1, 2, 3 John, by J. E. McDermond, 2011
Revelation, by John R. Yeatts, 2003

Old Testament Editors
Elmer A. Martens, Mennonite Brethren Biblical Seminary, Fresno, Calif.
Douglas B. Miller, Tabor College, Hillsboro, Kan.

New Testament Editors
Willard M. Swartley, Anabaptist Mennonite Biblical Seminary, Elkhart, Ind.
Loren L. Johns, Anabaptist Mennonite Biblical Seminary, Elkhart, Ind.

Editorial Council
David W. Baker, Brethren Church
W. Derek Suderman, Mennonite Church Canada
Christina Bucher, Church of the Brethren
John R. Yeatts, Brethren in Christ Church
Gordon H. Matties (chair), Mennonite Brethren Church
Jo-Ann A. Brant, Mennonite Church USA

Believers Church Bible Commentary

Deuteronomy

Gerald E. Gerbrandt

HERALD PRESS
Harrisonburg, Virginia
Kitchener, Ontario

Library of Congress Cataloging-in-Publication Data

Gerbrandt, Gerald Eddie.
  Deuteronomy / Gerald Gerbrandt.
    pages cm. — (Believers church Bible commentary)
   ISBN 978-0-8361-9970-3 (pbk. : alk. paper) 1. Bible. Deuteronomy—
Commentaries. I. Title.
  BS1275.53.G46 2015
  222'.15077—dc23

                                                              2015016716

Scripture quotations, unless otherwise indicated, are from *New Revised Standard Version Bible*, copyright © 1989, Division of Christian Education of the National Council of the Churches of Christ in the United States of America. Used by permission. All rights reserved. Other versions briefly compared are identified with Abbreviations.

© 2015 by Herald Press, Harrisonburg, Virginia 22802
   Released simultaneously in Canada by Herald Press,
   Kitchener, Ontario N2G 3R1. All rights reserved.
Library of Congress Control Number: 2015016716
International Standard Book Number: 978-08361-9970-3
Printed in United States of America
Cover and interior design by Merrill Miller

All rights reserved. This publication may not be reproduced, stored in a retrieval system, or transmitted in whole or in part, in any form, by any means, electronic, mechanical, photocopying, recording, or otherwise without prior permission of the copyright owners.

To order or request information, please call 1-800-245-7894 or visit www.heraldpress.com.

19 18 17 16 15   10 9 8 7 6 5 4 3 2 1

To my family:

Esther,
my invaluable love and support for more than forty years;

our children,
Nathan and Angela,
Bradley and Natalie,
Virginia and Andrew;

and their children,
Ruby, Zachary, James, and Daphne

But take care and watch yourselves closely,
so as neither to forget the things that your eyes have seen
nor to let them slip from your mind all the days of your life;
make them known to your children and your children's children.
—Deuteronomy 4:9

Abbreviations

*	The Text in Biblical Context
+	The Text in the Life of the Church
ANE	ancient Near East(ern)
ANET	*Ancient Near Eastern Texts Relating to the Old Testament.* Edited by James B. Pritchard. 3rd ed. Princeton, NJ: Princeton University Press, 1969. Now online.
AT	author's translation
BCE	before the Common Era (= BC, before Christ)
CE	Common era (= AD *anno Domini*)
cf.	*confer,* compare
ch(s).	chapter(s)
ed(s).	edition, editor(s)
e.g.	*exempli gratia,* for example
emph.	emphasis
esp.	especially
ESV	English Standard Version
ET	English translation or versification
et al.	*et alia,* and others
etc.	et cetera, and the rest
HWB	*Hymnal: A Worship Book.* Edited by Rebecca Slough et al. Elgin, IL: Brethren Press; Newton, KS: Faith & Life Press; and Scottdale, PA: Herald Press, 1992.
i.e.	*id est,* that is
KJV	King James Version of the Bible
lit.	literally
MBCF 1999	*Confession of Faith: Commentary and Pastoral Application.* Winnipeg, MB: (Mennonite Brethren) Board of Faith and Life, and Kindred Productions, 2000. http://www.mbconf.ca/home/products_and_services/resources/theology/confession_of_faith/detailed_version/.
MCF 1995	*Confession of Faith in a Mennonite Perspective.* Scottdale, PA: Herald Press, 1995, http://www.mcusa-archives.org/library/resolutions/1995/index.html.
MPML	*A Mennonite Polity for Ministerial Leadership: A Statement by the Joint Committee on Ministerial Leadership.* Newton, KS: Ministerial Leadership Services of the General Conference Mennonite Church; Elkhart, IN: Mennonite Board of Congregational Ministries of the Mennonite Church, 1996.
mg.	marginal reading
NABRE	New American Bible, Revised Edition, 2010
NASB	New American Standard Bible, 1995
NEB	New English Bible, 1970

NIV	New International Version, 2011
NIV84	New International Version, 1984
NJB	New Jerusalem Bible, 1990
NJPS	New Jewish Publication Society Translation of the Tanakh, 1999
NKJV	New King James Version, 1982
NRSV	New Revised Standard Version, 1989
NT	New Testament
OT	Old Testament
par.	parellels, i.e., in the Synoptic Gospels
pl.	plural
re:	regarding
RSV	Revised Standard Version, 1952
sg.	singular
TBC	Text in Biblical Context (in the commentary)
TEV	Today's English Version, 1976
TLC	Text in the Life of the Church (in the commentary)
v(v).	verse(s)
vol(s).	volume(s)
YHWH	Yahweh, the personal name for God

Pronunciation Guide for Certain Transliterated Hebrew Consonants

ʾ	(not pronounced)
ʿ	(not pronounced)
ḥ	ch (Scottish *loch*)
ṣ	ts
ś	s
š	sh
ṭ	t

Contents

Abbreviations..7
Pronunciation Guide 8
Series Foreword 15
Author's Preface 17

Introduction to Deuteronomy..........................19
A Sermon for *Today* 21
Theological Themes in Deuteronomy 22
Torah: Sermon, Not Law 26
The Structure and Logic of Deuteronomy....................29
Deuteronomy and the Scandal of Violence...................31
Deuteronomy and a Hermeneutics of Suspicion 35

Part 1, First Speech (1:1–4:43): Retrospect and Prospect . . . 37

1:1-5 Introduction 41
    *Israel at the Boundary 45
    +The People of God at Boundaries........................46
1:6-18 Retrospect: Dividing the Load 47
    *Responsibility for Justice..............................54
    +Justice Is the Bottom Line.............................55
1:19–2:1 Retrospect: Rebellion at the Border 57
    *An Imperfect Story.....................................66
    +Inordinate Confidence 67
2:2-23 Retrospect: Peaceful Encounters.......................68
    *God and the Nations....................................74
    +Theology versus Practice...............................77
2:24–3:11 Retrospect: Hostile Confrontations..................79

*Sihon and Og as Symbols............................87
  *The Gift of Land within Scripture......................89
  +Misreading the Story............................91
  3:12-29 Retrospect: Final Arrangements for Crossing the
    Jordan............................93
  *At Rest, and Yet Not............................100
  +Living on the Way to Full Rest......................101
  4:1-43 Prospect............................102
  *The Greatness of Israel............................116
  *Distress and Repentance............................117
  +Theological Images............................118

Part 2, Second Speech (4:44–28:68): Preaching Torah 121

2A Introduction, 4:44-49............................125

2B The Horeb Covenant, 5:1-33......................127
  *The Ten Commandments beyond the Pentateuch.........151
  +The Ten Commandments on Display....................153

2C Preaching the Foundational Commandment, 6:1–11:32..156
6:1-9 Yahweh Is One—Yahweh Alone......................158
  *Loving God............................164
  +Centrality of the Shema............................165
6:10-25 Remembering Yahweh in the Land..................167
  *Biblical Creeds............................172
  +A Story Provides the Meaning......................173
7:1-26 Chosen to Be a Holy Possession....................174
  *Why Did God Choose Israel?........................181
  *Election, Separation, and Mission......................182
  +The Church and Separation........................184
8:1-20 Remember! Do Not Forget!......................186
  *God's Nurture............................191
  *The Peril of Prosperity............................192
  *Jesus in the Wilderness............................192
  +Land as Blessing *and* Temptation....................193
9:1–10:11 Israel: Stubborn, Not Righteous..................195
  *Human Nature—God's Nature........................204
  *Interceding with God............................205
  +Original Sin............................206
  +The Power of Prayer............................207
10:12–11:32 A Midcourse Review......................208

   *Stark Alternatives 218
   +A Works Righteousness? 218

2D Preaching the Moab Covenant, 12:1–26:19 221

2D Unit 1 Exclusive Worship of the One God, 12:1–14:21 . . 227
12:1-32 Worship at The Place 228
   *Centralization in Israel and Scripture 242
   +Deuteronomy 2 and Contemporary Middle Eastern
      Politics 245
   +Right Worship 246
13:1-18 Purging Apostasy 247
   *One Way, and the Consequences of the Other Way 253
   +Capital Punishment or No Discipline 255
   +Worshiping the Family? 256
14:1-21 Cleanliness and Purity for a Holy People 257
   *Dietary Regulations: Symbols of Jewish Identity and
      Christian Universalism 267
   +Visible Reminders: Respect for All Life 270
   +Identity versus Mission 272

2D Unit 2 Justice in Israel: The Community, 14:22–15:18 . . 273
14:22-29 The Annual Tithe 274
   *Tithing versus Generosity in Scripture 279
   +Tithing and Celebration 281
15:1-18 A Sabbatical Release 282
   *Old Testament Release Regulations 294
   +"True Evangelical Faith" 295
   +Liberation Theology, Preferential Option for the Poor,
      Jubilee 2000 297
   +Breaking the Cycle 298

2D Unit 3 Festivals and the Cult, 15:19–16:17 300
   *Festivals and Renewal 311
   +A Communal Church Year 311
   +Drama versus Word 312

2D Unit 4 Leadership and Judicial Procedures, 16:18–19:21 . . 314
16:18–17:13 Judges and Judicial Procedures 316
17:14-20 The King 325
   *Torah, Moses, and Leadership in Israel and the New
      Testament 335

 *Kings and Kingship in Scripture 337
 +Of Kings and CEOs...................................339
 +Nation versus People 340
18:1-8 Levitical Priests 341
 *Priests, and a Royal Priesthood 347
 +Leadership and the Church............................348
18:9-22 Prophets..349
 *True and False Prophecy..............................357
 +Prophets Today? 359
19:1-21 Further Judicial Procedures 360
 *Jesus, Prophets, and Justice 368
 *Jesus, and an *Eye for an Eye* 369
 +*Eye for Eye*, or Reconciliation?.........................370

2D Unit 5 War, 20:1-20 372
 *War in the Old Testament and "Pacifism" in the New
  Testament..380
 +Making Use of Deuteronomic War Passages 383

2D Unit 6 Miscellaneous, 21:1-25:19 384
 *Does God Remarry a Previously Divorced Bride?.........429
 *Divorce in Scripture 430
 *God Shows No Partiality 431
 +The Church and Divorce 432
 +Syncretism 433

2D Unit 7 Theology through Worship, 26:1-19 435
 *The Two Greatest Commandments......................445
 +Thanksgiving as a Remembrance Day 446
 +Participation 446

2E Covenant Renewal, Blessings and Curses 27:1-28:68 ...448
 *Blessing and Curse, Reward and Punishment.............459
 +Secret Sins 460

Part 3, Third Speech (29:1-30:20): The Covenant in Moab ...463

Making a Covenant, 29:1-30:20 465
 *Seeing and Seeing, Hearing and Hearing.................481
 +The Doable Law 482
 +Deuteronomy as Altar Call 484

Part 4, Transition (31:1–34:12): Toward a Moses-less People . . 485

Preparation for Transition 31:1-30 489
  *When God Gives an Assignment 497
  *Inclined to Forsake, but 498
  *From Direct Speech to Written Word 499
  +Discerning Gifts and Calling 499
The Song of Moses 32:1-52 501
  *Punishing the Nations 509
  *The Vindication of God 510
  +The Power of the Song 511
The Blessing of Moses 33:1-29 512
  *The Last Words of a Leader 518
  +Security and Prosperity 519
The Death of Moses 34:1-12 521
  *Moses after the Pentateuch 525
  +Moses Made Public 526
  +Martin Luther King Jr. Speaks in Memphis 527

Outline of Deuteronomy 529
Essays 539
  Biblical Monotheism 539
  Chiasm 540
  Christians and Old Testament (as) Law 541
  Composition of Deuteronomy 543
  Cult 546
  Deuteronomistic History 547
  Deuteronomy, Covenant, and Political Treaties 547
  Deuteronomy and the Reform of Josiah 549
  Dietary Regulations 550
  Ḥerem 552
  Holy, Holiness 553
  Law 555
    Contemporary Law, Ancient Law 555
    Apodictic and Casuistic Lawlike Materials 557
  Peoples and Places in Deuteronomy 558
  Sacrifices and Offerings 565
  Yahweh War 566

Map of Palestine for Deuteronomy 570
Map of the Ancient Near East for Deuteronomy 571
Bibliography 572

Selected Resources......................................585
Index of Ancient Sources...............................587
The Author...599

Series Foreword

The Believers Church Bible Commentary series makes available a new tool for basic Bible study. It is published for all who seek more fully to understand the original message of Scripture and its meaning for today—Sunday school teachers, members of Bible study groups, students, pastors, and others. The series is based on the conviction that God is still speaking to all who will listen, and that the Holy Spirit makes the Word a living and authoritative guide for all who want to know and do God's will.

The desire to help as wide a range of readers as possible has determined the approach of the writers. Since no blocks of biblical text are provided, readers may continue to use the translation with which they are most familiar. The writers of the series use the *New Revised Standard Version* and the *New International Version* on a comparative basis. They indicate which text they follow most closely and where they make their own translations. The writers have not worked alone, but in consultation with select counselors, the series' editors, and the Editorial Council.

Every volume illuminates the Scriptures; provides necessary theological, sociological, and ethical meanings; and in general makes "the rough places plain." Critical issues are not avoided, but neither are they moved into the foreground as debates among scholars. Each section offers "Explanatory Notes," followed by focused articles, "The Text in Biblical Context" and "The Text in the Life of the Church." This commentary aids the interpretive process but does not try to supersede the authority of the Word and Spirit as discerned in the gathered church.

The term *believers church* has often been used in the history of the church. Since the sixteenth century, it has frequently been applied to the Anabaptists and later the Mennonites, as well as to the Church of the Brethren and similar groups. As a descriptive term, it includes more than Mennonites and Brethren. *Believers church* now represents specific theological understandings, such as believers baptism, commitment to the Rule of Christ in Matthew 18:15-20 as crucial for church membership, belief in the power of love in all relationships, and willingness to follow Christ in the way of the cross. The writers chosen for the series stand in this tradition.

Believers church people have always been known for their emphasis on obedience to the simple meaning of Scripture. Because of this, they do not have a long history of deep historical-critical biblical scholarship. This series attempts to be faithful to the Scriptures while also taking archaeology and current biblical studies seriously. Doing this means that at many points the writers will not differ greatly from interpretations that can be found in many other good commentaries. Yet these writers share basic convictions about Christ, the church and its mission, God and history, human nature, the Christian life, and other doctrines. These presuppositions do shape a writer's interpretation of Scripture. Thus this series, like all other commentaries, stands within a specific historical church tradition.

Many in this stream of the church have expressed a need for help in Bible study. This is justification enough to produce the Believers Church Bible Commentary. Nevertheless, the Holy Spirit is not bound to any tradition. May this series be an instrument in breaking down walls between Christians in North America and around the world, bringing new joy in obedience through a fuller understanding of the Word.

—*The Editorial Council*

Author's Preface

What a privilege it has been to live with Deuteronomy for the past decade plus! It truly is an inspiring book. I am intrigued at how often I am involved in some discussion, and suddenly a verse or passage from Deuteronomy comes to mind, a passage that so directly speaks to the issue under conversation.

My interest in Deuteronomy goes back to the late 1970s, when I was commissioned to write Sunday education curriculum for high school students. The result was *Clues for Gracious Living*, a title that so well reflects the central message of this choice Old Testament book. We all have a desire to live in a manner that leads to blessing and life, for ourselves, for our family and friends, indeed for the larger community around us. That is what Deuteronomy is about. This fullness of life can never be grasped or taken by force, but continuously remains a gift from God and is offered to us if we live in a generous, open-handed fashion.

One of my challenges in this project was working at it in spurts, interrupted by my other commitments. I must confess that I was insufficiently disciplined to make much progress on the commentary during the times I was working in administration at Canadian Mennonite Bible College (CMBC) and then Canadian Mennonite University. My writing thus was largely done in three blocks of time separated by a number of years: during two sabbaticals (1994–95 at the Institute for Ecumenical and Cultural Research in Collegeville, Minnesota; 2002–3 at Acadia Divinity College in Wolfville, Nova Scotia), and since retiring in 2012. No doubt this shortcoming has resulted in some unevenness in the final product.

Although my name is on the spine of the volume identifying me as "author," that is somewhat misleading. At various points I do name those whose ideas and perspectives I borrow or interact with, but really, virtually all of what I say is influenced and stimulated by the words of others, oral and written. My interest in Old Testament was initially sparked by Waldemar Janzen, my Old Testament professor at CMBC in the 1960s. He has remained a mentor and friend ever since. I cannot name all my other teachers who impacted me at the schools after CMBC, but their role also is substantial. Although my doctoral dissertation was not narrowly on Deuteronomy, my work at Union Theological Seminary in Virginia on the Deuteronomistic History with my adviser, Sibley Towner, played an important role.

And then there are all the writers: writers of other commentaries, writers of monographs, and writers of articles, people who became my constant companions and friends on my journey with Deuteronomy. Often I would have loved to sit down with them in person to discuss or debate a particular point or nuance. I trust I have not misused their words, and that they have contributed to a distinctive, perhaps even peculiar combination in my work which is true to the believers church tradition, and even more important, true to the biblical story of God's love for the world.

Others were more personally involved in the commentary project itself. The two editors with whom I worked, Elmer Martens and Doug Miller, provided valuable counsel. Likewise, I wish to express my gratitude to David Garber for his thoughtful copyediting and for saving me from a number of errors. I appreciate so much those who read a draft of the commentary and then gave their feedback to me: Rudy Baergen, Adelia Neufeld Wiens, and Lynn Jost. My family, to whom I dedicate this volume, was always with me on the journey. Thank you to all of you—professors, writers, friends, family, and institutions that generously give sabbaticals.

I pray that through this commentary Deuteronomy's "clues for gracious living" become more accessible, more understandable, and more potent.

—Gerald E. Gerbrandt
Winnipeg, Manitoba

Introduction to Deuteronomy

Deuteronomy—a book full of life, full of the story of God's people, full of a vision for walking in the way of God. It is a book that has been called "The Gospel according to Moses," a celebration of divine grace rivaled only by John's gospel. It is the book Jesus quoted in a time of great testing and quoted again when asked about the heart of Israel's faith.

When Jesus is tempted in the wilderness, three times he turns to Deuteronomy as a source for his response (Matt 4:1-11). When a lawyer asks Jesus which commandment is the greatest, Jesus quotes from Deuteronomy: *You shall love the LORD your God with all your heart, and with all your soul, and with all your might* (Deut 6:5; Matt 22:34-40; cf. Mark 12:28-34; Luke 10:25-28), a passage still recited daily by faithful Jews. In the New Testament as a whole, Deuteronomy is cited more than any Old Testament book except Isaiah and the Psalms.

For a long time, students of Scripture have known the vitality and force of Deuteronomy. Walter Brueggemann submits, "It is impossible to overstate the importance of the book of Deuteronomy for the shape and substance of Israel's faith in the Old Testament" (2001: 17), calling it "the theological center of the Old Testament" (1982: 37). Siegfried Herrmann goes even further by naming it the "center of biblical theology" (1971). Deuteronomy effectively articulates the tradition and themes that Judaism came to recognize as its center and lifeblood. As does the letter to the Romans for the New Testament, Deuteronomy presents "the most systematic presentation of theological truth" in the Old Testament (Block 2011: 25).

All of this may come as a surprise, for Deuteronomy has suffered from a bad reputation, as legalistic, violent, and perhaps even most harshly, as boring or irrelevant, a "dead book" (Block 2011: 59). Such stereotypes discourage readers from immersing themselves in what is arguably the most influential book of the Old Testament, one that is endlessly challenging and remarkably relevant for today.

The place and influence of Deuteronomy within the story of Israel and the Bible as a whole signals its significance. On the one hand, Deuteronomy is the *capstone* and climax of the Pentateuch, the first five books of the Old Testament. These books were the first part of the Old Testament recognized as canonical by Judaism and are still considered to be the most sacred part of Scripture for that tradition. It follows naturally after the book of Numbers, with Israel having arrived at the border of the Promised Land for a second time. Forward progress is put on hold as Moses addresses the people on the plains of Moab in preparation for entering the land. Deuteronomy reviews what has happened, returning to themes and legal material in the earlier books of the Pentateuch.

On the other hand, Deuteronomy serves as the first book in, or *introduction* to, that early monumental history of Israel known as the Deuteronomistic History *[Deuteronomistic History, p. 547]*. Joshua, Judges, Samuel, and Kings tell the story of Israel from the point of entering the Promised Land until Israel's exit from the land after the destruction of Jerusalem by the Babylonians in the early sixth century BCE. Not only does Deuteronomy set the stage for this history; it also provides the *theological lens* through which the history views events and developments. Deuteronomy thus is situated at the center of 40 percent of the Old Testament, serving as a hinge joining the Pentateuch to the Deuteronomistic History.

Further links connect Deuteronomy with Old Testament prophetic books, although here the direction of influence flows both ways. It is probable that the preaching of Israel's early prophets, especially Hosea, inspired those who produced early versions of Deuteronomy. At the same time many Old Testament interpreters detect Deuteronomic impact on the formation and final editing of the prophetic books. Deuteronomic elements may also be present in Genesis through Numbers, Psalms, and other parts of the Old Testament. It therefore is not surprising that Deuteronomy plays such an important role in the New Testament.

With Deuteronomy we thus are entering the center the of Old Testament and of biblical theology. This book influenced much of

Scripture and can be a life-giving resource to the Christian community today.

A Sermon for *Today*

Not with our ancestors did the LORD *make this covenant, but with us, who are all of us here alive today* (5:3, emph. added).

Deuteronomy is a book riveted on *today*. Fifty-nine times it uses this word. No other biblical book uses it more than thirty times (1 Samuel), and it occurs only thirty times in the whole New Testament. Israel's past is important, but only as it impacts the present. As reflected in the verse above, the past is collapsed into the present. The listener or reader is eternally addressed "today," as the future looms ahead. Each new generation and time has to determine "today" how to respond to the vision. Obedience "today" is critical for the people's future.

Deuteronomy employs a variety of rhetorical techniques, appealing to both heart and mind in order to persuade the listener to respond *today*. Learning from the past is important, so it regularly challenges Israel to remember God's past actions (e.g., 15:15). *Remember* as a directive is used fifteen times in Deuteronomy, more frequently than any biblical book other than the much longer book of Psalms. Israel is not to forget its past experience (e.g., 4:9), so *forget* also is used more often than in any book other than Psalms. The regulations of chapters 12–26 are not dispassionate law but incessantly supported with motivation clauses, sometimes based on potential consequences, sometimes based on obligation, but always with the goal of coaxing positive response *today*.

This focus on today contributes to making Deuteronomy enduringly relevant and continuously fresh. It fits well with the literary setting of the book as the words of Moses delivered to the people of Israel, at the border of the Promised Land and with their future at stake. Joshua will lead the people across that border into the land, but in this book the border between today and the future is never crossed. Deuteronomy serves as an "altar call" at that border, with its call a never-ending challenge for the audience: *I call heaven and earth to witness against you today that I have set before you life and death, blessings and curses. Choose life so that you and your descendants may live* (30:19).

This call takes on a new urgency during heated clashes over the faithful worship of the God of the exodus, the God heard at Horeb. These debates were particularly intense in the ninth to seventh centuries BCE, when the oral traditions of Moses may have been converted into a written document [*Composition of Deuteronomy, p. 543*]. In that setting it challenges the people to respond *today*, with their continued survival in the land in question. And again during the exile, as the community struggles over foundational questions of identity and faithfulness, Deuteronomy raises its clarion call: *today* they must worship only God and live rightly.

It is no different today, for our twenty-first-century world. In the face of apathy and amnesia and countless competing modern-day gods, Deuteronomy calls for the exclusive worship of the one God, with a reminder of what that God has done for us. In the face of the individualism and greed of our time, it presents a vision for a community of brothers and sisters who treat each other with justice and generosity. If ever a biblical book reflects the saying "Today is the first day of the rest of your life," it is Deuteronomy, the gospel of Moses.

Theological Themes in Deuteronomy

Foundational to Deuteronomy's vision is the concept of **election**: God has chosen Israel as God's very own possession (e.g., 4:20; 7:7-8). A special, unique relationship exists between God and the people of Israel. Election goes back to the story of Abraham and Sarah, with God promising to make a people of them and give them the land. It takes on a new reality when God delivers those descendants out of Egyptian slavery and makes of them a people at Mount Horeb. Now God is about to confirm and cement this relationship by giving them the land (see TBC at end of ch. 7).

Covenant is the primary metaphor for this relationship. God and Israel are bound together by covenant, a term that covers both the promises God made to the ancestors (e.g., 4:31) as well as the more conditionally shaped relationship associated with Mount Horeb. International treaties of the day provide a helpful model for speaking of that particular relationship between God and Israel.

Despite using the international treaty format as a model for speaking of covenant, the result is not a cold or calculated relationship. Rather, it is a warm, intimate bond with God and each other. This is already hinted at by the emphasis on how God loves Israel. The term "love" may have a treaty background, but in Deuteronomy it also evokes loving familial connotations. When Israel was in the wilderness, God carried it, *just as one carries a child* (1:31). One is reminded of Hosea's comparison of God's relationship with Israel to that between husband and wife (chs. 1–3) or parent and child (11:1-4).

Although Deuteronomy consistently affirms Israel's election, it is quite vague when providing a basis for it. What is clear is that Israel did not deserve to be chosen: Israel was neither a great or large people (7:7) nor is it a righteous people (9:5-7). Rather, we read, God *set his heart on you* because God *loved you* (7:7-8). This may be simple yet unsatisfying, for it leaves unanswered the natural follow-up question, "But why did God love Israel?" The answer remains a mystery, but the conviction that God did choose Israel as God's special possession is pervasive and omnipresent in the book.

Integral to the God-Israel relationship is the **land**, first promised to the ancestors and now about to be possessed. In fulfilling the promise made to the ancestors, the land confirms the covenant. Now that it is being given, it reflects the covenant. But land has an unusual two-sided character in Deuteronomy. It is a bounteous land, *flowing with milk and honey* (6:3; 11:9; 26:9, 15; 27:3; 31:20), a land *where you may eat bread without scarcity, where you will lack nothing* (8:9), a truly blessed land through which Israel will be blessed. At the same time, its very fertility and wealth has the threat of dulling Israel's memory of what God has done and how dependent the people are upon God. The land is both gift/blessing and responsibility/temptation (Brueggemann 1977).

It is the temptation and responsibility of living in the land that becomes a primary agenda for Deuteronomy. Once in the land, Israel will be tempted to forget God and to think that it deserves the land, with its bountiful resources (8:11-20). Remaining in the land will require that Israel *fear the* LORD *your God, to walk in all his ways, to love him, to serve the* LORD *your God with all your heart and with all your soul* (10:12). To fear God, to walk in his ways, to love God, to serve God with their total being—all this has implications in two directions.

On the one hand, it requires **exclusive loyalty to Yahweh**, the one God of the exodus, as represented in the first commandment as well as the Shema (6:4-9). Not only are Canaanite and other foreign gods rejected, but also any practices or worship objects that might compromise Yahweh's position as the sole God of Israel are to be eradicated. Most distinctively, Deuteronomy demands that sacrifice to this one God take place only at one location (cf. ch. 12). Deuteronomy does not name the location, but in monarchic Judah as well as the exilic and postexilic community, the only option for this is Jerusalem. The phrase "One God, One People, One Worship Site" is too simple a summary of Deuteronomy, but it does reflect crucial interrelated themes of the book. This may not reflect theoretical monotheism, but it represents a major step in that direction

[Biblical Monotheism, p. 539]. The only appropriate response to God—who chose Israel for his possession, then delivered the people from Egyptian slavery, and gave them the blessed land—is exclusive loyalty and allegiance.

It is this demand for exclusive loyalty that lies behind the most troubling element of the book. For Deuteronomy, the original inhabitants of the land loom large as a source of temptation. Their gods and their religious practices threaten to undermine Israel's devotion to the God of the exodus. The way this threat is countered is by speaking of Israel as exterminating the Canaanites. Despite this language, Deuteronomy itself provides evidence that this eradication did not happen: regularly we read of foreigners and aliens living in the land among Israel. But the seriousness of the threat results in Deuteronomy painting a picture in which these people are eliminated (see discussion of ch. 7). Yet when addressing how Israel is to treat aliens who actually are in the land, Deuteronomy does not call for their elimination but rather for them to be treated generously, even allowing them to become part of the covenant people (29:10-13).

On the other hand, to love God requires **the practice of justice**. Of special interest for Deuteronomy is the treatment of resident aliens, widows, and orphans, three traditional categories of individuals who for different reasons are vulnerable or socially weak (14:29; 16:11, 14; 26:12, 13). Along with them, Deuteronomy includes the Levites in the towns who did not receive an allocation of land and thus are dependent upon others. More than any other book of the Old Testament, Deuteronomy builds a safety net for those in need.

Similarities between this concern of Deuteronomy and the prophetic call for social justice reflect a profound agreement. Deuteronomy spells out an ethic aimed at all heads of households, not only political or religious leaders. The cult, Israel's ritual practice of its faith, does receive attention in Deuteronomy, but with little detail *[Cult, p. 546]*. The way one member of the community treats the other, however, receives great detail. Some speak of desacralization in Deuteronomy, a shift from cult to ethics (Weinfeld 1972). Deuteronomy does not reject the cult or religious ritual and continues to call for cultic purity, but its focus is on ethics: it is through ethics that Israel will become a light to the nations.

This call for justice in the way community members treat each other highlights a further aspect of Deuteronomy's vision. Israel is a community in which all members have mutual commitments and obligations to each other. In the NRSV we regularly read about *a member of the community* (e.g., 15:2), language that more literally is translated *brother* (as in RSV). Israel is a family, chosen by God, in which each member has responsibilities for the rest. It may be debated at what point Israel became a people with such a strong identity, but in Deuteronomy that is the plea. This emphasis is so consistent in Deuteronomy that one can speak of the book as an **ecclesiology**, a reflection on what it means to be one people as the people of God. Deuteronomy has a constitutional quality, but not for a political Israel narrowly understood. Rather, it presents a unified people of God, a people who models its life after the God who delivered it from slavery.

The themes of election and an in-group ethic for Israel raise questions about how Deuteronomy views God's relationship to other peoples. Its emphasis on Israel as God's special possession, combined with its rhetoric against the Canaanites, may suggest that Deuteronomy is interested only in Israel. Yet there are hints that challenge such a view. We read that the God of Israel also has chosen other peoples and given them their land (e.g., 2:5, 9, 19), and that Israel's ethic will be a witness to other nations (4:5-8). People of Edomite and Egyptian background are allowed to worship as part of the assembly of Israel (23:7-8), and perhaps most surprisingly, the alien has the potential to enter into the covenant between Israel and God, thereby becoming part of the chosen people (29:10-13). Deuteronomy, though a primary expression of Jewish faith, at the same time includes elements that question the exclusivity of the relationship between God and Israel.

Appropriate **leadership** is necessary for this people of God. Pervasive throughout the book is the theme that Moses, the exiting leader and key mediator between God and Israel, will die at the end. Moses thus needs to be replaced. This theme enters the conversation early when Moses installs leaders to help him in his role as judge (1:9-18); it receives further attention in chapters 16–19 as various leadership roles are introduced; and then it takes center stage in the final chapters of the book. Perhaps most striking in Deuteronomy's discussion of leadership is the very minor role for the king. Deuteronomy does not appear to be able to imagine an Israel in the land without a king, so a king is part of the vision. But the king has no particular responsibility other than to study and uphold the book of instruction that Deuteronomy places in the hands of the priests (17:18-20).

Above all, and providing the foundation for each of these themes, stands Yahweh, the God of the exodus and Horeb. Deuteronomy's interest is not some abstract monotheism *[Biblical Monotheism, p.*

539], but at its center is an **absolutely unique and supreme God**, Yahweh, beside whom *there is no other* (4:39). The character of this God must be derived indirectly.

There is a **transcendence** to God in Deuteronomy. God may be near to Israel (4:7), but not physically nor in a way that can be controlled. Unlike in Exodus, where God dwells in the sanctuary (25:8), in Deuteronomy God dwells in heaven (26:15), with God's name present at *the place* that God will choose (e.g., 12:5). The ark that in other places appears to serve as a throne for God (e.g., Exod 25:22) becomes a container for the tablets of the covenant (Deut 31:26). At Mount Horeb God speaks to Israel from the midst of the fire, but they do not see him (4:36).

Nevertheless, this transcendent God is **directly active** in Israel's story, with **humanlike feelings**. God's election of Israel and care for the people is based in God's love, a love like that of parents for their children (e.g., 1:31). This God can be trusted for he is fully faithful to his ancestral promises, having multiplied this people as the *stars of heaven* (1:10, cf. Gen 15:5; 22:17; 26:4), having fought for them in Egypt (1:30), having cared for them in the wilderness (1:31), and is now giving them the Promised Land (e.g., 1:8). This *mighty and awesome* God is model of justice, with a particular concern for the weak and the stranger—whose actions in freeing Israel from Egyptian slavery model the way Israel is to treat the weak (10:17-19). His love for Israel is reflected in jealousy when the people turn to other gods, leading to punishment (e.g., 6:15). But punishment is not the last word, with God's love for Israel so profound and deep that in the end, God's mercy prevails (4:31; 30:1-10).

With this characterization Deuteronomy reflects a paradox. The very existence of Deuteronomy is a gift to Israel, evidence of God's love for them as it spells out how they are to live in a manner that leads to life. It challenges Israel and each new audience to respond to the existential need for decision *today*, a decision that determines life or death. And yet, at the same time, Deuteronomy recognizes that the tendency to forget God and choose death is so pervasive that only God's merciful response can save the people. God thus will circumcise the human heart *so that you will love the LORD your God with all your heart and with all your soul, in order that you may live* (30:6).

Torah: Sermon, Not Law

Scholars frequently debate what type of literature Deuteronomy is. Deuteronomy speaks of itself as *torah* (e.g., 1:5; 29:21), but what is that? The most common translation of the Hebrew word *torah* is "law." At first glance this fits. After all, it is the capstone of the Pentateuch, or books of law. Its central chapters (chs. 12–26) consist largely of material with a legal style. This appears to justify calling it a "second law," the literal meaning of the Greek *deuteronomion*, the basis of our English name for the book. It thus is not surprising that Deuteronomy is popularly perceived as a *book of law*, or even a legal code. Yet the Greek reflects a misunderstanding of Deuteronomy 17:18, which speaks of the king needing to have a <u>copy of this law</u> written for him (emph. added), not a second law. More significantly, this reflects a too-narrow interpretation of torah, especially when the term "law" is freighted with its modern English connotations *[Law, p. 555]*.

Translating *torah* as *law* may not be wholly inaccurate, yet *law* misrepresents torah's spirit. Deuteronomy is not detached instruction or teaching; rather, it is the passionate vision of a preacher making use of every rhetorical technique available to motivate and encourage his listeners to respond. Law depends on sanctions and structures of enforcement to achieve its goal and so is less dependent upon forceful rhetoric; a sermon aims to persuade its audience. Deuteronomy is a plea to the people as a whole to live in the only way that can lead to life (cf. Deut 30:15-20). The essence of Deuteronomic torah, I suggest, is best captured by our notion of *sermon*. More than fifty years ago, Gerhard von Rad proposed that Deuteronomy was based on rural Levitical preaching (1953: 60–69). It is striking that Matthew depicts Jesus as the new Moses, preaching from a mountain, and that we call it the Sermon on the Mount.

The Hebrew title for the book, although accidentally, points in this direction. Consistent with the practice of naming a book after its opening words, Deuteronomy is called ʾ*elleh haddebarim*, or *These are the words*. Deuteronomy is all words, with very little action (cf. Exod 19:6; Deut 29:1; Jer 1:1; Amos 1:1). Its words are carefully chosen and arranged for maximum rhetorical impact, whether reviewing past events or presenting directions for life as a community. Richard Nelson helpfully describes this style:

> The mood is homiletic and didactic, with exhortations addressed directly to the audience in second-person language. Incessant repetition aims for rhetorical effect and ease of retention. The language seeks to arouse emotions and stimulate memory of the tradition in order to motivate acceptance and action.... The "presentation of evidence from history," which sets forth Yahweh's historical acts, calls on the audience to "know" their theological import, and then draws out the implications of this knowing. (Nelson 2002: 2)

Patrick Miller draws attention to features of Deuteronomy commonly found in effective preaching:

> (1) frequent reference to "this day" or "today," (2) the use of "we" in the credos and elsewhere, (3) frequent emphatic use of second-person pronouns ("you"), (4) repeated summons to hearing, (5) numerous vocatives, (6) appeal to memory as a way of actualizing the past in the present, (7) use of threat and promise to motivate hearers to respond, and (8) use of illustration. (P. Miller 1990: 12)

Other literary forms fill out the meaning of Deuteronomy as sermon. The proposal that Deuteronomy is a *constitution* helpfully highlights how Deuteronomy presents a comprehensive vision for how Israel might live together as a united community (McBride 1987). Like a constitution, Deuteronomy is concerned with the people as a body, with a comprehensive vision for how that people might live together in a manner consistent with the will and direction of God.

Another window into Deuteronomy is that of *catechesis*, "the process of education in faith from one generation to another based on a distillation of essential tradition" (Olson: 11). The term helpfully captures the foundational nature of Deuteronomy's teaching, with appropriate reference to passing on faith from one generation to another. One is reminded of the way catechism used to be preached annually in some congregations, blurring the line between preaching and teaching.

Although not a treaty document itself, ancient *political treaty* patterns and formulations have impacted the language and style of Deuteronomy [*Deuteronomy, Covenant, and Political Treaties, p. 547*]. There is little action in Deuteronomy, with Israel at the border of the Promised Land both at the beginning and end of the book. But Deuteronomy has a strong *historical* interest, with stories from Israel's past used as illustrations in a sermon.

It is also important to view Deuteronomy as the *final testament* of a great leader. Shortly before his death, Jacob calls together his sons and gives them his final words before leaving them (Gen 49). Joshua's climactic action is to lead the people in a covenant recommitment service where he makes his notable pronouncement, "As for me and my household, we will serve the LORD" (Josh 24:15). Similarly, Samuel leads the people in a covenant renewal after Saul replaces him as the leader of Israel (1 Sam 12). In this same tradition, Jesus gathers his disciples on the evening before his death and gives them lengthy guidance for the time when he will no longer be with them (John 13–17). Likewise in Deuteronomy we find Moses giving his final instructions before his death. These words have come down in a process difficult for us to recover. Rather than referring to the author or editor, I will speak in terms of the book itself: ultimately the authority of Deuteronomy to speak God's word to us is rooted in God and not in the original author(s) nor in the process by which it has come to us.

The commentary will treat the book as a whole as a post-587 document addressed to a Moses-less people, challenging them to faithfulness in their day, whether in hope of returning to the land (if placed during the exile), or remaining in the land (if placed in postexilic Judah). At the same time the older, traditional setting in the plains of Moab, and the battles over monotheism in the eighth and seventh centuries, will remain in view. Whatever the setting, Deuteronomy calls for faithfulness *today* [*Composition of Deuteronomy, p. 543*].

All of these literary analogies supplement and help fill out the spirit of Deuteronomic torah, a sermon originally directed to the people of Israel, with continuing relevance for contemporary followers of that God of Israel. Such is the nature of Deuteronomy.

The Structure and Logic of Deuteronomy

Three parallel introductory formulae (1:1; 4:44; 29:1) from the hand of a narrator divide the bulk of Deuteronomy into three speeches of Moses. The phrase *These are the words [of] Moses* (1:1) introduces the opening speech and sets the tone for the book as a whole. The **first speech** (chs. 1–4) consists of three chapters reviewing how Israel came to be where it is at the border of the Promised Land, and one chapter calling upon Israel to follow God's teaching once in the land.

The opening of the **second speech** (chs. 5–28)—*This is the law [torah] that Moses set before the Israelites* (4:44)—identifies its focus. Here is the heart of the Deuteronomic torah. Through the use of further introductory formulae (4:45; 6:1; 12:1; 27:1), this torah is subdivided into four parts. Chapter 5 presents the Decalogue, the content of the Horeb covenant that God spoke directly to Israel. The second part of the second speech (chs. 6–11) zeroes in on and expounds the first and most important commandment: the command to worship only Yahweh. The Shema rewords this expectation for Israel, *Hear, O Israel: The LORD is our God, the LORD alone* (6:4). The third part (chs. 12–26) continues the preaching style but does this through the presentation of specific regulations speaking to practical life in the land. The second speech then concludes with instructions for covenant renewal later in the land (chs. 27–28).

But before they enter the land, Moses leads the people in a covenant ceremony, the focus of the **third speech** (chs. 29-30). The narrator introduces this with *These are the words of the covenant that the LORD commanded Moses to make with the Israelites in the land of Moab* (29:1). The last chapters of the book (chs. 31-34) do not fit neatly into the speech format. Sometimes regarded as merely appendix, they are more than that, making an important contribution to the book. Bound together by the theme of Moses' death rather than a common literary style, they are about **transition**. They prepare for and begin the move into the time when Moses, God's great teacher and prophet, will not be with them any longer. The formula used to introduce the three major speeches is used here to introduce the blessing of Moses in 33:1: *This is the blessing with which Moses . . . blessed the Israelites* (cf. 31:1; 32:1). The basic overall structure of Deuteronomy thus is as follows:

First Speech, chapters 1-4
Second Speech, chapters 5-28
Third Speech, chapters 29-30
Transition, chapters 31-34

The speech organization is primary in Deuteronomy, but other structural features overlap or interact with it. Some scholars detect a chiastic structure for the book as a whole, highlighting the centrality of the core (chs. 12-16), with its preaching on the basis of regulations. Christensen, for example, proposes that chapters 1-3 and 31-34 serve as an outer frame, with chapters 4-11 and 27-30 an inner frame (2001: lviii). Although this commentary places greater emphasis on the speech format, the chiasm proposal appropriately highlights the central core, with its preaching of the Moab covenant *[Chiasm, p. 540]*.

The influence of ancient political treaties is evident on at least two levels *[Deuteronomy, Covenant, and Political Treaties, p. 547]*. First, it is likely that Deuteronomy's use of the covenant metaphor, as well as some of its language for speaking of God's relationship with Israel, is influenced by the world of political parallels. Second, some larger structural elements may also be impacted by treaties. For example, Deuteronomy's use of history as the basis for expecting response reminds one of these treaties (esp. chs. 1-3), and the blocks of blessings and curses (chs. 27-28) may very well have been modeled after those in treaties.

Covenants are a critical feature of Deuteronomy's larger logic. Deuteronomy speaks of two types of covenants. Foundational to Deuteronomy is the ancestral covenant of Genesis, essentially a unilateral promise from God to bless the ancestors and give their descendants the land. Israel as a people, however, is formed by and lives under a series of conditional covenants. Distinct to Deuteronomy is the way these are understood.

The initial covenant between God and Israel takes place at Mount Horeb, with the Decalogue as its content (Exod 20; Deut 5). Here Israel becomes the people of God. Deuteronomy then describes a second covenant between God and Israel mediated by Moses on the plains of Moab, at the border of the land (chs. 29–30). The Decalogue remains an integral part of it, but now it is expanded to include the whole Deuteronomic torah. Additionally, Deuteronomy directs the people to regularly hold a covenant-renewal ceremony once they are settled in the land (27:1-8; 31:9-13). This covenant logic is central to Deuteronomy and its torah.

Deuteronomy and the Scandal of Violence

Deuteronomy is a wonderful book, and yet it contains some of the most difficult and, to a sensitive contemporary reader, most embarrassing passages of the Bible. This is especially true for someone approaching the book with a commitment to nonviolence or pacifism. For some this scandal is so great that the book, and indeed Scripture as a whole, loses its appeal and power. After all, what does one do with the directive of 7:2?

> When the LORD your God gives them [the original inhabitants of the land] over to you and you defeat them, then you must utterly destroy them. Make no covenant with them and show them no mercy.

Or the one in 25:19:

> When the LORD your God has given you rest from all your enemies on every hand, in the land that the LORD your God is giving you as an inheritance to possess, you shall blot out the remembrance of Amalek from under heaven; do not forget.

It is understandable that these words are experienced as "texts of terror" (Trible) or examples of "disturbing divine behavior" (Seibert 2009).

Adding to their offense, Deuteronomy and texts like this have been used to justify acts of horrible violence. Early European settlers in America understood themselves as the new Israel, with a divine right to displace the Native Americans. In 1689 Cotton Mather "inspired" the troops to effect total vengeance and destruction upon the indigenous population, for "they are Ammon, Amalek, an indigenous population who will be displaced and disinherited by divine decision to make way for the new Israel" (Niditch: 4). Similarly, Afrikaner leaders in the early twentieth century used Deuteronomy; they understood themselves as Israel, with a right to all of South Africa, and codified the charge not to mix with the original inhabitants (Deist). More recently the Amalekite command was used as justification for a Jewish terrorist attack upon Muslim worshipers in their mosque in Hebron, and when "asked to explain the hard-line attitude of Israeli Prime Minister Benjamin Netanyahu toward the nation of Iran, one of his advisers told a U.S. journalist, 'Think Amalek'" (Jenkins: 19).

Scholars of widely diverse theological perspectives argue that this is an illegitimate use of such texts. In *Show Them No Mercy: Four Views on God and Canaanite Genocide*, four conservative scholars give quite divergent views on how to understand these texts, including efforts to justify why God commanded murder of innocents. But all agree that these commands cannot be transferred to the Christian era (Cowles et al.). More helpfully, Millard Lind's influential *Yahweh Is a Warrior* argues that central to Israel's "war theology" is the conviction that Yahweh is the warrior, with the crossing of the Red Sea and the defeat of the Egyptians the model for Yahweh war *[Yahweh War, p. 566]*. Israel's role is only to trust God to deliver (Exod 14). Such a theology undercuts any effort to make use of Deuteronomy to justify contemporary military action.

The emphasis on God as the divine warrior may effectively counter any use of Deuteronomy to justify genocide or other violence in our day, but it does not resolve the theological challenge: are we really called to worship a God whose character allows the killing of innocent women and children? Or perhaps the way some people put it, how can the violent God of the Old Testament also be the God of Jesus, who called on us to love our enemies? (yet see Yoder Neufeld's chapter "'Violence' and the 'New Testament'" [1–15]).

This is a tough issue that has confounded and disturbed thoughtful Christians for centuries. A number of recent publications have struggled with it, each contributing some helpful perspectives, but each still ultimately less than fully satisfactory. Notice the following titles from the last few years: *Disturbing Divine Behavior: Troubling Old Testament Images of God* (Seibert 2009); *The Immoral Bible: Approaches to Biblical Ethics* (Eryl Davies 2010); *Is God a Moral Monster? Making Sense of the Old Testament God* (Copan 2011); *Laying Down the Sword: Why We Can't Ignore the Bible's Violent Verses* (Jenkins 2011); *The Violence of Scripture: Overcoming the Old Testament's Troubling Legacy* (Seibert 2012); and *Holy War in the Bible: Christian Morality and an Old Testament Problem* (Thomas, Evans, and Copan 2013).

The present commentary takes up this difficult challenge and discusses key passages carefully. In anticipation of tackling the text of Deuteronomy, some observations may be helpful.

First of all, our inability to fully explain God and the questions of war and violence reminds us that we can never fully grasp and describe the mystery of God. In fact, the commentary will suggest that assuming we fully know God and God's will risks breaking the commandment against making images (see TLC for ch. 4, and the discussion of 5:8-10). Paul says, "For now we see in a mirror, dimly, but then we will see face to face. Now I know only in part; then I will know fully, even as I have been fully known" (1 Cor 13:12). Waldemar Janzen addresses this helpfully in his response to Eric Seibert's *Disturbing Divine Behavior*:

> In my view, the "disturbing" or "offensive" aspects of *both* Testaments lie at a deeper level than that of texts which, if used on the human plane (nonmetaphorically), would offend us. That deeper level is the level of God's mystery and our human inherent inability to understand the existence of evil (violence, suffering, sickness, etc., and ultimately mortality) in the Bible's monotheistic affirmation of God's complete control of creation *together with* God's character as ultimate love. Polytheism does not have that problem; there are good gods and evil gods, and sometimes one side wins, sometimes the other. Marcion knew that and sacrificed monotheism. (2011: 290)

Some years ago, Rabbi Harold Kushner struggled with the premature death of his son due to an early aging disease. He concluded that God could not be both all powerful and all loving, and so he resorted to "belief in an always understandably benevolent but limited God. . . . Such attempts to resolve this 'overwhelming and daring paradox,' although appealing at first glance, remain superficial and inadequate" (W. Janzen 2011: 190).

This leads into a second observation. The problem of violence in Deuteronomy is part of the much larger problem of evil, one that faithful followers of one God have struggled with from the beginning. Put most simply, if God is all-loving and all-powerful, how can God allow evil in our world? This is the issue with which Rabbi Kushner was wrestling.

Third, we must remember that the biblical text was not written first of all to answer contemporary questions but rather to address issues and to effect response in ancient Israel. Or as Wilma Bailey puts it, "The question is not just, What does the text say? but, What does the text intend to accomplish? What was and is the expected response of the reader or hearer to these stories?" (2011: 164). In responding to this question, we must take into consideration that the writers spoke out of and to a culture dramatically different from our own.

Fourth, war was very much part of the culture out of which and to which biblical writers spoke. Other than soldiers, contemporary North Americans have limited (if any) personal experience with war. We read about it, we see movies about it, but for most of us it is not part of our daily lives. Refugees from war-torn countries have their stories of terror. Veterans may experience posttraumatic stress disorder from their experiences. But despite an event like September 11, 2001, North America today remains a comparatively peaceful corner of the globe. How different the world of biblical Israel was, a world in which violence and war were inescapable aspects of everyday life. Life was harsh and brutal, a daily struggle for survival. War was an ever-present threat.

It thus should not surprise us that ancient people, including Israel, wrote about war. And given the conviction that they understood God as supremely in charge of the world, and integrally active in all aspects, it should not surprise us that Israel spoke of war and God at the same time. This was the way cultures of the day spoke of war and god. In ancient Near Eastern religions, violent gods were common. For example, the "Enuma Elish," the Babylonian story of creation, sets creation within a battle among the gods. The prevalence of violent gods in ancient culture "helps explain why ancient Israelites thought that their God was capable of brutal violence" (Bailey 2011: 165). Biblical writers vigorously struggled with bringing together their monotheistic conviction with the world as they experienced it. Deuteronomy and the stories of war in the Old Testament reflect or speak to that struggle. Even today the emotional impact of these biblical stories is very different in settings where war and violence are experienced more immediately.

This commentary will attempt to deal with difficult passages from a standpoint within the world of ancient Israel's day, asking what the passage is about and how it would have communicated to its audience. This will not fully satisfy our questions nor alleviate all discomfort, but it respects the mystery of God and participates in the ongoing search for insight. (For further discussion, see esp. on 2:24–3:11; 7:1-26; 20:1-20; and the essay *Yahweh War, p. 566*.)

Deuteronomy and a Hermeneutics of Suspicion

The introduction above presents Deuteronomy as advocating for the disadvantaged, as providing social and economic protection for those most vulnerable to abuse and oppression by the powerful forces of a competitive society. With the growing power of a central state, especially in the Northern Kingdom of the ninth century BCE, life could become harsh and trample over people. This is what Samuel warns about in his speech on the "ways of the king" (1 Sam 8:11-18). The eighth-century prophets in both Israel and Judah (notice Amos, Hosea, Isaiah, and Micah) indict the people for their behavior and call for a new commitment to social justice. Consistent with the preaching of these prophets, but moving beyond them, Deuteronomy advocates concrete practices and protocols that serve to protect the weaker members of society, thereby improving their situation.

Some recent interpreters challenge such an understanding of Deuteronomy. Rather than a progressive agenda with a preferential option for the poor, Harold Bennett proposes that Deuteronomy serves the interests of those in power:

> I argue that widows, strangers, and orphans were part of a strategy to regulate the behavior and to shape the ideas of local peasant farmers regarding the distribution of goods in ancient Israel. Specifically this project argues that Deut 14:22-29; 16:9-12, 13-15; 24:17-18, 19-22; and 26:12-15 exacerbated the plight of widows, strangers, and orphans—a category of socially weak but politically useful persons in the biblical communities—positioning intellectual elites to stave off potential uprisings by local peasant farmers in the North during the ninth century BCE. (Bennett: 11)

The laws and regulations of Deuteronomy may speak of the disadvantaged, but according to Bennett they most benefit those with influence and affluence.

Referring to the hermeneutics of suspicion, Douglas Knight warns, "If we take a written, canonical law at face value, we may miss a hidden agenda that caused it to come into being or that manipulated it through self-interest" (2). Those in positions of authority who draft laws can easily do so in a manner that hides the ultimate impact of their actions. This is a helpful reminder. None of us are consistently altruistic, with absolutely pure motives for our actions. The same reality applies in biblical times. Suspicion must be part of our toolbox when approaching the biblical text.

And yet the work of Bennett and Knight is not persuasive. Simply taking texts at face value may be problematic, but committing ourselves to an entirely hypothetical context or explanation is equally unsound. Bennett appears to force all the evidence into a model in which Deuteronomy comes from those in power, those with the authority to draft laws that are to be enforced. Thus he views the laws as regulations that strengthen the positions of the wealthy. This commentary finds in Deuteronomy a genuine effort to develop programs and protocols that actually help the poor and disadvantaged. This is consistent with the conjecture that Deuteronomy arose within a reform movement influenced by the social justice preaching of the prophets, a movement committed to historic Yahwism (the worship of Israel's God, Yahweh) with a hopeful vision for the future [*Biblical Monotheism*, p. 539].

Thus the reminder to approach the biblical text with suspicion remains legitimate and important but perhaps in a manner different from the way it is typically done. Even as it is appropriate to wonder what really motivated those behind the text, it is necessary to ask what factors influence the way we approach and understand the text. As Ellen Davis puts it, "Whenever we pick up the Bible, read it, put it down and say, 'That's just what I thought,' we are probably in trouble" (16). A healthy hermeneutics of suspicion warns us to be suspicious whenever our encounter with the text simply affirms traditional understandings, previously held positions and predispositions, or our status in society. Perhaps then we have not heard God speaking through the text.

Deuteronomy is an amazing book, a crucial slice of the canon. With its repeated reference to *today*, it invites us into a struggle, a struggle between (1) our own inclination to rationalize and justify and (2) the God who speaks through the text. This commentary is written to assist in that conversation, as we enter it with humility and repentance, open to being changed.

Note: The commentary pays most attention to the NRSV and NIV (2011) versions. All translations of Deuteronomy are given in italics, including those of the author (AT). Unless otherwise noted, translations of the Bible appear as NRSV. For a helpful identification of names in the book, see the essay "Peoples and Places in Deuteronomy," p. 558.

Part 1

First Speech: Retrospect and Prospect

Deuteronomy 1:1–4:43

OVERVIEW

Deuteronomy, the book of speeches by Moses, sets the stage for its central instruction (chs. 5-28), using a series of historical flashbacks (1:6-3:29) and a projection into the future (4:1-40). History can sometimes be boring, but when stories are told skillfully, with an eye to how they reflect and explain present reality and identity, they can be educational and engaging.

The Retrospect (1:6-3:29) sets the tone for the book as it selectively reviews a few key events between Israel's departure from Mount Horeb and its second arrival at the Promised Land. The first story (1:6-18) prepares the way for a shared leadership. Leadership is not to be monopolized by one person. The story of the first arrival at the Promised Land (1:19-2:1) reminds Israel of the consequences of losing faith. The account of the second arrival (2:2-3:11) gives Israel evidence of God's faithfulness in keeping his promise. Israel receives the first installment in the fulfillment of the promise of land, even as it includes the reminder that the God of Israel is the God of all peoples. The Retrospect concludes with specific directions for an Israel living in the land (3:12-29).

Through a nuanced retelling of these stories—all have been told previously in the book of Numbers and are assumed to be known by the audience—Deuteronomy raises a key question: will Israel trust and follow God once it has received the land? In the process of raising this question, it introduces the main characters of the book:

- God—the one who delivered Israel and who is giving Israel the Promised Land;

- Israel—a people to whom God is giving the Promised Land, a people who at points follows God faithfully but also demonstrates an uncanny tendency to lose faith and rebel at the wrong time; and

- Moses—the go-between, relating God and Israel; the "speaker" of Deuteronomy, who will expound torah to Israel even as he and we know he will not enter the Promised Land.

In the Prospect, the field of view changes from the past to the future as Deuteronomy begins its more explicit teaching or preaching. The past is not forgotten, but now it is used as a canvas for reflecting how God and Israel may relate in the future. The didactic style of Deuteronomy becomes evident as God through Moses warns and cajoles Israel to acknowledge God and keep his instructions for life in the land.

The Retrospect and Prospect are framed by an Introduction (1:1-5) and a short concluding passage on the cities of refuge in the Transjordan (4:41-43).

OUTLINE FOR PART 1
Introduction, 1:1-5
Retrospect, 1:6-3:29
Prospect, 4:1-43

Deuteronomy 1:1-5
Introduction

PREVIEW
How does one start a book? Biblical authors use widely diverse styles. Genesis begins with a summary statement. Ruth has virtually no introduction and moves directly into the story. Like a good-news report with a no-nonsense style, Deuteronomy begins by answering the essential questions of who, what, where, and when. Readers need to be alerted to transitions, movement, and change. Deuteronomy is Moses expounding torah to Israel, as God commanded, in the plains of Moab in the fortieth year after leaving Mount Horeb. But these straightforward answers are more than mere data. They also announce that the words of Moses are simultaneously the word of God, and they situate Deuteronomy geographically and historically (plains of Moab, fortieth year).

OUTLINE
A^1 *These Are the Words That Moses <u>Spoke</u>.*, 1:1a
    B^1 *Place: Beyond the Jordan...*, 1:1b
        C^1 *Time: Eleven Days...*, 1:2
            D *Moses <u>Spoke</u>... as the* LORD *Had <u>Commanded</u>*, 1:3
        C^2 *Time: After He Had Defeated...*, 1:4
    B^2 *Place: Beyond the Jordan...*, 1:5a
A^2 *Moses Undertook to <u>Expound</u> This Law...*, 1:5b

EXPLANATORY NOTES

Deuteronomy opens with the narrator speaking. The narrator does not speak often in Deuteronomy, at least not in the three main speeches (chs. 1-4, 5-28, 29-30). In this opening paragraph the narrator makes two key points. First, Deuteronomy conveys the words of Moses, but words that have been commanded by God. Second, these words are situated in a specific context, both in time and space. The seven-part concentric or chiastic structure highlights these two emphases [Chiasm, p. 540].

Not only does the first part (A¹) match the last part (A²); it also corresponds with the middle part (D). The words Moses speaks are the words God commands and thus also the words of God. Here is the central thrust of this opening passage. Parts B (B¹ and B²) and C (C¹ and C²) then locate Deuteronomy in time and space.

Deuteronomy as the Words of Moses 1:1a, 3, 5b

The first two words of Deuteronomy in Hebrew are, literally, *these the words*. In Hebrew, Deuteronomy is named after its opening words, *'elleh haddebarim*. Deuteronomy is a book of words, of many words. Three times (1:1a, 3b, 5b) this point is made in these five verses.

But Deuteronomy is not merely words. These words are organized into a series of distinct speeches, as reflected in the structure of the book and in its style and language. Interpreters have long recognized that the majority of Deuteronomy divides into three major parts, each having the form of a separate address or sermon, with its own introduction. The didactic or sermonic nature of Deuteronomy is also reflected in its literary style, using every rhetorical device available to persuade the listener or reader to respond (see "Torah: Sermon, Not Law" in the introduction).

But the introduction does not only speak of Deuteronomy as *words*; it also designates them as words of Moses. Here the text introduces an element of ambiguity. In the first clause it simply calls them *the words that Moses spoke to all Israel*. In verse 3 (part D, at the center of the introduction) this is expanded to *Moses spoke to the Israelites just as the* LORD *had commanded him to speak to them*. That language gives the impression that Moses is merely a mouthpiece, reporting the dictated words of God. The last clause of the introduction (part A²) then reads, *Moses undertook to expound this law as follows*. Now Moses comes across as a teacher who explains and clarifies something that has been received and may in fact be public information, but that may not be fully understood. The role of the educator is to help people understand by using techniques like explanation, analogy, and application. The implication is that Moses goes well beyond what he has received in an effort to make *this law* clear.

These verses thus warn against distinguishing too closely between divine and human words, or in this case, separating God's words from those of Moses. Deuteronomy is simultaneously words that Moses uses to explain the law to Israel and words that God commands Moses to speak. At points Deuteronomy does distinguish between words God gives directly to Israel and words that Israel receives indirectly through God's servant, Moses (cf. 4:9-14 and 6:22-27), but in the introduction this distinction is absent.

Deuteronomy is the word of God, with all the authority this implies, to Israel and to the contemporary church. But it comes in human form—one might compare this to the miracle of the incarnation in the New Testament—and so is at the same time a human word, with all the limitations intrinsic to language. For most readers of this commentary, this reality is made more complex by the fact that they have access to these words only through English translation.

A similar ambiguity arises when the phrase *words that Moses spoke* is unpacked with regard to the authorship of the book. Tradition is clear that Moses wrote the book of Deuteronomy as well as the rest of the Pentateuch. German translations of the Bible imply this with their designation of Deuteronomy as the "fifth book of Moses." Yet many contemporary scholars consider Deuteronomy to be an eighth- or seventh-century document. Both options are inadequate if taken literally or simply *[Composition of Deuteronomy, p. 543]*.

The opening verse directs the words to *all Israel* (v. 1). Strikingly, the last verse in Deuteronomy contains the same expression (34:12). The *all Israel* of Deuteronomy transcends the people gathered in the plains of Moab to hear the sermon of Moses. It includes the Israel of the seventh century, the Israel in exile, as well as all later Israels. As a people grafted into Israel, the church also is included (cf. Eph 2:11-22).

The concluding clause of the introduction includes the phrase *this law*. The Hebrew term *torah*, rendered *law* by most English versions, has a meaning much beyond or even different from that suggested by the English word "law" *[Law, p. 555]*. The ancestral stories of Genesis are torah. The account of Israel's escape from Egypt in Exodus is torah. All of Deuteronomy is torah, including narrative and exhortation. A recent Jewish commentary on Deuteronomy consistently translates *torah* as "Teaching," with a capital T (Tigay). Another writer suggests that Deuteronomy may be considered catechesis, or catechism, the foundational instruction that one generation of God's people gives to the next (Olson: 7-14). Deuteronomy uses *torah* in an expansive manner. To help remind us that the Hebrew means something other than law, this commentary will use *torah* for this broad meaning of the word, both when speaking of the teaching or sermon of Deuteronomy, as well as when referring more generally to God's instruction of Israel.

Deuteronomy in Time and Space 1:1b-2, 4-5a

Parts B (B[1] and B[2]) and C (C[1] and C[2]) place these speeches of Moses into a particular context. The exact location of some of the place names is unclear, but the general locale is straightforward—somewhere in the Transjordan, opposite Jericho in the plains of Moab (see map on p. 570). The phrase *beyond the Jordan* points to the Transjordan, from a vantage point on the west side (vv. 1b, 5a). The Transjordan may have already received a first installment of the gift of land as a sign of what is to come (see comments on 2:24-3:11), but the primary focus is the land west of the Jordan. Deuteronomy is a sermon at the border of the Promised Land.

The chronological context fits the geographical context. The significance of the surprisingly detailed dating probably lies more in the sequence than in the exact numbers. Looking backward, the book is placed a generation after the exodus (forty years signifies one generation), after the events at the mountain where they experienced God and were made a people through covenant (a place normally called *Horeb* in Deuteronomy and generally *Sinai* elsewhere), and after the years of wandering in the wilderness and the death of a whole generation due to their loss of faith upon first arriving at the Promised Land (cf. 1:34-36).

Looking forward, the occupation of the Promised Land still lies in the future, with all its dangers and potential, both for faith and loss of faith. The previous generation had experienced God's deliverance in the exodus, but when it had come to the Promised Land, it lost faith, and as a result perished in the wilderness (1:19-2:1). Now the present generation is the focus of attention. The defeat of the two Amorite kings reminds them that God is still powerful, still in control, and still wanting to give the people the land. As the previous generation had been, the present generation of the book is at the border of the Promised Land. The question is, will it have more faith than the previous generation, and receive the land God has given it?

THE TEXT IN BIBLICAL CONTEXT
Israel at the Boundary

The plains of Moab, a generation after the exodus, represent a critical juncture in the story of Israel. Ever since Genesis 12, the story has been looking forward to this point. Abraham and Sarah received the promise of land, but fulfillment for them was limited to a small plot that Abraham purchased for their burial (Gen 12:7; 24:7; 23:1-16; 25:7-11). Isaac and Jacob wander about in the land, but they do not settle down, and the promise is repeated (Gen 26:3; 28:13-15; 35:12). Jacob is even forced to take the family to Egypt, far away from the land, in order to survive the famines that inflict the area. His actions may secure life, but they also set the stage for slavery under a pharaoh who does not know Joseph. Hope for life, much less for the Promised Land, grows dim. But, the story says, God hears them in the land of slavery and calls Moses to lead them out. Now they are out, and the children of those who escaped are at the border, on the verge of receiving what had been promised so long ago. Throughout Deuteronomy this strategic location in time and in space cannot be forgotten. At this strategic location Moses gives Israel directions on how to live after it has received the land.

But the "border" or "boundary" is not a onetime location (Brueggemann 1977; P. Miller 1990). The power and force of Deuteronomy are bound up in the fact that many times later (continuously?) Israel again is at a boundary, at a point in its existence when the future lies open before it. The seventh century BCE was such a time. The Northern Kingdom had been defeated, and Judah had to determine how to respond to this new situation. Later the times of exile and restoration were such crises. Jerusalem and the temple had been destroyed. The foundations of Judah's faith had been undermined. Each time the sermon of Deuteronomy calls out to them.

The New Testament presents another such border time. John the Baptist calls on the people to repent "for the kingdom of heaven has come near" (Matt 3:2). Shortly thereafter Jesus begins his ministry with a similar proclamation: "The time is fulfilled, and the kingdom of God has come near; repent and believe in the good news" (Mark 1:15). Like Deuteronomy, Jesus presents his hearers with the challenge to respond now in their border situation.

THE TEXT IN THE LIFE OF THE CHURCH
The People of God at Boundaries

Not all of life is of the same significance for the future. There are times in the life of the people of God, or times in the lives of individuals, that have extraordinary import for their future. A congregation may need to reassess its identity and approach as its demographics change or the community within which it is located changes. Families have new opportunities and challenges when they relocate in a new community. At key points in life, individuals face potentially life-changing circumstances.

The church of the early twenty-first century may be in such a boundary situation. In her book *The Great Emergence*, Phyllis Tickle suggests that the church is in the midst of a massive rummage sale, an occurrence that happens roughly every five hundred years. This is a time of upheaval and overhaul as everything is under review, with the possibility of being rethought, radically reoriented, or even jettisoned entirely. The previous such great rummage sale was the Protestant Reformation of the sixteenth century. During the five hundred years leading up to the current shakeup, the institutional church has become so calcified, so set in its ways, that only a giant rummage sale can engender revitalization (2008; cf. 2012).

In the midst of the sale, everything is in a state of upheaval and confusion, but Tickle assures us that, once we have passed through the turmoil, the result is a revitalized and renewed older or former church and a dynamic new form of Christianity. Brian McLaren has a similar sense of our times. In his numerous books he attempts to paint what that new form of Christianity might look like, as reflected in titles like *A New Kind of Christian* and *A New Kind of Christianity*.

For young adults the transition from being dependent children in the homes of their parents to independent adults, with their own relationships, lifestyle, and career, is a unique boundary position. They must decide who their friends will be, how they will earn and spend their own money, how or if they will relate to the church, whom they will marry, and other matters. One might push this analogy even further by suggesting that they are about to enter the promised land, when their skills and education will provide for their livelihood and become the source of new blessing. They are at a critical boundary.

Into such boundary situations Deuteronomy presents the words of God through Moses. Just as these words were to guide Israel as it passes over the boundary into the Promised Land, so these words address people and church in their boundary situations today.

Deuteronomy 1:6-18
Retrospect: Dividing the Load

PREVIEW

Leadership, hierarchy, delegation of authority and administration are issues in every social organization. Businesses, church denominations, and countries all must deal with these. Israel is no exception. The first story of Deuteronomy retells the tradition of Israel receiving a very rudimentary organizational structure, in the process highlighting three realities. First, Israel needs this development because God has *multiplied you, so that today you are as numerous as the stars of heaven* (v. 9). Indirectly the passage reminds the reader that God has fulfilled his promise to the ancestors to make of them a great nation (Gen 12:2).

Second, despite Moses' greatness and unparalleled role within Israel (cf. Deut 34:10), he cannot do everything himself (1:9). A more efficient and effective administrative system is needed. Moses may be God's representative and have God's ear, but he is not God. The delegation of authority in this passage begins the process of dividing up the role of Moses, preparing Israel for the time when Moses will no longer be with them, an important theme in Deuteronomy.

Third, it is significant that the first structure for Israel is a judicial system. A central concern of Deuteronomy is the exclusive worship of Yahweh, the God of the exodus (ch. 12). But for Deuteronomy the faithful worship of God necessarily includes a way of living with fellow humans: it means treating others the way God treats Israel.

Worshiping God is not limited to the cult or religious ritual but integrally relates to everyday life [Cult, p. 546]. The statutes and ordinances of chapters 12-26 give this conviction concrete form. Placing a story concerned with the administration of justice at the head of the book sets the tone for this emphasis.

OUTLINE

Instructions to Leave Mount Horeb, 1:6-8
The Appointment of Judges, 1:9-18
    1:9-15   Selection of Judges
    1:16-17   Charge to the Judges
    1:18   Conclusion

EXPLANATORY NOTES

Instructions to Leave Mount Horeb 1:6-8

The story opens with God instructing Israel to leave Horeb and resume the journey (v. 6). Each of the vignettes in the Retrospect opens in a similar manner, with God directing Israel to move forward (1:19; 2:2-3, 24). Israel is a people on the move, on a journey directed by God. At each point in the journey, Israel faces challenges (administrative overload, entering the land, opposition from hostile kings), with each challenge raising the question: how will Israel respond?

God pronounces that Israel has lived at the mountain *long enough*. The exact location of Mount Horeb is unknown, but the text places it somewhere in the desert region between Egypt and Canaan. It will not have been an especially fertile or pleasing site, but it was safe from Egyptian threat, and it was where Israel had met God. Israel may have been tempted to settle down at the mountain, short of their promised goal (cf. Peter, James, and John on the Mount of Transfiguration, Matt 17:1-8). But Israel had not been freed from Egypt to become permanent inhabitants of the desert, even at the mountain of God.

The goal is the land of the Amorites and Canaanites, two of the names Deuteronomy uses for the people of the land. The boundaries given here (v. 7) are not exact, but they do encompass a huge region. In the south it includes the Negeb (southern part of Palestine, north of the Sinai Peninsula and the Wadi of Egypt; Num 34:5). The land extends up the Arabah (the geographical depression extending from the Gulf of Aqaba up to the Sea of Chinnereth/Galilee). The *hill country of the Amorites* is a portion of the Transjordan region. The *great river* is the Euphrates (in modern-day Iraq) in the far north. In other words, this verse speaks of the land as extending from Egypt in the south up through Lebanon to Mesopotamia in the north, and also west across the breadth of that land through the Jordan Valley to the Mediterranean seacoast (see map on p. 571).

At no point did Israel control this broad expanse of land. During the reigns of David and Solomon, and for a short time in the ninth century BCE, Israel, or Israel and Judah, had some influence over the peoples and nations in this territory, yet never was it all theirs. But Deuteronomy is not providing data for cartographers. Even in these opening chapters with their historical reminiscing, Deuteronomy's primary concern is not history or geography but theology. With this language Deuteronomy follows the tradition of Genesis 15:18, where Abraham is told, "To your descendants I give this land, from the river of Egypt to the great river, the river Euphrates" (cf. Deut 11:24; Josh 1:4). The land that Israel is about to receive is a great land, a gift beyond all measure and comprehension.

These verses mention three things about the land: (1) it is given to Israel, (2) Israel has to take possession of it, and (3) it had been promised to Israel's ancestors (v. 8; P. Miller 1990: 26–27). Of these three, the last is foundational. Deuteronomy, especially in its second sermon (chs. 5–28), emphasizes the covenant associated with Mount Horeb, and the expectations or responsibilities it places upon Israel. But priority is given to the covenant God made with Abraham and Sarah, and then confirmed with their son Isaac and grandson Jacob. Deuteronomy, as the larger story of God and Israel, begins with God's unconditional promise (cf. Gen 12) and action.

Unfortunately, the first characteristic is lost in some translations. The Hebrew translated *I have set the land before you* (Deut 1:8 NRSV, RSV) uses the simple perfect or past form of the verb "to give." It is the same verb and tense translated *has given* a few verses later (1:21). The NIV more helpfully translates verse 8, *I have given you this land* (similarly NABRE, NJB). The expression likely has a legal background, as property is transferred from one party to another. The verse thus not only announces what will happen but already reflects the official transfer (Mayes: 120).

The first two qualities reflect a paradox consistent in Deuteronomy. On the one hand, Deuteronomy affirms that God has given Israel the land—Israel cannot earn it. God freely and graciously gives it to Israel. The land never loses this gift quality. In fact, a critical question will be whether Israel will remember that the land is a gift and not a commodity it can do with what it wants. But on the other hand, it is not a gift forced upon Israel. Israel will only receive the land if it steps out in trust to take possession of it. The next story in this chapter (1:19-2:1) demonstrates what happens when Israel fails to do this. A cooperation or synergism between God and the human is expected. The passage giving journey instructions already sets the tone for the whole book.

The Appointment of Judges 1:9-18

The story of Moses delegating his authority interrupts what may previously have been a continuous travel narrative (v. 19 picks up directly from v. 8), but its strategic location highlights its paradigmatic significance. The Old Testament relates this story three times—here, in Exodus 18:13-27, and in Numbers 11:11-17. It is possible that the audience of Deuteronomy knew the earlier two stories and so heard the Deuteronomic version in light of them. Variations thus become significant windows into the interests of Deuteronomy.

The phrase *at that time* serves as a structuring device in the story (vv. 9, 16, 18). It opens the narrative, placing the story at Horeb, after the receipt of the commandments but before leaving the mountain as instructed in verse 7. Then, after the main story (a problem is introduced, a solution is proposed, the proposed solution is accepted, and the judges are selected, vv. 9-15), it introduces Moses' charge to the newly named judges (v. 16), and concludes the narrative (v. 18).

1:9-15 Selection of Judges

The Great Burden: Numerous as the Stars, 1:9-12. Each of the three accounts relates the need to delegate authority to the size of the people and the enormity of the task, but the tone they give this reality is very different. In the Exodus version Moses comes across as a somewhat inept administrator, who works from morning until night judging the people, risking burnout without noticing it, until his observant father-in-law, Jethro, draws it to his attention: "What you are doing is not good. You will surely wear yourself out, both you and these people with you. For the task is too heavy for you; you cannot do it alone" (Exod 18:17-18). In Numbers, Moses is very aware of the problem. Indeed, he appears to be overwhelmed by it as he protests in frustration to God, "Why have you treated your servant so badly? Why have I not found favor in your sight, that you lay the burden of all his people on me? . . . I am not able to carry all this people alone. . . . If this is the way you are going to treat me, put me to death at once" (Num 11:11-15).

The background is the same in Deuteronomy, but the thrust is very different. Moses is neither inept nor complaining when he admits that he cannot do it all himself. The cause of the problem is interpreted only positively—it is evidence that God has blessed the people and multiplied them as promised to the ancestors (cf. Gen 22:17; 26:4; Exod 32:13; Deut 10:22; cf. Exod 1:7). Moses' appeal to God to continue this increase *a thousand times more* only emphasizes its positive bias (v. 11). The foundational nature of the ancestral covenant with its promises once more comes to the fore (cf. 1:8). These verses subtly make the point: the "great nation" part of the promise has been fulfilled. Now they can look forward to the fulfillment of the second part, the gift of land. Moses' dilemma thus serves as a visible sign that God can be counted upon, that Israel can trust God to fulfill his promises.

Moses is the great, unparalleled leader of Israel, and yet he will die before the book ends. This story already begins the movement to his death. Moses recognizes the limits of what he alone can do and dies to an exclusive claim on authority and the hoarding of power. He begins to share and trust others with it (Olson: 24). Moses recognizes that in changed circumstances (increased people, movement into the land) the old administrative structure that placed all power in his hands is no longer adequate. New structures are required, and so Moses institutes them. Preparations begin for the time when God's living voice will no longer be with the people. Implicitly the story suggests to its audience that new times, even when the result of blessing, may require adaptation and adjustment. Freedom, indeed encouragement, is given to the people to continue this direction.

The Solution, 1:13-15. Moses, the wise leader and teacher, recognizes the problem, and proposes the solution (in contrast to Exodus, where an outsider, Jethro the Midianite, suggests the new organization). The people respond positively and immediately implement the new structure.

Two aspects of the solution are striking, especially when compared with the Exodus account. First, the characteristics of the judges to be appointed have a decidedly secular ring to them. They are to be *wise, discerning, and reputable* (v. 13), and again, *wise and reputable individuals* (v. 15). The RSV translates the last characteristic in both sets with *experienced*, suggesting relevant knowledge rather than authority and influence among the people. The latter is implied by the NRSV wording, though the tone remains similar in either case. The qualifications focus on the ability of the judges to make astute and perceptive judgments. In contrast, in Exodus the qualifications have a moral or even religious quality to them. The judges are to be "men who fear God, are trustworthy, and hate dishonest gain" (Exod 18:21).

Second, it is the people themselves who select their own judges, not as in Exodus, where Moses, the voice of God in the community, does the choosing (cf. Exod 18:25). The people will have to accept the authority of the judges, and so the people are to determine for themselves who those judges will be. One might suggest that a more democratic approach has entered the text.

These differences may reflect a wisdom influence upon Deuteronomy. Proverbs (8:12-16) considers wisdom the key to the king's ability to judge well. The absence of any reference to priests—given the significant role that priests played in the administration of justice in Israel, even within Deuteronomy—is consistent with this (cf. 17:8-13). This may reflect a secularizing trend in Deuteronomy (Weinfeld 1972), but more important, these qualifications and way of choosing judges reflect Deuteronomy's consistent emphasis on the responsibility of the people as a unity of brothers and sisters before God. The people evaluate the plan as a *good one* (v. 14); they select the judges; they later will also receive Moses' charge to them (v. 18).

The *officials* are probably assistants to the judges. They may very well have been scribes, or in modern terms secretaries or administrative assistants (v. 15; cf. *officials of* 16:18). The reference (similar in Exodus and Numbers) to the judges becoming *commanders of thousands, commanders of hundreds, commanders of fifties, commanders of tens* appears odd since the normal context for such language is the military (cf. 1 Sam 8:12; 17:18; 22:7; 2 Kings 1:9, 11, 13; Isa 3:3). This may point to a composite background to the story and tradition, but in its present context it has the effect of merging the judicial and martial roles, with the judicial role dominant. As is clear from the concluding charge, the story is about the appointment of judicial figures in an effort to lighten Moses' workload (vv. 16-17).

1:16-17 Charge to the Judges

As part of their installation, a formal charge is given to the judges, a convention known from the ancient Near East (Weinfeld 1991: 138). Central to the charge is the call to judge fairly and rightly (KJV speaks of judging *righteously*; the NABRE speaks of *true justice*). The warning against showing partiality literally says, *Do not recognize faces*. Later Deuteronomy will give the job description for judges as *Justice, and only justice, you shall pursue* (16:20). Much of this instruction is cast in typical ancient Near Eastern language. When Thutmose III appointed Rekhmire as his vizier, he instructed him, "He is the one who does not make himself a friend of anyone. . . . It is an abomination of God to show face. This is an instruction: . . . regard him whom you know like him whom you do not know, him who is near you like him who is far from you" (Weinfeld 1991: 141). Israel borrowed from the wisdom of its day in its understanding of justice and the responsibility of judges.

Yet that wisdom is not simply borrowed. For example, the reference to the resident alien is unusual. The *resident alien* (1:16; KJV, *stranger*) is an outsider, someone who is not a full member of the Israelite community but who in some way lives within the bounds of that community. This may be a traveler, a servant in a household, or possibly even a foreigner who has settled in the region but has not become a full member of the community. The charge to the judges requires that the resident alien and Israelite be treated equally. Deuteronomy gives special attention to those elements of Israelite society not in a position to protect themselves, like the resident alien, the widow, and the orphan (cf. 24:17-22).

Moreover, even when no obvious change is evident, the whole is changed when it is brought into the larger story of Yahweh and Israel. All nations of the day expected their rulers to implement justice. Israel felt quite free to draw from the language of other nations. But once that expectation becomes part of Israel's story, it is colored by that story. God's special concern for the weak and powerless—as represented most clearly in God's response to the cries of oppressed slaves in Egypt, along with the conviction that, in the end, *the judgment is God's* (v. 17)—fills borrowed language with distinctive content. Similarly, Proverbs incorporates diverse sayings and maxims into Israelite theology by placing them under the "fear of the LORD" (1:7).

The Hebrew term behind both *members of the community* and *citizens* literally is *brothers* (v. 16; cf. KJV et al.). The term is a key one in Deuteronomy for representing unity of the people, for this consisted of brothers and sisters with responsibility for each other and to God.

1:18 Conclusion

The story opens and closes with a verse including the phrase *at that time*. The *you* of this verse refers again to the people as a whole and not to the judges alone. This reflects Deuteronomy's concern that the united people together share responsibility for justice and the need to respond.

THE TEXT IN BIBLICAL CONTEXT
Responsibility for Justice

The Old Testament depicts Moses as the comprehensive leader of Israel. During the time of Israel as a political state, or two states, a specialization of leadership roles developed. Deuteronomy reflects this when it identifies key leadership roles and assigns responsibilities to them (16:18-19:21). In that text, judges receive a further mandate (16:18-20). But the administration of justice is too important an issue to be left to the judges alone. The king also has a special responsibility for justice.

The Deuteronomic law of the king may hint at this when it requires that the king is to *have a copy of this law [torah] written for him. . . . It shall remain with him and he shall read in it all the days of his life* (17:18-19). The king's responsibility for justice becomes even more explicit in other Old Testament books. When God offers to grant Solomon any request he desires, Solomon humbly asks for "an understanding mind." Such a mind has the ability to "discern between good and evil" (cf. Deut 1:13), so as to be able to "govern this your great people" (1 Kings 3:9); the Hebrew term translated *govern*, used twice in the verse, has the same root as the noun "judge." God is pleased with Solomon's request and gives him "a wise and discerning mind" (1 Kings 3:12). Later a restructuring of the judicial system is attributed to King Jehoshaphat of Judah (2 Chron 19:4-11). As in our passage, leadership is bound up with the administration of justice, with primary emphasis given to wisdom and understanding.

This obligation of the king takes center stage in Psalm 72, a psalm probably used at a king's coronation:

> Give the king your justice, O God,
>   and your righteousness to a king's son.
> May he judge your people with righteousness,
>   and your poor with justice. (Ps 72:1-2)

Proverbs also connects the administration of justice with the king, and grounds it in wisdom:

> By me [wisdom] kings reign,
>   and rulers declare what is just;

> by me [wisdom] rulers rule,
> and nobles, all who govern [judge] rightly. (Prov 8:15-16)

Leadership, the administration of justice, and wisdom form a close trio (note also 1 Kings 10:9; Ps 99:4; Prov 29:4; Jer 23:5).

The New Testament proclaims Jesus as the fulfillment and goal of the Old Testament, the one who clarifies its meaning (e.g., Luke 24:27). In his inaugural address in Nazareth (Luke 4:16-21), Jesus identifies himself as the one of whom Isaiah 61 says:

> The Spirit of the Lord is upon me,
> because he has anointed me
> to bring good news to the poor.
> He has sent me to proclaim release to the captives
> and recovery of sight to the blind,
> to let the oppressed go free. (Luke 4:18)

After Jesus heals a man's withered hand on the Sabbath, Matthew interprets this as fulfilling the words of Isaiah, and quotes from Isaiah 42, where twice we read of the servant proclaiming or bringing about justice. Like the kings of Israel, Jesus the Messiah is responsible for justice.

THE TEXT IN THE LIFE OF THE CHURCH

Justice Is the Bottom Line

Martin Luther says of this passage: "Before He gave laws He established judges, in order to impress equity upon us. For judges are living laws or the soul of the law. Therefore they are before and above laws" (Luther: 20). This order is not a coincidence but reflects true Deuteronomic (and OT) understanding of law. Judges do not administer the law but rather secure justice. Laws are just one of the forms used by Scripture to paint a picture of what justice is. Other forms are stories, proverbs, and songs. But above all of these stands God and God's way of justice—as is noted in 1:17, *the judgment is God's.*

When regulations or traditions are found to be inconsistent with God's justice, they must be changed. In the remarkable story of the daughters of Zelophehad, Moses concedes that the tradition of passing on the father's inheritance only to sons is unjust, and so a "statute and ordinance" is established (Num 27:1-11). The role of the judge thus is to represent or make visible this righteous justice of God in a judgment, and not merely to "apply" some law.

Since administering justice is much more than a mechanical application of regulations, it becomes even more critical that those who participate in the process are people of wisdom, discernment, and experience. The religious and moral qualifications included in the Exodus account (18:21) are assumed, but they are insufficient. Deuteronomy goes beyond these and calls for people of acumen and prudence. In this passage, the process itself is placed under the jurisdiction of Moses, the principal leader of the people.

Leaders today, whether congregational, institutional, or denominational, might take note. The bottom line is not financial, nor whether the budget is balanced, but whether righteousness and justice are practiced. The temptation to cover up mismanagement or even abuse remains. The bottom line is whether the leader cultivates and upholds God's justice in all actions.

Deuteronomy 1:19–2:1

Retrospect: Rebellion at the Border

PREVIEW

A boundary location presents opportunity and risk. Beginning a new job, leaving home to start university studies, entering a marriage covenant—all these are contemporary examples. The opportunity is to enter the future in trust and receive that which God is giving. The risk is more complex. Too little faith in God may lead to overly cautious action; too much confidence in one's own ability may lead to reckless decisions. The story of Israel's first arrival at the Promised Land exhibits both possibilities in dramatic fashion.

Deuteronomy abbreviates and revises the story of the spies from Numbers 13–14. When Israel arrives at the border, Moses directs them not to be afraid but to take possession of the land that God promised them and now has given them (v. 21; cf. v. 8). Three times, however, the people blow it. First, instead of simply entering the land, they determine to send spies *ahead of us* to explore the land. Already the question is hinted: does Israel truly trust God?

When the spies return from their mission, they laud the land: *It is a good land that the* LORD *our God is giving us* (v. 25). But they also report on the power of its inhabitants and the strength of its defenses, and so the people become afraid. They lose faith, they refuse to enter the land, they wish to return to Egypt.

Then, when God announces the consequences of their refusal to enter the land, the people abruptly change approach and resolve to enter the land even though God has already announced they are to return to the wilderness. Their new effort is futile, and they return to the camp, defeated and dejected.

In between, Moses and God speak to the people, reminding them of the promise, of God's earlier actions on their behalf, and encouraging them to have faith. But to no avail. God promises and leads, but the people must put their trust in that God, otherwise the very death they fear will come upon them. The result is years of aimless wandering and the death of the first generation to see the land.

OUTLINE

Arrival at the Given Land, 1:19-21
Spies Sent to Explore the Land, 1:22-25
Rebellion: Refusal to Enter the Land, 1:26-33
    1:26-28   Refusal to Enter
    1:29-31   Moses' Entreaty
    1:32-33   Continuing Refusal to Trust
Yahweh's Verdict, 1:34-40
    1:34-36   Adult Generation Denied Entrance
    1:37-38   Moses Shares the Fate of the People
    1:39-40   The Little Ones Reprieved
Rebellion: Presumptuous Attempt to Enter Land, 1:41-45
    1:41   Decision to Enter
    1:42   Yahweh's Entreaty
    1:43-44   Disastrous Effort to Enter Land
    1:45   The Closing of Yahweh's Ears
Outcome: Aimless Wandering, 1:46–2:1

EXPLANATORY NOTES

Arrival at the Given Land 1:19-21

The travel narrative interrupted by the account of the appointment of judges now resumes (cf. vv. 6-8). Somewhat schematically, the text identifies three locations: Horeb, the starting point; Kadesh-barnea, the goal of the journey on the southern border of the Promised Land (cf. v. 2); and the wilderness in between (see comments on v. 31).

At the edge of the Promised Land, Moses calls the people to attention (v. 21, *See*; RSV, *Behold*) and then largely repeats the speech God made earlier (vv. 20-21; cf. vv. 6-8 and comments there). All three characteristics of the land identified in verse 8 are noted: the land has been given to Israel, Israel must take possession of the land, the land had been promised to them. Although the NRSV now uses the phrase *has given the land* (v. 21), whereas earlier it used the phrase *have set the land*, in the Hebrew both verses use the same verb, the past form of "to give." The location of Kadesh-barnea, however, puts new weight on the second characteristic. Israel has *reached the hill country of the Amorites*, the goal of its long journey, and the practical question now is whether Israel will act in faith and take possession of it.

An important addition at the end of verse 21 marks the new situation. Instead of ending the speech with the reference to the promise to the ancestors, the speech now continues with *Do not fear or be dismayed* (v. 21; cf. v. 8). These words are more than merely general encouragement. They alert the informed reader that the following narrative is to be understood within the framework of Yahweh war, with God the divine warrior, the one who fights on behalf of Israel *[Yahweh War, p. 566]*. In so doing it introduces the central issue of the passage: will Israel trust God, or will Israel become afraid and lose faith?

The instruction not to be afraid is a frequent element in passages reflecting Yahweh war theology (cf., Deut 1:29; 7:21; 20:3; 31:6, 8; Josh 8:1; 10:25). As we will notice below, further language characteristic of this complex of ideas is used in the story of the spies. Deuteronomy 1:21 thus informs Israel (and us) that God is about to intervene on behalf of Israel as a divine warrior and defeat its enemies. Israel's role is to have faith in God.

Spies Sent to Explore the Land 1:22-25

At first glance the short description of the decision to send spies, the account of their undertaking, and their final report appears to be fairly neutral. As in other stories the spies are sent to reconnoiter a land before military action (cf. Josh 2:1-7; 7:2-3; Judg 18:1-6). A comparison with the Numbers account, however, raises some unsettling questions. Numbers says that God initiates the sending of the spies, but in Deuteronomy the proposal comes from the people (vv. 22; cf. Num 13:1-2). The people want assurance that *they* will be able to defeat the inhabitants of the land. The language describing Moses' affirmation of the suggestion is reminiscent of the people's affirmation of Moses' proposal on appointing judges (v. 23; cf. 1:14), but the reverse order is troubling. Without any explicit comment, the text begins to place in the reader's mind some key questions: Is this God's plan? Or are the people, including Moses, beginning to try to take over and develop their own strategy for taking the land? Are they beginning to be afraid?

After exploring the land up to the Valley of Eshcol (exact location unknown, but probably in the southern part of the land), the spies report, *It is a good land that the* LORD *our God is giving us.* The report is positive but appears truncated (cf. Num 13:27-33). Surely they would have said more than *It is a good land.* The formulaic nature of the report raises the question whether the text is reporting all that the spies said (see below). Something is not quite right. Already the verses send a warning.

Rebellion: Refusal to Enter the Land 1:26-33

1:26-28 Refusal to Enter

Instead of responding to the positive report of the spies by immediately entering the Promised Land (as in other OT spy stories), the people are *unwilling to go up*: they *rebelled* and *grumbled* (vv. 26-27). One is reminded of Israel murmuring and complaining in the wilderness before and after Horeb (Exod 15:22-26; 16:1-3; etc.). At first no reason for the negative response is given other than that it is rebellion *against the command* [lit., *mouth*] *of the* LORD *your God* (v. 26). Then comes the explanation: *Our kindred* [i.e., the spies] *have made our hearts melt by reporting, "The people are stronger and taller than we; the cities are large and fortified up to heaven! We actually saw the offspring of the Anakim!"* (v. 28). Apparently the spies' report had been more extensive than originally suggested by the text (v. 25b).

This explanation is especially striking for employing language normally associated with Yahweh war (cf. v. 21). Rahab informs the spies who come to explore Jericho that the people are aware of God's and Israel's previous victories, and that "as soon as we heard it, our hearts melted, and there was no courage left in any of us" (Josh 2:11). Similarly, Joshua 5:1 reports that after the kings of the Amorites heard what God had done for Israel, "their hearts melted, and there was no longer any spirit in them." Such language is typical of Yahweh war passages.

The possibility of receiving the land by allowing God to give the victory still is there in verse 21, but now the language is reversed and used against Israel. Now it is not the enemy whose hearts have melted, nor is it fear of Israel that causes the melting. Instead, it is fear within Israel brought on by the report of the spies. Yahweh war is not possible when fear in Israel is so great that its own hearts are melted (cf. 20:8). Fear is a powerful and at points even a destructive force.

The reference to the inhabitants of the land and their cities reflects a similar inversion. Four further times in the first half of

Deuteronomy the nations of the land are described as *greater and mightier* than Israel (4:38; 7:1; 9:1; 11:23), once with *great cities, fortified to the heavens* (9:1). But each of these is within a passage praising God for defeating these more powerful enemies on behalf of Israel. Again, Yahweh war language is subverted, with the Anakim (legendary giants of the land, as in 2:11) named as the reason for fear.

The encouragement and reassurance of Moses has not been heeded (v. 21b). Instead of trusting God to bring to completion the gift of the land promised, they have become afraid. They have lost faith. Both Moses and the people have the same facts: it is a good land occupied by strong people. Moses, however, focuses on the promise and power of God while the people are overwhelmed by the might of the Amorites.

The people's perspective leads them to a distorted picture of God's nature. For them God becomes an enemy rather than a friend (1:27). They interpret God's leading them out of Egypt as an action motivated by hate rather than by love. The people's words are countered directly a few chapters later (4:34-37). Fear and sin blind the people to the truth, leading to the ultimate distortion.

1:29-31 Moses' Entreaty

Moses' entreaty to Israel to have faith employs two quite different images for God. First, Moses speaks of God as the divine warrior, the one who fights for Israel against vastly superior enemies. As in Yahweh war, Israel is to *have no dread or fear* of the inhabitants even if they are *stronger and taller* (vv. 28-29; cf. v. 21). Israel is to trust in the powerful God who has delivered them only a short time previously.

The second image derives from a different perspective on the same exodus experience: not God as a fearsome warrior, but God as a tender, loving parent (v. 31). The NRSV translation (*as one carries a child*; RSV, *as a man bears his son*), in its effort to make the text gender inclusive, loses the biological relationship shown in the Hebrew. The wilderness is a place of threat, danger, and potential death. When Israel traveled through the wilderness, the fire and cloud represented God's providential care (v. 33). To speak of God as a warrior was not uncommon in the world of the day, nor is it in the Old Testament. To this image, however, Deuteronomy adds the picture of a caring parent. The term "love" is not used, but the verse looks forward to later passages that speak of God as loving Israel (e.g., 4:37; 7:8). One is reminded of the popular poem by Mary Stevenson, "Footprints in the Sand," which notices that God was walking with a person; but when the situation became especially desperate, the second set of footsteps disappeared, because God had carried the person.

The basis for Moses' plea is that Israel has seen for itself what God has done (v. 30, *before your very eyes*; v. 31, *where you saw*). Deuteronomy follows the maxim "Seeing should be believing" (cf. 3:21; 4:3, 9, 34, 35; 5:24; 6:22; 7:19; 9:17; 10:21; 11:7; 29:2-3). Israel had seen and experienced God's deliverance and thus should not be afraid. It is when this experience is forgotten that the enemy seems to be overwhelming.

1:32-33 *Continuing Refusal to Trust*

Despite Moses' plea the people do not change their mind. The essence of the issue is tersely identified: *You have no trust in the LORD your God*. Despite what Israel has seen and experienced, and despite Moses' words of assurance, the people lack trust. The refusal is not merely obstinacy but has grounds much deeper than that. The concluding reference to God's prior leading and care through the *fire* and the *cloud* (cf. Exod 13:21-22; 40:38; Num 14:14) only reinforces the theme.

Yahweh's Verdict 1:34-40

1:34-36 *Adult Generation Denied Entrance*

God has given the land (1:8, 21), but God does not force Israel to accept the gift. The irony of the punishment is that Israel is prevented from receiving that which it refuses to receive. In the wilderness Israel will experience the very death it feared.

The willingness to punish is part of the nature of God in Deuteronomy. The reference to God's wrath (v. 34) reminds one of Israel's earlier accusation that God hated Israel (v. 27). But the two are very different. Whereas hate and love may be opposites, anger and love are not. Israel's loss of faith leads to God's anger, but the love of God that lies behind the original election of Israel is not lost. The very next verse (1:35) again includes a reference to the ancestral covenant and the promise of land (v. 35). The purpose of the punishment is to make fulfillment of the promise possible.

Caleb and Joshua now enter the story with no introduction (vv. 36, 38). Deuteronomy may assume the audience knows the fuller version of the story in Numbers. After the ten spies have given their pessimistic report, Caleb and Joshua give a minority report that concludes with more encouraging words, "Let us go up at once and occupy it, for we are well able to overcome it" (Num 13:30). Because of his trust, Caleb (and later Joshua) is exempted from the punishment. Caleb and his family eventually settle in the region around Hebron (Josh 14:6-15). Caleb's faithfulness and consequent receipt of the land confirm the point: following after God leads to land and blessing; failure to follow after God leads to death.

1:37-38 Moses Shares the Fate of the People

Caleb's exemption from the punishment only accentuates the difficulty the text has with the fact that Moses is not able to enter the Promised Land. That Moses will die short of the land is a crucial reality for Deuteronomy, especially in the concluding chapters (cf. 3:26-29; 4:21-22; 31:1-2; 32:48-52; 34:1-12). In fact, Deuteronomy can be understood as a book that prepares Israel for life without Moses, without someone who serves as a direct voice of God in their midst (cf. 34:10). But the Deuteronomic explanation for the death is far from straightforward.

The immediate context of the first reference to Moses' death may be taken to intimate that Moses, like Israel (and unlike Caleb), is unable to enter the land because of his sin. Such an explanation would be consistent with that given in Numbers (20:12; 27:12-14), and even with a passage later in Deuteronomy (32:51). But this passage itself appears to contest such an explanation when it states that God was angry with Moses *on your account* (1:37; cf. 3:26). The intended inference is that Moses dies outside of the land not because of his own misdeed but out of solidarity with the people. Moses had done everything he could to persuade the people to enter the land, but they had been afraid and lost faith. Their punishment is to die in the wilderness. Moses, the passage suggests, now participates in this punishment.

Despite this language one must distinguish between suffering and dying *on account* of the people and suffering and dying on behalf of the people. Moses' death does not prevent the people from dying. This is not the substitutionary suffering as envisioned in Isaiah 53. Rather, it recognizes that when a people sin and rebel, the innocent, whether leader or merely part of the people, suffer as well (cf. the fate of other OT prophets). For the people in exile, this becomes an important recognition.

Joshua, Moses' assistant (lit., *the one who stands before you*), is designated his replacement as leader of the people (see 3:28; 31:7-8; 34:9-12).

1:39-40 The Little Ones Reprieved

Yet punishment is not the final word. Judgment is the necessary prelude to life. The people used their children as an excuse for not entering the land. Now the text announces that they are the ones who will eventually receive the land. This promise puts the punishment of 1:34-35 into perspective. The gift of the land had been grounded in God's eternal promise to the ancestors (vv. 8, 21, 35), a promise that God had confirmed with an oath (v. 8). God's new oath (v. 34 contains the same word as v. 8) does not cancel the old, even though it delays it for one generation, but rather renews the promise. Punishment is real, but the power of the original promise is greater. Perhaps there is even a subtle reminder that just as God carried Israel like a child in the wilderness, so God will continue to carry and protect Israel's *little ones, . . . your children*, or perhaps that in order to receive that protection, Israel must become trustful like children (cf. v. 31; cf. Matt 19:14; Luke 18:16). Again, words of hope for an exilic audience.

Rebellion: Presumptuous Attempt to Enter the Land 1:41-45

Israel recognizes its error—*We have sinned against the LORD!* (v. 41)—but does it really? Deuteronomy's account of its further action exposes the repentance as either not genuine or at least lacking understanding. For despite Israel's confession, the story reports that Israel *rebelled against the command of the LORD* (v. 43; cf. v. 26). At first rebellion was caused by fear, but now it is due to presumption (v. 43). But the judgment is the same.

The similarity in structure between this paragraph (vv. 41-45) and the one describing the previous act of rebellion (vv. 26-33) is instructive. Both begin with the people taking an independent position. In the first they accuse God of hating them and refuse to enter the land. In the second they express confidence and decide to enter the land on their own. Both times their position is a rejection of God's direction. Yet both times God gives them a further chance, inviting them to reconsider: Moses announces, *Have no dread or fear of them* (v. 29), and God says, *Do not go up and do not fight* (v. 42). But the people ignore the warnings and act on their original position. Deuteronomy's overall picture of Israel as a people who finds rebellion more natural than faithfulness is coming into focus.

The use of Yahweh war motifs confirms the message of the passage. In Yahweh war the people need not fear since God goes before them and fights on their behalf (cf. 1:30; 6:19; 7:1; etc.). But when

God is not in their midst (v. 42), Israel is bound to fail. Israel does not listen and tries to take the promise into its own hands, just as Moses did when he slew the Egyptian (Exod 2). The logic and message is consistent even if the second rebellion appears to be the opposite of the first. Israel does not defeat any enemy—God does. If Israel tries to confront the inhabitants of the land on its own, failure is the inevitable result. Israel is completely overwhelmed by the Amorites and returns to camp, weeping. But to no avail—presumption has its repercussions.

Outcome: Aimless Wandering 1:46–2:1

The story of the spies begins and ends with a travel narrative, but what happens in between changes everything (1:19; 1:46–2:1). The opening verse is full of hope and anticipation. Israel arrives at the land, ready to take possession. In the concluding verses Israel is headed back into the wilderness and the Red Sea, to wander around Mount Seir (southeast of the Dead Sea). God still dictates Israel's travel plan, but now it is a "journey in reverse" (McConville 2002: 82), or an "Anti-Exodus" (Moran 1969). Israel's loss of faith at the border results in Israel traveling again, but with no place to go. The awkward language (*You stayed at Kadesh as many days as you did*, 1:46), and the absence of any destination despite the reference to a lengthy journey (*we journeyed back into the wilderness . . . and skirted Mount Seir for many days*, 2:1) highlight the aimlessness of the wandering. For the next thirty-eight years Israel wanders in the wilderness, not too far from Kadesh-barnea and the Promised Land (cf. 2:14). The land remains in sight but is lost to this generation.

Looking Ahead

Deuteronomy 1:19–2:1 represents one side of the coin. It is a story of rebellion grounded in fear and presumption that leads to aimless wandering rather than possession of promised and given land (1:8, 21). Moses shares the fate of his people, whether because of his own sin or the sin of the people. Sin has its consequences, for those who commit it and for those around them. Despite this negative reading, however, the ancestral promise is not canceled or abrogated. It was foundational at the beginning of the story, and it remains effective at the end. A one-generation delay is significant, but when viewed against the centuries it is largely an interruption. Deuteronomy looks back at the story from such a later perspective.

To the exiles the story presents both hope and warning. The destruction of Jerusalem and the ensuing exile was another loss of land. The story of the spies anticipates that later loss and helps the people to cope with it. Rebellion and disobedience have their dire aftermath, with both innocent and guilty suffering. The earlier loss had been for one generation. Deuteronomy may here be hinting that there is hope for the exiles. The ancestral promise is more powerful than the rebellion of this story and, Deuteronomy suggests, remains in force.

THE TEXT IN BIBLICAL CONTEXT
An Imperfect Story

The Bible is not written in praise of people but in praise of a God who works with deeply flawed people. Unlike some national stories, the story of the people of God in Scripture is not some ideal and sanitized version but a narrative that recognizes error and shortcoming. The direction is already reflected in the stories of the ancestors, as Abraham and Sarah deceive Pharaoh (Gen 12:10-20), and Jacob is depicted as a rogue and liar. Exodus and Numbers speak of Israel murmuring and complaining against God on the way to the Promised Land (cf. Exod 15:24; 16:2; Num 11:1; 14:2; etc.). The Deuteronomistic History explains the defeat of both the Northern Kingdom and the Southern Kingdom as due to Israel's sin (2 Kings 17:7-18; 21:16; 23:26-27). The prophets regularly indict Israel for failing to do God's will.

Jesus, Stephen, and Paul all note the shortcomings of Israel (Luke 11:47; Acts 7:35-41; 1 Cor 10:1-5). The coming of Christ may inaugurate a new era, a new kingdom, but the people of God remain very human, with serious blemishes. Members intentionally mislead (Acts 5:1-11), widows are neglected (6:1), and Paul faces a variety of battles. The story of God's people confirms the verdict of Paul, "All have sinned and fall short of the glory of God" (Rom 3:23; cf. Eccl 7:20).

And yet God continues to work with this people. For that care, God receives rich praise. Psalm 106 is a lengthy hymn that begins with "Praise the LORD!" but devotes most of its verses to recognizing the sin of Israel. Appropriately, this psalm refers to the story of Israel's first arrival at the border:

> Then they despised the pleasant land,
>   having no faith in his promise.
> They grumbled in their tents,

and did not obey the voice of the LORD.
Therefore he raised his hand and swore to them
   that he would make them fall in the wilderness,
and would disperse their descendants among the nations,
   scattering them over the lands. (Ps 106:24-27)

THE TEXT IN THE LIFE OF THE CHURCH

Inordinate Confidence

The Jesus movement has always struggled with how to think about war, especially since the time of Constantine, when church and state essentially became one. Before that time, Christians tended to be pacifist. But once the responsibilities of statehood merged with those of the people of God, the pressure to find a way of accommodating war became overpowering. The result is the just-war tradition, a convention going back to Augustine, taught by Aquinas, and still held by the Roman Catholic Church as well as most other Christians. Basically, proponents of the just-war tradition try to describe conditions or circumstances under which war is justifiable as the lesser evil than other alternatives.

There is no official list of the criteria for judging a war to be just; each denominational or theological tradition nuances it in its own particular way. But in addition to including some reference to a just cause, its proponents generally include the condition that the prospects of success are probable and that the outcome will be a just peace. Both of these latter criteria require the ability to be able to assess the consequences of entering into armed conflict. As the wars to establish peace in Iraq and Afghanistan have once again demonstrated, this is notoriously difficult to do.

What is striking about the story of the spies is how Israel also failed at this. First, it judges its foes to be too strong and therefore chooses not to enter. After a reprimand, Israel presumes that God now will fight for Israel and grant victory. Both are miscalculations. The two reactions share in common an inordinate confidence in the human ability to assess reality along with the consequences of our actions. Both are attempts, based on human analysis, to project what will happen and then act on that basis, rather than placing confidence in God.

Deuteronomy 2:2-23
Retrospect: Peaceful Encounters

PREVIEW

It is possible to become so absorbed in one's own world that one loses sight of the larger picture. Deuteronomy is sometimes accused of this as it concentrates so heavily on Israel as the chosen people of God. But as it describes Israel's return to the Promised Land, it reminds Israel and us of the larger picture.

After wandering aimlessly *long enough* (2:3), time enough for the generation that lost faith at the first arrival at the land to perish, Israel sets out once more toward the Promised Land. The journey moves forward at God's direction (2:3-6, 9, 13a, 18-19, 31; 3:2), with repeated references to Israel passing over or across areas (some form of the verb "to cross" occurs thirteen times in the passage).

The resulting travelogue zeros in on encounters with five different peoples: descendants of Esau, 2:2-8; Moab, 2:9-15; Ammon, 2:16-23; Sihon and the Amorites around Heshbon, 2:24-30; and Og and the Amorites of Bashan, 3:1-7. In schematic fashion, prompted by theological concerns, Deuteronomy characterizes these five encounters as consisting of two distinct groups. The first three encounters are peaceful, with Israel passing through or by the regions occupied by the peoples. Yahweh may be the God of Israel but also has been active in the affairs of these peoples, giving them their land just as God is about to give Israel its land. Israel negotiates with Edom, Moab, and Ammon for food and water, but there is no conflict. The lands of

Sihon and Og, in contrast, are part of the land designated for Israel. These thus are battle reports in which God gives victory, with the land as down payment for or foretaste of what is to come.

Edom, Moab, and Ammon were three recently established nation-states east of the Jordan River. Surprisingly, in its description of Israel's encounters with them, Deuteronomy announces loud and clear: these nations have a right to exist. The God of Israel and the exodus has given them their land; Israel must not try to take it away from them. Each subsection (2:2-8, 9-15, 16-23) has at its center a pronouncement of God: *I have given Mount Seir to Esau as a possession* (2:5); *I have given Ar as a possession to the descendants of Lot* (2:9); *I have given it to the descendants of Lot* (2:19). Since animosity and tension existed between Israel and each of these states at various times throughout their history, these are unexpected and radical announcements.

Reflection on the wilderness years provides a secondary theme within this section. Each of the individual stories contains at least one comment on this time (2:7, 14-15, 16). The response is paradoxical. These years are described as a time when God led and protected Israel, but also as a time when God's hand was against the generation that had rebelled upon first arriving at the border.

OUTLINE

Crossing the Land of Esau, 2:2-8
    2:2-6   God's Instructions
    2:7   Review of Wilderness Period
    2:8   Travel Report
Crossing the Land of Moab, 2:9-15
    2:9   God's Instructions
    2:10-12   Historical Interruption
    2:13a   God's Instructions Continued
    2:13b   Travel Report
    2:14-15   Review of Wilderness Period
Bypassing the Land of Ammon, 2:16-23
    2:16   The End of the Wilderness Period
    2:17-19   God's Instructions
    2:20-23   Historical Interruption

Note: The Explanatory Notes for 2:2-23 have been organized as follows:
    God Directs the Way 2:2-6, 9, 17-19
    The Rationale for the Directions 2:5, 9, 19

The Wilderness Review 2:7, 14-15, 16
Historical Interruptions 2:10-12, 20-23

EXPLANATORY NOTES

God's command to Israel to *Head north* signals a new start (2:3). The reference to having skirted the *hill country long enough* appears to be an intentional reference back to the first start when God commanded Israel to *resume your journey* after having stayed at Horeb *long enough* (1:6). The opening directive includes no rebuke or hint of anger for the earlier failure at Kadesh-barnea. God even selects an alternative route to the land. God and Israel are ready for a new beginning, a new chance at taking possession of the land (see Brueggemann 2001: 34-35).

At first glance the journey account describes the return with amazing geographical and historical detail: the passage refers to sixteen different peoples and twenty-eight different geographical locations. Comparison with the Numbers version of the trip, translation ambiguities (e.g., 2:18), and the formulaic way peoples and places are named warn against trying to trace the route too exactly. Yet the general outline of the journey is clear: after wandering in the wilderness in the region of Mount Seir, Israel returns to the Promised Land by traveling around the Dead Sea (on the east side), through Edom and Moab, arriving in the Transjordan, where it captures the kingdoms of Heshbon and Bashan. Entrance into the land will be across the Jordan from a location near Beth-peor (3:29) rather than from the south at Kadesh-barnea, as in the first attempt (see map, p. 571). The journey is described in such detail not so that the exact route can be traced but rather that in the telling of it, Israel can learn about God and Israel and the nations.

The first three nations Israel encounters are all distant relatives. They had settled in their areas shortly before Israel arrived, and peoples by these names continued to live in this region even after the end of Judah. Numbers also records Israel's encounter with Edom and Moab (but not with Ammon), as well as with kings Og and Sihon, but with different emphases (Edom refuses Israel passage; Moab sends Balaam to curse Israel) and in different order (the defeat of Og and Sihon occurs between Israel's encounter with Edom and Moab; Num 20-24). In Deuteronomy these stories are placed into starkly contrasting groups to highlight its central interests.

Notice the systematic pattern into which the peaceful encounters are placed. The structure of the pattern draws attention to the central interests of the passage. Its regularity suggests that details have all been made subservient to those central concerns.

Esau, 2:2-8	Moab, 2:9-15	Ammon, 2:16-23
Then the LORD said to me (v. 2)	The LORD said to me (v. 9)	The LORD spoke to me (v. 17)
God's instructions (vv. 3-6)	God's instructions (vv. 9b, 13a)	God's instructions (vv. 18-19)
Be very careful not to engage in battle with them (vv. 4-5)	Do not harass Moab or engage them in battle (v. 9)	Do not harass them or engage them in battle (v. 19)
I will not give you . . . of their land (v. 5)	I will not give you any of its land as a possession (v. 9)	I will not give the land . . . to you as a possession (v. 19)
I have given Mount Seir to Esau as a possession (v. 5)	I have given Ar as a possession to the descendants of Lot (v. 9)	I have given it to the descendants of Lot (v. 19)
wilderness review (v. 7)	wilderness review (vv. 14-15)	wilderness review (v. 16)
travel report (v. 8a)	travel report (v. 13b)	
	historical interruption (vv. 10-12)	historical interruption (vv. 20-23)

God Directs the Way 2:2-6, 9, 17-19

Each leg of the return trek is initiated by explicit instructions from God. These include the ones in the chart above on how Israel is to respond to the peoples it meets, but also detailed directions on what route to follow, such as *Now then, proceed to cross over the Wadi Zered* (2:13). Regularly the text records that Israel follows the directives. This command-obedience dynamic pervades the story, and without explicitly drawing attention to it, emphasizes God's continuing care and control over Israel. The sovereignty of God, over Israel and indeed the other nations, is a quiet but moving assumption. God's word moves the story forward. God initiates the events, and Israel follows. Israel's repeated compliance already hints that in contrast to the first arrival, this time Israel will remain faithful, overcome its fear, and enter the land.

At the center of each segment are instructions from God concerning those other peoples. Israel is not to harass the people of Edom, Moab, and Ammon. Indeed, Israel is to *be very careful* that confrontation does not occur even accidentally. Numbers 20 speaks of Edom as rejecting Israel's request for permission to pass through its territory, requiring Israel to make a lengthy detour around it; but here Edom is afraid of Israel. God is sovereign, and God's people instill fear in those they meet. If Israel passes through the land of Edom peacefully, it is because God has determined it that way. Even the peaceful encounters reflect God's dominion.

The Rationale for the Directions 2:5, 9, 19

But why is Israel not to contend with these peoples? The text gives two reasons (P. Miller 1990: 38). First, these people are Israel's kin (2:4, 8 RSV, *brethren*), part of Israel's larger family. Edom, the national name of the first people, is not even named in the account. It simply speaks of the people as *the descendants of Esau*, the brother of Jacob, the ancestor of Israel (see Gen 36:1-8 for the correlation of descendants of Esau with the land of Edom). The people of Moab and Ammon are both identified as descendants of Lot, a nephew of Abraham. In these three segments Israel thus is directed not to initiate conflict with family.

Identifying these people as kin may make Israel's effort at peaceful relations appear less remarkable. It is true that both Old and New Testaments call on people to remember who their brothers and sisters are. As Patrick Miller states, "There is a fundamental assumption throughout the Bible that relationships count for something and affect the way the persons in those relationships live and act and think. To exist as brother or sister is to have a claim on but also a responsibility for another" (1990: 38). This passage participates in that understanding.

But the family dynamic is insufficient to explain these passages. After all, the Old Testament recounts many stories in which family members battle, beginning with Cain and Abel (Gen 4). Kinship certainly does not guarantee friendly relations. Further, mutual respect and familial hospitality did not characterize the historical relations between Israel and these Transjordan peoples. Jeremiah (49:7-22) and Obadiah (8-21) both reflect considerable hostility between Israel and Edom; Moab and Judah perennially battled over control of the area north of the Wadi Arnon; and Judges 11 speaks of war between Ammon and the tribes of Israel. Although Edom, Moab, and Ammon may be kin, the peaceful encounters of

Deuteronomy 2:2-23 remain noteworthy, both because of the dynamics that so frequently typify kinship relations and because of the antagonism that characterized the history between these countries and Israel. The Deuteronomic version stands in the face of historic relations between Israel and these nations.

The reason Israel is not to confront or fight these Transjordan states is simple yet striking. God has not given their land to Israel: Yahweh, the God of Israel, has given these people their own land. We may have a hard time grasping the radical nature of this confession. Remember that this comes from a time when monotheism was not the norm. Each people or land was understood to have its own national god. At points Deuteronomy itself appears to recognize the existence of gods other than the God of Israel *[Biblical Monotheism, p. 539]*. Yet here Deuteronomy makes the unexpected and radical claim that the peoples of Edom, Moab, and Ammon have received their land from the same God who was in the process of giving Israel its land. Frequently Deuteronomy uses some form of the root "to possess/inherit" for the manner in which Israel receives its land. The first chapter alone uses it three times. But now, in the space of twenty-two verses, it is used nine times (2:5, 9 [twice], 12 [twice], 19 [twice], 21, 22), not of Israel but of these other nations. Just as Israel is to *take possession* of its land (1:8, 21), so God has given possession of their lands to the descendants of Esau and Lot.

The Wilderness Review 2:7, 14-15, 16

As noted in the chart, each segment of the passage contains some mention of the previous years of wandering in the wilderness. Although 2:14-16 might be considered a unit belonging to the second segment of the passage, thus leaving the segment on Ammon without a reference to the wilderness, the grammatical structure at the beginning of verse 16 suggests a new paragraph (as in NRSV, RSV). The three short comments about those years consist of two very different and almost conflicting perspectives on this period, both picking up threads from the previous story.

Deuteronomy 2:7 is a continuation of the emphasis of 1:31, 33, where we read *in the wilderness, where you saw how the* LORD *carried you, just as one carries a child*. The present passage speaks of God blessing Israel, God knowing Israel, and climaxing with *These forty years the* LORD *your God has been with you;* you have lacked nothing. Wilderness is a place of hunger and thirst, of helplessness and death. It is a place where the people's dependence on God becomes obvious. Once settled in the land, the people will produce their own food through agriculture, but then they will be tempted to think that they are responsible for their own well-being (cf. 8:11-18). But that is not an option in the desert. And yet, the text says, during this time they *lacked nothing*. God's providential care for the people God chose and led out of Egypt is basic to Israel's thinking about God.

But God's providential care does not negate the possibility of consequences for overt rebellion. The next two references to wilderness remind us of what happened when Israel first arrived at the land (1:19–2:1). Notice how 2:7 speaks of forty years of care by God, and 2:14 speaks of thirty-eight years of wandering. During this time death comes to the generation that was overcome by fear of the Amorites and Canaanites rather than the fear of God. Consistent with the perspective of that story, these verses continue to use Yahweh war language against Israel to depict this death: it is a generation of *warriors* (2:14, 16) that perishes, and it perishes because *the LORD's own hand was against them* (2:15) *[Yahweh War, p. 566]*. Now that generation has died, and a new start is possible. The last two comments on the wilderness period (2:14-15 and 2:16) prepare the way for a renewed bid to receive the land.

Historical Interruptions 2:10-12, 20-23

The historical interruptions reinforce God's gift of land with the use of some traditional material. Edom, Moab, and Ammon are not the original inhabitants of their lands. Previously the Horim occupied the land of Edom; the Emim, also known as the Rephaim, lived in the land of Moab. Rephaim also lived in the land of Ammon, although there they were called Zamzummim. Two of these are compared to the Anakim, legendary giants (cf. 1:28). The text notes that the current residents have in each case replaced the earlier populations. The insertions emphasize that Edom, Moab, and Ammon do not have a natural right to their lands but rather live there due to special action by Yahweh, the God of Israel. Without explicitly referring to the events of chapter 1, the story reminds its audience of Israel's earlier unfounded fear of the *stronger and taller* inhabitants of the land, which even included the Anakim (1:28).

THE TEXT IN BIBLICAL CONTEXT

God and the Nations

A central claim of Deuteronomy is that God has chosen Israel as a special people (e.g., 7:7-8). Deuteronomic theology is sometimes summarized as one God, one people, and one worship center. But such a slogan risks the temptation to turn the theological affirmation of "only Yahweh" into a political or ethnocentric claim for "only Israel." When affirmed together, the twin themes of monotheism and election can easily seduce a people into making distorted claims for itself and its understanding of God. Israel of the Old Testament fell prey to that temptation; the church of today commits the same error (Brueggemann 1998).

This passage, early in a book that emphasizes God's election of Israel, challenges such a misunderstanding. The God who led Israel out of Egypt, and now will give it the Promised Land, is also the God who gives other nations their land, and by implication is the God over other peoples as well. Amos similarly "seeks to undermine the assured mono-ideology of Israel ... by introducing a radical pluralism into the character of Yahweh, a pluralism that subverts Israel's self-confident mono-faith" (Brueggemann 1998: 20). To an audience believing that its election protected it, Amos proclaims, "Are you not like the Ethiopians to me, O people of Israel? says the LORD. Did I not bring up Israel from the land of Egypt, and the Philistines from Caphtor and the Arameans from Kir?" (9:7). God acts not only in Israel's story, but also in the stories of other nations.

This dominion of God over all nations has two sides to it: both sides are present in Deuteronomy, and both are vital biblical themes. On the one side, God's sovereignty is reflected in God's care for peoples beyond Israel, with the desire that all be blessed, as reflected in this passage. On the other side, this care means that other nations also will be punished for their transgressions (for consideration of this side, see TBC at ch. 32; cf. Amos 1–2). At their foundation both sides have the biblical story of creation, the account that sees God as the creator of all things and all peoples. Those early chapters of Genesis contain some of the most carefully reflected theology of all Scripture. They should not be read without seeing that if God is the creator of all, then that God also must be the God of and for all peoples, not only the God of one people.

Genesis 1–11 characterizes humanity as having the inevitable tendency to consider itself supreme, in the process rebelling against the God of creation. It is this reality that lies behind the selection of one family in Genesis 12 as a special people. The purpose of this selection is not just for the benefit of the people chosen, but also for the benefit of all. This is clear in God's call of Abraham and Sarah, "In you all the families of the earth shall be blessed" (Gen 12:3), and repeated later, "By your offspring shall all the nations of the earth gain blessing" (22:18). This promise only makes sense coming from a God who is God of all peoples.

At times the Israel of the Old Testament appears to forget this purpose of its election. It thinks of its God as a God whom Israel possesses for its own benefit. Deuteronomy itself places primary weight on the side of Israel's election and the punishment of other nations, even though at points it hints at a larger vision (e.g., 29:10-15). Israel's prophets remind the people of the universal aspect of God's reign. The prophetic oracles concerning nations other than Israel or Judah assume a God over all peoples. The story of Jonah wonderfully reminds Israel that other nations also can repent and turn to God. The book of Ruth highlights a Moabite woman who accepts the God of Israel as her God. Perhaps the clearest expression of this theology comes from the Isaianic prophet of the exile who announces concerning God's servant:

> It is too light a thing that you should be my servant
>   to raise up the tribes of Jacob
>   and to restore the survivors of Israel;
> I will give you as a light to the nations,
>   that my salvation may reach to the end of the earth. (Isa 49:6)

It is this tradition and emphasis that Jesus fulfils in his mission on earth. In his inaugural sermon at Nazareth, Jesus draws attention to the prophets Elijah and Elisha; both of them mediated God's saving mercy to people outside of Israel, Elijah to the widow of Zarephath, and Elisha to Naaman the Syrian (Luke 4:14-30). It is only at that point in the story that the Sabbath worshipers became "filled with rage" (Luke 4:28). Although Jesus himself devoted primary attention to the people of Israel, his last words to his disciples were a challenge to become witnesses of what they had heard and seen "to the ends of the earth" (Acts 1:8). In response to this direction, Paul then becomes the missionary to the Gentiles.

Deuteronomy may not contain the more fully developed theology of Isaiah 49 or the New Testament, or perhaps even of those wonderful stories of Ruth and Jonah. Deuteronomy remains interested first of all in God's special relationship to Israel. Yet at various points it undermines a too-simplistic reading of this emphasis. Israel's torah and relationship to God give witness to other nations (4:5-9, 32-34); Deuteronomy consistently calls for generosity toward the alien, even allowing the alien to become part of the covenant people (29:11-13). As Deuteronomy tells the story of Israel returning to the Promised Land, it highlights at least three other peoples who received their land due to their God's special action. Israel may be God's special possession (e.g., 7:6), but Yahweh is not Israel's possession: this story challenges any such understanding. Deuteronomy must be read with this reminder constantly in mind, along with the larger biblical story.

THE TEXT IN THE LIFE OF THE CHURCH

Theology versus Practice

The Christian church has sometimes contrasted the Old Testament with the New Testament by characterizing the God of the Old Testament as working only with one people, with Israel, whereas the God of the New Testament opens up the gospel to all peoples. Such a contrast is unfortunate, overly simplistic, and at least to some extent inaccurate.

Not only does the Old Testament understand the God who elected Israel as the God of all creation and all peoples; it also insists that God chose Israel as an instrument through which blessing and salvation are to flow to all peoples. As both the Old and New Testaments reflect, however, Israel developed into a Judaism that was more concerned about distinct identity, drawing clear lines between itself and others, and ritual purity than about being a light to the nations (e.g., Ezra 10; Neh 13; Matt 9:10-13; 12:1-14). The temptation was to focus only on its special relationship to God, and not on what that entailed for other peoples.

Jesus challenges this development and calls on the people of God to be faithful to God's desire that his salvation reach to the ends of the earth (Matt 28:18-19; Acts 1:8; cf. Isa 49:6). Thereby Jesus reaffirms the mission given Israel at its election: God is God of all peoples and nations; God's blessings, or the gospel, are not to be saved for a few select groups but are for all peoples.

When the Old and New Testaments are inappropriately contrasted as above, the contrast may be between the theology of the New Testament and the way in which Israel fulfilled its mandate. But is the Christian church really that different from Israel? Does not the Christian church all too often also fall into the temptation of forgetting that God truly is God of all peoples, traditions, and nations? Does the church become concerned primarily with its own salvation? The theology may be there, but is the practice consistent? We may accept a Ruth (someone who marries one of "us") into our midst, or even the occasional Rahab (Josh 6:25), but would we respond differently from Jonah if a city of outsiders responded to the gospel? It is so easy to compare our theology and ideals with the practices of others.

Deuteronomy 2:24–3:11

Retrospect: Hostile Confrontations

PREVIEW

So far so good. But what if the indigenous population is not as accommodating, comes across as fearsome, or threatens violence? The struggle to obtain or to defend a homeland echoes down the millennia of recorded human history. People desperate for resources are willing to kill to accomplish their needs. For the people of Israel, the Wadi Arnon marks the transition from peaceful encounters with distant relatives to violent confrontations with kings whom they totally destroy (2:2–3:11). Within the larger story of Israel, this passage depicts the beginning of an important new stage in its history with God. The long history without land, beginning with Abraham and Sarah, and continuing through the period of Egyptian bondage and wilderness wandering, is finally over. Israel has returned to the Promised Land and now begins to receive it. The lands of Sihon and Og become the first installment, or firstfruits, of the land promised to Israel's ancestors. The language—the rhetoric of Yahweh war—underscores that it is God *giving* the land. For Israel of the Old Testament, the story of these two encounters draws attention to the faithfulness and generosity of Yahweh [*Yahweh War, p. 566*].

For a modern reader, however, this part of the story raises serious questions. Was Israel really as warlike as this passage suggests? Did God really require Israel to destroy its enemies? Is this the same God whom Jesus represents in the New Testament? Inevitably, questions like these insert themselves into the discussion.

The passage ends with Israel once more at the boundary. A silent question arises: will this arrival end differently than the previous one (1:19–2:1)? The victories over Sihon and Og demonstrate to this generation that God as divine warrior can deliver, but then the previous generation similarly had experienced God in the exodus.

OUTLINE

Begin to Take Possession, 2:24-25
The Defeat of Sihon, King of Heshbon, 2:26-37
    2:26-30   Unsuccessful Peace Negotiations
    2:31   Yahweh Announces Victory
    2:32-36   The Victory Report
    2:37   Ammon Obediently Bypassed
The Defeat of Og, King of Bashan, 3:1-7
    3:1   Og Confronts Israel
    3:2   Yahweh Announces Victory
    3:3-7   The Victory Report
Concluding Summary, 3:8-11

Note: The Explanatory Notes for 2:24–3:11 have been organized as follows:
    Begin to Take Possession, 2:24-25
    Defeating Sihon and Og 2:26–3:7
        2:26-30 Unsuccessful Peace Negotiations
        2:31–3:7 Two Kings Defeated
        The Defeat of Sihon and Og as Yahweh War
        Battle Reports as Theology
    Concluding Summary 3:8-11

EXPLANATORY NOTES

Begin to Take Possession 2:24-25

"Get up! Get going! Cross the Wadi Arnon!" With these words Deuteronomy ushers in a new, exciting era in Israel's story. The Hebrew of the verse opens with three consecutive imperatives, giving the verse an abrupt start, an element that is lost in the smooth translation of the NRSV, *Proceed on your journey and cross the Wadi Arnon* (v. 24).

The tendency of translations not to begin a new paragraph at this point hides the fact that this verse represents a key juncture in the narrative. The period of wilderness wandering is over. The report of the death of all the warriors who had lost faith at the first arrival at the land signals the end of the previous generation (2:16). Now Israel is to get going. Finally, after hundreds of years of waiting, according to the logic of the story, Israel will receive the land. The new era begins now!

A fourth imperative calls Israel to attention—*See* [RSV, *Behold*], *I have handed over to you King Sihon . . . and his land*. This is the third use of the imperative *See* in Deuteronomy (cf. 1:8, 21), and it is used again later in the passage (2:31). In all four instances it is within direct speech of God, in each case opening a speech in which God announces that he has given Israel the land, and that Israel is now to take possession of it. The previous generation failed to respond in trust (1:19-45), but this is a new generation. "Watch carefully!" Be especially observant, the new generation is alerted.

Land is at the center of this passage, and indeed, all of Deuteronomy. Deuteronomy as a speech of Moses is placed at the edge of the Jordan, at the boundary of the main body of land promised Israel. Israel has already received a structure for the administration of justice in the land (1:9-18). After a disastrous first arrival at the land (1:19-2:1), the three peaceful encounters bring Israel to the land once again, even as they signify that there is land that has not been given to Israel but to other peoples (2:2-23). The two hostile confrontations begin the process of giving the land (2:24-3:11). After the travel reports of this passage cease, there is no more physical movement of Israel in the book of Deuteronomy. The history has been brought up to date: the Promised Land has been reached, with the remainder of Deuteronomy giving Moses' final charge to the people. The focus of that charge is life on the land, or more accurately, how to live in the land so as to enjoy its blessings.

One peculiarity about Deuteronomy's understanding of the Promised Land is that it includes the Transjordan. In most Old Testament traditions (e.g., boundary list of Num 34), the Promised Land is the land west of the Jordan River. The crossing of the Jordan, then, becomes the critical, almost cultic entrance into the Promised Land (cf. Josh 3-4). In those traditions the Transjordan is settled by Israel, but it does not hold the same status as the land west of the Jordan. For Deuteronomy, however, it is the crossing of the Wadi Arnon (2:24) that symbolizes the entrance into the land. Moab and Edom south of the Arnon are not part of the land; Ammon to the east of the kingdoms of Sihon and Og is not part of the land. But the Amorite kingdoms of Sihon and Og, located north of the Arnon in the Transjordan region and just east of the Jordan, are part of the land (see map, p. 570). The command to cross the Arnon thus is immediately followed by *I have handed over to you King Sihon the Amorite of Heshbon, and his land.*

Three further imperatives conclude the verse: *Begin! Take possession! Contend with him in battle!* (v. 24 AT). The last verb highlights the contrast between what lies ahead and the encounters Israel has had with Edom, Moab, and Ammon. Each of those narratives stress that God commands Israel *not* to contend (2:5, 9, 19) with those peoples. But those lands had not been given to Israel.

The battles, however, are not first of all between Israel and the armies of Sihon and Og, but between God and these enemies of Israel. Cultic Yahweh war language and motifs dominate the description *[Yahweh War, p. 566]*. God has *handed over to you* King Sihon, and God will put *dread and fear* in these people so that *they will tremble and be in anguish because of you*. In the story of the spies (1:19–2:1), Yahweh war language is directed against Israel (Israel fears the inhabitants of Canaan); here such language is used in a more traditional manner, with God on the side of Israel. The stories of the confrontations themselves (2:26-37; 3:1-7) continue this emphasis.

Defeating Sihon and Og 2:26–3:7

2:26-30 Unsuccessful Peace Negotiations

Setting the stage for the battle reports is a narrative relating Israel's request for peaceful passage through the land of King Sihon (vv. 26-30). Although attached to the Sihon story, it provides context for both confrontations. The text presents the hostile confrontations as beginning in a manner similar to the peaceful encounters, with Israel offering to pass through the land without any hostile intentions, wishing only to buy food and water.

The two requests are explicitly compared (v. 29), with Israel's offer to Sihon characterized as *terms of peace* (v. 26). The difference between the two sets is not in how Israel initiates the meeting but in the response of the other side. Whereas Edom and Moab accept Israel's peaceful proposal, Sihon (and by implication, Og) rejects it. Indeed, both kings take the initiative in coming out to meet Israel in battle (2:32; 3:1). The opening paragraph defends Israel against the possible accusation that it initiates the battles or that it enters the lands of Sihon and Og with unfriendly intentions. Israel is not the aggressor.

But is Sihon (or Og) the aggressor? Verse 30 concludes with *For the* LORD *your God had hardened his spirit and made his heart defiant in order to hand him over to you, as he has now done.* This assertion appears to make Sihon a pawn in God's hand, thus freeing him from responsibility for his actions—suggesting that Sihon is innocent and God is guilty. But such a verdict also is too simplistic. As it often does so elsewhere, Deuteronomy is reminding its audience of the events of the exodus, here with particular reference to the confrontation between God and the man/god Pharaoh (Exod 7–14).

Seventeen times Exodus speaks of Pharaoh's heart being hardened. But these expressions are of three distinct types:

1. God hardens Pharaoh's heart: Exod 7:3; 9:12; 10:1, 20, 27; 11:10; 14:4, 8.

2. Pharaoh hardens his own heart: Exod 8:15, 32; 9:34.

3. Pharaoh's heart is hardened (without specification as to who caused the hardening): Exod 7:13, 14, 22; 8:19; 9:7, 35.

All three formulations speak of the same reality, but if taken strictly as written, for a modern reader they represent a contradiction.

A characteristic of Hebrew poetry, but also prose, is to repeat the same thought in parallel lines or sentences, using different words or metaphors. Of the seventeen cases that speak of Pharaoh's heart, only one (10:1) is not accompanied by a statement of action on Pharaoh's part. Each of the other sixteen speak of Pharaoh's heart being hardened and in the same breath mention an action of Pharaoh that reflects or leads to that assessment. Notice the following example: "<u>He sinned once more</u> and <u>hardened his heart</u>, he and his officials. So <u>the heart of Pharaoh was hardened,</u> and <u>he would not let the Israelites go</u>" (Exod 9:34-35).

Six of the passages link Pharaoh's hardened heart to his refusal to listen to Moses and Aaron (7:3-4, 13, 22; 8:15, 19; 9:12), seven note his refusal to let the people leave Egypt (7:14; 8:32; 9:7, 35; 10:20, 27; 11:10), two refer to his pursuing Israel into the sea (14:4, 8), and one says, "He sinned once more" (9:34). Israel observed Pharaoh's refusal to listen to Moses and Aaron and experienced Pharaoh's refusal to let Israel leave. Based on its faith that God indeed was leading Israel out of Egypt, Pharaoh's actions could only be understood as rebellion against God, as sin, and as a reflection of a hardened heart. Given Israel's understanding of the sovereignty of God over all of history, the hardening of Pharaoh's heart had to have been God's doing as well. In speaking of this hardening in these different ways, the biblical text allows ambiguity. These statements are not arguing that God did it and not Pharaoh, but rather that Pharaoh did it but, given God's sovereignty, God also must have been involved. These texts are not taking a side in a debate between free will and determinism. The sovereignty of God and the free will of the human are both affirmed.

This is the world of the Deuteronomic report. The account of the peaceful encounters has emphasized God's supreme sovereignty over all. The text could not in the next few verses speak of Sihon's (and by implication, Og's) militant response as merely their exercise of free will. It was that, but it also was part of God's action in the world. Deuteronomy opens the section on the hostile confrontations by drawing attention to Israel's offer of peace, by noting Sihon's arrogant rejection of this offer, and by placing the whole under God's sovereignty.

2:31–3:7 *Two Kings Defeated*

These may be two separate reports and parts in the outline, but their parallel nature and structure suggest that they are one, two traditions shaped into one pattern, combined into one account. The following draws attention to the parallel language:

Deuteronomy 2:31-36	Deuteronomy 3:1-7
See, I have begun to give Sihon and his land over to you. (2:31)	For I have handed him over to you, along with his people and his land. (3:2)
Sihon came out against us, he and all his people, (2:32)	Og of Bashan came out against us, he and all his people, (3:1)
for battle at Jahaz. (2:32)	for battle at Edrei. (3:1)
The LORD our God gave him over to us; (2:33)	The LORD our God also handed over to us King Og. (3:3)
we struck him down. (2:33)	We struck him down (3:3)
At that time we captured all his towns; (2:34)	At that time we captured all his towns, (3:4)
in each town we utterly destroyed men, women, and children. (2:34)	We utterly destroyed them, . . . in each city utterly destroying men, women and children, (3:6)
We left not a single survivor (2:34)	until not a single survivor was left. (3:3)
Only the livestock we kept as spoil for ourselves, as well as the plunder of the towns. (2:35)	But all the livestock and the plunder of the towns we kept as spoil for ourselves. (3:7)
Reference to height of walls (2:36)	Reference to the height of the walls (3:5)

The Defeat of Sihon and Og as Yahweh War

The first half of each account gives the basic outline: God announces he has given the enemy king and his land into Israel's hand (in the Og account this is accompanied by the command *Do not fear him*; 3:2; cf. 1:29); it reports that the enemy king and his people come out to meet Israel for battle at a particular location; the confrontation is summarized by saying that God gave the enemy king to Israel; and it states, *We struck him down*. This is Yahweh war, with God the divine warrior winning the battle for Israel even if Israel participates in the final phase *[Yahweh War, p. 566]*.

The second part of each account begins with *At that time* (2:34; 3:4) and then presents a more detailed yet still stylized battle report. Behind the phrases translated *utterly destroy* (2:34; 3:6) and *utterly destroying* (3:6) lies a form of the Hebrew *ḥerem*, a term that suggests a ritualistic offering to God, with the implication that all is destroyed (2:34; 3:3). That military victories were understood as due to the work of God was not unique to Israel. As a sign of praise and thanksgiving to the god who had given the victory, that which was conquered and taken must be offered to the god through sacrifice as a burnt offering. The action thus has the quality of a cultic sacrifice about it. The god of the victory receives the spoil of the victory *[Cult, p. 546]*.

The Deuteronomic version of the ban is derived from this tradition (both here and in Deut 20) but tends to have a somewhat different emphasis. Little of the cultic devotion remains. One might even suggest a more pragmatic concern has taken over. In Deuteronomy, Israel's greatest temptation is to go after the gods of the original inhabitants of the land. Israel's later exile is attributed to Israel having fallen prey to this temptation. Deuteronomy's most drastic and radical policies or regulations are directed against this temptation (cf. Deut 13). The destruction of Sihon and Og and their peoples, according to Deuteronomy, is a "necessary step to ensure that Israel is not lured into paganism by the indigenous population of Canaan" (Cairns: 46).

In other words, Deuteronomy's concern is the exclusive worship of God and not how Israel goes to war (cf. 7:1-5). This also explains why the people are to be destroyed, but their cattle and possessions may be retained as booty (2:35; 3:7; over against the expectations of 20:16)—the temptation to follow other gods does not come from animals or noncultic property but from people. The accounts of the confrontations between Israel and the two Transjordan peoples thus have this framework. The tradition of Yahweh war, along with that of the ban, or *ḥerem*, is used to support Deuteronomy's central concern *[Ḥerem, p. 552; Yahweh War, p. 566]* (see discussion of 7:1-5).

Battle Reports as Theology

The parallel nature of the Deuteronomic descriptions of the two confrontations, combined with the extensive use of formulaic Yahweh war language, gives this passage a somewhat artificial quality. This becomes even more striking when the Deuteronomic passage is compared to the Numbers version of the confrontations.

In Numbers, the defeat of Sihon has a quite different character (Num 21:21-32): Moses plays no role in the confrontation; God is not mentioned at all, with no reference to God giving Israel the land; it reports that Israel "put him [Sihon] to the sword" with no reference to the destruction of people; there is no mention of livestock and booty; and it concludes with a taunt song against Moab. It is a secular battle report between two ancient powers. In contrast, the Numbers version of the defeat of Og, albeit short (only four verses, Num 21:32-35), includes key elements of the Deuteronomic version: Og comes out to meet Israel, God assures Moses not to be afraid for Yahweh has given Og into his hand, and a brief summarizing report is given stating that Israel killed all until no survivor remained, although without explicit reference to the ban.

It thus appears that Deuteronomy has reformulated the tradition (from Numbers or elsewhere) so as to emphasize the parallels between Sihon and Og and to make the strongest theological claims possible. Details and distinctions are lost. All is subordinated to its theological concerns. First, the account highlights God's faithfulness to his promises. God had been ready to give the land to the previous generation, but that generation lost faith. By implication, Deuteronomy is reminding its audience that they can continue to have confidence in God's promises.

Second, through the use of Yahweh war language, Deuteronomy underscores the sovereignty and power of its God. The kings and powers of the land, strong as they may be (e.g., *fortress towns with high walls, double gates and bars*, 3:5), are quite unable to obstruct God's will. The Israel of the eighth century BCE, facing Assyrian threat, as well as the Israel of the exile—both are reminded that they can trust in God: neither Assyria nor Babylon can thwart God.

Third, later Deuteronomy uses the tradition of *ḥerem* in support of its call for the exclusive worship of God (7:1-6). The ancient Near Eastern custom of the ban, the total devotion of the enemy to God, is adapted so that its cultic connotations fade into the background and it becomes a way of warning Israel to resist the temptation of serving the gods of the land. It is these concerns that are at the center of our passage, not the actual defeat of two early Amorite kings called Sihon and Og.

The last verse of the first account (2:37) ties these two conquest stories to the previous peaceful encounters as well as to the story of the spies (1:19-45). In contrast to the generation that arrived at the land the first time, this generation is depicted as faithful to God. It peacefully traverses the lands of Edom and Moab, and it does not encroach on the land of the Ammonites; it does not fear the kings Sihon and Og, *just as the LORD our God had charged*. Submission to the will of God is the way to blessing. It is intimated here, and it will be emphasized later in the book.

Concluding Summary 3:8-11

The last brief section surveys the land that Israel receives through the defeat of the Amorite kingdoms of Sihon and Og, again in parallel style. The land is first described in terms of its natural boundaries (v. 8), and then largely in terms of political regions (v. 10). The Transjordan is divided into three traditional parts: the central plateau, or *tableland*; Gilead, the region north of the plateau up to the Wadi Yarmuk; and Bashan, a rich agricultural area north of the Wadi Yarmuk (map, p. 570).

The passage concludes with a reference to the size of Og's bed (according to most translations). This is commonly taken as a reference to his sarcophagus (a stone coffin), with the term *iron* referring to black basalt, a stone used in the region for coffins. Maria Lindquist defends the literal translation and suggests it has as its background the Neo-Assyrian tradition that when it defeated Babylon, it captured as a war trophy the bed of the Babylonian god Marduk, which also happened to measure nine cubits by four cubits (roughly 4.5 x 3.5 meters). God here has defeated no mere human, but another god, or a legendary giant (Rephaim). The giants, and even gods of the land, so feared in the earlier story of the spies, have been defeated. A new era is open before them (Lindquist).

THE TEXT IN BIBLICAL CONTEXT

Sihon and Og as Symbols

Sihon and Og receive more attention in the Old Testament than one might expect. Excluding references to them in the stories of their defeat in Numbers 21 and Deuteronomy 2-3, Sihon is mentioned twenty-one times and Og sixteen times. The majority of these references are of two distinct groups. On a number of occasions Sihon and Og are mentioned where the gift of the land and its division are described (Sihon, in Josh 12:2, 5; 13:10, 21 [two times], 27; Og, in Deut 3:13, Num 32:33; Josh 12:4; 13:12, 30, 31). In ten other cases Sihon and Og are named together, frequently in the same sentence in parallel form, as the two Amorite kings defeated in the conquest. This style, present in Deuteronomy (1:4; 4:47-48; 29:7; 31:4), and also found in the Deuteronomistic History, that story of Israel influenced by Deuteronomy (Josh 2:10; 9:10; 1 Kings 4:19), becomes even more common in Israel's later literature (Neh 9:22; Pss 135:11; 136:19-20).

The way Deuteronomy speaks of these two kings appears to set the direction for these later passages. Their interest is not historical detail but symbolic value: they represent God as defeating the powers of the Promised Land. The two psalms referencing Sihon and Og are salvation-history psalms that survey the story of Israel as grounds for praising the God who provides deliverance. Notice the reference in Psalm 135:

> He it was who struck down the firstborn of Egypt,
>   both human beings and animals;
> he sent signs and wonders
>   into your midst, O Egypt,
>   against Pharaoh and all his servants.
> He struck down many nations
>   and killed many kings—
> Sihon, king of the Amorites,
>   and Og, king of Bashan,
>   and all the kingdoms of Canaan—
> and gave their land as a heritage,
>   a heritage to his people Israel. (Ps 135:8-12)

Immediately preceding the Sihon and Og reference is mention of the exodus from Egypt. Following is a short word of praise (Ps 135:13-14), and then comes a longer section discounting the gods of the nations as idols made by human hands.

Psalm 136 moves from the exodus to the wilderness to the defeat of Sihon and Og and the gift of land, and then concludes with a short section praising God for his providential nature. Nehemiah 9 has a short piece on the exodus (9:9-11), a lengthy section on the whole wilderness period (9:12-21), and then a passage on the entrance into the Promised Land (9:22-25) in which Sihon and Og are the only specific kings or places mentioned. In each of these three passages, Sihon and Og provide the sole references for Israel's entrance into the land. Surprisingly, the capture of Jericho and Ai, two stories that play such an important role in the conquest in the book of Joshua (and in contemporary consideration of the entrance), are not mentioned. Sihon and Og have become the primary symbols, one might almost say ciphers, for the faith that God has given Israel the land.

This dehistoricizing of Sihon and Og continues in Jewish tradition (Ginzberg et al. 1: 160; 3: 339–48). Sihon and Og appear as descendants of fallen angels who were five hundred years old by the time Moses confronted them. They have both become monstrous giants (cf. Deut 3:11). In such lore, Og already lived at the time of the flood but was so huge that he could not fit into Noah's ark, so he had to sit on top. Later Og attempts to get Abraham killed so he can have his wife, Sarah. The cities of Sihon and Og also have grown in these legends. Og supposedly founded sixty cities, each surrounded by high walls, the lowest of which was sixty miles in height. Og meets his end when a mountain he is carrying on his head slides down over his neck, thereby imprisoning him, and Moses leaps high in the air, strikes his ankle, and kills him. The armies of Sihon kill each other after God draws masks on their faces and they mistake each other for Israelites (cf. Judg 7:9-23). Any historical Sihon and Og gradually disappear as the stories highlight their symbolic value, a development already evident in Deuteronomy.

The Gift of Land within Scripture

In a book titled *The Land: Place as Gift, Promise, and Challenge in Biblical Faith*, Walter Brueggemann argues, "Land is a central [theme], if not *the central theme* of biblical faith" (1977: 3). The whole book then systematically surveys the theological significance of land in Scripture, both Old and New Testaments. He may overstate the point, but there is little question that land is an important biblical theme.

Israel understands its story as beginning in a promise of land to Abraham and Sarah, who left their land at the request of God (Gen 12). Abraham and Sarah travel to the land that God promised them, but throughout their lives they remain sojourners, without real ownership of land. Eventually their descendants settle in Egypt, but it becomes a land of slavery. God does deliver them from Egypt, but a whole generation of wandering in the wilderness passes away before the promise to the ancestors is finally fulfilled and Israel receives the land. Genesis to Deuteronomy is moved forward by anticipation of land, and looks forward to the fulfillment of the promise. The story of Deuteronomy 2:24–3:7 represents a first installment of this fulfillment, with Joshua the account of its completion.

The story of Israel in the land—as told in Judges to Kings, retold in 1 and 2 Chronicles, and reflected in a number of the prophetic books—is a checkered story at best. The Old Testament recognizes some high points, such as the reign of David, the building of the temple by Solomon, the reigns of Hezekiah and Josiah, and the faithfulness of the prophets; but on the whole it is a story of a gift abused. The final verdict is that Israel failed in its obligation to be faithful to the God who had given the land; its life on the land was not consistent with the true nature of that land as a gift from God. Both 2 Kings and 2 Chronicles record Israel's loss of land, first as Assyria overthrows the Northern Kingdom and then as Babylon defeats Judah and destroys Jerusalem, including the symbol of God's presence, the temple. Exile to Babylon is the consequence. Once again the people find themselves in a foreign country, far away from the land given them. Once again they dream of a return to their land.

When the return happens, a community reestablishes itself over the ruins of Jerusalem. It constructs a new temple, with Ezra and Nehemiah instrumental in the development of a strong sense of identity based on a commitment to the torah that God gave them. The national state was not revived, but the people were back on the land. Eventually Jewish communities flourished, with Jerusalem as their center, until Jerusalem was again destroyed, this time by the Romans in 70 CE. This gift of land is front and center for the Old Testament.

Jesus came into this context. Against the common tendency to understand the New Testament as having spiritualized the Old Testament's teaching on land, Brueggemann makes a strong case for greater continuity than is usually acknowledged. Christ and the early church recognized that God was concerned with the real things of life—freedom, health, food, and so forth—all of which are only possible on the land. The same challenge also applies in the New Testament: a grasping for land leads to loss of land, and treating land as gift leads to realizing the blessings of the land. Jesus' beatitude "Blessed are the meek, for they will inherit the earth" (Matt 5:5) is consistent with this.

Our passage thus addresses a central biblical theme: land is a gift of God. The Yahweh war ideology within which this passage is written does create a challenge for the modern reader, but it guards against Israel ever thinking that it possesses the land due to its military strength or superior cunning or righteousness or whatever other reason one might imagine (Deut 9:4-6). Israel has use of the land for only one reason, and that is because God has given it. This is the crucial starting point for the theology of Deuteronomy.

THE TEXT IN THE LIFE OF THE CHURCH
Misreading the Story

The stories of Israel's conquest have been an embarrassment to some and the source of considerable satisfaction to others. Crusaders in the eleventh to thirteenth centuries used these stories to justify their efforts at conquering the Holy Land, American settlers used these stories to support their actions, Afrikaner leaders used them to justify the displacement of the black population in South Africa (see "Deuteronomy and the Scandal of Violence" in the introduction).

But these are all misuses. Within the Old Testament, stories of Yahweh war were not used to *justify* a particular course of action (such as initiating war against an enemy), but rather to *explain* a particular situation (Israel's presence in the land) and to *encourage* greater faith and obedience. Israel did not deserve the land or win it; instead, Israel was given the land. These stories do not justify aggression but rather call for living with land and possessions in a manner that truly recognizes God and God's gifts. This is the spirit of Deuteronomy.

Duane Christensen puts it this way:

> It is important to remember that this account of Israel's conquest of Transjordan, as well as the subsequent summons to take Cisjordan (3:18-22), is presented in the language of Holy War. It is difficult to move from these pages directly into history per se. This is schematized history, presented as theology to encourage obedience and trust on the part of each new generation who celebrated these events. YHWH, the God of Israel, is a God of might and power who will deliver those who place their trust in Him. In terms of Deuteronomic theology we are to face the future in confidence, with full awareness of what God has already done for us in the past. (2001: 61-62)

Approaching these stories in this way does not resolve all theological difficulties. As with the problem of evil (how can an all-powerful, all-loving God allow humans to inflict violence upon each other?) and the problem of judgment and punishment (how does one relate God's merciful, gracious nature to judgment?), simple answers are inadequate. In fact, these narratives draw attention to the challenge and complexity of speaking about God as working in our world. But they cannot be used to justify actions that do violence to fellow human beings. Such use is in tension with the role these stories play within Deuteronomy, or within the Old Testament as a whole, and most clearly it is in conflict with the revelation of Jesus Christ.

Deuteronomy 3:12-29
Retrospect: Final Arrangements for Crossing the Jordan

PREVIEW

Sometimes, just before we head out on an important trip or other venture, we pause to review. We may feel ready to move forward but then discover that a few things still need to be taken care of. Likewise for the people of Israel. This Retrospect (1:6–3:29) concludes with four brief paragraphs tying together loose ends, each set off and introduced by the phrase *at that time* (3:12, 18, 21, 23). Unfortunately, most translations do not follow the signal of this key phrase and divide the section into fewer than four paragraphs. A verse situating Israel geographically concludes the section.

The four paragraphs (1) allocate the Transjordan to the tribes of Reuben, Gad, and half of the tribe of Manasseh; (2) challenge these three tribes to represent their unity with the other tribes by sending their warriors across the Jordan to assist their kin in taking possession of the land west of the Jordan; (3) portray Moses encouraging Joshua as he prepares to lead the tribes across the Jordan; and (4) report one more futile appeal to God by Moses to be allowed to cross the Jordan with the people. The chapter concludes with Israel camped *in the valley opposite Beth-peor*, ready to cross the Jordan. But according to the logic of Deuteronomy, first it must hear the final instructions, or testament, of Moses.

OUTLINE

Allocation of the Land beyond the Jordan, 3:12-17
    3:12-13a   Allocation of Land to Reuben, Gad, and Half of Manasseh
    3:13b   Historical Interruption
    3:14-17   More Detailed Description of Allotments
Solidarity for the Crossing, 3:18-20
Charge to Joshua: *Fear Not!* 3:21-22
Moses Denied Permission to Cross the Jordan, 3:23-28
    3:23-25   Moses' Request: *Let Me Cross*
    3:26-28   Yahweh's Response: *No*
Geographical Location: Valley opposite Beth-peor, 3:29

EXPLANATORY NOTES

Allocation of the Land beyond the Jordan 3:12-17

After presiding over God's defeat of the Amorites in the Transjordan (2:24–3:11), Moses allocates their land to the tribes of Reuben, Gad, and half the tribe of Manasseh. The logic and process is parallel to the book of Joshua, in which chapters 1–5 concentrate on crossing the Jordan (cf. crossing of Wadi Arnon in Deut 2:24), chapters 6–12 cover the conquest of the land west of the Jordan (cf. defeat of Sihon and Og in Deut 2:26–3:7), and chapters 13–19 distribute the land among the tribes (cf. Deut 3:12-17).

In contrast to Numbers and Joshua, Deuteronomy treats the Transjordan as part of the Promised Land. After lengthy negotiations, Numbers only allows Reuben and Gad to settle east of the Jordan (Num 32); and in Joshua the tribes west of the Jordan speak of the Transjordan as "unclean," with land on the west side "the LORD's land" (Josh 22:19). In these books the Transjordan is not fully part of the Promised Land, so the crossing of the Jordan becomes the critical event (note emphasis in Josh 1–5). In Deuteronomy the defeat of the kingdoms of the Transjordan becomes the first stage in the giving of the Promised Land, with its allocation beginning the fulfillment of the promise. The Retrospect of Deuteronomy 1:6–3:29 thus ends with two and half tribes having received their portion of the promise. This first installment, or firstfruits, is a sign of what the other tribes also will experience.

As reflected in the outline, the paragraph summarizes the allocation twice, first briefly (3:12-13a), and then in more detail (vv. 14-17), assigning Reuben and Gad to the southern half of the Transjordan, the plateau area north of the Wadi Arnon and the southern half of Gilead; and putting the half tribe of Manasseh in the northern half, with Bashan going to Jair and the northern half of Gilead to Machir. The passage understands Jair and Machir to be two descendants of Manasseh, or parts of that tribe, although at some point Machir may have been a separate tribe (cf. Judg 5:14). The phrase *to this day* reminds us that considerable time has passed between the allocation and the time of Deuteronomy.

The success of the victory over Sihon and Og and of allocating the land to the tribes raises hope that this generation is more faithful than the one that arrived the first time (1:19-45). Whereas accounts of the victory consistently speak of God as acting, now God is not mentioned, and Moses is the main actor. In the space of these few verses, four times we read, *I gave* . . . The allocation of the land to specific tribes makes the possession concrete, but it remains secondary after the primary action of conquest (Brueggemann 2001: 44).

Solidarity for the Crossing 3:18-20

After allocating the Transjordan to Reuben, Gad, and half of Manasseh, Moses addresses these tribes (the *you* of v. 18) and requests that they accompany the rest of Israel as it crosses the Jordan into the main part of the Promised Land. They may have received a first installment of the land, but Israel's task is complete only when *all tribes* have received their portion and *rest* on the land (v. 20). Here is a further example of Deuteronomy's emphasis on the unity of all Israel (cf. the *all Israel* of 1:1). Recent studies on the early history of Israel, supported by the biblical text (e.g., Josh 22; Judg 5:17-21), make it clear that early Israel was far from a unified, peaceful people. For Deuteronomy, however, Israel is one. Regardless of how Israel came to be historically, regardless of the intertribal tensions and even warfare that took place over the years, Deuteronomy treats Israel as one people, united through its covenant with its God, Yahweh.

This theological conviction of Deuteronomy has practical implications. Even after they have received their share of the inheritance, the Transjordan tribes are expected to contribute to the larger good and well-being of the people. Fulfillment of the promise is complete only once all tribes have received their share. This need to place the welfare of the larger community above that of individual members or small groups, as represented here, becomes an important principle in later instructions of the book. "The prosperity and blessings we receive turn sour unless they prompt us to ensure that our fellow human beings also receive their share" (Cairns: 49).

Unlike the Numbers version of the story, with its negotiations, the charge here is straightforward and appears to be well received (Num 32:16-27; cf. Josh 1:12-16). Deuteronomy's emphasis on the goodness of the land, and the bounty and wealth that the conquest gives Israel (cf. 6:10-11), also means the tribes do not need to build their own sheepfolds and towns, but simply occupy those that Moses has *given to you* (3:19; cf. Num 32:16).

A further important Deuteronomic concept is introduced in verse 20 with the words *When the LORD gives rest to your kindred* (cf. 12:9-10; 25:19). For Deuteronomy, the term *rest* basically means salvation. It cannot be spiritualized as referring to a vague peace of mind, but as Gerhard von Rad suggested in an important study years ago, it is the "tangible peace granted to a nation plagued by enemies and weary of wandering" (note 12:10). It can only be a gift from God. "The life of the chosen people in the 'pleasant land,' at rest from all enemies round about, the people owning their love for God and God blessing his people—this is the epitome of the state of the redeemed nation as *Deuteronomy* sees it" (Rad 1933: 95). The tribes of Reuben, Gad, and half of Manasseh have received their rest, or at least the first stage of it; the remaining tribes still look forward to it. Only after all the tribes have received their share of the land and are at peace will Israel truly have its rest.

Deuteronomic rest theology provides both hope and encouragement, as well as challenge, to its earliest audiences. If one imagines the people hearing Moses on the plains of Moab, the reference to rest is fairly straightforward: soon all of the tribes will have received their inheritance and Israel's wandering will cease. For a later Israel receiving this message, its essence is more complex. Enemies remained a threat after the entrance and indeed throughout the time of the monarchy. Some sense of security may have been achieved during the time of David (cf. 2 Sam 7:1), but with the defeat and exile of the Northern Kingdom, even that "rest" is significantly undermined. At that point Deuteronomy may be reminding Israel of the rest it has received, even as it subtly suggests that this rest cannot be taken for granted; continuing disregard of the instructions of Deuteronomy risks the possibility of losing this rest. To a sixth-century audience in exile, the hope element of the passage comes to the fore once again. When read together with passages like 30:1-5 (*God will bring you into the land that your ancestors possessed, and you will possess it*, 30:5), the references to rest take on new meaning. The land has been lost, but God continues to want rest for his people. It is the will of God that people receive rest in their "land." After the return from exile, the challenge aspect of the passage would again become prominent.

Charge to Joshua: *Fear Not!* 3:21-22

References to Moses' death and his succession by Joshua appear throughout the opening and closing chapters of Deuteronomy. Eight times attention turns to Joshua as the future leader of Israel (1:38; 3:21-22, 28; 31:3, 7-8, 14-23; 32:44; 34:9-12), always in close proximity to some mention of Moses' death. Deuteronomy is preparation for the future, for life in the land under God. But this future will come about only through suffering and death, first the demise of the generation that died in the wilderness, and second, the death of Moses himself.

This charge to Joshua assumes both the conclusion of the following verses (3:23-28), in which Moses is refused permission to cross the Jordan, and the command of God to Moses (3:28). The Hebrew term translated *charge* is translated "commission/ed" in the parallel Numbers passage (27:19, 23). The different translation may be justified, however, since the Numbers passage has other signs pointing to a formal ceremony. In Numbers, Moses places his hands on Joshua's head before Eleazar the priest and the gathered people. Some of Moses' authority is given Joshua, and "he shall stand before Eleazar the priest, who shall inquire for him by the decision of the Urim before the LORD" (Num 27:21). The exact nature of this last action is unclear, but the passage as a whole suggests a religious ceremony commissioning someone to a formal office. In Deuteronomy the more formal commissioning takes place later (31:7-8, 14-15, 23). The emphasis here is encouragement.

Just as the book as a whole is teaching for Israel, these verses are Moses' counsel for Joshua, with the language and logic typically Deuteronomic. First is the reference to learning from experience. Joshua has seen what Yahweh has done. Regularly Israel is reminded of what it has seen (1:30, 31; 4:3, 9, 34, 35; 5:24; 6:22; 7:19; 9:17; 10:21; 11:7; 29:2, 3). References to the past serve to encourage Israel, and here Joshua, for the future. Second, typical Yahweh war language is used to encourage Joshua in preparation for his future role: *Do not fear them* [cf. 1:21, 29; 3:2], *for it is the LORD your God who fights for you* (3:22). Just as Israel is not to fear, so Joshua is not to fear.

Moses Denied Permission to Cross the Jordan 3:23-28

After encouraging Joshua, Moses makes one further emotional plea to be able to *cross over to see the good land beyond the Jordan* (v. 25). God had already disclosed to Moses that this was not to be (1:37). As part of the generation that lost faith upon first arriving at the land, even though individually not guilty, Moses is to share in their punishment. But that whole generation had *perished from the camp* (2:14, 16), yet Moses continues to lead the people. Is it possible that God has changed his mind about Moses?

The present passage at least hints that Moses may have thought so. One more time he entreats God to be allowed to cross the Jordan and see the land. The Hebrew term translated *entreated* (3:23) literally means he appeals to God to treat him with grace, or favor. The request is certainly not unreasonable. God is known to change his mind in response to the prayers of his people. Abraham negotiated hard and long for the city of Sodom (Gen 18:16-33), and more than once Moses successfully appealed to God on behalf of Israel (e.g., Exod 32:11-14; Num 14:13-25). Here he prays that he be allowed to see the completion of what God has started.

The prayer is an extraordinary combination of humility and boldness. The opening phrase, *O Lord GOD*, is used only twice in Deuteronomy, both times in prayers of Moses appealing to God to change his mind (cf. 9:26). The God he is praying to is his master and lord. Consistent with this stance of meekness, Moses identifies himself as *your servant.* Verse 25 contains a Hebrew expression translated *I pray* in the RSV (omitted from the NRSV). Yet he does not shy away from making his case as strongly as possible. God's greatness and might (language mostly used of the exodus, yet here also including God's actions against the Transjordan kingdoms) and uniqueness (cf. 4:7-8, 32-39) are appealed to in an effort to convince God to allow him to *cross over to see the good land.* God's answer (*Enough from you! Never speak to me of this matter again!* v. 26) suggests that Moses has been persistent in his request. The prayer is a brave plea from someone who has served God well and has dared to challenge God before.

Despite the plea, the answer remains "no." The expression used for God's anger is strong (v. 26). In Psalm 78 it is used twice, first as in "he was full of <u>wrath</u>" (v. 59), and then again in verse 62: "He gave his people to the sword, and vented his <u>wrath</u> on his heritage." Simply inserting that sense into our passage may be too harsh since the specific word choice may well have been influenced by the immediate context. The term itself is based on the same Hebrew root as the verb "to cross." These verses thus involve a wordplay, or a pun, on the term "cross." The passage begins with Moses requesting permission to "cross the Jordan." The response then could be translated, *but the* LORD *was cross with me* (v. 26 AT), with the continuation, *for you shall not cross the Jordan* (v. 27). God does not grant Moses' request, but the passage does not imply that the request, or even Moses' persistence, were inappropriate. God's answer to prayer cannot be a guaranteed "yes."

Yet God's response is not only negative. Moses' request involves two components, to *cross over* and to *see the good land beyond the Jordan* (v. 25). Although perhaps not as intended by Moses, the second part is granted. God commands Moses to ascend to the top of Pisgah, from which he is to raise his eyes over the whole land, and *Look well!* (AT, lit., *see with your eyes*; cf. v. 25), and concludes with the phrase *the land that you will see* (v. 28). Moses may not be allowed to cross the Jordan, but he is given permission to see the land.

Behind this language lies the story of Abraham and Lot (Gen 13). After Abraham and Lot separate, with Lot settling in the cities of the plains and Abraham in Canaan, God says to Abraham, "Raise your eyes now, and look from the place where you are, northward and southward and eastward and westward; for all the land that you see I will give to you and to your offspring forever" (Gen 13:14-15). At that time Abraham was promised the land, but he could only behold it and sojourn in it. Similarly, now Moses is asked to survey the land. Like Abraham, he is unable to settle down on it, but he is able to see the land. In ancient legal custom, a formal seeing the land was a form of accepting the grant (cf. 1:8). The land had been promised to the ancestors, and it was given formally at the beginning of Deuteronomy (1:8); in viewing the land, Moses now accepts it. All that remains is the actual taking possession of that which has been given.

With Moses now definitely denied permission to cross the Jordan, attention turns to Joshua. His is the role of leading Israel across the Jordan into the land and taking possession of it. Moses is asked to encourage and strengthen him for the task (cf. 1:38; 3:21-22; 31:3, 7-8, 14-23; 32:44; 34:9-12). (For further discussion of the theme of Moses' death, see comments on 1:37; 4:21-24; 31:1-6; 32:48-52; 34:1-8.)

Geographical Location: Valley opposite Beth-peor 3:29

The introduction to Deuteronomy (1:1-5) opened and concluded by placing Israel *in the wilderness, on the plain opposite Suph,* and *beyond the Jordan, in the land of Moab*. The Retrospect has told the story of how Israel came to that location, beginning from its stay at Mount Horeb. The Retrospect concludes by once more locating Israel geographically, this time identifying it as *the valley opposite Beth-peor*.

Across the Jordan from Beth-peor is Shittim, the place where Numbers reports, "Israel yoked itself to the Baal of Peor" (Num 25:1-5). Is Deuteronomy subtly warning the audience that Israel is ready to cross the Jordan, but that the crossing is fraught with danger and temptation (Brueggemann 2001: 46)? In order to survive the crossing and life in the land, Israel will need to heed the instructions it will receive from Moses in the remainder of the book.

THE TEXT IN BIBLICAL CONTEXT
At Rest, and Yet Not

The Israel of Deuteronomy is situated on the banks of the Jordan, with two and a half tribes having received their portion of the Promised Land, and the remainder still looking forward to that milestone. A portion of Israel has reached its rest; the majority still anticipates it. The tension between having received rest and looking forward to receiving it does not end with the account of Israel crossing the Jordan and taking possession of the land. Rather, the tension reflected by the location of the Israel of Deuteronomy is lasting. Deuteronomy freezes the moment and in so doing paints a picture of reality as Israel experienced it, and as the New Testament depicts it.

After Israel crosses the Jordan, it does receive the land, and the biblical text does say, "And the LORD gave them rest on every side" (Josh 21:44), but enemies remain and peace is elusive. The book of Judges has story after story of Israel tyrannized by assorted peoples of the region. Finally, under David, a level of security is reached, and we read, "Now when the king was settled in his house, and the LORD had given him rest from all his enemies around him" (2 Sam 7:1). Israel had to wait generations after entering the land before this rest arrived.

Yet even then rest is not complete. Israel still awaits a unifying religious center. The building of the temple under Solomon addresses this need, and 1 Kings 8:56 announces "Blessed be the LORD, who has given rest to his people Israel according to all that he promised." Rest appears to be achieved in stages, with each new stage revealing that rest has not been fully achieved: true rest always remains in the future, a vision that inspires and fills the present. The defeat of the Northern Kingdom and later the destruction of Jerusalem, exile, and return continue this pattern. God wishes his people to have rest, but human sinfulness interferes, sometimes allowing only a partial rest, sometimes causing removal from the land and the rest it has the potential to provide.

That same tension continues in the New Testament with kingdom language. John the Baptist introduces Jesus with language borrowed from the unnamed prophet of Israel's exile who centuries earlier announced Israel's return to the land and its rest (Matt 3:3; cf. Isa 40:3). Through his teaching, healings, and death and resurrection, Jesus brings in this new kingdom, this new rest. With language reminiscent of Deuteronomy, he offers those who are weary rest (Matt 11:28-30). Yet even its full realization remains elusive. Sin and evil continue to disrupt and obstruct the full reality of the kingdom. The book of Hebrews continues this conversation on entering rest (esp. ch. 4). The church thus looks forward and prays as Jesus taught his followers, "Your kingdom come" (Matt 6:10). Deuteronomy, as Jesus did, will paint a picture of what life can be and should be like once rest has been received, even if not in its fullness, with the faithful invited to already live in that rest today.

THE TEXT IN THE LIFE OF THE CHURCH
Living on the Way to Full Rest

Most Christians in North America have received rest, but not completely. We may have much—home, job with security, family, friends—but full rest remains elusive. All human relationships have their tenuous quality: despite modern technology, sickness has not been defeated. As represented by Israel on the plains of Moab, and even as experienced by Israel in the Promised Land, the rest we do have is incomplete and points ahead to a fuller rest that God holds before us in the future, a rest that only God can provide. The New Testament thus speaks of Christ returning and of a new heaven and a new earth in which there will be no more sorrow. We thus only live in a state of partial rest, or anticipated rest. Deuteronomy invites us to worship God wholly (chs. 5–26), expressing this worship in a particular manner of living (chs. 12–26).

Yet even in North America, and perhaps especially elsewhere, many do not share in that partial rest that the privileged few have. Poverty, abuse, illness or death, or broken relationships may have taken over to the extent that all sense of rest has been displaced. Like the Israel in the wilderness or the Israel in exile, rest is only a faint glimmer in the distance. But, Deuteronomy says, the hope for rest remains. God wants rest for his people. And as will be announced later in the book (e.g., 30:1-10), God will provide that rest.

Deuteronomy 4:1-43
Prospect

PREVIEW

One can stay in the past only so long without neglecting the responsibilities and opportunities of the hour. Good preaching addresses and challenges the present even as it speaks of the past and for the future. We followed Israel as it journeyed from Horeb to Beth-peor in the plains of Moab, with the Transjordan representing the firstfruits of the gift of land. But before the land is fully taken, the journey halts for the people to receive guidance on how to live in the land. The Retrospect, Moses' opening words during this pause (1:6–3:29), already is part of that guidance. Now for the people at the boundary, the focus shifts from the past to the present and then stretches out into the future. The first speech of Moses concludes by placing that future in the land under the rubric of "Obey, or else!"

The shift in focus is matched by a shift in style. Historical survey changes to exhortation. The more subtle teaching of the Retrospect, through its nuanced telling of stories, changes to explicit preaching as the hortatory style with its "do's" and "don'ts" vocabulary so often associated with Deuteronomy takes over. Imperatives are characteristic of this sermonizing, such as these: *Give heed* (4:1). *You must neither add anything . . . nor take away anything, . . . but keep the commandments* (4:2). *See* (4:5). *You must observe them* (4:6). *But take care and watch yourselves closely* (4:9). This style dominates the first part of Moses' second speech (chs. 5–11), and remains prominent for the rest of the book.

The message is simple, yet complex. The simple side is reflected in the repeated and consistent correlation of obedience with long life in the land (cf. 4:1, 5, 23-24, 40). Israel may be unique (vv. 4-8), and Yahweh, the God of Israel, may be unique (vv. 32-39), but a blessed life for Israel in the land is contingent upon remembering and obeying. Disobedience will lead to exile, with Israel scattered among the peoples (e.g., 4:26). The second commandment, the prohibition of images, takes center stage in the discourse (vv. 9-31). Obey, or else!

Yet it is not that simple. Even as the address warns Israel that its fate will be determined by the people's response to the torah, it raises questions about that very emphasis. Disobedience does lead to exile, but that is not the last word. God's determination is more powerful. God will not forget the ancestral covenant; life will overcome death. A fascinating interplay between God's mercy and God's judgment results (4:23-31).

OUTLINE

Opening Challenge, 4:1-4
The Uniqueness of Israel, 4:5-8
Preaching against Graven Images, 4:9-31
    4:9-14   Basis of the Command
    4:15-22   Expounding the Command
    4:23-31   Consequences of Disobeying the Command
The Uniqueness of the God of Israel, 4:32-39
Concluding Challenge, 4:40
Appendix: Designating Cities of Refuge, 4:41-43

EXPLANATORY NOTES

The discourse has three major elements arranged in chiastic structure [Chiasm, p. 540]: an outer frame consisting of the introduction and conclusion (A^1 and A^2); an inner frame consisting of two expressions of uniqueness, first of Israel and then of Yahweh, the God of Israel (B^1 and B^2); and a central section of preaching on the basis of the second commandment (Olson). The central section is also divided into three parts, with the actual explanation of the second commandment (D) surrounded by arguments for the commandment, one based in history (C^1), and one in the negative consequences of disobedience (C^2). The structure, as reflected in the diagram below, draws attention to the central significance of the second commandment.

A^1 Opening Challenge, 4:1-4
    B^1 The Uniqueness of Israel, 4:5-8

  C¹ Basis of Command: Yahweh, without Form, Declared
            Covenant at Horeb, 4:9-14
    D Expounding the Command, 4:15-22
  C² Consequences of Disobeying the Command: Exile, but
              Also Mercy, 4:23-31
 B² The Uniqueness of the God of Israel, 4:32-39
A² Concluding Challenge, 4:40
  Appendix: Designating Cities of Refuge, 4:41-43

The opening *So now* both indicates a significant new start and connects what follows with the preceding three chapters. The historical survey remains very much in mind even as attention turns forward to life on the land and beyond. The references to Israel's past continue, but now they are used as evidence for particular arguments (vv. 3-4, 10-14, 15, 20, 33-38).

The next phrase sets the tone for the whole chapter: *Give heed to the statutes and ordinances that I am teaching you to observe.* Exhortations of this sort govern the spirit and structure of the discourse. They function as key markers of the six main units (1-4, 5-8, 9-14, 15-22, 23-31, 32-39), as each unit begins with summoning Israel to specific action: *Give heed* (v. 1). *See* (v. 5). *But take care and watch yourselves closely* (vv. 9, 15). *So be careful not to forget the covenant* (v. 23). *For ask now about former ages* (v. 32). And finally, *Keep his statutes and commandments* (v. 40).

Opening Challenge 4:1-4
Concluding Challenge 4:40

The first three chapters of Deuteronomy may have sounded like mere storytelling, if there ever is such a thing, but with the Prospect the nature and purpose of Deuteronomy becomes quite transparent. This longer passage is framed by verses 1 and 40, both of which outline the key elements of the book. Deuteronomy is the *teaching* of *statutes and ordinances* to *Israel* so that Israel will *observe* them, with the goal to *live* long in *the land* God is *giving* it (4:1). Each of the key terms is included in the first verse, and each plays an important role in the theology of Deuteronomy.

Deuteronomy presents Moses as the supreme *teacher*, a role intimated in the introduction to the book (*Moses undertook to expound this law as follows*, 1:5), and now made explicit (4:1, 5, 14; according to vv. 5 and 14, at the express command of Yahweh). Deuteronomy uses some form of the Hebrew root *lmd* (translated "teach" or "learn," depending on the exact form used) seventeen times, more often than any other book of the Old Testament except the much longer book of Psalms (e.g., *learn* in Deut 5:1; *teach* in 6:1). Since Moses is the teacher, Deuteronomy may be called teaching. A recent book on Deuteronomy suggests that the most helpful category within which to understand Deuteronomy is catechesis, "the process of education in faith from one generation to another based on a distillation of essential tradition" (Olson: 11). In Deuteronomy Moses the great teacher shares the essentials of Yahwism with the next generation just before he dies.

The specific content of that teaching is *statutes and ordinances*. Deuteronomy uses a series of terms for the substance of the teaching: statutes, ordinances, commandments, and testimonies are most common. In 4:1-43 alone *statutes* is used six times (vv. 1, 5, 6, 8, 14, 40); *ordinances* appears four times (vv. 1, 5, 8, 14), always as a pair with *statutes*. Although it is likely these two terms (as well as *commandments* and *testimonies*) originally each had its own connotations, in Deuteronomy they become virtually interchangeable synonyms. Generally they refer to the central section of the book, chapters 5-28, with its exhortation (chs. 5-11), teaching through specific regulations (chs. 12-26), and the instructions for covenant renewal (chs. 27-28), but they can also be a broad reference to the contents of the book of Deuteronomy as a whole, including its narratives and other miscellaneous material. This is the torah of Deuteronomy. The book does distinguish between the Ten Commandments and this whole torah (see discussion of 5:22-27), but all is designated by the phrase *statutes and ordinances*, along with its parallel terms in the book.

The warning to *neither add . . . nor take away anything from it* refers to this whole torah. Similar warnings are found elsewhere (cf. Deut 12:32; Prov 30:6; Eccl 3:14; Jer 26:2; Rev 22:18-19). The differences between the Decalogue in Deuteronomy and the Decalogue of Exodus clarify "that the reference is to the *essence* of the law, not the *letter* of the law" (Craigie 1976: 130). The background to such expressions is the larger world of the day, with its political treaties, official documents, and prophetic literature, that used similar injunctions.

Moses' teaching is directed at *Israel*, that people chosen by God for a special mission (cf. Gen 12:3). More than most books of the Old Testament, Deuteronomy emphasizes the uniqueness of Israel and the special relationship it has with God (cf. 4:4-8; 7:7-11; 33:26-29). Israel receives the teaching not because it only applies to Israel—God's torah given to Israel reflects a righteousness that pertains to all peoples (4:4-8)—but because through Israel's obedience to it other peoples may come to recognize its God.

More immediately, however, the teaching is given with the invitation that Israel *observe* it in order that it may *live*. Just as Deuteronomy uses a number of terms as synonyms for the content of the teaching, Deuteronomy uses a host of terms to describe faithful response to it. The speech of chapter 4 alone uses *give heed* (v. 1), *observe* (vv. 1, 5, 6, 13, 14), *keep* (vv. 2, 40), do not *forget* (vv. 9, 23). Later passages add to this list (see esp. 10:12–11:1). Deuteronomic style is to pile up words for key themes without making sharp distinctions among the terms. It is the overall impression they make—in this case faithful response to Moses' teaching—that is important.

The people's response to this teaching will determine, at least on a first level (cf. 4:23-31), whether they live or die (cf. 30:15, *See, I have set before you today life and prosperity, death and adversity*). A historical example of this reality is given immediately (4:3-4). At Baal-peor many within Israel worshiped the local Baal and suffered death as a result, whereas those who *held fast to the* LORD *your God are all* alive *today* (cf. Num 25:1-9). Later in the chapter it is announced that Israel will suffer exile for its disobedience (4:23-31). God will not forget his unconditional covenant with the ancestors (v. 31), and Deuteronomy sees hope beyond death (cf. the generation currently at the boundary, succeeding the one that earlier had lost faith upon first arriving at the land), but this does not cancel the fact that faithful response to the teaching is the condition for life.

God is *giving* (or, *has given*) Israel the *land* (cf. 1:8, 21). Appropriate response to the teaching is not conditional for entering the land, but its goodness and blessing will only be experienced fully through obedience.

After three chapters of narrative, the introduction thus signals the change in style; although not touching on the content of the teaching, it briefly presents the nature and thrust of the book of Deuteronomy as a whole. The concluding challenge (4:40) essentially repeats the essence of this opening verse (4:1), only now expanding it to future generations.

The Uniqueness of Israel 4:5-8
The Uniqueness of the God of Israel 4:32-39

The inner frame consists of two passages marked by rhetorical questions (vv. 7-8 and 33-34), a worldwide stage, and a sense of amazement at the uniqueness of Israel (vv. 5-8) and its God (vv. 32-39). The two claims to uniqueness serve as theological affirmations behind the general appeal of the outer frame (vv. 1-4, 40), and the more particular preaching around the second commandment of the central section (vv. 9-31).

The first segment begins with language that is largely a continuation of the introductory section: when in the land, keep and do the statutes and ordinances that Moses has taught (vv. 5-8). Quickly, however, a surprising shift takes place (v. 6). In contrast to the outer frame, where Israel is called to obedience *so that you may live* (4:1) and *for your own well-being* (4:40), here the arena is the larger world of nations, and the language used is at home in international wisdom (*for that will be your wisdom and your understanding,* 4:6 RSV). Obedience is not only so that Israel may live but also in order that the attention of other nations will be drawn to it. Earlier, Deuteronomy spoke of God's actions as taking place in the sight of Israel (e.g., *just as he did for you in Egypt before your very eyes,* 1:30; cf. 3:21); now it is the nations that will see the wisdom of this great people.

Israel is a *great nation*, a phrase used three times (vv. 6-8). But it is an unusual greatness. Just as today, the tendency then was to consider a nation great if it had immense size or massive military or economic power. But none of those apply to Israel (cf. 1:28; 4:38; 7:7). The grounds for Israel's greatness are twofold: (1) the nearness of its God (v. 7) and (2) the justness of its torah (v. 8).

In the religions of that period, it was not uncommon to have a high god who reigned above, along with intermediary and less powerful gods who related to people on a more personal level. For Israel, however, the God who has redeemed it from Egyptian slavery and now is giving Israel the land is the same God who cares for his people like a parent cares and loves a child (cf. 1:31). Israel's God is so near that whenever it calls upon God, God is present (cf. 1 Kings 8:27-53). This nearness of its God is shown most clearly in God giving Israel *this entire law* (4:8). Just as God has given Israel land (cf. 1:8, 21), God is now giving Israel directions for life in the land, directions that will lead to blessing and that other peoples will recognize as reflecting great wisdom and understanding.

The statement that no nation has *statutes and ordinances as just* [RSV, *so righteous*] *as this entire law* is a radical and unusual claim. Normally people are judged on the basis of whether or not they are obedient to the law. The law thus is the norm. This statement evaluates the law itself. This is possible only if it is assumed that there is a standard or measure of righteousness even above the law. The particular regulations thus are not the measuring stick of true justice, but examples of what that true justice might look like in particular situations. The Hebrew term here translated *just* normally is reserved for speaking of appropriate relations between humans. Israel's greatness lies in having received torah that more perfectly points to true righteousness and life-giving relationships, within society and also between God and humans.

The second segment of the inner frame moves from the uniqueness of Israel to the uniqueness of Yahweh, the God of Israel (4:32-39). Again, the context within which the claim is made is broader than Israel. All time (*since the day that God created human beings on earth*, v. 32) and space (*from one end of heaven to the other*, v. 32) are considered. The rhetorical questions that follow, with their reference to *any people* and *any god*, emphasize the worldwide frame of reference (vv. 33-34).

Even on such a worldwide stage, Israel's God is alone, a statement made both at the center of the passage (v. 35) and again at its climax (v. 39): *The LORD is God in heaven above and on the earth beneath; there is no other.* In the polytheistic world of the ancient Near East, all peoples had their gods. The real questions were how one related to these powers and which ones the people worshiped. The Old Testament consistently demands that Israel worship only Yahweh. But it is much less clear on the more theoretical question of what to make of the gods that other peoples worshiped. Most of Deuteronomy appears to accept the existence of these other gods. Even the first commandment is probably more accurately understood in this way (see comments on 5:7). It is because there are other gods that worshiping them becomes such a temptation. Yet this passage moves in a monotheistic direction. Gods worshiped by other peoples are in fact no gods. Their representations are *objects of wood and stone that neither see, nor hear, nor eat, nor smell* (4:28), Together with the Isaianic disciple of the exile (cf. Isa 43:10-13; 44:6; 45:6-7, 20-23) and the first story of creation (Gen 1:1–2:4), this passage leaves no room for other significant powers or gods. Yahweh, the God of Israel, stands alone.

This claim is based historically or experientially, not philosophically. Verse 35 begins with *To you it was shown so that you would acknowledge* [or perhaps more literally, *know*, as also in v. 39] *that the LORD is God*. The rhetorical questions zero in on the two primary pieces of evidence for the affirmation: an experience of revelation (Mount Horeb, v. 33) and an experience of redemption (exodus and the gift of land, v. 34). The rest of the passage refers back to these events (vv. 36, 37, 38). Israel heard God's voice at the mountain and yet lived (cf. vv. 9-14). Israel has been taken by its God *from the midst of another nation, by trials, by signs and wonders, by war, by a mighty hand and an outstretched arm, and by terrifying displays of power* (v. 34). The piling up of images and terms emphasizes the greatness and power of God in delivering a people. Although each term or phrase is used of God's work of redemption in other parts of Deuteronomy and the Old Testament, this is an unusual concentration of exodus images. The basis of God's action is nothing more nor less than God's love for this people (v. 37; cf. 7:7-11). The second segment of the inner frame thus moves from Israel's experience to knowledge about God, knowledge that can never remain mere head knowledge but must be taken *to heart* (v. 39). It must become the basis of response or action, as is featured in the central passage of the larger oration.

Preaching against Graven Images 4:9-31

The outer frame (A^1, 4:1-4; A^2, 4:40) calls on Israel to keep the *statutes and ordinances* that Moses is teaching the people. The inner frame (B^1, 4:5-8; B^2, 4:32-39) stresses the uniqueness of Israel as a people whose wisdom is displayed in their obedience of these statutes and ordinances that are more righteous than those of any other nation, and the uniqueness of the God of Israel, who created Israel and gave it those statutes and ordinances. Within this central discourse (4:9-31) the second commandment represents those statutes and ordinances. The heart of the passage is a warning against worshiping images, including a rationale for the command (vv. 9-14) and a warning about the consequences of disobedience (vv. 23-31).

4:9-14 *Basis of the Command*

Again a new unit begins with an exhortation, *But take care and watch yourselves closely*. The immediate issue, however, is not obedience to the torah, even though that remains the final concern. Instead, two supporting directives are given: (1) Israel is not to forget what it has seen, and (2) Israel is to make known what it has seen to following generations. Both play an important role for Deuteronomy. The theology of Deuteronomy is carefully grounded in Israel's experience with God. It is not coincidental that the book begins with three chapters of story. Now story is no longer the primary format for communication, but Israel's experience remains close to the surface. Regularly the book uses incidents from experience as a way of motivating response or as a key element of an argument.

In order to motivate obedience, experience must be recalled. It must be part of Israel's *mind* (RSV, *heart*). Memory determines self-understanding. How Israel understands the past and God's actions in it will govern Israel's response to God. Repeatedly Deuteronomy calls Israel to remember what Yahweh has done, or not to forget what it has seen. The first such call comes here, but it becomes a regular feature (4:9; cf. 4:23; 5:15; 6:12; 7:18; 8:2, 11, 14, 18, 19; 9:7, 27; 15:15; 16:3, 12; 24:9, 18, 22; 25:17; 32:7). The most important memory for Israel is God's act of redemption, God's deliverance of a slave people from Egypt. The frequent references to God's actions taking place before their eyes, or in their sight (4:9; cf. 1:30; 3:21; 4:6, 34; 6:22; 7:19; 9:17; 10:21; 11:7; 28:67; 29:2, 3), reflects the book's emphasis on experience and its role in motivating faithful response to God's action.

A people's memory is predicated on education. Moses, the last one of the generation that had experienced the exodus and Mount Horeb, teaches the next generation its story and what life lived as part of that story is. Each generation must learn this anew; otherwise the people may perish. Religious festivals as well as informal times in the home become important settings for this teaching. Verse 9 introduces this theme, verse 10 calls on the people to teach their children, and the larger passage ends (4:40) with a reference to these descendants, expressing the hope that *you may long remain in the land*. Deuteronomy understands memory of experience as crucial in motivating response (cf. 6:7, 20-25; 11:19; 31:12-13; 32:46), and thus the story must be passed on to each new generation.

The key event is the theophany at Horeb, an experience of a mountain blazing with fire and *shrouded in dark clouds* (4:11). The RSV better catches the mystery intimated by the Hebrew with its series of nouns at the end of the sentence—*darkness, cloud, and gloom*. Important to Deuteronomy's argument is that although Israel saw fire and darkness, the people did not see God, or even a form. God's most significant revelation happens without the aid of physical representation. Therefore Israel is not to make any images of God.

Covenant, an important word for Deuteronomy, is used for the first time in this context (v. 13) *[Deuteronomy, Covenant, and Political Treaties, p. 547]*. The term is used with different referents, however, so each time it is used one must ask to what it is referring. Here it refers to the event at Horeb, where Israel received the Ten Commandments (lit., *ten words*). The Horeb covenant placed obligations upon Israel. It emphasized the expected response of Israel to God's prior actions. Israel could break the Horeb covenant by not keeping it. Deuteronomy also uses covenant for God's unconditional promises to Israel's ancestors (cf. 4:31; 7:12; 8:18), and later of the relationship confirmed between God and Israel on the plains of Moab, as represented by the book of Deuteronomy (29:1, 9, etc.). When Josiah's workmen find what was probably the core of Deuteronomy, they call it "the book of the covenant" (2 Kings 23:2). The covenant theme is supported with the introduction of the *two stone tablets* (cf. 5:22; 9:11; 10:1-5). This probably indicates two copies of the commandments, "not several commandments on each, as commonly assumed," analogous to the two copies of ancient political treaties (Christensen 2001: 88; cf. Nelson 2002: 66; Kline: 13-26).

The section concludes with God's charge to Moses to teach Israel *statutes and ordinances*. Later Deuteronomy makes a distinction between the Decalogue, which God himself announced to Israel at Horeb, and the teaching of Moses (see comments on 5:22-33), but here *statutes and ordinances* refers to the whole torah that Israel is to observe.

4:15-22 Expounding the Command

Since you saw no form, . . . do not act corruptly by making an idol (RSV, *graven image*) *for yourselves* (vv. 15-16). This, in its briefest form, is a summary of these verses placed at the heart of this whole discourse. All else is expansion and elaboration. The initial concern, and probably the original focus of this prohibition, was that Israel not make any images or figures of Yahweh, its God. The logic of the argument, that Israel saw no form of God in the theophany at Horeb, moves in this direction. But as in the second commandment (cf. 5:8-10), this prohibition is enlarged or expanded: first, into a ban on making images not only of God, but also of humans, animals, birds, or fish, or any part of creation that might be used to represent God or substitute for the true God; and second, into a proscription against worshiping the great bodies in the heavens. Three distinct stages thus are present: (1) images of God are disallowed, (2) images of created beings are disallowed, and (3) the nature gods of the surrounding nations are disallowed. By the end its meaning is quite similar to the first commandment, *You shall have no other gods before me* (5:7).

The rejection of images was one of the unusual characteristics of Israel's religion. Surrounding nations made physical representations of their gods, out of wood, stone, or metal. These "idols" carried some of the power of the god, with their owners then having special access to these gods and their strength. Some Old Testament passages appear to reflect this understanding (e.g., when Jacob and his family flee from Laban, Rachel takes along with her the "household gods"; Gen 31:33-35). The very need to reject such practice is evidence that at least some in Israel were tempted to make images of God. The direction of the Old Testament is clear: any human-made representation of God is rejected. Yahweh, the God of Israel, is a sovereign God who cannot be limited, contained, or controlled in any way.

Yet God is not without image on earth. The creation story states that God created man and woman in the image of God, with the responsibility to represent God on earth (to "have dominion over...," Gen 1:26-27). No further representation is required or allowed even though the human only imperfectly reflects God. The tension between God's transcendence (God's presence above and beyond all creation) and God's immanence (God's presence within creation) is maintained by hinting at some distance between God and humans. This is done, first, by using a number of words for the representation ("Let us make humankind in our image, according to our likeness," Gen 1:26; emph. added); and second; in the use of the plural pronouns. If humans, made in the image of God by God, only reflect God incompletely, how much more this is true of human-made representations. Our Deuteronomy passage, using terms also found Genesis 1:26, awkwardly but exhaustively rejects all reproductions—*by making an idol for yourselves, in the form of any figure* (Deut 4:16). Four different Hebrew terms used for images are strung together in a series to make the point.

After presenting the prohibition in principle, the text expands on it by listing representative categories that stand for all of created life: human, and animals of land, sky, ground, and water (cf. categories of the second commandment, in 5:8; 14:3-20; also Gen 1:20-25). Five times the term *likeness* is used (Deut 4:16b-18). The Egyptians and Canaanites did represent their gods as animals. The falcon, representing the god Horus, and the cow, representing the god Hathor, both played important roles in Egyptian religion; and each of the Canaanite gods Baal, El, and Anath were depicted as a bull.

The repudiation of the worship of the heavenly bodies receives separate attention (v. 19), probably influenced by the important place these had in ancient worship. The beauty, power, and significance of the sun for life on earth resulted in it frequently being honored as a god. The moon and stars shared in this stature and were considered lesser divine beings. This passage even seems to lend some legitimacy to this (*things that the LORD your God has allotted to all the peoples everywhere under heaven*, v. 19; cf. 32:8-9). Many in

Israel were tempted to do the same. The creation story emphasizes that God made and assigned roles to the "greater light" and the "lesser light," but does not even name them, perhaps as a way of avoiding the use of terms that had become known as names for gods (Gen 1:16). As part of God's wonderful creation, the heavenly lights reveal "the glory of God" and proclaim "his handiwork" (Ps 19:1; cf. Ps 8), but they remain part of the created world and thus are not to receive worship themselves. The distinction is important yet forgotten in some of today's adoration of nature. Israel is different from the nations of its day. A people redeemed by God from the *iron-smelter* of Egypt, to be God's *very own possession* (v. 20), must only worship that God, and do so only directly, not via some image of any created object.

Once more the text notes that Moses is not allowed to cross the Jordan, this time as a warning that he will not be present with the people of Israel when they are faced with the temptations of the land, especially the temptation to make or honor images (cf. 1:37-40; 1:37-40; 3:23-28; 31:1-2, 16-22; 32:48-52; 34:1-12).

4:23-31 *Consequences of Disobeying the Command*

At first glance, and as suggested by the outline, this passage plays a fairly straightforward role. It, together with 4:9-14, encloses and supports the central warning of the chapter (4:15-22): the opening frame (vv. 9-14) gives the logic or rationale for the warning against images; the closing frame (vv. 23-31) presents the negative consequences of ignoring the warning—making images will lead to exile.

But there is much more to this passage than that. It contains a nuanced and carefully constructed discussion of the character of God and how God relates to his people. Two themes, or aspects of God's character, are presented in dialogue with each other. On the one hand, there is Yahweh, the jealous God who is like a devouring fire. On the other hand, there is Yahweh, the merciful God who does not forget the covenant he swore to Israel's ancestors. The passage begins by putting all weight on the first quality but by the end the emphasis has shifted, and the jealous God has been superseded by the merciful God. The language and images emphasize this exchange and contribute to the blended picture.

Once more Israel is called to *be careful not to forget* (v. 23; cf. v. 9), this time with emphasis on the covenant made at Horeb, with its obligations and responsibilities representatively reflected by the commandment against images. Then comes an unusually harsh statement, *For the* LORD *your God is a devouring fire, a jealous God* (v. 24).

To be jealous is to be strict, but not necessarily unfair or heartless. As the theological affirmations of the inner frame attest, *the LORD is God; there is no other besides him* (4:35; cf. v. 39); furthermore, this God loved Israel and gave it statutes and ordinances more righteous than any other. God's uniqueness, and the uniqueness of Israel's relationship to God, justifies God demanding an exclusive relationship, one that has no room for other gods, or even images. God's love for Israel and God's jealousy are two sides of the same coin. The image of a *devouring fire* already hints at the destructive consequences that can result from violating the relationship between Israel and this God.

The threat is complacency in the land (cf. 8:11-17), or amnesia. The consequences of such forgetting of who God is and what God has done is death: Israel *will soon utterly perish from the land*; it will not *live long on it, but will be utterly destroyed* (4:26). Twice in this verse the infinitive absolute follows verbs of death and destruction, thereby intensifying the meaning of the verb. Surely Israel will experience devastation, leading to a scattering *among the peoples*. Only a remnant will survive, and they will serve powerless idols. Exile is the consequence of God's jealous character and of Israel's forgetting the covenant.

The reference to *heaven and earth* witnessing against the people reflects the covenant context of the passage. In the polytheistic world of the day, gods normally served as witnesses of covenants or treaties between nations or kings. These witnesses then were responsible for enforcing the treaty and applying its curses. But in the covenant between God and Israel, the only God recognized was a party to the covenant and thus could not function as a witness. Here heaven and earth take on that role (cf. 31:19, 26; 32:46). They have witnessed the treaty, and now they witness the desolation that falls upon the covenant partner that has broken its side of the agreement. The theme of Yahweh the jealous God reaches its climax with these verses. Israel is devastated, scattered, futilely serving *gods made by human hands* (4:28; cf. vv. 32-39; Isa 40:18-20; 44:18; 45:20-21; 46:5-7).

But with that, the second theme of the passage breaks into the scene. Whereas the first theme is introduced by a statement in principle (v. 24), and then with a description of what it means for Israel, the second theme is presented in the reverse order. First comes a sketch of how this aspect of God's character touches Israel, and then comes the statement in principle. The passage thus is enclosed by two abstract declarations, with the story in between exemplifying both assertions: *The LORD your God is a devouring fire, a jealous God* (v.

24); and *The LORD your God is a merciful God* (v. 31). The parallel language emphasizes that the two should be seen in relationship to each other.

The passage concludes by depicting the implications of this merciful nature of God. Although Israel is devastated, scattered, futilely serving nongods, this is not the end. The story of God with his people does not end in failure. The remnant in exile *will seek the LORD your God, and you will find him; . . . you will return to the LORD your God and heed him* (vv. 29-30). The outer frame, with its emphasis on God's nearness *whenever we call to him* (v. 7), has helped prepare for this. The passage does include *If you search after him with all your heart and soul* (v. 29), but the tone of the passage makes a strong suggestion that this *will indeed happen*, because the sovereign God is a merciful God and wills it to happen. Later Deuteronomy again speaks of this scattering and announces that God will *circumcise your heart and the heart of your descendants, so that you will love the LORD your God with all your heart and with all your soul, in order that you may live* (30:6). Exile is not the end but is the means to the end. Punishment is not the goal; instead, it is the disciplining required to purify the people so that they will truly love God.

The climax of the passage presents the final word on the subject (v. 31). God is a jealous God, but in the end this characteristic is overlaid or overcome by God as a merciful or compassionate God. The Hebrew term here translated *merciful* is related to the common word for a woman's womb. God relates to his people like a mother relates to her child, whom she has carried for nine months in her womb (cf. 1:31). Such love is present not because of what the child does but in spite of, or regardless of, what the child does. The last part of the verse explains this further with the help of language used in the first part of the passage, but now with new meaning (v. 31). God *will neither abandon you nor destroy you*. The term translated *destroy* is the same one earlier used for Israel acting *corruptly* (v. 25). Whereas Israel acts in a self-destructive manner, God will not respond in kind and destroy Israel. God *will not forget the covenant* (v. 31)—earlier Israel is warned *not to forget the covenant* (v. 23). But now the covenant of Horeb, with its requirements and conditions, has been overlaid by the covenant that God made with the ancestors, with its unconditional promises. The last verse picks up images and themes used in the first part of the passage, but whereas earlier they were used in a context of covenant breaking and punishment, now they emphasize God's mercy. The statement on God's jealous nature is not negated—the warning remains very real—but it is not God's final word.

With this interlacing of the two themes, the text develops the power to be God's word in radically diverse contexts. To Israel during its history on the land, as it was confronted by the practices of the Canaanites, the passage provides a forceful warning and argument against making images. Such a forgetting of the covenant and its expectations can only be destructive. To the exiles in Babylon, the warning remains—the gods of the Babylonians now are the threat—but the word of hope shines through as gospel. God has not forgotten them or his promises. God will not abandon them. The death of exile will be overcome by life. Their role is to return to God with their total being.

Appendix: Designating Cities of Refuge 4:41-43

The first major speech of Moses has ended, but before the second one is introduced, three cities of refuge are established in the Transjordan region (cf. Josh 20:8). Its location here is probably because it is connected to the narratives on occupying the Transjordan and on its distribution to the tribes of Reuben, Gad, and half of Manasseh (cf. 2:24-3:17). Each of these tribes receives its own city of refuge (see discussion of 19:1-13 for further on the cities of refuge).

THE TEXT IN BIBLICAL CONTEXT
The Greatness of Israel

It is highly unusual for the Old Testament to speak of Israel as a *great nation*. True, God promises Abraham that he will make of him "a great nation" (Gen 12:2), and later this promise is repeated to Jacob as he and his family prepare to move to Egypt (Gen 46:3). But only Deuteronomy speaks of Israel as actually being great, and it does so at only two places. In Deuteronomy 26 the faithful Israelite presents firstfruits to God, and in a liturgical response offers a stylized summary of the history of Israel with God. This historical credo refers to Israel's ancestors, who entered Egypt *few in number and there ... became a great nation, mighty and populous* (v. 5). The promise to the ancestors has been fulfilled.

The only other references to Israel as a *great nation* are found in our present passage, where the phrase is used three times (vv. 6-8). The more common tendency in the Old Testament is to emphasize Israel's smallness, or its insignificance in the world of nations (cf. 7:7; Amos 7:2, 5). Given this larger picture, the way these verses speak of Israel becomes even more striking. Israel's greatness lies in its wisdom and discernment, as reflected in the nearness of its God and in the justness of its *entire law* (Deut 4:6-8).

Isaiah (2:1-5) and Micah (4:1-5) also speak of other peoples recognizing in Israel a way of life that leads to peace and blessing.

> In days to come
> > the mountain of the LORD's house
> shall be established as the highest of the mountains,
> > and shall be raised above the hills;
> all the nations shall stream to it.
> > Many peoples shall come and say,
> "Come, let us go up to the mountain of the LORD,
> > to the house of the God of Jacob;
> that he may teach us his ways
> > and that we may walk in his paths."
> For out of Zion shall go forth instruction,
> > And the word of the LORD from Jerusalem. (Isa 2:2-3)

The correlation between Israel's greatness and the witness of its law made in Deuteronomy 4, and the prophetic emphasis that other nations will come to the God of Israel for instruction in the word of God—together these suggest that another look at the Genesis 12:2 passage may be helpful: "I will make of you a great nation, and I will bless you, and make your name great, so that you will be a blessing." On one level the announcement that Israel will become a great nation is fulfilled when it becomes large and numerous. Exodus proclaims, "But the Israelites were fruitful and prolific; they multiplied and grew exceedingly strong, so that the land was filled with them" (1:7). Deuteronomy 26:5 is consistent with that reading.

But Deuteronomy 4:5-8 suggests that Israel's greatness is in more than size and includes its impact upon the nations, thereby connecting the promise of greatness with the promise of being a blessing. Yes, God will make a great nation out of Abraham and Sarah because their descendants will become numerous as *the stars of the heaven* (Deut 1:10; cf. Gen 15:5), but there is more. Israel will also become great because other nations will be blessed through its wisdom and justice due to the torah, God's major gift. Deuteronomy 4:5-8 thus expands the meaning of the promise found in Genesis 12.

Distress and Repentance

Crying to God in a state of distress or crisis is a natural reaction, mentioned regularly in Scripture and echoed countless times today even by people not especially religious. Deuteronomy's statement that in exile Israel will seek God thus is not especially striking. What is notable is the confidence Deuteronomy expresses that God will respond favorably even when the suffering itself is punishment for sin. Punishment thus is not the goal, or the last word, but has a purpose beyond itself, and that purpose is to return people to God.

Deuteronomy is far from alone in expressing this certainty. Jeremiah, in a letter to the exiles, asserts:

> Then when you call upon me and come and pray to me, I will hear you. When you search for me, you will find me; if you seek me with all your heart, I will let you find me, says the LORD, and I will restore your fortunes and gather you from all the nations and all the places where I have driven you, says the LORD, and I will bring you back to the place from which I sent you into exile. (Jer 29:12-14)

In a similar vein at the dedication of the temple, the prayer attributed to Solomon speaks of Israel coming to its senses in the land of their captors, returning to God in repentance, and God in heaven hearing its prayer. The book of Lamentations grieves the defeat and destruction of Jerusalem, and in so doing it emphasizes the trauma of the time. When Israelites question whether Israel has irrevocably broken the covenant God had made with Israel at Horeb, Deuteronomy and others respond that God's mercy is more powerful and will, in the end, prevail. Israel will return, and God will receive it back.

Jesus' story of the father with two sons (Luke 15:11-32) reflects this same message in a powerful way. The younger son asks for his inheritance and then squanders it away. Desperate, he cries out to God in repentance and returns to his father, who accepts him back and celebrates his return.

THE TEXT IN THE LIFE OF THE CHURCH
Theological Images

In June 1524, the Council of Zurich issued a decree that all images and idols be removed from Zurich churches. Over the next few weeks, a group led by the city's three priests systematically purged the local churches. Statues of the saints were destroyed; paintings were burned; murals were scratched from the walls; and all images, crucifixes, and holy objects were removed. The preaching of Zwingli and others against images had been effective and won the day. An important argument in this preaching was the second commandment. In a pamphlet written against images, Ludwig Hätzer's initial thesis is "God our Father and Spouse forbids us to make images." In a later disputation, Leo Jud claims all other arguments are based on the second commandment. Much more recently, some Mennonite groups have rejected the use of photographs of people because they are considered to be transgressions of the second commandment. In both of these worlds, the second commandment has a clear practical meaning.

Most Christians consider both of these actions as strange and unnecessary responses to the second commandment. In their own practice, however, they essentially ignore the commandment because they are not sure what it means in a day when, in their view, as Walter Harrelson writes, making images of God is "something our generation has certainly not the slightest temptation to do" (6).

But might theological images of God present such temptations for us today? Theology, whether done by scholars or laypeople, is an effort to better describe and understand God. Through detailed study of Scripture, careful reflection on experience, and systematic logic, God is captured, so to speak, in word pictures. Might these portraits be contemporary images, the work of human "hands," that can give a false sense of security? Patrick Miller notes, "Theology is a very dangerous game and always teeters on the brink of idolatry, with the tendency, intentional or not, of seeking to get at God for our own well-being and programs" (2009: 58).

Part 2
Second Speech: Preaching Torah

Deuteronomy 4:44–28:68

OVERVIEW

All of Deuteronomy is torah—a sermon with a vision for how Israel is to live in the Promised Land. This includes the narrative review and challenge of the first speech (chs. 1–4), and it includes the differing components of the second speech (chs. 5–28).

After an introduction that once more situates Deuteronomy geographically and chronologically (4:44-49), this second speech is divided into four segments reflecting the basic logic of Deuteronomy. The first segment presents the covenant revealed to Israel at Mount Horeb, where *God spoke with* them *face to face* (5:4) and gave them the Decalogue (ch. 5; cf. 4:13). Here the Decalogue is repeated for the people. The second segment then is extensive preaching stimulated by the first or foundational commandment (chs. 6–11).

The third segment (chs. 12–26) is still preaching, but now it makes use of *statutes and ordinances that you must diligently observe in the land that the* LORD, *the God of your ancestors, has given you* (12:1). God is still the source of this instruction, but it is mediated to the people via Moses (cf. 1:5, *Moses undertook to expound this law*). At first glance these regulations may appear to be written for use or application by Israel's judicial system, but more careful reflection suggests that this is not so *[Law, p. 555]*. That this is preaching rather than directions for the court is confirmed by the extensive use of motive clauses in these regulations, trying to *persuade* the people to allow themselves to be shaped by them. This becomes the covenant in the land of Moab that confirms this people, a second covenant, reaffirming the one made at Horeb.

In the fourth segment of the speech (chs. 27–28), Moses directs Israel to renew the covenant once they have entered the Promised Land. An extensive list of blessings, and especially curses, are included to encourage a positive response.

OUTLINE FOR PART 2

Introduction, 4:44-49
The Horeb Covenant, 5:1-33
Preaching the Foundational Commandment, 6:1–11:32
Preaching the Moab Covenant, 12:1–26:19
Covenant Renewal, Blessings and Curses, 27:1–28:68

Deuteronomy 4:44-49
Part 2A
Introduction

EXPLANATORY NOTES

The narrator introduces the second major speech with an introduction similar to the first, situating what follows in space and time (cf. 1:1-5)—*beyond the Jordan* and after the defeat of Kings Sihon and Og (4:46-49). The reference to the defeat of the two Amorite kings is expanded to highlight that their lands now have been occupied (cf. 1:4; 2:23-3:17). A foretaste of the fulfillment of the promise to the ancestors has been received. The two references to Egypt (4:45, 46) remind the audience of God's past actions on their behalf. And yet the concern of the second speech is not the past but the future, when Israel has received the full land. Israel is at the border of that land, at a critical juncture in the story, where all action pauses as Moses addresses the people.

As in the first introduction, that teaching is labeled torah (4:44; cf. comments on 1:5). Three further terms supplement the general designation of torah: *the decrees* [RSV, *testimonies*] *and the statutes and ordinances* (4:45). These terms are largely synonyms within Deuteronomy even though originally they may have had distinct connotations. The specific regulations included in chapters 12–26 are designated by these terms, but so are the Ten Commandments (5:1, 6-21), the Shema (6:1, 4-9), and the sermonizing of chapters 5–11. The geographical description encompasses the whole of the Transjordan and as such emphasizes that Israel has begun to experience the gift of the land. Pisgah has earlier been used as a boundary marker for the Transjordan region (3:17), but in Deuteronomy it is also the place from which Moses surveys the Promised Land and where he dies (cf. 3:27; 34:1). By concluding this passage with a reference to Pisgah in verse 49, the narrator subtly reminds us: Moses, the one here teaching on behalf of God (though God is not named in vv. 44-45; cf. 1:1-5), will die shortly. Accountability for response to the torah thus resides with the people.

Deuteronomy 5:1-33

Part 2B
The Horeb Covenant

PREVIEW

It is doubtful that any part of the Old Testament is recited more or known as well as the Ten Commandments, or Decalogue. In times past young people learned them in Sunday school or catechism, and their elders knew them from youth. They were posted on the walls of public courthouses. They were deemed God's will for the larger society, not narrowly Christian or Jewish or Muslim. Times have changed, but even today many with scant church association know of them and may even be able to identify a few of the commands. The Ten Commandments, one might say, are public property.

For most Christians the Ten Commandments transcend the usual limitations of Old Testament law. Judaism, using the term Ten Words, also gives it high significance. This and the Shema (6:4-9) are the most important texts in what is Scripture for both Jews and Christians. Postexilic Jews daily read these two passages in the temple in Jerusalem. It is possible that already during the time of the Israelite monarchy, part of the Festival of Weeks (Pentecost) consisted of Israel celebrating the gift of the law. At this time the Decalogue would be read, and Israel would recommit itself to follow it. Weinfeld suggests that Psalms 50 and 81 reflect such a ceremony (1991: 264).

The Ten Commandments already have a unique and central place within the Old Testament, even if this exact title is never used.

The term *Decalogue* (lit., *Ten Words*) reflects the way this passage is referenced elsewhere: Moses "wrote the words of the covenant—the Ten Words" (Exod 34:28 NJB; also Deut 4:13; 10:4). The very fact that it is included twice in the Old Testament in virtually the same form (Deut 5:6-21; Exod 20:2-17) is a sign of its importance. It has a special place in the story of Israel: both Deuteronomy and Exodus distinguish between the Ten Commandments that God speaks directly to Israel and then writes on stone with his finger (Deut 4:13; 5:22; 9:10; Exod 31:18), and the rest of the law that is mediated through Moses (Deut 5:22-33; Exod 20:18-21). Only the Decalogue is placed in the ark of the covenant (Deut 10:5; 31:24-26).

Practical factors contribute to this prominence: the Decalogue has concise formulations (making it easy to memorize), it has a nice round number (ten—one command for each finger of the two hands), it is applicable to all Israelites, and it is absolute yet general in format. The Decalogue symbolizes the covenant and special relationship between God and Israel.

And yet its significance can be exaggerated or misrepresented. It is neither foundational for the rest of Israel's law nor a summary of it. It remains a sampling of life that is faithful to God. The Decalogue does not touch on all aspects of life, nor does it cover all other laws in the Old Testament. Most of its individual laws are presented in other parts of the Old Testament as well. Nor is it the only series of prohibitions or regulations found there that appear to have been abstracted for teaching purposes (cf. the holiness regulations of Lev 19; the twelve curses of Deut 27:15-26; the liturgical regulations of Exod 34; the list of crimes of Ezek 18:5-9; and the series of positive qualities found in Pss 15 and 24).

The Decalogue presents one outline of what life in a community faithful to the God of the exodus looks like. The general absence of consequences for disobedience takes away the utility of the statements for the actual administration of justice, but Israel can ignore its content only at grave peril. The terms are nonnegotiable, even if their practical implications are endlessly negotiable (Brueggemann 2001: 79). For if Israel disregards the covenant that God gave it at Horeb, disaster and death are inevitable. The Decalogue may not be law in a modern sense, but it embodies the key to life for Israel.

OUTLINE FOR PART 2B

A Covenant for *Today*, 5:1-5
The Content of the Horeb Covenant, 5:6-22
    5:6   Prologue

5:7-21   The Commandments
5:22   Conclusion
Moses Appointed Mediator, 5:23-33
5:23-27 Israel Asks Moses to Serve as Mediator
5:28-31 God Confirms Moses as Mediator
5:32-33 Concluding Exhortation

EXPLANATORY NOTES

A Covenant for *Today* 5:1-5

Ritual and ceremony play a prominent role in religion. Festivals were joyous occasions in the ancient world: people gathered from great distances to fellowship, celebrate, and worship together. At these assemblies huge dramatic reenactments could take place. These were not dramas performed by a small group of people whom the crowds watched, but events in which all participated through action and liturgical responses. In Israel historical events played a significant role in these festivals. The Passover commemorated the escape from Egypt; the Festival of Booths reminded the people of their time of wandering in the wilderness; and, at least in later Israel, the Festival of Weeks (called Pentecost in the NT) celebrated the gift of law at Mount Horeb.

The language of the opening paragraph suggests such an assembly. *All Israel is convened* (RSV, *summoned*) for the occasion (cf. *all Israel* in 1:1). The covenant originally proclaimed at Mount Horeb then is declared to the people. The speech itself begins with the typically Deuteronomic exhortation *Hear, O Israel* (cf. first verse of the two larger sections surrounding this passage, 4:1 and 6:4, as well as 9:1; 20:3; 27:9). The text makes it clear that to hear means more than merely to listen; it includes learning and observing (5:2). The entreaty to hear covers the whole second speech (chs. 5–28), as indicated by the language of *statutes and ordinances*; but quickly the focus narrows to the Horeb covenant, with its primary content, the Decalogue (cf. 4:10, 13). Here is reflected the larger logic of Deuteronomy: At Horeb, God created Israel through covenant, with the Decalogue representing its content. In Moab, Moses renews the covenant, with the preaching of Deuteronomy representing its content (cf. 29:1).

The assertion that the Horeb covenant was made with *all of us here alive today* (5:3), with its awkward construction (lit., *With us! We! Those here today! All of us! Alive ones!*), highlights a key element of Deuteronomic theology. According to the story line of Deuteronomy, those present at Horeb (with the exception of Moses, Caleb, and Joshua) have died in the wilderness. It is a new generation at the border of the Promised Land, listening to Moses. Nevertheless Moses proclaims, *The LORD our God made a covenant with us at Horeb* (v. 2). And in case the people miss the significance of the statement, it is expanded further: *Not with our ancestors did the LORD make this covenant, but with us, who are here alive today* (v. 3).

Taken literally, this is not true—and the audience of Deuteronomy knows that—but the point is made. Patrick Miller says, "The time gap and the generation gap are dissolved in the claim that the covenant at Sinai, the primal revelation that created the enduring relationship between the people and the Lord, was really made with the *present* generation. The covenant is not an event, a claim, a relationship of the past; it is of the present. The time between the primal moment and the present moment is telescoped, and the two are equated" (1990: 67). The awkward Hebrew emphasizes the immediate reality of the covenant; no one could miss the point. Its truth would remain for all later readers or participants in festivals commemorating the gift of the covenant, and it endures throughout time. The covenant is always made *today*, with us.

For discussion of verses 4-5, see on 5:22-33 (cf. 4:12, 33).

The Content of the Horeb Covenant 5:6-22

The prominent role of the Ten Commandments within Israel and the Old Testament is beyond question, but the history and development of the Decalogue are much debated. Was there an original list consisting of ten short statements, all in the negative? Or is the Decalogue a combination of various groups of prohibitions that only later coalesced into a neat grouping of ten? Does either the Exodus or Deuteronomy version of the Decalogue represent an older tradition? This commentary is not the place to enter into a lengthy discussion on the background of the Ten Commandments: for extended treatment of these questions, see the volumes by Stamm and Andrew; Nielsen; Harrelson; and Weinfeld (1990).

Although the number "ten" is used, there is no consensus on how the Decalogue divides into ten words or commandments (see explanation for *Decalogue* in the Preview above). Dispute takes place at three points. Is the statement of self-expression (*I am the LORD your God* . . .) opening the passage to be considered one of the "words," or is it an introduction to them (5:6)? Are the statements about no other gods (v. 7) and about making idols (vv. 8-10) two commandments or one? Are the two statements about coveting and desiring (v. 21) two commandments or one? Disagreement over how these questions are answered results in several variations in the numbering of the Ten Commandments. This commentary will follow the numbering of the Reformed tradition, at points noting reasons for the variations.

Statement	Judaism	Roman Catholic	Lutheran	Reformed, Anglican, Other	Orthodox, Other
I am the LORD your God who brought you . . . (v. 6)	1		Preface	Preface	1
You shall have no other gods . . . (v. 7)	2	1	1	1	
You shall not make . . . an idol (vv. 8-10)			(omitted)	2	2
You shall not make wrongful use of the name . . . (v. 11)	3	2	2	3	3
Observe the sabbath . . . (vv. 12-15)	4	3	3	4	4
Honor your father and your mother . . . (v. 16)	5	4	4	5	5
You shall not murder (v. 17)	6	5	5	6	6
Neither shall you commit adultery (v. 18)	7	6	6	7	7
Neither shall you steal (v. 19)	8	7	7	8	8
Neither shall you bear false witness . . . (v. 20)	9	8	8	9	9
Neither shall you covet your neighbor's wife (v. 21a)	10	9	10	10	10
Neither shall you desire . . . (v. 21b)		10	9*		

*Martin Luther followed the Exodus 20 sequence for commandments 9 and 10.

It is common to note that the commandments deal with both the vertical relationship (God-human) and horizontal relationships (human-human). The commandments then are divided between those that focus on God (first four) and those that focus on social relationships (the last six, or possibly commands six to ten, with the fifth commandment functioning as a transition). Some see the reference to the commandments as recorded on two tablets of stone reflecting this division into two arenas (5:22; Exod 32:15; although see comments on 4:13). Patrick Miller consistently speaks of "first table" and "second table" with these connotations (2009). Such a division may conform to Jesus' summarizing of the law with the two commands to love God and neighbor, but it also can mislead since it separates the two spheres too sharply. Israel and the Old Testament understood all of life in a more unified fashion. All sin was ultimately against God.

5:6 Prologue

Whether God's self-identification (5:6) is treated as the first of the ten "words," as the Jewish tradition does, or whether as the introduction to the Decalogue, as some Christian traditions have, it is an integral part of the Decalogue itself. The NRSV highlights the connection between God's self-identification and the Decalogue by translating verses 6-7 as one sentence and setting them apart as a separate paragraph (in contrast, KJV, NABRE, NIV, and even RSV have them as separate sentences). The unity of the prologue with the first two commandments is also highlighted: only in them does God speak in the first person: elsewhere in the Decalogue, God is spoken of in the third person.

The language of self-identification (*I am the LORD your God*) occurs frequently in Scripture, suggesting that in Israel it was a formulaic way to speak of God (cf. Exod 16:12; 20:2; Lev 11:44; 18:2, 4, 30; 19:3-4, 10; Num 10:10; 15:41; Deut 29:6; Judg 6:10; Isa 43:3; Ezek 20:5, etc.). It also points to the call of Moses, where God first introduces the name Yahweh to Moses. The story of Exodus 1-15 very much informs the connotations of the prologue. In Hebrew the first phrase of this verse consists of three terms without a verb (lit., *I, Yahweh, your God*), thus allowing either the usual translation, *I am the LORD your God*, or *I, the LORD, am your God* (cf. comments on 6:4, first verse of the Shema).

This statement of self-identification presents the world within which the Decalogue is to be heard and understood. The Decalogue is given by a *particular* God, Yahweh, to a *particular* people, Israel, with whom that God has a *particular* relationship. The reference to the name—*I am the* LORD (i.e., Yahweh)—reminds us of the call of Moses, where this name is introduced to Moses. But at that point the name still has little content. That content is supplied by the events that follow, God's deliverance of Israel from Egypt.

Two connotations of that story are important here. First, the Decalogue is given to a people who has already experienced deliverance, a group of slaves that has been freed from bondage to Pharaoh. At Horeb this group of liberated slaves becomes "a priestly kingdom and a holy nation" (Exod 19:6). The regulations are not conditions for receiving liberation but directions for how to live as a liberated and liberating people, a holy nation of God. In the language of this theology, grace comes before law, salvation comes before response. Second, deliverance is not to absolute freedom, but into a new relationship. Yahweh, the God of Israel, replaces Pharaoh as the one to whom they owe allegiance: Israel is now subject to Yahweh, as emphasized by the repeated use of the phrase *your* God (244 times in Deuteronomy alone!). In the New Testament, 1 Peter invites us to "live as free people," yet calls us "servants [or "slaves"] of God" (2:16).

The Decalogue is not some universal set of rules for all humanity that can be abstracted out of the specific context in which it is given.

> We should resist the trend to isolate them, understand them as self-authenticating principles, make them into comprehensive schemes of embracing the total realm of ethics, or even equate them with universal moral law that can equally well be discerned in classical Greece, Buddhism, and in many other places. The Decalogue remains part of the story that shaped the ideal underlying it, and it loses its character and authority when detached from that story. (W. Janzen 1994: 100)

The prologue is an integral part of the Decalogue, giving nuance to the expectations, placing them within a particular story and relationship (cf. the way Deuteronomy opens with three chapters of historical review, with the story of Israel regularly referenced in its later preaching).

5:7-21 *The Commandments*

The First Commandment: Other Gods, 5:7. The most important and most radical commandment, at least within the world of that day, is the first: Israel is not to have any other gods (lit.) *before my face.* The language may reflect an earlier concern that Israel not set up idols or images in the temple (i.e., before the face of Yahweh), but now the prohibition clearly is against any worship of other gods. All such worship is utterly repudiated. Yahweh, the God of the exodus, expects exclusive loyalty.

This commandment is not participating in a philosophical debate about the existence of God or gods. It is not attacking the notion of polytheism or even of atheism. Only fools question the existence of higher powers (cf. Ps 14:1). The charge is not an abstract or metaphysical statement about reality but a practical directive dealing with the dynamics of daily life for Israel. Once in the land, Israel will be sorely tempted to worship indigenous gods whom the Canaanites regard as an integral part of agricultural technique. Later, good arguments could be made for worshiping the gods of the Assyrians and Babylonians, the powerful nations that captured Samaria (722 BCE) and Jerusalem (587 BCE). It should not surprise us that many within Israel, perhaps the majority (Cook 2004), sought their security by supplementing the worship of God with the worship of other gods (cf. the story of Elijah and the prophets of Baal on Mount Carmel, in 1 Kings 18). The Decalogue forbids the practical recognition of any power other than Yahweh. Among ancient peoples such an exclusive understanding of God was highly unusual, if not unheard of. At Horeb, God created a truly alternative community, one that was expected to wholly live and orient itself toward their God.

This radical, exclusive expectation permeates the whole of Scripture; only a few examples can be given here. It is confirmed by the Shema (Deut 6:4) and repeated many more times in Deuteronomy, in positive formulation (e.g., 11:13) and in negative warnings (e.g., 6:14), with chapters 6–11 preaching on this commandment. The Pentateuch and historical books contain countless stories of its breach, the Psalms direct praise only to this God of the exodus (e.g., 81:9-10), and the Prophets indict Israel for going after other gods (note esp. Hosea). Jesus affirms this commitment when he rejects his temptation (Matt 4:10; Luke 4:8) and when he identifies the Shema as the most important commandment (Deut 6:5; Matt 22:37-38; Mark 12:29-30). The church's conviction that this one God was present in the incarnate Jesus does not change its commitment to the first commandment, and so Paul affirms, "For us there is one God, the Father, from whom are all things and for whom we exist" (1 Cor 8:6).

In the face of this absolutely consistent conviction, Scripture recognizes gods or powers that threaten this exclusive allegiance. In the Old Testament these may have been Canaanite or even Assyrian gods. Jesus speaks of the impossibility of serving two masters, and then identifies "wealth" (NRSV) or "mammon" (KJV, RSV) as competing gods (Matt 6:24).

Today as well, the commandment is best treated not as a speculative statement of doctrine but as a call for total reliance upon the God of Israel and Jesus Christ. The question is whether faith in God is foundational only for Sunday religion, or whether it determines all of life and how we live it. Any passion or ideology or system that undermines absolute loyalty and obedience to the God of Jesus Christ is a god against which the first commandment warns. Lust for possessions, excessive confidence in ourselves, allegiance to a particular political or economic system—these are a few examples. It is so tempting to add some other commitment to faith in God, thus "limping with two different opinions" (1 Kings 18:21). The radicality of the first commandment for today, even as the polytheism of ancient Israel is no longer believable, cannot be exaggerated.

The Second Commandment: Idols, 5:8-10. The close relationship of the second commandment to the first makes it unsurprising that some traditions merge the two statements into one. It may begin on a different note from the first, but it then returns to the same concern. The commandment has three distinct parts, possibly reflecting historical development, but now closely bound together.

The command opens, as traditionally understood, *You shall not make for yourself an idol.* The term *idol* may mislead, for the concern here is physical representations of God, the one giving the direction (the RSV's *graven image* may be more helpful; similarly KJV; cf. ESV, NKJV, *carved image*; NJPS, *sculpted image*). Although the Old Testament gives examples of God's people violating this expectation, Israel was unusual in the ancient world with its Yahwistic tradition that persistently rejected images, even of its own God.

Elsewhere Deuteronomy supports this command by drawing attention to the theophany of Horeb, where Israel *heard the sound of words but saw no form* (4:12). This historical justification may suggest that the focus of the command is the manner of God's revelation, which is through word and the dynamics of history, not through objects made by human hands. And yet the commandment again is much more than an abstract theological statement: it speaks to the practical question of how to worship. Worship cannot include images of God that may be understood to give the worshiper special power or control over God. God's sovereignty, freedom, and even mystery is protected. The absence of any likeness of God for worship is a constant reminder to Israel that its God can never be fully captured or understood (for further discussion of this command, see comments on 4:9-22). Any practice that limits this freedom of God is to be rejected.

The middle part of the commandment significantly broadens the focus and relates it to the first commandment (5:8b-9a). Not only is Israel to refrain from making images of Yahweh; it also is to resist the temptation to make representations of the multitude of natural objects that played a central role in the religion of the Canaanites and other peoples of the day. In its opposition to this practice, Israel sharply distinguished itself from its neighbors. The phrase *You shall not bow down to them or worship them* (RSV, *serve them*) is one of the many phrases Deuteronomic literature uses for the worship of foreign gods (cf. Exod 23:24; Josh 23:7, 16; 2 Kings 17:35) and suggests that the expansion has returned to the theme of the first command. Israel's exclusive loyalty to Yahweh must not be undermined by the worship of other gods, or even by the worship of images, either of Yahweh or the elements of nature.

Here the danger of seeing God in nature is also rejected. The transcendence of God the Creator from all that God has created, be it sun and moon or the animals, is maintained. The one exception to this emphasized distance is the human, that part of creation explicitly made in the image of God (Gen 1:26). This commandment not only prohibits making images but also has a positive dimension as well, for it calls on the people of God to "portray the presence of God in daily life" (Harrelson 1980: 70). We are the divinely sanctioned image of God. Nature may point to God (e.g., Ps. 19), but it is not an image of God. This may warn against the contemporary tendency to see God in nature rather than in the image that God supplied for us.

The close connection or even overlap between transgression of the first commandment and the prohibition of images is reflected in the story of the golden calves erected at Bethel and Dan by Jeroboam after the division of the kingdom. The calves were probably originally intended as thrones for the invisible God who had delivered them from Egypt (note the language of 1 Kings 12:28; cf. Aaron's golden calves, Exod 32). But over time these instruments for promoting worship became objects of worship themselves. This raises questions for our own worship: Is it possible for a worship pattern to become such a time-honored tradition that it is treated as sacred in itself, and thus becomes like a banned image? Might creative efforts at shaping or leading worship of God today become an image that impinges upon God's freedom?

The command concludes by giving motivation for obedience (vv. 9b-10). The reference to God's punishing action and God's mercy is a common biblical theme (cf. Exod 34:6-7; Num 14:18; Jer 32:18; Nah 1:2-3). But as in the previous mention of this in Deuteronomy 4:25-31, here God's mercy is greater. Only three or four generations (the number of generations alive at one time) experience the punishment, but thousands of generations experience God's *steadfast love*. Later, Deuteronomy revises the typical language and limits the negative consequences of sin even more to *those who reject him* (7:10). As part of the Decalogue, however, this verse deals with community dynamics. It recognizes that regardless of what might be considered fair, the truth is that sin negatively affects the larger body, resulting in even the innocent suffering (cf. Moses dying prior to crossing the Jordan). Weinfeld suggests that the Hebrew term translated *jealous* might better be translated *impassioned*, understood as foundational both for God's punishment and for God's love (1991: 293-96).

The Third Commandment: Name of Yahweh, 5:11. Israel is not allowed to make an image of the divine, but God has given it a gift that it can use for approaching God: the name of God, Yahweh. Twice Exodus records God announcing the name to Moses (Exod 3:13-16; 6:2-3). The Decalogue opens with God announcing, *I am the* LORD *[i.e., Yahweh] your God* (Deut 5:6; cf. Exod 20:2).

In the culture of the day, names represented the character or essence of a person. When we are introduced to Nabal (meaning "fool"), the husband of Abigail, we are informed that he is *surly and mean* (1 Sam 25:3). Abram and Sarai's names are changed to Abraham and Sarah to represent their new status as covenant partners with God (Gen 17:5, 15). In Deuteronomy, God's name becomes an important way of speaking of the essence and presence of God. Israel shall worship at *the place* God chooses to put his name (12:5, 11, 21; 14:23, 24; 16:2, 6, 11; 26:2); Israel's priests and prophets minister in the name of God (18:5, 7, 19, 20, 22); Israel is to be known by the name of God (28:10) and fear that awesome name (28:58). The name of God thus fully represents the holiness and power of God.

This is true even though the full meaning of God's name remains veiled. When Moses asks who is sending him to Egypt, God's response is the ambiguous "I AM WHO I AM," or alternatively, "I WILL BE WHAT I WILL BE" (Exod 3:14 mg.). God's independence is protected. The events of the exodus and Mount Sinai/Horeb provide primary content or meaning for the name, and yet there is always an open-endedness and freedom to God. Capturing God in an image is denied, but the community of the redeemed is given the name with which it can access God, even if the name retains a certain quality that cannot be captured.

Deuteronomy elsewhere frees Israel to swear and bless by that name (6:13; 10:8, 20; 21:5), and consistent with the first commandment, by that name only. The third commandment thus does not prohibit its use but warns Israel to use it carefully. Clearly this prohibition includes swearing falsely (cf. Lev 19:12; Jer 7:9), but within the Decalogue lying is more directly rejected by the ninth commandment. The phrases used in the NRSV, *wrongful use* and *misuses* (KJV, *in vain*; NIV, *misuse/misuses*), although somewhat free translations, get at the heart of the matter. The name of God is not to be misused, either too lightly or casually, without fully recognizing its gravity, or for personal purposes or benefit. In the ancient world, with its very dynamic understanding of the power of God, the second temptation probably was the greater. The name of God was understood to be a powerful force that could be used selfishly or destructively in a curse on someone else.

Both directions of the commandment address today. That which is called swearing or cursing is an example of using the name of God too lightly, but so may be prayers that are trivial or unconsidered. Such speech is an affront to God because it fails to recognize the seriousness of God's name and its use. Church people today may not use a curse to harm someone, but religion has been so used, even if unintentionally, in ways that have been destructive. Consider when people are made to feel so guilty that they become emotionally disturbed, when religion is used to excuse oppression, when church leaders announce peace when there is no peace, when war is justified because God is on our side, or when theology is used to support power politics in the church. Whenever God is invoked for human causes, the power of God's name is corrupted. Together with the second commandment, the third points to appropriate worship of God, in which praise of God's name is central. Christian trinitarian theology understands Jesus to be one with God, with his name thus covered by this commandment as well.

The Fourth Commandment: Sabbath, 5:12-15. After three commandments that define God's exclusive claim on Israel, the fourth and fifth serve as a transition to the directives dealing primarily with social relationships and identity. Within Judaism, keeping the

Sabbath became a primary symbol of its distinctive identity as a community different from the surrounding culture.

The history and origin of the Sabbath in Israel is unclear. Surrounding peoples had days when it was considered unlucky to work, and they had festive days, usually related to the lunar cycle, but nothing quite like Israel's Sabbath. The Old Testament grounds the seven-day cycle in the order of creation, with the Exodus version of the fourth commandment (20:11) specifically making this connection. The Deuteronomic version of the commandment deletes direct reference to creation, but its ancient audience was surely aware of the connection. The God who created the world in six days and then rested is the model for Israel. Like the first three commandments, the fourth begins with God, but it goes on to speak directly to social dynamics within the community of Israel.

At the heart of the command is a double requirement: to keep and hallow the Sabbath, and to cease working on that day, with the latter having the implication of expecting all to work for six days each week. Israel developed an extensive sacrificial system for the Sabbath, but no reference to the cult is made within this command [*Cult, p. 546*]. The only positive expectation comes in the opening sentence: Israel is to *keep it holy*. Genesis speaks of God blessing the Sabbath and hallowing it (Gen 2:3; cf. Exod 20:11). Lohfink says, "'To keep holy' means to remove something from the sphere of the normal, the common, the profane, and then to place it in relation to God through (for example) ritual or prayer or worship" (1982: 209). Consistent with this, the day is spoken of as *a sabbath to the* LORD *your God* (v. 14). The day stands as a regular reminder that work and the provision of daily necessities, important as they may be, are not all there is to life. Above all stands the God upon whom life ultimately depends. During the Sinai theophany, Moses spends six days waiting for God. On the seventh day God calls to Moses out of the cloud and invites him into "the glory of the LORD" that was like "a devouring fire" (Exod 24:15-18). The Sabbath calls on Israel regularly to turn its attention from the mundane and the everyday to the fire of God, within which the structure of life is to be found.

The second expectation is reflected by the name itself, Sabbath, which simply means "to stop" or "cease." Deuteronomy's substitution of *Observe* (v. 12) for the "Remember" of Exodus (20:8) and its addition of *keep the sabbath day* (v. 15) do not change its essential meaning. In the ancient world outside Israel, the amount of work one did was a key sign of one's stature or class. Slaves worked, masters had leisure. A common theme of creation stories was to see humans as created to serve the gods so that the gods would have more leisure time. Into this world the Sabbath command makes a radical statement: like God, all are expected to work; and like God, all, including slaves and aliens and even animals, are to have the opportunity to rest. Through Sabbath practice, a community is fostered in which all participate; one not defined solely by utility and production (Brueggemann 2001: 68–75).

Deuteronomy's version of the commandment further highlights its humanitarian and even broader concerns. Here the ox and donkey are specifically named as among the "livestock" mentioned in Exodus. After listing the members of the Hebrew household excused from work on the Sabbath, Deuteronomy adds, to make sure the point is not missed, *so that your male and female slave may rest as well as you* (v. 14). Then, in the most significant revision of the Exodus version, it substitutes a reference to the exodus from Egypt (now the term *Remember* is used) for the reference to creation. This change grounds the commandment in the particular story of Israel (cf. prologue to the Decalogue, v. 6). The people of Israel had been slaves, and thus should have empathy for those with less freedom. God has redeemed Israel from slavery, reflecting God's interest in the weak. The background to the Sabbath may be the order of creation, but the motivation given for keeping it in Deuteronomy is God's liberation of slaves. The language of the commandment continues to assume the presence of slaves, but it begins to undermine the very foundations of slavery (Lohfink 1982: 204), forming a community that practices an "emancipatory ethic" (Brueggemann 2001: 66). This humanitarian concern is so prominent that Patrick Miller speaks of a sabbatical principle "because the commandment opens up a large trajectory of social justice" as reflected in later regulations. The sabbatical principle thus is "one of the primary manifestations of God's provision for justice and compassion in the human community" (2009: 134; see comments on ch. 15).

Jesus repeatedly challenges a legalistic approach to the Sabbath (e.g., Mark 2:27-28), but at the same time, his ministry reflects this core thrust of what might be called a sabbatical principle. In his inaugural sermon in Nazareth, Jesus reads from Isaiah with its reference to proclaiming "release to the captives" (Luke 4:18). When he is challenged for healing on the Sabbath, he asks, "Ought not this woman . . . be set free from bondage on the sabbath day?" (Luke 13:16). As Marcus Bockmuehl puts it, "To sanctify the Sabbath means to save life and do good, not just to rest, but to *give rest* to others" (116).

For a long time the "Christian Sabbath," Sunday, was recognized in North America by two practices: church attendance and the proscription of most work and certain public entertainment. With the rise of pluralism and an emphasis on rights, together with a decline in the church's influence on society, Sunday has become "everyday." It is incumbent on the church to ask anew how the Sabbath might be hallowed and the sabbatical principle effected. The danger of defining life by work remains pronounced. Both those who identify themselves primarily through their occupation and those who feel they have lost their identity because of unemployment or retirement—such people need to be reminded that our true identity is determined by our response to God. Work is part of the created order that God calls "very good" (Gen 1:31): humankind is given the mandate to care for and "have dominion" over the rest of creation (1:28), "to serve and keep" our home (Gen 2:15 AT). But work can become idolatrous and oppressive. It can invade all, even when the Sabbath is formally kept (cf. Amos 8:5). The Sabbath relativizes all human work and serves as a safeguard against these tendencies (W. Janzen 1999: 1-10). The fourth command in Deuteronomy calls on us to *observe* it and *keep* it, and to *remember* God's acts of liberation.

The Christian shift to Sunday as a day for remembering the resurrection and God's new act of redemption is in line with this. The Sabbath is a gift from God that guards the first three commandments, directing our attention to the work of God, even as it sets the stage for the social justice of the latter commandments. Its role as a mark of God's people, a community in contrast to larger society, becomes even more significant as its place in general society is lost.

The Fifth Commandment: Father and Mother, 5:16. The fifth commandment is not directed at unruly teenagers or younger children challenging their parents' authority. The general tenor of ancient society, coupled with the formal control parents had over younger children, already strongly discouraged children from defying their parents. The provision allowing the execution of a rebellious son, although probably seldom if ever applied, gives some sense of the milieu (Deut 21:18-21). Like the rest of the Decalogue, the fifth commandment is directed at adults. Strikingly, father and mother are treated equally in the commandment; here, as well as at other points, Deuteronomy raises questions about the strong patriarchal conventions of the day.

The term translated *Honor* comes from a root meaning "to give weight" and is the opposite of cursing or taking lightly. With its feet in the first part of the Decalogue, this commandment challenges adult children to take seriously that which the parents are entrusting to them, the story of God's covenant with Israel. Deuteronomy regularly calls on parents to teach their children what God has done for Israel (e.g., 4:9-10; 6:7, 20). Here is the other side: children are invited to accept and live this covenant faith. The promise in the commandment is consistent with the numerous other references insisting that long life and well-being in the land depend on keeping the statutes and ordinances (e.g., 4:40). Each generation must receive this tradition and live by it. God and parents then are honored.

Yet there also is a more practical side. The commandment calls on adult children to respect and care for parents later in life, when their contribution to the community no longer is as obvious. The way Joseph treats Jacob and the way Ruth relates to Naomi are wonderful models of what it means to honor a parent, or even a parent-in-law. In a time when the only security available in old age was care by one's children, this responsibility was especially important. Sirach in the Apocrypha includes an exposition of this commandment:

> Do not glorify yourself by dishonoring your father,
>   for your father's dishonor is no glory to you.
> The glory of one's father is one's own glory,
>   and it is a disgrace for children not to respect their mother.
> My child, help your father in his old age,
>   and do not grieve him as long as he lives;
> even if his mind fails, be patient with him;
>   because you have all your faculties do not despise him. . . .
> Whosoever forsakes a father is like a blasphemer,
>   And whoever angers a mother is cursed by the Lord. (3:10-13, 16)

The promise fits this expectation. As adult children help provide well-being for their aged parents, they also model for their own children how to honor parents, thus increasing the possibility that they will receive similar treatment in their own old age (cf. Eph 6:2). As with the Sabbath commandment, this commandment envisions a community in which production and practical usefulness do not limit a person's meaning; thus honoring parents benefits the ongoing community.

With its starting point in the particular story of God and Israel and with its social concern, this commandment (as well as the fourth) provides a transition to the last five commandments. Disrespectful treatment of parents in the home, a setting where contempt and abuse are easily possible, easily leads to mistreatment of other community members, especially those who are weaker or more vulnerable to abuse. A healthy community requires that the most vulnerable are protected.

Patrick Miller reports that during the Reformation turmoil, both Luther and Calvin extended the meaning of this commandment to call for obedience to civil authorities. Luther understood all authority as "derived and developed out of the authority of parents" (2009: 208). The primary exegetical ground for this move is the supposed connection between this command and the Deuteronomic material on leadership roles (16:18-18:22). Despite the absence of any reference to parents in these chapters, it is suggested that "they share with the commandment honoring parents a basic set of values concerning the role and purpose of authority" (Olson: 78). But such an extension of a directive understood to protect vulnerable parents is at best awkward and appears to be moved more by an effort to apply these commandments to civil society rather than within a particular community of redeemed slaves.

In Mark, Jesus endorses this command and then reprimands those who attempt to escape its practical implications with the justification that (in its place) they are making an offering to God (7:9-13). Jesus' words about hating father and mother (Luke 14:26-27) thus are "not an attack on the commandment to honor parents but an insistence that following him means letting go of all things that matter, . . . setting discipleship above all devotions, caring more about obedience to the Lord, or following Jesus, than anything else" (Miller 2009: 215).

The Sixth Commandment: Murder, 5:17. The last five commandments deal with community life; within both Jewish and Christian tradition, they have been understood as practical implications of the commandment to love neighbor as self (cf. Lev 19:18, 34; Matt 22:39-40 and parallels). The Deuteronomic version of the Decalogue (in Hebrew) binds these five commandments together into one sentence, beginning each new directive with *neither* (NRSV, RSV; lit., *and*; entirely ignored by NIV). Despite dealing with matters of human interaction, these commandments still are not laws for the judicial system. They say nothing about possible punishment, nor do they make the fine distinctions necessary for criminal law (e.g., they do not distinguish between intentional homicide and accidental killing; they do not help determine when an action is to be understood as stealing). Thus they remain general descriptions of the kinds of actions that lead to a more blessed life in the community.

As Wilma Bailey observes in her important study, around the middle of the twentieth century a subtle shift took place in the translation of this verse (2005). Whereas previously it tended to be translated *Thou shalt not kill* (KJV; similarly ASV, RSV, etc.), it now became *You shall not murder* (NRSV, NASB, NIV, NKJV, etc.). Whereas the term *kill* could include all taking of human life, the term *murder* limits it to unlawful killing, whether first-degree murder (i.e., premeditated, intentional homicide) or manslaughter (i.e., unintentional or accidental homicide). With that change of wording, killing in war, capital punishment, and self-defense are abruptly exempted from the prohibition.

The stated reasons for this change are the claims that (1) the key Hebrew term in this commandment elsewhere means "murder" and (2) to translate it as *kill* puts this commandment in tension with other passages in which God allows or even commands the taking of life in war or capital punishment. And yet as Bailey shows, the first claim is incorrect (e.g., Num 35:30; Deut 4:41-42; Prov 22:13), and the logic of the second claim is faulty (scholars do not normally change translations in order to produce an absolutely consistent God or text). She goes on to suggest that this change in translation is more due to theological and political considerations: "Most people either support killing traditions such as war and capital punishment or are resigned to them. A 'you shall not murder' translation fits their theological or political commitments better than a 'you shall not kill' translation" (2005: 20).

Some details of her argument may be debated, but her overall approach to the Decalogue and its role is instructive. The Decalogue is not a legal code to be implemented, which then can be debated in lawyerlike fashion to determine what is allowed and what is not. Rather, it is a "pedagogical tool," presenting a window into a life of faithfulness (Bailey 2005: 83). The commandments characterize the grateful life of a redeemed community, and as such, they are principles that invite refining and clarifying, "deepening and broadening," within that community (cf. J. Yoder and his similar language).

The related regulations and directives of the New and Old Testaments reflect such development and expansion, with both Christianity and Judaism continuing this refining process. The responsibility for exacting blood revenge is removed from the family or clan and lodged in the larger covenant community. The Old Testament, and rabbinic texts after the biblical period, put increasing limits on capital punishment by exempting accidental killing (Num 35:22-28; Deut 19:1-10), by requiring two witnesses (Num 35:30), by excluding cultic and other crimes, and by placing increasingly strict regulations on the trial process and thereby making its application unusual if not impossible. Talmudic literature requires not only two witnesses but also that they need to testify that they have witnessed the act and had warned the person "beforehand that if he carried out the act he would be executed, and he had to accept the warning, stating his willingness to commit the act despite his awareness of the consequences." Circumstantial evidence was not allowed, nor even the criminal's own confession (Jacobs: 67). In the story of Cain and Abel, God does not find the death penalty necessary for murder (Gen 4).

Jesus continues this process further when he fulfills the law by applying the command even to motive (Matt 5:21-22) and by enlarging the target people to include even the enemy (5:43-44). Jesus allowed himself to become the victim of a violation of the sixth commandment, demonstrating the supreme application of his own teaching (cf. J. Yoder: 397). For the first few centuries the Christian church understood the essence of the sixth commandment to imply the rejection of all killing, including that of capital punishment and war. Thus they counted all killing as a form of playing God—the basic sin of humankind. For behind the sixth commandment lies not some abstract principle on the sacredness of life, but rather the conviction that questions of life and death belong to God, that all human bloodshed is a taking over of the prerogative of God, and that such presumption is destructive of human community.

The Seventh Commandment: Adultery, 5:18. Numerous Old Testament passages reflect Israel's concern with a broad range of sexual matters. Formally, the seventh commandment has a more narrow focus, with an interest in the dynamics of a marriage relationship rather than sexual conduct in general. It is often suggested that a dual standard existed in Israel, allowing sexual activity between a married man and a single woman or a prostitute, in some cases, but prohibiting sexual relations between a married or engaged woman and any man outside her marriage (cf. 22:28-29). It is true that in Israel, standards for men and women were not identical. Yet the general nature of the term *adultery*, combined with the fact that these commandments were addressed to the community as a whole, suggests a broad application. Further, as was the case with the previous commandment on murder, approaching this commandment as a law that can be mechanically applied or can become the basis for legal reasoning represents a misappropriation of the Decalogue. The seventh commandment is another sweeping statement, without careful definitions or distinctions and without any consideration of consequences or possible punishments for disobedience. It presents a basic reality or truth about life in community: breaking a marriage covenant is destructive to marriage and as such it is unfaithfulness to the partner; it violates the neighbor's marriage, harms the community, and is a sin against God (cf. Gen 39:7-9).

Numerous Old Testament stories and laws confirm the seriousness with which Israel took the issue of adultery (e.g., Sarah, Abraham, and Abimelech, Gen 20; Joseph and Potiphar's wife, Gen 39; David and Bathsheba, 1 Sam 11–12; regulations of Deut 22:22-27; Lev 18:20; 20:10). Consistent with this, adultery becomes one of the most powerful metaphors for Israel leaving its exclusive commitment to Yahweh and including other gods in its worship (cf. Hos 1–3; Jer 3:6-14; 13:27; Ezek 16; 23). It is common to identify political treaties as the background for Israel's understanding of its covenant with God, yet the marriage covenant plays a more explicit role in the Old Testament. It also provides color for the references to God's jealousy in response to Israel breaking the first commandment, with its expectation of exclusive commitment (Deut 4:23-24; 5:9; 6:14-15; 32:21). Conversely, the use of the marriage metaphor for God's relationship with Israel highlights the significance of the marriage covenant. The world of the day provides the context within which the principle was originally understood (e.g., polygamy is not rejected, patriarchy is accepted), but the faithful marriage relationship is considered one of the cornerstones of a healthy people of God.

Jesus' expansion of this commandment to lust or the thought of adultery (Matt 5:27-28) is already anticipated in the Decalogue itself; the tenth commandment in Deuteronomy opens with the prohibition of coveting *your neighbor's wife* (Deut 5:21). Jesus also expands the range of this commandment to include marrying someone who is divorced (Matt 5:32; 19:9; Mark 10:11-12; Luke 16:18), thereby protecting further the marriage covenant. Jesus does offer grace to the woman caught in adultery, even as he names the act sin: "Go . . . and from now on sin no more" (John 8:11; cf. Hosea speaking of God taking adulterous Israel back, in 2:14-23).

The Eighth Commandment: Stealing, 5:19. It is possible that the original focus of this commandment was the stealing of persons, kidnapping. Other laws in the Old Testament show this as a problem (e.g., Exod 21:16; Deut 24:7), with the story of Joseph just one example. Such an interpretation would fit with the Old Testament's concern for people over property. Stealing another person for personal gain, possibly for selling into slavery, would undermine the well-being of the community and be a breach of the spirit of this commandment.

There is no need, however, to limit the scope of this commandment to kidnapping: instead, all theft is covered. Yet its primary concern is not a modern notion of private property, but rather the protection of those unable to defend themselves against the designs of the more powerful. The story Nathan told David about the rich man who stole the only lamb of a poor neighbor represents this concern very well (2 Sam 12). Further, the Old Testament makes it clear that stealing is not limited to physically taking something that belongs to someone else but also happens in diverse ways. The Deuteronomic prohibition of moving a neighbor's boundary marker is one example (19:14) but so are provisions controlling the use of property taken as pledges (24:10-13), prohibiting the charging of interest (23:19-20), and withholding wages from the poor (24:14-15). One might also include here the expectation that the Israelite is expected to watch out for a neighbor's straying animals (22:1-4).

Israel's prophets repeatedly indict Israel's leaders for not protecting the poor and for devoting all energy to accumulating wealth. Jesus may not directly refer to this commandment, but his ministry is very much one of good news for the poor (cf. Luke 4:18). Patrick Miller concludes that the commandment is "a fundamental instruction with broad-ranging applications protecting the lives of members of the community from oppression and exploitation." He quotes John Calvin in support:

> Since charity is the end of the Law, we must seek the definition of theft from thence. This, then, is the rule of charity, that every one's rights should be safely preserved and that none should do to another what he would not have done to himself. It follows, therefore, that not only are those thieves who secretly steal the property of others, but those also who seek for gain from the loss of others, accumulate wealth by unlawful practices, and are more devoted to their private advantage than to equity. (quoted in Patrick Miller 1990: 92)

The Ninth Commandment: False Witness, 5:20. The language of this commandment has as its background Israel's judicial system. Trials or legal matters were often settled at the city gate by a quorum of citizens, stopped on their way to and from their fields (cf. Ruth 4). Modern investigative procedures and technology obviously were absent, with the integrity of the verdict largely dependent on the truthful word of the accuser, the accused, and the witnesses. Deuteronomy highlights the connection with the third commandment by using the same Hebrew word in each, traditionally translated *vain* in the third commandment (KJV, RSV), but as *false witness* (KJV, RSV, NRSV) or *false testimony* (NIV) in the ninth.

Lives and reputation were at stake. Old Testament laws dealing with witnesses (e.g., Exod 23:1-3; Deut 17:6; 19:15-21), the stories of Naboth's vineyard (1 Kings 21), and the accusation of Potiphar's wife against Joseph (Gen 39), and psalms that lament false accusations (e.g., Ps 27:12)—all point to potential abuse in this area. Order in society, both ancient and modern, is very much dependent upon people's confidence in the judicial system. As Charles Swezey says, "The duty not to bear false witness is a cornerstone of the court because it forbids inflicting harm. The institutionalization of this practice is a social condition for the survival of society" (407).

But the import of this commandment is in no way limited to the legal process. Words can be powerful weapons with destructive impact, whether used to distort the legal system or elsewhere. Sissela Bok observes, "Deceit and violence—these are two forms of deliberate assault on human beings" (quoted by Miller 1990: 345). Lying can destroy a reputation, and it can be used as a way of gaining property from others, most commonly from the poor or powerless. Today truth is distorted through euphemism, spin, misrepresentation, and doublespeak, all hurting the neighbor and the community.

The prophets thus regularly accuse the people of lying (e.g., Hos 4:2; Jer 51; Mic 6:12). Jesus warns the people not to swear falsely, but to "let your word be 'Yes, Yes' or 'No, No'" (Matt 5:33-37). Integrity cannot be maintained in the court system if it is trampled on in the rest of life. Life is not divided that neatly. The ninth commandment depicts life within the covenant community as characterized by truthfulness, both in formal or judicial contexts and in daily life. The words of Ephesians well reflect its spirit: "So then, putting away falsehood, let all of us speak the truth to our neighbors, for we are members of one another" (Eph 4:25).

The Tenth Commandment: Coveting, 5:21. The tenth commandment is unique in that it is the only one that deals with an attitude or motivation rather than a concrete action. This uniqueness—and the fact that the term here translated *covet* may in some passages imply a desire that has already resulted in taking something—has led some to argue that the last commandment prohibits the stealing of property, with the eighth one forbidding kidnapping (see discussion of 5:19).

Such a conclusion is unnecessary. The commandments are "addressed to the believer and not to the lawyer" (Weinfeld 1991: 316). The commandments are not civil law but a confession of faithful response to Yahweh. The fact that covetousness is an internal desire and cannot be controlled by the courts or punished, then, is not a problem. The Deuteronomic version of the Decalogue makes this more explicit by using a different term in the second clause of the verse, translated *desire* (in Exodus "covet" is simply repeated in the second clause), a term that even more clearly refers to an inner attitude.

The last commandment zeroes in on the root cause of breaking all the other commandments: a desire or inclination of the heart. This does not eliminate the distinction between thought and deed but highlights the truth that action arises out of thought, or habits of thought, or the very character of a person. This commandment warns against allowing oneself to become overwhelmed by passion, greed, or obsessions about other people and what they have. Deuteronomy's vision is for an alternative community in which both actions and attitude matter.

The two clauses of the last commandment distinguish the two spheres in which coveting is most likely to occur: (1) matters of sexuality and personal relations, and (2) a neighbor's possessions, especially those contributing to economic productivity. The first clause does reflect that on one level the audience of the Decalogue is the adult male head of the house, but the larger context of Deuteronomy presents God as proclaiming the Decalogue to the whole community, including women. Old Testament stories, as well as prophetic indictment, confirm the significance of these two categories. David lusts after Bathsheba (2 Sam 11); Ahab longs for Naboth's vineyard (1 Kings 21); and Micah indicts the wealthy for coveting more fields (2:1-2). In these examples the line between legal and illegal pursuit of the object of desire fades away. Uncontrolled desire for that which is someone else's is the first step in the spiral of immorality and ruin. The initial sin in Scripture begins with misplaced desire (Gen 3:6).

With this move to the inner being, the Decalogue sets the stage for Jesus' approach to the commandments (Matt 5:21-37). For Paul, the command against coveting becomes the illustration of how inordinate desire has the potential to transform even that which is good into sin (Rom 7:7-13): "None of the other commandments could uncover what sin does as clearly as the last one" (P. Miller 2009: 411). James points to coveting and "cravings" as the foundation for conflict and war (4:1-2). A heart or character formed so as not to covet is the way to the covenant faithfulness of the Decalogue, to God, and to community.

5:22 Conclusion

Verse 22 concludes the giving of the Horeb covenant, with the Decalogue as its core and the accompanying wonders of nature: *He added no more.* Later the phrase *the day of the assembly* becomes a formal designation for this event (cf. 9:10; 10:4; 18:16). The two stone tablets receive considerable notice in Deuteronomy (cf. 4:13; 9:8-21; 10:1-5)

Moses Appointed Mediator 5:23-33

The account of the Horeb covenant concludes with a passage introducing Moses as the mediator. In the process a clear distinction is made between (1) the Decalogue, the content of the Horeb covenant; and (2) the rest of the Torah as taught by Moses on behalf of God. This passage has three distinct scenes distinguished from each other by who is on stage. The first scene features Moses and the representatives of Israel (vv. 23-27), the second God and Moses (vv. 28-31), and the third has Moses addressing the people (vv. 32-33).

5:23-27 Israel Asks Moses to Serve as Mediator

The awesomeness of the theophany, with God speaking and the phenomena of fire and darkness, prove too much for people. Earlier this experience was used as evidence for the uniqueness of Yahweh and Yahweh's relationship to Israel (4:33), but now Israel wishes no more of it. After all, no one can see God and live (cf. Exod 33:20). Israel has seen no form (Deut 4:12), but it has *seen* God speak (5:24; cf. v. 4). Consistent with 4:9-14, the text continues to emphasize God's speaking at Horeb. Six times a form of the verb "to hear" is used, four times it notes that God spoke, and four times the voice of God is mentioned (5:23-27). The people promise to obey, but they request of Moses that from now on he represent them before God (5:27; cf. Exod 24:7).

5:28-31 God Confirms Moses as Mediator

God supports the request of the people for a mediator and affirms their commitment to obey. The narrative quickly jumps forward from Horeb to Israel at the border (6:1), but the reader knows that this commitment was short lived since the people made a golden calf at the foot of the mountain (cf. 9:9-29). Deuteronomy simultaneously calls Israel to obedience and recognizes that ultimately this will only happen once the people's hearts have been changed (the term translated *mind* more literally is *heart*, in Israel understood as the center of thinking; cf. 15:9 KJV, RSV) and they truly fear God (30:1-5; cf. Jer 32:39-40; see Deut 10:12–11:1 for discussion of the Deuteronomic emphasis on fearing God). The *return to your tents* (v. 30) formally excuses the people from further immediate responsibility. Moses has become their mediator. Moses is to hear the commandments, the statutes, and the ordinances; then he is to teach them. It is striking that in this important passage commissioning Moses as mediator, the primary content for his role is that of teacher/preacher. This fits with the nature of Deuteronomy as torah or sermon (cf. 1:5).

By distinguishing in this way between the Decalogue and the remainder of the Torah, Deuteronomy confirms the special place of the Decalogue. But this does not give the Decalogue some general universal status as is sometimes argued; it remains firmly rooted in the particular story of Israel. The Ten Commandments, as the content of the Horeb covenant given directly by God and supported by its unconditional style, receive a priority and unique status that remains throughout the biblical story and beyond.

5:32-33 Concluding Exhortation

In the last two verses Moses again addresses the people. In language by now familiar to us, the verses summon Israel to do what God has commanded so that it will go well with them in the land that they are about to possess.

THE TEXT IN BIBLICAL CONTEXT
The Ten Commandments beyond the Pentateuch

For many Christians the Ten Commandments are a summary of Old Testament law, Old Testament law condensed into a nutshell. It thus may be surprising to learn that the Decalogue as such does not play a major role in Scripture. Torah, usually translated as *law*, is mentioned frequently, and individual prohibitions from the Decalogue are referenced regularly, but the Ten Commandments as a distinct unit (named only in Exod 34:28; Deut 4:13; 10:4) is never explicitly named after Deuteronomy *[Law, p. 555]*.

There are biblical passages that, with their reference to prohibitions included in the Decalogue, may have the Decalogue in mind. Jeremiah does refer to stealing, murder, adultery, and swearing falsely, as well as going after other gods (7:9), and Hosea indicts the people for "swearing, lying, and murder, and stealing and adultery" (4:2). These may be allusions to the Decalogue, but they may also reflect a general or popular sense that these actions were wrong, a common conviction that influenced both. Consistent with this, Leviticus 19 presents a longer series of commandments or responsibilities as explication of the rationale, "You shall be holy, for I the LORD your God am holy" (19:2). The series includes most of the commandments of the Decalogue, but many others as well. There thus is no unequivocal evidence that the Decalogue as such played a prominent role in Old Testament Israel.

It does appear that by New Testament times the Decalogue had become representative of Old Testament law. When the rich ruler asks Jesus what he must do to inherit eternal life, Jesus refers to the commandments, and then continues "You shall not murder; You shall not commit adultery; You shall not steal; You shall not bear false witness; Honor your father and mother; also, You shall love your neighbor as yourself" (Matt 19:18-19; cf. Mark 10:19; Luke 18:20). Most commentators interpret Jesus as here quoting five of the commandments of the Decalogue, and then adding the command to love the neighbor from Leviticus 19:18.

In a similar way, other New Testament passages may be references to the Decalogue. James mentions murder and adultery, although in reverse order (2:11). Ephesians includes the clearest references to the Decalogue, for after it cites the command to honor father and mother, it adds, "this is the first commandment with a promise," an observation that appears to have the Decalogue in mind (Eph 6:2). In Romans, Paul references the commandments against adultery, murder, stealing, and coveting, but his summarizing "Love your neighbor as yourself" suggests he may not be thinking of the Decalogue as a whole (Rom 13:9).

But the story of Jesus and the ruler, as well as the epistle references, is revealing. If Jesus' response is a quotation from the Decalogue, it is interesting that the commandments are not given in their biblical order, and that the command to love the neighbor is included, with no distinction between it and the previous commands. Further, it is striking that, although the story is told in all three synoptic gospels, the order of the commandments varies, and even what is cited varies. The Markan version includes "You shall not defraud" (often interpreted as a substitute for the command not to covet, but really quite different) and omits the command to love the neighbor (10:19). The Lukan version exchanges the order of the first two commandments and has no reference either to defrauding or loving the neighbor. Assuming that Jesus is here referring to the Decalogue, these variations suggest that the Decalogue with a particular order may not have been as distinct and set as we may think.

Perhaps as interesting is the way Jesus uses these commands. Jesus' response may quote five commands from the Decalogue, but he adds to them an additional one from Leviticus and, at least in Mark, the command not to defraud. Donald Hagner suggests: "Thus Jesus here neither lists all the commandments, nor does he put them in order of importance. He points instead to some of the commandments as representative of the whole" (557). When the ruler responds that he has indeed followed them (i.e., not these particular examples but the commandments as a whole), Jesus goes beyond them and says, "Go, sell your possessions, and give the money to the poor" (Matt 19:21; Mark 10:21; Luke 18:22). This reminds one of how Jesus, in the Sermon the Mount, expanded the thrust of the commands against murder, adultery, and swearing falsely (Matt 5:21-37).

As in Deuteronomy, these commandments are treated as neither comprehensive nor to be taken legalistically, but as a partial painting of what a faithful life looks like. Deuteronomy includes both the Decalogue and tithe regulations, yet still exhorts Israel to be generous. Torah is God's direction for Israel, with the Decalogue the most prominent sampling of it; but it remains representative rather than foundational or exhaustive.

THE TEXT IN THE LIFE OF THE CHURCH
The Ten Commandments on Display

Roy Moore, chief justice of the Alabama Supreme Court, generated enormous controversy in 2003 when he refused to remove a stone monument of the Ten Commandments from the front of the Alabama Judicial Building, disregarding a direct order from a federal judge to do so. As a result he was removed from his position by the Alabama Court of Judiciary (in 2012 he was reelected), and the monument was taken away. The dispute, however, drew attention to the prominence of the Ten Commandments in public places in the United States and the arguments used in support of it.

Although there is a long history of references to the Decalogue by U.S. political leaders, the practice of setting up monuments with the Ten Commandments on them, or placing them on the wall of a courthouse, is generally a more recent practice. In the 1950s the Fraternal Order of the Eagles (FOE) energetically distributed pamphlets with the Ten Commandments. When Cecil DeMille heard of this, he proposed an informal partnership with FOE for constructing and distributing stone monuments of the Decalogue. These were then used to promote his new movie, *The Ten Commandments*, with actors on hand for the dedication. In 1956 Charlton Heston said the following at the dedication of such a monument at the International Peace Gardens on the Manitoba-North Dakota border: "The Ten Commandments have become the basis for the whole code of human law.... It is appropriate that on the border between the two countries, the United States and Canada, the Ten Commandments have an important place to show how men can live in peace" (Hoffman). Another six-foot monument of the Decalogue, set up by the FOE in 1961 at the state capitol in Austin, Texas, entered the news recently when the U.S. Supreme Court narrowly agreed to allow it to remain there. Interestingly, the court considered it to serve a mixed but primarily nonreligious purpose.

The arguments for placing the Decalogue in public settings tend to be twofold. Moore and others see this as a public witness to the sovereignty of God, a way of symbolizing U.S. dependence on God, perhaps analogous to the "In God We Trust" on U.S. currency. In the face of strong separation of church and state commitments in the U.S., however, a second argument becomes more prominent. In this approach the Decalogue is considered essentially nonreligious, but serving as the historic and moral foundation of U.S. and even English common law. Historians challenge the validity of this argument. For example, most of the Ten Commandments have never been part of U.S. law, even if they may be considered by many to reflect a moral ideal. We may affirm that it is good to honor our parents, or that adultery is wrong, or that coveting is destructive, but these do not become legislated. The opening commandments on worshiping only God, or the prohibition of images, also are not part of Western legal tradition. Perhaps one might even compare this with the Old Testament itself, in which the Decalogue is neither the foundation of torah nor a summary of it, even if it may be the most prominent sampling series.

From the standpoint of biblical tradition, however, this second argument is striking for an entirely different reason. It was noted above that the Decalogue, indeed all of the Torah, is inextricably bound up with Israel's particular story. The God who freed Israel from Egyptian slavery entered into a covenant with them at Horeb that bound the people to him, that made them his *treasured possession* (Deut 7:6; cf. Exod 19:5). Within that covenantal relationship, God gave them torah, instructions for how to live as God's people in the Promised Land. The Decalogue is not some abstract, self-interpreting legal code, but a window into torah that is given concrete content through the particular story of God and the people of God. Later we will see how God's way of dealing with them as slaves in Egypt provides the model for what it means to love God, and how to relate to the alien in the land (e.g., Deut 10:19, *You shall also love the stranger, for you were strangers in the land of Egypt*; cf. 24:17-18).

Deuteronomy 6:1-11:32

Part 2C
Preaching the Foundational Commandment

OVERVIEW

After introducing the Horeb covenant, Deuteronomy continues by preaching on its foundational expectation: Israel is to worship only one God, Yahweh of the exodus. The Shema (6:4-9) at the heart of the first section (6:1-9) is a reformulation of the first commandment, along with an expansion of it. Not only is Israel to have only Yahweh as God; the Israelites are also to love this God with their total beings. The remainder of this unit then considers who this God is, who Israel is, and what this relationship means. The key here is the theme of election: God chose Israel to be his special people, a choice based not on merit but on God's gracious love (7:1-26). Indeed, Israel tends to be a stubborn people, inclined to go its own way (9:1-10:11). It thus is critical that Israel remember and not forget its God (6:10-25), especially when they have become settled in the land and *lack nothing* (8:1-20, esp. 9). The significance of this foundational expectation is summarized in the "Midcourse Review" (10:12–11:32): whether Israel experiences blessing or curse when in the land is entirely dependent upon whether it *loves*, *fears*, and *serves* this God, whether it *walks* in his ways and *keeps* his commandments.

OUTLINE FOR PART 2C
Yahweh Is One—Yahweh Alone, 6:1-9
Remembering Yahweh in the Land, 6:10-25
Chosen to Be a Holy Possession, 7:1-26
Remember! Do Not Forget! 8:1-20
Israel: Stubborn, Not Righteous, 9:1–10:11
A Midcourse Review, 10:12–11:32

Deuteronomy 6:1-9
Yahweh Is One—Yahweh Alone

PREVIEW
We love debates about what or who is number one. Is athlete X the greatest baseball player ever, or is it athlete Y? Is family the most important value, or is it serving others? Perhaps the scribe who asked Jesus, "Which commandment is the first of all?" (Mark 12:28), was participating in such banter. When Jesus answers by citing Deuteronomy 6:4-5, the scribe agrees. The foundational nature of this passage is evident within the book of Deuteronomy as well. After a brief introduction (6:1-3), the Shema, or great commandment (Matt 22:34-40), is presented.

OUTLINE
Introduction, 6:1-3
The Foundational Commandment, 6:4-9

EXPLANATORY NOTES
Introduction 6:1-3
The opening three verses of chapter 6 serve as an introduction and bridge, most specifically to the Shema (6:4-9) but also to the rest of the long second speech that follows, both the exposition of this foundational commandment (chs. 6–11) and the preaching of the Moab covenant (chs. 12–26). The Horeb covenant, with the Decalogue

at its center, has been presented (5:6-22), its present relevance has been proclaimed (5:1-5), and Moses has been commissioned as God's teacher and mediator (5:23-33). Now Moses begins his teaching task, the assignment given in 5:31.

The content of this teaching is *the commandment—the statutes and ordinances* (6:1). The NRSV translation of this somewhat unusual phrase (one singular noun coupled to two plural nouns, as also in 5:31; 7:11) suggests that the term "commandment" is a comprehensive term for the whole teaching of Deuteronomy, similar in meaning to torah. Alternative proposals include that the singular term "commandment" refers (1) to "the same principle underlying all the law" (Craigie 1976: 167; Christensen 2001: 135); or (2) to the first commandment of the Decalogue, the "basic demand for loyalty that is actually expounded in 6:4–11:30," with the statutes and ordinances referring to the regulations of chapters 12–26 (Weinfeld 1991: 327; Olson: 50); or (3) to the Decalogue as a whole over against the regulations (implied by P. Miller 1990: 66–70). Although the distinctions suggested are present and important in Deuteronomy, it is doubtful any of them can be derived from this admittedly unusual phrase.

The remainder of the introduction consists largely of stock Deuteronomic phrases and themes: Israel is to observe this teaching in the land; concern for children and grandchildren; the goal that this generation and those following will fear God all their lengthy lives, so that it will go well with them, and so that they will multiply greatly in the land, a land flowing with milk and honey. The phrase *milk and honey* highlights the fertility of the land compared to Egypt; likely the milk is from goats and the honey a paste from dates. All is traced back to God's original promise to the ancestors. All has been heard previously and will be heard again. For a discussion of the various Deuteronomic terms for obedience, see comments on 10:12–11:1.

The Foundational Commandment 6:4-9

Judaism and Christianity agree in designating this passage, commonly called the Shema (on the basis of the Hebrew of the first word, *Hear!*), the most important text in the whole of the Old Testament. Some years ago while flying across the Atlantic, I observed an Orthodox Jew faithfully praying the Shema at the rear of the plane. Observant Jews recite this prayer every morning and every evening. And when Jesus is asked which commandment is first or greatest, he responds by quoting from the Shema. The significance of the Shema for Deuteronomy is clear from its location at the head of Moses' teaching after the account of the covenant at Horeb, and by the regular references to it in other parts of Deuteronomy (e.g., 10:12; 11:1, 13, 18-22; 13:3; 30:6). In this passage we are at the center of Deuteronomy's theology and at the heart of biblical faith.

Integral to the Shema's power is its combination of a confession of faith (v. 4) with a statement expressing an expected response (vv. 5-9; cf. the prologue and the commands of the Decalogue, 5:6-21). The Shema contains the "fundamental truth of Israel's religion" and "the fundamental duty founded upon it" (Driver: 89). The truth is contained in the phrase immediately following the opening call to listen, a phrase that in the Hebrew consists of four words: *Yahweh/our God/Yahweh/one*. Although the meaning of each individual term is clear, the translation of the phrase is much disputed, both because a verb or two needs to be supplied and, perhaps even more significantly, because the connotations of the last term are not obvious. Most English versions draw attention to this by including two or three alternative readings in a footnote. Two primary options are *The LORD our God, the LORD is one* (NKJV, NIV; cf. RSV, KJV) and *The LORD is our God, the LORD alone* (NRSV).

The first half of the phrase claims Yahweh to be the God of the community. The name Yahweh was revealed during the call of Moses before the exodus (Exod 3:13-15) and ever afterward remained a constant reminder of that event. The prologue to the Decalogue opens with Yahweh identifying himself as *your God* and then referring to the supreme act of deliverance. The Shema thus hints at this as well. The personal nature of the relationship is intimated by what in Hebrew is one word: *our God*. The significance of this relationship for Deuteronomy is marked by more than 240 references to *your God* (well over half of such references in the whole OT), and a further twenty-four references to *our God*. Any confession of faith for Israel begins with this assertion.

The second half of the phrase continues the confession. The NRSV's *the LORD alone* probably is implied by the passage and fits Deuteronomic theology. From beginning to end, Deuteronomy emphasizes that God redeemed Israel and that in response Israel owes Yahweh *uncompromising exclusive* allegiance. Recognizing the political treaty background for the term "love" would support such a reading (below). This translation then becomes a positive expression of the first commandment, which calls on Israel to worship only God: the affirmation of the Shema has Israel accepting that claim. It may not reflect abstract monotheism (see comment on 5:7), but it is an expression of total commitment. Given the Deuteronomic context of the Shema, this significance certainly is part of the assertion.

The alternative translation, *The LORD our God, the LORD is one*, may be a more straightforward reading of the Hebrew but is less clear in meaning. What does it mean for God to be one? At least two options are possible. The first has its background in Israel's worship of God under different names and in different places. Israel's ancestors built altars throughout the land and used multiple names for their God (e.g., *El Shaddai*, translated "God Almighty," Gen 17:1). When the name Yahweh is revealed to Moses, the narrative stresses that this is the same God as the one the ancestors worshiped, even though they knew him by a different name (Exod 6:2-3). During the tribal period as well as during the time of the monarchy, Israel continued to worship Yahweh at various holy sites. Deuteronomy's strong opposition to such many-sites practice (cf. Deut 12) is evidence that it was considered a problem. Given the polytheistic world of the day, the danger of seeing these as different gods no doubt existed. Over against this possibility the opening phrase of the Shema asserts that God is one: the God worshiped by the ancestors under a different name, and the God worshiped by Israel throughout the land is one God, and that God is Yahweh, the God of the exodus.

But there is a second and perhaps more significant meaning of the phrase. A real question for Israel was whether God was consistent, whether God could be trusted. When the spies return and give their report on the Promised Land, the people respond by accusing God of hating them (1:27). The accusation, made against the background of the exodus event, can only "imply either Yahweh's inconsistency or Yahweh's deceptiveness, in both cases a form of double-dealing and thereby of moral doubleness" (J. Janzen 1987a: 283). Over against such a possibility, the Shema affirms God's moral integrity and unity. God is one in the sense that God's nature is always loving and merciful, not sometimes loving and sometimes hating. And God is also one in that there is a "unity between desire and action, between intention and execution" (J. Janzen 1987a: 287). God can be counted on to act in the future in a manner consistent with his redemption of Israel as his people in the past. Because of this unity, Israel can trust God and his promises. As a statement of God's character, it enforces the frequent reminders of God's promise to the ancestors. The Shema opens with a statement of faith, an affirmation that begins by acknowledging Yahweh, the God of the exodus, as Israel's God; accepts God's claim of exclusive worship; acknowledges the unity of God despite the various names and holy sites; and, what is most important, affirms the unity and integrity of God's nature.

The second part of the Shema (vv. 5, 6-9) then presents the response that God expects of the people he redeemed from bondage. The key term is *love*. Love is not just some warm emotion or feeling, although it includes that (cf. 1:31), but basically a commitment of total loyalty, a response that can be commanded. As signified by the language of the second commandment (*those who love me and keep my commandments*), its closest synonym in Deuteronomy is obedience (see on 10:12–11:1). Although the parent-child metaphor for Israel's relationship to God plays an important role in Deuteronomy (cf. 1:31), and shapes the connotations of the term *love* as well, the more significant background for Deuteronomy's call to love God is probably the world of politics and international relations (Moran 1963). Ancient Near Eastern treaties use this term for the total loyalty expected from subjects to their king, or from the king of a vassal nation to the king of the nation to which it was subservient. Prior to the exodus, the people had been slaves of Pharaoh, king of Egypt. God has freed them from bondage to Pharaoh, but not for a freedom without direction or for a modern sense of self-determination. Rather, they were freed for service to God. Repeatedly Moses calls on Pharaoh, "Let my people go, <u>so that they may worship me</u>" (lit., "<u>serve me</u>," Exod 7:16, emph. added; cf. 8:1, 20; 9:1, 13; 10:3). Through the exodus and the Horeb covenant, Israel now has a new master. Pharaoh has been replaced by Yahweh. The people now owe Yahweh their total response. "Love" is the term Deuteronomy uses to signify that unqualified response to God.

But this is not a one-way street. The God whom Israel is called to love has loved first, in the election of Israel itself and in the exodus (cf. Deut 4:37; 7:7, 12; 10:15; 23:5; 33:3 mg., KJV; see TBC "Election, Separation, and Mission" at the end of ch. 7). It is a reciprocal love. The content of the term "love" may be colored by its use in political treaties, but God's own action is based on gracious mercy. The God whom Israel is to love is not some petty tyrant but a God who, it has been affirmed, is one.

The combined reference to *heart, soul,* and *might* emphasizes the totality of the response. The separate words appear to have distinctive connotations elsewhere. The term translated *heart* is associated with intellect and decision making, and could even be translated *mind*. Pharaoh's heart is hardened (Exod 7:13; etc.), and Solomon requests a "wise and discerning heart" (1 Kings 3:12 NIV). McConville translates the Hebrew behind NRSV's *soul* as *being*, as referring to the whole person, especially the person's life and vitality (2002: 137; cf. Judg 12:3; Ps 6:4; etc.). The term *might* is also translated *strength* (NIV) and suggests the total capacity of the person, including wealth and possessions.

Consistent with this, some Jewish interpretation has understood these three terms as referring to different ways of demonstrating love toward God: *heart* implies undivided loyalty; *soul* stands for loving God to the point of death, including the possibility of martyrdom; and *might* represents the person's wealth and property, all of which is dedicated to God. Christian exegesis, on the other hand, has tended to view the three terms as representing attributes of the human personality: *heart* is the mind or intention, *soul* is the soul of the person, and *might* suggests spiritual and moral power.

But here these divisions are less significant than their combined meaning. The total being of the community and its members now must turn toward the one who has redeemed them. Deuteronomy 6:5 is

> not a statement of early Greek psychology nor does it seem likely that precise modes of expressing love were intended by the three terms. They were not meant to specify specific distinct acts, spheres of life, attributes, or the like, but were chosen to reinforce the absolute singularity of personal devotion to God. (McBride 1973: 304)

Love of God means loving and obeying God with one's total being; thus each term represents the whole person in some way.

This means not only the total being but also the total life. The confession of faith and the appropriate response of love are to become part of the heart, the very essence of the person (v. 6); they are to set direction at home and away, from morning till night (v. 7b), and as many ways as possible must be employed to continually remind the person of the central significance of the affirmation and response (vv. 8-9). Some Jewish groups take these last few verses quite literally, leading to their reciting the Shema morning and evening, and even binding actual copies of the Shema to arms and foreheads and to doorframes of the house. Archaeology provides evidence that such practices were not unheard of in the ancient world, thus suggesting that these verses may very well have been intended literally. But even taken figuratively, they emphasize the all-encompassing nature of the expectation. Love of God is to infuse and inform the whole life of the individual and community.

Finally, this central teaching is to be taught to the children (v. 7a). As has been noticed previously (4:9-10), and will be emphasized again at the end of this chapter (vv. 20-25), Deuteronomy regularly returns to the theme of transmitting the faith to the next generation. The timeless *today* of Deuteronomy requires that each generation has to reaffirm its allegiance to the God who loved first.

THE TEXT IN BIBLICAL CONTEXT
Loving God

That God loved Israel is not a particularly pervasive theme in the Old Testament. It is important for Hosea, who speaks of it directly (3:1; 9:15; 11:1; 14:4) and through story (chs. 1–3), and it is noted by Isaiah (43:4), Jeremiah (31:3), and Malachi (1:2). But the only references outside of Deuteronomy to God loving Israel prior to the Psalms (47:4) and the Prophets are placed in the mouths of foreigners, the Queen of Sheba (1 Kings 10:9; 2 Chron 9:8) and King Hiram of Tyre (2 Chron 2:11).

To summarize, Israel's expected response to God with the term *love* is a uniquely Deuteronomic contribution. Both Judaism and Christianity have developed this Deuteronomic emphasis into a central theme. Around the time of Christ, the Shema already held a special place in the worship of Jewish groups. More recently it has been called "the Jewish confession of faith par excellence," and "the fundamental doctrine of Judaism." Rabbinic sources speak of the person reciting the Shema as "receiving upon oneself the yoke of the kingdom of Heaven (God)" (McBride 1973: 276). Consistent with Deuteronomic theology, this phrase describes the Shema as an oath of allegiance to God, the suzerain who has replaced Pharaoh.

Although the Shema came to be understood as the central conviction of Judaism, this was not always so in Israel. Struggle over this central claim is evident throughout much of the story of Israel. Elijah stands out as one who challenged Israel for "limping with two different opinions" (1 Kings 18:21). On that day on Mount Carmel, the people reaffirmed their loyalty, "The LORD indeed is God; the LORD indeed is God" (18:39), but the battle was far from over. As Deuteronomy reminds us, it is so easy to forget this commitment.

Christian emphasis on the passage goes back to the words of Christ himself. All three synoptic gospels contain the story of Jesus and the first, or great, commandment. In what is possibly the earliest account (Mark 12:28-34), a scribe asks Jesus, "Which commandment is the first of all?" Jesus responds by quoting Deuteronomy 6:4-5 and adding to it the command to "love your neighbor as yourself" (from Lev 19:18). Then Jesus declares, "There is no other commandment greater than these." The dialogue appears to reflect a contemporary Jewish debate. The scribe supports Jesus' position in the debate. Interestingly, his response, "He is one, and beside him there is no other" (Mark 12:32), implicitly affirms both translations discussed earlier.

In the Matthew account, Jesus adds, "On these two commandments hang all the law and the prophets" (Matt 22:40). The addition fits the structure and theology of Deuteronomy. The teaching of the Horeb covenant begins with the Shema, a reformulation of the first (and second) commandment(s) of the Decalogue. The remainder of chapters 6–11 is an exposition of that most fundamental teaching, with chapters 12–26 providing regulations, or what might be called illustrations of what the fundamental command means for daily life in community, in interaction with neighbor.

THE TEXT IN THE LIFE OF THE CHURCH

Centrality of the Shema

Martin Luther and the early Anabaptists disagreed on some key matters. But their affirmation of the Shema as having a binding claim on the Christian was similar. Luther speaks of it as a second assertion of the First Commandment, with a slightly different emphasis: the first touches faith, the Shema touches love:

> No one can have one God unless he clings to Him alone and trusts in Him alone: otherwise he will be snatched off into a variety of works and will devise various gods. The second touches love, which follows from the first. For when we repose all faith in Him to whom we cling and understand that all things flow from Him alone and that we are in His care, then sweet love toward Him has to follow. (Luther: 68)

Luther also states that the command to love this God with our total being is literally impossible since we all have weaknesses. The command thus assumes that God's forgiveness is available to the saints.

Menno Simons does not devote detailed attention to the Shema but does cite it at a few points and draws two emphases from it. First, he equates the love of God charged by the Shema with obedience to the commandments, in a manner similar to what Jesus did in his response to the lawyer (657; cf. Matt 22:34-40). Second, he focuses on the last half of the Shema, with its emphasis on teaching the faith to our children (388).

Mennonite confessions also regularly cite the Shema in support of the affirmation of only one God. For example, Dirk Philips writes,

"In the first place, we believe and confess that there is one God and Lord Jesus as is basically contained in all Scripture and expressly stated in writing"; Deuteronomy 6:4 is the first verse given in support of this assertion (62). It is used similarly in confessions from different geographical wings of the early Anabaptist family (Koop: 52, Swiss/South German; 138, 172, Waterlander; 172, 270, Frisian, Flemish, and High German). In one interesting example it is also used as biblical support for the unity of God (177).

The use of the Shema in support of the confession that there is only one single, unified God raises an intriguing question. In so doing early Anabaptist leaders, among others, were taking the verse beyond its original significance within the world of ancient Israel, where it was not speaking to the theoretical question of whether or not only one God truly existed. What might such expansion of the verse mean in the contemporary world, especially one in which the religions of Judaism, Christianity, and Islam are often in conflict with each other despite their agreement that there is only one God? Although not overtly based on the Shema, the Islamic creed, or Shahada, similarly states, "There is no god but God," and then adds, "Muhammad is the messenger of God." What does Paul mean when he writes to the Christians in Rome, "Or is God the God of Jews only? Is he not the God of Gentiles also? Yes, of Gentiles also, since God is one" (Rom 3:29-30a)? Or, how does Paul's identification of the God of Jesus Christ with the unknown god of the Athenians relate to the Shema (Acts 17:23)?

Deuteronomy 6:10-25
Remembering Yahweh in the Land

PREVIEW

We all remember some things; we all forget some things. But what people remember and what they forget differs, raising the question of how we determine what we remember and what we forget. After restating the foundational commandment in the Shema, Deuteronomy turns its attention to the land that Israel is about to enter, and to the danger of forgetting God in the land. Israel is about to receive a land with cities and vineyards ready for use. In the land, Israel will be tempted to forget God and God's directions for them. In the Shema, Israel is charged to recite its words to the children; now the children ask, *What is the meaning?* The answer lies in the story, the story of God's deliverance from Pharaoh, along with God's gift of torah.

OUTLINE

Two Warnings for the Land, 6:10-19
    6:10-15   The Gifted Nature of the Land
    6:16-19   The Danger of Testing God
The Story Provides the Meaning, 6:20-25

EXPLANATORY NOTES

Two Warnings for the Land 6:10-19

6:10-15 *The Gifted Nature of the Land*

This unit (6:10-25), as well as the next three, begins with a reference to Israel entering the Promised Land (v. 10; cf. 7:1; 8:1; 9:1). The torah that Moses is teaching the people is the path into the land, and as such it is the key to the good life for Israel. The first concern after the foundational commandment is presented (6:1-9) is how to understand the land. Repeatedly Deuteronomy has spoken of the land as given by God (1:8, 20, 25, 35, 36, 39; 2:29, 31; 3:20; 4:1, 21, 38, 40; 5:16, 31). Now that emphasis takes center stage. The passage begins with one of the formulaic ways Deuteronomy expresses this theme, *the land that he swore . . . to give you* (6:10), then continues with a poetic description of what they will receive in the land (v. 11):

fine, large cities	*that you did not build*
houses filled with all sorts of goods	*that you did not fill*
hewn cisterns	*that you did not hew*
vineyards and olive groves	*that you did not plant*

The land is bountiful (cf. 8:7-10) and will result in their being filled (v. 11; cf. 8:12), but the repeated phrase *that you did not . . .* draws attention to the main point: they are not, nor ever will be, responsible even for the physical improvements of the land. It is all part of God's gift to them. Although in its literary context these verses refer to cities, houses, and other things constructed or planted by the Canaanites, for a later audience during the monarchy this was no longer literally the case. And yet the truth of the passage remains. As the rest of Deuteronomy makes clear, the people can never treat the land and what it provides for them as their own possession: it always remains a gift from God. In a comparable way the New Testament proclaims, "For by grace you have been saved through faith, and this is not your own doing; it is the gift of God—not the result of works, so that no one may boast" (Eph 2:8-9). Salvation and the gifts of God are never the work of our own hands but due to the mercy and grace of God (P. Miller 1990: 106).

The danger, according to Deuteronomy, is that when the people receive this gift, they will eat and be filled and forget God (Deut 6:12; cf. 8:11-20). In the world of Israel, to forget is more than a mental lapse; it includes an action component (see comments on Deut 8). The warning is emphasized by the first phrase in verse 12, which literally reads *Watch yourself.* If they forget God, they will forget who they were (slaves of Pharaoh) and who they now are (slaves of God). The use of the same root in *house of slavery* and in the phrase *him you shall serve* draws attention to this exchange of masters. Instead of forgetting, they are to *fear* God. To fear God is an alternative way of expressing the great commandment (Lohfink 1968). In 10:12–11:32, the lengthy summary of chapters 5–12, the first answer to the question *What does the LORD require of you?* is *to fear the LORD your God* (10:12). Swearing by the name God reflects such ultimate dependence. When the last half of the passage largely quotes from the first and second commandments (6:13-15; cf. 5:7-10), it is essentially repeating this expectation. Forgetting that the land and its blessings come as a gift is the first step away from fearing God and beginning to go after other gods. The very land that God gives them thus can become that which tempts them to forget God. Forgetting will result in the reversal of the gift, expressed as perishing from earth, or land.

6:16-19 The Danger of Testing God

As with the reference to Baal of Peor in 4:3-4, this short passage uses an incident in Israel's past to highlight a point. The incident is quite clear: Exodus 17:1-7 describes how, during their journey through the wilderness, the people quarrel and complain to Moses because they are thirsty. God responds by having Moses strike a rock, thus providing water for the people. The account closes with "He called the place Massah and Meribah, because the Israelites quarreled and tested the LORD, saying, 'Is the LORD among us or not?'" (v. 7). The name Massah is a form of the Hebrew verb "to test."

The relevance of this episode for chapter 6 relates to the question asked by the people: "Is God really among us?" The question reflects a loss of faith. Earlier in the Exodus account, this loss of faith is represented by the people accusing God of delivering them from slavery only to kill them in the desert (Exod 17:3). In a similar way Israel accuses God after the spies return with their report (Deut 1:27). These accusations impugn the integrity of God's character and question God's constancy, or unity (see comments on 6:4). Such a testing of God is a rejection of the confession with which the Shema begins—*The LORD our God, the LORD is one* (6:4 NRSV mg.)— and the first step in transgressing the commandments. "Obedience, on the other hand, is a tacit declaration that God does not need to be 'proved.'" (Cairns: 87). In Psalm 78:56 the term "test" is used in parallel construction with "rebelling against" God, and with "not observing" his decrees. The Deuteronomy passage continues by calling on Israel to *keep the commandments* so that the people may fully experience *the good land*.

The Story Provides the Meaning 6:20-25

At the center of the Shema is the command to *recite* (RSV, *teach*) *them* (the words of the Shema) *to your children* (6:7). The last passage in chapter 6 picks up this theme and zeroes in on the education of children (cf. 4:9-10; 11:19). Deuteronomy, despite its repeated reference to past events, is not history written for an archives: instead, it is teaching for *today* (see on 5:1-5)! The concern is always the present. Each new generation must be taught in order that it might enter that *today* and respond to that electing God in a manner consistent with the Shema and its implications.

Three aspects stand out. First, a question from a child instigates the teaching moment. Children naturally ask questions. Unusual expectations (*the decrees and the statutes and the ordinances*) inevitably raise questions. Israel's daily life provided countless teaching opportunities. This was true when Israel was in the land, yet even more so during the exile, when Israel's ways and customs distinguished it from its Babylonian neighbors. Such a context naturally raises the questions "Why are we different from everyone else? Why do we have to follow all these rules when others don't?" Judaism formalized this approach by incorporating the questions of children into the ritual of its festivals.

Second, the answer is a story, a carefully formulated survey of Israel's past with God (cf. 26:5-10). Obviously the story is greatly abbreviated, focusing on that part of the story most significant for present identity. It is one story, but it has two distinct parts. The first part highlights God's deliverance from Egyptian slavery. Stereotypical language describes the events: God accomplishes this deliverance *with a mighty hand* and with *awesome signs and wonders*; the goal of the deliverance is *to give us the land*, as promised to the ancestors; this is all done *before our eyes*, as the Exodus account of these events emphasizes, in order that the people might "know that I am the LORD your God" (Exod 6:7). When the sea is crossed, it is reported: "Israel saw the great work that the LORD did against the Egyptians. So the people feared the LORD and believed in the LORD and in his servant Moses" (Exod 14:31). Through this event, Israel comes to know God.

But the answer to the child's question does not end with the account of the exodus. The second part incorporates the Horeb covenant into the story. At that mountain Israel received the Decalogue and entered a covenant with God (Exod 20, 24) through which it became the people of God (cf. Exod 19:4-6). Our passage's description of the event is striking. It speaks of God as commanding Israel *to observe all these statutes* and *to fear the LORD our God*. Again obedience is treated as synonymous with fearing God (cf. 6:2, 13; 10:12-11:1). The outcome of obedience is *for our lasting good, so as to keep us alive* (6:24). Obedience is not requested in order to make God feel good, or as a token of appreciation for the deliverance, or even to satisfy some overarching order in which receipt of divine favor (deliverance) must be balanced by a comparable response (obedience). The answer of the text is that observing the statutes leads to good life for the people. No wonder Deuteronomy points to its statutes and ordinances as its *wisdom and discernment* before the nations and asks, *What other great nation has statutes and ordinances as just as this entire law?* (4:6-7). With this concluding statement (6:21-24), the answer returns to the original question. The *meaning of the decrees and the statutes and the ordinances that the LORD our God has commanded* (6:20) is found in the story, a story that begins with promise to the ancestors, continues with deliverance, and reaches its climax in the giving of direction, all done *for our lasting good.*

It is too simple to distinguish the two parts of the answer as revelation in history and revelation of word, or as salvation and response, although such a distinction contains some truth. The story shaping the child is the story of salvation; but for Israel, salvation includes *both* deliverance *and* direction for life. The structure of the answer may be summarized as follows:

What is the meaning of the decrees . . . ?

Action	**Goal**	
exodus deliverance	*to give us the land*	Salvation
statutes, commandment	*our lasting good, so as to keep us alive*	

Third, the pronouns of the passage demand some attention. The introduction to the passage, with the question and directive, contains five second-person pronouns (vv. 20-21a), four as singular. Unfortunately, the English language hides this since it does not distinguish between "you/your" (sg.) and "you/your" (pl., "you-all"). The NRSV, in its effort to use inclusive language, loses this effect even more as it changes the singular nouns to the plural ("son/

child" becomes *children*, 6:20). But the scene depicted by the Hebrew is an individual young Israelite asking a parent the question.

The response of the parent again makes heavy use of pronouns, but they now shift to first person and plural (*we, us,* or *our,* fifteen times). This significantly impacts the tone of the story (cf. 26:5-11). The second-person pronouns of the question hint at distance—the faith of the parents still is not the faith of the children. The question is that of a semi-outsider. The first-person plural pronouns not only contribute to making the story contemporary, as was called for in 5:1-5—God not only redeemed our ancestors: God also redeems *us* and gives *us* directions; the plural pronouns also invite each succeeding generation into the story. The use of the plural prevents the story from being heard as that of some individual; instead, it is the story of a people. Through this double shift each child is invited to become part of "we," to enter into a community that pledges absolute loyalty to the God who first loved it.

THE TEXT IN BIBLICAL CONTEXT
Biblical Creeds

Expressing the faith of the community in narrative form is a regular feature of the Old Testament and can be found in the New Testament as well. Later in Deuteronomy a similar summary is recited by the Israelite offering a basket of firstfruits in the temple (26:1-9). After Israel enters the Promised Land, when Joshua challenges the people to choose God, he supports the challenge with a survey of God's relations to Israel. Again the account becomes the occasion for inviting Israelites fully to enter that story themselves and worship God in a manner consistent with that story. Psalms 135 and 136 are confessions of this story within the context of worship. Nehemiah 9 recounts how Ezra, at a critical point in the community's life after some returned from exile, reviews that story for the people. Scholars sometimes call such a brief summary of Israel's story a "credo," Israel's creed (cf. Rad 1966: 1-13). They are Israel's expressions of faith.

The New Testament may not highlight such historical credos as obviously, but the basic approach remains. The most significant part of the New Testament is the Gospels—surveys of the life, death, resurrection, and teachings of Jesus—rather than a systematic presentation of theology. Jesus interprets himself through the story (Luke 24:27). The book of Acts continues the story beyond the life of Christ. When Stephen faces martyrdom, he proclaims his confession of faith with a summary of the Old Testament story (Acts 7). The hymn of Philippians 2 can be viewed as summarizing the story of Christ in its briefest form. Both Old and New Testaments call on the people of God to walk in the way of God, with both the meaning and motivation for this walk to be found in the account of God's unprecedented, unmerited actions on behalf of that people. The story highlights this: the story invites others to enter that narrative.

THE TEXT IN THE LIFE OF THE CHURCH
A Story Provides the Meaning

Some years ago a prominent journalist interviewed a Canadian author on a national radio program. At one point the interviewer asked, "You're a Mennonite, aren't you? What do you Mennonites believe?" The response was striking: "We trace our story back to the sixteenth century, to the city of Zurich, and the reforms of Zwingli...." In a few sentences he presented the basic outline of the Anabaptist story. One can quibble with the content, but the manner of the response was consistent with the answer Deuteronomy 6 gives to the child's question.

A weakness of that author's response lies in beginning the story in the sixteenth century. Although Anabaptism as a separate movement originates in the sixteenth century, "our story" goes back much further: it begins where the biblical story begins, with the promise to the ancestors recorded in Genesis, and continues through the Old and New Testaments, climaxing in the incarnation of Christ; then our story continues in the story of the church, in New Testament times, in medieval times, through the Reformation and the origin of our specific movement, up till today. The challenge for Anabaptism (as well as any other Christian tradition) is to learn to tell its story in such a way that the distinctive elements of the tradition are recognized, yet simultaneously so that it is always clearly part of that larger story of God's people, as inaugurated by God's undeserved merciful action. Summarizing the Christian faith through telling the story is more true to the nature of Scripture than the tendency to do so with creeds or systematic expressions of belief. It is doubtful that any form of education of the next generation will be more effective or more faithful to this biblical model than telling the story.

Deuteronomy 7:1-26

Chosen to Be a Holy Possession

PREVIEW

Is chapter 7 instructing Israel on what to do when it arrives at the Promised Land? Or is it a metaphorical exposition of God's love for Israel and what God expects in return? Metaphors can be confusing or even deceptive when taken literally. The key for unlocking the content of the chapter, the window through which one must view it, is verse 6. It presents the central premise of the chapter, election (*God has chosen* [elected] *you*), and proclaims its implications: on the one hand, separation (*You are a people holy*); and on the other hand, abundance and safety (*to be his people, his treasured possession*).

The three principal words of the verse (*holy, chosen,* and *treasured possession*) thus provide the structure for the chapter. The opening verses spell out what it means to be *holy*: to live as a holy people requires separation from the neighboring peoples and their religious ways (vv. 1-5). The central portion of the chapter declares that Israel has been *chosen*, or elected, yet clarifies that that this relationship was initiated by God and is based not on merit but solely on God's undeserved love (vv. 7-11). If Israel remains true to its election, it will be blessed beyond all measure (vv. 12-16), it will be God's *treasured possession* in the land that God is giving (vv. 17-26).

The question provoking this chapter is not what policies Israel is to follow for entering the land, but what it means to be chosen as God's people. Patrick Miller's title for the chapter, "The Election of

Israel," zeroes in on its essence (1990: 110–14). Craigie's title, "Israel's Policy of War," unfortunately misrepresents and misleads (1976: 175).

OUTLINE

Election Requires Separation, 7:1-5
Election and Its Basis, 7:6-11
    7:6   Israel's Election
    7:7   Rejection of Erroneous Explanation
    7:8   Election Grounded in God's Love
    7:9-11 Therefore Yahweh Your God Is God
Faithfulness to Election Leads to Blessing, 7:12-26
    7:12-16 Outline of Blessing
    7:17-26 Blessing and the Awesome God

EXPLANATORY NOTES

Election Requires Separation 7:1-5

The opening paragraph spells out what it means to be *holy*. It does this by calling upon Israel to *ḥerem* (*utterly destroy*) the people of the land (vv. 1-2a), followed by three directives that expand upon or explain the first (vv. 2b-5) *[Ḥerem, p. 552]*. The Old Testament contains some twenty-seven lists of the earlier inhabitants of the land (Weinfeld 1991: 362), some with as many as ten nations (Gen 15:19-21), most with six or seven. The lists with seven emphasize the totality of the peoples. The formulaic style immediately warns us that the focus is less on the nations as historical entities than on their symbolic value. These are not contemporary enemies of Israel, but peoples of long ago (cf. Sihon and Og, ch. 3).

Exactly what is to happen to these *seven nations* is unclear. After suggesting that God will clear away these nations from before Israel, the text continues by saying that *God gives* these nations over to Israel to be defeated, and then concludes by calling upon Israel to *ḥerem* them, a Hebrew term translated *utterly destroy* (7:2; cf. 2:34; 3:6). After translating the text as *destroy them totally*, the NIV acknowledges the ambiguity of the term with a footnote: "The Hebrew term refers to the irrevocable giving over of things or person to the LORD, often by totally destroying them" (7:2 mg.). According to the NJPS, Israel is to *doom them to destruction,* without identifying the instrument of destruction. In the book of Joshua the NIV simply renders this term "devoted to the LORD" (e.g., 6:17, 21). It clearly involves more than simple destruction and has a "mysterious air about it," with a "'sacrificial' or 'sacral' character to it," as something is offered to God (Earl 2010: 54). Not coincidentally, both *holy* and *ḥerem* have as their background the world of the cult *[Cult, p. 546]*.

That the command to ban, or *utterly destroy*, those nations was not understood literally is consistent with the three directives that follow, which would not have been relevant if all the nations had truly been destroyed. It is also consistent with Exodus 23:20-33, after which this passage in Deuteronomy may have been patterned, which similarly calls upon Israel to remain separate from the original inhabitants but without any reference to *ḥerem*.

Israel is to *make no covenant* with the peoples (v. 2b; cf. Josh 9) nor to intermarry with them (vv. 3-4). For the audience of Deuteronomy— whether a weak Judah under Assyrian pressure or a small exilic community surrounded by Babylonian peoples—the passage is not promoting a policy for invading Israelite troops but instead emphasizing God's call for separation and holiness. Treaties with other peoples present multiple problems. Not only do they ally Israel with peoples who might lead Israel astray, but also the very making of the covenant commonly entails the recognition of the gods of both parties. In the world of real politics (e.g., a treaty between Israel and Moab in the face of Assyrian threat), leaders formed strategic alliances not based on trust in God. The paragraph thus opens by making an absolute call for separation.

From the world of political relationships, the text turns to a more practical day-to-day issue. The biblical narrative has a number of stories that exemplify the dangers of marrying outside the faith circle (e.g., Solomon, 1 Kings 11:1-13; Ahab, 1 Kings 16:31). Deuteronomy's call for separation recognizes this as a major temptation and speaks out unambiguously against it (but cf. 20:14; 21:10-14). This includes political marriages but is not limited to them.

Additionally, Deuteronomy calls upon Israel to destroy the cultic objects of Canaanite religion. The *pillars* were stone monuments, probably associated with Canaanite fertility practices. The *sacred poles* (KJV, *groves*; Hebrew, *'ašerim*) appear to have been wooden objects or statues representing the Canaanite goddess Asherah. Each of these was common in Canaanite religion, but as the Old Testament story makes clear, they also were incorporated by many into the Israelite cult. Deuteronomy's rejection of such syncretism is repeated and expanded later (e.g., 12:2-3).

Israel's election calls forth a *holy* people, a people committed to exclusive worship of God as proclaimed by the first commandment and the Shema (6:4-9). As Moberly suggests, with a metaphoric use of the term *ḥerem*, Deuteronomy calls for total loyalty to the Shema, a loyalty that requires complete separation (1999). Disregard of this holiness is most explicitly represented by covenants with other peoples, intermarriage, and the cult of the Canaanites.

Election and Its Basis 7:6-11

7:6 Israel's Election

Israel's election theology is summarized by this verse, a verse repeated later (14:2). The principal terms of the verse tell the story. Here Deuteronomy claims that God has *chosen* Israel. The theme of election is common in the Old Testament (see TBC below), but Deuteronomy especially highlights it, introducing the term "choose" for the act of election (cf. 4:37; 10:15; 14:2). Later Deuteronomy also speaks of God choosing a king (17:15), the Levitical priests (18:5; 21:5), and, most frequently, a place for worship (12:5, 14, 18, 26; 14:25; 15:20; 16:7, 15, 16; etc.). God's election of a people takes priority, however, and remains foundational for everything else.

Israel's election makes it a *holy* people. The Hebrew term here translated *holy* means "separated," or "set apart." Israel's election sets it apart from other peoples. Exodus speaks of Israel as a "priestly kingdom and a holy nation" (19:6), using two terms, both of which imply a national state; here Deuteronomy removes Israel from the political sphere by employing the more general term *people* (Weinfeld 1991: 367). As verses 1-5 emphasize, for Israel to be holy requires sharp separation, a distinguishing from the peoples round about. Through this election, Israel becomes God's *treasured possession* (one word in Hebrew). The term emphasizes that Israel belongs to God—it is not free or independent—even as it underscores the special status of Israel.

Chapter 7 is an exposition of this verse and its three key terms:

verses 1-5	Israel as a holy people
verses 7-11	Israel as a chosen people
verses 12-26	Israel as a treasured possession

7:7 Rejection of Erroneous Explanation

Election may be a central biblical concept, but it contains within itself the potential for misuse or abuse. One of its most insidious temptations is to think that election is deserved. Deuteronomy recognizes the power of this temptation for Israel by confronting it immediately. Yes, Israel is chosen by God, but Israel should never begin to think that this selection is based on merit. In fact, Israel is one of the least deserving of all nations.

7:8 Election Grounded in God's Love

If Israel does not deserve election, then why did God choose it? On one level Deuteronomy's answer is clear and straightforward: God loved Israel (cf. 4:37; 7:13; 10:15; 23:5). The term "love" includes both the connotations of political loyalty and familial or even tender affection. This love lies behind God's promise to the ancestors, and God's integrity (cf. 6:4) ensures that God is true to those promises. The exodus events are visible confirmation of God's faithfulness.

But really, this is no answer because it simply raises the next question: why did God love Israel? The "why" of the second question can mean either of two things: (1) Why did God love Israel *out of all the peoples on earth*? or (2) For what *purpose* did God love Israel? The Old Testament elsewhere speaks to the second option (e.g., Gen 12:3; Isa 49:6). But neither form of the question consumes Deuteronomy.

Rather, Deuteronomy's concern is to confront and reject any misunderstanding of election that might ground it in Israel's merit. Election is simply based in God's undeserved love. The gracious basis of this love is incomprehensible: it remains a mystery, indeed must remain a mystery. But its reality is fundamental. Israel is bound to God through God's love. The question before Israel is whether it will return that love to God (cf. v. 11; 6:4-9).

7:9-11 Therefore Yahweh Your God Is God

The consequence of election is a relationship—or in the language of Deuteronomy, a covenant (e.g., 5:2)—with a redeeming God. To *know* (7:9) is much more than merely intellectual awareness: it includes making the reality fully part of one's total being, both thought and action. The phrase *your God*, used more than 240 times in Deuteronomy, highlights the relationship in this passage and is a reminder of it whenever used in the book. God's faithfulness to the covenant means that Israel can count on God. If Israel responds faithfully by loving God and keeping the commandments (not two different responses but one and the same), its blessings will be endless (cf. vv. 12-16). Disobedience is not merely disregard of regulations but basically a personal rejection of God. And rejection has consequences. The language here recalls that of the second commandment (5:9-10), which contrasts the infinitely greater effect of God's love with God's discipline. The twice-used phrase *repays in their own person*, with its use of the singular noun, also suggests that the punishment is more limited than God's *covenant loyalty*, which applies to a *thousand generations*. The only appropriate response thus is diligent observance of the Torah (v. 11).

Faithfulness to Election Leads to Blessing 7:12-26

Election leads to Israel as God's *treasured possession*. To be a treasured possession implies both that Israel is bound to God and that Israel has a special status. The focus of the last section of the chapter is on the benefits of election, here called blessings, but it is framed by two verses that stress obligation (vv. 12, 26). Although the first word of verse 12 is translated either *If* (e.g., NRSV) or *Because* (e.g., RSV), its meaning is quite clear: the favors outlined in the following verses are conditional upon Israel's obedience, with *because* intimating that Israel will obey. The conditional nature of this passage does not contradict earlier statements emphasizing God's integrity or the unconditional nature of the ancestral covenant. Israel's election and God's faithfulness to his promises are not conditional upon Israel's obedience. In Deuteronomy, however, the fate of Israel in the land is very much dependent upon the nature of its response (cf. curses of Deut 28), with obedience leading to blessing.

7:12-16 Outline of Blessing

As outlined clearly in these verses, blessing is not some vague notion of well-being but a concept with concrete connotations (Westermann 1978; Mitchell). First, especially in the Pentateuch, blessing means fertility, fertility of the human womb, fertility of the flocks and herds, and fertility of the soil. All three are explicitly emphasized in verses 13-14, and all are mentioned later, in the covenant blessings and curses (28:4, 11, 18). The first use of the term "blessing" in the Bible, in the creation story, reflects this meaning (Gen 1:22, 28). Genesis 12–50, a block of material that opens with God announcing to Abraham and Sarah that he will multiply them into a great nation (i.e., fertility of the womb; cf. Deut 7:13) and bless them, has blessing as a central theme. Westermann suggests that the stories of Abraham and Sarah revolve around the question of whether they will have a son (fertility of the womb), the story of Jacob emphasizes fertility of flocks and herds, and the story of Joseph concerns fertility of the fields (1962: 19–53). After introducing the theme with the summary statement that God will *bless you* (v. 13), the passage refers to multiplying the people, a sign that the Genesis stories are in purview. Obedience in the land will lead to prosperity as the people grow, as the herds reproduce, and as grain, grapes, and olive trees, the three major agricultural products of the land, bear fruit. In ascribing this fertility to God, the passage is simultaneously rejecting any notion that the Canaanite fertility gods are responsible.

Second, blessing means good health. Exodus 23:25 reads, "I will bless your bread and your water; and I will take sickness away from among you." This aspect may not receive the same emphasis, but it is easy to understand how this would have been a major concern in the ancient world, and here Deuteronomy includes it as a necessary ingredient of the blessed life in the land (7:15).

Third, blessing means protection from the enemy. That deliverance from the foe is an important aspect of blessing is clear from the long list of blessings and curses in chapter 28. When Israel is blessed, *The LORD will cause your enemies who rise against you to be defeated before you* (28:7); when Israel is cursed, *The LORD will cause you to be defeated before your enemies* (18:25). In the present passage this element of blessing is portrayed with the cruel language associated with Yahweh war (see discussion of 2:24–3:11), together with the distinctive Deuteronomic challenge not to serve the gods of the land. The context of the verse is important. Verse 16 comes in a chapter considering Israel's election. The opening phrase of verse 16 thus is more likely to be understood as a promise than as a command: God *will give* the enemies over to Israel, and Israel will devour them. The last part of the chapter presents a vision of what it means to be God's *treasured possession*. In a land regularly crossed by foreign armies, this had to include the element of protection from the enemy. Using stock phrases and images of the day, Deuteronomy emphasizes that God will give other peoples over to Israel, and Israel will be safe.

7:17-26 *Blessing and the Awesome God*

The final paragraph of the chapter expands and throws further light on the third aspect of blessing. In this expansion the imagery and language of Yahweh war remain prominent (cf. 2:24–3:11). The overarching theme is *Do not be afraid of them* (vv. 18, 21; cf. 1:21, 29; 2:25; 3:2). Israel's experience of God in the exodus reminds the people that they can count on God's protection. The *great and awesome God* who made himself known to Israel in those events *is present with you* (7:21). God will give their enemies over to them, will *throw them into a great panic,* and will *hand their kings over to you* (vv. 23-24). The focus is not on what Israel is to do but on what God does on behalf of

Israel. After all, Israel is *the fewest of all peoples* (v. 7), and the nations are *more numerous* (v. 17; cf. v. 1). When confronted by an enemy, especially one of superior might, the natural reaction is fear. In some cases there may also be a false confidence in one's own military strength. Upon arriving at the land the first time, Israel's two responses reflect both of these attitudes (1:19-45). Both are "wrongful worship of the false god of militarism." This chapter, rather than promoting military aggression, is a warning against "bowing down to the god of military might" (Olson: 53-54).

The passage climaxes by emphasizing the need for Israel to reject the religion of the land, its gods, and all its cultic objects—a major theme in Deuteronomy. For Israel to allow these gods and their representations to become part of its life is *abhorrent* to God. The last verse twice uses the Hebrew term *ḥerem*, earlier used of people, now directed at cultic objects *[Ḥerem, p. 552]*. Foreign cultic objects, whether Canaanite or Assyrian, must be destroyed, for they are "banned." If Israel keeps them, then Israel will be "banned." The centrality of the first commandment and Shema comes through even in a passage portraying the potential blessings of election. Faithfulness to the election and its implication of exclusive loyalty result in blessing; disregard can lead to Israel itself being "banned," or *set apart for destruction* (7:26). This is the promise and warning of this paragraph.

THE TEXT IN BIBLICAL CONTEXT
Why Did God Choose Israel?

Deuteronomy may give the theme of election greater emphasis and use theologically laden terms (e.g., *love, chose*), yet the conviction that Israel has a special relationship with God is foundational for the vast majority of the Old Testament (the exception may be parts of the wisdom tradition, e.g., Job). With Genesis 1-11 as a background, Genesis 12 to the end of Malachi surveys and considers various aspects of that special relationship. Modern sensitivities regarding fairness make one uncomfortable with this theme—was it fair or just of God to choose one nation from all the rest? Or, why did God love, or choose Israel? If the question has in mind why God chose Israel rather than some other nation, or the issue of fairness, the biblical text provides only a negative answer: not because Israel deserved it. But any attempt to give a positive answer is avoided. Even the remark that God chose Israel because God loved Israel (7:8) is no real answer, since it leaves open the question of why God loved Israel. On this level the selection can only be accepted and not explained. Perhaps one might compare it to the challenge of justifying theologically why some people are born into privileged settings (the West?), and others into settings of poverty. If, however, the question is *for what purpose* did God chose Israel, the biblical text is not silent. Israel is to be a blessing to all peoples, a light to the nations (Gen 12:3; Isa 42:6; 49:6; cf. Deut 4:5-8; for discussion see TBC on Deut 2:2-23).

Election, Separation, and Mission

Although most of the Old Testament assumes the theme of election, there is not uniformity on what this means for relations with other peoples. On the one side, a number of Old Testament passages call for virtually total separation from other peoples (e.g., Deut 7), with the practical implication of disallowing intermarriage with "outsiders." This tendency is reflected in the story of Abraham sending a servant to Nahor to find a wife for son Isaac among his kin so that he would not marry a Canaanite (Gen 24). The accusation that Israel was intermarrying with the Canaanites in the time of the judges fits here (Judg 3:6). The indictment of Solomon for marrying foreign women (1 Kings 11) and the condemnation of Ahab for marrying the foreign Jezebel (1 Kings 16:31) are further examples. Intermarriage will lead to the worship of foreign gods and thus is rejected. This direction reaches a climax in the restoration community of Ezra and Nehemiah, when they not only prohibit intermarriage (Ezra 9:2), but even send away foreign wives (Ezra 10:2-5, 10-11, 18-19; Neh 10:30; 13:23-27).

But the Old Testament admits a strong countertendency as well. Moses, the great teacher of Deuteronomy, married a Midianite woman and is nowhere censured for this. Ruth, the wife of Boaz and great-grandmother of David, was a Moabite woman. Bathsheba, one of the wives of David, and the mother of Solomon, was probably a Hittite. Even Deuteronomy is not entirely consistent (see 20:10-14). It is likely that for most of Israel's history, intermarriage with "outsiders," although possibly not common, was accepted. In fact, it is probable that the sharp line between Israel and other peoples assumed by some passages only developed during the exile and later.

In this dialogue Deuteronomy 7 reflects a harsh stance, through the use of the term *ḥerem* as well as through its specific demands. Absolute loyalty to God trumps everything else. Although on a surface level the book of Joshua narrates the fulfillment of Deuteronomy 7, with its martial account of Israel's entrance into the Promised Land, it may actually be qualifying "the discourse and assumptions of Deut 7 by making the questions of separation and of exclusion from the community of Israel more problematic than Deut 7 envisages" (Earl 2009: 46). In Joshua, Rahab the Canaanite prostitute is not banned but instead accepted into Israel, becoming in the New Testament a model of faith (Josh 6:22-25; cf. Heb 11:31; James 2:25). Conversely Achan, a "birthright" Israelite, is executed for his disobedience, placing him under *herem* (Josh 7). Joshua 8:30-35 includes aliens in the covenant renewal ceremony (cf. Deut 29:11), and Joshua 9 records Israel entering into a covenant with the Gibeonites, allowing them to remain in the land. The book ends with Joshua upholding the call of Deuteronomy 7 for absolute loyalty to God, with total separation from the gods of the land. But in light of the stories of Rahab and Achan, separation is based "on responsiveness to Yahweh, rather than with rigid regard to genealogy or geography" (Earl 2010: 94).

The responsibility of Israel to be a source of blessing for all peoples (Gen 12:3) and a "light to the nations" (Isa 49:6) also challenges building too high a wall between Israel and other peoples. It is hard to imagine what total separation means when the nations will stream to the "mountain of the LORD's house" to be instructed by God in the ways of peace (Isa 2:1-4).

The New Testament carries this conversation forward. Like Deuteronomy, Jesus calls for total loyalty to God, as reflected in his response to the question about inheriting eternal life. But he immediately adds to the first commandment a second, which with the story of the good Samaritan counters a narrow exclusivism (Luke 10:25-37). Perhaps more significantly, Jesus begins his ministry by referring to stories of Elijah and Elisha reaching out beyond Israel (Luke 4:25-30), the great commission is to "all nations" (Matt 28:19), and the promise of the Holy Spirit brings witness to the ends of the earth (Acts 1:8). Paul in 2 Corinthians 6:14-18 sounds very much like Deuteronomy 7, but then elsewhere he appears to qualify this (e.g., 1 Cor 7:12-14; 8:1-13), and his ministry was predominantly to the Gentiles.

The New Testament thus retains election theology (e.g., 1 Pet 2:9) with a concern for separation, or perhaps one might rename it "distinction" (e.g., the call to be in the world but not of it, John 17:15-16; the warning not to "be mismatched with unbelievers," 2 Cor 6:14); yet this is always colored by the call to be agents of blessing and witness. Separation and mission are not mutually exclusive in either testament.

THE TEXT IN THE LIFE OF THE CHURCH
The Church and Separation

Some years ago H. Richard Niebuhr tried to analyze the major options available to the church as it confronts larger society in a work titled *Christ and Culture* (1951). In this volume he identified Mennonites as well as Catholic monastic orders as representing the "Christ-against-culture" type. This approach emphasizes the evils of society and sees the only faithful approach to be complete separation from, or opposition to, society. Deuteronomy 7, with its absolute rejection of any significant contact with other peoples, might be cited as support for such a position. Neither making covenants with them nor intermarriage with them are permitted, for fear that Israel will be contaminated.

Niebuhr rejects this option and appears to favor a Christ who transforms culture. This approach recognizes that Christ and culture are not identical, but then advocates not separating from that culture while attempting to convert or transform it. A British Catholic has written a book consistent with this approach in which he calls on a reenergized church to re-create Christendom, "a society where the historic Christian faith provides the cultural framework for social living, as well as the religious form of the State" (Nichols 1).

The question of Christ and culture, of how the people of God respond to and relate to their larger context, is one of the most complex and critical issues for the church. John H. Yoder as well as people like Stanley Hauerwas and William Willimon accept neither Niebuhr's categories overall nor his preferred option in particular. Instead, they call upon the church to be a radical alternative to society, a "community of the cross" witnessing in their context as a body of "resident aliens" (Stassen, Yeager, and Yoder; Hauerwas and Willimon). Such a people has a distinct identity and vision, offering an alternative to the usual options.

To suggest this as the model envisioned by Deuteronomy is too bold, but Deuteronomy does appear to imagine Israel as a distinct people living a countercultural ethic among the nations of the day. This fits especially well if one pictures the audience of Deuteronomy as the exilic or postexilic community. It appears that Israel understood this issue differently at different times. For example, the Israel of David's kingdom experienced this issue very differently from the exiles in Babylon. Similarly, the nuances and configuration of the discussion change significantly when one moves from the United States to Chile or China. No one simple answer can become absolute.

The invitation is to retain the conviction behind Deuteronomy's call for separation—that exclusive loyalty to God is of ultimate significance, and that nowhere is this loyalty more likely to be undermined than through the seduction of blessing *and* larger society—even as one remains faithful to the call of both testaments to be God's way of providing blessing and to be God's witnesses within those cultures.

Deuteronomy 8:1-20

Remember! Do Not Forget!

PREVIEW

Can something be both a gift from God and a source of temptation? Being an amazing athlete, having a charming and charismatic personality, or possessing phenomenal business sense could work that way. Blessing may be what Israel desires and longs for and what God has promised, but here it is identified as the potential root of Israel's greatest danger. Chapter 7 highlights the blessings that Israel will receive when it is faithful to its election (note esp. 7:12-16). Chapter 8 picks up the theme of blessing and emphasizes the goodness of the Promised Land. It is a land of great natural resources, a land in which they will become wealthy, a land in which they will be filled and lack nothing. But this very abundance, this outcome of their election, has the possibility of dulling their memories. It can lure them into forgetting the God who has led them out of Egypt and provided for all their needs in the wilderness. The contrast between the obvious dependence upon God in the wilderness and the danger of perceived self-sufficiency in the land plays a key role in the argument. The chapter opens by reminding Israel that observing God's commandment will result in life and increase (v. 1); it closes by warning the people that forgetting God leads to worshiping other gods, with death the result (vv. 18-20).

OUTLINE
Introductory Entreaty, 8:1
Remember! 8:2-10
Do Not Forget! 8:11-17
Concluding Warning: Remember! Do Not Forget! 8:18-20

EXPLANATORY NOTES

Some commentators argue for a prolonged redaction and editing behind Deuteronomy 8 (e.g., Mayes: 189-94). They may be right, but the end product is a complex literary structure with a high level of thematic integrity. At least three patterns or techniques are intertwined in the chapter, each contributing to the theological emphasis of the chapter (Lohfink 1963: 194-95; Weinfeld 1991: 397; Olson: 54-55). First is the overarching theme, the call to Israel to remember and not forget its God when it experiences the blessings of the Promised Land. The two key words, *Remember* (vv. 2, 18) and *forget* (vv. 11, 19), become the markers of a linear structure as outlined above and depicted below. In two sequences Israel is called first to remember, and then not to forget.

I. Remember! Do Not Forget! 8:2-17
8:2, <u>Remember</u> *the long way that the* LORD *your God has led you . . .*
8:11, *Take care that you do not* <u>forget</u> *the* LORD *your God . . .*

II. Remember! Do Not Forget! 8:18-20
8:18, <u>Remember</u> *the* LORD *your God . . .*
8:19, *If you do* <u>forget</u> *the* LORD *your God . . .*

Second, Israel's experience in the wilderness serves as the basis for the warning not to forget God in the Promised Land. A chiastic pattern *[Chiasm, p. 540]* supports this argument:

A¹ Introduction, 8:1
  B¹ God's Discipline in the *Wilderness*, 8:2-6
    C¹ The Goodness of the *Land*, 8:7-10
      D Central Exhortation: *Do Not Forget*, 8:11
    C² The Temptation of the *Land*, 8:12-14
  B² God's Care in the *Wilderness*, 8:15-17
A² Conclusion, 8:18-20

The outline of this chiastic pattern is slightly different from the linear structure based on *remember* and *forget*, but the overlap is significant.

By having at its center the call not to forget, it strongly enforces the central theme of the first outline and the chapter as a whole.

Third, the chapter also contains a regular alternation between action and effect. Over and over the chapter speaks of some action of Israel, then follows by identifying its consequence. As the chart below indicates, both the linear structure of remember/do not forget, and the chiastic pattern of land and wilderness are reflected in this configuration.

Action	Consequence
8:1a, observing the commandment	8:1b, life and increase
8:2-5, remembering God's care in wilderness	8:6, keeping the commandments
8:7-9, remembering God in the land	8:10, blessing God
8:11-13, forgetting God in the land	8:14, exalting oneself
8:15-16, forgetting God's care in wilderness	8:17, seeing success as produced by self
8:18-19, forgetting God	8:20, perishing

Deuteronomy 8 warns Israel not to forget God once it experiences the goodness of the land. Basic to the chapter is the Deuteronomic faith that Israel's fate in the land is determined by its response to God. The repeated correlation of action and consequence reflects this conviction. The discipline of the wilderness experience should convince the people of their dependence on God even in the land, a dependence more hidden yet vital.

Introductory Entreaty 8:1

The chapter opens with a call for obedience to the commandment similar to others in Deuteronomy, motivated by *so that you may live and increase in the land* (cf. 4:1; 6:1). The sermon of Deuteronomy addresses the people before they enter the land, but the *today* of the verse collapses time, both for Israel and Deuteronomy's modern readers.

Remember! 8:2-10

A call to remember God's leading in the wilderness opens the first larger section of the chapter (vv. 2-10). Wilderness, or desert, is a land of danger and desolation, where hunger and thirst threaten life itself. Yet, the text stresses, Israel had all it needed: the people's clothes did not wear out, their feet did not swell, they had enough to eat (vv. 3-4; cf. 2:7, *you have lacked nothing*).

Through this experience God *humbled* the people (vv. 2-3; cf. 16), *testing* them (vv. 2-3; cf. v. 16) *as a parent disciplines a child* (v. 5). The wilderness experience was not merely a delay along the way to the Promised Land but an important time of preparation for life in the land. The passage suggests two different purposes. Through testing, God learns to know Israel better, to see what *was in your heart* (v. 2). But it is the second objective that is more important in the chapter. The wilderness experience is a time of discipline. Discipline must be distinguished from punishment. Punishment is penalty for past sin; discipline is training or schooling for the future. The discipline of the wilderness is to change Israel's *heart* (v. 5). The second reference to *heart*, preceded by the imperative (*Know*), may suggest God had learned that Israel's heart was not ready for life in the land. The Exodus accounts of the wilderness period demonstrate that at times Israel responded to adversity without the trust and obedience God desired (e.g., Exod 16:1-36; 32:1-35). This passage puts the whole in the context of the love of a parent for a child. God, like a parent, expresses love both by carrying and protecting (cf. 1:31) and by preparing for the future. Through the wilderness experience, God makes clear to Israel its utter dependence on God.

This lesson is explicitly noted in verse 3: *in order to make you understand that one does not live by bread alone, but by every word that comes from the mouth of the LORD*. The contrast "is not spiritual versus material food but trust in the Lord's provision and obedience versus reliance upon self" (P. Miller 1990: 116). The term translated *word* in the NRSV is the simple particle for "everything." The RSV more accurately and helpfully translates it *by everything that proceeds out of the mouth*. In the wilderness Israel had to rely on God for everything: food, water, and direction. Jesus' confidence that he would be preserved by God allows him to reject Satan's temptation to turn stones into bread, and so he quotes this verse (Matt 4:1-4). For Israel to trust God in a similar way means it will *keep the commandments* (v. 6).

It is the lesson of the wilderness that Israel must remember in the land. And a good land it is. Verses 7-10, with their poetic quality, may very well come from a hymn extolling the richness of the land. While the desert is barren and dry, the good land has an abundance of water, thereby allowing Israel to plant and harvest a wide variety of agricultural products. The land has mineral resources that can be mined. These verses may exaggerate the wealth of the land, yet compared to the surrounding wilderness, it truly was a land of plenty, of milk and honey. The song thus praises the land that will provide everything Israel needs: *a land where you may eat bread without scarcity, where you will lack nothing* (8:9; cf. 2:7).

But this is exactly the source of tension or temptation. In the wilderness Israel lacks nothing because, as it was taught, God provides. In the land Israel again lacks nothing but now all is provided by the goodness of the land. If Israel remembers the lesson of the wilderness (cf. v. 2), then when it is in the land and has eaten until full, it will *bless the* LORD *your God for the good land that he has given you* (8:10). Here is the climax of the first section.

Do Not Forget! 8:11-17

The second part of the chapter covers ground similar to the first, only now it is introduced by the negative form of the summons to remember: *Do not forget.* Forgetting God is paralleled by not keeping the commandments (v. 11). We are reminded of Deuteronomy 6, where *the decrees and the statutes and the ordinances* become the occasion for teaching the story of God and his people (6:20-25). Remembering and obedience cannot be separated: they are inextricably bound together.

Again the goodness of the land is emphasized. The threefold reference to multiplying (v. 13) points to the essence of blessing (cf. 7:13). The two descriptions of the land together contain four phrases emphasizing satiation: *without scarcity* (v. 9), *lack nothing* (v. 9), *eat your fill* (v. 10), *eaten your fill* (v. 12). The contrast between this good land and a menacing wilderness is made even more vivid here in the second round, with its reference to the *terrible wilderness, an arid wasteland with poisonous* (NIV, *venomous*; RSV, *fiery*) *snakes and scorpions* (v. 15). And yet again, it stresses God's leading and providing. In the face of death the God of the exodus provided water (cf. Exod 17:1-6) and manna (cf. Exod 16:4-36). As in the first part, the testing of Israel in the wilderness is given a positive goal: *in the end to do you good* (Deut 8:16).

Whereas remembering leads to obedience and the blessing of God (v. 10), forgetting leads to exalting oneself (v. 14) and beginning to think that *My power and the might of my own hand have gotten me this wealth* (v. 17). Within a short phrase three first-person singular pronouns are used. Here is the central concern of this passage. Blessing and success easily bring on poor memory and a concentration on oneself. Amnesia is the greatest threat. A loss of memory equals a distorted sense of reality. In the death-threatening wilderness,

Israel accused God of leading it out of Egypt in order to kill it through hunger and thirst (Exod 16:3; cf. Deut 1:27), but it was not tempted to forget God. The temptation to forget is most powerful when all is well, when one has eaten one's fill. It strikes hardest in the midst of blessing.

Concluding Warning: Remember! Do Not Forget! 8:18-20

The closing paragraph reiterates the dominant concern of the chapter and connects it to the central theme of chapters 5–11. The *Remember* and *If you do forget* pick up the key words of the two main sections (vv. 2, 11). Even when the remark of verse 17 (*My power and the might of my own hand . . .*) has some truth in it, it is really not true, as verse 18 responds. God gives the land, and God gives Israel the power to harvest the abundance of the land. Although the focus of the chapter has been on the danger of replacing confidence in God with pride and self-confidence, the conclusion takes the next logical step for Deuteronomy and speaks against following, serving, and worshiping (three separate terms used for emphasis) other gods. Not only may hubris itself be another god; it also easily leads to the recognition of new gods, gods that the peoples of the land serve in their quest for prosperity and security. Breaking the first commandment then becomes a temptation as well.

The final verse and a half complete the gradual transition of the chapter. The introduction speaks of living in the land as the consequence of obedience. The middle two sections cover similar ground, but the first does it positively (remembering, which leads to blessing God), and the second does it negatively (forgetting, which leads to pride). The chapter concludes by underscoring the supreme consequence of forgetting: Israel will perish from the land (vv. 19-20) like the nations that occupied the land previously. The warning comes *today* (cf. 5:1-5) and always remains a present reality.

THE TEXT IN BIBLICAL CONTEXT

God's Nurture

As a mother and father love their child, so God loves his people. Deuteronomy uses this imagery, as does the prophet Hosea, who very well may have influenced Deuteronomy. Nurture is a prominent element in this relationship.

> When Israel was a child, I loved him,
> and out of Egypt I called my son. . . .

Yet it was I who taught Ephraim to walk,
> I took them up in my arms;
> but they did not know that I healed them
I led them with cords of human kindness,
> with bands of love. (Hos 11:1, 3-4a)

In a similar vein Proverbs reads,

My child, do not despise the LORD's discipline
> or be weary of his reproof,
for the LORD reproves the one he loves,
> as a father the son in whom he delights. (3:11-12)

But Israel did not fully learn its lesson and forgot God. Hosea speaks of luring Israel back into the wilderness, where God will "speak tenderly to her." Once back in the wilderness, it will recognize that God provides all, and "there she shall respond as in the days of her youth" (Hos 2:14-15).

The Peril of Prosperity

Once Israel was firmly established in the land and a strong political structure had developed, a wealthy class gradually evolved. This development reached its peak in the eighth century, during a time of stability and relative prosperity. In both the north and the south, God called prophets to confront the affluent. Amos denounces those who "lie on beds of ivory, and lounge on their couches" (6:4), and Micah castigates those who "covet fields, and seize them" (2:2). Hosea sees the apostasy of the people and announces, "My people are destroyed for lack of knowledge" (4:6). Each of these prophets envisions a time when Israel's forgetting God will lead to a loss of the land God gave it. An exile will come that may be seen as a new wilderness, a time when Israel can learn anew to place its trust wholly in God.

Jesus in the Wilderness

The connection between Deuteronomy 8 and the account of Satan tempting Jesus is extensive (Matt 4:1-11; Luke 4:1-13). Not only does Jesus quote Deuteronomy 8:3 (as well as 6:13, 16), both accounts speak of testing, both take place in the wilderness, both use the number forty (days and nights, years), and both deal with hunger. The contrast comes in the response. Although Israel in the wilderness regularly lost faith and in the land frequently forgot God and the lesson of the wilderness, Jesus came through the test without blemish. It is easy to allow our convictions around Jesus' divinity to diminish the reality of his test. The New Testament, however, shows that it was very real; each time Jesus was confronted, he rejected the offer and relied entirely on God to take care of the present as well as the future. Jesus becomes the model. This also is the concern of Deuteronomy 8. Truly remembering and knowing God, who God is and what God has done, is at the heart of Jesus the model.

THE TEXT IN THE LIFE OF THE CHURCH

Land as Blessing *and* Temptation

In his book *The Land*, Walter Brueggemann characterizes the Promised Land with four terms: as *gift*, as *temptation*, as *task*, and as *threat*. The first two especially reflect the thrust of Deuteronomy 8. Deuteronomy is rhetoric at the boundary, speaking of the land as "pure gift, radical grace. There is no hint of achievement or merit or even planning" (1977: 48). The result is "satiation." With the land, Israel receives the "apparatus of satiation—cities, houses, cisterns, vineyards and trees—not just food, but the instruments of production" (49). But this very gift, this wealth, this potential to generate food and blessing on their own, dulls the memory and risks the temptation to forget that life is dependent upon God and upon worshiping God.

Israel fell prey to that temptation, was seduced by the gods of the nations, and lost the land. But was land and blessing and wealth all wrong? Our believers church tradition has focused its ethical reflection on living away from power. Many have felt vindicated as Christendom fades away in our day, as the church loses its influence in society. After all, for them, Christendom and Constantinianism are associated with the fall of the church.

But does this take seriously enough Deuteronomy as a theology for managing land? Deuteronomy regularly speaks about the goodness of land and its blessings. These are gifts from God. Deuteronomy paints a vision for community in the land, where prosperity is prominent and justice prevails as brother and sister take care of each other. This is shalom. Has our criticism of Christendom, our sometimes demonizing of wealth, perhaps not allowed for this? Is it easier to develop an ethic for the landless than for the landed?

Schlabach suggests, "The Deuteronomic problem is the problem of how to receive and celebrate the blessing, the *shalom*, the good, or 'the land,' that God desires to give, yet to do so without defensively and violently hoarding God's blessing" (451). Deuteronomy 8 assumes that God's gift of land is blessing and that it remains blessing even if it becomes the soil of temptation.

Deuteronomy 9:1–10:11

Israel: Stubborn, Not Righteous

PREVIEW

From young ages, children are taught to be fair. But is God fair? If God is fair and just, how can God take the side of one people over another? For the second time in three chapters, Deuteronomy appears to struggle with justifying God's actions on behalf of Israel (cf. 7:7-11). Again the explanation it gives is not fully satisfying. After declaring that Yahweh is a *devouring fire* who *crosses over before you*, who defeats and subdues the peoples of the land (9:1-3), Deuteronomy continues by accounting for this action of God (vv. 4-6). The proposed explanation takes three directions. God is doing this to *fulfill the promise that the* LORD *made on oath to your ancestors* (v. 5; cf. v. 3). God is doing this because the nations are wicked (vv. 4-5). But most of all, God *is not doing this* because Israel is righteous. In fact, Israel is a *stubborn people* (v. 6; cf. vv. 4-5). The negative or nonanswer receives most attention.

The remainder of the passage supports the negative answer by retelling the story of Israel making a golden calf while Moses is on Mount Horeb, receiving the law (cf. Exod 32). This incident of stubbornness is not an exception (Deut 9:22-24) but rather typifies Israel's ongoing rebellious response to God. As in chapters 1–3, Israel's history provides content for teaching material. A significant subtheme is Moses' role as intercessor for Israel before God.

OUTLINE

Explaining God, Characterizing Israel, 9:1-6
    9:1-3   God, the Devouring Fire, Crosses Over before Israel
    9:4-6   Justification: Not Because of Righteousness, for Israel Is Stubborn
Israel's Stubbornness Epitomized at Horeb, 9:7-10:11
    9:7-8   Introduction
    9:9-14   Moses on Horeb
    9:15-29   Moses Intercedes on Behalf of the People
    10:1-5   The Covenant Renewed
    10:6-9   Interruption: Death of Aaron, Designation of Levites
    10:10-11   Return to the Journey

EXPLANATORY NOTES

Explaining God, Characterizing Israel 9:1-6

The basic argument of this larger passage is presented in the opening two paragraphs (vv. 1-3, 4-6). God is giving Israel the Promised Land, but it is not because Israel is righteous; rather, Israel is a stubborn people.

9:1-3 God, the Devouring Fire, Crosses Over before Israel

The opening paragraph is a combination of phrases and themes common to Deuteronomy, underscoring God's gracious but powerful intervention on behalf of Israel in defeating the peoples of the Promised Land. The call *Hear, O Israel!* (cf. 5:1; 6:4; 20:3) means more than to just listen; it includes making what is heard part of one's mind and action. Once Israel crosses the Jordan, it will be confronted by mighty nations, with superior defenses (cf. 1:28; 4:38; 7:1; 11:23). The Anakim, legendary giants of the land (cf. 1:28; 2:11), receive special attention. But Israel is not to fear. It is to know (cf. 4:39; 7:9; 8:5) that Yahweh is crossing the Jordan before it (cf. 31:3). Earlier the image of God as a *devouring fire* illustrated God's jealousy for Israel with regard to exclusive worship (4:24). Its connotation here remains similar: God has the power to consume those who in some way withstand him; but now that fire is turned on the inhabitants of the land. Israel is called upon to *dispossess and destroy*, but first it says God *will defeat them and subdue them* (9:3; cf. 7:1-2; 11:23; 19:1; 31:3). The two are treated as essentially one, but the focus is on God's action. As was proclaimed at the beginning of Deuteronomy and the beginning of their journey from Horeb, God is giving them the land in fulfillment of his promise (1:8, 21): Israel only has to take possession.

9:4-6 Justification: Not Because of Righteousness, for Israel Is Stubborn

But how is Israel to understand this action of God? The modern discomfort with Israel's election and its negative implications for the original inhabitants of the land (cf. vv. 1-3) may have been felt by Israel as well. Some explanation is required. Deuteronomy 7 argued that Israel's election could not be attributed to Israel's greatness or military might, for they were *the fewest of all peoples*. God's choice could only be explained on the basis of God's unexplainable love for Israel (7:7-8). Deuteronomy 9 returns to this matter—perhaps because the answer given previously did not entirely satisfy, perhaps because of significant concern within Israel—and proposes three further explanations.

First, and this emphasis is present throughout the book, including the previous discussion of the problem, God is giving Israel the land *in order to fulfill the promise . . . to Abraham, to Isaac, and to Jacob* (9:6; cf. 1:8, 21, 35; 6:10, 18, 19, 23; 7:8, 12, 13; 8:1, 18; etc.). Obviously this does not resolve the problem. It simply raises the question to another level: why did God promise this to Abraham, Isaac, and Jacob? But it does place the giving of the land into a larger historical context, and it does draw attention to God's faithfulness.

Second, God's action of defeating and subduing the nations, thrusting them out before Israel, is attributed to the wickedness of the nations (vv. 4-5). God's sovereignty over all creation extends to punishing other nations for their sin. Their defeat thus is an act of judgment (cf. Gen 15:16). This rationale is consistent with the general Old Testament condemnation of Canaanite religion and cult (cf. Deut 18:9-14; Lev 20:23-24; 2 Kings 17:8; etc.). In other words, Deuteronomy implies, the original inhabitants of the land deserved their fate. As Deuteronomy warns Israel over and over again, ignoring the will of God does have negative consequences. For Deuteronomy, this explanation has a two-sided aspect to it. Even as it provides an explanation for why the original inhabitants of the land were dispossessed, it hints that Israel's possession of the land also is not unconditional. Israel must know that it also may be replaced if it rejects God.

Although justifying God's action on the basis of the nations' wickedness has its grounds, it receives little stress in Deuteronomy and is immediately undermined as an entirely adequate answer. For if the nations lost the land because of their wickedness, then one might extrapolate that Israel is receiving the land because of its righteousness. The terms "wickedness" and "righteousness" have as their natural context the court setting. Since judicial cases of the day commonly involved settling disputes between two parties, the judge, or the people's representatives, had the task of determining which party was right and which was wrong, which was righteous and which was wicked. The references to the nations' wickedness thus naturally could lead to the conclusion that in this story the other party, Israel, was righteous, or innocent.

But Deuteronomy immediately rejects this corollary. The Canaanites may be guilty and deserve their fate, but in no way does this imply Israel's innocence. In rejecting this corollary, Deuteronomy is indirectly questioning the explanation it just gave. Rejecting such a possible misinterpretation of election then becomes the major focus of the chapter and leads to Deuteronomy's third way of responding to the question. After warning Israel that it should not claim to be righteous (v. 4), Deuteronomy twice emphasizes, *It is not because of your righteousness or the uprightness of your heart* (v. 5; cf. v. 6); indeed, *you are a stubborn people* (v. 6; cf. vv. 13, 27). The Hebrew phrase translated *stubborn* literally means "stiff-necked." Its opposite is to "turn the ear," or to bend the neck in order to listen (cf. Deut 10:16; 31:27; Exod 32:9; 33:3, 5; Jer 7:26; 17:23; Weinfeld 1991: 406). To be stubborn does not mean to have strong convictions, but to be obstinate by rejecting the direction of God. Regularly Deuteronomy opens passages with the call *Hear, O Israel!* (5:1; 6:4; 9:1; 20:3); to be stubborn is to disregard this charge.

Israel is to know and have confidence that God is crossing over the Jordan before it (v. 3), but Israel also must know that God's gift of land is not because of its own righteousness (v. 6). The election claim remains, but its grounds ultimately are unfathomable. The passage's focus on the stubborn and rebellious nature of Israel then serves to accentuate the graciousness and mercy of a God who elected Israel and gave it the land.

Israel's Stubbornness Epitomized at Horeb 9:7-10:11

Deuteronomy's account of Israel's sin at Mount Horeb does not follow a neat chronological sequence, thus making reconstruction difficult. The five references to forty days and forty nights (9:9, 11, 18, 25; 10:10) only complicate the picture. Likely these references are to two (or at most three) separate forty-day periods. The first and second references (9:9, 11) refer to the forty days Moses is on the mountain receiving the covenant from God, as described in 9:9-14. During this period the people construct the calf. At verse 15 Moses descends from the mountain, sees the sin of the people, prays to God on behalf of the people for forty days (9:18, 25), and then destroys the calf

(v. 21). This is described in 9:15-21, with 9:25-29 presenting the prayer noted briefly in 9:18-19, now in greater detail. The last reference to forty days (10:10) may be a third mention of this same forty-day period of prayer, adding the information that it took place upon the mountain. Or it may refer to a third forty-day period following the destruction of the calf, when Moses returns to the mountain to receive the second set tablets.

9:7-8 Introduction

Both sides of the warning, *Remember* and *do not forget*, are used to introduce the story of Israel and the golden calf at Mount Horeb. In chapter 8 Israel was called to remember God's deliverance from Egypt and his providence in the wilderness (cf. 8:2, 11, 18, 19), but the negative must be remembered as well. No story better illustrates Israel's stubbornness than that of its making a golden calf even as Moses is receiving God's directions for Israel. Although possibly an extreme example, it reflects more the rule than the exception (v. 7).

9:9-14 Moses on Horeb

Israel's great sin takes place at the very time Moses is on the mountain receiving the covenant. The two tablets of the covenant are the two copies of the Decalogue that God had earlier pronounced to Israel (cf. discussion at 4:9-14). The present passage recalls Deuteronomy 5: after Israel heard these words, it became afraid and appealed to Moses to represent it before God. God grants Israel's wish, but adds *If only they had such a mind as this, to fear me and to keep all my commandments always* (5:29). Moses spending forty days and forty nights without food and water marks his total dedication and subservience to the task, and likely also supernatural sustenance from God. The number "forty" denotes that it was "the proper time for the completion of a lengthy process" (Tigay: 99).

The solemn account of Moses receiving the tablets is interrupted by the announcement that the people have *acted corruptly* (9:12). Soon after Moses is out of their sight (*They have been quick to turn from the way that I commanded them*, v. 12), they forget the commandments they have received and *cast an image for themselves* (v. 12). Moses' earlier judgment of the people is now confirmed in the words of God: *This people is indeed a stubborn people* (v. 13). The speech of God also reflects a distinct distancing between God and the people. Israel is called *this people* (v. 13), and even more significantly, they are designated *your people whom you have brought from Egypt* (v. 12). No longer is Israel *his* (referring to God's) *treasured possession* (7:6). Everywhere else in Deuteronomy it is always God who has brought the people out of Egypt. The later suggestion that God will destroy the people is already anticipated.

Consistent with Deuteronomy's lack of interest in ritual detail, it devotes little attention to the offense itself. The object Israel has made is simply called an *image* (v. 12), and then *an image of a calf* (v. 16), or *the calf* (v. 21). Deuteronomy may assume that its audience is familiar with the more complete story told in Exodus 32–34 in which Aaron gathers gold from the people in order to make an image of a calf, or a god of gold.

That Deuteronomy (and Exodus) understands the making of the molten calf as a transgression of the commandments is clear, but the exact nature of the violation is less clear. Archaeology confirms the prominent use of bull or calf images in the world of the day. In Canaanite religion the bull was associated both with El and Baal, and it represented qualities of strength and fertility. Our present story, together with the report of Jeroboam constructing calves at the two northern cultic centers of Bethel and Dan (1 Kings 12:26-29), show that some form of a calf cult entered Israelite religious practice. But neither tradition is clear on exactly how the image is understood. Was the calf understood as representing a god distinct from the God of Israel so that by worshiping it Israel was breaking the first commandment? The fact that Exodus 32 (v. 4) and 1 Kings 12 (v. 28) have both Aaron and Jeroboam connecting the image to the exodus from Egypt makes this doubtful. Or was the calf understood as an image of Yahweh, the God of the exodus? If so, Deuteronomy 9 highlights how quickly Israel disregarded the second commandment.

But it is also possible, perhaps even likely, that the calf was intended not to represent a god itself, but like the cherubim of the ark, as the throne or the footstool of the invisible Yahweh. If this is correct, then the exact nature of the transgression becomes even more difficult to articulate. The calf then is not a clear transgression of either the first or second commandment. As a symbol of fertility, however, the calf may have become an entry into Canaanite fertility rites and cult prostitution. The calf of Aaron and the calves of Jeroboam may have led Israel into idolatry. Given the significance of the calf in Canaanite cult, it also is easy to see how the people may have started to worship the image itself even if it originally had not been intended for this purpose. Hosea speaks of the people kissing the calves and making sacrifices to them (Hos 13:2; cf. Hos 8:5-6; 10:5; Ps 106:19-20; Neh 9:18). These objects then serve as an example of syncretism that leads Israel into violation of possibly both the first and second commandments. Clearly, for Deuteronomy the people's action at Horeb is a rejection of the direction God has given Israel only a short time previously. Within the context of later Israel, the passage lives on as a forceful condemnation of the royal cult practiced at Bethel and Dan.

God's *Let me alone* (Deut 9:14) appears as a preemptive effort to prevent Moses from interceding on behalf of the people (see vv. 18-21 below). The rejection of God by the people has been so quick and so massive that God suggests starting over again, this time with Moses. The reference to *their name* brings to mind, on the one hand, the original promise to Abraham, I *will make your name great* (Gen 12:2), and on the other hand, the reference to blotting out the name of the kings of the land (Deut 7:24). God's promises can be counted upon, but Israel has the possibility of rejecting God to such an extent that its fate may become the same as that of the nations whom it is to displace upon entering the land.

9:15-29 Moses Intercedes on Behalf of the People

With the mountain still *ablaze* (cf. 4:11, 24, 36; 5:22-27) with the presence of God, Moses descends to the people. Once Moses sees the sin of the people for himself, he takes the drastic step of smashing the *two tablets of the covenant*. This is not a spontaneous act of uncontrolled temper but a symbolic statement representing what Israel has done to the covenant through its mutinous action. It announces to the people that they have violated the covenant. It may be compared to formally tearing to shreds a contract that has been broken. The reference to doing this *before your eyes* suggests the legal nature of his action (Mayes: 200), but it also ties it to those many other events that Deuteronomy uses to teach Israel about God (cf. 1:30; 4:3, 9, 34; 6:22; 7:19; etc.).

Moses rejects God's offer to start over again with him; true to the role of a prophet (see TBC), he prays to God on behalf of the people. Again, his refraining from eating and drinking represents his total dedication to the task (v. 18; cf. v. 9). Aaron has not been mentioned previously in the Deuteronomic account, but the Exodus report places him at the center of the crime (note esp. Exod 32:1-5).

As he did with the tablets, Moses destroyed the calf idol, *burned it with fire and crushed it* (v. 21). Striking is the absence of any reference to punishment, a significant element of the Exodus account. In Exodus the destruction of the calf takes place before Moses' final appeal to God, with Israel having to drink the water into which the gold powder has been scattered (Exod 32:20). Likely this is understood to play some role in the punishment. In Deuteronomy the calf is only destroyed after God has relented, with the powder thrown into a stream that runs down the mountain (cf. 1 Kings 15:13; 2 Kings 23:12). The matter has been resolved, and pollution is removed from the camp. All detail is subservient to the central point of the section: Israel's apostasy at the mountain is the foremost illustration of its persistent stubbornness. The story provides a permanent reminder that Israel should never understand its receiving the land as a reward for righteousness.

Inserted into the narrative is a brief reference to other occasions when Israel rebelled against God (vv. 22-24). Each geographical reference denotes some incident (Taberah, Num 11:1-3; Massah, Exod 17:1-7 and Deut 6:16; Kibroth-hattaavah, Num 11:4-34; Kadesh-barnea, Num 13–14 and Deut 1:19-45). All support Deuteronomy's contention that Israel has *been rebellious against the* LORD *as long as he has known you* (9:24; cf. 9:7).

Moses employs three arguments in his prayer of intercession (alluded to in 9:18-19; recounted in detail in vv. 25-29). His opening petition rejects God's distancing himself from the people as reflected in the language of verses 12-13. Moses again calls Israel *your very own possession*, and reminds God that it is God, not Moses, who redeemed the people and brought them out of Egypt (v. 26). This past relationship cannot simply be ignored. The affirmations of 7:6 cannot be disregarded. Next the prayer names Abraham, Isaac, and Jacob. There is no explicit mention of God's promise to them, but the frequent references to God's oath to the ancestors in Deuteronomy make it impossible to read their names without seeing in the names an allusion back to the promise. Deuteronomy has said that God is faithful to his promises: here Moses indirectly reminds God of that. To the people Moses emphasizes their history of faithlessness. To God, Moses emphasizes his faithfulness.

Finally, Moses moves beyond Israel to the world of nations. God's actions are not merely played out before Israel but also on a worldwide stage (cf. 4:5-8, 32-39). Regardless of the justification God might have in destroying Israel, Moses argues, it will be interpreted either as failure (*Because the* LORD *was not able to bring them into the land*) or as a sign of God's duplicity (*because he hated them, he has brought them out to let them die in the wilderness*) (v. 28). The first challenges God's sovereignty (see comments on 2:2–3:11), the second questions God's integrity (see on 6:4-9). God's very reputation is at stake, Moses charges. The prayer concludes with a further reference to the people as God's *very own possession,* and a further mention of God's great historic actions on Israel's behalf (deliverance from Egypt). Moses uses every argument he can muster to persuade God to continue working with the people God has chosen. God listens to the voice of his prophets, and so *the LORD listened to me that time also* (v. 19).

10:1-5 The Covenant Renewed

The prayer of Moses has been heard: God has relented. The graciousness of God is demonstrated in the renewing of the covenant (cf. Exod 34). Just as the breaking of the covenant was accompanied by a symbolic action, so the renewal of the covenant calls for a symbolic action. Again God calls on Moses to prepare two tablets of stone, and again God writes on them the ten words, or *ten commandments* (Deut 10:4; cf. 4:10, 13; 5:22; 9:10-11). The correspondence between the account of the original inscribing of the tablets (9:9-11) and the present passage emphasizes that the covenant has been fully renewed.

The new element is the introduction of the *ark of wood,* as it is called here. This is the first mention of the ark in Deuteronomy. Within Deuteronomy the ark functions exclusively as a container for the two tablets containing the Decalogue (cf. 1 Kings 8:9), the content of the Horeb covenant (cf. 4:13). As such, it fulfills a role similar to the religious shrines of that day in which copies of political treaties would be kept (Craigie 1976: 199). It thus is called the *ark of the covenant* (10:8), a title used largely by Deuteronomy and those books heavily influenced by Deuteronomy (as in 31:9, 25; Josh 3:6, 8; 4:7, 18; etc.). Later Deuteronomy places the book of the law next to the ark (31:26). With this emphasis Deuteronomy appears to counter those tendencies in Israel that give the ark a much more glorified or hallowed role as the throne of God, or the symbol of his real presence within Israel. As a sign of God's presence, the ark was understood to guide Israel through the desert (cf. Num 10:35) and give its armies strength for battle (e.g., Num 14:42-44; Josh 3-6; 1 Sam 4:1-9). Weinfeld sees this as an example of Deuteronomy's consistent tendency to secularize or demythologize cultic or ritual traditions. He argues that Deuteronomy, as a product of royal scribal schools, radically reforms Israel's religion by curtailing and circumscribing the role of priests, sacrifice, temple, and all aspects of cult, with a vision for an abstract, rational religion. Deuteronomy's concern is for faithfulness to God as reflected in obedience to the Torah (Weinfeld 1972: 191-243; 1991: 37-44, 417-18; cf. below on 12:1-27; 14:22-29). Here the ark enters the picture in relationship to the renewed covenant.

10:6-9 Interruption: Death of Aaron, Designation of Levites

Two short passages interrupt the narrative at this point. The first (vv. 6-7) is a fragment from a travel report (cf. Num 33:30-33). Its reference to Aaron dying at Moserah (cf. Num 33:37-38) confirms that the intercession Moses made on his behalf (Deut 9:20) was fruitful. Not only did he live, but also his son succeeded him. God's forgiveness is again demonstrated.

Perhaps triggered by the reference to the ark (vv. 1-5), a second insertion reports the designation of the tribe of Levi for special service to God (vv. 8-9). According to Exodus 32:25-29 it was the Levites' zeal in punishing those who had succumbed to the temptation of the calf that occasioned their designation to God's service. The background is omitted here, but the commission remains. Their assignment has three components: *to carry the ark of the covenant* (cf. 31:9, 25), *to stand before the* LORD *to minister to him*, and *to bless his name*. The second and third of these are priestly duties. Deuteronomy does not distinguish between priests and Levites and thus allows the Levites to participate in the service of God as well (Abba; Cook 2011). For more on the *inheritance* of the Levites, see comments on 18:1-8.

10:10-11 Return to the Journey

Deuteronomy's account of the sin of Horeb concludes with a return to the journey. The sin has been forgiven, the covenant has been renewed, Israel is back on its way to the Promised Land. By showing how God once again listens to Moses' plea, the story simultaneously highlights God's gracious, forgiving nature and Israel's stubbornness.

THE TEXT IN BIBLICAL CONTEXT
Human Nature—God's Nature

Deuteronomy depicts Israel as a *stubborn people* (9:6), consistently rebellious *from the day you came out of the land of Egypt until you came to this place* (9:7). Perhaps even more negatively, despite receiving God's gift of the torah, Deuteronomy harbors little hope that Israel will avoid continuing this behavior, thereby avoiding the covenant curses (chs. 27–30). Just as with the original election, hope for the future is not based on Israel's merit in becoming fully faithful, but on God's mercy. Only when God takes the initiative and circumcises their hearts will they *love the* LORD *your God with all your heart and with all your soul* (30:6).

In this logic Deuteronomy is by no means unique. This is also the story of Genesis 1-11, where humankind consistently ignores God's life-giving direction, choosing to go its own way. The result is punishment—although harsh, nevertheless a form of discipline—yet each time God enters the story with a sign of hope. Adam and Eve receive clothing from God and are sent from the garden, preventing their eating from the tree of life; Cain receives a mark protecting him from vengeance; after the great flood, God places a rainbow in the sky, promising never again to send such a flood. The remainder of Scripture then tells the story of how God responds to humanity's tendency to be stubborn and rebellious.

Within that story the climax comes in the sending of Jesus Christ, who came to "seek out and to save the lost" (Luke 19:10). In him "the Word became flesh and lived among us" (John 1:14); through him "we have all received grace upon grace" (1:16). Paul expresses the theology of Deuteronomy as follows: "All have sinned and fall short of the glory of God; they are now justified by his grace as a gift, through the redemption that is in Christ Jesus" (Rom 3:23-24). The vision of Deuteronomy is for a community of stubborn slaves mercifully redeemed by God and living an alternative ethic shaped by the way of that gracious God.

Interceding with God

At the center of our story is Moses prostrating himself before God, praying to God on behalf of Israel. This was not a singular occasion for Moses. The book of Numbers suggests that there were a number of times when the people's rebelliousness demanded a harsh response, and Moses intervened on behalf of the people before God (e.g., Num 11:1-3; 12:9-16; 14:1-25; 21:4-9). Perhaps the classic example of someone praying to God on behalf of others is Abraham in Genesis 18. Repeatedly Abraham appeals to God for the citizens of Sodom. Each time the number of righteous requested for deliverance decreases—first fifty, then forty-five, forty, thirty, twenty, and finally ten. Each time God accedes to the appeal. The wickedness of the city is not in question, only the magnitude of God's mercy.

Prophets also prayed to God on behalf of Israel. Old Testament prophets are sometimes characterized as harsh, almost as if they gloried in the punishment they were announcing. But virtually without exception they feel the pain of their own indictments and cry to God for the deliverance of the people. When God reveals to Amos a vision of Israel's fate, Amos responds, "O Lord GOD, forgive, I beg you! How can Jacob stand? He is so small" (Amos 7:2; cf. 7:5).

And we read, "The LORD relented concerning this" (Amos 7:3). Isaiah 53 says of the suffering servant, "yet he bore the sin of many, and made intercession for the transgressors" (Isa 53:12). It is the character of God's servants to pray to God on behalf of others, even when their sinfulness is great, and it is the character of God to listen to those prayers. Jesus' prayer on the cross, "Father, forgive them; for they do not know what they are doing" (Luke 23:34; cf. Acts 7:60), is in this Old Testament tradition.

THE TEXT IN THE LIFE OF THE CHURCH
Original Sin

The doctrine of original sin has played an important role in the history of Christianity. *The Catholic Encyclopedia* speaks of it as "(1) the sin that Adam committed; (2) a consequence of this first sin, the hereditary stain with which we are born on account of our origin or descent from Adam" (11:312). Evangelicals, also influenced by Augustine, tend to speak of the "fall" of Adam and Eve as resulting in all humanity being "born in sin." The primary scriptural text in support of this doctrine is from Paul; "Therefore, just as sin came into the world through one man, and death came through sin, and so death spread to all because all have sinned" (Rom 5:12).

More recently, however, voices from different wings of the church have expressed their discomfort with the doctrine, or with the impact it has had. The Dominican priest Matthew Fox is quoted in the *Living the Questions* curriculum:

> Jesus never heard of "Original Sin." The term wasn't even used until the fourth century, so it's "strange to run a church, a gathering, an *ekklēsia*—supposedly on behalf of Jesus—when one of its main dogmatic tenets, Original Sin, never occurred to Jesus." Sadly, Western Christianity is dependent on and chronically "attached to Original Sin—but what they're really attached to is St. Augustine."

After a meticulous study of Romans 5:12, John Toews concludes that although Augustine's interpretation of it became the dominant one for Western theology, it is based on a mistranslation of the text (150–67). He adds that "sixteenth-century Anabaptists consistently rejected Augustine's notion of original sin" (400). Similarly, Brian McLaren, speaking from within the emergent church movement, observes that nowhere in the Old Testament does it speak of original sin. He also warns against viewing Jesus through the lens of Paul and Augustine and later confessions (33–40). The debate is intense and will continue, with side conversations on related issues like the atonement and infant baptism.

As on the issue of the existence of other gods, Deuteronomy appears less interested in abstract doctrine than on ethical response. Consistent with this, Elie Wiesel declares in the *Living the Questions* curriculum that the notion of original sin is alien to Jewish thinking. For Deuteronomy, Israel has been, remains, and is projected to be in the future a stubborn people. Recent confessions issued by both the Mennonite Brethren and Mennonite Church take a similar approach.

> Mennonite Brethren: "We believe that the first humans yielded to the tempter, and fell into sin. Since then, all people disobey God and choose to sin." (MBCF 1999: 45)
> Mennonite Church: "We confess that, beginning with Adam and Eve, humanity has disobeyed God, given way to the tempter, and chosen to sin." (MCF 1995: 31)

Neither refers to original sin, both use a form of "to choose," and both speak of people disobeying God. This is consistent with the emphasis of Deuteronomy.

The Power of Prayer

One of the characteristics traditionally ascribed to God is that God is immutable, or unchangeable. This means that God can be counted on to have integrity. The Deuteronomic emphasis that God's promises can be trusted is consistent with this. God's word is sure. God always has been a gracious, loving God, and God always will be a gracious, loving God.

But a negative consequence of this way of speaking or thinking about God is that it contributes to an impression that God's plan for the future is all set, that God's mind is made up and nothing can change it. Such an understanding is roundly challenged by the passages about people interceding with God on behalf of others. In the Exodus account of the golden calf, the text reports, "And the LORD changed his mind about the disaster that he planned to bring on his people," or as the RSV reads, "And the LORD repented . . ." (Exod 32:14). The biblical accounts are consistent in depicting God as listening to the prayers of his people, and when God listens, the possibility of God changing his mind is real. Otherwise, petitionary prayer is meaningless.

Deuteronomy 10:12–11:32

A Midcourse Review

PREVIEW

Tradition has it that when an older, renowned preacher was asked what made his preaching so effective, he responded, "First I tell them what I am going to tell them, then I tell them, and then I tell them what I told them." I suspect that preacher had read Deuteronomy.

Before moving to preaching based on specific regulations, Deuteronomy reviews the emphases of its preaching thus far. First, the foundational expectation is reworded—to fear, love, and serve God by keeping his commandments and walking in his ways (10:12–11:1). The past can provide invaluable lessons (11:2-7) for knowing how to live in and enjoy the land of milk and honey (11:8-17). The review moves to a climax by borrowing language from the Shema (6:4-9) to call on Israel to absorb God's words into *heart and soul*, to hold these words always before them, to teach them to the next generation (11:18-25), for their response will determine whether their future is one of blessing or curse (11:26-32).

OUTLINE

God's Requirement, 10:12–11:1
    10:12-13   God's Requirement Pronounced
    10:14-15   The Wonder of Election
    10:16-19   The Justice of God
    10:20–11:1   God's Requirement Repeated
Lessons from the Past, 11:2-7

Enjoying the Land of Milk and Honey, 11:8-17
    11:8   Call to Obey
    11:9-12   A Land Cared for by God
    11:13-15   The Fruit of Obedience
    11:16-17   The Consequence of Apostasy
A Reminder of the Great Commandment, 11:18-25
The Alternatives: Blessing and Curse, 11:26-32

EXPLANATORY NOTES

God's Requirement 10:12-11:1

10:12-13 God's Requirement Pronounced

The *So now, O Israel* of verse 12 (cf. 4:1, starting the last part of the first speech) marks the beginning of a new section yet at the same time connects it with the previous one. Here it introduces an extended review of the first half of Deuteronomy's second speech. Not surprisingly, the review contains considerable repetition and overlap with the preceding chapters. This is meant to be a summary of God's basic expectation, as made clear by the opening question: *What does the LORD your God require of you?* (cf. Mic 6:8).

Deuteronomy answers with five key terms or phrases, each of which has been previously used in Deuteronomy, and each of which will be used again many times over. Although the phrases each have slightly different connotations, they do not refer to different aspects of the response but are largely synonyms. Altogether they paint a picture of the absolute allegiance that God expects from Israel, a loyalty based in the inner being but made manifest in action and obedience. God requires these not simply for his pleasure, but especially for Israel's *own well-being* (v. 13; cf. 8:16).

*to **fear** the LORD your God—4:10; 5:29; 6:2, 13, 24; 10:12, 20; 13:4; 14:23; 17:19; 25:18; 28:58; 31:12, 13; notice also the references to Israel not fearing its enemies (1:21, 29; 3:2, 22; 20:3; 31:6, 8), and the references to Israel's enemies fearing it (2:25; 11:25).

Fearing God is not a state of terror but arises from a full recognition of the awesome nature of God and the gravity of the human relationship with God. It does not paralyze but leads to trust and action. The most common use of the term "fear" in Deuteronomy is in reference to fearing God (at least fourteen times). But it is also used in two other related ways. Israel is regularly assured that it does not need to fear its enemies (at least seven times): after all, God is acting on its behalf. Further, Deuteronomy declares that Israel's enemies will fear it. These three usages are integrally related in Deuteronomy, although in a somewhat paradoxical manner. Israel shall fear God, not its enemies; its enemies will fear it, especially when Israel fears God. This Deuteronomic theme might be summarized thus: "If one truly fears God, one has nothing to fear; if one does not fear God, then one truly should fear." In a similar manner, Paul exhorts the Philippians to "work out your own salvation with fear and trembling" (Phil 2:12; cf. Acts 9:31; 13:16, 26; 2 Cor 5:11; 7:1). As shown in the present context, the meaning of the Deuteronomic call to fear God is parallel to and not distinct from loving God and obeying his will.

*to walk in all his ways—5:33; 10:12; 11:22; 13:4, 5; 19:9; 26:17; 28:9; 30:16.

The teaching of Moses is presented to Israel as the way to life (cf. 30:15). It thus invites Israel to walk in it. Psalm 119 opens with a beatitude that introduces this same metaphor: "Happy are those whose way is blameless, who walk in the law of the LORD. Happy are those who keep his decrees, who seek him with their whole heart, who also do no wrong, but walk in his ways (vv. 1-3). The psalm regularly returns to this image of "the way" (e.g., vv. 27, 59, 105). Perhaps influenced by Deuteronomy, Jesus uses a similar image, "I am the way, and the truth, and the life" (John 14:6).

*to love him—5:10; 6:5; 7:9; 10:12; 11:1, 13, 22; 19:9; 30:6, 16, 20; notice also the references to God's love for Israel (7:7, 13; 10:15).

The middle phrase of the five, and possibly the most important, calls on Israel to love God. As in the comments on 6:4-9, for its background Deuteronomy's use of the term may have political treaties, where "love" denotes political allegiance, but its familial connotations cannot be disregarded. Important for Deuteronomy is the reciprocal nature of this love: God loved Israel first, and now Israel is expected to return this love. Similarly, we read in the New Testament, "We love because he first loved us" (1 John 4:19).

*to serve the LORD your God—6:13; 10:12, 20; 11:13; 13:4; 28:47; notice also numerous references to serving other gods (re. serve/worship, cf. RSV: 4:19, 28; 5:9; 7:4, 16; 8:19; 11:16; 12:2, 30; 13:2, 6, 13; 17:3; 28:14, 36, 64; 29:18, 26; 30:17; 31:20).

The most basic identifying characteristic of God is that God has redeemed Israel from *the land of Egypt, out of the house of slavery* (5:6). Yet deliverance is not for the purpose of unrestricted freedom but for service of God (the same Hebrew root stands behind *slavery* and *to serve*). Absolute freedom is not a real option. The option is to serve the God of the exodus or to serve other gods, the gods of Egypt, the gods of the ancestors, or the gods of the land (cf. Josh 24:15). The phrase *serve/serving other gods* is Deuteronomy's primary way of speaking of such apostasy.

*to <u>keep</u> the commandments of the LORD your God—4:2, 40; 5:29; 6:2, 24-25; 5:10, 29; 6:17; 7:9, 12; 8:2, 6, 11; 11:1, 8, 13, 22; 13:4, 18; 17:19; 26:17, 18; 27:1, 10; 28:9, 45; 30:8, 10, 16.

The final phrase binds it all together. Those who love God, fear God, walk in his ways, and serve God—such people demonstrate this by keeping his commandments, or torah. No separation between attitude and action is possible. The frequency with which Deuteronomy uses this phrase or comparable wording highlights this emphasis.

10:14-15 *The Wonder of Election*

God's election of Israel, reflected in multiple covenants, has been a common theme in Deuteronomy thus far, and not surprisingly, is picked up in this review. The key terms *chose* and *love* are both used in 10:15. Twice previously Deuteronomy has wrestled with the basis for Israel's election, and then simply attributed it to God's love. Deuteronomy 7:7-11 emphasizes that Israel was not a large or powerful people and thus did not deserve to be elected on that basis. Rather, election was based on God's love (4:37). Deuteronomy 9 continues in this manner, justifying God's action in terms of the wickedness of the Canaanites and the promise to the ancestors, but then again makes it clear that Israel did not deserve its election because it is a stubborn people (9:1-6). The present passage again affirms the fact of election, relates it to God's love, but then places it within a context of God's sovereignty over all. All creation belongs to God—everything, whether in the highest heavens or anywhere on earth. The phrase *heaven and the heaven of heavens* is probably to be understood as a form of the superlative (cf. 1 Kings 8:27; Ps 148:4). No further effort at explanation is attempted. God's dominion over all gives God the right to elect whomever God wishes (cf. Neh 9:6-7; Isa 45:12-13; Jer 27:5-6). One is reminded of the book of Job. After repeated efforts by Job to have God explain himself, God responds by pointing to the mystery and greatness of creation. Finally Job can only accept his lot and repent of his audacity (Job 42:1-6). God's sovereignty means that Israel's election cannot be fully explained. Its wonder and mystery can only be accepted, with the responsibility to live accordingly (see the TBC "Election, Separation, and Mission" after ch. 7).

10:16-19 The Justice of God

Once the wonder and mystery of the election are accepted, response must follow. The form of the response suggested here goes beyond review of what has been emphasized thus far in Deuteronomy and begins to prepare for the last half of the second speech and for the rest of the book. The metaphor *Circumcise, then, the foreskin of your heart* builds on the Israelite rite of circumcising infant boys. In Israel's story this rite sealed the election of the ancestors (Gen 17). During the exile it came to hold special significance as a distinguishing sign of membership in the Israelite community. But external compliance is inadequate. Deuteronomy and other Old Testament writings thus speak of circumcising the heart (cf. Jer 4:4), or of uncircumcised lips (Exod 6:12 mg., 30 mg.) and uncircumcised ears (Jer 6:10 mg.). Later, Deuteronomy will speak of God circumcising Israel's heart (30:6). To be a full member of the people of God requires that the inner being of the people be oriented toward God, that the people love God with heart, soul, and might (cf. 6:5; 10:12). It is the opposite of being *stubborn* (10:16; cf. 9:1–10:11) or stiff-necked.

God is the model for what it means to live with a circumcised heart. Using language that probably came from Israel's worship (cf. Ps 136:2), Yahweh is identified as *God of gods and Lord of lords* (Deut 10:17). Again a Hebrew superlative construction is used (cf. v. 14). With its reference to gods and lords, the language probably reflects a polytheistic background, but its meaning in the passage is clear: the God of the exodus (the terms *mighty and awesome* point to the exodus) is incomparable; Yahweh is the great king before whom the only appropriate stance is one of awe. This great God then is depicted as the supreme judge. In the ancient Near East, justice was the responsibility of the king (cf. Ps 72). The king had responsibility for ensuring that justice be fair (*is not partial and takes no bribe*, Deut 10:17; cf. 1:17) and that the *orphan*, the *widow*, and the *stranger*—three elements of society that in the usual process have least access to the judicial system—be protected. The reference to God supplying these people with *food and clothing* highlights that not only does God protect them but also goes the next step, providing them with essentials for life. God's greatness is represented most particularly by this concern and help for the poor. To live with a circumcised heart thus means to *love the stranger* (RSV, *sojourner*): after all, God cares for the stranger, and the people of Israel experienced this care when they *were strangers in the land of Egypt*. This last directive is especially interesting because here the stranger is not an Israelite but a foreigner, possibly even a descendant of the original inhabitants of the land. Subtly, earlier commands to remain separate are put into question. With this characterization of God and the summons for Israel, the text begins to prepare for regulations (of chs. 12–26) that frequently demonstrate special concern for the weak and disadvantaged (e.g., 14:28-29; 16:9-15; 24:17-21; 27:19).

10:20–11:1 *God's Requirement Repeated*

God's requirement is repeated, using four of the five key terms noted in verses 12-13 (*fear, love, keep*; the term translated *worship* in v. 20 is the same root as was translated *serve* in v. 12). The first verse (10:20), basically taken from 6:13, adds two phrases: *to him you shall hold fast* and *by his name you shall swear*. The first of these two phrases is used in the creation story of the intimate relationship of a husband to wife (Gen 2:24; cf. 34:3; 1 Kings 11:2). In Deuteronomy and the literature dependent upon Deuteronomy, it becomes an important image for the close relationship that God desires with his people (cf. Deut 4:4; 11:22; 13:4; 30:20; Josh 22:5; 23:8; 2 Kings 18:6). Through election and covenant they have been united in a bond that is not to be broken. The reference to swearing by God's name may be referring to an oath of loyalty to God (cf. Isa 45:23), but even if not, swearing by the name of another god would imply allegiance to that god and is thus to be rejected. A true worshiper of Yahweh must only swear by that name (cf. 5:11; Lev 19:12; Ps 63:11; Isa 48:1; Jer 4:2; 5:2).

Praise is generally not a central theme in Deuteronomy, but recollecting what God has done naturally leads to glorifying and extolling God (v. 21). The *great and awesome things* are God's actions in the exodus. Again it is stated that *your own eyes have seen* God's deeds (cf. 4:9; 7:19; 11:2-7; 29:3). In the older tradition the number *seventy* suggested the totality of the group that entered Egypt (cf. Gen 46:27; Exod 1:5). Here, however, it emphasizes the modest size of the group, which God has increased so they have become *as numerous as the stars in heaven* (cf. Deut 1:10; 28:62). Appropriate response to this God is fear, love, and obedience, but also praise and worship.

Although this passage largely builds on what has been said previously, its location immediately following the verses on God's justice begins to broaden its meaning. Until now the primary focus in Deuteronomy has been the first two commandments, and clearly they are assumed here as well. But even in the review there is the hint that to love God and to *keep his charge* (11:1) will require that Israel treat fellow human beings in a manner not unlike the way God has treated them.

Lessons from the Past 11:2-7

History is an important teacher for Deuteronomy, especially in the first speech (chs. 1-4), but also here in the first half of the second. The review now reminds the readers of God's lessons in the past. The term *discipline* is used (v. 2), but much more than punishment is meant (cf. 4:36; 8:5). It is God preparing Israel, nurturing Israel, training them for life in the land. God's education includes both acts of correction as well as acts demonstrating God's power and nature, deeds of deliverance, and deeds of judgment. The three cited examples reflect both aspects of discipline.

Of prime importance is the exodus. Again a number of the Deuteronomic code words for that complex of events associated with Israel's deliverance from Egypt are used: *his greatness* (cf. 3:24; 9:26), *his mighty hand* (3:24; 4:34; 5:15; 6:21; 7:8, 19; 26:8; 34:12), *his outstretched arm* (4:34; 5:15; 7:19; 9:29; 26:8), *his signs* (4:34; 6:22; 7:19; 26:8; 29:3; 34:11). To this list is added an allusion to the plagues (*deeds that he did in Egypt*, 11:3; cf. Exod 7-12), and Deuteronomy's only explicit reference to the confrontation with Pharaoh's army at the Red Sea (11:4; cf. Exod 14-15). All credit is given to God. In Exodus this series of events is introduced by God's announcement, "You shall know that I am the LORD your God, who has freed you from the burdens of the Egyptians" (Exod 6:7), and concludes with the statement, "Israel saw the great work that the LORD did against the Egyptians. So the people feared the LORD and believed in the LORD and in his servant Moses" (14:31). Here is God's basic lesson.

The second historical reference is to the period of wilderness wandering (Deut 11:5). As Deuteronomy has earlier emphasized, although the desert is generally a place of great danger, for Israel this has been a time when it *lacked nothing* (2:7; cf. 8:2-6, 15-16). God led Israel, protected it, and gave it food and water. In the wilderness Israel learned that it was totally dependent upon God.

The third historical illustration demonstrates that although discipline is more than correction or punishment, it does include the element of judgment. The story of Dathan and Abiram as told in Numbers 16 concerns rebellion against God and God's representative, Moses. The end result is death. The warning is clear: forgetting the lessons of the exodus leads to death.

The historical lessons are encased by two typical Deuteronomic themes. Verse 2 directs attention to the present generation. Although Deuteronomy 5:1-5 emphasizes that God's covenant is not limited to the ancestors but is also *with us, who are all of us here alive today* (5:3), this passage turns in the other direction. Education of the children, the next generation, is important (cf. 4:9-10; 6:6, 20-25), but the call is always addressed to the present: *It is you who must acknowledge his greatness* (11:2). The time for decision is always now. The passage concludes with a further reference to Israel having seen those lessons from history with its own eyes (cf. 3:21; 4:9; 7:19; 10:21; 29:2).

Enjoying the Land of Milk and Honey 11:8-17

The strategy Israel must follow to fully experience and enjoy the land of milk and honey is obedience to *this entire commandment*, the totality of what Moses is teaching. This has been emphasized in Deuteronomy thus far and is stressed again in this midcourse review.

11:8 Call to Obey

As at some other points in Deuteronomy (cf. 4:1), this verse appears to make Israel's original entrance into the Promised Land conditional upon obedience to the law. The remainder of the passages makes it clear, however, that the primary focus is on the actual life in the land. Faithfulness will lead to blessing in the land (vv. 13-15); unfaithfulness will lead to loss of blessing and death (vv. 16-17).

11:9-12 A Land Cared for by God

Again we have a passage extolling the wonders of the land that God is giving Israel (cf. 6:10-15; 8:7-10). The direction the passage takes, however, may very well be influenced by the story of Dathan and Abiram, mentioned a few verses earlier (11:6). In their rebellion against Moses, Dathan and Abiram speak of Egypt as "a land flowing with milk and honey" and accuse Moses: "It is clear you have not brought us into a land flowing with milk and honey, or given us an inheritance of fields and vineyards" (Num 16:12-14). This passage in Deuteronomy begins by calling the land promised the ancestors *a land flowing with milk and honey* (11:9) and then contrasts it with the land of Egypt. Whereas in Egypt a bountiful harvest depends upon backbreaking work, in the Promised Land God provides the required moisture through *rain from the sky* (v. 11). Although the precise nature of the work assumed by the phrase *irrigate by foot* is not clear (building dams for water? digging irrigation ditches? operating lifting devices?), it likely refers to some type of irrigation. In a land of *hills and valleys*, irrigation is viable primarily for small vegetable gardening (Weinfeld: 445). But instead of seeing this as a problem, the passage emphasizes that here God waters the fields.

It is admitted that the contrast "has a touch of theological exaggeration about it" (Cairns: 115). As the stories of the ancestors reflect (e.g., Gen 12:10-20; chs. 41–47), Egypt was the breadbasket of the world of that day, comparable to *the garden of the* LORD (Gen 13:10). Irrigation might be hard work, but with rich soil and a plentiful water supply, it virtually assured sufficient food. But the point of the comparison is that in the Promised Land Israel is dependent upon God and not on human technique. The land God is giving Israel is a land that God *looks after*, a land upon which the *eyes of the* LORD *are always* present. The care of God may be compared to "the care of the scholar lovingly poring over the sacred text or the researcher examining a case conscientiously, the care that counts the hairs of the head and keeps an exact inventory of the sparrows (Luke 12:6-7)" (Cairns: 115). Not only the people of Israel but also even the land it is receiving are given a special place in God's providence.

11:13-15 *The Fruit of Obedience*

If Israel *heeds* (lit., "hears") the commandment, then it will experience the blessings of the land generated by plentiful moisture. The commandments are represented here with a reference back to the Shema (6:4-9). The *early rain*, coming in late fall, softens the soil baked hard by the summer sun, thereby making seeding possible. The *later rain*, coming in spring, provides the moisture needed for the final maturation of the grain. When these rains come, harvests are bountiful and pastures provide ample feed for the herds; when these rains come, Israel will eat its fill (cf. 8:10). Truly enjoying the land comes only through obedience.

11:16-17 *The Consequence of Apostasy*

The opposite of obedience is not simply disobedience but *serving other gods* (cf. 10:12). The repeated declaration that God provides the rain (vv. 11-12, 14), ensuring abundant harvest, is a direct challenge to Canaanite religion in which Baal, a god of fertility, sends the rain. The danger in the land is that Israel will become so "open-minded" (a possible translation of the Hebrew; Craigie 1976: 210) to the culture and religion of the Canaanites that it begins to accept the worship of Baal as a normal part of agricultural practice in the land. As Elijah's confrontation with the prophets of Baal makes clear, Israel fell prey to exactly this seduction (1 Kings 18). When that happens, Deuteronomy proclaims, God's control of nature and fertility will become evident: God *will shut up the heavens, so that there will be no rain* (v. 17; cf. drought announced by Elijah before his showdown with the prophets of Baal; 1 Kings 17:1). In a land in which hills and valleys make irrigation a huge challenge, drought can only lead to death. God will give Israel the land, but it is not a gift that can be taken for granted. Forgetting and forsaking God, serving and worshiping other gods—all such lead to the loss of that gift.

A Reminder of the Great Commandment 11:18-25

As is suggested by the heading this commentary has given Deuteronomy 6–11, "Preaching the Foundational Commandment," these chapters are an exposition of the Shema and its demand for exclusive loyalty. They begin with its proclamation (6:4-9), and now they conclude with a final reminder of it. In this review Israel's fortune is tied to its response to the Shema's foundational expectation. When Israel is faithful in its response, God will drive out the nations, giving it the land.

The cycle is presented two times:
11:18-20   references to 6:4-9 (plus 4:9-10)
11:21   obedience leads to long life on the land (cf. 4:40; 6:2)
11:22   reference to 6:4-9 (plus 10:12-13; 10:20–11:1)
11:23-25   obedience leads to God giving full land (cf. 1:7-8; 4:1, 38; 7:23-24; 9:1; 11:8)

The Alternatives: Blessing and Curse 11:26-32

As good preaching is prone to do, Deuteronomy concludes the review with a passage once more emphasizing the intimate relationship between Israel's response to Moses' teaching and its fate in the Promised Land: a faithful response leads to blessing, or life; a faithless response leads to curse, or death (cf. 30:15). This includes a reference to a future covenant-renewal ceremony (repeated annually?) once in the Promised Land, where the alternative of blessings and curses is represented by the two mountains Gerizim and Ebal. For a more detailed discussion of covenant renewal, blessings and curses, see discussion of chapters 27–28.

THE TEXT IN BIBLICAL CONTEXT
Stark Alternatives

Deuteronomy has a tendency to articulate Israel's response with stark alternatives: either Israel heeds, fears, loves, and serves God, keeping torah—or Israel forgets God and goes after other gods. Israel must choose blessing or curse. The alternatives are hinted at in the beginning of our passage (10:12) and made explicit toward the end (11:26). The third speech concludes with a similar either/or appeal: *See, I have set before you today life and prosperity, death and adversity* (30:15). This is in good prophetic tradition (cf. Hosea's metaphor of adultery), as well as similar in tone to much of Jesus' teaching.

Consider the number of times Jesus uses similar stark alternatives. When speaking about the temptation of wealth, Jesus says "No one can serve two masters; for a slave will either hate the one and love the other, or be devoted to the one and despise the other" (Matt 6:24). We are encouraged to "enter through the narrow gate; for the gate is wide and the road is easy that leads to destruction" (7:13). Similarly, "every good tree bears good fruit, but the bad tree bears bad fruit" (7:17). And he teaches that when the Son of Man comes to judge, "he will put the sheep at his right and the goats at the left" (25:33). We recognize that there is often ambiguity in knowing what it means to serve God in a particular situation, but that does not erase the larger conviction that Israel, and the church, must choose between serving the God of the exodus and Jesus Christ, or serving the gods of the day. We cannot "go limping with two different opinions" (1 Kings 18:21).

THE TEXT IN THE LIFE OF THE CHURCH
A Works Righteousness?

A popular 1970 hymn composed by Sheilagh Nowacki, though based on Jeremiah 7:23, well represents a central thrust of Deuteronomy:

> Obey my voice, and I will be your God,
>   and you shall be my people,
> and walk in all the ways I have commanded you,
>   that it may be well with you, and I will be your God.
> Obey my voice, and I will be your God,
>   and you shall be my people.

Through the use of imperative verbs forms (*fear, walk, love, serve, keep, cleave, circumcise*), the midcourse review (10:12–11:32) repeatedly calls on Israel to respond so that all will go well once they are in the Promised Land. Is this then a "works righteousness," in which Israel earns its salvation through obedience and action?

The Anabaptist tradition has responded warmly to this side of the biblical message. After all, does Jesus not make it clear that we will be judged by how we act toward the hungry, the thirsty, and the naked (Matt 25:31-45)? Are we not told in James, "Be doers of the word, and not merely hearers who deceive themselves" (1:22)? We know that confession without action is empty.

Yet it is not that simple. Martin Luther, overwhelmed by guilt and inspired by the writings of Paul, stressed the role of grace and faith. After all, Paul highlights how Abraham was justified not by works but by faith (Rom 4:1-5); and to the Galatians, Paul writes,

> Yet we know that a person is justified not by the works of the law but through faith in Jesus Christ. And we have come to believe in Christ Jesus, so that we might be justified by faith in Christ, and not by doing the works of the law, because no one will be justified by the works of the law. (Gal 2:16)

Not surprisingly, Luther then was quite uncomfortable with certain words of James: "You see that a person is justified by works and not by faith alone" (2:24). Countless others like Luther have been racked with guilt from a sense that they have failed in their efforts at obedience.

The Christian church has struggled with this apparent grace-law opposition, with Anabaptists and Lutherans representing, at least in theory, the two extremes. Scripture can be used to support both, but it also includes passages that challenge pitting these two against each other. In the gospel of John, Jesus says, "Very truly, I tell you, the one who believes in me will also do the works that I do and, in fact, will do greater works than these, because I am going to the Father" (14:12).

In an interesting study of the story of Abraham ready to offer Isaac as a sacrifice, W. R. L. Moberly observes that after Abraham has passed the test, thereby becoming the model for Paul's emphasis on faith, God responds, "For now I know that you fear God" (Gen 22:12). Moberly suggests that "'fear of God' is the primary category within the Old Testament for depicting appropriate human response to God, and as such, it plays a role within the Old Testament somewhat analogous to that of 'faith' within the New Testament" (2003: 190).

Deuteronomy 10:11–11:32 feels very different if faith is included as a connotation of the term "fear." Perhaps faith and response cannot be separated as sharply as we have tended to do. Deuteronomy's use of the circumcision metaphor supports this. In the current passage Israel is called to circumcise its heart (10:16). Later Israel is assured that God will circumcise their hearts (30:6). Deuteronomy's persistent call to obedience must be placed alongside Deuteronomy's judgment that Israel is a stubborn people (9:6, 13) and ultimately must place its faith in God's covenantal promises.

Deuteronomy 12:1–26:19

Part 2D
Preaching the Moab Covenant

OVERVIEW

These are the statutes and ordinances that you must diligently observe in the land that the LORD, the God of your ancestors, has given you to occupy all the days that you live on the earth (12:1). Deuteronomy has reviewed the covenant given Israel at Mount Horeb (ch. 5) and expounded the foundational commandment as reworded in the Shema (chs. 6–11); now the book moves into the details of what this means. Although the phrase *statutes and ordinances*, found in the opening verse, applies to the whole of the second speech (12:1, but also 4:1; 5:1; etc.), it does fit chapters 12–26 especially well. Deuteronomic preaching now makes use of concrete regulations to paint a picture of what Israel's life in the land is to be like, what it means to love God with one's total being (cf. 6:4-9).

For many contemporary Christians, however, this shift also signals the end of their interest. Their reaction is both emotional and intellectual. Our immediate intuitive sense is that law, whether modern state law or biblical law, does not inspire. Factoring into this reaction is our experience with law today. The term "legalese" reminds us of lengthy legal jargon, formulated as precisely as possible to describe possible actions and their potential consequences. Courts and enforcement agencies require such precision so law can be applied or enforced equitably across the land [*Law, p. 555*]. We accept that law may be necessary, but for most of us it makes for dull and uninteresting reading.

This emotional response is supported by our impression that the New Testament, especially Jesus and Paul, regularly challenge the Pharisees and their legalistic use of their Scripture. After all, did Jesus not repeatedly offend the Jewish leaders of his day by "working" on the Sabbath and then defend it by responding, "The sabbath was made for humankind, and not humankind for the sabbath" (Mark 2:27)? Whether because of the way his opponents interpreted the law, or because the laws themselves were abrogated, we believe that Jesus moves beyond Old Testament law.

Deuteronomy 12–26 challenges such notions as it preaches to Israel a vision for responding to God's salvific action by making use of legal-like material. They may be *statutes and ordinances*, or even have a legal style, yet they are not legalistic and certainly not lifeless. They include statements that most today would consider to be arcane or meaningless (e.g., *You shall not wear clothes made of wool and linen woven together,* 22:11; *You shall not muzzle an ox while it is treading out the grain,* 25:4), but the section as a whole is still preaching. It appeals to the mind and heart, with the goal of *persuading* the listeners to respond by structuring their lives together around the vision revealed in the preaching. It is preaching designed to inspire Israel *to fear the* LORD *your God, to walk in all his ways, to love him, to serve the* LORD *your God with all your heart and with all your soul* (10:12), *so that* they might *live long in the land that the* LORD *swore to your ancestors to give them and to their descendants, a land flowing with milk and honey* (11:9).

Deuteronomy 12–26 and Old Testament Law

The reform movement that led to Deuteronomy did not creatively formulate a new religion but worked fully within the Mosaic monotheistic faith. The stories of exodus and wilderness wandering, as well as Israel's legal traditions, shaped its understanding of God and the vision for how Israel was to live. Deuteronomy thus incorporates or assumes earlier legal-like traditions (i.e., it does not need to state that which was known to be the case) and then supplements them, expands upon them, and adapts them. Its regular emphasis on *today* makes the point that *now* is the time to respond, yet it also hints that former regulations have been revised or updated so that they better fit the present (e.g., 4:8, 39).

The larger pentateuchal narrative has God proclaiming the law to Israel at Mount Sinai (Exod 19–Num 10), with Deuteronomy a recapitulation of that law by Moses on the plains of Moab. Scholarly research, however, sees in this large mass of material distinct traditions and blocks reflecting different historical periods and emphases. In addition to material attributed to the primary pentateuchal sources, scholars identify three distinct larger blocks: the Book of the Covenant, or Covenant Code (Exod 20:23–23:19), the Deuteronomic Code (Deut 12–26), and the Holiness Code (Lev 17–26). Of these three, the Book of the Covenant generally is considered to be the oldest, with the Holiness Code the latest, although the relationship between the last two is more complex than often thought.

The significant overlap in material between Deuteronomy 12–26 and the Book of the Covenant argues for a relationship between the two. If the historical order suggested above is accurate, then Deuteronomy is in dialogue with the earlier code, or the traditions behind it, editing and updating the regulations in keeping with its vision. The chart below (p. 224) reveals important similarities between these two collections (chart adapted from Patrick: 97; cf. Cairns: 120–24).

Structure of Deuteronomy 12–26

Despite the longtime, careful work of competent scholars, there is no consensus on how the material of chapters 12–26 is arranged. Already in 1924, A. C. Welch lamented, "While any order into which the laws may be placed is sure to be unsatisfactory, none can be quite so bad as the order in which they appear in Deuteronomy today" (24). The most common response to this reality by commentators is to move through the text passage by passage with minimal attention to larger structure (e.g., Craigie 1976; Cairns; Brueggemann 2001; Tigay; McConville 2002).

Over the years many proposals have been suggested. One of the earliest was that the regulations were arranged thematically around topics like cultic law, judicial laws, war laws, and so forth (Steuernagel). A Jewish scholar argues that the laws of Deuteronomy follow the narrative of the Pentateuch (Carmichael 1974). Others propose that although there may be no comprehensive structure for the whole block, the arrangement of the regulations themselves is a consequence of a combination of various Hebrew literary techniques, such as word association, length, chiasm, and thematic connections.

Parallels between Deuteronomy 12–26 and the Covenant Code

Deuteronomy	Exodus	Topic
12:1-28	20:24	altars, offerings, worship
13:1-18	22:20	false prophets and other gods
14:21a	22:31	eating carion
14:21b	23:19b	eating a kid boiled in mother's milk
15:1-11	23:10-11	sabbatical remission, fields, debts
15:12-18	21:2-11	sabbatical remission for slaves
15:19-23	22:30	offering firstborn of animals
16:1-17	23:14-17	three festivals
16:19-20	23:6-8	do not distort justice
17:2-7	22:20	worshiping/sacrificing to other gods
18:10b-11	22:18	sorcerers, diviners, soothsayers, etc.
19:1-13	21:12-14	cities of refuge
19:15-21	cf. 23:1-3	two witnesses, false witness
21:18-21	21:15, 17	rebelling against parents
22:1-4	23:4-5	caring for the neighbor's animals
22:28-29	22:16-17	violating a virgin
23:19	22:25	charging interest
24:6, 10-13	22:26-27	taking pledges for loans
24:7	21:16	kidnapping
24:17-18	22:21-24; 23:9	protecting the widow, the orphan, the resident alien
24:19-21	cf. 23:10-11	gleaning, food for the poor
26:1-11	cf. 22:29a; 23:19a	presenting first fruits

A proposal that has generated some interest in the past few decades, although remaining well short of consensus, is that the Decalogue provides the organizational principle for these chapters. Since its proposal in 1979 (Kaufman), a number of prominent Deuteronomy scholars have explored it further with their own variations (e.g., Braulik 1991; Millar; Olson). A recent commentary on Deuteronomy by Gary Hall follows the outline of Dennis Olson and organizes his consideration of Deuteronomy 12–26 around the commands of the Decalogue. Below is an adaptation of this proposal as developed by Olson and used by Hall:

Olson/Hall

Commandment	Deuteronomy
1 Have no other gods.	12:2–13:18
2 Make no images.	12:2–13:18
3 Use God's name rightly.	14:1-21
4 Keep the Sabbath.	14:22–16:17
5 Honor your parents.	16:18–18:22
6 Do not murder.	19:1–22:8
7 Do not commit adultery.	22:9–23:18
8 Do not steal.	23:19–24:7
9 Do not bear false witness.	24:8–25:4
10 Do not covet.	25:5–26:15

An advantage of this proposal is that it helpfully associates the opening portion of chapters 12–26 with the first commandment, *You shall have no other gods before me* (5:7). Along with the Shema (6:4-9), it is the foundational commandment providing the direction for the preaching of chapters 6–11, and it is the moving conviction behind the centralization regulation of chapter 12 and the denunciation of apostasy in chapter 13. Further, it also recognizes that the tithe regulation (14:22-29), the sabbatical release provisions (15:1-18), and the festival calendar (16:1-17) all make use of time categories and may be associated with the Sabbath command.

The limitations of the proposal remain significant, however. The Decalogue may be the most important legal grouping in the Old Testament, but it remains representative rather than foundational or exhaustive (see comments on 5:6-21). This proposal gives the Decalogue a foundational status for Israelite law beyond the evidence. But the larger difficulty is that although there may be some correlation between the first commandment and the first chapters of this section (12–13), and perhaps between the fourth commandment and chapters 15–16, the schema is quite forced when dealing with the later material.

Chapters 21–22 demonstrate this. Hall relates the first part (up to 22:8) to the murder command, and the second part (22:9-30) to the adultery command; yet the first part includes the passage on the rights of the firstborn (21:15-17), and the second part includes the prohibition against wearing clothes made of wool and linen (22:11). The very general statements used to defend this organizational proposal only confirm the difficulty scholars have in finding thematic coherence. Christopher Wright suggests that each of the five sections in chapter 21 deals "with a situation of human distress or misconduct and seeks either to rectify the wrong or to mitigate its worst effects" (1996: 232). A. D. H. Mayes speaks of most of chapter 22 as "concerned with respect for different forms of life" (306).

Crüsemann summarizes the discussion with "We have indeed barely uncovered the overall design of 12-26, and in any case it is not simply structured analogous to the ten commandments" (205). Brueggemann concludes, "This extended body of statutes is rather random and admits of no compelling structural analysis" (2001: 214). In the end the strongest argument for arranging chapters 12-26 on the basis of the Decalogue is the absence of any viable alternative.

The absence of any clear organization within these chapters then becomes a major challenge for a careful study of this section. Most of the material in chapters 12-20 can be treated under thematic headings, but in the absence of any clear organizational principles, chapters 21-25 are simply named Miscellaneous.

OUTLINE FOR PART 2D

Unit 1: Exclusive Worship of the One God, 12:1–14:21
Unit 2: Justice in Israel: The Community, 14:22–15:18
Unit 3: Festivals and the Cult, 15:19–16:17
Unit 4: Leadership and Judicial Procedures, 16:18–19:21
Unit 5: War, 20:1-20
Unit 6: Miscellaneous, 21:1–25:19
Unit 7: Theology through Worship, 26:1-19

Deuteronomy 12:1–14:21
Part 2D, Unit 1
Exclusive Worship of the One God

OVERVIEW

This may be a major new section with a different style, but its theological thrust builds on earlier chapters. The call for the exclusive worship of the God of the exodus as required by the first commandment of the Decalogue, and reformulated positively in the Shema (6:4-9), drives the opening chapters of this section as well.

This block includes three subthemes. First, the exclusive worship of the one God is understood to require Israel to worship God only at *the place that the LORD your God will choose out of all your tribes as his habitation to put his name there* (12:1-32). Here is one of the most unusual expectations in the whole book. Not only is Israel to destroy the worship sites of the former inhabitants (12:2-3), taking great care not to be lured into worshiping their gods (12:29-31), but Israel also is to worship its God *only* at *the place that God will choose* (e.g., 12:5). Here is Deuteronomy's centralization expectation, an expectation not expressed so directly anywhere else in the Old Testament, although assumed by the Deuteronomistic historian's critique of the Northern Kingdom.

After presenting the implication of the first commandment for worship, Deuteronomy turns to the possibility of some within Israel not only disregarding the first commandment and worshiping other gods, but also encouraging fellow Israelites to follow suit. Chapter 13 considers three such scenarios. Prophets, family members, and *scoundrels* all have the potential to say, *Let us go and worship other gods* (13:13; cf. 13:2, 6). In each case Deuteronomy pronounces the death penalty on those who speak such treason. The exclusive worship of God is a life-and-death matter (cf. 30:15).

Third, as *a people holy to the* LORD *your God* (14:2, 21), with a unique relationship to the one God, Israel is expected to live in a distinct, separate manner. God's election of Israel has made it a holy people. Israel's identity as a holy people shapes and affects all of life. Deuteronomy's version of dietary regulations, with its distinction between clean and unclean animals, is the model example of this (14:1-21) *[Dietary Regulations, p. 550]*.

Passages later in Deuteronomy continue this emphasis on Israel's distinct identity, and may be considered related to the theme of the exclusive worship of the one God: 21:1-9, 22-23; 22:5, 9-11; 24:8-9.

OUTLINE
Worship at The Place, 12:1-32
Purging Apostasy, 13:1-18
Cleanliness and Purity for a Holy People, 14:1-21

Worship at The Place
Deuteronomy 12:1-32

PREVIEW
Where do you most long to be? At home? At church? At a ball game? For at least some in ancient Israel, The Place had that special status: "My soul longs, indeed it faints for the courts of the LORD; my heart and my flesh sing for joy to the living God" (Ps 84:2).

Just as the Covenant Code begins with an altar law (Exod 20:24), so does the legal section within Deuteronomy. Deuteronomy 1–11 repeatedly emphasizes that the God of the exodus has chosen Israel as his special people (e.g., 4:34; 7:7-8) and that Yahweh is the only God for Israel (first commandment, the Shema): One God, One People.

Now Deuteronomy teaches that this unique relationship requires Israel to worship and bring sacrifice to that one God only at *the place that the* LORD *your God will choose out of all your tribes as his habitation to put his name there* (12:5, 11, 14, etc.). Israel is not to worship where the former inhabitants worshiped nor wherever it pleases. To One God, One People is added One Place. Here may be Deuteronomy's most unusual but far-reaching teaching (see TBC).

Chapter 12 sets centralization of worship within a framework rejecting the cultic practices of the Canaanites (vv. 2-3, 29-31) *[Cult, p. 546]*. Centralization becomes the implication of, or obedience to, the first commandment, the central theme in chapters 6–11. Thus Deuteronomy 12 considers the implication of centralization for eating meat as part of Israel's daily life, leading to permission for secular slaughter. The logic of the chapter may be summarized as follows:

1. Obedience to the first command requires the rejection and destruction of Canaanite worship.

2. Rejection of Canaanite worship requires one worship center.

3. One worship center requires a new approach to butchering animals for food.

OUTLINE

A¹ Introductory Exhortation: *Diligently Observe*, 12:1
  B¹ Demolish the Places of the Nations, 12:2-3
    C Seek The Place, 12:4-28
      Presentation of the Directive, 12:4-7
      Expansion of the Directive, 12:8-28
  B² Do Not Imitate the Worship of the Nations, 12:29-31
A² Concluding Exhortation: *Diligently Observe*, 12:32

EXPLANATORY NOTES

Structure

Even a cursory reading of this chapter exposes its repetitious nature. Phrases and themes are repeated over and over as it hammers home its central point. The usual explanation is that our current text is the end product of a complex and long history of literary development. Scholars then focus on tracing the history of that literary growth (are vv. 13-19 the earliest version of the command?) or attempt to reconstruct the historical development of Israel's centralization thrust. These efforts can be creative, technically complicated, and possibly even accurate: it is very likely that the present form of this passage does have a long history behind it. But in the process they may miss the power of the rhetoric in its present form. As any good preacher knows, repetition is a key element of rhetorical style. Deuteronomy employs this technique throughout the book, and especially in this chapter.

The paragraph divisions of the NRSV suggest the passage consists of three distinct accounts of the basic directive (vv. 2-7, 8-12, 13-19), with the last part of the chapter an expansion of the command. But this loses the important role that the opening and concluding verses play in providing a framework for the central portion, and misses the chiasm of the chapter (see Outline) *[Chiasm, p. 540]*. Nor does it draw attention to the framework within which the central directive is placed (opposition to the cultic practices of the other nations, vv. 2-3, 29-31), or the careful construction of the central thrust (vv. 4-28).

Deuteronomy tends to present a command or directive in a fairly simple manner, then to expand upon it through repetition, explanation, greater clarification, and motivation to obey. That style comes into play in this chapter, with verses 4-7 presenting the directive regarding worship at The Place in its most simple and direct form, with the remainder of the central block serving as expansion of the directive (Tigay: 118-27). This expansion consists of five sections that alternately repeat the substance of the centralization directive (vv. 8-12, 17-19, 26-28) and consider the implication of the directive for the slaughter of domestic animals for food (vv. 13-16, 20-25). The command to seek *the place* thus receives priority attention. It is the focus of the initial presentation (vv. 4-7) and is presented three times in the expansion, including the all-important central position.

Like chapter 7, chapter 12 focuses on Israel as a holy people, receiving blessings from God. Even though Israel is not called "holy" in chapter 12, its emphasis on worshiping only at *the place* God will choose certainly gives Israel a set-apart status. Further, both chapters place this central thrust within a framework calling for the destruction and rejection of all Canaanite worship (cf. 7:1-6, 17-26). These connections with chapter 7 highlight that the third section (chs. 12-26) of the second speech has the same foundational concern as the second (chs. 6-11): the exclusive worship of Yahweh, the God who blesses Israel, and the rejection of all aspects of Canaanite worship.

Introductory Exhortation 12:1
Concluding Exhortation 12:32

The opening verse serves double duty, as the chapter's opening exhortation matched by the concluding exhortation, and as a superscription for the larger section, Preaching the Moab Covenant (chs. 12–26). The combination *statutes and ordinances* in Deuteronomy regularly identifies key transition points—the opening of the important chapter 4 (4:1), the beginning of the second speech (4:45), the chapter presenting the Horeb covenant (5:1), the beginning and ending of the block "Preaching the Foundational Commandment" (6:1; 11:32)—and will be used again near the end of this larger section (26:16). Some interpreters limit the meaning of this combination to chapters 12–26, with its use in earlier chapters looking forward to the presentation in these chapters, but it is doubtful Deuteronomy makes this kind of a careful distinction (Nelson 2002: 159). Deuteronomy is presenting instruction for how Israel is to live in the land and uses multiple synonyms for its content: commandments, statutes, ordinances, and law. The phrase *statutes and ordinances* combines two of these broad and all-inclusive terms for the whole teaching of Deuteronomy as found in chapters 5–26.

At key junctures Deuteronomy reminds the reader that Israel is to *diligently observe* these directions in the land *all the days that you live on the earth*; thus *obedience* is integrally connected with life on the land. This is one of the few places in Deuteronomy where this gift of land is spoken of with the perfect tense, as in God *has given* the land, rather than with a participle, as in God *is giving* the land (cf. *has given* in 1:21; 3:18; 8:10; 28:52). The text visualizes Israel already in the land, experiencing its blessings, but also facing the existential challenge of whether or not to obey.

The concluding verse of the chapter and outer frame expresses a similar exhortation with the identical *diligently observe*, but substituting for one of the synonyms the broad but all-encompassing phrase *everything that I command you*. (For discussion of the phrase *Do not add to it or take anything from it*, see 4:2.)

Demolish the Places of the Nations 12:2-3
Do Not Imitate the Worship of the Nations 12:29-31

The inner frame (vv. 2-3, 29-31) arises directly out of the central concern of the preceding chapters. The presentation of the Decalogue (5:6-21) led to the Shema (6:4-9), a positive expression of the first commandment, followed by a longer section of preaching on this foundational commandment. The practical implication of the first commandment and Shema for a people living in a land occupied by the Canaanites was perfectly clear. Chapter 12 may be the start of a new larger block, but the passion of Deuteronomy remains on the same target: Israel is to eliminate all signs and remnants of the religion of the previous inhabitants of the land (cf. 7:1-6, 17-26). The right worship of the true God cannot have anything in common with the worship and cult of the people of the land [*Cult, p. 546*].

The plural term *places* provides striking contrast with the core of the chapter. Israel is to destroy the *places where the nations whom you are about to dispossess served their gods*, and instead seek *the place* (sg.) that God chooses. The phrase <u>all</u> *the places* may also include the nuance that the Canaanites worshiped anywhere and everywhere.

Mountains (or hills) and trees were popular locations for Canaanite worship sites. Mountains and hills were closer to the heavens and may even have been understood as places where the gods lived. Pilgrimage to these sites and worship of the gods there ostensibly brought the worshiper closer to the god. Deuteronomy does not use the phrase "high places" here or elsewhere, but in later Old Testament writings it becomes a common code word for illegitimate worship sites, especially in literature influenced by Deuteronomy (e.g., 1 Kings 3:2; 12:31; 2 Kings 12:3; 2 Chron 14:3; 33:17; Jer 19:5; Ezek 6:3; Hos 10:8; Mic 1:3). It is not hard to understand how a healthy tree with bountiful green leaves might become a symbol of fertility and life, a concern prominent in Canaanite religion. These places were probably open sites, without a temple or enclosed place of worship, but where *altars, pillars, sacred poles,* and *idols* were erected, sites to which people would come repeatedly for worship and sacrifice (see discussion of 7:5 for consideration of these). When Israel entered the land, these cultic objects were to be destroyed.

Not only is Israel to destroy the sites; they also are to eradicate all evidence (*name*) of these former religions. This may be a reference to renaming these sites after Israel entered the land (cf. Num 32:38). Again, the contrast with the central thrust of the chapter is clear: the names of the gods of the nations are to be removed forever. Instead, Israel is to go *the place* where God chooses to put his name.

The concluding frame (vv. 29-31) returns to and expands the theme. Again, the text assumes that the nations have been dispossessed, with Israel now living in the land. But now the focus is not on destroying the Canaanites cultic sites but rather on a warning not to be lured into worshiping the gods of these peoples. The term *abhorrent* (NIV, *detestable*; KJV, RSV, *abomination*), first used in 7:25-26, now becomes a common term in Deuteronomy for designating that which is especially reprehensible to God, frequently because of its connections with Canaanite cultic practices. The two parts of the framework (vv. 2-3, 29-31) provide the negative contrast to the central directive of the chapter.

The history of Israel tells us that all too often Israel did not follow this command and indeed continued to worship in ways borrowed from these peoples. With similar language 2 Kings explains the destruction of the Northern Kingdom as due to this transgression:

> The people of Israel secretly did things that were not right against the LORD their God. They built for themselves high places at all their towns, from watchtower to fortified city; they set up for themselves pillars and sacred poles on every high hill and under every green tree; there they made offerings on all the high places, as the nations did whom the LORD carried away before them. (17:9-11)

Seek The Place 12:4-28

The central portion of the chiasm opens by presenting the directive in its most direct form (vv. 4-7). Then in a further chiastic structure, it rephrases the centralization expectation (vv. 8-12, 17-19, 26-28), inserting its implications for the slaughter of domestic animals (vv. 13-16, 20-25).

Centralization, 12:8-12
   Secular Slaughter, 12:13-16
      Centralization, 12:17-19
   Secular Slaughter, 12:20-25
Centralization, 12:26-28

A helpful entrance into this passage is to focus on the phrases and themes that appear repeatedly. All of these except for the permission for secular slaughter appear in the initial presentation of the directive, and more than once in the later expansion.

Centralization as an Alternative

Three times the call to seek *the place* is set over against an alternative, with the first perhaps the most illuminating: *You shall not worship the LORD your God in such ways* (v. 4). The importance of centralization for Deuteronomy, especially given how little a role it played in Israel's history, raises difficult questions about its logic or

Deuteronomy	Initial Presentation 12:4-7	Expansion 12:8-28
Centralization as an alternative	12:4	12:8, 13
Centralization formula: *the place*	12:5	12:11, 14, 18, 21, 26
Listing of offerings to be presented	12:6	12:11, 14, 17-18, 26-27
Eating and rejoicing at *the place*	12:7	12:12, 18
Call for inclusiveness (invite Levites)	12:7	12:12, 18, 19
Permission for secular slaughter	—	12:15, 20-22
Reference/hint of blessings/rewards	12: (2), 7	12:9-10, 15, 20, 25, 28

history: Why is centralization so important for Deuteronomy? How and when did this expectation develop? The closest Deuteronomy comes to providing a rationale for the call comes in the expressions that reject the alternative (see TBC).

The first such statement (v. 4) sets it over against the worship practices of the previous inhabitants of the land. Instead of worshiping like the Canaanites, Israel is to seek *the place*. . . . This contrast casts centralization as a key strategy in the battle with idolatry and the worship of foreign gods. The Canaanites worshiped their gods in *all places*—Israel is to worship its God in only one place. Yet this statement does not fully explain the logic. Were numerous worship centers rejected simply because multiplicity of worship sites was a Canaanite characteristic, perhaps comparable to the way some other practices and objects were rejected primarily on the basis of their association with worship of other gods? Or was a single site promoted because it would make possible central control of worship practice and the Yahweh cult, thereby making it easier for Israel's religious leaders to protect and maintain a faithful worship of Israel's God of the exodus?

The alternative of the second and third statements (vv. 8, 13) is not the religion of the Canaanites but the ways of the Israelites. Israel is to seek *the place* instead of acting *as we are acting here today, all of us according to our own desires* (v. 8), instead of offering *your burnt offerings at any place you happen to see* (v. 13). The term *today* at this point (v. 8) should not be taken as a historical reference, whether to Israel gathered on the plains of Moab (when it really does not fit: Israel probably had a more unified cult there than at any other point), or to Israel under the late monarchy (when it could fit), but must be interpreted in light of Deuteronomy's repeated use of the word *today*. Deuteronomy repeatedly uses *today* to highlight that Israel must decide now, in the present moment, how to respond (e.g., 4:8, 39, 40; 5:1, 3), with the present moment timeless, always stretching into the future. The *today* of this passage, although timeless and always present, also hints at the negative, the reality that today is also the time when Israel is acting *according to its own desires* rather than the way of God. Today is not only the "first day of the rest of your life"; it is also the last day of your life until now.

The reference to their *own desires* (v. 8; cf. *any place you happen to see*, v. 13) draws attention to Israel's volition in determining where it worships; such irregular choice is in sharp contrast with what Israel is called to do: go where *God* determines (see discussion of *choose* below). Here the use of *our own desires* reminds one of the chapters at the end of Judges, where Israel is twice indicted because "the people did what was right in their own eyes" (Judg 17:6; 21:25). This was not the way it should be. In Judges these verses are part of a passage that argues for a king who will guide them. Here they set the stage for the centralization command.

The ambiguity in Deuteronomy regarding a rationale for the centralization requirement has not stopped interpreters from proposing possible motivations for it. Centralization could foster political unity, and so it is suggested that political leaders of the day instigated it as a way of strengthening the nation against foreign pressures. Centralization could boost economic activity at the center, so the economic elite may have promoted it as a way of increasing their own wealth. Centralization could give greater prestige to central authority, so kings may have promoted it.

Significant changes like this seldom have a single or simple motive. But for Deuteronomy, the goal is expressly and only theological.

> Deuteronomy explicitly advocates centralization as a way of disrupting popular but problematic religious practices (12:2-4, 29-31), making supervision by an orthodox, central authority possible. This may have been a power play, but it was a theological power play, intended to eliminate religious behaviors viewed as unorthodox. (Nelson 2002: 149–50)

The problematic rejected practices are first of all those of the former inhabitants; this is stated directly in the opening part of the framework (vv. 2-3) and hinted at by the first expression of the alternative (12:8). But they also include other objectionable practices of Israel, as indicated by the second and third of these statements (vv. 8, 13).

The Centralization Formula

Some variation of the centralization formula occurs six times in this chapter. The elements common to all six are underlined below:

- 12:5—*Seek the place that the* LORD *your God will choose out of all your tribes as his habitation to put his name there.*

- 12:11—*To the place that the* LORD *your God will choose as a dwelling for his name.*

- 12:14—*Only at the place that the* LORD *will choose in one of your tribes.*

- 12:18—*At the place that the* LORD *your God will choose.*

- 12:21—*If the place where the* LORD *will choose to put his name.*

- 12:26—*The place that the* LORD *your God will choose.*

Most simply, the directive is that Israel worship only at *the place . . . the* LORD *. . . will choose*. Negatively, *the place* of the formula is in explicit contrast to *the places* of verse 2, where the Canaanites worshiped and which Israel is to destroy. Beyond that, Deuteronomy says little about *the place*.

The term *the place* is tantalizing since it gives no hint of specific location and almost seems a deliberate avoidance of the usual terms for a worship center (e.g., temple, house, shrine). The tendency not to use technical language for the holy and the cult, especially in comparison with Exodus, is typical of Deuteronomy's lack of attention to cultic detail *[Cult, p. 546]*. But in this case it also opens the door to a richer meaning for the word. Earlier the term *place* has been used for the Promised Land, the place God has given Israel (1:31; 9:7; 11:5, 24). Now within that larger *place*, God will choose another place for the dwelling of his name. In both cases Israel is to follow God's direction.

Within the larger story of Israel, *the place* clearly is a reference to Jerusalem. Why then does the text not make this identification? An obvious and old answer is that this would be inconsistent with the historical context given the book of Deuteronomy, with Israel camped in the land of Moab before entering the land. This may be accurate, but it also is inadequate. At other points Deuteronomy quite comfortably moves ahead in time to when Israel is settled in the land (e.g., law of the king, 17:14-20). Israel did understand this place as Jerusalem, but there also is evidence that other centers functioned as primary worship sites for Israel prior to David making Jerusalem the capital and bringing the ark of the covenant to the city, thereby making it the religious center (see TBC). Jeremiah seems to understand Shiloh as having been such a worship center where God's name dwelled (Jer 7:12; cf. 1 Sam 1–4, which has the ark located there), and Gilgal and Bethel have been suggested as other possible early centers. A simple identification of *the place* with Jerusalem thus does not fit the story.

McConville makes the further argument that "the silence concerning the name of the place is intended to resist the making of the wrong kind of claims about any particular temple institution" (2002: 220), that "the namelessness of the place has an irreducible openness" (232). Deuteronomy is not making an "irreversible claim on Jerusalem's behalf" (232) with the law of centralization, even if Jerusalem is assumed to be the location Deuteronomy has in mind. By not naming it, Deuteronomy is withholding its stamp of approval on an unconditional Zion theology that assures Israel that God has permanently established Jerusalem and the Davidic line. The absence of any reference to the ark—a striking omission given the centrality of the ark in establishing Jerusalem as Israel's worship center (cf. 2 Sam 6; 2 Kings 8)—may support this. Deuteronomy's language allows for an openness to the future, a future in which God may choose to remove his name from that place (cf. Jer 7:11-15).

The above discussion assumes that Deuteronomy 12 does indeed require that worship be limited to *one* place. Is it possible to read the text as allowing for more than one worship site? Some interpreters argue that the grammar of the text indeed does allow for more than one place to be chosen by God, either consecutively or simultaneously (e.g., McConville and Millar 1994; yet McConville in 2002 seems to pull back from that position). But this is not persuasive. If Deuteronomy had more than one center in mind, why the emphasis on distance from the center in the provisions for secular slaughter? The difference between Deuteronomy and the Exodus altar law, a regulation quite possibly behind this one, also is significant. Exodus allows Israel to erect an altar "in every place where I cause my name to be remembered" (20:24, emph. added), but Deuteronomy clearly uses the singular of *place* for where Israel must worship, here and everywhere else in the book. Reading Deuteronomy 12 as requiring the centralization of cultic worship only at the one place that God will choose remains the most convincing reading.

The absence of any specific location allows the passage to focus on the most important characteristic of The Place: God will choose it. The Place is not just any place: it is not a place Israel *desires* (v. 8) or just *any place you happen to see* (v. 13), nor is it even necessarily a place with an important historical memory. Right worship means allowing God to choose and determine where, not choice by the Canaanites or Israel. The term *choose* has its background in Deuteronomic election theology. God *chose* Israel as his special possession (4:37; 7:6, 7; 10:15; 14:2). Later Deuteronomy gives Israel permission to have a king, but only one *whom the LORD your God will choose* (17:15). In language similar to that used in the centralization directive, God *has chosen Levi out of all your tribes to stand and minister in the name of the LORD* (18:5). For Deuteronomy, the otherwise general phrase *the place* becomes a code phrase for this central worship location, occurring twenty-one times in the book (12:5, 11, 14, 18, 21, 26; 14:23, 24, 25; 15:20; 16:2, 6, 7, 11, 15, 16; 17:8, 10; 18:6; 26:2; 31:11). That the central thrust is God's choosing rather than the nature of The Place is indicated by the fact that in each of these references the term is linked with some form of the word *choose*.

In contrast to the names of the Canaanite gods, which are to be blotted out from the land (12:3), the name of the God of Israel will dwell at The Place. Three times the chapter makes this claim (vv. 5, 11, 21). This language may be influenced by "the practice of kings immortalizing their names on memorials and monuments in order to demonstrate possession and sovereignty (cf. 2 Sam 12:28)" (Nelson 2002: 153). Deuteronomy is making the claim that The Place (just like the other *place*, the Promised Land; e.g., 1:31) is owned by God through God's choice. The land has new ownership, with a new God in control. Replacing the names of the Canaanite gods with the name of the God of Israel makes this changeover public.

But the name of God also had specific, historical connotations within Israel. Israel did understand its God to have a proper name (YHWH, likely pronounced Yahweh, translated LORD in the NRSV, NIV, et al.). God revealed this name to Moses during his call at the burning bush (Exod 3). When Moses asks what the name means, God's answer is ambiguous at best. The exodus events that follow then give the name its content. Yahweh, the God of Israel, is known through his action of redeeming a slave people. The name becomes a cipher for that story, always reminding the people of what God has done for them. The dwelling of the name of God at The Place serves a similar function, pointing the worshipers back to the exodus and those early nation-shaping events and times.

When Deuteronomy speaks of God's *name* dwelling at The Place, it may also be countering a theology that understood God's earthly dwelling to be physically at the temple. For Deuteronomy, God lives in heaven, with only God's name dwelling at The Place. The prayer of Solomon at the dedication of the temple (2 Kings 8:14-61) implies such a distinction:

> But will God indeed dwell on the earth? Even heaven and the highest heaven cannot contain you, much less this house that I have built.... [We pray] that your eyes may be open night and day toward this house, the place of which you said, "My name shall be there." ... Hear the plea of your servant and of your people Israel when they pray toward this place; O hear in heaven your dwelling place; heed and forgive. (1 Kings 8:27-30)

If God dwells anywhere, it is in heaven above (1 Kings 8:30, 32, 34, 36, 39, 43, 45, 49; cf. Deut 26:15).

Deuteronomy's language may fit such a distinction, but it is doubtful that is its primary point. Deuteronomy's regular reference to *before the* LORD or *in the presence of the* LORD (both translations of the same Hebrew phrase), three times within this chapter alone (12:7, 12, 18), raises questions about such an emphasis. "The present text is not directly concerned with conceiving the nature of God's Presence, and it is wrongly used in pursuit of such arguments.... The point is simply that Israel must worship at the location Yahweh himself has chosen to be present" (McConville 2002: 221-22). It is God's election of The Place and God's presence at The Place that the text affirms.

Offerings to Be Presented

Israel is to bring all its offerings to The Place. In this chapter, Deuteronomy names *burnt offerings* (vv. 6, 11, 14, 27), *sacrifices* (vv. 6, 11), *tithes* (vv. 6, 11), *donations* (vv. 6, 11, 17, 26), *votive gifts* (vv. 6, 11, 17, 26), *freewill offerings* (v. 6, 17), *firstlings of your herds and flocks* (vv. 6, 17), and the *tithe of your grain, your wine, and your oil* (v. 17) [*Cult, p. 546*].

The absence of any reference to sin offerings is probably explained by Deuteronomy's consistent lack of interest in the details of Israelite worship and ritual. Neither in this chapter nor anywhere else does Deuteronomy provide any detail on the precise role of priests with sacrifices at The Place. There also is no reference at all to the role of the king or royal officials in such practices, a noteworthy omission given the central role royalty normally played in major festivals (cf. 17:14-20). This may suggest that Deuteronomy is shifting emphasis in the sacrificial system from king and priest to the household, but one should be careful not to overinterpret these silences. Deuteronomy is not spelling out an alternative cultic system but rather looking away from cultic detail to larger issues, the exclusive worship of God and its implications for community life. Thus Deuteronomy is passionate about its central point: in this chapter the implication of faithful worship of the one true God is that Israel shall worship that one God only at the one place God will choose. Everything else is subservient to that foundational commitment.

Eating and Rejoicing at The Place

Deuteronomy 12 highlights two further themes. First, worship is a time for eating and rejoicing. Three times in the chapter the expected centralization calls on Israel to rejoice when it comes to The Place to offer the various sacrifices and tithes (vv. 7, 12, 18). Israel's sacrificial system may have been about sin and communion with God; yet for Deuteronomy, communion within the community, celebration, and joy are also inseparable from communion with God. As Deuteronomy's directives regarding festivals will reveal (see comments on 14:22-27; 16:1-17), festivals are a time when the community celebrates before God.

An Inclusive Celebration

This emphasis on eating and rejoicing leads quite naturally to a second concern of Deuteronomy: no one is to be excluded from these celebrations. Repeatedly in this chapter there is a call for inclusiveness (vv. 7, 12, 18, 19), consistent with the theme of the Sabbath command (5:12-15). This is striking since it would not have been unusual for only the head of the household to participate in these joyous events.

The language is interesting: *you, your sons and daughters, your menservants and maidservants, and the Levites from your towns* (vv. 12, 18 AT; cf. 5:14). The opening *you* (pl.) of the directive includes both husband and wife, not only the head of the household as might normally have been the case (cf. command to honor father and mother, 5:16). The whole household is to be included, husband and wife, daughter and son, even the slaves. Deuteronomy's larger concern for justice in the community informs even the description of worship at The Place.

The inclusion of the Levites in these lists, with separate attention in verse 19, requires comment. Levites did not receive a portion of the land for their own possession (12:12; 14:27, 29) but were expected to serve in the cult [Cult, p. 546]. With the centralization of all cultic worship at The Place, Levites serving in worship centers elsewhere would have lost their means of making a living. Centralization of worship has major consequences for them. Many Levites (at least those who do not take up the option allowed for in 18:6-8 to move to The Place and serve the cult there) would join the ranks of the deprived. Chapter 12 deals with the centralization of the cult, and so Deuteronomy highlights their plight and warns not to neglect them. In the rest of the book they are regularly included in the more common list of the powerless: the stranger/sojourner, the widow, and the orphan (14:29; 16:11, 14; 26:12, 13).

Permission for Secular Slaughter

In ancient cultures, including Israelite, the killing of domestic animals for food was a "sacred" act, or sacrifice, and possibly done on an altar. Centralization of worship presented a problem since it disallowed all sacrifice away from The Place chosen by God. Unless some concession were made, eating the meat of sheep, goats, and cattle other than at The Place would become impossible. Deuteronomy responds by giving permission to eat meat away from The Place by introducing what might be called secular slaughter or profane killing, the butchering of animals for food. Such killing then becomes similar to the way clean wildlife like the gazelle or deer (12:15, 22) were treated previously. The phrase *as I have commanded you* (v. 21) suggests that Deuteronomy knows more detailed instructions for such killing but, consistent with Deuteronomy's tendency to avoid detail, simply assumes them.

Since this secular slaughter is no longer a cultic act, it now becomes possible for the ritually unclean to participate along with those who are ritually clean (vv. 15, 22). Israel, like other peoples of the day, designated some people as "unclean," whether because they suffered from some skin condition, had experienced the discharge of some bodily fluid, or because they had come in contact with a dead body or unclean animal or bird (Cairns: 130; see 14:3-20). Those designated ritually unclean could not participate in cultic activities. Consistent with Deuteronomy's concern for inclusion, the book makes a point of stating that even those unclean are welcome to eat of meat slaughtered for the purpose of eating and celebrating.

The one restriction Deuteronomy places on such killing is that the blood of the animal, representing its life (v. 23), must receive special attention. It is not to be eaten but must be poured on the ground (vv. 16, 23-25), just like the blood of animals brought to The Place for sacrifice to God (v. 27). This continues the prohibition God gave Noah after the flood: "Every moving thing that lives shall be food for you.... Only, you shall not eat flesh with its life, that is, its blood" (Gen 9:3-4), as well as the cultic legislation in Leviticus (17:10-13). This restriction remains in effect in the New Testament for the compromise developed at the Jerusalem Council. Gentile converts are no longer bound by Jewish laws on clean and unclean animals, but they are expected to "abstain from what has been sacrificed to idols and from blood" (Acts 15:29).

Blessings and Rewards

Repeatedly this chapter makes direct references to, or hints at, the blessings and rewards Israel is about to receive. God will bless Israel (vv. 7, 15) and give it the land, in the process dispossessing the nations who have lived there (v. 2). God will give Israel rest from its enemies (vv. 9, 10) and enlarge its territory (v. 20). Once in the land, Israel is mandated to worship only the God of the exodus, and that only in *the place . . . God will choose*. If Israel will *obey all these words*, it will go well, in the present and in the future (v. 28), and it will continue to enjoy these blessings.

THE TEXT IN BIBLICAL CONTEXT

Centralization in Israel and Scripture

Although many Old Testament directives are repeated in multiple places (e.g., the Decalogue in Exod 20; Deut 5), the centralization directive occurs only in Deuteronomy, even if it is assumed elsewhere, especially in the Deuteronomistic History. Given its impact upon the Old Testament and the later development of Judaism, Deuteronomy 12 is one of the more significant chapters for the whole Old Testament.

Surprisingly, there little evidence of this centralization expectation through most of Israel's story. That Israel's ancestors (i.e., before the time of Moses and Israel's entrance into the Promised Land under Joshua) sacrificed to God in a variety of places may come as no surprise. Abraham, for example, built altars and worshiped God at Shechem (Gen 12:6-7), Bethel (12:8), Hebron (13:18), Moriah (22:1-19), and Beersheba (26:23-25 NIV).

But after the exodus and Israel's entrance into the Promised Land, leaders continue to build altars and worship God throughout the land, without any direct or implied condemnation. Immediately after the entrance, Joshua builds an altar on Mount Ebal (Josh 8:30). Gideon sacrifices to God in his home town of Ophrah (Judg 6:24). Manoah, the father of Samson, offers sacrifice in his home tribal area of Dan (13:16-19). The people of Israel as a whole sacrifice to God at Bethel (21:2-4). Shortly before the rise of kingship, "at Shiloh" is a "temple of the LORD" (1 Sam 1:9), where the priest Eli serves, where Elkanah offers sacrifice, and where Samuel ministers. Later Samuel builds an altar at Ramah (1 Sam 7:17). After the army of Saul defeats the Philistines, Saul builds an altar, apparently on the field of battle (14:35). Early in his reign Solomon travels to Gibeon "to sacrifice there, for that was the principal high place" (1 Kings 3:4). There God appears to Solomon in a dream, offering to grant Solomon whatever he wishes.

Admittedly, most of these occur before the building of the temple at Jerusalem confirms Jerusalem as The Place of worship for Israel. And it is true that a few of these examples could fit with an interpretation of Deuteronomy 12 as allowing only one worship place at one time, but with the possibility that that worship place could move about, with the presence of the ark representing that one place (e.g., Joshua's altar on Mount Ebal; the sanctuary in Shiloh, where the ark resided during the time of Eli and Samuel; 1 Sam 3:3). But some of the instances above clearly do not fit such an explanation (e.g., Gideon and Manoah); at the time when Gibeon is identified as the "principal high place," the ark is already in Jerusalem.

Even after Solomon's construction of the magnificent temple in Jerusalem, the existence of worship centers and altars outside of Jerusalem continues. When the nation divides after the death of Solomon, Jeroboam, king of the Northern Kingdom, has the challenge of maintaining the loyalty of the people even as they travel south to Jerusalem to worship at the temple. His response is to establish Bethel and Dan as northern worship centers (1 Kings 12:25-31). In addition he also "made houses on high places, and appointed priests from among all the people" (12:31). The ninth-century prophets Elijah and Elisha make no protest against these centers even though they are not hesitant to attack the kings of their day. Elijah's dramatic showdown with the prophets of Baal climaxes with God sending down fire upon the altar Elijah has erected on Mount Carmel (1 Kings 18:17-40). In the eighth century BCE, Amos gives scathing condemnation of the social injustice in his day, and of a cult that does not require justice, but he does not reject in principle the worship centers at Bethel and Dan. Hosea does mention the wickedness of Bethel (10:15), but whether this is related to the centralizing expectation of Deuteronomy 12 is unclear.

Although the dominance of Jerusalem makes competing shrines and centers in Judah less obvious, the later references to worship at the high places in the Southern Kingdom indicate that Jerusalem was not the only worship place in the south. Isaiah (eighth century BCE) emphasizes the holiness of Jerusalem, but he makes no point of condemning worship outside of the Jerusalem.

The first evidence that worship outside of Jerusalem is a violation of God's law comes from the reign of King Hezekiah, when he "removed the high places, broke down their pillars, and cut down the sacred pole" (2 Kings 18:4). According to 2 Chronicles 30 he also sponsored a nationwide Passover celebration in Jerusalem. Roughly a century later King Josiah, after finding the book of the law in the temple (possibly an early version of Deuteronomy), also destroys the high places and holds a Passover in Jerusalem "as prescribed in this book of the covenant" (2 Kings 23:21) [*Deuteronomy and the Reform of Josiah, p. 549*]. For the first time in the Old Testament story, a written document shapes action, with its centralizing requirement playing a role.

It is the Deuteronomistic History, finished during the exile, that makes the centralization expectation a critical element of its assessment of the story of Israel. It forcefully condemns Jeroboam's building worship centers at Bethel and Dan as a transgression of the Deuteronomic demand for centralization. Since none of Jeroboam's successors in the Northern Kingdom eliminate these centers, it judges them as continuing in the sin of Jeroboam (e.g., 1 Kings 15:15-26). After Assyria defeats the North, the Deuteronomistic History concludes that this is because Israel continued to worship at the high places (2 Kings 17).

The Deuteronomistic History judges the kings of Judah with two criteria: First, do they walk in the way of the law, often with David as the model? And second, do they eliminate the worship of God or gods at the high places? Only two kings are counted fully righteous: Hezekiah and Josiah, the two kings who actively demolished worship centers outside of Jerusalem. For the Deuteronomistic History the centralizing expectation of Deuteronomy 12 is a central theological criterion for judging what happens in Israel. This conviction also explains its account of the heavy static arising when the Transjordan tribes build an altar near the Jordan (Josh 22). Chronicles then builds on the direction established by the Deuteronomistic History.

Josiah's reforms were not entirely successful, neither in eradicating cultic activity outside of Jerusalem (Jer 10:11-16; Ezek 8:1-18) nor in preventing God's punishment for Israel's sin (2 Kings 23:26-27). During the exile and afterward, however, the conviction that faithful sacrifice to God could only be offered at one place, with that being Jerusalem, became orthodoxy.

This conviction informs the story of Jesus and the Samaritan woman. The Samaritans accept that God requires worship at only one place, as set forth in Deuteronomy 12. But for them, that one place is Mount Gerizim, where the Samaritans constructed their own temple, not at Jerusalem. When the woman perceives that Jesus is a prophet, she immediately attempts to have him settle this contentious issue. Jesus responds, "Woman, believe me, the hour is coming when you will worship the Father neither on this mountain nor in Jerusalem. . . . The hour is coming, and is now here, when the true worshipers will worship the Father in spirit and truth" (John 4:21-23).

THE TEXT IN LIFE OF THE CHURCH

Deuteronomy 12 and Contemporary Middle Eastern Politics

At some point—exactly when may be debated—Israel came to understand Deuteronomy 12 as requiring cultic or sacrificial worship at only one place, with that one place the Jerusalem temple. When the Babylonians destroyed the temple early in the sixth century BCE, Israel's sacrificial system ceased. During the exile the practice of gathering for prayer in what came to be called synagogues gradually developed. When the temple was rebuilt, synagogue worship continued, but Jerusalem and the temple as the only place for sacrifice again became the absolute center. The New Testament narratives reflect this reality. No accusation against Jesus was more emotionally effective than the one that he predicted the destruction of the temple (cf. Matt 26:61; etc.).

A generation later, Rome did destroy the temple, and sacrifice ceased for a second time. Again synagogues increased in importance as the place where the local community gathered, with prayer and Scripture replacing sacrifice. But they could never quite replace the temple. Although the Jewish sacrificial system has now been on hold for nearly two thousand years, many religious Jews continue to look to Jerusalem, and to the Temple Mount, as The Place that God has chosen for them, and they look forward to the day they will once again be in control of this sacred location, be able to offer sacrifice there and practice right worship of God as called for in Deuteronomy 12.

Present-day Middle East tensions cannot be fully appreciated without recognizing the emotional and religious power of this chapter and its role in the life of the Jewish people. Simultaneously, Middle East tensions cannot be understood without recognizing the powerful conviction of Islam that it was from this same location that Muhammad ascended to heaven, thereby making it their holy place as well.

Right Worship

How important is right worship of God today? Deuteronomy 12, as well as much of chapters 14–16, deals with Israel's worship and cult [Cult, p. 546]. Faithful and right worship of God is very important to Deuteronomy, a key aspect and implication of what it means to love God with our whole being (6:4-9). And yet the church has largely ignored this suggestive chapter, perhaps out of a general disregard for Old Testament legal material, perhaps influenced by the response of Jesus to the Samaritan woman he met at the well and told, "God is spirit, and those who worship him must worship in spirit and truth" (John 4:24).

At least three elements of this chapter may raise questions for us. First, there is the centralization call itself, a means of protecting the purity of Israel's worship. If worship takes place anywhere and everywhere, the potential for falling prey to the ways of the people of the land are too great. Limiting worship to one location allows central priests to exercise more oversight. Dispersed worship did develop through the synagogue, but the centralization thrust remained part of the tradition. The Roman Catholic Church has its Rome, which despite allowing diversity in worship practice, nevertheless serves as a formidable center, rallying point, and symbol for the church. The Anglican Communion and Episcopal Church have their Book of Common Prayer, which in a different way curbs widely divergent worship. Might "centralization" for the sake of worship "purity" and identity have a role for traditions that highly value congregational autonomy?

Second, here and elsewhere, Deuteronomy emphasizes that The Place is God's choice. Deuteronomy demonstrates little interest in cultic detail, choosing instead to focus on central matters. Contemporary worship often places much value on creative and "meaningful" ways of worshiping God, with "worship wars" fueling intense debate. Do these ever reflect worshiping *according to our desires*?

Third, rejoicing and inclusion play an important role in Deuteronomy's vision for worship: all in the community are to be included so all can celebrate the wonderful gifts of God. Do we need this reminder as well?

Deuteronomy 13:1-18

Purging Apostasy
Deuteronomy 13:1-18

PREVIEW
Toleration is wonderful, right? After all, we know how cruel and violent religious wars can be, and we hear of the dangers of religious fundamentalism. But is all toleration the same? At points, Deuteronomy and other Old Testament voices come across as quite intolerant.

Upon entering the Promised Land, Joshua gathers the tribes at Shechem and presents them with a challenge: "Choose this day whom you will serve, whether the gods your ancestors served in the region beyond the River or the gods of the Amorites in whose land you are living; but as for me and my household, we will serve the LORD" (Josh 24:15). Despite responding on that day with one accord, "We will serve LORD," the story of Israel shows that the people frequently acted differently. When Elijah in a similar vein confronts the people on Mount Carmel, "How long will you go limping with two different opinions? If the LORD is God, follow him; but if Baal, then follow him" (1 Kings 18:21), they are silent, unwilling to commit themselves.

Deuteronomy 13, with the first and second commandments and the Shema (6:4-9) as a background, proclaims a similar message: exclusive allegiance to the one God of the exodus is a life-and-death matter. Three scenarios are developed. Verses 1-5 consider the possibility of a prophet or religious official promoting the worship of other gods. In verses 6-11 the source of temptation is someone close and intimate. In verses 12-18 it is the whole town that goes astray. In each case, the verdict is death.

OUTLINE
If a Prophet Leads You Astray, 13:1-5
If Anyone Close to You Leads You Astray, 13:6-11
If a Town Goes Astray, 13:12-18

EXPLANATORY NOTES
Introductory Comments
The chapter introduces three potential scenarios of Israelites leading each other into apostasy, each requiring capital punishment. Each

paragraph has a casuistic style, as reflected by their common opening, *If* (vv. 1, 6, 12), followed by a description of the crime, and then a pronouncement of punishment *[Law, p. 555]*. But this is rhetorical technique, not case law for the court. It remains preaching that uses every argument available to persuade the audience to choose a particular path of action.

Each scenario is presented with a common structure:

1. Identification of a <u>source of temptation</u> (vv. 1, 6, 12). Each paragraph opens with some individual or group leading the people astray. The examples cover an unusual breadth of temptation. Each case makes a specific point: together they stand for all possible sources of apostasy.

2. A set phrase for the <u>invitation to stray</u>: *Let us follow/go worship/ go and worship other gods* (vv. 2, 6, 13). The temptation is in direct speech, beginning with the important words *Let us*. With these words someone entices or attracts others to join in a particular direction. The language of following, or worshiping, or going after other gods is typically Deuteronomic. The text does not make clear whether the invitation is to have these gods replace Israel's God, or whether the invitation is to worship these gods alongside God. But ultimately this distinction makes no difference: both are clear transgressions of the first commandment and thus rebellion against God.

3. A reference to the <u>gods as previously unknown</u> (vv. 2, 6, 13). It is striking that each invitation includes some reference to these gods as previously unknown. The term "know" implies relationship and experience, not merely awareness of them. Hosea, a prophet whose theology has numerous contacts with Deuteronomy, repeatedly uses the term in his characterization of God's relationship to his people. He addresses a people God "know[s]" (Hos 5:3), but which has demonstrated a lack of "knowledge of God" (2:8; 4:1, 6; 5:4; 11:3), yet in the future will once more "know the LORD" (2:20; 6:3). Deuteronomy emphasizes that the God of the exodus has loved and chosen Israel (e.g., 7:7-8), that Israel has seen with its own eyes what God has done (e.g., 1:30; 3:21; 4:9, 34; 6:22) and thus should know this God. Notice 4:35—*To you it was shown* [i.e., *you were made to see*] *so that you would acknowledge* [i.e., *know*] *that the LORD is God; there is no other besides him.* Israel has a God it knows; the repeated portrayal of the gods in this passage as ones Israel has not known emphasizes the enormity of their fickleness. Israel has no excuse.

4. <u>Identification of God</u> with exodus and gift of land (vv. 5, 10, 12). Each scenario at least once, directly or indirectly, declares that it is Yahweh who led them out of Egypt and is giving them the land.

Through God's actions on behalf of Israel, in the exodus and in the gift of the land east of the Jordan, Israel has experienced God's nature and has come to know God. The tone of exasperation is clear: how can Israel now turn its back on the God who has demonstrated through these past actions his love and care for the people? How can they go after unknown gods?

5. A <u>verdict of death</u> (vv. 5, 9-10, 15-16). The matter of whom Israel worships is a life-and-death matter. Death is the consequence of rebuffing the God of life.

6. An <u>interpretation of outcome</u> (vv. 5, 11, 17-18). Each account concludes with a statement of motivation or interpretation, consistent with this not being case law.

With this common structure and uniform conclusion, the case is made. Through election and deliverance, Israel is bound to its God. Substituting the worship of some other god, or even adding the worship of other gods alongside the worship of Yahweh, has fatal consequences. It is a clear either/or situation.

If a Prophet Leads You Astray 13:1-5

The first scenario considers the possibility of a prophet leading the people astray. The reference to *those who divine by dreams* (repeated in v. 5) of itself does not have negative connotations since Israel understood dreams as a legitimate way for God to communicate with his people. Israel's leaders received God's word through dreams (e.g., Abimelech, Gen 20:3-7; Joseph, Gen 37:5-11; Solomon, 1 Kings 3:5-9), as did Israel's prophets. God tells Aaron and Miriam, "When there are prophets among you, I the Lord make myself know to them in visions; I speak to them in dreams" (Num 12:6). Isaiah (6:1-13), Amos (7:1-9), and Ezekiel (1:1) each hear from God through a vision. The *prophets* and *those who divine dreams* thus are potentially legitimate messengers from God who might be expected to have special access to God's will for the people.

Not only do these religious leaders receive their word in an acceptable manner: what they announce takes place. Later Deuteronomy identifies the fulfillment of a prophet's pronouncement as the key criterion for determining whether the prophet truly speaks on behalf of God (18:21-22). That test would support the authenticity of the prophet in our passage. Yet the content of their word, the invitation to go after other gods, is in direct conflict with what Israel knows to be true. Here is a further and more significant test of a faithful leader. Results are an insufficient indicator. In addition, the word and action of the prophet or leader must be based in the faithful tradition of the community.

Israel understands difficult times as a test from God (cf. 8:16; Job). Each challenge or hardship is a test, determining whether or not the people will be faithful, whether or not the people love God and God alone, as commanded in the Shema (Deut 6:4-9). According to Deuteronomy, the future of Israel is dependent upon how it does in this test. From the standpoint of the exile, Israel has failed this test. But, as 4:23-31 assures them, this is not God's final word.

The rhetoric of 13:3b-4 states the positive expectation of Deuteronomy with passion and fervor. Again we have preaching: Deuteronomy pleads with the people to walk in faithfulness to their God. The phrase *whether you indeed love the LORD your God with all your heart and soul* (v. 3) refers back to the Shema, highlighting its primary expectation that each person shall love God with the total being. The last half of verse 4 includes six verbs, in parallel form, all favorite Deuteronomic expressions, hammering home what God expects: *You shall follow* (cf. 5:33), *You shall fear* (cf. 4:10; 5:29; 6:2, 13, 24; 10:12, 20), *You shall keep* (cf. 4:2, 40; 5:12, 15, 29; 6:2, 6, 17; 8:2, 6, 11; 10:13; 11:1, 8), *You shall obey* (cf. 8:20; 11:27, 28), *You shall serve* (cf. 6:13; 10:12), *You shall hold fast* (cf. 4:4; 10:20; 11:22). Deuteronomy 10:12-11:32 uses each of these same words and phrases, providing the background to the expectation here.

Any prophet or leader within Israel who, despite everything God has done (v. 5b) and despite the clarity of God's expectation (vv. 3b-4), invites people to reject this story in favor of some unknown god—that speaker has committed *treason* (v. 5). Although *rebellion* (RSV, NIV) may be a more common translation of the Hebrew here, the term *treason* more fully captures the spirit and emotion of the text. Such a person has betrayed the very nature of their own identity as a member of God's people. Such an action puts at risk the survival of the larger people, with the punishment for treason being death; even today some nations punish treason with death. The phrase *put to death* is common Old Testament language for the ultimate punishment (cf. Gen 26:11; Exod 19:12; Lev 19:20; Deut 17:6; etc.).

The closing sentence then presents an explanation for the verdict. Although this is the first time the phrase *purge the evil* is used in Deuteronomy, it becomes common in this book (cf. 17:7, 12; 19:13 [*purge the guilt*], 19; 21:9 [*guilt*], 21; 22:21, 22, 24; 24:7). The Hebrew term translated *purge* is based on a verbal root that means "to burn out," or "to cauterize." The logic of the passage is that the sin of going after other gods is such that the people as a whole can be poisoned by it, "so that unless the offender is 'excised,' the covenant is threatened and the communal life placed in jeopardy (cf. Josh. 7)" (Cairns: 136), that is, like surgery to remove cancerous growth.

If Anyone Close to You Leads You Astray 13:6-11

The second scenario moves from the leaders of Israel to the household and community of the person. Whereas the temptation of the prophet probably was a public situation, here the text draws attention to the secretive or private nature of the enticement. This fits the listing of people identified. The list itself is not exhaustive but rather representative of those with whom one is especially close: siblings, children, spouse, or friend. The close relationship is highlighted by the portrayals of *wife* and *friend* as *the wife you embrace* [lit., *wife of your bosom*], and *your most intimate friend* [lit., *your friend who is as your own soul*]. These are the people one most trusts, in whom one places greatest reliance. The passage imagines a scene in which one's closest confidant surreptitiously makes an invitation to stray.

The source and context of the temptation may be different from the first scenario, but the temptation itself is the same: "*Let us go worship other gods,*" *whom neither you nor your ancestors have known.* The temptation of verse 2 here is expanded to universal proportions, including any gods, be they of the people nearby or far away, anywhere on earth (v. 7).

As in the first scenario, and as in good preaching, repetition is a key element of the rhetoric. In staccato-like fashion, the text uses five consecutive verbs, each preceded by the Hebrew particle of negation, to speak the warning. In an apparent effort to produce a smoother reading the NRSV hides some of this. Here is a more literal translation: *You shall not yield to him, nor shall you listen to him, nor shall your eye pity him, nor shall you have compassion upon him, nor shall you condone him* (AT). The last verb is rendered *shield* or *conceal* in most versions, with the implication that the Israelite is not to hide the enticing person but report that person to the proper authorities. Levinson argues that *nor condone* is a better translation, continuing the thought of the previous two verbs, speaking to how the person is to be treated directly (1996). The nature of the crime is such that no compromise is possible.

The proximity of the source of seduction leads to a heightened emphasis on the punishment. Not only is the verdict death, but also the lured family member initiates executing the verdict.

The concluding comment stresses the impact of the case upon the larger community. Its language does not come from the realm of holiness and purity, as in the first scenario, but rather from the world of instruction to the community. The verdict is a sign and warning to the community that apostasy leads to death.

If a Town Goes Astray 13:12-18

The basic plot is the same: people in Israel succumb to the temptation to go after other gods, and the verdict is death. The source of the temptation now is *scoundrels* (RSV, *base fellows;* NIV, *troublemakers;* lit., *sons of worthlessness*). This may refer to people on the edge of society, those who have no real place in the community and thus nothing to lose by advocating something new or different. Yet it is also possible that the language already is a judgment on their role in leading the village astray. Clearly, anyone doing that could legitimately be considered good-for-nothing, worthless.

That the central characters are not totally on the margin nor without influence is suggested by the success they have. Unlike the first two scenarios, this one includes that the seductive invitation is heeded. The *scoundrels* may not have the status of religious leaders nor be as trustworthy as an intimate family member, but they are effective. The text raises the possibility that a whole town may fall prey to the seduction of other gods. When Israel entered the Promised Land, at least some Canaanite villages remained intact within the boundaries of the land, especially in the northern regions. This case may have such communities in mind; yet the common format of these passages, with its emphasis on a source of temptation to worship gods previously unknown, suggests it is speaking of Israelite peoples.

A significant new feature is that an *investigation* is required (v. 14). Presumably the public pronouncements of a prophet, or the enticement of someone close, albeit expressed in secret, would have been unambiguous. The opening phrase *If you hear it said*, however, suggests a rumor or other indirect information. Here Deuteronomy shows its concern for justice and due process, even in (or perhaps, especially in) a case as foundational and emotional as this one. Even though this is a life-and-death matter, lynching is prohibited: due process must be followed with integrity. Before any action can be taken, a <u>thorough</u> *investigation* is required to determine whether *such an abhorrent thing* has taken place. The term *abhorrent* is common in Deuteronomy, in most cases referring either to the worship of other gods or to the religious practices of the Canaanites (cf. 7:25, 26; 12:31; 13:14; 18:9, 12; 20:18; 23:18; 27:15; 32:16).

The punishment (vv. 15-16) places the whole within the realm of Yahweh war, with the application of the ban, or *ḥerem* [*Ḥerem, p. 552; Yahweh War, p. 566*] (cf. 2:24-3:11). This is unusual since normally *ḥerem* applies only against external enemies. By its action in going after other gods, the town—whether originally Israelite or Canaanite—has become like an external enemy. Its actions threaten the life and existence of the total Israelite community. All is sacrificed to God in a community cultic event [*Cult, p. 546*]. This cultic language also raises the question of whether the punishment was meant literally. God's compassion for his people remains (v. 18), but Israel is expected to be faithful to God, especially to the foundational commandment to worship only God.

THE TEXT IN BIBLICAL CONTEXT

One Way, and the Consequences of the Other Way

The Deuteronomic conviction that the God of the exodus expects exclusive worship, although perhaps expressed more explicitly and repeatedly in Deuteronomy than elsewhere, is characteristic of Scripture as a whole. Hosea's indictment of Israel playing the harlot when it worshiped Baal instead of, or in addition to, Yahweh may be the most picturesque way of expressing this, but it is present explicitly or implicitly throughout Scripture.

The Judaism of Jesus' day had largely accepted this conviction, so Jesus did not address the question in the categories of Deuteronomy and the Prophets. But the sense of exclusivity remains integral to his preaching and being. Now, however, Jesus himself becomes part of this exclusive expectation. In a response to a question from Thomas, he thus says, "I am the way, and the truth, and the life. No one comes to the Father except through me" (John 14:6). His warning on the temptation of wealth expresses the same truth in a more general way: "No one can serve two masters; for a slave will either hate the one and love the other, or be devoted to the one and despise the other" (Matt 6:24).

The Deuteronomic passion that the people's response to this expectation is an all-or-nothing matter, with life-and-death consequences, also is pervasive in Scripture. The Deuteronomistic Historian's verdict that the destruction of both the Northern Kingdom and the Southern Kingdom were caused by disregard of this expectation (2 Kings 17:7-9; 23:26-27) is consistent with stories within that history, earlier stories (e.g., the story of Aaron and the golden calf, Exod 32), as well as the message of the prophets. In the New Testament, Jesus speaks of the narrow and broad way (Matt 7:13-14), or the sheep and the goats (Matt 25:31-46). It is the ultimate significance of our response that moves Paul to speak of working out our "own salvation with fear and trembling" (Phil 2:12).

The case-law style of Deuteronomy 13 may suggest that the chapter is not only expressing these convictions but also providing the community with some practical guidelines on how to respond when someone, or some group, from its midst chooses to follow and serve some god other than the God of the exodus and Jesus Christ. There is limited historical evidence for how Israel or later Jewish groups understood this expectation. Jezebel has Naboth executed on the trumped-up charge of having "cursed God and king," but whether it was the alleged apostasy or political insubordination that led to the capital punishment is unclear (1 Kings 21:10). After the exile the reforms of Ezra and Nehemiah placed great emphasis on separating returning people from the peoples of the land, to the extent that foreign wives were even sent away. Those who did not participate in this renewal were banned from the community (substitute for capital punishment?), but capital punishment does not appear to have been used to enforce the law.

Some New Testament stories suggest that capital punishment may have been practiced within Judaism in Jesus' day, but one of the few stories touching on it directly has Jesus delivering the woman caught in adultery from her accusers, who were about to stone her (John 8:1-11). Two words of Jesus may be relevant. Within the Sermon on the Mount, Jesus says,

> If your right eye causes you to sin, pluck it out and throw it away; it is better that you lose one of your members than that your whole body be thrown into hell. And if your right hand causes you to sin, cut it off and throw it away; it is better that you lose one of your members than that your whole body go into hell. (Matt 5:29-30 RSV)

A similar principle appears to be at work when Jesus speaks of the crime of leading little children astray: "If anyone puts a stumbling block before one of these little ones who believe in me, it would be better for you if a great millstone were fastened around your neck and you were drowned in the depth of the sea" (Matt 18:6). In both sayings Jesus suggests excising a member of the body if it puts at risk the health of the larger body (cf. 1 Cor 5:6-13).

Deuteronomy 13 must be read within this larger framework. Our response to God has life-and-death consequences. The negative consequences do not affect or poison only the one making the choice but inevitably draw others into the circle of evil and death. Both testaments use language or imagery of purging evil, or plucking out the offending member. It is doubtful that either Deuteronomy 13 or the words of Jesus were intended to be implemented literally. Both are preaching to the community, preaching that has as its goal the recognition of the awesomeness of the choices people make, and the consequences of those choices for themselves and the community around them, with the goal of persuading their audience to love and serve the one God with their total being.

THE TEXT IN THE LIFE OF THE CHURCH
Capital Punishment or No Discipline

Deuteronomy 13 raises the difficult question of discipline within the church community, a critical one for and within the Anabaptist tradition. On the one hand, the early Anabaptists experienced the harsh side of discipline as the established churches of the day tried to purge this movement from the church, in effect putting it under an extreme ban. Most of the leaders were killed in the early years of the movement. On the other hand, the Anabaptists themselves emphasized church discipline, and debated it at great length, although consistently rejecting the death penalty as a means of discipline.

Menno Simons suggests that the death penalty was exercised within Judaism until the time of the Roman period, and then was replaced by the ban since the Jews did not have the authority to execute. He then goes on to advocate for the use of the ban as a crucial instrument of church discipline (Menno: 723-34). His last tract, a long defense of absolute shunning in the church, even within a marriage relationship, opens by citing Deuteronomy 13:6-10 (1001-15). All contact and relationship is denied. The goal of such an extreme ban was protecting the community from evil, as well as the return of the guilty party to faithfulness.

Excommunication, without absolute shunning, remained an option for church discipline in many traditions until recently, and is still employed by some as a way of maintaining the purity of the body (cf. 13:5), as well as to send a message to the rest of the community (cf. 13:11). Concern about the harsh nature of such action, however, has led to its being abandoned by most, often leaving the church unsure of how to exercise any form of discipline.

Using Matthew 18 as direction setting, Marlin Jeschke has written an excellent resource on church discipline, or as he speaks of it, "discipling" in the church. Sin within the people of God is not to be ignored: it must be confronted head-on. The goal in confronting sin, however, is redemption and forgiveness more than maintaining some abstract purity in the community: "If another disciple sins, you must rebuke the offender, and if there is repentance, you must forgive" (Luke 17:3). The story of Jesus and Zacchaeus reflect these words put into practice (19:1-9).

The goal may be restoration, but as implied by Matthew 18, and as directed by Paul in his letter to the Corinthians (1 Cor 5:1-13), there may be times when an individual rejects the rebuke of the brother or sister, and some form of sanction or excommunication may be necessary. Even then, Jeschke argues, the goal is redemption (74–89). That this step is only taken as a last resort is consistent with Jesus sharing bread and wine with Judas at the Last Supper (John 13:21-30), as well as his parable of the wheat and the weeds, with the instruction to leave the weeds among the wheat "for in gathering the weeds you would uproot the wheat along with them" (Matt 13:29); they will be separated in "the harvest" (13:30).

The tension between the call to purge evil from our midst, as reflected by Deuteronomy 13 and elsewhere, and the repeated biblical emphasis on grace, forgiveness, and redemption—these are not simply resolved, nor should they be. It is the responsibility of the people of God to struggle within this tension over how to appropriately name and recognize the poisonous impact of serving other gods, whatever they may be, along with being a people of grace and love.

Worshiping the Family?

The second scenario in Deuteronomy 13 raises the prospect that someone from one's own family may tempt one to go after other gods. We live in a time when, perhaps because of the severe pressures families experience and the resulting breakup and disintegration of so many families, there is a tendency to privilege the nuclear family above virtually all else, almost to the point of worshiping the family. Everything is sacrificed for the family, everything is compromised for the family. It is through one's family experience that one determines right and wrong, be it the issue of marriage and divorce, homosexuality, or other challenging issues.

Deuteronomy 13 does not negate the role of experience in ethics, nor does it downplay the significance of family. In fact, it is the intensity of the family relationship that makes temptation from within it so powerful and so seductive. The family is important, but Jesus' teaching, like Deuteronomy, makes it clear that even more important than the biological family is the family of faith. He thus warns his followers that his teaching could set "a man against his father, and a daughter against her mother" and that "whoever loves father or mother more than me is not worthy of me" (Matt 10:35, 37). The church today, caught in battles over the family, also must remember that warning. The temptation from the inside is often more subtle and compelling than enticement from a distance.

Cleanliness and Purity for a Holy People
Deuteronomy 14:1-21

PREVIEW
Whoever travels to a dramatically different culture—for North Americans this could be to China or to Africa—quickly learns to be careful in interpreting other people's actions. God's instructions detailing how the tabernacle is to be built (Exod 26–31), exactly what constitutes "the ritual of the sacrifice of the offering of well-being" (Lev 7:11), and how lepers are to be purified (Lev 13–14)—such texts show how different the Old Testament world is from ours. Weinfeld speaks of Deuteronomy as "demythologizing" Israel's traditions, with a tendency toward "secularization" (1972), making the book feel more modern at some points. Deuteronomy's vision, he suggests, is for an abstract, rational religion that has moved beyond priests, sacrifice, temple, and a ritualistic cult (1972: 191–243).

Still, Deuteronomy very much remains an ancient document, speaking to the concerns and categories of ancient Israel. This point is driven home by a series of passages that at first glance may appear to fit better into a book like Leviticus, with extensive instructions for priests on how to maintain a proper cult [Cult, p. 546].

Deuteronomy's dietary regulations reflect this very different world (14:1-21). As does Leviticus 11, Deuteronomy here instructs Israel regarding clean and unclean animals, identifying which may be eaten and which are prohibited. As in the creation story of Genesis 1, the animal world is divided into three categories—animals of the land, animals of the sea, and animals of the air. Significant for the passage are its opening and closing, emphasizing the holy nature of Israel. Incorporated within the framework are a few additional prohibitions: against participating in certain mourning rites (14:1b), against eating animals that have died of themselves (14:21a), and against boiling a kid in its mother's milk (14:21c).

A Christian steeped in the modern world has to overcome multiple hurdles in order to appreciate these regulations as Scripture. Ancient notions of holiness and purity are foreign to those raised in post-Enlightenment times, with its faith in reason and science, combined with a quite modern sense that everything is equally and only physical. Societies in the ancient world understood the divine as intertwined with the physical world; they understood objects and people as potentially holy, with mysterious power; they understood the world as requiring a certain kind of order. As is the church today, Israel was very much part of the world of its day. Although the way it understood God and God's relationship to the world may have been different from its neighbors, in many ways it participated in this larger understanding of reality.

Added to this modern tendency to reject anything that does not immediately fit into a particular model of logic is the common Christian impression that Jesus and the New Testament rejected all Old Testament ritual regulations. After all, Jesus said, "'Do you not see that whatever goes into a person from outside cannot defile . . . ?' (Thus he declared all foods clean.)" (Mark 7:18-19). And the early church, influenced by the experiences of Peter and Paul, decided not to require Gentile converts to follow Jewish food laws (Acts 15). With this as a background, it becomes difficult for a Christian to take these regulations seriously. So what is the issue?

It is helpful to remember that for many faithful practicing Jews today, the dietary regulations remain crucial for their identity and have not been abolished. For them, these regulations continue to be important and are not meaningless tradition or legalism, but something of power and value. Christian bias against these regulations makes it hard to appreciate Jewish respect for them and undermines our ability to understand them.

In this passage we come across preached instructions that are more detailed than typical of Deuteronomy. Here Deuteronomy is likely applying to the people as a whole instructions originally written for priests, whether the passage is based on Leviticus 11, or whether both go back to a common source (both positions are advocated). In the process the central focus shifts from attention to the minutia and more technical details of the instructions to the overall role these directives play within the people.

In addition to this passage, a number of those in the "Miscellaneous" section (21:1-25:19) also deal with matters of holiness and purity (21:1-9, 22-23; 22:5, 9-11, 12; 24:8-9).

OUTLINE

Introduction, 14:1-2
Do Not Eat Any Abhorrent Thing, 14:3-20
    14:3   Summary Prohibition
    14:4-8   Clean and Unclean Life of the Land
    14:9-10 Clean and Unclean Life in the Sea
    14:11-20 Clean and Unclean Life in the Sky
Conclusion, 14:21

EXPLANATORY NOTES

Introduction 14:1-2

Conclusion 14:21

Again in chapter 14 we have a chiastic structure in which an introduction and conclusion, with common features, frame a central passage *[Chiasm, p. 540]*. Both elements of the frame include the identical sentence *For you are a people holy to the* LORD *your God* (vv. 2, 21), and both include a pair of prohibitions (vv. 1, 21) beginning with *You must/shall not . . .* (NRSV, *must* in v. 1, *shall* in v. 21, yet the Hebrew repeats identical wording; cf. RSV, *shall* in both cases). The framework presents the overall concern within which the instructions on clean and unclean animals must be read. Following the dietary regulations will reflect Israel's holiness.

Before the common elements of the framework appear, however, the chapter opens with a sentence that may catch us by surprise: *You are children of the* LORD *your God* (lit., *sons of . . .* , as in RSV, etc.). Deuteronomy has previously used parent-child imagery, but this is the first time in Deuteronomy, indeed in the whole Old Testament, where Israel is simply called *children of the* LORD *your God,* even if it is implied elsewhere (e.g., Exod 4:22-23). Deuteronomy may have been influenced in this language by the prophet Hosea, who uses parent-child imagery for God's love of Israel (Hos 11:1), and speaks of a time when Israel shall be called "children of the living God" (1:10). If Hosea is the source of influence, then the reference here draws attention to the intimacy of the relationship between God and the people God has chosen. They are like his own blood, with all the emotional connotations this entails.

But it is also possible that here Deuteronomy is influenced by the political treaty language of the day, in which the vassal may be called the "son" of the suzerain king *[Deuteronomy, Covenant, and Political Treaties, p. 547]*. This would emphasize the responsibilities or obligations that the "son" has to the "father." Perhaps one need not choose between the two: both connotations are present. The people of Israel are children of God, both because this represents a tender and intimate relationship and because this relationship places responsibilities on Israel to live in a particular manner.

Other biblical writers pick up this theme even if not with identical language. Exodus speaks of God commanding Moses to tell Pharaoh on behalf of God that "Israel is my firstborn son" (Exod 4:22-23; cf. Jer 31:9; Ezek 16:21; Isa 43:6; 45:11). Jesus says "peacemakers . . . will be called children of God" (Matt 5:9), and Paul regularly uses this language to emphasize the close relationship God has with his people (Rom 8:14, 16, 17, 19, 21; 9:8, 26; Gal 3:26; Phil 2:15). God chose this people because God loved them (cf. Deut 7:7-8). They are like his children. When they are in need, he carries them on his back (1:31); when they need discipline, he provides that (8:5). And yet it is a relationship that cannot be understood without recognizing its practical implications for life.

Both parts of the frame include a pair of prohibitions for Israel. The two within the introduction, *You must not lacerate yourselves or shave your forelocks for the dead* (lit., *make yourself bald between your eyes*), have as their background mourning rituals of the time. Ancient texts of the region (Craigie 1976: 230-31) and the Old Testament (Isa 3:24; 15:2; 22:12; Jer 16:6; 41:5; 47:5; Ezek 7:18; Amos 8:10; Mic 1:16; etc.) provide evidence that self-mutilation (lit., *cutting oneself*) and shaving one's hair were common practices associated with mourning rites. The logic of the practice, however, is not transparent. It may have been motivated by an effort to change one's appearance so that the potentially harmful spirits of the dead could not recognize the person, or it may have been an effort to place on one's body a lasting reminder of the deceased (Cairns: 139). Cutting one's hair may have had a similar motivation.

Nor is it entirely clear on what grounds Deuteronomy and also Leviticus (19:28) reject it, especially since some of the Old Testament passages that name these practices do not give them negative connotations. There is nothing in the verse itself suggesting that the prohibitions are based on respect for the body, although this cannot be entirely eliminated. Paul's invitation to "glorify God in your body" since it "is a temple of the Holy Spirit" (1 Cor 6:19-20) could fit such an interpretation, but the text of Deuteronomy does not point in this direction.

More likely the problem is the connection of these practices with Canaanite religion, and not merely their role within the mourning rites of the region. Perhaps the *dead* of verse 1 refers to a dying fertility god within the cult of Baal (Cairns: 139). The story of Elijah and the prophets of Baal on Mount Carmel supports there being a connection between self-laceration and Canaanite religion. When Baal does not immediately respond to the call of his prophets, "they cried aloud and, as was their custom, they cut themselves with swords and lances until the blood gushed out over them" (1 Kings 18:28). Whether the custom originally was a mourning rite that had evolved into a religious ritual, or vice versa, is not important. In either case, self-laceration or shaving oneself bald had become a sign of participation in the Baal cult. Deuteronomy's rejection of it thus is consistent with the preceding chapters and their call for exclusive worship of Yahweh. It also fits well with the immediate context of verses 1-2, with its emphasis on Israel's holy character and the connotation of being distinct from all other peoples.

The two prohibitions in the conclusion both relate to eating, and thus connect more directly to the dietary regulations central in the chapter. The rationale for the prohibition against eating *anything that dies of itself* (v. 21a) is not clear. Such meat may be forbidden because it is unhealthy or hazardous, perhaps because it contains a disease that caused the animal's death, or perhaps if killed by some other animal (the reference to dying *of itself* probably means not killed by a human being), it may have spoiled from lying out in the heat. Contemporary hesitance to eat such meat is based on factors like that, combined with a general aversion to eating such meat.

But the permission to give such meat to the alien living in their midst, or sell it to a foreigner passing through, weighs against health considerations. Deuteronomy consistently demonstrates concern for the alien (e.g., *You shall not deprive a resident alien or an orphan of justice; you shall not take a widow's garment in pledge*; 24:17), at some points making no distinctions in treating the alien and the fellow Israelite (e.g., 5:14; 14:29). Even in this passage the permission to give such meat to the *alien* may be a way of helping the disadvantaged in their midst. The *foreigner* does not receive the same consideration in Deuteronomy; this is reflected here when it is stated that the meat is *given* to the alien but *sold* to the foreigner. That Deuteronomy allows this meat to be eaten by the alien or foreigner suggests that Deuteronomy does not see anything inherently wrong or unhealthy about this meat.

More likely this prohibition has a ritual basis: since the animal died on its own, it has not been slaughtered according to ritual requirements, with its blood drained from it. This prohibition then is the practical corollary of Deuteronomy's permission to kill meat for consumption away from the central altar, with the condition that Israel not eat its blood (see on 12:15-27, esp. vv. 16, 21, 23). Even this explanation is not without difficulty, for the basis of the blood prohibition in 12:15-27 is the prohibition found in Genesis 9:4, given to Noah and all his descendants, not to eat flesh with its blood.

Perhaps a way through this is to recognize that although the prohibition of Genesis 9:4 does include all humanity in its purview, including all humanity in the prohibition does not appear to have been important for Deuteronomy. Despite the universal claim of Genesis 9:4, it appears that the surrounding nations in the world of Israel had no qualms about eating blood, or meat with blood in it. On a practical level, Israel's avoidance of meat with blood in it thus served to distinguish it from those around. "Because impurity does not matter outside the 'holy people' of the worshiping community, one may donate this meat to the (often poor) resident alien within one's town" (Nelson 2002: 181). The law thus not only supports Deuteronomy's concern to keep Israel holy, with a definite boundary between it and others, but also contributes to Deuteronomy's social vision of justice for the disadvantaged.

The background to the last prohibition in the passage, *You shall not boil a kid in its mother's milk* (also found in Exod 23:19; 34:26) is lost, with scholars suggesting a variety of reasons for it. Was the practice prohibited because of its connections with the worship of other gods, perhaps in fertility rites? Ian Cairns suggests that both the newborn kid and the milk were "powerful symbols of natural fertility," and may have been part of rituals meant to enhance the fertility of fields and flocks (143). If so, then the practice may be prohibited because it again brings foreign religion into Israel's life: Israel is to trust God for blessings and not attempt to magically ensure fertility of fields and herds through formulaic practices. Or is there some humanitarian concern behind the prohibition, a concern that a young kid should not be eaten for pleasure but should be allowed to become full grown? Or did the practice represent an unacceptable mixing of life—as represented by a kid and the mother's milk, meant for continuation of life—and death (Hall: 218)? Or does the prohibition connect the milk to blood, either because it does have some blood in it from the birth, or because some ancient peoples regarded milk as a kind of equivalent of blood, and thus eating a kid boiled in milk was a transgression of the command not to eat blood (Christensen 2001: 288)?

Whatever its background, this particular directive continues to have ongoing significance for Jewish kosher practice: it serves as the basis for keeping meat products separate from milk products. The lack of a clear, rational explanation for it contributes to it being understood simply as a command from God. Following it thus represents a total subjection of oneself to the greater wisdom and knowledge of God, rather than trusting human understanding.

The parallel nature of the frame is highlighted further when both the introduction and the conclusion characterize Israel with the identical sentence *For you are a people holy to the LORD your God* (vv. 2, 21). As in Deuteronomy 7:6 (a verse identical to 14:2), Israel's holiness is a by-product of its undeserved election, not something it achieves. This election is from *all the peoples of the earth*, thereby drawing attention to Israel's unique status, as reflected in the phrase *his treasured possession* (see comments on 7:6). The introduction and conclusion thus place the dietary regulations within a context of living in a manner consistent with Israel's identity as a holy people *[Holy, Holiness, p. 553]*.

Israel *is* a holy people. It is a standing they have received: it is not something they must earn through obedience. In contrast, Leviticus appears to make holiness something Israel aspires to: "For I am the LORD your God; sanctify yourselves therefore, and be holy, for I am holy. You shall not defile yourselves with any swarming creature that moves on the earth. . . . You shall be holy, for I am holy" (Lev 11:44-45; cf. 19:2; 20:26). In Deuteronomy, Israel is holy and thus is urged to live in a manner consistent with that nature. As implied by the meaning of the word *holy*, this points to it being distinct or separate from other peoples. Both its worship life (the concern of chs. 12-13) and its daily life (as reflected in the dietary regulations) are to reflect this difference. Both contribute to building a clear boundary between Israel and other peoples.

Do Not Eat Any Abhorrent Thing 14:3-20

14:3 Summary Prohibition

A short, succinct prohibition opens the central section of this passage: *You shall not eat any abhorrent thing.* The Hebrew consists of only four words: a negative particle, a verb that includes the second-person pronoun, and the object with the prefix "any" or "all" attached to it. One is reminded of the concise form of the negative commands in the Decalogue. The term *abhorrent* (NIV, *detestable*; RSV, KJV, *abominable*) involves cultic and ethical evaluation and is not simply emotional. In Deuteronomy it is regularly, but not exclusively, used of customs and practices associated with the religion of gods other than Yahweh (cf. 7:25-26; 12:31; 13:14; 17:4; 18:9, 12; 20:18; 27:15; 32:16). In 24:4 it is used of impermissible remarriage, and in 25:16 of fraudulent business practice. Something is *abhorrent* if God in God's wisdom rejects it, if it "defiles and breaks one's relationship with Yahweh" (Nelson 2002: 179).

General Comments

The key terms in this passage are *eat* (occurring eleven times in these verses, plus twice in v. 21) and *clean* (twice) and *unclean* (four times). How Israel eats is an important part of its faithfulness to God. The importance of eating correctly was evident already in chapter 12, in discussing the implications of a central sanctuary, even if the concern there was very different (i.e., that *all* eat together in a celebrative manner), but now it is the central focus. The terms *clean* and *unclean* are not hygienic categories but instead ritual terms very much related to the category of holiness, which requires cleanliness and purity. To be clean is not the same as to be holy, but to be holy and unclean are mutually exclusive categories. In other words, anything ritually unclean is in direct tension with holiness: it pollutes that which is holy.

As a holy people, Israel must be careful about what is unclean. This is the logic of Deuteronomy 14. On the whole the categories of clean and unclean do not play a major role in Deuteronomy. Outside of this chapter the term *clean* is used only three times in the NRSV (12:15, 22; 15:22), and the term *unclean* five times (12:15, 22; 15:22; 23:10; 26:14); without exception, the Hebrew terms involved (each is actually used four times) are employed to speak about people as clean and unclean rather than food. In comparison, the term *clean* occurs forty times in Leviticus, and the term *unclean* eighty-five times. Deuteronomy's concern in chapter 14 is not some abstract concern for ritual purity, but that Israel's eating habits be consistent with its identity as a holy people.

Deuteronomy thus incorporates Israel's eating practices into its sermon to Israel. Most cultures have eating taboos. Generally one's own eating taboos make emotional sense whereas the next person's feel illogical. North American sensitivities against eating dog or cat surely fall into this category. Israel's dietary regulations may have developed out of such eating taboos, but within the biblical text and Jewish tradition, they have move beyond that *[Dietary Regulations, p. 550]*.

More significant than determining on what basis these various animals were originally designated clean and unclean is the understanding the biblical writers had of these dietary regulations. Considerations of purity and holiness are more central for Leviticus than Deuteronomy, but for both books, dietary regulations are directly tied to holiness, even if the relationship is slightly different. Leviticus concludes its section on clean and unclean animals with the words "You shall be holy, for I am holy" (11:45). Later it gives an even more explicit interpretation,

> You shall therefore make a distinction between the clean animal and the unclean, and between the unclean bird and the clean; you shall not bring abomination on yourselves by animal or by bird or by anything with which the ground teems, which I have set apart for you to hold unclean. You shall be holy to me; for I the LORD am holy, and I have separated you from the other peoples to be mine. (20:25-26)

Deuteronomy frames the dietary regulations with the statement *For you are a people holy to the LORD your God*, and adds in the introduction, *it is you the LORD has chosen out of all the peoples of the earth, his treasured possession*. The dietary regulations thus are not the way to holiness, but they reflect and represent this holiness. Although concern for order and completeness may have been a factor in their original development, in Deuteronomy these regulations distinguish Israel from others: they set the boundaries between Israel as a holy people and the profane nations surrounding it.

14:4-8 *Clean and Unclean Life of the Land*

The listing of clean and unclean animals is organized by larger categories similar to the creation story of Genesis 1—land, sea, and sky—beginning with animals of the land. The passage opens on a positive note by naming three domesticated animals (*ox, sheep,* and *goat*) and seven wild animals that can be eaten. After naming the clean animals, the text presents the two criteria that these meet (they have split hooves and chew their cud). It only names some unclean animals that meet only one of these two criterion (or at least appear to, such as the hare) and thus conceivably might be ambiguous. Many other animals of Israel's world would not have met either of these two criteria and thus would have been unclean, such as rodents, horses, donkeys.

14:9-10 Clean and Unclean Life in the Sea

Very little is said about animals of the sea. In Old Testament times Israel was not a marine people. Fish and other sea animals, although known by Israel, were not a common part of the people's diet. The fact that no specific sea animal is even mentioned here suggests that the writers may not have known of many examples, either of the clean or unclean. In fact, no specific fish is named in the whole Old Testament. The need to be comprehensive, however, requires that this part of creation is covered as well. It is possible that the criterion of order plays a role here. A normal sea animal is a fish with fins and scales. Sea animals without these tend to be animals that creep along the bottom, and these may have been considered unclean for other reasons as well. Also eliminated by this criterion are eels, rays, and lampreys, common in the waters of the Mediterranean (Craigie 1976: 232).

14:11-20 Clean and Unclean Life in the Sky

This longer passage is framed by sentences that at first glance give the impression that they will introduce criteria for distinguishing between clean and unclean (*You may eat any clean birds.... You may eat any clean winged creature*; vv. 11, 20). But they do not. Instead, what we have is largely a listing of flying creatures that are prohibited, some twenty of them. A comparison of different English translations shows that scholars are quite uncertain about the identification of a number of the birds named.

The passage itself has two subunits, the first dealing with birds (vv. 11-18), the second dealing with insects (vv. 19-20). Although it gives no criteria, most, if not all, of the unclean birds identified are carnivorous and either would catch animals for their food or would be scavengers (e.g., vultures). These are rejected both because they have touched dead carcasses (another form of impurity) and because they have eaten blood. Birds considered clean based on other Old Testament passages include quail, doves, and pigeons.

After naming the unclean birds, the text moves on to insects (vv. 19-20) but provides neither clear criteria for distinguishing between clean and unclean nor examples. Leviticus 11, in contrast, gives criteria for distinguishing between clean and unclean (generally insects that walk upon four legs are unclean, with the exception of those that have jointed legs and that hop on the ground), and it names some clean insects (the locust, the bald locust, the cricket, and the grasshopper).

Differences among versions draw attention to an ambiguity. At first the NRSV appears to prohibit all winged insects (v. 19) but in the next verse allows *clean winged creatures*. The Hebrew word translated *insects* and *creatures* is commonly translated "fowl" or "birds." Both NIV 1984 and KJV, influenced by the adjective preceding the noun in verse 19, interpret it as a particular type of insect—*flying insects that swarm* (NIV84) or *creeping thing that flieth* (KJV)—with the implication that some flying insects are unclean whereas others are not. The NIV 2011 deleted the phrase *that swarm*. Whether this was enough to actually help an Israelite distinguish among clean and unclean insects is doubtful. More likely Deuteronomy here is speaking of taboos the readers all know about, placing them within its larger theological agenda.

THE TEXT IN BIBLICAL CONTEXT

Dietary Regulations: Symbols of Jewish Identity and Christian Universalism

It is easy to exaggerate the significance of dietary regulations for the Old Testament. Leviticus 11 and Deuteronomy 14 both present them in some detail, but even within these two books they do not play a major role. Deuteronomy never mentions them again, and Leviticus has only one other passage that gives them attention, and that in a fairly general manner. Leviticus 20:22-26 is a summarizing passage that includes the expectation "You shall therefore make a distinction between the clean animal and the unclean, between the unclean bird and the clean" (v. 25), with no further comment. That there were clean and unclean animals is also recognized by Numbers 18:15, where Israel is asked to redeem the "firstborn of unclean animals," but the context of the verse is sacrifice and not eating.

Beyond the Pentateuch there is little indication that Israel even had dietary regulations. The angel announcing to the wife of Manoah that she will become the mother of a son (whom she names Samson) instructs her "not to drink wine or strong drink, or to eat anything unclean" (Judg 13:4, also 7, 14), but the sense is that she receives this instruction because of the special calling of her son, not simply because she is part of a holy people (cf. Deut 14; Lev 11). Hosea warns that when the people go into exile "in Assyria they shall eat unclean food" (9:3). Although Hosea does not go into any detail, there is the recognition that Israel has dietary expectations that distinguish it from other people. Because the food the king is giving is problematic, "Daniel resolved that he would not defile himself with the royal rations of food and wine" (Dan 1:8). Despite the prominence given dietary regulations in Leviticus and Deuteronomy, they play very little role in the remainder of the Old Testament.

The story of Daniel, although not giving specifics, begins to reflect the emphasis evolving Judaism placed on dietary regulations during the exile and later. During this time dietary expectations, along with practices like circumcision and strict adherence to the Sabbath, became key characteristics identifying the Jewish people, distinguishing them from their neighbors. In the Apocrypha, 2 Maccabees 6 provides a moving testimony to the role that food regulations played during a time of Syrian persecution. After describing the execution of two women who had circumcised their sons, and the burning of others who had observed the Sabbath, it presents in great detail the story of Eleazar (6:18-31). When pork is forced into his mouth, he spits it out. Bystanders suggest that he pretend to eat the pork and therefore live. However, he steadfastly rejects this in case it would send the wrong message to the young, who might suppose "that Eleazar in his ninetieth year had gone over to an alien religion, and through my pretense, for the sake of living a brief moment longer, they would be led astray because of me, while I defile and disgrace my old age" (vv. 24-25). He stands firm and is executed: "So in this way he died, leaving in his death an example of nobility and a memorial of courage, not only to the young but [also] to the great body of the nation" (v. 31). The very next chapter (2 Macc 7:1-41) tells the story of the systematic torture and execution of seven brothers and their mother for their refusal to "partake of unlawful swine's flesh" (v. 1). Their spokesman proclaims, "For we are ready to die rather than transgress the laws of our ancestors" (v. 2).

Stories like these shaped the Jewish community of New Testament times. These stories were passed on from generation to generation, no doubt together with the warning to remember the God of the exodus, who calls on his people to be faithful to what he has commanded, regardless of the consequences. The dietary regulations, along with observance of the Sabbath and circumcision, became key practices identifying and protecting the community, in the face of hostile persecution or the more subtle temptation of assimilation to the predominant Greek culture. They were God's commands. They prescribed faithful Jewish response to the law. They distinguished Judaism from the nations.

And yet, by the end of the first century these dietary regulations played a limited role in the Christian community, by then largely Gentile, even though it had developed out of Judaism and included many who had Jewish background. This transition did not take place easily. As Walter Houston says, "Though Jesus cannot be seen as originating the abandonment of the dietary laws, there were certainly features of the movement that he created radical enough to make its evolution into a purity-free Gentile mission intelligible" (1993: 276). According to Matthew, Jesus sharply attacks the Pharisees for the great care they demonstrate for ritual cleanliness even as they are filled with greed and self-righteousness (Matt 23:23-28). By placing greater emphasis on the moral aspects of the law over against ritual, Jesus is in good Old Testament tradition (cf. Amos 5, esp. vv. 21-24). In Mark, Jesus says, "Then are you also without understanding? Do you not see that whatever goes into a man from outside cannot defile him, since it enters, not his heart but his stomach, and so passes on?" (7:18 RSV). Without further comment Jesus proceeds from there to heal a Syrophoenician woman (not a Jew and thus unclean; 7:24-30). Mark, however, adds his own and the later church's interpretation: "Thus he declared all foods clean" (7:19).

Jesus may have set the direction, but the issue was far from resolved. Jesus continued to work primarily with his own people (e.g., Matt 15:24), with the earliest church essentially Jewish. Christianity began as a kind of "party" (cf. Pharisees, Essenes) within Judaism that recognized Jesus as the anticipated Messiah, a community that remained faithful to Jewish law. Although Philip baptizes an Ethiopian eunuch (Acts 8:26-40), this does not change the basic nature of the church. When Peter experiences his direction-setting vision and is presented with a menagerie of animals and the command, "Get up, Peter; kill and eat," Peter responds in horror, "By no means, Lord; for I have never eaten anything that is profane or unclean." Despite having followed Jesus throughout his ministry, and despite having experienced the birth of the church at Pentecost, the Peter of this verse responds very much in the tradition of Eleazar of the Maccabean period. The response of the heavenly voice, however, is equally clear, "What God has made clean, you must not call profane" (Acts 10:10-16). After experiencing the vision, Peter goes to Joppa, where he presents the gospel to Cornelius, the Roman centurion. His actions are sanctioned by God as the Holy Spirit comes on all those who have heard the message. The story of the vision becomes a major argument when Peter defends his actions before the church leaders in Jerusalem (Acts 11:1-18).

The vision of Peter and the conversion of Cornelius inaugurate a new era. Shortly thereafter Paul begins his mission to the Gentiles. Acts 15 describes a conference in Jerusalem where the leaders debate how to treat those who join their community from a Gentile background. Although the focal point in the debate is the question of circumcision, the final agreement shows that Jewish ritual dietary regulations also are an issue. The conference determines that Gentile converts do not need to take Jewish ritual law upon themselves, neither circumcision nor the dietary regulations. The new converts are, however, expected to abstain "from things polluted by idols and from fornication and from whatever has been strangled and from blood" (Acts 15:20). Although this sidelines the expectations of Deuteronomy 14, it continues the Deuteronomic emphasis on exclusive worship of God (abstain what is polluted by idols), purity in sexual matters, and the universal requirement not to eat blood.

This became general church practice. The followers of Jesus were a community bound together through their focus on the Jesus who had come preaching to the Jews, but with a vision for a larger, universal mission. The de-emphasis of Jewish purity regulations that had played such a critical role in representing Jewish identity became symbolic of a new movement that, although still including Jews, had a universal scope.

THE TEXT IN THE LIFE OF THE CHURCH

Visible Reminders: Respect for All Life

Even if the rationale behind specific dietary regulations is elusive, their role in the life of a community can be substantial. In multiple places Jacob Milgrom argues that the dietary regulations have an ethical function (1963; 1990). His focus is not on getting behind the biblical sources to why certain animals were allowed and others not—a sleuthing task that he says cannot be successful—but on their function or role for Israel and Judaism.

The Old Testament, he observes, begins with the understanding that humanity is vegetarian (see Gen 1:29). Allowing humans to kill animals for food is a concession to human desire (9:3-4). But along with this concession comes the first commandment in Scripture, a commandment not given to Israel alone but to all humanity, the prohibition against eating blood: "Only, you shall not eat flesh with its life, that is, its blood" (9:4). Animals, although clearly not having the same status as humans in Scripture, nevertheless have a close relationship to them. The prohibition against eating blood, with the Israelite practice of returning it to God in a ritualistic manner, becomes a constant reminder that killing animals is a form of violence that needs to be curtailed and reconciled.

The dietary regulations limiting which animals Israel can kill for food, then, are part of this larger system.

> The Bible has evolved a system of dietary restrictions that teach the Jew to have reverence for life by (1) reducing his choice of flesh to a few animals, (2) limiting the slaughter of even these animals to the most humane way and by the few who can qualify, and (3) prohibiting the consumption of blood, as acknowledgement that bringing death to living things is a concession of God's grace and not a privilege of man's whim. (Milgrom 1963: 293)

In Deuteronomy the second restriction is altered in light of its call for centralization of worship, but the first and third remain in force.

This combination of restrictions, Milgrom argues, distinguished Israel from its idolatrous neighbors, thereby contributing to the theme of holiness. The reference to holiness occurs more frequently in relationship to dietary regulations than any other commandment (cf. Deut 14:2, 21). The dietary limitations serve to identify Israel as a holy people, separate and distinct from other nations, chosen by God. Simultaneously, they teach reverence for life and warn against violence, not only violence against animals but also against fellow human beings. The daily reminder that the people of God are not able to eat anything they desire reminds them that human power is not limitless or absolute, that life belongs to God. Daily kosher practice continues to contribute to such a Jewish identity today.

Christopher Wright moves in a similar direction:

> The food laws were thus a daily reminder to Israel of their status and role in God's purpose and of the consequent call to holiness in other more morally significant areas of personal and social life. Holiness was woven into everyday life. Every meal should have reminded the Israelite family of God's commitment to them and their commitment to God. A God who governs the kitchen should be not easily forgotten in the rest of life. (1996: 182)

The early church's departure from these dietary regulations may be an appropriate response to the call for mission, but at the same time, it presents the church of today with a challenge. The call to be holy and thus distinctive remains: "You are a chosen race, a royal priesthood, a holy nation, God's own people" (1 Pet 2:9). A question the dietary regulations pose to the church is whether it has comparable symbols or rituals that can continuously remind it of its holy identity, that can model a reverence for life, as the dietary regulations have done for the Jewish people.

Identity versus Mission

During the exile in Babylon, the Jewish community developed and highlighted those elements of its faith and tradition that distinguished it from its neighbors: circumcision, dietary regulations, and observance of the Sabbath. These practices enforced identity and raised the wall between it and others. They represented holiness and separateness. These practices contributed to their surviving exile when so many other peoples forced into exile disappeared as distinct peoples. After the exile, Judaism continued to emphasize these ritual practices. They helped it become a vibrant community back in Judah, and they helped it withstand oppression and persecution during the centuries prior to the New Testament.

But this emphasis on identity-supporting practices and a clear boundary between it and its neighbors also undermined their ability to fulfill the mandate God gave Abraham, to be a blessing to all peoples. Identity with clear boundaries and fulfillment of mission beyond one's boundaries inevitably are in some tension with each other. Jesus' clashes with the Pharisees were often related to the tension between holiness and mission.

This tension is recognized rather than simply resolved. The Jesus movement in its own way developed identity-fostering practices. The prohibition of Acts 15 not to eat meat presented to idols remained a distinguishing practice, even if qualified somewhat by 1 Corinthians 10:25-30. The early church's rejection of service in the military was a powerful statement. The ceremonial breaking of bread also played a role. It developed a new way of living faithfully in the tension.

Deuteronomy 14:22–15:18

Part 2D, Unit 2
Justice in Israel: The Community

OVERVIEW
Patrick Miller identifies three themes in Deuteronomy 12–26: (1) the worship of God, (2) care of the needy and weak, and (3) a system of leadership. The first part of chapters 12–26 calls for faithful and exclusive worship of Yahweh. After forcefully presenting this, Deuteronomy moves to life in the community. Deuteronomy's concern for justice, especially as it impacts the weak and powerless within the community, quickly comes to the fore. The tithe regulations (14:22-29) point the direction, with Deuteronomy 15 "the definitive chapter for discerning the centrality of Deuteronomy's concern that access to the blessing of God be available to all members of the community, including those who, out of need and position, are least likely to enjoy that blessing" (P. Miller 1987: 22, 25).

A number of passages in other areas of Part 2D (12:1–26:19) also relate to the theme of justice in the community of Israelite brothers and sisters: 19:14; 22:1-4, 6-8; 23:15-16, 19-20, 24-25; 24:6-7, 10-22; 25:1-4, 11-19.

OUTLINE
The Annual Tithe, 14:22-29
A Sabbatical Release, 15:1-18

The Annual Tithe

Deuteronomy 14:22-29

PREVIEW

Benjamin Franklin first observed, "Nothing is certain but death and taxes." Neither is desired by most people. Tithes easily sound like taxes and, when required of people, are really not that different. The distinction between tithes and taxes was even less in the ancient world, where state and religious bureaucracy were interconnected and where people were "taxed" for the support of public personnel, whether religious, political, or military. When Israel asked for a king, Samuel warned the people that a king would take their sons and daughters, plus one-tenth (a tithe) of their grain and vineyards and their flocks. Then the people *will cry out* against their king (1 Sam 8:11-18). Taxes and tithes take away independence as hierarchical structures take control. It is doubtful that taxes and forced tithes were any more appreciated in Israel than today.

Nevertheless, Deuteronomy's vision for a people faithful to the God of the exodus includes a tithe requirement. Astonishingly, although Deuteronomy recognizes that the people need to support priests (e.g., 18:3), the concern of its tithe requirements is not political or religious personnel. Rather, its focus is on communal celebration at The Place (the annual tithe) and on the use of the tithe for supporting the poor (the third-year tithe). Its tone is represented by the surprising statement: *Spend the money for whatever you wish— oxen, sheep, wine, strong drink, or whatever you desire* (14:26). The tithe may have an element of unwanted taxes—after all, the farmers do lose control of the third-year tithe that is assigned to the poor—but the overall mood is one of eating, drinking, and rejoicing in the presence of Yahweh, the God who has redeemed them and now is blessing them (14:29).

OUTLINE

The Annual Tithe Command, 14:22
The Annual Tithe of Celebration, 14:23-27
The Third-Year Tithe of Assistance, 14:28-29

EXPLANATORY NOTES

Perhaps due to word association, Deuteronomy places the tithe regulations immediately following the dietary regulations (14:1-21).

Food and eating are central to the tithe regulations and thus continue the food interest of the dietary regulations. The reference to the (*resident*) *alien* (14:21 RSV, 29) also ties these two passages together. Placing the tithe regulations next to the dietary regulations, however, also has thematic implications. The dietary regulations opened and concluded with the statement *for you are a people holy to the* LORD *your God*. Israel's special status and place is symbolized by these provisions. The way in which Israel tithes thus also becomes a mark of its holiness.

The tithe regulations serve as a transition from the first part of chapters 12–26, with its focus on the exclusive worship of God, to the chapters that follow. Typically tithes in the larger ancient Near East were the domain of king and cult personnel. They thus begin the move from an emphasis on exclusive worship to consideration of Israel's festivals and other cultic regulations (ch. 16, "A Festival Calendar for The Place"). But the way in which Deuteronomy envisions the tithe's functioning points to a radically different understanding of community relationships; as such it prepares the way for chapter 15, with its release provisions, and the many other later passages that outline Deuteronomy's social vision.

The following treats verses 22-27 and verses 28-29 not as two separate pieces of legislation (as in paragraphs of NRSV), the first dealing with the annual tithe and the second with a tithe expected every three years, but as an integrated whole. The opening verse presents the basic regulation or directive, with the following verses consisting of explanation or application.

The Annual Tithe Command 14:22

The basic expectation is stated in the opening verse. All were familiar with the general practice, so no background explanation is needed. Whether tithe or tax, state bureaucracy requires income. The king and his court, the cult and its personnel—all need resources to survive and implement their programs. Since the king was chosen by God, the line between religious and political is blurred. Deuteronomy, like Leviticus (27:30-33) and Numbers (18:21-32), assumes that tithing is part of life.

Other Old Testament passages reflect this reality. Abraham gives one-tenth to Melchizedek (Gen 14:20), Jacob speaks of giving one-tenth to God (Gen 28:22), and Amos refers to Israel bringing its tithes to Bethel (Amos 4:4). Samuel warns that a king will take the best of their fields, one-tenth of their grain, and one-tenth of their herds and flocks (1 Sam 8:15, 17). The term "one-tenth" in 1 Samuel

8 is based on the same root as the one translated *tithe* in Deuteronomy 14:22, a variation of the Hebrew word for ten. The tithe expectation of verse 22 fits well into the larger ancient Near Eastern and Israelite world.

The Annual Tithe of Celebration 14:23-27

The distinctive nature of Deuteronomy's regulation is highlighted when it is compared with the parallel expectation in Leviticus and Numbers. Leviticus focuses on God—the tithes "are the LORD's; they are holy to the LORD"—and then outlines how an Israelite might "redeem any of their tithes" by adding "one-fifth to them" (27:30-33). This likely means that they can choose to keep the animal or produce being tithed, and instead of the tithe give to the Lord (to the temple?) an amount equivalent to the value of the tithe plus 20 percent. The tithe of Numbers protects the Levites: "To the Levites I have given every tithe in Israel for a possession in return for the service they perform" (Num 18:21). The Levites then give one-tenth of what they receive to the priests ("a tithe of the tithe," 18:26). In Deuteronomy the emphasis falls on the community as a whole eating together and celebrating at the central sanctuary.

Instead of viewing these three tithe requirements as reflecting different historical periods, it is more likely that there was a common tithe tradition that each book then presents in a manner consistent with its particular concerns or theological emphases. Deuteronomy does not reject that the tithe is holy, belonging to God (in fact, the NRSV's opening phrase, *Set apart*, is consistent with this), nor that the Levites should benefit from the tithe (notice Deut 14:27). In its Deuteronomic dress, however, the tithe regulation becomes an unusual directive with a distinct tone to it.

A tithe quite naturally draws to mind thoughts of giving away, of sacrificing, of losing. And yet the striking feature of this passage is that its tone is best captured by the term *rejoicing* rather than by a sense of giving away or sacrifice. For Deuteronomy, the tithe is a tithe of celebration.

The distinctive interest of Deuteronomy is evident already in verse 23. With the directive to eat the tithe at *the place that he will choose as a dwelling for his name*, Deuteronomy reminds us of chapter 12. In three consecutive verses, God's choice of *the place* is mentioned (vv. 23, 24, 25), the second of which specifies God choosing The Place as a dwelling for his name. Deuteronomy's tithe expectation is fully integrated with its call for a central sanctuary. The opening phrase of verse 23, *in the presence of the LORD your God* (lit., *before the* LORD *your God*), also points back to chapter 12, with the phrase occurring twice in each passage (12:7, 18; 14:23, 26; cf. 26:13). The two verses with the phrase in chapter 12 signal two themes prominent in Deuteronomy's tithe expectation.

First, the tithe is a response to God's blessing. Not only does verse 24 refer to God's blessing (cf. 12:7); it also makes this point more vividly by listing what Israel is to tithe: *the tithe of your grain, your wine, and your oil, as well as the firstlings of your herd and flock* (14:23). Here is an echo of Deuteronomy 7, with its focus on Israel's election. After declaring Israel's election (7:6) and its basis (7:7-11), the chapter turns to how it benefits Israel (7:12-26). The key verse there is verse 13: *He will love you, bless you, and multiply you; he will bless the fruit of your womb and the fruit of your ground, your <u>grain</u> and your <u>wine</u> and your <u>oil</u>, the increase of your <u>cattle</u> and the issue of your <u>flock</u>, in the land that he swore to your ancestors to give you*. Each example of blessing in chapter 7 now is repeated in the same order, with the exception of the reference to multiplying *you* (*herd* replaces *cattle*). Tithing is possible because of God's blessing, and it is a reminder of that blessing.

Second, in chapter 12 both references to *the presence of the* LORD *your God* speak of the community eating and rejoicing before God (vv. 7, 18). The tithe expectation of chapter 14 gives this theme concrete content. The tithe provides provisions for the annual celebration that the whole *household* (14:26) enjoys at the central sanctuary. The inclusive nature of the feast is highlighted in 12:18 with the listing of the household members: *you together with your son and your daughter, your male and female slaves, and the Levites resident in your towns*.

The accommodation that Deuteronomy includes for those who live too far from the sanctuary contributes to the tone of inclusive celebration. To ensure that all are able to celebrate together the blessings from God, Deuteronomy allows those from a distance to sell their tithe in their local community, and then purchase at The Place of God's choosing *whatever you wish—oxen, sheep, wine, strong drink, or whatever you desire* (14:25-26). Again one hears echoes of chapter 12, where three times Israel is told that it may eat meat *whenever you (have) desire* (12:15, 20, 21). Even the distance is interpreted positively as a direct outcome of God's blessing. God's abundant blessing is to be enjoyed; Deuteronomy gives Israel a freedom and encouragement to do so, with the tithe a means of accomplishing this.

Not surprisingly, the celebration of God's bountiful blessing provides an opportunity for exhortation and instruction. The eating is done *so that you may learn to fear the* LORD *your God always* (14:23). This may suggest that the presentation of the tithe is associated with a reading of the law (so Mayes: 245), but not necessarily so. The very act of tithing is a reminder of God's blessing, a call to remember that Israel is experiencing this blessing because of what God has done. Deuteronomy has previously exhorted Israel to remember and not forget what God has done (e.g., 6:12; 7:18), with the danger in mind that Israel may begin to think that it is responsible for producing its own wealth (8:17). The tithe challenges any such misreading of reality. The required response is to fear God (see on 10:12–11:32, which repeatedly calls Israel to fear God; 10:12, 20). The tithe feast of chapter 14 brings together an emphasis on rejoicing with a didactic purpose.

Even though it introduces a new element, verse 27 is part of this section rather than the following verses (as is suggested by the NRSV paragraph divisions). Since the Levites have no allotment in the land, they need special consideration (cf. 18:1). Numbers assigns the total tithe to the Levites with the expectation that they contribute one-tenth of it to the priests (18:21, 26). Deuteronomy may adjust this expectation but does not cancel it entirely. Even if the tithe celebration at the central sanctuary is lavish, at least for ancient times, there still is food left over. This verse reminds the people that despite the distinctive thrust of these verses, with all celebrating the blessing, the more traditional understanding of the tithe remains: the Levites must not be neglected (cf. comments on 18:3-5).

The Third-Year Tithe of Assistance 14:28-29

The last two verses of the chapter present a third-year variation for the annual tithe (cf. 26:13-15). Every third year (probably understood as the third and sixth year of a seven-year cycle) the tithe is stored in the local community as a "food bank" for those in need, *the Levites, because they have no allotment or inheritance with you, as well as the resident aliens, the orphans, and the widows in your towns.* A tithe in support of the cult was common both in Israel and among other peoples, but this version is unusual.

Although it is a *good land* (a phrase that occurs ten times in the first eleven chapters of Deuteronomy) that will allow most citizens to prosper and be self-sufficient, inevitably there will be some who will not benefit as fully from the blessings of the land. The resident aliens, the orphans, and the widows represent this disadvantaged group (for discussion of these categories, see on 24:17-18). The third-year tithe supports this group. The food designated for them is not merely enough to prevent them from starving, but they are invited to *come and eat their fill*. Earlier, when Deuteronomy described the bounty of the Promised Land (*a good land, a land of flowing streams and . . . of wheat and barley, of vines and fig trees and pomegranates, . . . a land where you may eat bread without scarcity, where you will lack nothing*; 8:7-9) it concluded with *You shall <u>eat your fill</u> and bless the LORD your God* (8:10). Similarly, in 14:29, the disadvantaged shall *eat their fill* and experience the blessings of the land. The passage concludes by connecting this sharing of the blessings with God's continued blessing *in all the work that you undertake* (14:29). Sharing blessings is the way to ensure continuation of blessings from God.

These two verses treat this expectation largely as a matter of social assistance. In chapter 26 Deuteronomy adds that after paying this third-year tithe, the Israelite *shall say before the LORD your God, . . . I have given . . .* (26:12-15). It is likely that saying it before God implies that the Israelite is to go to the central sanctuary and there publicly proclaim that he has met the expectation. Interestingly, in this context the tithe is called *the sacred portion* (lit., *the holy*, 26:13). Normally the best of the crops and herds belong to God. Here they are assigned to the disadvantaged. They are able to eat to their full on God's share.

By requiring a liturgical response at the sanctuary, and by designating the tithe as something holy, this passage closely connects even this tithe with the central cult and the exclusive worship of the God who takes care of his people when in need *[Cult, p. 546]*. The thrust of Deuteronomy is consistent with the preaching of the prophets, who also were unwilling to separate cultic response to God from justice in the community. Any simple or absolute categorizing of Deuteronomic material as cultic or moral is not possible. Providing for the disadvantaged is an integral aspect Israel's relationship to God.

THE TEXT IN BIBLICAL CONTEXT

Tithing versus Generosity in Scripture

Leviticus (27:30-33), Numbers (18:21-32), and Deuteronomy (12:6, 11; 14:22-29; 26:12-15) all require tithing, but the remainder of the Old Testament says little about the practice. Given the way Deuteronomy speaks of tithing, we may be surprised that it does not play a more prominent role in other parts of the Old Testament, especially the prophetic books. After all, the prophets also were concerned about justice for the disadvantaged.

The mood of celebration and generosity prominent in Deuteronomy tends to be absent in other Old Testament passages about tithes. Amos speaks of tithes ("Come to Bethel—and transgress; to Gilgal—and multiply transgressions; bring your sacrifices every morning, your tithes every three days"; 4:4), but in a context of indicting Israel for its diligent observance of cultic requirements even as it ignores justice and righteousness (cf. Amos 5:21-24). Malachi chastises the people for not bringing their full tithe to the cult, thereby robbing God (3:8-12). By the time of Nehemiah, the Levites have the responsibility of going about the community, collecting tithes for priests and temple personnel (Neh 10:35-38; 12:44; 13:4-5). In these passages the tithe sounds much more like the tax Samuel warned the people about when they demanded a king (1 Sam 8:11-18). Although kings no longer existed in the days of Malachi and Nehemiah, the temple could be equally demanding.

Postexilic Judaism did develop a complex system of tithes. In its effort to be meticulous in obedience to Scripture, it interpreted the variations among the different passages as requiring multiple tithes. The tithe of Deuteronomy, with its provision for celebrative eating at the central sanctuary, came to be understood as a tithe in addition to the one required for the support of the Levites in Leviticus and Numbers. The third-year tithe of Deuteronomy 14:28-29 was above and beyond these two, and thus a third tithe. No wonder the people struggled under this multiple taxation.

This may explain why the tithe plays minimal role in the New Testament. In words reminiscent of Amos, Jesus says, "Woe to you, scribes and Pharisees, hypocrites! For you tithe mint, dill, and cummin, and have neglected the weightier matters of the law: justice and mercy and faith" (Matt 23:23). At another point Jesus negatively compares a Pharisee who prides himself in his scrupulous obedience to the law, including tithing, with a tax collector who can only say, "God, be merciful to me, a sinner!" (Luke 18:9-14).

The New Testament may not make tithing compulsory, but the generous spirit of Deuteronomy's tithing regulations is present (e.g., 2 Cor 9:7). Acts characterizes the early church at Jerusalem as one in which all goods were held in common, in which people sold their possessions for distribution, leading to a situation in which "there was not a needy person among them" (Acts 4:34; cf. 2:44-45). Paul commends the church in Macedonia and Achaia for sharing of its resources with the poor in Jerusalem (Rom 15:25-28; cf. 1 Cor 16:1-3; Eph 4:28). The stories of Ananias and Sapphira (Acts 5:1-11) and of the neglect of the Gentile widows (6:1-6) point out that church members continued to struggle with the temptation of selfishness, but this is only to be expected. The new commandment Jesus gives is "that you love one another," with the consequence that "everyone will know that you are my disciples, if you have love for one another" (John 13:34-35). This love is only real if it is reflected in people sharing with each other. A strict or legalistic tithe system is replaced with an emphasis on a generous and giving spirit.

THE TEXT IN THE LIFE OF THE CHURCH

Tithing and Celebration

"Bring the full tithe into the storehouse, so that there may be food in my house" (Mal 3:10). Employing verses like this for support, many a preacher has challenged people to tithe to the church. To what extent Old Testament passages on tithing are decisive for the church, however, is much debated. Although most denominations have not tried to enforce it—one exception is The Church of Jesus Christ of Latter-day Saints—tithing passages are used to motivate financial contributions to the church.

Consistent with the logic of these passages, such giving has two distinct functions. First of all, it represents a symbolic acknowledgment that all belongs to God, who has entrusted us to be stewards of God's creation (cf. Lev 27:30-33). On the other hand, the resources themselves are significant because they are used to support the work of the church, both to pay its workers (cf. Num 18:21-32) and to support the disadvantaged (Deut 14:28-29). The Mennonite Brethren *Confession of Faith* summarizes this as follows:

> The Bible teaches cheerful, sacrificial, and proportional giving through the church in grateful response to God's goodness. Christians do not claim any of their possessions as their own, but manage all their resources, including money, time, abilities and influence, in generous ways that give glory to God. They do not despise the poor but practice mutual aid within the church and share what they have with others in need. (MBCF 1999: 22)

One of the elements of the Deuteronomic tithe regulations largely absent in more recent use of these passages is the prominence they give to joyful rejoicing in the presence of God. The key limitation placed on the celebration is that it be inclusive: the whole household participates in the celebration. Other than that, the tithe money can be spent on *whatever you wish* or *whatever you desire*. The vision of Deuteronomy is for a community with a strong social concern, but the voice of Deuteronomy is not that of a dour prophet who sees only the harshness of the responsibility. Rather, the voice is more like that of a cheerleader enthusiastically encouraging the people in unabashed celebration of the blessings of the land that God has given them.

The cross may be the primary Christian symbol, but the cross is defeated by the resurrection, an event that deserves celebration. Yet celebration does not even have to be of some important Christian event. The Passover commemorates the exodus, but the celebration of the tithe regulation refers to no historical event. It does not exist to commemorate some event but is celebration for the sake of community. Its inclusive nature ensures that.

A Sabbatical Release
Deuteronomy 15:1-18

PREVIEW

How often do we really wonder whether we will have enough to eat? Or a bed to sleep on? Or clothes to wear? We may not be rich, but most of us are not poor. In ancient Israel most people lived at a subsistence level, so survival was the primary concern. When misfortune came, whether through accident, poor health, or bad crops, there was little if any reserve to fall back upon. In severe situations this could necessitate borrowing from a community member to buy food or to purchase seed for next year's crop. Generally, borrowing was reserved for such times of crisis. The contemporary practice of borrowing money for investment, whether for furthering one's education, purchasing a home, or to pursue a business venture, was uncommon.

Borrowing then began a vicious cycle. With interest rates extremely high (as high as 50 percent) and the means of production limited, it was difficult to escape from this cycle. Patrimonial land could be mortgaged and lost; with no other alternative, people themselves could be assigned to a creditor, whether the male head of the family himself or one of his dependents (e.g., 2 Kings 4:1). Chattel slavery (e.g., slaves resulting from capture in war; cf. Deut 20:14) could happen, but debt slavery was much more common. As Israelite society became more complex and segmented, as state taxation increased, more and more Israelites lost everything, including their own personal freedom.

The sabbatical release of this passage works toward breaking the cycle of poverty, debt, and debt slavery that so easily ensnared people in its grip. God had given all of Israel the Promised Land. All of Israel was to benefit from this and experience the blessings of the land. Debt slavery prevented this. The Deuteronomic sabbatical release provisions do not take on the ancient economic system as such—to expect it to do that is unrealistic—but they undermine or ameliorate its worst effects, thereby beginning to raise questions about its very nature. The immediately preceding passage allocating the triennial tithe to feeding the disadvantaged (14:28-29) sets a direction that the Deuteronomic release provisions continue. They present the strongest expression of Deuteronomy's vision for social justice.

OUTLINE

The Sabbatical Debt Release, 15:1-11
 15:1 The Debt Release Command
 15:2-3 The Manner of Release
 15:4-6 Consequences of Obedience
 15:7-11 Exhortation: Give Generously to Those in Need
The Sabbatical Slave Release, 15:12-18
 15:12 The Slave Release Command
 15:13-14 The Manner of Release
 15:15 Exhortation: Remember
 15:16-17 An Escape Clause
 15:18 Concluding Exhortation

EXPLANATORY NOTES

The Deuteronomic release passage has two distinct albeit parallel provisions, the release of debts (vv. 1-6) and the release of slaves (vv. 12-18). The middle verses (7-11) are a general exhortation for generosity, but their reference to the seventh-year release (v. 9) clearly connect them to the debt release. In good Deuteronomic style (cf. 12:4-28), the first verse presents the basic directive: *Every seventh year you shall grant a remission of debts*. The following verses then provide further clarification of the directive (*This is the manner of the remission*) and motivation for obedience.

The language of the release provisions repeatedly point back to the Sabbath command of the Decalogue:

- In both passages the number *seven* (or *seventh*) plays a vital role (5:14; 15:1, 9, 12).

- Both passages refer to working for six units of time, with rest or freedom coming in the seventh unit (5:13; 15:12).

- Both passages emphasize various forms of the Hebrew verb "to work," translated *labor* (5:13) or *works* (15:12) and *slave* (5:14, 15; 15:15, 17).

- Both passages are grounded explicitly in the fact that Israel had been a people of slaves in Egypt when God redeemed it (5:15; 15:15).

- Both passages move in the direction of including the poor in the blessings of the land.

Observance of the Sabbath and concern for justice within society are inseparable for Deuteronomy, establishing what might even be called a Sabbath principle. Every Sabbath observance is a celebration of Israel's deliverance from Egypt (5:15), a reminder to a delivered people to treat the needy among them in a similar manner.

The Sabbatical Debt Release 15:1-11

15:1 The Debt Release Command

The passage opens with a terse apodictic command *[Law, p. 555]* calling for a release. The NRSV (*grant a remission*) and NIV (*cancel debts*) translations capture the spirit of the Hebrew, but the term *release* (RSV, KJV) renders the Hebrew more literally. The Hebrew term translated *release* is relatively rare, yet reflects a thought world beyond that of financial debts. In Exodus 23:10-11, a passage that may have influenced the Deuteronomic version (see TBC), it refers to the release of land, allowing land that has been worked for six years to rest and lie fallow. The first verse thus not only opens the portion of the passage dealing with debt release but already points ahead to the second portion, dealing with slave release. In Israel a new start becomes possible every seventh year.

The distinctive thrust of the Deuteronomic release provisions becomes more striking when read within its larger setting. As a way of meeting their responsibility to ensure justice for the weak and disadvantaged, kings throughout the ancient Near East would issue royal decrees of release. These edicts "were royal proclamations intended to release private debts and some form of public taxes" (Hamilton: 48). Not uncommonly a king might issue such a release proclamation at the beginning of his reign, although it could also happen at other times. Kings considered such an act to be a sign of their commitment to justice, one of their important achievements.

Israel thus lived in a world in which the occasional canceling of debts and freeing of slaves was known, in which this was considered a significant act of justice, and in which the king was the authority with the responsibility to make it happen. That the Old Testament includes reference to debt and slave release is not unique or especially radical within the world of the day. What distinguishes the Deuteronomic release from the occasional royal decrees of kings is their regular nature (every seven years) and their separation from the king. Their implementation is to be independent of the will or political calculations of the king. Release is at the heart of life in the community of Israel.

15:2-3 The Manner of Release

After an opening apodictic command sets the direction, Deuteronomy provides further clarification (vv. 2-3) and motivation for obedience (vv. 4-6). The clarification, or manner of release, has a chiastic structure [Chiasm, p. 540].

A^1 *Every creditor shall remit the claim that is held against the neighbor,*
    B^1 *not exacting it of the neighbor who is a member of the community,*
        C *because the* LORD's *remission has been proclaimed.*
    B^2 *Of a foreigner you may exact it,*
A^2 *but you must remit your claim on whatever any member of your community owes you.*

The A parts announce the practice of release, the B parts apply this release only to the community of Israel, and the C part bases the command in the God of Israel and the exodus. Both parts A and C include some form of the term translated *release*.

A literal reading of the first part of A^1 is *Every lord of the loan of his hand . . .* The audience for this instruction is the lords (*baʿal*) of the land, who have the wherewithal to lend money to those in need. The initial statement is not entirely clear as to what is released or remitted. Is it the loan itself? Is it the interest on the loan for a year, a kind of deferral of payments? Or is it even the pledge that has been given to guarantee the loan? The warning of verse 9, however, points to the loan itself. The property owner thus gives up any claim to receive payment on the loan.

Both parts A and B emphasize that the provision is regarding loans between members of the Israelite community. This is stated repeatedly within the context of 15:2-3. Twice the fellow Israelite is called a *neighbor*, twice a *brother* (KJV, RSV; NRSV, *member of the community*), and part B² explicitly exempts loans to a foreigner from the remission. Deuteronomy's vision for Israel is that of a community of brothers and sisters (Perlitt 1980). This emphasis may give the passage a somewhat parochial feel (cf. 14:21) but actually strengthens its central concern.

Financial loans in Israel tended to be crisis loans made for survival purposes. It is these loans that are to be canceled at the end of the seventh year. Loans made to foreigners (i.e., people living outside of Israel in contrast to aliens who were not Israelites but lived among them) were more likely to be commercial transactions. This is consistent with traditional Jewish interpretation that understood this call for release not to apply to "unpaid wages, bills owed to shopkeepers for merchandise, and certain types of secured loans" (Tigay: 143). The distinction between *a member of the community* and *a foreigner* may thus have more to do with the nature of the loan than the identity of the person making the loan. Deuteronomy is spelling out a vision for a community with an economic safety net that allows those who have been caught in the cycle of poverty to escape: it is not setting policies for commercial activity.

At the center of the chiasm (C) stands the phrase *because the LORD's remission has been proclaimed*. When compared with the release edicts of the day, it is striking that there is no mention of a king. The literary context for the book, with Israel in Moab before its entrance into the land (west of the Jordan), does not explain this omission. Later Deuteronomy explicitly allows Israel to have a king (17:14-20). Rather, this establishes the regulation by the authority of the God of Israel: protection of the weak is too important to make it depend on the whim or will of a king. Nor is release to be used by the king for political purposes. Release is grounded in the nature of God and in God's relationship to Israel, a relationship shaped by Israel having been released from Egyptian slavery by that God.

15:4-6 Consequences of Obedience

After clarifying the law of release (vv. 2-3, although even these verses have an exhortative quality about them), Deuteronomy makes a case for obedience. Motivation for obedience takes the form of exhortation (see vv. 7-11) and a description of the consequences of obedience and disobedience (vv. 4-6). These consequences are not legal penalties but a general characterization of what life will be like if Israel obeys or disobeys.

This speaks to the apparent contradiction between the statement in verse 4 (*There will, however, be no one in need among you*) and the statement in verse 11 (*Since there will never cease to be some in need on the earth*). To suggest that these two statements reflect some editor including contradictory passages from different sources does not respect the intelligence of that final editor or writer. The contradiction is as obvious to any ancient person as to us. Rather, the two statements have a different role or picture in mind.

Verse 4 is painting a picture of what will happen in Israel if it fully obeys: *if only you will obey the LORD your God by diligently observing this entire commandment that I command you today* (v. 5). Obedience leads to blessing in the land *God is giving you as a possession to occupy* (v. 4b; cf. v. 6a), leading to abundance for all. It hints that if Israel truly is faithful to the commands of God, the release regulations will become superfluous since the kind of crisis loans they are responding to will be unnecessary. God is giving Israel a good land, an abundant land, a land of milk and honey, through which God will richly bless Israel if only it is obedient to the directions God is giving it through this book. This is the utopian expression of Deuteronomic theology.

The blessings resulting from obedience will not only come to the poor but also the whole people will benefit. This is the logic of the last verse of this portion: *You will lend to many nations, but you will not borrow; you will rule over many nations, but they will not rule over you.* The link between financial wealth and power was recognized by ancient society as well. Debt inevitably brings a power differential between the two parties. This is true on an individual level, and it is true on a national level. In this idealistic depiction, obedience leads to blessing, which leads to no needy people, which leads to a wealthy corporate reality, which leads to national influence. Here is the crux: *If only* Israel *will obey* . . . (v. 5)!

15:7-11 *Exhortation: Give Generously to Those in Need*

At the center of the Deuteronomic sabbatical release provisions, and perhaps their most important element, is a stirring exhortation calling for generosity to those in need (vv. 7-11). After painting a picture of what Israel's world will be like if it is fully obedient to God's commands, the text moves to the real world of Israel. Needy people are part of that real world, and so Israel, or perhaps more accurately those within Israel who have the resources to do so, is exhorted to be generous in its dealings with the disadvantaged. Deuteronomy's instructions for living in the land are directed toward all of Israel, but the economic directions have special relevance for those with means, those in a position to make a difference.

The force and effect of the exhortation are achieved through a blend of rhetorical techniques. First, the passage includes a remarkable combination of carrot-and-stick statements: positive encouragement mixed with harsh warnings, rewards for obedience, and consequences for disobedience.

Opening context
If there is among you anyone in need, a member of your community in any of your towns within the land that the LORD your God is giving you . . . (15:7)

Statements of encouragement
- *You should rather open your hand, willingly lending enough to meet the need, whatever it may be.* (15:8)

- *Give liberally and be ungrudging when you do so.* (15:10)

- *I therefore command you, "Open your hand to the poor and needy neighbor in your land."* (15:11)

Statements of warning
- *Do not be hard-hearted or tight-fisted toward your needy neighbor.* (15:7)

- *Be careful that you do not entertain a mean thought, thinking, "The seventh year, the year of remission, is near," and therefore view your needy neighbor with hostility and give nothing.* (15:9)

Rewards of obedience
For on this account the LORD your God will bless you in all your work and in all that you undertake. (15:10)

Consequences of disobedience
Your neighbor might cry to the LORD against you, and you would incur guilt. (15:9)

Closing context
Since there will never cease to be someone in need on the earth. (15:11)

Second, Deuteronomy emphasizes the totality of the response invited through the prominent use of body language, much of it unfortunately lost in the NRSV (P. Miller 1990: 136; cf. C. Wright 1996: 190-91). Similar to the Shema, which called on the Israelite to love God with heart, soul, and mind (6:4), here *hand, heart,* and *eye* all are named. Attitude and action, emotion and will—all are involved in the generous response. Although the NRSV only uses *hand* twice in the passage, the Hebrew word for hand occurs five times, in verses 2 (AT, *the loan of your hand*), 3 (RSV, *but whatever of yours is with your brother your hand shall release*), 7 (*tight-fisted*), 8, and 11. It is used with four slightly different connotations, with the last and possibly most important sense used twice: the hand owns the loan (v. 2), it can release the loan (v. 3), it can refuse the loan (v. 7), and it can be generous (vv. 8, 11). The hand reflects and represents the power the wealthy have over the poor.

The *heart*, the place of decision making, is named thrice in the exhortation, each time with an ominous tone: *Do not be hard-hearted* (v. 7). *Do not entertain a mean thought* (v. 9; RSV, *Take heed lest there be a base thought in your heart*). *Give ... and be ungrudging* (v. 10; RSV, *your heart shall not be grudging when you give to him*). Each is a "warning against a malicious will. . . . Deuteronomy is well aware of the self-interest of those who wield economic power and dictate economic policy and realizes that justice for the poor requires a wholly different mind-set translated into personal and political willpower" (C. Wright 1996: 191). It is through the *eye* that the more prosperous Israelite sees the poor person (v. 9, <u>view</u> *your needy neighbor;* v. 18, *Do not consider it a hardship,* lit., *Do not make it hard/difficult in your eyes*). Deuteronomy calls for full obedience, and this requires that the total person responds.

Third, the passage employs rich relational language (P. Miller 1990: 136). The needy person is not far removed, but a *neighbor* (vv. 7, 9 [twice], 11), *a member of your community* (lit., *brother,* v. 7; cf. vv. 2, 3). The repeated use of personal pronouns reinforces this. Twenty-one times in this short passage some form of the second-person pronoun is used. The message comes from *your* God and is directed at *you.* The needy are *your* neighbors, *your* brothers and sisters, living in *your* land. If *you* open *your* hand to the needy, God will bless *you* and *your* work. This piling up of personal pronouns highlights the connection between the text and the audience, as well as uniting various groups and actions: God and the people, the well-to-do and the needy, action and consequence.

Fourth, Deuteronomy employs a Hebrew grammatical style that intensifies the force of a verb through the use of the imperfect followed by the infinitive absolute of the same verb. An example of this appears in a literal translation of verse 8: *But opening, you shall open your hand to him; lending, you shall lend enough to him for his needs that he needs* (AT). The NRSV misses the first example of this construction entirely and translates the second with the term *willingly*. Deuteronomy uses this technique more in this chapter than anywhere else in the book, thereby heightening the intensity of the exhortation.

Fifth, the passage warns Israel that if it does not obey, the needy person *might cry to the LORD against you, and you would incur guilt* (v. 9). Here is a reminder of their Egyptian slave experience, when "the Israelites groaned under their slavery, and cried out. . . . Their cry for help rose up to God," and God responded by delivering them from their oppressors (Exod 2:23). With this the text links the needy with the oppressed Israelites in Egypt and, perhaps more forcefully, links the person who begrudges help to the poor with the Egyptian oppressors. The prominence of the exodus story within Israel's thinking makes this an extremely persuasive argument. After opening with the brief apodictic law (15:1), followed by a short explanation of it (vv. 2-3), Deuteronomy devotes eight verses to an eloquent plea to the audience, calling it to respond in a manner consistent with God's will. This is not impersonal law but emotional preaching.

The Sabbatical Slave Release 15:12-18

In the ancient world debt could easily lead to the loss of personal freedom and to debt slavery. The sabbatical slave release provision thus is a natural follow-up to the debt release provision. It uses the same structure as the debt release provision, with an opening directive (v. 12), a clarification of the directive (vv. 13-14), followed by exhortations (vv. 15, 18). In addition it adds a short exception clause (vv. 16-17).

15:12 *The Slave Release Command*

Sabbatical release applies not only to debts but also to debt slavery that could so easily result when a person is unable to pay a debt. This passage envisions such a situation. Although both the debt release law (vv. 1-11) and the slave release law (vv. 12-18) speak of the *seventh year*, this need not be the same year. Whereas the debt release law assumes a common year for the whole people (see v. 9), the timing of the slave release law is triggered by the date someone becomes a slave. Any year can be a year for slave release.

The double reference to Hebrew is noteworthy. Not only is the one sold into slavery *a member of your community* (lit., *your brother*, cf. vv. 2, 7), the person also is a *Hebrew man or a Hebrew woman* (only here in Deuteronomy). Perhaps to our surprise, Israelites are not often called "Hebrew" in the Old Testament: only thirty-five times in all, and only five times after 1 Samuel (1 Chron 24:27, "Ibri"; Jer 34:9 [twice, as in Deut 15:12, for male and female Hebrew slaves]; 34:14; Jon 1:9). Although there is considerable debate on the issue, it is possible the term "Hebrew" is related to the word *ḫābiru*, a term used in the ancient Near East for a lower class of people without roots, without land, who sold their services to whatever country or lord would employ them (Moore, Bishop, and Kelle: 109–10, 125). The descendants of Jacob, living in Egypt and building storehouses for Pharaoh, may have been such *ḫābiru*. It probably is no coincidence that it is in Exodus where Israelites are most often called Hebrews, fourteen times. At some point the term "Hebrew" came to be used of Israelites as a people, with ethnic connotations.

C. Wright proposes that in this verse the term has this earlier meaning, one with class connotations rather than ethnic meaning (1996: 192). This slave release law then does not govern Israelites as much as those considered to be *ḫābiru*. In light of Deuteronomy's heavy emphasis on the unity of the people, however, this proposal is not persuasive. The passage is addressing the loss of personal freedom resulting from economic disparity among the people, not foreign slaves who have been captured or purchased (notice the distinction in Lev 25:39-46). With this term Deuteronomy is once again making use of Israel's story. It then becomes an emotionally charged term, reminding the audience that the person selling oneself into slavery as well as the one buying that person both at one point were without land and means, *ḫābiru* in a foreign country.

The passage explicitly includes both man and woman. The inclusion of women in the provision is reinforced later, in the last sentence of verse 17. The equality of men and women within the Deuteronomic slave release law is in contrast to the older slave release law of Exodus 21:2-11 that exempts female slaves from the release (although see the treatment of this passage by W. Janzen 2000: 291–93). Deuteronomy does not directly challenge the ancient Near Eastern institution of slavery, but it does undermine it, raising unsettling questions about the system.

15:13-14 The Manner of Release

The manner of release portion does not spell out in detail conditions that govern when a slave is released, which might open up loopholes for the slave owner or refine or clarify the law in any way—what is not said may be as significant as what is said—but it exhorts the slave owner not to send out the newly freed person *empty-handed*. A person in debt slavery would have lost all personal resources, including access to the land, the source of the blessing. A freed slave then would have virtually no alternative but to once more sell oneself into a new cycle of slavery. Simply implementing the law in a legalistic manner achieves little. Deuteronomy follows up the basic law with a challenge to the slave owner to make it possible for the newly freed person to really start over, with the potential of being successful.

The phrase *provide liberally* is a further example of the double verb construction (imperfect with infinitive absolute) noticed in verses 7-11. The verb is based on a word that means "garland" or "necklace," a term that can signify honor and extravagance (McConville 2002: 263). With this language the text makes the point that the newly freed slave shall not leave penniless, with a bad reputation, but as someone with new potential. One is reminded of Israel's escape from Egypt, when the people received jewelry and clothes for their new start (Exod 12:35-36; cf. Ezra 1:6-11). The supplies to be given, *out of your flock, your threshing floor, and your wine press*, represent the major categories of agricultural products: animals, grains, and fruits (cf. 7:13). Each is directly dependent on the land, the gift of God to all. Through encouragement to the former slave owner, the provision works toward helping the freed person become free and independent, to begin receiving blessings from the land. If this is followed, then the *bounty with which the LORD has blessed you* will remain.

15:15 Exhortation: Remember

The exhortation opens with a key Deuteronomic term, *Remember* (see ch. 8), and returns to a favorite theme, Israel's deliverance from Egyptian oppression. This reminder has special force within the context of the slave release law. After all, Israel as a whole has been enslaved in Egypt, until God redeemed them and brought them to the Promised Land. Every time a slave is released within Israel, a new exodus takes place. How can an Israelite who knows the story of the Egyptian bondage and deliverance refuse to release a fellow Hebrew who has been forced to sell oneself into servitude?

15:16-17 An Escape Clause

Normally slaves will only too joyfully accept their freedom and receive the gifts the slave owner will give them. But the text does allow for the exceptional situation where a slave (and again, both male and female slave are explicitly identified) finds the current situation sufficiently attractive that instead of risking the freedom of independence, the slave prefers to remain bound to the master. If that happens, a special ceremony is required to formalize this relationship.

The slave release law in the book of Exodus introduces this ceremony with the direction *Then his master shall bring him before God* (Exod 21:6), implying that the ceremony takes place at a sanctuary. Deuteronomy's elimination of all sanctuaries other than the one at The Place makes this impractical (cf. Deuteronomy's approach to animal slaughter, 12:15-27). The absence of any reference to place allows the ceremony to occur at the home of the slave owner. The meaning of the ceremony itself, with the piercing of the *earlobe into the door*, is unclear. It may have the connotation that the slave is to listen to the directions of the master. An Egyptian word for slave literally means "listener" (Tigay: 150). It may also be a way of marking the slave by putting a tag through the ear. Or thrusting the awl through the ear *into the door* may represent the slave's attachment to a particular household. Ancient ceremonies and customs, not unlike modern ones, can have multiple meanings, some of which are lost over time. Whatever the sense, through some symbolic ceremony the slave—and notice that it is the slave's initiative and decision—makes a commitment to remain with the master.

The reference to the slave loving the master, especially when used within the context of a ritual ceremony, reminds one of its use in political treaties of the day *[Deuteronomy, Covenant, and Political Treaties, p. 547]*. Emotional connotations, however, are not to be dismissed. Its use here may suggest a formal covenant with mutual obligations.

When the slave chooses to remain with the master, it is *forever*. Traditional Jewish exegesis interprets this to mean until the death of the master, or until the next Jubilee (Lev 25:39-46), whichever comes first (Tigay: 150). If correct, this places a significant limitation on the *forever*, for the arrangement is a permanent *personal* relationship, without the slave having become property that can be passed on as part of the master's estate. This fits the tone of the passage. The norm is that in the seventh year the slave owner will release the slave and provide the freed slave with generous provisions, making a new start possible. On those rare occasions when the slave chooses to remain with the master, this is permissible, but even then the slave does not become property.

15:18 Concluding Exhortation

The concluding exhortation speaks to the feelings or attitude of the slaveholder releasing the slave. The effort to persuade the slave owner that releasing the slave is the right thing to do is consistent with the regulations being voluntary. The appeal is to the economic fairness of the release. The master should not consider the release *a hardship* (lit., *Do not consider it a hard thing in your eyes*) because for six years the debt slave has served the master well. Differences in translation expose an ambiguity in the Hebrew. Has the slave given value equal to that of *hired labors* (as implied by the NRSV), or has the slave given double value (implied by NIV, KJV, RSV, etc.)? In either case, even when judged economically, the slave release law is fair. Additionally, following it will result in God blessing *you in all that you do*. The slave owner thus should take this step happily, with no hard feelings.

THE TEXT IN BIBLICAL CONTEXT

Old Testament Release Regulations

Three other passages in the Old Testament speak to some type of release, all of them linked to the Sabbath or the seven-day cycle. The oldest is likely the regulation requiring that all land be left fallow every seven years (Exod 23:10-11). It explicitly gives its purpose "that the poor of your people may eat." It is very possible that Deuteronomy has expanded upon this requirement in its release provisions. The Exodus passage is the only other provision that uses the Hebrew term translated *release* in Deuteronomy 15. Exodus also includes a slave release decree (21:1-11). The year of Jubilee passage of Leviticus is the most extensive and may be an expansion of the Deuteronomic provision. It requires, among other matters, that land be returned to its original owners, that it be left fallow, and that slaves be freed (Lev 25:8-55).

Despite the considerable debate on the subject, there is no consensus on how these passages relate to each other. The differences between them make it difficult to attempt to harmonize them into one consistent set of regulations (note the effort of C. Wright 1996: 197). They may reflect different historical eras, with the Exodus passages the oldest and the Leviticus passage the most recent.

Theologically it is more important to notice the distinctive elements of the Deuteronomic versions in order to get at their central concern, rather than to use these as a way of reconstructing the history of the practice in Israel.

When compared with the other regulations, three elements stand out in the Deuteronomic version. First, Deuteronomy makes a point of including male and female slaves equally in the regulation. Deuteronomy does not represent some contemporary understanding of equal rights, but by twice emphasizing that both male and female are to be released (vv. 12, 17), Deuteronomy begins to challenge the tendency of the time to treat women simply as property. Both men and women are to benefit from the blessings God has given Israel via the land.

Second, the exhortation to give liberally to the released slave is unique to Deuteronomy. Both the Exodus and Leviticus versions stop at the release itself. Deuteronomy goes beyond the release to call for generous treatment of the one released. Justice is not legalistic, nor simply following regulations, but includes treating disadvantaged people in a way that allows them to escape a cycle of poverty, debt, and loss of freedom.

Third, the Deuteronomic version is filled with preaching, with words of encouragement, warning, motivation, and rationale for the actions outlined. In fact, exhortation seems to play a more important role than the regulation itself. This is consistent with the previous comment. Deuteronomy is not a document setting forth law in any modern sense as much as a presentation of a vision for what a faithful community would look like.

Outside of the Pentateuch these release provisions become virtually invisible. This raises the question of whether they were ever practiced. Jeremiah's indictment of Judah for not "granting a release to your neighbors and friends" (34:17) indicates that among some, the release provisions were considered realistic and not merely utopian, at least during a time of severe crisis; this is true even if it also makes clear that they were not followed by all or generally (for a discussion of the larger question of justice in Scripture, see the TBC following 19:1-21).

THE TEXT IN THE LIFE OF THE CHURCH
"True Evangelical Faith"

Menno Simons loved to quote Scripture, and his thematic verse was 1 Corinthians 3:11, "For no one can lay any foundation other than the one that has been laid; that foundation is Jesus Christ." But he understood that building on this foundation had social and economic implications. He thus also wrote, "True evangelical faith . . . cannot lie dormant, but . . . clothes the naked, . . . feeds the hungry, . . . shelters the destitute" (Menno: 307). In other words, making Jesus the church's foundation has practical implications for how we live our lives. This is more than an abstract commitment to social justice. As the quote from Menno highlights, it must be translated into concrete terms that serve those in need. Menno may not have quoted Deuteronomy 15, but his approach is entirely consistent with it.

Early Mennonite pioneers in the Canadian prairies had a unique way of giving their faith concrete content. When a group of families settled in a particular region, they would soon construct a house for worship. The architecture of these buildings tended to be quite plain, both for financial and theological reasons. But it was common to include a large loft, well supported by strong beams. Into this loft the farmers would carry valuable grain from their fields that would be made available for those in need. The church building became both a place of worship and a food bank. Here was an almost literal application of the Deuteronomic third-year tithe requirement. Those early communities also established credit unions, which were used for mutual aid.

Those customs have largely disappeared as Mennonites have integrated into larger society and as support of the disadvantaged is understood more as a societal responsibility administered by the government. But these examples from the past, especially when viewed in light of the biblical trajectory from tithe to benevolence, raise an important question: Is the generally acknowledged responsibility of the "haves" in the church to support those in need most faithfully met through structured programs or "taxes" that attempt to ensure that this happens—or through consistent encouragement to charity and generosity?

Deuteronomy's tithe is an example of a structured program, based on an assumption of general bounty, with the goal of ensuring that all in need can eat their fill. But other biblical passages hint that tithes could become obligatory taxes, with people complying, yet in as mechanical a manner as possible. Or they might attempt to escape the tithe entirely by finding loopholes in the expectation. In either case justice and righteousness are not served, and the communal rejoicing called for by Deuteronomy is lost. Structured programs also run the risk of being controlled by the religious leadership, which can manipulate them for their own benefit. Yet when a nonprogrammatic approach results in widows being neglected, the early church develops a program to rectify this (Acts 6:1-6). The Bible thus presents us with both sides. Perhaps particular times and places require a structured approach, and other times call for an approach based more in an inspired generosity. What approach best fits our time and the global village we inhabit?

Liberation Theology, Preferential Option for the Poor, Jubilee 2000

The writings of Gustavo Gutiérrez and other liberation theologians of the late twentieth century are a sharp challenge to the dominant theology of the day. Although criticized by some, their emphasis on a "Preferential Option for the Poor" is generally recognized as a legitimate appropriation of the biblical gospel. Catholic social teaching now incorporates the liberationist moral test concerning how our most vulnerable are faring.

Perhaps not surprisingly, liberation theologians have tended not to make extensive use of Deuteronomy in their writings. Their favored texts come from Exodus, with its focus on the deliverance of Israel from Egyptian slavery and oppression, and the classical prophets, with their indictments of society for abuse of the weak. Liberation theology is created out of oppression, whether economic, racist, or other.

Like liberation theology, Deuteronomy raises up the story of the exodus as the clearest window into the identity of God and what God does. Yet Deuteronomy is not addressing an Israel in Egypt, but an Israel that has been liberated from Egypt and has received the blessing of the Promised Land. In that land, Deuteronomy calls on Israel to live in a manner consistent with the will of the God of the exodus.

Inspired especially by the call for a fiftieth-year Jubilee in Leviticus (chs. 25-27)—an expansion of the Deuteronomic release provisions—an international Jubilee 2000 movement arose in the 1990s with the goal of wiping out $90 billion of debt owed by the world's poorest nations. Although initiated within church settings, it quickly caught the imagination of activists and became a worldwide campaign, with leaders like Prime Minister Blair of Great Britain expressing support for debt forgiveness. Although falling short of its initial goal, some significant debt releases took place. After 2000, the movement continues through national organizations like Jubilee USA. Remarkably, an Old Testament vision for justice and the reduction of poverty has become relevant once again.

Deuteronomy, however, goes beyond liberation, debt release, and opposing injustice. It imagines a new society that incorporates practices preventing oppression and undermining the natural harshness of society. Gutiérrez recognizes this when he says, "It is not simply a matter of denouncing poverty," and then repeatedly references Deuteronomic provisions that help provide for the disadvantaged (167). The vision of Deuteronomy is for a community of brothers and sisters in which concrete provisions protect those most vulnerable from exploitation. It provides clues as to what a preferential option for the poor might look like in a particular context.

Breaking the Cycle

In many ways the world of our day is quite different from the world of Deuteronomy. But in one way it is all too similar: once a family or community has become trapped in a cycle of poverty, it is extremely difficult to escape. The Christian Reformed Church describes the cycle of poverty as a "phenomenon where poor families become trapped in poverty for generations. Because they have no or limited access to critical resources, such as education and financial services, subsequent generations are also impoverished." Sadly, despite all the wealth and development in the western world, the bars imprisoning people in this cycle are becoming stronger and harder to break.

It is exactly such a cycle that Deuteronomy's release provisions attack. All in Israel are brothers and sisters, members of the community God has redeemed, with the gifted land an inheritance and token of that blessing. The vicissitudes of life can wreak material havoc on a family. The sabbatical release provisions aim at preventing such setbacks from permanently trapping families in such a cycle of poverty.

Governments, not-for-profits, and Christian communities have initiated programs to similarly break the cycle of poverty. In 2009, Ontario's Ministry of Children and Youth Services launched a program called "Breaking the Cycle," with the goal of reducing poverty. With a vision to help people "experience God's love and unleash their potential to earn a livelihood," Mennonite Economic Development Associates (MEDA) creatively finds "business solutions to poverty" by providing entrepreneurial skills and economic opportunity that help people out of the cycle.

Some congregations in central Kansas are finding resources via social work organizations, such as Bridges out of Poverty and Circles USA, to help families escape the cycle, to "inspire and equip families and communities to resolve poverty and thrive" (Bridges; R. Payne et al.; Circles). There may be debate about what factors contribute to the cycle of poverty: no doubt a similar debate existed in the Israel of Deuteronomy. And yet Deuteronomy challenges us, *Open your hand to the poor and needy . . . in your land* (15:11).

Deuteronomy 15:19–16:17

Part 2D, Unit 3
Festivals and the Cult

OVERVIEW

When viewed through the lenses of belief, ritual, and ethics, ancient religions tended to place a heavy emphasis on cult, the ritual aspect of the religion *[Cult, p. 546]*. The important place of sacrifice is a prime example of that. Major festivals are a further example. The religion of biblical Israel is ancient and thus places considerable emphasis on the cult as well. The extensive regulations of Leviticus and Numbers reflect that reality *[Sacrifices and Offerings, p. 565]*.

But is the contemporary church that different? Consider how your congregation practices child dedication, or the Lord's Supper, or how funerals are observed. Think of how difficult it may be to make a minor change in the order of worship, or to agree on when a program of the church meets. Ritual and tradition are integral to our life together. Not only do these rituals vary greatly from denomination to denomination, but also from community to community within a denomination. Sometimes the original rationale for the ritual is forgotten, yet the ritual continues. More often leadership at least has a clear theological explanation for the ritual, even if the ritual or explanation may be quite different in another community.

Deuteronomy has a number of passages that deal with Israel's cult and festivals. The significance of cultic ritual along with its ambiguities is reflected in Deuteronomy's mixture of regulations. Yet Deuteronomy demonstrates limited interest in the details of the cult. In this, Deuteronomy is different from some of the priestly writings in the Pentateuch. Whether Deuteronomy is describing how to offer the firstborn of the herds or flocks (15:19-23), or how to celebrate the great festivals of Israel's calendar (16:1-17), the book appears to take Israel's cultic life for granted, and then uses it to espouse its particular theological emphases. One can question whether Moshe Weinfeld's language of secularization fully captures the nuance (1972), yet it seems indisputable that Deuteronomy represents a significant step away from a primarily cultic religion to one that places comparatively greater emphasis on ethics, on how Israel lives as the people of God.

Later passages continue this discussion of the cult: 16:21-17:1; 23:1-8, 17-18, 21-23.

OUTLINE

Consecrating the Firstborn, 15:19-23
A Festival Calendar for The Place, 16:1-17
    16:1-8   Passover and Unleavened Bread
    16:9-12   Festival of Weeks
    16:13-15   Festival of Booths
    16:16-17   Concluding Summary

EXPLANATORY NOTES

Consecrating the Firstborn 15:19-23

Firstfruits belong to God, the firstborn from the human womb, the firstborn from herds and flocks, and the firstfruits of the fields and orchards (Exod 13:2, 10-16; 22:29-30; 23:19; Lev 27:26-27; Deut 12:6, 17; 14:23; 26:2-10). Reflecting the patriarchal culture, this means male both for humans and animals, even if not always stated explicitly (cf. Exod 13:2 with 13:11-16). Originally this custom may have been understood as a gift to God, a kind of "rental" payment to God as the owner of the land.

But Israel has moved beyond this. All reproduction, whether of seed or of animal, is a product of God's blessing. Returning the *firstling male born of your herd and flock* to God acknowledges this reality (Deut 15:19). By consecrating (i.e., recognizing as holy) the animal, the Israelite worshiper is setting the animal apart from the rest, removing it from profane use. Moreover, in Exodus it is converted into a reminder of Israel's deliverance from Egypt: the firstborn of the Egyptians died in the tenth plague (Exod 13:11-16) while Israel's were redeemed. The practice thus combined a gift of thanksgiving to God for blessings received with a commemoration of God's foundational redemptive act.

Deuteronomy's audience knows and understands this tradition. Deuteronomy thus states the expectation succinctly (v. 19a) and then offers its particular contribution in the expansion (vv. 19b-23). In its present context the passage serves as a transition between the sabbatical release provisions (15:1-18) and the festival calendar (16:1-17; cf. the role of the tithe provisions, 14:22-29). The reference to work (v. 19; cf. 15:12), the motif of giving away that to which one could have a claim, and the symbolic reminder of the exodus—all recall the social concern of the immediately preceding release provisions.

Deuteronomy's particular interest appears in the expansion (vv. 19b-22). Whereas in Exodus the firstling is offered to God on the eighth day, presumably at a location within the local community, Deuteronomy's centralization requirement makes that impossible. In Deuteronomy the presentation of the firstling becomes an annual event (*year by year*), for which Israel comes to the central sanctuary (*at the place that the* LORD *will choose*, v. 20). Here each *household* eats together *in the presence of the* LORD, perhaps in connection with one of the major festivals that are celebrated at The Place (16:1-18).

The prohibition not to work the animal or shear it (v. 19b), a prohibition not needed if the animal is offered to God on the eighth day, prevents the farmer from receiving any economic benefit from the animal during its life since it belongs to God (Nelson 2002: 200). The term translated *work* (v. 19b) also yields the term "slave." Not working the animal during this time represents the freedom Israel has received. The holy animal in their midst serves as a visible reminder to the people that they also have been made holy, or consecrated, and redeemed from slavery in Egypt.

Once the animal has been presented to God at The Place, God returns it to the community. God does not need the offering for food and shares it with the household in another festive banquet. Taking the animal to the sanctuary may be an extra chore, but it also gives the event greater importance.

The passage concludes by exempting all defective firstborn animals from the regulation (vv. 22-23). Blindness and lameness make the animal incomplete, lacking sight and the ability to walk. Giving God an offering with a shortcoming is an affront to God and "incongruent with the character of YHWH, who has given generously to Israel and who cannot receive back from Israel an offering unworthy of that generosity" (Brueggemann 2001: 171). Deuteronomy calls on Israel to offer only its best.

Deuteronomy makes no provision for the redemption of a flawed firstborn but simply stipulates that it may be eaten within the local community. Since it has not been consecrated to God, the ritually unclean are welcome to participate in the communal benefit. The one condition is that they must refrain from eating its blood (see on 12:15-27).

A Festival Calendar for The Place 16:1-17

Festivals and celebrations play an important role in all societies. Consider the significance of national independence celebrations for countries, or harvest festivals in an agricultural community. For the church, Christmas and Easter are central in its calendar. At those times the identity of a people is reflected and reinforced, the rhythm of the year is marked, and work takes a backseat to food, fellowship, and custom.

If anything, festivals were even more significant in ancient societies, where the daily grind of routine and survival was so all-consuming. Each year Israel celebrates three such festivals: (1) Passover and Unleavened Bread, in spring; (2) Feast of Harvest, or Weeks, in summer; (3) Feast of Ingathering, or Booths, in fall.

The importance of these festivals is reflected in the number of times they are introduced or prescribed: Exodus 23:14-17; 34:18-24; Leviticus 23:4-44; Numbers 28–29; Deuteronomy 16:1-17. In addition, much of Exodus 12–13 deals with the Passover and Unleavened Bread celebration.

The festival calendar of Exodus 23:14-17 likely informs the Deuteronomic version (e.g., Nelson 2002: 203). The points of contact are striking: each commands Israel to *observe* (Deut 16:1; Exod 23:15-16), each speaks of not appearing before God *empty-handed* (Deut 16:16; Exod 23:15), and each summarizes the expectation with virtually identical language, *Three times a [in the] year all your males shall appear before the* LORD *God* (Deut 16:16; Exod 23:17). Deuteronomy is not introducing these festivals to Israel but giving its particular interpretation of celebrations well known by its audience.

Even a cursory comparison between the Exodus and Deuteronomic passages draws attention to one significant difference: whereas Exodus 23 introduces them as three quite parallel festivals, Deuteronomy divides them into two groups. In Exodus each celebration is introduced by the same phrase, "You shall observe the festival of . . . ," and each is then named, followed by a brief description. The introduction to the passage, "Three times in the year you shall hold a festival for me" (Exod 23:14), fits their parallel nature. In

Deuteronomy, Passover with Unleavened Bread receives considerably greater attention (eight verses) than Weeks (four verses) and Booths (three verses). In Deuteronomy, Passover with Unleavened Bread is the most important event of the year. The more detailed descriptions confirm this first impression.

16:1-8 Passover and Unleavened Bread

The first verse summarizes the basic instruction: the command to observe, the general time of the event, its identification as Passover, the command to keep the event for *the LORD your God*, and the historical connection. The next seven verses then expand upon this.

The term *observe* (v. 1) immediately reminds us of the Sabbath command that similarly opens with the command to observe, or keep (5:12). Moreover, the four other festival calendars in the Old Testament either include Sabbath instructions (Exod 34:18-24; Num 28-29) or give them immediately before the festivals (Exod 23:12-17; Lev 23:3-44). Further, both the Sabbath command and the Deuteronomic festival calendar include the reminder *Remember that you were a slave in [the land of] Egypt* (5:15; 16:12). The weekly cycle, climaxing in the Sabbath, is central to the rhythm of cultic life in Israel: the festivals build on that foundation. This connection also reminds one of the Sabbath principle, the inseparable relationship between observing the Sabbath and a concern for social justice (see on 5:14-15; 15:1-18).

This first festival occurs in the month of Abib. The Jewish calendar is based on a lunar cycle, beginning in early spring. Abib, the first month of the year, overlaps our March and April. The Passover and Unleavened Bread celebration thus is not only the first major event of the year; it also inaugurates the year. The grammar of the verse, with its command to *Observe the month of Abib* (i.e., the whole month), supports this direction. The new beginning that Israel experienced in the exodus from Egypt sets the tone for each new year (cf. Exod 12:2, "This month shall mark for you the beginning of months; it shall be the first month of the year for you").

Deuteronomy's lack of interest in cultic detail is reflected already in this opening verse. Unless the Hebrew behind *month* (NRSV, NIV, KJV, etc.) is given the unlikely translation of "new moon," the verse does not give a specific date for the Passover. Exodus 12-13 instructs the Israelite to select a lamb on the tenth day of the month, and then keep it until the fourteenth day. On that evening the lamb is to be slaughtered, "roasted over the fire with unleavened bread and bitter herbs" (Exod 12:8). It is not to be eaten "raw or boiled in water" (12:9). The dearth of detail in Deuteronomy is not evidence of disagreement but a sense that the audience already knows the festival and its details.

The lack of detail does not weaken its clear pedagogical role: to commemorate Israel's foundational saving event. The opening verse connects it with God's deliverance from Egypt (16:1), and verse 3 identifies the goal: *so that all the days of your life you may remember the day of your departure from the land of Egypt*. Even the name *Passover* makes the connection, with *pesaḥ* (possibly "to skip" or "to limp") reminding Israel of the angel of death passing over those doors with blood on the lintel and doorposts as part of the tenth plague (Exod 12:12-13).

The *unleavened bread* is called *the bread of affliction* and represents the *great haste* with which Israel had to flee Egypt (v. 3). On that night there was no time to wait for the bread to rise. Unleavened bread thus was the answer. Even today it is sometimes the bread of choice when a meal must be prepared quickly. But the absence of leaven also symbolizes a new beginning. Today yeast is normally used as leaven, but in ancient times bread would be leavened by some dough from a previous batch that had been left to ferment. Bread with leaven in it thus represented continuity with past; unleavened bread represented a new future (W. Janzen 2000: 159).

The awe-inspiring escape from Egypt initiated a new phase in the story of Israel and its God. Passover and Unleavened Bread is the first and foundational observance in Israel's cultic calendar, but rejoicing is muted as they remember the slavery from which God has delivered them. Given Deuteronomy's emphasis on rejoicing when the community gathers at The Place, the absence of any such reference in this passage cannot be accidental. Instead of rejoicing, the climax to the event is a *solemn assembly for the* LORD *your God* (v. 8). Although Deuteronomy calls on Israel to keep the *festival of weeks* (16:9-12) and the *festival of booths* (vv. 13-15), it does not in a parallel way invite Israel to keep the festival of the Passover. The concluding summary does speak of the *festival of unleavened bread* (v. 16), but the absence of the term *rejoice* in the more extensive description of the Passover is consistent with the more somber mood Deuteronomy gives this first event in the calendar compared to the other two (vv. 1-8).

Consistent with the centralizing requirement of chapter 12, the Passover celebration is to be kept only *at the place that the* LORD *will choose as a dwelling for his name* (16:2). Verses 5-7 return to this theme: *You are not permitted to offer the passover sacrifice within any of your towns. ... But at the place that the* LORD *your God will choose, ... only there shall you offer the passover sacrifice*. Deuteronomy may not be concerned with cultic details, but precisely *where* the Passover is kept is of critical importance. Within the space of eight verses, the centralization formula occurs three times (vv. 2, 6, 7), with four verses highlighting this expectation (vv. 2, 5, 6, 7).

The original Passover event in Egypt may have taken place in homes, and its celebration during the time of the monarchy appears to have been in household units within local communities. Nevertheless, for Deuteronomy it is to be a national celebration at the central sanctuary (as in 2 Kings 23:21-22; cf. 2 Chron 30:1-27). Family and households might still celebrate it together (cf. Jesus and his disciples coming to Jerusalem for the celebration, but then having the Last Supper in the upper room), but centralization places greater central control on overall practice and abolishes rural and variant customs that could develop. Deuteronomy's concern that Israel's worship remain faithful to the only God is evident here as well.

The Deuteronomic chronology for the event may not be entirely clear, but the outline is there. The rhythm of the seven-day cycle and its connection with the Sabbath are evident. Israel is to eat unleavened bread for seven days (16:3). Later we read it is to eat unleavened bread for six days, and then *on the seventh there shall be a solemn assembly for the* LORD *your God when you shall do no work* (v. 8). On the basis of Exodus, we know that the Passover sacrifice took place on the evening of the fourteenth day of Abib. These verses suggest that for the following six days Israel continued the celebration by eating unleavened bread, concluding with a communal assembly on the seventh day. This last day, as on every Sabbath, Israel is to refrain from work. Just as each Sunday is a minicelebration of Easter and the resurrection of Jesus, so each Sabbath is a commemoration of the exodus and the deliverance from hard work forced upon them by Egypt.

The account does raise a few questions. The directive that there be *no leaven . . . in all your territory for seven days* (16:4) is unusual, with its significance unclear. Since leaven could also be a symbol of corruption, Hall suggests, "There was a sort of purity symbolism in the feast as well as the reminder of the Exodus" (264). Further, the note that after eating the Passover they *may go back to your tents* (v. 7) also is not clear. Again, does this reflect a time when the celebration was taking place in the local communities? Or does this simply assume that the people have made their pilgrimage to the central sanctuary, and now return to their temporary dwellings around the sanctuary?

Perhaps most complex is the historical challenge. The opening verse identifies the celebration as *Passover*. But when the festival calendar is summarized at the end of the passage, it is called *the festival of unleavened bread* (16:16). It is possible that Passover and Unleavened Bread had quite separate origins, with Passover an early, premonarchic commemoration of the exodus, and Unleavened Bread an agricultural celebration at the beginning of the barley harvest. The language of Deuteronomy 16, as well as other Old Testament passages that speak of one without mentioning the other, may support such an explanation (e.g., Exod 23 speaks only of Unleavened Bread without any reference to Passover). Alternatively, it is possible that the two were originally joined, but then became separated as Passover fell into disuse, or became a home-based celebration.

Change in practice and understanding of festivals should not surprise. Over time celebrations evolve, with even their core experiencing substantial change. Our Christmas celebration provides an example in which "Christianity interpreted an old Germanic solstice festival with its emphasis on light (the return of the sun) into Christmas, the birthday of Jesus Christ, 'the light of the world' (John 8:12)" (W. Janzen 2000: 157). Similarly, the way festivals in Israel were celebrated and understood changed over time.

From our present vantage point we can affirm the following:

1. The variety of ways the Old Testament speaks of Passover and Unleavened Bread suggests a complex history for these celebrations.

2. Despite the best intentions of scholars, it is doubtful that the history of these celebrations will ever be fully and satisfactorily reconstructed.

3. Within the biblical story these two celebrations are merged into one larger festival, even if the details of how they fit together may not always be clear.

The last statement reflects the emphasis of Deuteronomy. Although verse 1 only speaks of Passover, and verse 16 only speaks of Unleavened Bread, Deuteronomy envisages a combined, centralized Passover and Unleavened Bread as the most important celebration for Israel, one that it is to keep *for the LORD your God* as a commemoration of God's bringing *Israel out of Egypt by night* (v. 1).

16:9-12 Festival of Weeks

Deuteronomy calls the second festival of the calendar year the *festival of weeks* (cf. Exod 34:22; Num 28:26). Other Old Testament passages speak of it as the festival of harvest (Exod 23:16; cf. 34:22) or the time of firstfruits (Exod 23:16; 34:22; Num 28:26). The festival calendar of Exodus 34 combines all three elements with its description of the event as "the festival of weeks, the first fruits of wheat harvest" (v. 22). Eventually the name Festival of Weeks came to dominate.

Each of these names represents an important element of the festival. Seven weeks after the beginning of the barley harvest in the spring, Israel is to *keep the festival of weeks*. At this point the wheat harvest normally begins. As an expression of thanksgiving, Israel presents the firstfruits of the harvest to God.

An earlier Canaanite harvest festival probably lies behind Israel's Festival of Weeks. After having worked in slave labor camps in Egypt and then wandering in the desert for a generation, Israel entered the land not as experienced farmers. They then learned agricultural technique from the locals, in the process adopting other elements of the agricultural year, probably including a harvest festival. The Deuteronomic description of the festival as well as other accounts suggest that at least for the period of the monarchy, this celebration remained primarily an agricultural festival. In the postexilic period the Festival of Weeks became a commemoration of God's giving of the law at Mount Horeb. Jewish tradition interprets Exodus 19:1 as implying that Israel arrived at Horeb on the fiftieth day after choosing a lamb for the first Passover.

The Deuteronomic version of the festival is quite sparse. Leviticus 23:15-21 and Numbers 28:26-31 give detailed description of the timing of the festival and the rituals involved: each Israelite (family?) is asked to "bring from your settlements two loaves of bread as an elevation offering, each made of two-tenths of an ephah. . . . You shall present with the bread seven lambs a year old without blemish, one young bull, and two rams" (Lev 23:17-18).

In contrast, Deuteronomy simply identifies four themes in typically Deuteronomic dress. First, Israel is to contribute *a freewill offering in proportion to the blessing that you have received from the* LORD *your God* (v. 10). This *freewill offering* is not identified as firstfruits (likely grain), but possibly should be understood as such, connecting the passage with the earlier tithe directives (14:22-29; 26:12-15) and the passages on firstfruits (15:19-23; 18:3-5; 26:1-11). The Festival of Weeks is a time when Israel returns to God a portion of that which God has given it through blessing the harvest.

Second, the dominant tone of the festival is inclusive celebration (cf. ch. 12, plus 14:22-27; 15:19-23). Both elements, *inclusive* and *celebration*, are important. A command to rejoice may sound strange, but that is what verse 11 gives: *Rejoice before the LORD your God*. Typical of Deuteronomy, this rejoicing includes the whole community, men and women, parents and children, free and slave, well-off and disadvantaged. All are part of the community that is experiencing the blessings of the land God has given Israel.

Third, the celebration occurs *at the place that the LORD your God will choose as a dwelling for his name* (v. 11; cf. ch. 12). Since it is very possible that this festival had its background in Canaanite agricultural tradition, the danger of incorporating elements of Canaanite religion is real. Centralizing the festival makes it more likely that it remains true to the God of the exodus.

Finally, Deuteronomy concludes the description of the Festival of Weeks by urging, *Remember that you were a slave in Egypt, and diligently observe these statutes* (16:12). Again we see Deuteronomy's emphasis on remembering. This one reference does not convert this festival to one focused primarily on history—it is still an agricultural celebration—but it begins a move in that direction. The reference to observing the statutes prepares for when Israel will celebrate this festival as a commemoration of God's gift of the law. For Deuteronomy, all celebration is in some way connected to faith in a God who acted in the particular story of Israel. Israel is always to remember that its present blessings are in striking contrast with its earlier experience as slaves. The transition from oppression to blessing is solely God's doing.

16:13-15 Festival of Booths

The third festival, here called Festival of Booths, is also known as the Festival of Ingathering (Exod 23:16; 34:22). As the alternative name implies, originally this also was an agricultural festival, marking the end of the harvest year with special emphasis on the completion of the grape harvest. Fruits (e.g., dates, figs, olives, and grapes) were the last crop to be harvested before the fall rains arrived. This festival thus celebrates the end of the agricultural year.

The term *booths* (unhelpfully rendered *tabernacles* in NIV and KJV) probably refers to a primitive hut constructed out of branches and leaves, providing temporary shelter for the farmers as they camped in the vineyard during the harvest. At some point, however, Israel's story of redemption became the central focus of this festival. The booths then came to represent the tents within which Israel slept during its journey from Egypt to the Promised Land (cf. Lev

23:43). Again, an agricultural festival is reinterpreted to commemorate Israel's story of salvation.

It is possible that the Old Testament passages referring to a "yearly festival" (Judg 21:19) or a "yearly sacrifice" (1 Sam 1:21) are referring to this festival. The end of the harvest year is a time of great joy and celebration: the crops are in, and enough food for the winter has been harvested. Grapes and wine can also lead to exuberant celebration. The Judges passage includes a reference to women coming out for dancing (Judg 21:19-21), and Eli's suspicion that Hannah was drunk at this annual celebration intimates this as well (1 Sam 1:13; cf. v. 9).

Deuteronomy's description of this festival is even more sparse than the previous one. Whereas Numbers devotes twenty-seven verses to describing the sacrifices and ritual required during these seven days (Num 29:12-38), Deuteronomy simply identifies typical themes. The whole community is to participate in the festivities (16:14), the festival is to be kept at The Place (16:15), an atmosphere of rejoicing is to dominate. This last element receives particular attention. The expansion of the initial directive begins with *Rejoice during your festival* (v. 14) and concludes with *and you shall surely celebrate* (v. 15). Perhaps surprising by its absence is any reference to Israel's history, especially given how this festival evolved, and Deuteronomy's later directive to Israel to read the book of the law every seven years at the Festival of Booths (31:9-13). But in this context the emphasis is on the joyful celebration of the people before God at The Place God has chosen for his name.

16:16-17 Concluding Summary

A summarizing exhortation concludes Deuteronomy's festival calendar. Two elements of the brief summary are surprising. First, the expectation that *Three times a year all your males shall appear before the* LORD *your God* is quite unexpected, especially given the emphasis in previous verses that the whole community is to participate in the celebrations, including daughters, female slaves, and widows (vv. 11, 14). Some attempt to explain this by suggesting that whereas women are welcome, or even encouraged to come, only the men are required to attend. But this does not treat with sufficient seriousness the consistent call of Deuteronomy, here and elsewhere, to include all in these celebrations, not just the male head of the household.

The second surprise comes with the naming of the festivals. Here the first celebration is called *festival* (this term is not used in its description in vv. 1-8), and it is called the *festival of unleavened bread*, whereas the opening description used the term *Passover* as the name of the event (v. 1), and in the expansion thoroughly joined the two. These two surprises suggest that a traditional summary of the festivals may simply been inserted into Deuteronomy here.

THE TEXT IN BIBLICAL CONTEXT
Festivals and Renewal

Despite the harsh words of Amos, "I hate, I despise your festivals, and take no delight in your solemn assemblies" (5:21), festivals were the high points of Israelite life. They were times when the community celebrated together, and they probably were the primary way priests and religious officials taught the content of Israel's faith to the next generation.

It thus is not surprising how frequently festivals, especially the Passover, play a key role in times of renewal or reform in Scripture. The two kings most prominently involved in reform—and a return to historic biblical monotheism and the worship of Yahweh as the only God—are Hezekiah and Josiah [*Biblical Monotheism, p. 539*]. Both mark their reforms with a renewed celebration of the Passover festival. It is so important for Hezekiah that he even moves it to the second month since the priests first need to be consecrated. The invitation to the people to come to Jerusalem for the event opens with "return to the LORD" (2 Chron 30:6). Similarly, Josiah's reform climaxes with "the passover to the LORD your God as prescribed in this book of the covenant" (2 Kings 23:21). The Passover celebration also served as a dedication of the new temple, finally finished by those who had returned from exile (Ezra 6:19-22).

The Passover ritual then also becomes the framework within which early Christianity understood the death of Christ. Jesus' death occurred at the time of the Passover celebration, with Christ understood as the Passover lamb (e.g., 1 Cor 5:7). As God redeemed Israel from Egyptian slavery, so Christ's death delivers people from slavery to sin. The church also was born at the time of a festival, although now it is the festival of Pentecost, or Weeks, that provides the setting.

THE TEXT IN THE LIFE OF THE CHURCH
A Communal Church Year

Although believers church groups have tended to place limited emphasis on formal liturgy or ritual, traditionally they have emphasized special days like Christmas, Easter, Thanksgiving, and often Pentecost and Ascension Day, both through worship and family celebrations. But this is evolving. On the one side, many congregations are showing more appreciation for the liturgy of the full church year. It is not only Christmas but also Advent that is recognized, not only Good Friday and Easter but also Lent. This is a positive direction, one that is consistent with our passage even though not a literal application of Israel's festival calendar.

On the other side, developments in family life have significantly impacted the family celebrations that formerly were so central. Increased mobility resulting in families divided and scattered throughout the land, the significant growth of melded and nontraditional families complicating a simple family celebration, and the growing tendency to place greater emphasis on affinity groupings rather than family identity—all these have contributed to undermining the place of these family celebrations. There are reasons why many people count these times of festivities as the loneliest times of the year. One response to this reality is to develop structures and programs that attempt to reinvigorate the traditional family.

These may be good, but a case can be made that the Deuteronomic vision moves in a somewhat different direction. Even though it regularly refers to households, these households include slaves or servants as well as resident aliens, and even the Levites are incorporated. In other words, these are not simply biological families, neither nuclear nor extended. These truly are communal and inclusive celebrations. It is to this side of the church festivals that twenty-first-century congregations may need to give more attention. The high days of the Christian year are times to commemorate God's great acts of deliverance, yet they also are times when the people of God celebrate joyfully together. These celebrations must be communal and not divisive.

Drama versus Word

Ancient Near Eastern festivals were filled with drama and pageantry. In Babylon the celebrating community participated in a massive dramatization recognizing the reign of Marduk over the city and the land. Israel's festivals also incorporated drama. The account of the ark crossing the Jordan river (Josh 4) may reflect a corporate reenactment of the earlier crossing of the sea as the Egyptian army pursued them (Exod 14–15). Through these huge participatory dramas, the people of Israel came to know the story of God.

Reformed and Anabaptist churches have tended to deemphasize symbol and liturgy, both inherently dramatic, with greater attention to the preached word. The two primary exceptions to this are the celebrations of baptism and communion. In both, the people of the church participate in dramatic reenactment of what God has done for us. But perhaps the church should include more dramatic action in its worship life. It is generally recognized that learning takes place most effectively when people participate and not only listen to the spoken word. Perhaps Israel understood more of educational philosophy than the church today.

Deuteronomy 16:18–19:21

Part 2D, Unit 4
Leadership and Judicial Procedures

OVERVIEW

A healthy, well-functioning community has laws and regulations, yet it also has structure and organization. In Israel each person was part of a household or extended family, part of a clan consisting of a number of families, part of a tribe consisting of a number of clans, and part of the nation or people as whole. These different groupings are not ever systematically introduced, but simply assumed. In contrast, Deuteronomy gives the leadership roles envisioned for such a society overt attention.

After highlighting some implications of the exclusive worship of God for Israel's cultic life (12:1–13:18; 15:19–16:17) and communal interaction (14:22–15:18, etc.), Deuteronomy turns to the roles of judge, king, priest, and prophet. Despite their significance in Israel, Deuteronomy largely assumes the role of elders. There is no clear textual break at 16:18 to mark a new unit, but the common subject matter of 16:18–18:22 leads most interpreters to treat it as a distinct block, "a self-contained section dealing with state and religious officials, the local court and its processes" (Nelson 2002: 213).

Against the background of Israel gathered in Moab prior to their entrance into the Promised Land, Deuteronomy presents a leadership plan for later Israel. Within the context of Israel's monarchy

—the passage does seem to reflect considerable experience as a people in the land—it fits well with the hopes of a major reform movement. If one imagines the time of exile, the passage looks forward to a reconstitution of Israel after its return. Depending on the setting, the passage presents a vision for organizing, reforming, or reorganizing Israel around a particular vision and model.

This leads some interpreters to speak of this passage as a constitution for Israel, perhaps comparable to the U.S. Constitution (Halpern 1981: 226-33; P. Miller 1990: 141). McBride gives this block special prominence in his case for viewing the whole of Deuteronomy as a national constitution rather than a legal code, a position already promoted by Josephus in the first century (1987: 229, 241).

But to interpret Deuteronomy as here presenting a political agenda insufficiently appreciates the comprehensive nature of the vision Deuteronomy is painting, nor the primacy of the theological foundation shaping that vision, "to establish a people under the authority of Torah and governed by 'righteousness'" (Block 2012: 19). There is no sharp separation between cultic matters and civil matters, nor between religious personnel or political offices. For Deuteronomy, all of life is constructed around the exclusive worship of the one God who led Israel out of Egypt (first commandment together with its prologue, 5:6-7; cf. the Shema, 6:4-5).

Just as Deuteronomy is vague on cultic detail, it does not here present precise job descriptions for each office. Rather, based on its theological convictions, Deuteronomy continues the work of painting the big picture for the type of people Israel is to be. This fits with the somewhat idealistic or utopian impression of the passage. These are not detailed directions for political administration but part of a theologically shaped vision One God, One People, One Place—all three remain central themes and shape the way these leadership positions are understood.

The chiastic structure of the block highlights its two major components: the introduction of key leadership positions, framed by instructions on judicial procedures *[Chiasm, p. 540]* (Christensen 2001: 353). Priests are given prime place at the center (C). Although it is doubtful that Deuteronomy arose within the priestly community *[Composition of Deuteronomy, p. 543]*, priests do receive significant emphasis in Deuteronomy. They are mandated to *stand and minister in the name of the* LORD (18:5; cf. v. 7) and are given responsibility for maintaining the book of the law (17:18). The inner frame (B^1 and B^2) partners the king and the prophet, a connection not emphasized within Deuteronomy but significant in the Deuteronomistic History, the story of Israel influenced by the book of Deuteronomy. The outer frame (A^1 and A^2) encompasses all with a consideration of judges and judicial procedures. Realizing the just society envisioned by Deuteronomy will require a wise and honest justice system (cf. 1:9-18). Deuteronomy thus opens and closes the block of 16:18–19:21 by giving attention to this critical aspect of society.

OUTLINE
A^1 Judges and Judicial Procedures, 16:18–17:13
   B^1 The King, 17:14-20
      C Levitical Priests, 18:1-8
   B^2 Prophets, 18:9-22
A^2 Further Judicial Procedures, 19:1-21

Judges and Judicial Procedures
Deuteronomy 16:18–17:13

PREVIEW
Justice, and only justice serves as a kind of rallying cry for the introduction to this block (16:20). Judges who will render just decisions are the road to achieving this. Living a life of blessing in the land depends upon the faithful worship of God and upon a communal life shaped by justice. As Christopher Wright puts it, "The integrity of the judicial system was (and still is) basic to the preservation of society. Any society will have some levels of crime and some levels of injustice, but if the means of restitution and redress themselves become corrupt, then there is only despair. Justice itself turns to wormwood (Amos 5:7, 10)" (1996: 205). Guidelines for judicial procedures continue in 19:1-21.

OUTLINE
Appointment of Judges and Officials, 16:18-20
Two Instructions for the Cult, 16:21–17:1
Judicial Procedures, 17:2-13
    17:2-7   Local Courts
    17:8-13   The Court at The Place

EXPLANATORY NOTES

Appointment of Judges and Officials 16:18-20

The opening paragraph calls on Israel to appoint *judges and officials throughout your tribes*. Although the term translated *judge* is used in more than one way in the Old Testament (in the book of Judges, it refers to Israel's charismatic leaders), in this passage the term clearly refers to those with responsibility for judicial matters. Who *officials* are is less clear, but possibly they are assistants or scribal administrators.

This instruction reminds us of the earlier passage where Moses lightens his own heavy workload by having the people select for themselves *leaders* who are to *judge rightly* among the people (1:9-18; cf. Exod 18:13-27). Now the text returns to the theme even if in a somewhat different style. That there are two such passages in the book underlines the significance of the administration of justice for Deuteronomy.

Perhaps the most surprising term in this short passage is the one that comes first in most English versions (it is not first in Hebrew): *You shall appoint* . . . This passage is addressed to the people as a whole, as one body (*you* is a collective singular, not plural). It is the people who appoint or elect these judges, not the king or some other representatives of the central administration, as normally would be the case. In the world of the day, including Israel (note Pss 72:2; 89:14), kings are responsible for justice. One should not read into the verse a contemporary understanding of democracy, but nevertheless it does represent a distribution of authority.

The *you* at the beginning of the longer block also makes the point that judges, indeed the whole structure, are the responsibility of the people. Deuteronomy is a book addressed not only to priests or some other elite group. Elsewhere it challenges all the people to obey God; here it calls upon all to take responsibility for their life together, including the leadership roles. Consistent with this, these judges are to *render just decisions for the people* (v. 18).

Although the text calls on the people to put these judges in place, it does not give any directions for how this is to be done (e.g., is this to happen in each community, or centrally?). The absence of specifics does not imply that Deuteronomy is giving each community freedom to do this in whatever manner it prefers but again reflects Deuteronomy's tendency not to spell out details. These are not regulations that can be mechanically implemented. This tendency to avoid detail may also explain the absence here of any reference to *elders* even though elsewhere they play a role (e.g., 19:12; chs. 21–22).

Two other terms in the first verse lose their nuance in translation. The term translated *appoint* (NRSV, NIV; KJV, *make*) is a form of the verb "to give," the term Deuteronomy consistently uses to speak of God *giving* Israel the Promised Land. The verse thus begins by speaking about God giving them the land, and then it continues by calling on the people to "give" themselves judges, with verse 20 once more referring to the giving of land. Likewise in chapter 1 the appointment of judges is associated with God's blessing. The Hebrew behind *towns/cities* is more commonly translated as *gates* in the Old Testament. The translation *towns/cities* is not wrong, but it loses the reference to the gate, the setting where questions of justice commonly were settled in Israel. When Boaz needs a legal question resolved, he goes to the gate, where ten elders review the case and render a verdict (Ruth 4:1-12).

The task of the judges is to pursue righteousness and justice. Each of the three verses in this short passage make this central point. The Hebrew translated *just decisions* is simply two nouns placed next to each other, the first commonly translated *judgment* or *justice*, the second commonly as *righteous* or *righteousness* (Deut 16:18) The first refers to the right or appropriate verdict in a case and as such refers to process. The second speaks to content, the quality that determines justice (McConville 2002: 287). The prophet Amos uses these same two terms in his preaching to Israel:

- Hate evil and love good, and establish justice in the gate. (5:15; justice is to happen at the "gate")

- Let justice roll down like waters, and righteousness like an ever-flowing stream. (5:24)

The three prohibitions of Deuteronomy 16:19 then give further directives, making use of a style much like that of the short commands of the Decalogue (cf. 1:17; Exod 23:6-8; Lev 19:15):

- *You must not distort justice.*

- *You must not show partiality.*

- *You must not accept bribes.*

Each of these undermine justice and betray the essence of what it means to be a judge. Bribes are rejected by recognizing that *a bribe blinds the eyes of the wise and subverts the cause of those who are in the right* (again a form of the word "righteous"). Here is the first of a number of connections with 1 Samuel 8–12, which reports that the sons of Eli "took bribes and perverted justice" (8:3). This overall direction is then summarized in the closing verse with a motto-like call: *Justice, and only justice, you shall pursue.* Similarly Jesus challenged the Pharisees: "For you tithe mint, dill and cummin, and have neglected the weightier matters of the law: justice and mercy and faith" (Matt 23:23).

After addressing the people as a whole, verses 19-20 may reflect a shift in audience (e.g., McConville 2002: 286), with the newly appointed judges now the intended addressees. But the more communal connotation does not disappear. Justice and righteousness remain a concern for the people as a whole. Responsibility for maintaining justice is communal (Nelson 2002: 218).

The passage closes with one further reference to the land. At first glance this is simply another expression of a typical motif: faithfulness and obedience are associated with good life in the land. A more careful examination of the phrase draws attention to an ambiguity. The direction to appoint judges *throughout your tribes, in all your towns* assumes that Israel is already living in the land. The final verse, however, appears to make the occupation itself, an event in the future, conditional upon having followed the provisions. Deuteronomy holds in tension "occupation of the land as a decisive event in history and as permanent future possibility, which has its obverse in the possibility of loss" (McConville 2002: 286). This contributes to Deuteronomy continuously having a present quality. It speaks to Israel during the time of the monarchy, and it speaks to Israel in exile: the hearers and readers of Deuteronomy are always at some *today*, where they are confronted by the challenge of how to respond to God's exclusive claim and its implications (cf. 5:1-21).

Two Instructions for the Cult 16:21–17:1

Immediately following the call to appoint judges come three verses dealing with Israel's cult (16:21–17:1) *[Cult, p. 546]*. Their placement may exemplify the kinds of cases over which the judges would preside. Even though the judges are local and civil appointments, their responsibility can include matters of cult and religious ritual, perhaps prosecuting cases where Canaanite cultic objects have been employed (16:21-22), or determining when an animal's defect was such that it could not be sacrificed (cf. 17:1). Alternatively, their inclusion here may signal that the appointment of judges is not merely civil administration but integrally bound up in faithful worship of God. Given the absence of a sharp line between religion and politics in the ancient world, this second suggestion is certainly true: the appointment of judges is a religious matter. But whether the placement of these verses here make that point is uncertain.

Elsewhere Deuteronomy calls for the destruction of Canaanite cultic objects like the *sacred pole* (NIV, *Asherah pole*) and *stone pillar* (NIV, *sacred stone*; cf. 7:5; 12:3; 16:22). This brief passage, however, envisions a new possibility, that Israel might itself construct such objects right next to the *altar that you make for the LORD your God*. This is no longer a matter of allowing Canaanite practice to continue but a question of incorporating elements of Canaanite worship into the cult and worship of Yahweh, the God of Israel. Israel is not to "'baptize' any of the pagan symbols and bring them into their own worship" (Hall: 274).

Yet that is exactly what happened. Repeatedly 1 and 2 Kings refers to sacred poles and stone pillars, in Samaria and in Jerusalem, with even kings setting them up (e.g., 1 Kings 16:33; 2 Kings 21:3). According to 2 Kings 17 the destruction of the Northern Kingdom at the hand of the Assyrians occurred because the people "walked in the customs of the nations whom the LORD drove out (17:8) and had set up for themselves pillars and sacred poles on every high hill" (17:10).

This brief passage concludes with a passionate denunciation: these are *things that the LORD your God hates* (v. 22). With the word *hates* we are brought back to Israel's covenant with God. The proper relationship within the covenant is one of love: God loves Israel, and Israel is called to love God (cf. 7:8; 6:5). For God to hate something means that something interferes with and undermines the covenant relationship. Canaanite worship objects in the cult of Israel do exactly that.

The next verse (17:1) repeats the directive of 15:21 that animals with defects are not to be offered to God. The only new element is the surprisingly strong statement: *for that is abhorrent to the LORD your God*. Although the offering of a flawed animal does not appear to have any necessary connection with the worship of other gods (a common context for the word *abhorrent*), the use of the term here emphasizes the significance of the concern. Malachi says offering a blind animal to God is despising the name of God, and he compares it to offering God polluted food (1:6-8).

Judicial Procedures 17:2-13

After an interruption of three verses dealing with cultic matters (16:21-17:1), the text returns to the subject of the judicial system. The first paragraph (vv. 2-7) presents a sample case that the local courts would need to adjudicate. The second (vv. 8-13) introduces a court at *the place the* LORD *your God will choose*. Together the two paragraphs give a sense for how justice is to be established by the courts and address the relationship between the administration of justice *in one of your towns* (17:2) and by the central court at The Place (17:8).

17:2-7 Local Courts

With focus, language, and structure reminiscent of chapter 13, this passage presents a sample case for the local courts. Both deal with apostasy in a casuistic format (*if . . . then . . .*), speak of apostasy in terms of worshiping other gods (17:3; cf. 13:2, 6, 13), refer to hearing about the charge and then making a thorough investigation of it (17:4; cf. 13:12, 14), climax in execution (17:6; cf. 13:5, 9, 15), and speak of the purpose of the action: *so that you may purge the evil from your midst* (17:7, cf. 13:5). Hence this paragraph is often treated as a fourth case in the series of chapter 13, a case that at some point in the transmission of Deuteronomy was displaced to the present position.

And yet there are differences. As does chapter 13, this passage speaks about the worship of other gods (v. 3; cf. 13:2, 6, 13), but adds a reference to worshiping *the sun or the moon or any of the host of heaven* (17:3). A more significant difference becomes evident when our present passage is compared with the second case in chapter 13, the one most similar to it. In that case the source of the temptation is a member of the family, with the required response upon discovery being *You shall surely kill them*. It appears to allow for a summary execution, with no hint of due process. The central concern in chapter 13 is the terrible nature of apostasy and its destructive consequences. In chapter 17 emphasis shifts from the apostasy itself to considering *how* Israel is to deal with such apostasy. The case of 17:2-7 may have chapter 13 as background, but its focus is process (Levinson 1997: 98-143).

The apostasy of chapter 17 occurs *among you*, an apparent recall of the opening verse of chapter 13 that speaks of a prophet appearing *among you*. But 17:2 follows up *among you* with *in one of your towns*. The additional phrase may appear redundant but draws attention back to the short passage introducing the call for judges that also uses the phrase *in all your towns* (16:18). The opening verse also moves beyond the language of chapter 13 in speaking of the apostasy as a transgression of God's *covenant*. The formal relationship established through covenant has been transgressed, so the court needs to determine how to deal with this transgression. The introductory verse thus begins to shift the focus from apostasy to judicial process.

Before considering the safeguards that the passage places upon the judicial process, notice the setting for the process in relationship to the nature of the case. The discovery of the apostasy takes place *among you, in one of your towns* (cf. 16:18, where judges are appointed *throughout all your tribes, in all your towns*), with no hint that the matter is taken elsewhere for processing. In other words, the sample case demonstrates that the local courts have responsibility for the most severe cases, even apostasy. There is no division here between sacral courts (i.e., those dealing with cultic or religious matters) and civil courts (i.e., those dealing with economic or interpersonal matters such as theft or assault).

The passage continues by giving directions to the local courts (C. Wright 1996: 206):

1. The process requires *thorough inquiry*, with punishment not implemented unless the *charge is proved true* (v. 4). Similar language is used in 13:14, but the wording of 13:6-11 appears to allow for a summary execution by the one discovering the crime. Throughout, this passage emphasizes the importance of due process, safeguarding the rights of one charged with a crime, thereby ensuring that the innocent are not falsely punished.

2. The process is public, from beginning (17:4, *a thorough inquiry*; NIV, *investigate it thoroughly*) on through to punishment (17:5, *at the gates*). The gate, as the place through which people exit and enter the city, is an ideal place for gathering people to consider important issues. This clarifies what may be ambiguous in 13:6-11.

3. The passage emphasizes that *two or three witnesses* are required to render a guilty verdict (17:6). In a world without the science of forensic evidence, witnesses become the primary means of determining guilt or innocence, with the validity of a verdict largely depending upon the integrity of the witness. This explains the prominence given to the need for two or three witnesses (cf. 19:15) and the severe punishment for giving false testimony (cf. 19:16-21; cf. 5:20).

4. Requiring the witnesses to take the lead in implementing the punishment further discourages a false charge (17:7). The requirement appears to be in some tension with 13:7-11, where the accuser is the one to begin the punishment, but this difference is more apparent than real: the accuser could simultaneously be a witness. The

difference in language may simply reflect a different interest. In chapter 13's concern, apostasy is such a serious sin that even family relationships should not prevent its exposure, whereas here the concern is due process.

5. Three times the passage uses the phrase *man or woman*, drawing attention to the fact that both men and women are equally accountable for their actions (vv. 2, 5 [twice]). This is not a contemporary commitment to equal rights but is consistent with other passages where Deuteronomy treats women as real people with a place in the community (cf. the fifth commandment, 5:16; the clear inclusion of women in the *you* of many of the regulations, as in 14:26; etc.).

The people as a whole are responsible for administering justice. They do this by appointing judges and officers (16:18-20), but even then their role is not finished. They continue to participate in the local judicial process as witnesses and presumably as people who contribute to the thorough investigation. When these safeguards are followed, this local process has authority over even the most serious cases, including those with a possible capital punishment. In this way the people contribute as they *purge the evil from their midst* (17:7).

17:8-13 *The Court at The Place*

The second paragraph introduces the court at *the place that the* LORD *your God will choose* (v. 8). Cases that are *too difficult* are to be taken to the court at the central sanctuary. Presumably the *levitical priests and judges* at The Place are more highly trained than local judges and thus more qualified to handle difficult cases. But the text does not clarify what makes a case too difficult (cf. 1:9-18; McConville 2002: 291).

A passage in the Covenant Code may contribute some insight. The case involves an Israelite who has given some money or other possession to a neighbor for safekeeping (Exod 22:7-8; cf. v. 11). While under the neighbor's protection, this property is stolen. In this case the usual method for determining guilt (the use of witnesses) does not work. Since suspicion naturally falls on the owner of the house from which the property has been stolen, the only way the owner can be freed of this is to take an oath of innocence "before God" (W. Janzen 2000: 304).

Perhaps that is the logic of these two paragraphs. If judgment of wrong in a particular case, regardless of its nature or the severity of punishment, can be determined through usual judicial procedures, then the local judicial system has full authority to administer the case. If, however, the case is *too difficult*, meaning that it cannot be resolved through the usual judicial process of considering statements from witnesses, then it must be brought to The Place

(Levinson 1997: 98-143). The Hebrew translated *too difficult* literally is *too wonderful*, with the connotation of relating to the divine. "Such 'wonderful' cases are beyond human knowledge (Job 42:3; Ps 131:1; Prov 30:18; cf. Gen 18:14) and thus require priestly intervention" (Nelson 2002: 221). At The Place the priests and the judge then would determine how to proceed, perhaps through divine oracle, perhaps through the use of the Urim and Thummim (instruments given the priests to determine God's word/direction), or perhaps in some other manner (cf. Exod 28:30; Deut 33:8).

Deuteronomy's centralization thrust, with its consequent limiting of what may be called sacred activity to The Place, fits such an interpretation, even if the central court is not limited to using sacral means for arriving at a verdict. The judicial procedures section in chapter 19 supports this both-and approach. The text there speaks of a *malicious witness*, implying that there are witnesses on both sides of the issue, otherwise the local court could give the verdict. When the case then is brought to the central court, the priests and the judges are to *make a thorough inquiry*, a process that implies more than simply seeking the word of God (19:16-18).

Likely the local judge would have to make the referral to the central court. Since the central court is not an appeals court, it is doubtful that the one ruled against in the local setting could make the appeal. We must remember, however, that procedures in the ancient world were not as systematically governed by regulations as they are today, so it is possible that on occasion disputants, especially if they lived near the central sanctuary, might decide to take their case to the central court (cf. stories in Samuel and Kings about people taking their cases to the king: 2 Sam 15:1-6; 1 Kings 3:16-22).

The overall thrust of the passage is twofold. First, as part of the larger passage on judicial procedures (17:2-13), it outlines a two-court system, local courts and a central court at The Place, with local courts limited to using nonsacral procedures.

Second, the passage emphasizes the importance of accepting the verdict determined by the central court. This concern is expressed in multiple ways:

- The call to accept the verdict is repeated: *Carry out exactly the decision* (v. 10), *diligently observing everything they instruct you* (v. 10). *You must carry out fully the law* (v. 11). *Do not turn aside from the decision* (v. 11).

- The verdict of the central court is divine authority: The

Hebrew term translated *consult* (v. 9) may be used of coming before God to seek a word from God (cf. Exod 18:15; Deut 4:29; 12:5; 1 Sam 9:9). The decision is announced *from the place the LORD will choose* (v. 10). The priests have been *appointed to minister there to the LORD your God* (v. 12).

- The text tries to be comprehensive in that which is to be accepted as it speaks of *the decision* (v. 10), *the law that they interpret, the ruling that they announce to you, the decision that they announce to you* (v. 11).

- Punishment for disregarding the verdict is severe: *That person shall die* (v. 12).

Confidence in the judicial system depends upon its being effective. Deuteronomy's vision for society includes a judicial system driven by *justice, and only justice* (16:20), yet also one that is effective because people will abide by its rulings. Disobedience of a verdict derived from God is a rejection of God. To reject God is to act *presumptuously* (17:13), to be arrogant. In a sense it is the original sin of determining that one does not need to follow God but instead can follow one's own assessment or judgment (cf. Gen 3). In so doing one has replaced God with oneself. Disobedience thus is like apostasy, a disregard of the foundational commandment, and so Israel is directed to *purge the evil* from its midst (17:12; cf. v. 7).

(TBC and TLC for this section are located after comments on 19:1-21.)

The King

Deuteronomy 17:14-20

PREVIEW

Who will lead this people? In the world of Israel, before democracy, before prime ministers and presidents were elected by the people, a king was an attractive possibility. After introducing judges and the judicial system, Deuteronomy thus turns to the role of the king. This surprising order alerts us that something unusual is taking place. Unless the order of presentation of leadership positions is entirely haphazard, and this is doubtful, one would expect the king to be first as the supreme leader in Israel, or last as the climax to the list, or perhaps in the center of this chiastic structure (see Overview). But instead the king is presented second in the list of four leadership roles—judge, king, priest, and prophet.

This unusual treatment of the king is further highlighted by the observation that of the four offices, it is the only one that is discretionary. The people are commanded to appoint judges, God assigns the role of priest to the tribe of Levi (18:1), and God will raise up prophets (18:15-22), but Israel need only set a king over itself *if* it requests to do so. Whereas judge, priest, and prophet are required, a king is optional. That this passage presents an unusual view of a king's role is general consensus, but debates continue over what that view is.

OUTLINE

Permission to Have a King, 17:14-15
Directives for the King, 17:16-20a
    17:16-17   Restrictions on Royal Policies
    17:18-19   A Torah Scholar
    17:20a   An Obedient *Brother*
The Outcome: A Dynasty, 17:20b

EXPLANATORY NOTES

Permission to Have a King 17:14-15

The directive opens with two conditions for establishing a monarchy: first, Israel must already be in the land; and second, Israel must demand a king for itself. The first is so common for Deuteronomy that it is easily disregarded. But here it provides additional meaning. Land reflects God's blessing, which leads to property and possessions that must be managed and administered. During the time of the desert wanderings, Israel needed leadership that kept the people focused on their goal of reaching the Promised Land; but once in the land, the nature of the required leadership changes. Now leadership is necessary that will manage the land and its blessings in a particular manner (Brueggemann 1977). Even today the leadership needs of a business or large institution are different from the needs of a group or organization with no property. The opening reference thus not only provides a setting for the passage but also implicitly connects the passage with land and blessing and the need to organize life and property in the land.

Nevertheless, Israel will only have a king if it demands one. The second condition suggests that kingship is not absolutely necessary: it is not part of the fabric of reality but a contingent arrangement, an optional institution. By contrast, in Mesopotamia the people believed that the gods gave kingship to humanity; in Egypt the king himself was counted as a god. By grounding Israel's kingship in the people's request, Deuteronomy is already distinguishing Israel's kingship from what is common in its world.

On a practical level this optional quality may be more apparent than real. Once Israel has *taken possession* of the land *and settled in it* (v. 14), the development of monarchy is a natural next step. The people whose land Israel took over had kings (2:24–3:11). In the world of that day, it is difficult to imagine transitioning from a wandering people to a nation with land without adopting the standard leadership structure. There thus is an element of inevitability in this projection. A Deuteronomic audience during the time of the monarchy surely considers a king natural and necessary; an audience during the exile certainly associates any return to the land with reestablishing the monarchy. The initiative for the king may be Israel's, but it is to be expected and perhaps is inevitable.

And yet the language and tone of the second condition places the institution of kingship under a cloud, already warning that a distinctive understanding of kingship is necessary. After all, the ways of *all the nations* are generally forcefully rejected in Deuteronomy (17:14; cf. 18:9; etc.). The sense of foreboding, with permission coming only with a caveat, becomes more acute when this passage is considered in light of Israel's experience with kings, and in light of the debate over kingship in the Old Testament, especially 1 Samuel 8–12. The request for a king in 1 Samuel 8 includes similar language: "appoint for us, then, a king to govern us, like other nations" (1 Sam 8:5, emph. added; cf. v. 20), but then adds to it the expectation that this king will "go out before us and fight our battles" (v. 20). This request is a rejection of God "from being king over them" (v. 7). It is not necessary to assume the full debate of 1 Samuel 8–12 behind our passage, but the obvious connection between the two highlights the warning present in our passage. God grants the request—after all, this is how nations administer land—but simultaneously the request sharply forewarns that there are potential pitfalls in having a king (cf. the "ways of the king," 1 Sam 8:10-18). As the story develops, these are pitfalls into which Israel and its kings did fall.

The permission to have a king comes with two requirements (Deut 17:15): first, that God *choose* the king, and second, that the king must be a *brother* (AT; NRSV, *one of your own community*), stated in three different ways (lit., *your brother, . . . not a foreigner . . . who is not your brother*). Both requirements are significant. Although the request for the king may come from the people, unlike choosing judges, the people cannot select their king. This language puts the king in select company: in Deuteronomy, God chooses Israel (7:7; etc.), The Place (12:5; etc.), the king, and the tribe of Levi as priests (18:5); here the language is most similar to that used for God's choice of the central worship site. The role of the king may be conditional and have restrictions, but nevertheless the king is chosen by God and as such has a special place.

The manner of choice is not addressed. In the story of Israel, this frequently happens through designation of a prophet; thus Samuel anoints Saul and David (1 Sam 10:1; 16:13) and Ahijah designates Jeroboam (1 Kings 11:26-40). But it may also take place by lot (Saul is selected, 1 Sam 10:17-24) or the charismatic demonstration of leadership (e.g., David's actions following his anointing but prior to becoming king, 1 Sam 16–26).

The second requirement is that the king must be an Israelite. This is a theological statement, not one concerned with ethnicity. As the later directives make clear, Israel's king is to place himself under the law as a member of the covenant community (Deut 17:18-19). This is a radical position in the world of that day. When Naboth rejects Ahab's offer to purchase his vineyard, Ahab returns home to sulk. When Queen Jezebel, a foreigner from Sidon, discovers Ahab sulking, she asks rhetorically, "Do you now govern Israel?" (1 Kings 21:7), with the implication that if he truly were king, he could do as he wishes: a commoner like Naboth could not turn him down. This is the way of kings in the ancient Near East, but it is not to be the way of kings for Israel, where the king is to be one of the covenant community, a people of former slaves who worship the one true God, a people called upon to treat the weak and the poor in a manner modeled after the way God has treated them.

Directives for the King 17:16-20a

Israel receives permission to have a king, but it is an unusual kind of king, fitting for an unusual people. After emphasizing that the king must be a "brother" chosen by God, the passage gives directives for the king. It is striking that the "you" of the passage, or the audience, continues to be the people as a whole. The king is only spoken of with the third-person singular masculine pronoun. The people remain responsible for the overall structure, and by implication, even for ensuring that these directions for the king are followed.

The structure for these directions is relatively simple and can be outlined as follows:

Negative: Restrictions on Royal Policy
- He must not acquire many horses.
- He must not acquire many wives.
- Silver and gold he must not acquire in great quantity.

Positive: A Torah Scholar
- He must *have a copy of this law* that he *shall read* and be *diligently observing.*

Negative: An Obedient *Brother*
- He shall be *neither exalting himself above other members of the community*
- *nor turning aside from the commandment,*

End Result: A Dynasty
- *so that he and his descendants may reign long over his kingdom in Israel.*

17:16-17 *Restrictions on Royal Policies*

The three restrictions denounce exactly those characteristics of a king that normally would have been considered evidence of success.

1. The first is a rejection of success through military might. *Horses* in the world of Israel have only one purpose: for the chariots and cavalry of the armed forces. The use of horses for agriculture and other domestic work only comes later. Since a king has responsibility for defending the nation from enemy forces, it is only to be expected that one of his priorities is building strong armed forces, and this requires an abundance of horses. As even contemporary dynamics show, there never are enough resources for the defense felt needed by the chief commander.

The restriction is supported with the further comment that he also must not *return the people to Egypt to acquire more horses, since the* LORD *has said to you, "You must never return that way again."* This may simply be a reference to Egypt as the logical nation from which to obtain these horses, a country known to be an exporter of horses. But within the story of Israel it is much more than that. Egypt is the land from which Israel has been delivered. Deuteronomy regularly reminds Israel of this (1:27; 4:20; etc.). God's identity is wrapped up in this defining action. The Decalogue introduces God as the one who *brought you out of the land of Egypt, out of the house of slavery* (5:6); and before its entrance into the Promised Land, Israel is assured that *The LORD your God, who goes before you, ... will fight for you, just as he did for you in Egypt before your very eyes* (1:30). To speak of a return to Egypt intimates a reversal of the exodus, a cancellation of God's deliverance.

But there is more. The quotation *You must never return that way again* (17:16), although not a literal translation, appears to be based on a passage from Exodus where Moses reassures Israel at the edge of the Red Sea, "Do not be afraid, stand firm, and see the deliverance that the LORD will accomplish for you today; for the Egyptians whom you see today you shall never see again. The LORD will fight for you, and you have only to keep still" (Exod 14:13-14, emph. added). These words are spoken in the face of "all Pharaoh's horses and chariots," including at least "six hundred picked chariots" (14:9, 6). After the Egyptian chariots and horses have been covered by the sea, the people of Israel "feared the LORD and believed in the LORD and in his servant Moses" (14:31). The reference to not returning people to Egypt brings that whole story to mind, a story in which the horses of the mighty nation Egypt have been defeated by Yahweh of Israel.

The restriction also brings to mind the account of the rise of kingship in 1 Samuel 8-12. Again Israel is afraid of an enemy, this time the Philistines. The people come to Samuel with the request that he appoint a king for them "so that we also may be like other nations, and that our king may govern us and go before us and fight our battles" (1 Sam 8:20, emph. added). To multiply horses is the same sin as to request a king to fight our battle: both are a rejection of the God who has demonstrated through the exodus that deliverance does not occur through armies and horses but through obedience to that God. The prophet Isaiah indicts the "house of Jacob" because "their land is filled with horses, and there is no end to their chariots" (2:7; cf. Mic 5:10).

2. The second and third restrictions address the typical actions of a king in the political and economic realms. The prohibition that *he must not acquire many wives* (17:17; RSV, *he shall not multiply wives for himself*) is not addressing the king's sexual practices nor defending monogamy; instead, it is a theological critique of political or economic practices. In the ancient world, arranged marriages were a common way of formalizing political alliances and trade

agreements with other nations, as well as of consolidating power internally. They were public symbols and representatives of international and economic partnerships. The passage rejects multiplying wives since through them *his heart will turn away*. This rationale echoes the earlier direction to the people as a whole that they should not intermarry the previous inhabitants of the land *for that would turn* [the same root as in 17:17] *away your children from following me, to serve other gods* (7:3-4). The first concern of the prohibition thus appears to be that marriages to women from foreign countries will lead a king to worship their gods. Solomon had many "foreign wives," who "turned away his heart after other gods" (1 Kings 11:1-8, esp. v. 4); Ahab, in the Northern Kingdom, married Jezebel of Sidon and then built a house for Baal in Samaria, the capital city (1 Kings 16:31-33). The foundational commandment to worship only God remains direction setting.

Yet likely the prohibition against multiplying wives also has internal considerations in mind. After all, the text itself does not specify "foreign" wives but prohibits *many wives* of any kind. Internal alliances with powerful families, "signed" and sealed through marriages, had the potential to undermine the king's place as one of the community. This was true both because it would give key families undue influence, thereby making it difficult for the king to promote justice for all, and because it would reflect a wealth and status well above that of the common people (Nelson 2002: 224).

3. With this concern we move to the third prohibition, the warning against accumulating too much *silver and gold*. At least three Deuteronomic themes underlie this limitation. First, great wealth contributes to a king forgetting that everything he has is a result of God's blessings and not his own achievement (cf. 8:11-20). Second, such wealth on the part of the king tempts him to distinguish himself too sharply from the people, thereby *exalting himself above other members of the community* (v. 20). And third, the major way in which a king could gain such wealth is through heavy taxation. Such taxation is in tension with the care for the weak for which Deuteronomy consistently calls (cf. how 1 Sam 8:10-18 warns against heavy taxation in "the ways of the king").

17:18-19 A Torah Scholar

The one positive directive to the king is that he become a scholar of *this law*, or *torah*. The first task of a king upon enthronement is to *have a copy of this law written for him in the presence of the levitical priests*. Versions differ on whether the king himself is to write out the law (KJV, NIV, RSV) or whether he is to commission others to do it (NRSV), yet the prominent role of the priests in relationship to the law is clear (cf. 31:9).

This verse is the source of the common English title for our book of Deuteronomy. Deuteronomy is derived from the Greek (Septuagint) translation of this verse, which misunderstood the Hebrew phrase now translated *copy of the law* as "second law." The teaching of Moses in Moab may be understood as a second law in addition to the original given at Mount Horeb, but here the phrase is better translated as *a copy of this law*. Missing from many translations, including the NRSV, is the phrase *in a book* (as in KJV, RSV; NJPS, *on a scroll*). The combination *this torah* with *in a book* points to the book now called Deuteronomy: whether to the whole book or to the central section of regulations in chapters 12–26 may be debated (it is common to argue that the reference is only to chapters 12–26; Tigay: 168; McConville 2002: 295; etc.).

This requirement may be influenced by the ancient practice of having documents or texts "specially written for royal instruction" (Nelson 2002: 225). But the torah or law that the king is to copy and then read *all the days of his life, so that he may learn to fear the* LORD *his God*, is not directed only to the king: the same law and instruction is given to all of Israel. The directive is reminiscent of the opening exhortation in chapter 6 immediately preceding the Shema: *This is the commandment . . . God charged me to teach you to observe in the land, . . . so that you and your children and your children's children may fear the* LORD *your God all the days of your life, . . . so that your days may be long* (6:1-2). Common to these two passages are references to observing the torah all the days of life so that there will be a long life (cf. 17:20). In its own way the Shema calls on the Israelite to keep the law in mind everywhere, all the time (6:4-9).

By giving the king this one responsibility, the text makes two striking points. First, the king is not above the law but subservient to it. His throne is built upon the foundation of the law: "If one thinks in political terms, Deuteronomy claims a constitutional status as a written legal document, to which even the king is subject" (Nelson 2002: 225). This Israelite conviction allows prophets to indict kings on the basis of the law (e.g., Nathan confronts David on his sin, 2 Sam 12). Second, it makes the king the prototypical Israelite, the ideal citizen. Through study and diligent obedience, the king models for Israel what it means to live on the basis of the law.

17:20a An Obedient Brother

The final directives are summarized in two statements, both in a negative format. On the surface the two statements have different directions, one the community (*neither exalting himself above other members of the community*, lit., *his brothers*) and the other the law (*nor turning aside from the commandment, either to the right or to the left*). Yet both have the effect of creating solidarity between the king and his community as a people under torah. This passage does not deny that the king will have special responsibilities: that comes with being king. But the concern of Deuteronomy is that despite these, he must remain one with the people. Pharaoh exalted himself over the people (Exod 9:17), and this led to his doom. An Israelite king must not do that, through wives, wealth, or any other way. A warning not to turn *aside* from what has been commanded *to the right or to the left* has been used twice previously, once in a general command to the people: *Be careful to do as the* LORD *your God has commanded you; you shall not turn to the right or to the left* (5:32); the other was just a few verses earlier in the present passage, warning to obey the verdict of the central court (17:11; cf. 28:14).

The LORD gives Joshua a similar exhortation at his commissioning: "Be strong and very courageous, being careful to act in accordance with all the law that my servant Moses commanded you; do not turn from it to the right hand or to the left, so that you may be successful wherever you go" (Josh 1:7; cf. Deut 31:14-23). Joshua was then commanded to meditate on the "book of the law . . . day and night" (v. 8). King Josiah's introduction in Kings characterizes him as follows: "He did what was right in the sight of the LORD, and walked in all the way of his father David; he did not turn aside to the right or to the left" (2 Kings 22:2; cf. 2 Chron 34:2). It is not coincidental that Josiah, upon discovering the "book of the law" in the temple, makes the content of that book, also called the "book of the covenant," the basis for a major reform in Judah; this reform includes a ceremony of covenant renewal and a centralized Passover (2 Kings 22–23). He thus acts in a manner consistent with the Deuteronomic law for the king.

The Outcome: A Dynasty 17:20b

Solidarity with the people and obedience to God's instructions as represented by the book of Deuteronomy are the key to continued blessing in the land, for the people as a whole as well as for the king. The concluding phrase of the passage takes the characteristic

Deuteronomic promise of long life in the land and applies it more particularly to the situation of the king. Kingship and dynastic succession go hand in hand. Dynastic succession is a connotation of the term "king." Although the Deuteronomic law for the king sharply distinguishes the king from the typical ancient Near Eastern monarch, nevertheless it does allow for dynastic succession. But it diverges from the normal pattern because dynastic succession is not dependent upon military success or astute alliances, external and internal, or great wealth; rather, it depends on solidarity with the people and obedience to God's torah. This is an atypical form of kingship, even if the blessings are quite recognizable—a long reign for the king and his descendants.

The Responsibilities of the King

This last comment raises the question of what, if any, responsibilities Deuteronomy imagines for the king. The only task assigned the king is to study and obey *this law*. Interpreters commonly speak of the law as severely limiting or restricting what a king is normally expected to do. McConville says, "It is the limitations placed on the king (17:16-20) that make the laws on the administration of Israel so radical. The Deuteronomic picture of the king contrasts, in fact, not only with kingship as it was exercised in the ANE, but also with the reality of it in ancient Israel." Josiah thus is not an ideal king since even in his reform he "acts in a way that is incompatible with the Deuteronomic law; that is, he assumes total charge of the affairs of the state, including religion, while Deuteronomy's constitution clearly restricts the king's powers" (2002: 283-84).

This misses how radical Deuteronomy's vision is. The text does not assign formal responsibility to the king in any specific area, yet the king is still king. Whitelam speaks of a triple function: "the king's role in the protection of society as warrior, the guarantor of justice as judge and the right ordering of worship as priest are the fundamental roles that cover all aspects of the well-being of society" (130). The Deuteronomic restrictions do not so much limit his areas of responsibility as they shape the way he fulfills them. This is not a contemporary debate between democracy and kingship. Deuteronomy may not speak of the king's responsibility for justice, but this does not necessarily contradict the words probably pronounced at the coronation of each new king: "Give the king your justice, O God.... May he judge your people with righteousness, and your poor with justice" (Ps 72:1-2; McBride 1987). Although the king is given no formal responsibility within the cult, there is nothing in

Deuteronomy that challenges the king's authority to centralize the cult as called for in Deuteronomy 12 *[Cult, p. 546]*.

Deuteronomy's approach here may be compared with the way it speaks of the cult. The book assumes the cultic system and then challenges or addresses particular aspects, even foundational issues, without spelling out the cultic detail. Similarly, Deuteronomy's silence on the usual responsibilities of a king is not evidence that he rejects them, including the triple function identified by Whitelam: defense of the nation, the administration of justice, and the oversight of religious practice. Indeed, as Deuteronomy makes clear throughout the book, Israel's long-term future on the land depends upon its obedience of torah. It thus is not surprising that the way the king ensures Israel's security is related to his relationship to torah. The central thrust is that if there is a king in Israel, he must be one of the covenant community, one who does not exalt himself above his brothers and sisters, one whose life and reign are shaped by *this law*, and perhaps most radically, one who defends the nation not by building up armies with horses but by leading the people in obedience to the law of Deuteronomy.

THE TEXT IN BIBLICAL CONTEXT
Torah, Moses, and Leadership in Israel and the New Testament

Deuteronomy is torah given to the people of Israel for life in the land: whether the people thrive in the land is dependent upon their response to this torah. The audience of the book is "you," the people, or at least the heads of the households. At the same time, there is a secondary theme that rises to the surface at various points, and here in the middle of the book it takes center stage: the question of leadership, and how Israel responds to it, is a crucial aspect of the mix.

In Deuteronomy, Moses is the supreme human leader. After God proclaims the Decalogue to the people at Horeb, they become afraid and ask that Moses serve as mediator between them and God (5:23-31; 18:16). Not only does Moses do this at Horeb; the whole book of Deuteronomy reflects this role as he expounds the torah to them (1:5) and leads them in their ceremony of commitment to the Moab covenant (chs. 29-30). But Moses is more than instructor of torah. He is also their supreme administrative and military leader, as reflected in the confrontations with Kings Sihon and Og (2:24-3:11) and then in the division of land, and he is the supreme judge and mediator of disputes within Israel (1:9-18). Deuteronomy does not stress a priestly role for Moses, but in Exodus he is also the high priest as he leads Israel in sacrifice to God (Exod 24). Moses is the comprehensive leader for Israel, the one who fills all leadership functions.

But Moses will die. The "today" for which Deuteronomy is preparing Israel is a Moses-less tomorrow. The first hint of that comes in the opening chapter, where Moses accepts that he cannot bear the people by himself (1:9), so he gives up his exclusive role as judge and has the tribes appoint judges from among themselves. After that, at multiple points, we overhear dialogue between God and Moses about his impending death, a debate that in the last chapter climaxes with the account of his death outside the Promised Land. These chapters presenting Israel's key leaders are part of this conversation. In a Moses-less tomorrow, leadership is divided into multiple roles, with the Deuteronomic torah binding them together and standing above them.

This vision of Deuteronomy corresponds with Israel's historical experience. Moses is succeeded by Joshua and then by the charismatic judges (e.g., Gideon, Samuel), each of whom continues to provide a relatively comprehensive leadership. Although their responsibility for torah is not emphasized, the book of Judges repeatedly reports that when a judge dies, the people do "evil in the sight of the LORD" (Judg 3:12; 4:1; 6:1; 10:6; 13:1). Leadership is key to faithfulness by the people.

With the rise of kingship, the all-encompassing roles of Moses, Joshua, and the judges are gradually divided up and become more specialized. The king becomes responsible for the political or administrative realm; judges for the administration of the judicial realm, even if the king remains ultimately in charge (e.g., Ps 72:1); and priests for the cult. These roles are continuous or constant, with prophets as messengers of God more sporadic or occasional. This is consistent with Deuteronomy, which highlights that God will raise up prophets; whereas the people demand a king, the tribe of Levi are ongoing priests, and judges are selected by the people, only God can raise up a prophet to speak on God's behalf.

The significance of leadership and the paired role of kings and prophets comes out clearly in the Deuteronomistic History. The demise of the Northern Kingdom happens because the people "sinned against the LORD their God" (2 Kings 17:7-18, esp. v. 7); yet throughout the story the text emphasizes that each king followed in the ways of Jeroboam, who built worship centers in Bethel and Dan, thereby contravening the requirements of Deuteronomy 12. The demise of Judah, the Southern Kingdom, is directly attributed to the actions of King Manasseh (2 Kings 23:26). Effective leadership is key.

Within the Deuteronomistic History, prophets relate almost exclusively to kings. Prophets are God's voice in the process, designating kings (e.g., Samuel anoints Saul and David, Ahijah announces to Jeroboam that he will become king), proclaiming their rejection (Samuel announces this to Saul), and indicting them for their sin. The classical prophets also proclaim God's word into the story. Their audience may be the people as a whole, but in the process they highlight that Israel's leaders are not fulfilling their responsibility (e.g., Isa 1:10; Jer 2:8; Mic 3:1).

In the language of the early church, Jesus once again combines these various roles, even if in a very different manner from Moses. The New Testament thus speaks of Jesus as "priest" (esp. in Hebrews, e.g., 2:17; 3:1); as "prophet," with explicit reference to Deuteronomy 18:15 (Acts 3:17-26); as "king" (Acts 17:7; Rev 15:3); as the one who will "judge" all peoples (2 Tim 4:1, 8); and also as sage (Matt 12:42). Christ becomes the new model for leadership in the kingdom community, the one who presents and represents a new torah to the people.

Kings and Kingship in Scripture

A remarkable feature of Israel's story is that it retains the memory of intense debate around the rise of kingship. To be a nation means to have a king. And yet Israel remembers the transition to kingship as a contested event (1 Sam 8-12; for a more extensive discussion of these chapters, see Gerbrandt) and sees kingship as contingent and qualified. After all, God is king, the one who gives victory over enemies, the one who deserves absolute loyalty. Choosing a human king amounts to rejecting that role for God (1 Sam 8:7).

This ambiguity around kingship permeates the whole story. On the one hand, kingship is natural, integral to greatness, and blessed by God. Even the tradition most critical of it calls it the way of "other nations" (1 Sam 8:5; cf. Deut 17:14). Before the rise of kingship, "all the people did what was right in their own eyes" (Judg 21:25; cf. 19:1). God not only directs Samuel to consent to the people's request for a king (1 Sam 8:7, 9) but also has Samuel anoint the first king, Saul, as well as the second king, David, as a sign of his participation in the institution (1 Sam 9:1-10:16; 16:1-13). Kings are part of God's providential care for the people.

Israel's glory days then come with David and Solomon on the throne. Their success is directly attributed to God's presence: "And David became greater and greater, for the LORD, the God of hosts, was with him" (2 Sam 5:10; cf. the story of Solomon and his dream at Gibeon, 1 Kings 3:3-14). God substantiates his relationship to David by promising David an everlasting dynasty: "Your house and your kingdom shall be made sure forever before me; your kingdom shall be established forever" (2 Sam 7:16). This covenant becomes an important element of the Jerusalem cult (e.g., Pss 18:50; 89:3-4). At critical points in this story, God uses kings to lead the people back to God. Hezekiah "did what was right in the sight of the LORD, just as his ancestor David had done. He removed the high places, broke down the pillars, and cut down the sacred pole" (2 Kings 18:3-4a), as called for in Deuteronomy (16:21-22). Josiah leads the people in a recommitment to the covenant, along with a centralized Passover (2 Kings 22–23), again as called for in Deuteronomy (16:1-8). When the postexilic community is unable to reestablish kingship in Jerusalem, the Davidic promise becomes the foundation for messianic expectations, the anticipation that God will send a new king, or "anointed one," to deliver the people.

On the other hand, kingship does not escape the dark cloud that accompanied its birth. The reference to being *like all the nations* (Deut 17:14) already suggests danger. Although God commands Samuel to consent to the people's request for a king (1 Sam 8), at the same time he has Samuel warn the people of the "ways of the king." Kings tend to be ambitious and oppressive, taxing the people both of their goods and even their lives (1 Sam 8:10-18).

Israel's actual experience with kings only confirms the warning. Most individual kings receive extremely negative evaluations by the Deuteronomistic History, with the demise of the Southern Kingdom attributed to the sins of Manasseh (2 Kings 24:3). Even the "great" kings are not exempt from rebuke. David's sin with Bathsheba receives detailed coverage (2 Sam 11–12). The text highlights Solomon's love of foreign women and their gods (1 Kings 11:1-8, 33), as well as his oppressive internal policies (e.g., 1 Kings 5:13-18); both are a direct violation of Deuteronomy's law of the king (17:14-20). Repeatedly prophets confront kings, calling for their subservience to God and God's representatives. Kingship is normal, but the Old Testament calls for a radically transformed kind of kingship.

Jesus' proclamation of the kingdom of God participates in this same tension. Messianic expectations were widespread at the time. There was hope that once again God would act mightily, freeing the Jews from Roman control, once again establishing a national kingdom. Within this milieu Jesus announces the kingdom and accepts messianic designation. When Peter at Caesarea Philippi makes the bold assertion, "You are the Messiah, the Son of the living God,"

Jesus assents and even adds that this has been revealed to Peter by "my Father in heaven" (Matt 16:16-17). But when Jesus then continues to speak about his needing to suffer and die, Peter cannot accept that because he still thinks of the Messiah as a powerful king, a heroic David (Matt 16:21-23). Similarly, on Palm Sunday the crowds shout, "Hosanna to the Son of David," apparently anticipating a Davidic-type king (21:9). But that is not to be. Jesus the Messiah continues the trajectory reflected by the Deuteronomic transformation of ancient kingship in chapter 17.

THE TEXT IN THE LIFE OF THE CHURCH
Of Kings and CEOs

Israelite kingship has not fared well in liberal Western thought, much less in believers church circles. Kings are considered to be autocrats and demigods, quite in tension with our sense that democracy and priesthood of all believers are the ideal forms of organization, perhaps even God's way. The rise of kingship then is considered the "fall of Israel," similar to the fall of Christianity into Christendom. George Mendenhall writes, "The Old Testament Constantine, King David, represents a thoroughgoing reassimilation to Late Bronze Age religious ideas and structures" (1973: 16).

This assessment was not always so. Julius Wellhausen writes,

> In the eyes of Israel before exile the monarchy is the culminating point of the history, and the greatest blessing of Jehovah. . . . Under it the people dwell securely and respected by those round about; guarded by the shelter of civil order, the citizen can sit under his own vine and fig-tree. (253)

He believed that those Old Testament traditions critical of kings could only have arisen in late postexilic Judaism, when all the positive benefits of kingship had been forgotten (255). We now recognize that Wellhausen's perspective was influenced by his admiration for the strong leadership of Chancellor Otto von Bismarck. But he serves as a warning that what one sees in the text can be quite influenced by the political mood of the time.

A contemporary Western commitment to democracy risks biasing us to interpret passages like Deuteronomy 17 as supporting an antikingship bias, thereby hindering us from receiving a word from them. And yet, despite our rhetoric, there is in North America a longing for "kings," or as it is often expressed, a need for strong leadership. This is true on the political level, it is true in the church, it is true in business. Megachurches and such movements, whether conservative or liberal, tend to have leaders larger than life. Hugely successful businesses like the software giants have their creative genius leaders. We may espouse the power of the people, but we follow our kings. This is the way of the nations today.

Powerful leaders have the potential to achieve large results. That was true of Israelite kings, and it is true of powerful leaders today. Deuteronomy calls upon modern-day kings to remain rooted in their community; to abstain from typical power politics to achieve their goals; to be especially vigilant against the natural temptations of the role, whether financial or sexual; and, most of all, to give priority attention to studying torah, an artistic painting of what faithful following of God means. Whether in the role of charismatic pastor, dynamic institutional CEO, or strong business leader, the temptation to function in the manner shaped by *all the nations round about* is powerful. Only a transformed kingship, centered around torah, has the possibility of withstanding it.

Nation versus People

With the rise of kingship and the development of a royal court and standing armies, Israel became a fairly typical ancient Near Eastern state. Historians debate how strong a state it was, and they weigh the relative power of Judah in the south versus the Israel of the north; yet for some four centuries the Old Testament people of God were simultaneously a political nation. With the fall of Jerusalem in the early sixth century BCE, this synthesis fell apart. The Maccabeans revived it for a time, but by the time of Jesus, Jewish identity had become established as a distinct ethnic and religious entity within the Roman Empire (though Jews also lived elsewhere); the exilic period helped prepare it for this way of existing.

Christianity began as a minority movement within a powerful empire, but from Constantine onward, a Christendom evolved in which state and church merged. The Reformation may have been an earthquake in the story of the church, but mainline traditions continued to affirm this fusion of church and state. Although the U.S. formally rejected the notion of an established church, it for long understood itself as a Christian nation, with Protestantism the norm. Early in the twentieth century President Wilson could still speak of "America" as "born a Christian nation" (Marty: front pages), and the University of Michigan could serve as a model of a Christian university, even requiring chapel attendance of its students (Marsden: 167–80). This era of Christendom, however, is over.

The story of Deuteronomy fits into both settings, with its *today* always relevant. Whether at the border of the Promised Land, or during the time of kings, or in exile, its vision is relevant. Perhaps not surprisingly, John Calvin makes use of Deuteronomy when discussing the "duty of magistrates, its nature, as described by the word of God" (4.20.9-10). The organizational instructions of these chapters were considered applicable to the national structures of his day.

The believers church tradition has tended to understand the church as a people of God quite apart from national politics, with an emphasis on the separation of church and state. The church is the body of Christ, global, and above nation and state. But it consists of human beings, with its organization susceptible to the dynamics of any other organization. The vision of Deuteronomy is exactly for such a people of God.

Levitical Priests

Deuteronomy 18:1-8

PREVIEW

With our long history of lay leadership in the believers church tradition, we may forget that professionalism in the delivery of religious services is nothing new. Mesopotamia and Egypt had their cultic functionaries who derived their living from service to the gods and the cult, and Israel had its priests, who first served at open-air shrines and then in the temple in Jerusalem *[Cult, p. 546]*.

It thus is not surprising that priests are included in this unit. But the central concern of the passage is not the job description of the priests, which is assumed, but their status within Israel and the way in which they are supported. The argument is fairly simple. The tribe of Levi did not receive an inheritance or allotment when Israel settled in the Promised Land. Instead, God is their inheritance; hence the people are to provide for the priests' daily needs through their sacrificial offerings and the giving of firstfruits.

OUTLINE

Basic Principles, 18:1-2
The Dues Owed the Priests, 18:3-5
Levites at The Place, 18:6-8

EXPLANATORY NOTES

Deuteronomy's introduction of priests says little about their role or duties other than that they *stand and minister in the name of the* LORD (18:5; cf. v. 7). Within Israel, priests had two primary areas of responsibility: (1) the administration of the cult, especially the sacrificial system; and (2) the safeguarding and instruction of the law (Lev 10:11). Deuteronomy says little about the first, although at least two passages assume it (26:3-4; 33:10). Sacrifice and the work of a priest were so closely connected in the ancient world that it did not need to be highlighted.

Deuteronomy highlights the priest's responsibility for the law. The priests are responsible for the ark of the covenant, the place where the copy of the law is kept (10:1-5, 8); they are involved in the king's preparation of a copy of the law (17:18); and later Moses writes down *this law* and gives it to the priests, who then are commanded to read it to the people every seven years (31:9-13). The priests' role in Israel's judicial system may be understood as a practical implication of their responsibility for law (17:9, 12; 19:17; 21:5; 33:8). In addition, the priests had a role in Yahweh war (20:2-4).

Basic Principles 18:1-2

A comparison of different versions draws attention to an ambiguity in the Hebrew text. A literal translation of the key terms yields *to the priests, the Levites, the whole tribe of Levi* (18:1). The KJV is most similar and equally ambiguous: *The priests the Levites, and all the tribe of Levi.* The RSV and NRSV combine the first two terms into the phrase *levitical priests* (cf. 17:9, 18; 24:8; 27:9) and then interpret the third phrase to be a further reference or clarification to the same group (RSV, *the Levitical priests, that is, all the tribe of Levi*). The TEV resolves all tensions with its combination of these terms into one phrase: *the priestly tribe of Levi.*

These different translations highlight the ambiguity around the relationship of the category "priests" to the category "Levites." Does Deuteronomy equate Levites with priests, thereby implying that all Levites are priests or at least have the right to be priests (e.g., Emerton)? Or does Deuteronomy reflect the more general Old Testament position that God designated the whole tribe of Levi for special service (including responsibility for the law and other supportive services in the cult), but that not all within the tribe were priests (only the descendants of Aaron?). This much-debated issue cannot be resolved in a commentary like this (cf. Emerton; Abba; Nelson 1991; Cook 2011). Here Deuteronomy is not addressing what may have been a dispute between competing groups within Israel but rather is speaking to the more limited issue of how Israel is to understand and treat the whole tribe of Levi, whether all of them were priests (as may be implied by this verse), or only some of them (as reflected by Num 3 and possibly implied by Deut 10:6-8; 26:1-11 next to 26:12; 27:9 next to 27:14). Deuteronomy 18:1 TEV, although not literal, reflects this emphasis on the whole tribe even as it implies that all are considered priests.

The Hebrew of the last part of 18:1 also is obscure, with a literal rendering something like *They shall eat the fire of the LORD and his inheritance*. The term *fire* is probably a reference to offerings to God that are partially burned at the altar. These offerings are given to God (i.e., *his inheritance*) but not fully burned, therefore making it possible for the priests to receive what is left for their daily sustenance.

Despite these ambiguities, the overall thrust is clear. Since the tribe of Levi does not inherit a portion of the Promised Land (cf. Num 18:20), God is its inheritance. Practically, this means that they receive a portion of the gifts given to God. Deuteronomy uses the theologically charged term *inheritance* four times in these two verses (the second use, at the end of verse 1, is lost in translation), plus the term *allotment*. The Hebrew term, here translated *inheritance*, but in some other passages as *possession*, is used in three interrelated ways in Deuteronomy. First and foundationally, it is used of the Promised Land (4:38; 12:9; 15:4; etc.). This inheritance is *a land in which you will eat bread without scarcity, in which you will lack nothing* (8:9 RSV), a land so fruitful that not one of them will need to be poor (15:4). Second, Deuteronomy speaks of Israel as God's inheritance (4:20). And third, it is used of God as the inheritance of the tribe of Levi (10:9; 18:2). This use is parallel to the first, since in both cases the inheritance becomes the source of daily sustenance. It is true even if somewhat indirect for the Levites, through the Israelites' offerings to God. In this way they also participate in the blessings of the land.

Although the Levites do not receive land as their inheritance, they still are *members of the community* (i.e., *brothers*), living in their midst. In Numbers 35 the Levites throughout the land receive forty-eight cities, in which they can live and even keep their livestock (cf. Josh 21). The repeated reference in Deuteronomy to the *Levites who reside in your towns* (12:12, 18; 14:27; 16:11) may refer to these cities, although the language of Deuteronomy seems to suggest the Levites lived in the same towns as other Israelites. Without land they cannot provide for their own food. Because of this, Deuteronomy regularly lists them among the categories of people who need special consideration (cf. 14:29; 16:11, 14; 26:12, 13).

The Dues Owed the Priests 18:3-5

After summarizing the basic principles, the text zeroes in on what is due the priests. These verses only speak of *priests* (v. 3), but both the context and the language of verse 5 imply that the passage is still speaking of the whole tribe. Although the NRSV includes the proper noun *Levi* in verse 5, the Hebrew is simply the third-person singular masculine pronoun (RSV, *him*; NIV converts to the plural, *them*). The reference to *out of all your tribes* fits with the passage still speaking of the whole tribe. The whole tribe has the mandate to *stand and minister in the name of the* LORD, whether through officiating at sacrifice (a role Exodus limits to priests, 30:20) or serving in some other way, such as responsibility for the ark (Deut 10:8), taking care of the place of worship and its cultic objects (Num 1:50; 3:31), or through teaching and interpreting the law.

Deuteronomy identifies two types of dues for the priests: first, a portion of that which is sacrificed; and second, the firstfruits from the field and sheep. That a portion of sacrifices belongs to the priests is consistent with other passages (cf. Exod 29:16-18; Lev 7:28-34; Num 18:9-24). When one compares the details, however, differences emerge. For example, whereas Deuteronomy speaks of the priests as receiving *the shoulder, the two jowls, and the stomach* (18:3), Exodus speaks of the priest as receiving the breast and thigh (29:26-28). The account of Eli's sons gives a still different impression (1 Sam 2:12-17). These differences may reflect changes in practice over time, or they may represent the dues from different types of sacrifice. In any case, Deuteronomy's interest is not in the detail of what is due for the priest—after all, Deuteronomy is not giving priestly legislation, but preaching for the people—but instead is with the bigger issues. Levites are to receive compensation for the work they do on behalf of God.

Earlier Deuteronomy has called upon Israel to bring its annual tithes to the central sanctuary, where they are used for a communal celebration (14:22-27; cf. 12:6, 11; 26:11), with the third-year tithe remaining in the local communities for the sake of the *Levites, ... the resident aliens, the orphans, and the widows* (14:28-29). The earlier passage on tithes (14:22-29) as well as the later one on the presentation of firstfruits (26:1-11) both place the giving of these fruits to the priests within the context of a celebration that includes everyone, including widows, orphans, and the poor, as well as the Levites. They may assume that *the first fruits* are given to the priests, and thus are not in tension with this passage (18:4). For Deuteronomy, the land was a bountiful land that, if Israel obeyed, would more than supply all their needs.

These verses conclude by identifying the tribe of Levi as the fourth entity God has chosen for a special task or role. God *has chosen* Israel *out of all the peoples on earth* (7:6), God *will choose ... the place ... out of all your tribes* for worship (12:5), God *will choose ... a king* for Israel (17:15), and now it is stated that *God has chosen* the tribe *of Levi out of all your tribes* (18:5; cf. 21:5; 1 Sam 2:28). The similarity of language between this election and that of The Place reflects the natural connection between the two.

Levites at The Place 18:6-8

Debate over how (or whether) these verses relate to 2 Kings 23:8-9 has dominated discussion of this passage. Ever since the late nineteenth century, it has been common to argue that Deuteronomy is here defending the rights of rural Levites in the light of cult centralization. The argument is that the Levites living throughout the land previously would have had duties at the many local cultic sites and thus would have had sources of income. The Deuteronomic vision, however, eliminates these sites and centralizes cultic activity at one place, thereby taking away the rural Levites' livelihood. These verses then contend that if any of these rural Levites wish to move to the central sanctuary and minister there, they have the right to do so.

A tension then arises when this is linked to the report of Josiah's reform. As Deuteronomy demands, Josiah does rid the temple of Baalistic objects and customs (e.g., vessels made for Baal and Asherah), and he does defile and destroy the high places throughout the land (2 Kings 23:4, 8-10). But we read that although "he brought all the priests out of the towns of Judah ... , the priests of the high places ... did not come up to the altar of the LORD in Jerusalem, but ate unleavened bread among their kindred" (23:8-9). In other words, whereas Deuteronomy directs that the rural priests who have lost their livelihood through centralization be allowed to minister at the central sanctuary, Josiah's reform do not follow through on this provision. Although it centralizes the cult as required, it does not allow the former priests of the high places to serve at the Jerusalem temple.

The question of how Deuteronomy relates to the reform of Josiah is complex *[Deuteronomy and the Reform of Josiah, p. 549]*. There are good reasons, however, for questioning the approach described above, both in its interpretation of our present passage and in its understanding of the relationship of the two passages to each other. For example, whereas Deuteronomy 18:6-8 speaks simply of Levites and does not use the word "priests," 1 Kings 23 speaks only of priests and nowhere uses the word "Levites." Further, it is difficult to imagine that Deuteronomy, with its fervent rejection of anything related to pagan cult, would allow priests who had formerly served these gods at the high places now be allowed to serve in the worship of the God of Israel at The Place (Nelson 2002: 232; McConville 2002: 299). Our present passage thus needs to be approached on its own, albeit within the larger context of Deuteronomy. A key interpretive issue is the proper translation of these three verses. The three verses consist of three distinct phrases, and the first begins with *If* (Deut 18:6). This raises the question of where the consequent "then" is placed since it is not explicit in the Hebrew. Most versions place it before the second phrase (as introducing v. 7), and then consider the third phrase (v. 8) a new sentence (e.g., KJV, RSV, NRSV). This results in the traditional sense: *If a Levite from one of your towns comes to the place, then he may minister (and) he shall have equal portions* (AT, shortened to highlight its logic). But grammatically it is also possible that the "then" should be placed just before the third phrase, resulting in the following sense: *If a Levite from one of your towns comes to the place, and if he ministers there, then he shall have equal portions* (AT; thus Nelson 2002; McConville 2002; Christensen 2001; NEB). The focus of the passage, then, is not the right to serve at The Place, but the right to receive income when serving at The Place.

This latter reading fits much better with the immediate context (18:1-8) and the book of Deuteronomy as a whole. These verses are continuing the theme introduced in the opening verses of the passage (18:1-2) and expanded upon in the middle section (18:3-5). Deuteronomy regularly speaks of Levites as living in the towns throughout the land (12:12, 18; 14:27; 16:11). Since Deuteronomy does not allow any sacrifice away from The Place, these Levites would not be administering the sacrificial system, but they still could be active in teaching and representing the law. The point of this passage is that if such a rural Levite chooses to come to the central sanctuary and there does participate in the cult like the Levites there (whether as a priest or in some other duty), then that Levite should be recompensed appropriately. This applies whether the Levite is making a permanent move to The Place or if it is only temporary. A priest living in the country, perhaps in one of the priestly cities, might come to The Place for a time of service, and then after it was over he might return to his home community (cf. Zechariah shuttling between his home in the Judean hill country and Jerusalem for "his time of service," Luke 1:8, 23, 39-40; also 1 Kings 2:26).

The final phrase of the passage, *even though they have income from the sale of family possession,* is perhaps a surprise. Although the Levites as a tribe did not receive a portion of the land, they were assigned cities and thus may have had property. Despite this, Deuteronomy regularly categorizes the Levites among those who need special consideration (12:12, 18; 14:27, 29; 16:11, 14; 26:11, 11-13).

THE TEXT IN BIBLICAL CONTEXT
Priests, and a Royal Priesthood

Priests were a given in the larger world of Israel: other peoples and nations had them, and Israel had them. They served as institutionalized mediators between God (or gods) and people, with primary responsibility for religious practice, or the cult. Based on the blessing given the tribe of Levi in Deuteronomy 33:8-11, the book understands priestly responsibilities as focused on divination, instruction, and sacrifice (P. Miller 2000: 165). Elsewhere Deuteronomy highlights the priests' role in instruction by giving them responsibility for the ark, beside which the book of torah (i.e., Deuteronomy) rests (31:24-26), and the regular reading of the torah to the people (31:9-10).

In the postexilic period a threefold hierarchy of cultic officials became standard: a high priest, other priests, and Levites, the last serving as priestly assistants. Since there no longer were any kings in Israel, and the prophetic voice was silent, priests became the sole institutional mediators between God and the people, with the high priest not only the religious leader but also the political and economic leader. This was the world into which Jesus was born.

Given their significance, it is not surprising that the New Testament makes use of this language for understanding Jesus and the church. Hebrews addresses a community that may have been attracted to Judaism and its rituals to assure forgiveness. In response, Hebrews systematically makes the case that Jesus as high priest is superior in every way to the Aaronic priesthood of the Old Testament (Heb 2:17; 3:1; chs. 7–10, et al.). In fact, "Jesus takes on a double role, both that of mediating priest and sacrificial victim," thereby bringing to an end the need for animal sacrifice (Nelson 1993: 148).

The New Testament may speak of Jesus as priest, but perhaps surprisingly, it does not use the term "priest" "for a particular ministry among the people of God" (Marlin Miller: 721). Rather, it speaks of the church with priestly language. First Peter calls the early church community "a chosen race, a royal priesthood, a holy nation" (1 Pet 2:9; cf. Exod 19:6; Rev 1:6; 5:10). Especially those denominational traditions going back to the Reformation, including Mennonites, have tended to make use of this verse to argue for a "priesthood of all believers," with the implication that each believer has individual access to God, without the need for a mediating priest. Nelson helpfully observes that 1 Peter 2:9 is not about individual priests but about the church community as a whole.

> The community's collective designation as a priesthood is both a pledge of election and a summons to holiness, evangelism, and the Christian life.... Neither ritual prerogatives nor individual privileges are in view, but the shared election, holiness, and responsibilities of the whole people of God. (1993: 168)

The church serves as a mediating community between God and all peoples (note the excellent article on "Priesthood of All Believers" by Marlin Miller).

THE TEXT IN THE LIFE OF THE CHURCH

Leadership and the Church

The Reformation gave birth to the slogan "priesthood of all believers": all are priests, all are called to witness, all are ministers. Some have taken this to imply that there is something unbiblical about appointing a few to special leadership roles over the rest. The Protestant model of a solo pastor then is contrasted with the "New Testament model of universal ministry" (Elias: 86).

In response it is argued that that the New Testament does indeed allow for ministry offices. The statement on ministry produced by the Mennonite Church affirms "the ministry of all believers" even as it advocates for "calling out persons to offices of ministry." These offices of ministry then are categorized in a "threefold pattern," ministry that provides "oversight to the church," "ministry which provides prophetic, priestly and administrative service in a local and/or specific setting," and "ministry which represents the members of the congregation" (*MPML* 17-21). The categories are determined somewhat hierarchically rather than by role or function.

What is striking about this debate is that the Deuteronomic passages on leadership, or the Old Testament role of priest, tend to be entirely absent: conversation is largely based on New Testament texts like Ephesians 4:11-13; Romans 12:3-8; and 1 Corinthians 12:4-31. Even if one does not apply the Deuteronomic vision for the Old Testament people of God directly to the contemporary church, it still seems strange not to consider and even to ignore a portion of Scripture so explicitly focused on leadership within the people of God (this is an example of Text *Not* in the Life of the Church).

Two points of contact may be suggested. First, torah, or the instruction and word of God, is foundational and authoritative for each of the leadership roles introduced here in Deuteronomy (McConville 2002: 304-6). The prophet explains and expounds torah with Moses as the model: the judge administers torah, the king studies torah, and the priest preserves and teaches torah. This primacy of torah for all roles is instructive, showing the torah's qualities of justice and righteousness.

Considering the pastor as priest also points to a second observation. Whereas the roles of priest as well as of king and judge are ongoing offices, the role of a prophet is occasional, initiated by God in a time of particular need. This may put into question the tendency to think of or imagine pastors as prophets. Pastors, with their ongoing and official roles, are more like Old Testament priests, and possibly even kings, with some overarching administrative responsibilities. Rather than looking to the prophet as a role model, a pastor today might ask, "Has God raised, or whom has God raised, as a charismatic prophet around me to speak an unsettling word to me?"

Prophets

Deuteronomy 18:9-22

PREVIEW

Whom would you consider a prophet? Someone who predicts the future? Or someone who adopts an austere countercultural lifestyle? Or perhaps someone who is on the cutting edge of change? Or is it someone who forcefully confronts or indicts either church or society? Do they have to be Christian, or can they come from another faith or even be nonreligious?

For Deuteronomy, a prophet is someone who speaks God's words, like Moses. The climactic location of Deuteronomy's introduction of the prophet reflects the importance it gives this role. Although the place of the prophet in Israel may be less clear-cut than that of the judge (judicial system), the king (highest administrative leadership), and priest (cult and law), the prophet plays a key role in Deuteronomy's vision for a covenanted community. The prophet is one whom God raises, the one who speaks God's words to the community. Hence the people, the explicit audience of this passage, are to listen to the prophet.

Deuteronomy introduces the prophet with two distinct paragraphs. The first (vv. 9-14) rejects the ways nations of that day seek information about the future. Instead, God will raise up prophets through whom God will speak (vv. 15-22). The passage contrasts the rejected ways of the nations with the type of prophet Israel will have.

OUTLINE
Rejection of False Prophetic Practices, 18:9-14
A Prophet Raised by God, 18:15-22

EXPLANATORY NOTES

Rejection of False Prophetic Practices 18:9-14

The passage opens with language reminiscent of the text introducing the king, first by noting Israel's entrance into the land God is giving them (v. 9; cf. 17:14), and then by referring to the ways of the nations. King and prophet are leadership roles uniquely related to each other, particularly relevant for life in the gifted land. The relationship of king to land is obvious: when Israel is not in the land, there is no need for a king. The relationship of the prophet to the land may not be as direct, but it is striking that in Israel prophets play their most significant role during the time of the monarchy. Like the nations round about, Israel will have prophets, but the way Israel's prophets obtain their knowledge about God and the future is transformed (cf. the way kingship is transformed in Deuteronomy).

The opening reference to God giving Israel the land, followed by a reference to the practices of the nations in the land, is matched by the closing verse of the paragraph that speaks of the dispossession of the nations (i.e., Israel receiving the land) and again of their rejected practices, thus forming a frame for the listing of practices in the middle of the paragraph (vv. 9 and 14). Even as this frame instructs Israel how to live in order to experience God's blessings, it subtly warns that the ways of the nations previously in the land can be tempting, and that following them can lead to destruction (cf. v. 12). The final phrase of verse 14, *The LORD your God does not permit you to do so*, enforces this warning (lit., *the LORD your God has not given thus to you*). The NRSV loses the Hebrew play with the word "to give." God has given Israel the land, but God has not given Israel the practices of the people who were in the land. If Israel chooses to follow those practices, the gift of land will be put into question. Instead of learning the practices of the nations, Israel is to learn to fear God (4:10; 14:23; 17:19; 31:12, 13) and to obey God's commandments (5:1).

The text identifies seven or so techniques used by people in the ancient world to hear a word from God or to learn about the future. The uncertainty of ancient life leads to "a whole array of esoteric arts and practices, . . . with various kinds of experts in them," all with the goal of attempting to discover what God is saying or what the future holds (McConville 2002: 300). The Old Testament regularly denounces these methods (cf. Exod 22:18; Lev 19:31; 20:6, 27), and yet it recognizes that they were practiced within Israel and at points were even effective. When Saul wishes to know what will happen in an upcoming battle with the Philistines and cannot receive his answer "by dreams, or by Urim, or by prophets," he contacts the spirit of Samuel through a medium at Endor and correctly learns that Israel will be defeated and that he and his sons will die in the battle (1 Sam 28:3-25; cf. Jer 27:9; Mic 3:7). Our text, however, rejects these practices as *abhorrent to the LORD* (the term *abhorrent* is used three times within these six verses; cf. 7:25, 26; 12:31; 13:14; 14:3; 17:1, 4; 20:18; 22:5; 23:18; 24:4; 25:16; 27:15; 32:16).

The passage directly associates these practices with the ways of the nations whom Israel displaced, and it accounts for their loss of the land as due to these practices (18:12). But the mere fact that the nations employed them is insufficient grounds for rejection. Rather, the rejection is much more fundamental than that. These practices challenge Israel's conviction that God is in control and that there is a dynamic relationship between God and Israel (Brueggemann 2001: 193). The rejected practices tend to be manipulative, requiring special knowledge by those employing them. Most of the practices assume a closed future, one that is "set in stone," either by fate or the gods, with the goal of the technique being to discover what that future will be. This is in sharp contrast to the theology of Deuteronomy, and indeed of the whole Old Testament. Deuteronomy is a word for today (4:8, 26, 39, 40; 5:1; 6:6; 7:11; 8:1; etc.), whenever that "today" may be, when the audience is challenged to choose life over death (30:15). The future is dependent upon how the people respond.

The list of practices may not be exhaustive, but it is intended to be comprehensive. All the techniques nations use to discover the future are rejected. This is supported by the list including seven practices, with the number seven symbolizing a complete list.

- *who makes a son or daughter pass through fire*: This may refer to a divination practice rather than child sacrifice (cf. 2 Kings 17:17; 21:6), one in which a child is passed through a fire, with the child's survival or death providing a "yes" or "no" answer (Nelson 2002: 233).

- *divination*: This is a general term for seeking the divine will, including a wide variety of techniques beyond those cited in the list (e.g., hepatoscopy, the interpretation of the configurations of the liver of a sacrificial animal), yet also methods elsewhere accepted (e.g., the priestly use of the Urim and Thummim).

- *soothsayer*: The meaning is unclear, but in light of its Hebrew root (the word "cloud"), some suggest it may refer to the observation of clouds. The Old Testament speaks of the Philistines (Isa 2:6) and Manasseh (2 Kings 21:6) practicing it, with the classical prophets rejecting it (Isa 2:6; Jer 27:9; Mic 5:12).

- *auger*: Again the meaning is unclear, but apparently Joseph practiced this in Egypt through the use of a cup, perhaps by observing the "patterns formed when liquids of different density are mixed in a goblet, such as drops of oil added to water or the reverse (Gen. 44:5, 15)" (Tigay: 173).

- *sorcerer, . . . who casts spells*: These are probably forms of magic rather than divination; they attempt to affect or change the future through mysterious techniques. Exodus pronounces the death penalty on a person who practices sorcery (22:18). Pharaoh's sorcerers were able to duplicate some of the signs of Moses when he came to Egypt (Exod 7:11). The casting of spells may be used against enemies as a form of self-defense (Tigay: 173; cf. Ps 58:5; Isa 47:9, 12). Both of these practices assume that there is power in particular techniques unrelated to the power of God.

- *who consults ghosts or spirits, or who seeks oracles from the dead*: The effort to communicate with the dead (necromancy) on the grounds that the dead have knowledge of the future—this was common in the ancient world, with the story of Saul and the medium of Endor (1 Sam 28:3-25) indicating that although the practice was prohibited within Israel, it had a longstanding reputation and was considered to be effective.

Since these practices led to the expulsion of the previous nations from the land, (v. 12), the message is clear: if Israel follows these practices, it will put its life on the land in jeopardy (cf. 2 Kings 17:17; 21:6). In contrast, Israel *must remain completely loyal to the* LORD *your God* (v. 13). The term translated *completely loyal* is used of sacrifices that are unblemished (Exod 12:5; Lev 1:3; 3:1; etc.), leading to the common translation of *perfect* (KJV) or *blameless* (RSV). This is not abstract perfection but a righteous relationship with God (cf. Ps 18:23, "I was blameless before [God])." Similarly, Jesus calls on his followers to "be perfect, therefore, as your heavenly Father is perfect" (Matt 5:48). Neither is referring to absolute perfection but *complete* loyalty and unity of spirit. Full dependence upon God implies that Israel will not seek these alternative ways of discovering the future but will turn to God and God's messengers, the prophets.

A Prophet Raised by God 18:15-22

Whereas the nations *give heed* to *soothsayers and diviners* (v. 14), Israel is to *heed* (v. 15) the *prophet like* Moses. The use of the identical term in both places strongly connects the two verses, and it sets the second (what Israel is to do) in contrast to the first (what the nations do). The following verses then introduce the prophet, a focus highlighted even more in the Hebrew where *prophet* is the first term of the verse: *A prophet, from your midst, of your brothers, like me, he will raise for you, [namely,] the* LORD *your God* (18:15 AT).

The opening verse of the paragraph introduces three key themes: (1) the divine initiative for prophecy, (2) the nature of a prophet—like Moses—and (3) the need to listen to the prophet. First, a true prophet is one whom God raises up. This is stated in the opening verse of the paragraph (*God will raise up for you a prophet*, v. 15), is repeated a few verses later (*I will raise up for them a prophet*, v. 18), and then said again a third time in different words (*or who presumes to speak in my name a word that I have not commanded*, v. 20). The contrast between the nations' manipulative techniques—rejected in the first paragraph, all of which arise out of human curiosity or desire—is certainly intended. It may also be hinting at a contrast between the prophet whom God raises when needed, and judges and priests who fill ongoing roles. The emphasis on call stories in later prophetic books similarly highlights God's role in raising a prophet (e.g., Isa 6; Jer 1:1-13; Amos 7:14-15).

The opening verse may assign the initiative for raising a prophet to God, but the immediately following verse gives this a slightly different tone. Prophets are traced back to Mount Horeb, where, after receiving the Decalogue, the people fearfully request that God no longer speak to them directly but that Moses function as an intermediary between them and God (18:16; cf. 5:22-33). One may compare the account of the rise of kingship (1 Sam 8–10): in both cases the people come to God with a request, and God responds with a "yes, but." Israel may have a king, but only one whom God chooses (Deut 17:14-15); Israel may have intermediaries between itself and God, but only when God raises them up (18:15-18). Deuteronomy speaks of both king and prophet as needing to be a *brother* (17:15, 20; 18:15, 18) who comes *from among you* (18:15 RSV; the Hebrew term translated *from among you* in 18:15 is also present in 17:15, 20 and 18:18 even if versions mostly miss it). These connections are too great to be coincidental. Both king and prophet play an important role in Deuteronomy's vision for Israel, even though it may be possible to imagine society without them (cf. time of the judges). The roles are not necessarily in relationship to each other (although prophets frequently direct their messages at the kings), but they also cannot be entirely separated.

Second, Deuteronomy speaks to the nature or foundation of prophecy. This is done in two distinct but complementary ways. One, this is done historically by connecting the office of the prophet to the person of Moses and the events at Mount Horeb. And two, this is done more foundationally by emphasizing that the prophet is one who *shall speak to them everything that I command* (v. 18). The phrases *a prophet like me* (v. 15) and *a prophet like you* (v. 18) both connect the prophet with Moses. Although these are given in the singular, they need not be taken as referring to one future prophet—even though some New Testament passages appear to take them that way (e.g., John 1:21, 25; 6:14; 7:40; Acts 3:22)—but rather to prophets generally as needed (cf. 17:14-15, speaking of *a* king). The phrases also are not in tension with the later statement that *Never since has there arisen a prophet in Israel like Moses* (34:10). The present passage makes Moses the model for future prophets without implying that future prophets will be equal to Moses.

For Deuteronomy, Moses is the prophet par excellence, the model for all future prophets. Moses had a complex and comprehensive leadership role within Israel (see TBC for 17:14-20), but it is his role as mediator of the divine word, especially with regard to the torah, that gives content to the statement. At Horeb, God gave the law through Moses after the people became afraid. In Moab, Moses is again teaching the law, explicating what God has given (4:1, 13-14; 5:1; 6:1). Deuteronomy opens with Moses speaking *to the Israelites just as the* LORD *had commanded him to speak to them* (1:3; cf. 18:18, the prophet *shall speak to them everything that I command*). Moses' prophetic role includes that of suffering servant and intercessor (P. Miller 1990: 154), but it is his role as messenger of God's word, especially as it relates to torah, that is primary. The words may be about the future (cf. techniques for learning about the future rejected in vv. 9-14), but they address *today*.

This is confirmed through repeated references to word, speaking, or command in the passage:

- listen or hear: šamaʿ (NRSV, *give heed*), 18:15, 16, 19, 20

- say or speak: ʾamar, 18:16, 17, 21

- to request or ask for: šaʾal, 18:16

- word, or to speak: dabar, 18:17, 18, 19, 20, 21, 22 (a total of sixteen times, nine as a verb and seven as a noun, with the meaning of either *word[s]* or *thing[s]*)

- mouth: peh, 18:18

- command: ṣawah, 18:18, 20

Third, the passage provides motivation for obeying the prophet whom God raises up. This is done indirectly by the repeated references to the prophets speaking God's word, directly in the opening verse (18:15), and with the statement *Anyone who does not heed the words that the prophet speaks in my name, I myself will hold accountable* (v. 19). Disregarding the word of the prophet is the same as disregarding a word directly from God. Whereas the people are to punish someone who does not heed the verdict of the central court, consisting of judges and priests, here the punishment comes from God. The phrase *I myself will hold accountable* is unusual. The term translated *hold accountable* is a form of the word commonly used of people "seeking" or "inquiring" of God (4:29; 12:5; etc.). That meaning is now turned around. Instead of the people inquiring of God, God will come to inquire of the person or persons who are disregarding God's word as delivered by a prophet. This statement "establishes the prophet as the highest authority in the land, higher even than the king" (Tigay: 177).

The emphasis on obedience to the prophetic word not surprisingly raises the question of distinguishing between true and false prophets, the final theme of the passage (vv. 20-22). Two types of false prophets are identified: (1) one who *speaks in the name of other gods* or (2) one *who presumes to speak a word that I have not commanded the prophet to speak* (v. 20). The first type of false prophet is easy to recognize. This is a clear violation of the first and foundational commandment, whether the prophet is trying to persuade the people to worship that other god instead of or in addition to the God of Israel (as covered by the first case in ch. 13), or whether the prophet is addressing some other matter on behalf of a different god, thereby implicitly giving that other god independent authority and power. Both such false prophets are rejected and given a verdict of death.

The second kind of false prophet is more difficult to discern: *How can we recognize a word that the LORD has not spoken?* (v. 21). This is the critical question: *if* a prophet speaks falsely, that prophet is to be charged; on the other hand, *if* the prophet truly speaks on behalf of God, then that prophet is to be feared. The true prophet's words of doom are to be taken seriously, and that prophet is to be obeyed.

Deuteronomy thus suggests a three-stage testing process for validating a true prophet, reflected in the following questions. If the answer to any of these questions is no, the prophet must be rejected:

1. Is the prophet speaking on behalf of the God of Israel? A word from any other god is not acceptable (cf. 13:1-5).

2. Is the prophet soundly based in the tradition (esp. the story) of God working with his people and the teaching God has given the people in the past? Notice how Moses regularly refers back to the story of God and Israel and in his teaching explicates and adapts the law that God has given in the past for the present situation.

3. Does the prophetic word come to pass?

The test that Deuteronomy gives for distinguishing true and false prophets seems simple, but soon the difficulties with the test become obvious. First, the test works best in one direction: failure of any criterion can identify a false prophet. But as noted earlier, any one of the isolated criteria, such as fulfillment of a prophetic word, is not adequate proof that the prophet is true (cf. 13:1-5). In addition, the third criterion cannot be applied in any present situation since it requires time, perhaps considerable time, before it is evident whether the word has come to pass. Even when a prophet's track record over a longer period of time is being considered, this criterion is not entirely trustworthy (see TBC below).

The prophet who gives a word that God has not commanded *has spoken it presumptuously* (18:22). This term has been used thrice previously: (1) of Israel's action when it tried to enter the Promised Land on its own after losing faith in God (1:43) and (2) of someone who does not obey the verdict of the central court (17:12-13 [two times]). In all these cases a person is taking upon oneself a decision that is God's: this is presumptuous!

THE TEXT IN BIBLICAL CONTEXT
True and False Prophecy

Prophets speak on behalf of God. But how do the people of God discern who truly is speaking on behalf of God, and who is not, whether fraudulently or mistakenly, even though well intentioned? Israel struggled with this question as it received contradictory words from those claiming to be prophets of God. The criterion Deuteronomy 18 presents for distinguishing between true and false prophecy is ambiguous, an ambiguity also present in other Old Testament passages that continue the conversation.

The obvious difficulty with the Deuteronomic criterion is that it is not helpful in the moment when discernment is required. It can only come into play retrospectively. Jeremiah's denunciation of those "prophesying a lie to you" (Jer 27:14; the Hebrew text nowhere uses the phrase "false prophets," although the Septuagint at points translates the simple term "prophet/s" as "false prophet/s" when speaking of those deemed to be false, e.g., Jer 27:9; 28:1, 8), and in confrontation with Hananiah, highlights the challenge of the Deuteronomic criterion (Jer 28). When Hananiah, speaking on behalf of "the LORD of hosts, the God of Israel" (28:2), directly contradicts Jeremiah's pronouncement, Jeremiah can only respond, "Amen! May the LORD do so; may the LORD fulfill the words that you have prophesied" (28:6). After a further word from God, Jeremiah confronts Hananiah: "Listen, Hananiah, the LORD has not sent you, and you made the people trust in a lie" (28:15). Later readers can use the Deuteronomic criterion to assess Hananiah as a false prophet, but this does not help in the heat of the confrontation.

The criterion does not work cleanly even when used in retrospect. Ezekiel announces that God will conquer Tyre so that it will "never again be rebuilt" (Ezek 26:7-14), yet later he reports that this did not happen (29:17-20). When Jonah arrives in Nineveh, he proclaims that, because of "their wickedness" (1:2), "Forty days more and Nineveh will be overthrown" (3:4). When the people repent, "God changed his mind about the calamity" (3:10). One can explain this as demonstrating the dynamic nature of God's' plans, with God always willing to change when people respond, with prophetic announcements not written in stone. But as Christensen observes, "It would appear, at least in a surface reading of Jonah, that to be a true prophet may involve being a 'false prophet' according to Deut 18:22, for the words God gave Jonah to declare to the people of Nineveh did not in fact come to pass" (2001: 412).

The story of Micaiah raises another complexity. When called before the kings of Israel and Judah, Micaiah surprisingly supports the word of the four hundred other prophets who claim to be speaking for Yahweh. When challenged, Micaiah recounts that God was intentionally using a genuine prophetic word to mislead the kings, announcing that they would succeed in battle when in fact they would not (1 Kings 22). And yet, the canonical verdict clearly is that Jeremiah, Jonah, and Micaiah were true prophets of Yahweh, and their opponents were not.

Scholars scrutinizing the debate have tried to discern additional criteria that might be useful. Perhaps it is possible to distinguish based on rootedness in the Yahwistic tradition. Jeremiah could claim to be part of a long line of prophets of judgment, but then Hananiah could claim to be in the tradition of Moses at the Red Sea (Exod 14:13-14) or Isaiah's announcements of deliverance (e.g., Isa 37:6-7). Moberly proposes two additional criteria: (1) character or moral integrity of the prophet and (2) a message that reflects God's priorities, seeking "to engender unreserved engagement with God" (2006: 232-33). These may not be irrelevant, but as Epp-Tiessen observes, they do not appear to play a role in the confrontation between Jeremiah and Hananiah (36).

The issue does not disappear in the New Testament. The verdict of the New Testament is that Jesus is the true prophet, the eschatological prophet promised by Isaiah (Luke 4:16-30), the one who fulfills in a unique way the role of the prophet as spelled out by Deuteronomy 18 (cf. John 1:21, 25; 6:14; 7:40; Acts 3:22). But debate over true and false prophets continues. Jesus warns against false prophets who comes in sheep's clothing (Matt 7:15), false prophets who will lead people astray (24:11; cf. Matt 24:24; 2 Pet 2:1; 1 John 4:1), and he speaks of being able to recognize false prophets by their fruits (Matt 7:15-20). But as with the Deuteronomic criterion, this may take time to assess.

Epp-Tiessen suggests that the consensus among scholars is that Scripture gives us "no foolproof criteria" for discerning between true and false prophets, between those who truly speak on behalf of God and those who do not (2). Although true on a literal level, that need not be the last word. Moberly's second criterion should be considered: true prophets, whether announcing salvation or doom, engender genuine encounter with God, leading to repentance and righteous living. Nelson puts it as follows:

> Genuine prophets follow the pattern of being "like Moses," the profile for which is set forth throughout the book of Deuteronomy: accurate transmission of Yahweh's word, utilization of effective rhetoric, intercession in crisis, promotion of public and private ethics, and concern for the plight of the poor. (Nelson 2002: 236)

THE TEXT IN THE LIFE OF THE CHURCH

Prophets Today?

In Deuteronomy we read that *God will raise up for you a prophet like me* (18:15), but also that *Never since has there arisen a prophet in Israel like Moses* (34:10). At a time when the people sense God is no longer speaking through prophets, Joel announces, *Your sons and daughters shall prophesy* (2:28), a word that Peter understands to be fulfilled in his time (Acts 2:15-21). The early church understands Jesus to be the prophet projected by Deuteronomy (Acts 3:22), but also that God is continuing to use prophets among them (Acts 11:27; 13:1; 15:32; 1 Cor 12:28-29; Eph 3:5; 4:11). But what about today?

At the risk of oversimplifying, the church today has gone in three directions in response to this question. The instruction of Ephesians 4:11-12—"The gifts he gave were that some would be apostles, some prophets, some evangelists, some pastors and teachers, to equip the saints for the work of ministry, for building up the body of Christ"— is a key passage for those advocating a fivefold ministry model for the church, or APEST (Apostle, Prophet, Evangelist, Shepherd, Teacher). Allan Hirsch is a proponent of this approach, which places emphasis on an ongoing prophetic role in the church today. Although giving it a very different place, The Church of Jesus Christ of the Latter-day Saints speaks of God continuing to call out prophets, who then are key leaders of the church.

Over against this approach, some argue that the prophetic role was temporary. God spoke through prophets before the writing of Scripture and then again through Jesus Christ. Now that is no longer needed. "With the completion of salvation in Christ comes the cessation of revelation. Consequently the church now lives by a 'Scripture only' principle of authority" (White).

Yet there is another tradition within the church that picks up the social justice theme from the prophetic books. Modern-day prophets then are those who dramatically tackle political and social justice issues of the day. An Anglican church in Toronto recently announced a series on "prophets of the modern world," focusing on Thomas More, William Wilberforce, Dietrich Bonhoeffer, Martin Luther King Jr., and Oscar Romero, each greater-than-life figures of their day.

Striking about contemporary approaches is that often they do not build on the role that prophets played in Israel. Generally, Old Testament prophets were *messengers* of God, proclaiming the *word of God*, to the *people of God*, in a time of *crisis*, with a message of *indictment or hope*, calling for greater *faithfulness* to God. They appear to have been sporadic (when God raised them up), with a primary focus on Israel—in fact, often rebuking or guiding its leadership. The contemporary tendency to use the name "prophets" for those who address society is more a vestige of Christendom than a restoration of Old Testament prophets. Even the book of Jonah, although about someone who preaches to Nineveh, probably is a book addressed to Israel.

Further Judicial Procedures

Deuteronomy 19:1-21

PREVIEW

All too often significant conflicts are due to insufficient attention to following good process. That is true in judicial matters and in the church more generally. After introducing the various leadership offices in Israel, the text returns to the theme of judicial process (cf. 16:18–17:13).

The first part of chapter 19 deals with murder: its concern is not so much the crime itself as how Israel deals with it, and the importance of a judicial system that protects the innocent (*so that the blood of an innocent person may not be shed*, v. 10). The last part of the chapter continues this theme with its requirement of two witnesses (v. 15) and the punishment for a *malicious witness* (vv. 16-21). The two passages on judicial process (16:18–17:13; 19:1-21) provide a framework for Israel's leadership offices. All of Israel's leaders, including the king, priests, and prophets, are expected to function within a context that pursues *justice, and only justice* (16:20).

OUTLINE
Cities of Refuge, 19:1-13
The Neighbor's Boundary Marker, 19:14
Regulations Governing Witnesses, 19:15-21
    19:15   A Single Witness Is Insufficient to Convict
    19:16-21 Punishment for a Malicious Witness

EXPLANATORY NOTES

Cities of Refuge 19:1-13

The Old Testament provision for cities of refuge has as its background the ancient practice of blood vengeance. Even after ancient societies became nation-states with kings and had developed to the point of having a central judicial system, the vast majority of disputes and crimes were resolved locally, either through formal processes making use of local arrangements (local judges and elders) or informally, often within the extended family or clan. In such a context family members understood themselves to have the responsibility or even obligation to defend the lives of their kin. When someone was killed, their next of kin was expected to "redeem" that person's blood by putting the killer to death (Tigay: 179). The Old Testament includes the stories of Gideon and Joab exacting such blood vengeance (Judg 8:18-21; 2 Sam 3:26-30). "It is evident that in the heat of family honor, the 'redeemer' does not stop to ask if the initial death is accidental and indeed, does not care, for blood requires blood" (Brueggemann 2001: 198). Thus innocent people die. Even in cases where the first killing may have been murder, the practice could lead to family feuds and an ongoing cycle of violence. The Old Testament cities of refuge or asylum insert an element of restraint (cf. 16:20; on the need for this, see Gen 4:23-24; 34:25) into this ancient judicial context and the practice of blood vengeance (cf. Exod 21:13-14; Num 35:9-34; Deut 4:41-43; Josh 20).

The passage consists of two paragraphs speaking directly about cities of refuge (vv. 1-3, 8-10), along with two sample cases of killing that speak to how the cities are to function (vv. 4-7, 11-13). Earlier Deuteronomy identified three cities of refuge in the Transjordan region (4:41-43). To these Deuteronomy now adds three additional cities in the main part of the land. Deuteronomy does not name these cities, but according to Joshua they are Kedesh in the northern part of the country, Shechem in the central region, and Hebron the south (Josh 20:7). Each of these six cities also is a Levitical city (Num 35:6).

The primary criterion for these cities is location. They are spread throughout the land as evenly as possible (*calculate the distances and divide into three regions*, Deut 19:3) so as to improve the chances that someone fleeing to the city will arrive there before being caught by the one in pursuit (*but if the distance is too great, the avenger of blood in hot anger might pursue and overtake*, v. 6). There also does not appear to be any connection between these cities and the central court at The Place. The whole passage assumes that the judicial process is local, in the hands of the elders (v. 12).

Two cases or examples of killing offer criteria for distinguishing between murder and manslaughter (vv. 4-7, 11-13). This is an expansion of the distinction in Exodus between a killing that is "not premeditated" but a result of "an act of God," and that in which "someone willfully attacks and kills another by treachery" (Exod 21:13-14). The first case presents a scene where the death is entirely accidental, but given the often informal nature of ancient justice with its practice of blood vengeance, even such a killing could easily precipitate a rash action by a relative of the one killed. After all, *hot anger* easily clouds good judgment (Deut 19:6). The city of refuge protects the person who has accidentally killed someone.

The second case makes it clear that the city of refuge would not, however, permanently protect someone who has committed murder. Even then the city of refuge has a role to play: it serves as a place to protect the person during the time of the "trial," during the time that the community determines whether it indeed is a case of murder. Here the city of refuge protects due process. The account of the second case climaxes in a guilty verdict, resulting in the execution of the murderer. The passage accepts the practice of blood vengeance by having the *avenger of blood* (lit., *the one who redeems blood*) responsible for the execution (cf. 13:9; 17:7). The practice itself is not rejected, but the city of refuge places some significant safeguards upon it.

That the city of refuge could not protect the guilty person is emphasized by the concluding words of the case: *Show no pity; you shall purge the guilt of innocent blood from Israel, so that it may go well with you* (19:13). A similar statement concludes the passage instructing Israel what to do in the case of an unsolved murder (21:1-9). The conviction that a person's death causes guilt which must be dealt with is common to both passages. Some other ancient peoples also had places of asylum but did not distinguish between the innocent and the guilty. Tigay quotes Tacitus: "Temples in the Greek cities were filled with felons as well as debtors, all enjoying sanctuary" (182). Justice in Israel requires identifying the guilty and taking seriously the reality of bloodguilt.

Although the passage retains the concern that the guilty person be punished, this is given less weight than in the comparable passage in Numbers (cf. Num 35:6-34). In addition to going into much more detail on ways of distinguishing between intentional and accidental killing, Numbers explicitly rejects the option of ransoming "the life of a murderer," and includes a longer statement on not polluting or defiling the land (Num 35:31-34). In contrast, Deuteronomy focuses on protecting the innocent one. Cities of refuge are there *so that the blood of an innocent person may not be shed in the land that the* LORD *your God is giving you as an inheritance, thereby bringing bloodguilt upon you* (v. 10). Bloodguilt results not only from murder but also from the wrong execution of one who did not murder but killed accidentally.

The directive to add three further cities of refuge (thus producing nine in total) if and when God *enlarges your territory* reflects Deuteronomy's understanding that taking possession of the land is not an event that takes place at one point under Joshua, but a much longer, gradual process (cf. 7:22, *the* LORD *your God will clear away these nations before you little by little*). The concern that no one should live too far away from a city of refuge logically leads to the need for further such cities should Israel's territory be expanded to encompass the full area promised the ancestors, reaching to the Euphrates in the north. There is no evidence in the Old Testament that these last three cities were ever established.

Deuteronomy's tendency not to focus too much on detail is also evident in this passage. The text says little about how the community determines whether a person has committed murder or whether the killing was accidental other than the reference to previous *enmity*

(v. 11), although very probably witnesses played a significant role (cf. comments on 19:15-19). But what if the killing appears to have been accidental and yet there has been previous enmity? The passage does not specify any location within the city that has a special function with regard to the asylum process. The Exodus passage speaks of "my altar," probably meaning that any altar could function that way (centralization is not a theme in Exodus, so altars could be constructed "in every place where I cause my name to be remembered," 20:24). Perhaps more significantly, the passage says nothing about how long an innocent person is to remain in the city of refuge. Numbers requires that the person remain there until the high priest has died (35:25, 28). This may reflect the sense that the killing, even when accidental, did produce bloodguilt and did require some expiation (Tigay: 177). Again we notice that Deuteronomy is not instructions for the priests or the judges but preaching for the people as a whole. As such it does not provide a detailed manual but instead issues fundamental directions for the community. Cities of refuge are one way in which Deuteronomy protects due process and arrests the spiral of vengeance and violence that easily follows when justice is motivated by revenge.

The Neighbor's Boundary Marker 19:14

This verse is an intrusion into the unit on leadership and more directly relates to the theme of justice in Israel (cf. 14:22–15:18). Its terms *neighbor* (also in vv. 4 and 11 RSV, even if lost in the NRSV), *boundary marker* (also in vv. 3 and 8, again lost in the NRSV), and *property that will be allotted to you* (also in v. 10, there translated *inheritance*) may explain its present location. The goal of protecting each Israelite's ability to benefit from the blessings God is giving Israel through the gift of land connects it directly to Deuteronomy's emphasis on justice as introduced by the sabbatical release provisions.

The verse consists of two unequal parts. The first part is an apodictic command, expressed in Hebrew with four short words: *not/you move/boundary/your neighbor*. Its structure reminds one of the short commands of the Decalogue, even if it is more specific than those of the Decalogue. In the absence of modern surveying techniques, extensive official records, and long steel stakes, property boundaries were marked by items that were naturally available: stones or other similar moveable objects. By moving one of these markers, a boundary line could be changed, thereby stealing property from the neighbor. A prohibition like this one is common in the ancient Near East.

The second, larger part of the verse then imbeds the prohibition in the story of Israel. The property protected is not a commercial commodity but a possession *allotted to you in the land that the* LORD *your God is giving you to possess.* God has given Israel the land promised to the ancestors. This land has been allotted to Israel by tribe, clan, and family as its *property* (RSV uses the more emotionally freighted term *inheritance*). Israel experiences God blessing through the land (cf. 8:7-10). Patrimonial land both provides the means of survival for each family and represents God's election of them as God's *own possession*: the land is Israel's inheritance, Israel is God's inheritance (4:20). Moving a boundary marker is theft, yet much more than theft of property. It is stealing not only the means of survival but also a family's symbolic stake in God's election and the covenant. This conviction lies behind Naboth's response to King Ahab when the king offers him a *better vineyard* in exchange for his: "The LORD forbid that I should give you my ancestral inheritance" (1 Kings 21:3).

The significance of this particular theft is reflected by the number of biblical passages that treat it. Deuteronomy includes it in the list of curses in chapter 27, preceded only by curses for making idols and dishonoring parents (27:17). Proverbs address it (Prov 22:28; 23:10), Job considers it a characteristic of the wicked (Job 24:2), and prophets inveigh against it (Hos 5:10). An indictment of Micah suggests that the concern is not limited to the surreptitious moving of a marker at night but may include the illegal and even the technically legal machinations of the powerful as they find ways of increasing their property holdings at the expense of weaker elements in society (Mic 2:1-2; cf. Isa 5:8). This prohibition may suggest contemporary property rights, yet its primary concern is not protecting impersonal property but guarding the nature of the covenant community, in which the livelihood of all is important and each family has its own access to God's blessings. The verse reflects well the concerns of the sabbatical release provisions (15:1-18).

Regulations Governing Witnesses 19:15-21

19:15 A Single Witness Is Insufficient to Convict

The principle of requiring a minimum of two witnesses in order to establish a guilty verdict already appears in the earlier sample case for the local courts of the *man or woman who does what is evil* (17:2-7, esp. 2, 6). It now is repeated on its own in proximity to the passage on cities of refuge. A similar requirement is found in Numbers 35, also in the context of a passage on cities of refuge. Both are concerned with due process and the protection of one falsely accused. False testimony may result from a *malicious witness* (Deut 19:16-21), but may also be a case of misunderstanding or misperception or even a well-intended but inaccurate observation. To require two witness, although no guarantee that the result will be just (cf. the case of Ahab and Naboth's vineyard, which has two dishonest witnesses; 1 Kings 21:9-13), nevertheless is an effort at ensuring that the judicial process is fair and true. The New Testament picks up this safeguard when speaking about justice in the church: "Never admit any charge against an elder except on the evidence of two or three witnesses" (1 Tim 5:19; cf. Matt 26:60-11).

19:16-21 Punishment for a Malicious Witness

It is not possible to legislate against witnesses who unintentionally give testimony that is misleading. In such cases the requirement that two witnesses are needed to convict helps safeguard the judicial process. But what about a case of perjury, where someone intentionally gives false evidence in order to produce the wrong result? This is the situation envisioned by the last passage on judicial procedures, a passage clearly related to the ninth commandment: *Neither shall you bear false witness against your neighbor* (5:20).

The parallel structure between this passage and the earlier passage on judicial procedures (17:2-13) may help explain the logic assumed by our passage (Nelson 2002: 242).

Deuteronomy	17:2-7; 19:15	17:8-13; 19:16-21
Setting	local court	central court
Process	2 or 3 witnesses	(unclear witness)

The parallel nature of these passages is not exact (e.g., 17:8-13 speaks of *levitical priests and the judge*, and 19:16-21 speaks of *the priests and the judges*), but the similarities are too great to be ignored. This suggests that 19:16-21 assumes a situation in which someone has come forward with a false accusation, perhaps with the hope that someone else might support it. Since no one does support it, it becomes the kind of *judicial decision... too difficult* for the local court (17:8). It thus is brought *before the LORD*, where the central court (cf. *to the place*, 17:8), consisting of *the priests and the judges*, makes a thorough *inquiry* in an effort to determine whether the single witness or accuser is simply uncorroborated, or whether the person is *malicious* (lit., *violent*) in intention (19:17-18).

Much is left unsaid in this description. For example, no hint is given as to what happens if the central court is unable to determine whether the single witness has been malicious. Is it possible for the central court to find someone guilty on the basis of a single witness? Or are there cases that are simply left unresolved? Deuteronomy does not answer these questions.

Instead it closes the passage with one of the harshest responses to false witness possible: *If the witness is a false witness, and testified falsely against his brother, then you shall do to him as he plotted to do against his brother* (AT; cf. story of two false witnesses in the apocryphal book of Susanna, 50-62). The situation is one in which someone is trying to use the judicial system in order to harm or do violence to a fellow member of the covenant community. The law of equivalent retribution, lex talionis, then is included as an example of what this may mean, or as a proverbial way of expressing the basic principle. The apocraphal book of Susanna tells the story of two false witnesses receiving the capital punishment threatened. That it is only an example or statement of principle is clear because one can imagine many cases of false witness where the intended result is not a physical injury. In fact, more often than not it may involve theft or some personal offense (such as the example of moving a neighbor's boundary marker; 19:14).

Few if any Old Testament passages have "been the victim of more misunderstanding and exaggeration" than this law of retribution. "This verse, understood in the most literal and vengeful sense, has entered popular imagination as the summation of Old Testament ethics" (C. Wright 1996: 225; cf. P. Miller 1990: 146). In approaching this verse, a number of considerations must be kept in mind:

- The law of retribution is not a summary of Old Testament ethics or of the ethical vision of Deuteronomy. Significant for Deuteronomy's approach to justice (16:20) is concern for the weak and those unable to defend themselves, generosity to the poor and deprived, support for the brother and sister, and so forth.

- Although the law of retribution is cited three times in the Old Testament (Exod 21:23-25; Lev 24:19-20; Deut 19:21), each time in the context of a general statement, the principle is never used when designating a specific punishment for a specific crime other than in the case of murder. Mutilation as punishment for a specific crime is mentioned only once in Deuteronomy (25:11-12).

- The basic principle of the law of retribution is one of proportionality: "Let the punishment fit the crime." It is likely that *eye for eye* (etc.) was a recognized saying within Israel and elsewhere that the Old Testament incorporates, a proverbial saying not necessarily understood literally (cf. Jesus instructing, "If your right eye causes you to sin, pluck it out and throw it away; it is better that you lose one of your members than that your whole body be thrown into hell"; Matt 5:29 RSV).

- The intended purpose of the law of retribution is not to ensure that punishment is harsh enough (as it is often understood) but to protect the person being punished from punishment too severe. It is not intended to "condone rampant vengeance" (cf. Gen 4:23; Judg 19–21), but precisely the opposite (C. Wright 1996: 226). In a context of local justice that allows blood vengeance, consequences of crime can be extreme. The law of retribution limits these.

- The specific context in which Deuteronomy presents the law of retribution is not one that speaks of particular crimes but one that speaks of the misuse or abuse of the justice system itself. It is this system that is intended to protect the weak and innocent.

THE TEXT IN BIBLICAL CONTEXT
Jesus, Prophets, and Justice

Deuteronomy's call that *justice, and only justice, you shall pursue* (16:20) is consistent with the voice of the prophets and continues in the preaching of Jesus. When Jesus proclaims his mission in Nazareth, he uses words from Isaiah: "The Spirit of the Lord is upon me, because he has anointed me to bring good news to the poor. He has sent me to proclaim release to the captives and recovery of sight to the blind, to let the oppressed go free" (Luke 4:18).

The logic of Deuteronomy is also reflected in his debate with a lawyer and a rich young ruler, who asks, "What must I do to inherit eternal life?" (Luke 10:25). Jesus responds by pointing to the (OT) Scriptures. When the lawyer quotes from the command to love God and neighbor (Deut 6:5; Lev 19:18) and then asks who his neighbor is, Jesus tells the parable of the good Samaritan, who clearly goes beyond the minimum. The Samaritan—a follower of Abraham and Moses and yet not a Jew, but also not a complete outsider (cf. the *resident alien* of Deuteronomy)—gives generously to the *needy neighbor* (Luke 10:25-37; Deut 15:7-11). Similarly, when the rich young ruler asks about eternal life, Jesus refers him to the Decalogue. But Jesus' further response highlights that ultimately obedience even to this law is insufficient: "There is still one thing lacking. Sell all that you own and distribute the money to the poor, and you will have treasure in heaven" (Luke 18:22). In both cases the dialogue begins with reference to the law and then continues with the call to care for the needy much beyond the minimum required by regulation. Again, the form may be different, but the concern and conviction are the same.

Similarly, the prophets consistently and repeatedly accuse Israel of not taking care of the weak and not practicing justice. Amos in the Northern Kingdom and Micah in the Southern Kingdom, to name two, announce that punishment will come because the people "sell the righteous for silver, and the needy for a pair of sandals" (Amos 2:6) and because "they covet fields, and seize them; houses, and take them away; they oppress householder and house, people and their inheritance" (Mic 2:2). Both understand the oppression of the poor to be of national interest because the fate of the people as a whole will be determined by how those with influence and affluence treat those without. The form may be different, but the concern and conviction are similar.

In language similar to that of Deuteronomy 15:4, Acts speaks of the early church as having "not a needy person among them" (4:34; cf. 2:43-47; 4:32-37). Yet, as in Deuteronomy (cf. the transition from 15:4-6 to 15:7-11), this idyllic characterization is quickly spoiled by reality a few chapters later, where we learn that some widows are "being neglected in the daily distribution of food" (Acts 6:1). But this less than perfect picture is not the final word. Later, when the church in Jerusalem is suffering, we read that Christians in "Macedonia and Achaia have been pleased to share their resources with the poor among the saints in Jerusalem" (Rom 15:26). The ideal is never fully achieved in the communities from which Scripture comes, but there are foretastes of it.

Jesus, and *an Eye for an Eye*

Jesus' reference to the law of retribution must not be ignored (Matt 5:38-42). Strikingly, it comes shortly after the statement regarding plucking out one's right eye (5:29). Here Jesus uses this well-known saying to make the point that proportionality is not a principle to be used in interpersonal relations. Rather, these relationships are to be governed by nonresistance (turn the other cheek) and generosity (give the coat, go the second mile). The generosity is consistent with Deuteronomy's exhortation to *give liberally and be ungrudging. . . . Open your hand to the poor* (15:10-11). The nonresistance may reflect an emphasis different from Deuteronomy, but the contrast between it and Deuteronomy is not nearly as great as usually imagined (see comments on ch. 20).

THE TEXT IN THE LIFE OF THE CHURCH
Eye for Eye, or Reconciliation?
The lex talionis (*eye-for-eye*) passage (19:21) has taken on a life of its own, both in the church and in larger society. Those advocating for capital punishment, for example, regularly speak of it as a permanent prescription, as based in the nature of reality. Justice, it is argued, requires that crime be punished in a manner appropriate to the crime. Those opposed to capital punishment regularly respond to it, either by arguing that its original intention was to limit violence, or by citing Jesus' reference to it. Others recognize the challenge of eye-for-eye justice: if it were followed literally, as Tevye says in *Fiddler on the Roof*, "the whole world will be blind and toothless."

Two nations have consciously tried to work at the larger question of justice in a manner very different from a literal application of *eye for eye*. In 1995, South Africa established a Truth and Reconciliation Commission (TRC) to hear testimony, to record stories, and even to grant amnesty in certain situations to those who had committed human rights crimes during the horror of apartheid. The TRC's goal was genuine reconciliation in a country torn apart by racial violence. The church had significant impact in introducing the idea of "offering amnesty (forgiveness) in exchange for truth (confession)" (Graybill: 26). Graybill continues, "That theology would so thoroughly inform the working of the TRC mainly has to do with the personal role of Desmond Tutu as its chair." Bishop Tutu reminded the faith community that "reconciliation is . . . the central message of faith" (26).

No doubt influenced by the experience of South Africa, Canada established its own Truth and Reconciliation Commission as a way of responding to the legacy of the Indian Residential Schools and their destructive impact on First Nations people. Its goal is "to guide and inspire Aboriginal peoples and Canadians in a process of reconciliation and renewed relationships that are based on mutual understanding and respect." As Justice Murray Sinclair, chair of the commission, states, "There are no shortcuts" on the road to reconciliation. It is not about replacing justice with forgiveness, but about understanding justice as much more than a giant set of scales balancing crime and punishment. Instead, it means seeing justice as a way of working toward harmony and reconciliation, as establishing the kind of community that Deuteronomy envisions.

Deuteronomy 20:1-20
Part 2D, Unit 5
War

PREVIEW

"War is hell" (General William T. Sherman). Soldiers caught in the trenches of World War I, with poison gas floating down on them, experienced this. Civilians caught in the bombing of World War II, whether in Coventry or Dresden or Hiroshima, knew it. The television program M*A*S*H exposed harsh realities of the Korean War. Whether in Vietnam, Iran, Bosnia, or Syria, once war starts, a regard for right and dignity and morality seem to go out the window. War is hell.

Israel knew and understood war. For Israel, war was not some theoretical notion or report on the news but an ever-present reality, always accompanied by hunger, humiliation, and death. The small nation-states to the east of the Mediterranean (Israel, Edom, Moab, and Syria) regularly had conflicts with each other. And there was always the threat that one of the superpowers of the day (Babylon or Assyria to the northeast, or Egypt to the south) would impose its will on the land, wreaking havoc as it exercised its power over the region, or simply passing through it on its way to confront another superpower. The Northern Kingdom ended when Assyria captured Samaria, carrying away as captives many of its citizens (722 BCE); and the Southern Kingdom ended when Babylon sacked Jerusalem, taking many of its people into exile (587 BCE).

Deuteronomy comes out of a world at war: its audience knows what war is like firsthand. Recognizing this is necessary so we can grasp what the passage is really about rather than becoming caught up with what strikes us on the surface.

Chapter 20 consists of three distinct sections introduced by the identical *when/if you*, followed by an imperfect second-person masculine singular verb, intended as a collective to the people as a whole. The same construction is used in 21:10 and 23:10, marking these five passages as a series dealing with war. The first unit presents the basic logic or principles of Israelite war (20:1-9). The second section addresses how Israel is to treat its enemies, first those *far from you* (20:10-14), then those within the land (20:15-18). The last part of chapter 20 introduces an unusual consideration for the trees of a besieged town (20:19-20).

The series of war passages continues in 21:10-14, now with reference to war brides, and concludes with a passage highlighting the need to keep the war camp pure and clean (23:9-14).

OUTLINE

Foundational Principles of War, 20:1-9
    20:1-4   Trusting God for Victory
    20:5-9   Reducing the Militia
The Conduct of War, 20:10-18
    20:10-14   Distant Cities
    20:15-18   Cities of the Land
Consideration for Trees, 20:19-20

EXPLANATORY NOTES

Foundational Principles of War 20:1-9

20:1-4 Trusting God for Victory

Deuteronomy is theology through the lens of an inferior power. This is Israel's usual position. When Israel looked across the Jordan from the plains of Moab, it expected to encounter people who were *stronger and taller* than they were, with cities *large and fortified up to heaven*, as reported by the spies at Israel's first arrival at the land (1:28). During the time of the judges, Israel regularly fell under the power of other peoples. During the monarchic period, on more than one occasion neighboring nation-states exploited Israel, and Israel was never a match for the superpower of the day. Assyria may have been weakening during the time of Josiah, but it had already destroyed the Northern Kingdom, and Babylon was waiting in the wings. Despite the sometimes glorious ways in which the kingdoms of

David and Solomon are described, Israel remained a small player on the ancient Near Eastern scene. Israel's story is one of a small people confronted by *horses and chariots, an army larger than your own* (20:1).

Nevertheless, the confidence of the opening paragraph is clear and simple: do not be afraid because *it is God who goes with you, to fight for you* (20:4). The ideal model for war is Israel at the Red Sea: despite Egypt's massive army of horses and chariots, the most modern military technology available (Exod 14:5-9), God delivered Israel and gave the victory (Exod 14:5-9; cf. Deut 11:4). Horses and chariots do not bring victory, but God does. In addition to referring to the exodus directly, the paragraph uses stereotypical language to reassure Israel of God's presence and remind it of previous deliverance: *The LORD your God is with you, who brought you up. . . . For it is the LORD your God who goes with you, . . . to give you victory* (vv. 2, 4).

The words of the priest prior to facing an enemy thus become words of encouragement to trust God (cf. Moses' words to the people at the edge of the Red Sea in the face of Pharaoh's army; Exod 14:13-14). The opening *Hear, O Israel!* echoes the opening address of the Shema and the repeated call of Moses to listen to his words (Deut 20:3; cf. 5:1; 6:3; 9:1). The speech itself is reminiscent of Moses' words after Israel has heard the report of the spies upon arriving at the Promised Land for the first time: *Have no dread or fear of them. The LORD your God, who goes before you, is the one who will fight for you, just as he did for you in Egypt before your very eyes* (1:29-30; cf. 7:21-24). In the face of fear that is only natural when confronting a stronger enemy, with language reminding the people of God's exclusive claim upon them, Israel is encouraged to trust and not be afraid since it is God who gives victory.

The absence of any reference to the king is noteworthy. The passage is addressed to the people as a whole (*when you go out to war*, etc.), emphasizing that it is God's war in cooperation with the people. Normally in the ancient Near East, war was the king's responsibility. The people who request that God give them a king assume this ("that our king may govern us and go out before us and fight our battles," 1 Sam 8:20), and the narrative about David accepts this when it speaks of "the spring of the year, the time when kings go out to battle" (2 Sam 11:1). But Deuteronomy takes war away from the king. This is consistent with the law of the king that prevents the king from acquiring many horses for himself in order to prepare for war. The passage does assume that Israel will participate in war—anything else was unthinkable in that day—but it is God's war, not the king's, and the people's role is to trust God and not be afraid.

20:5-9 Reducing the Militia

Four times the word *troops* appears (vv. 2, 5, 8, 9). The Hebrew word so translated is the common word for "people" (thus *people* in KJV, RSV; but *army* in NIV). The NRSV may not be wrong, yet it hides the fact that the passage does not envision a standing or professional army, but men of the community who have left their normal occupations for a temporary period. It is a militia of untrained farmers and tradespeople, an army similar to the people who faced Pharaoh at the Red Sea. The RSV helpfully reflects this tone: *And when the officers have made an end of speaking to the people, then commanders shall be appointed at the head of the people* (20:9; contrast with NRSV). The RSV correctly implies that there are no standing commanders but that such leaders are appointed from the people at the point of the battle.

Yet even this group is too large or not right and must be reduced. The *officials*, probably not military people (the same people appointed as assistants to judges in 16:18?), achieve this reduction through four questions. The first three exemptions are derived from ancient "futility curses" found later in Deuteronomy (28:30). In each case there is a premature break in the normal relationship between an initial action and its natural completion or fulfillment. Building a new house is incomplete without dedicating it and living in it. Similarly, planting a vineyard or becoming engaged only become significant when concluded through harvest or marriage. Not completing these could have a destructive effect and certainly means that the benefits and blessings of life in the land are frustrated. A good life includes building houses *and* living in them, planting gardens *and* enjoying their fruit, marriage *and* having children (cf. Jer 29:5-6). In this passage Deuteronomy is employing both a practice (military deferments) and language (futility curses) from the world of its day.

Is the moving force behind these exemptions a fear of activating a curse? Or do they represent a humane ethic and the protection of the family? The passage may well reflect some of both, but their practical impact must be recognized. The kind of people most likely to build a house or plant a vineyard or become engaged are young adults, in this case young men. Leviticus indicates that one could only enjoy the fruit of a vineyard in the fifth year (19:23-25). In other words, the very people who normally become the core of a strong fighting force are allowed to exempt themselves from battle for up to five years or longer. The chapter thus envisions Israel's wars as fought not by a standing army but by a militia, yet a militia missing many if not most of the young men.

The final question is of a different sort: *Is anyone afraid or disheartened?* The negative impact on morale of having people within the army who are afraid is mentioned, but again one must ask whether this fully explains the exemption. War and the potential death that it brings produce fear in virtually all. It is true that the passage opens with the priest assuring the people they have nothing to fear, and yet how many would not admit some fear in battle? These are now exempted. The passage does not address the question of who is left. Who actually will do the fighting? The implicit answer of the passage is clear: God. It was God who defeated Pharaoh at the Red Sea, and it is God who now will *give the victory* (Deut 20:4).

God's victory at the Red Sea may be the archetypal battle, but verses 5-9 also remind us of the account of Gideon and the defeat of the Midianites. When Gideon musters the people for battle, he has thirty-two thousand troops. God responds, "The troops with you are too many for me to give the Midianites into their hand. Israel would only take the credit away from me, saying, 'My own hand has delivered me.'" Of the troops, twenty-two thousand are afraid and are allowed to return home. Finally the number is reduced to three hundred, with which God says, "I will deliver you" (Judg 7:2-7). Again the message is clear: Israel is to trust God to deliver with an army obviously unable to defeat the more powerful enemy in any other way.

Deuteronomy 20 assumes that Israel will participate in war, but it paints a peculiar picture of how Israel is to confront its more powerful adversaries:

- War is not given over to the king (according to the law of the king, he is not to have a standing army), who might be tempted to use war as a form of foreign policy.

- In the face of this greater enemy with its more advanced military technology, Israel gathers its militia under nonmilitary leadership.

- Even the militia is drastically reduced in size.

- In the face of a greater enemy, with a small and reduced militia, Israel is to trust God for the victory.

The Conduct of War 20:10-18

After presenting the foundational principles of war in Israel, the text continues by addressing how war is to be conducted. The passage consists of two distinct sections, the first dealing with *towns that are very far from you* (vv. 10-15), the second with *towns of the nations here* (vv. 16-18), with verse 15 joining these two sections together. Nevertheless, the two sections are not really as parallel as this suggests. As Richard Nelson puts it, "These verses [10-14], taken by themselves without vv. 15-18, could be understood to refer to all wars, local ones as well as campaigns outside the land of promise" (2002: 250).

Read on their own, the first five verses sound more like a general rule for the treatment of all defeated populations rather than only for those at a distance (Tigay: 188). Consistent with this, Israel did on occasion impose forced labor on local Canaanite people (cf. Josh 9:3-15; Judg 1:28, 33, 35; 1 Kings 9:20-21). The second part, in contrast, is a typical Deuteronomic call for the destruction of all inhabitants of the land lest they tempt Israel to worship other gods. It is verse 15 that links these two together and produces the present parallel effect.

Some suggest that the first paragraph is based on older sources, and the second is a "secondary insertion" into the text (Nelson 2002: 246). McConville does not address the question of composition but speaks of the first section as "quite different from the kind of warfare commanded in 7:1-2," as applying "to ordinary warfare conducted by people after settlement in the land"; he counts the second section as "clauses concerning 'holy war'" (2002: 320, 317). Interpreters who suggest a different literary history for these two sections may well be correct, but there are no grounds from within our present text to distinguish between "ordinary warfare" and "holy warfare." Regardless of what sources Deuteronomy may have used, the present chapter places all warfare, whether nearby or at a distance, within the same category, one in which God gives the victory (20:4; cf. 20:13-14).

20:10-14 Distant Cities

The starting point for negotiations with a distant town is offering *terms of peace* (*shalom*). War is only to be commenced if and when this offer is rejected. It is true that the offer itself is a demand for full submission, but the text clearly begins with negotiation. The *forced labor* of the passage does not necessarily imply enslavement but probably refers to the imposition of work responsibilities (a kind of labor levy) on the community.

The alternative to submission is abject defeat. Once the surrender has taken place or the city is overthrown, the warriors of the city, meaning the males, are killed. This is not the devotion to destruction of verse 17 but should be considered strategic. The rest—women, children, and booty—are taken and enjoyed as spoil (for further detail on how women taken in such battle are to be treated, see on 21:10-14).

Taken by itself, this section reflects fairly typical ancient Near Eastern war practice, strategy, and rhetoric. Even the act of attributing the victory to God is far from unique. War is a convention by which a people or nation with the power to do so uses that power for its own benefit. Negotiations that result in a tribute of goods or labor may be the first step; yet when talks are unsuccessful, military confrontation may take place, presumably with the expectation of victory and the enjoyment of spoils, again consisting of people and goods. The Israel Deuteronomy is addressing has experienced such war. But remember the summary of foundational principles above (at end of comments on 20:5-9). Those principles make it hard, if not impossible, to imagine putting this section into practice: Deuteronomy undermines the potential of such war even as it continues to speak of it (cf. just war tradition, see TLC below).

20:15-18 Cities of the Land

Although still placed under the foundational principles of the opening verses (20:1-9), the section on *towns of the nations here* has a very different tone to it from the one on *towns that are far from you* (20:15). The driving force is no longer material benefit for Israel but concern for the purity of Israel's worship of the one God. The language and themes shift from that of typical war strategy (e.g., *offer it terms of peace, forced labor, besiege it*; vv. 10-12) to that of religion. Israel is to utterly "devote" or "ban" or *destroy* all the previous inhabitants of the land (a double use of the Hebrew ḥerem; v. 17).

Ḥerem is "a kind of sacrifice to God" (McConville 2002: 321) [*Ḥerem, p. 552; Yahweh War, p. 566*]. The accounts of the defeat of Heshbon and Bashan in the Transjordan (2:26–3:7), and Jericho and Ai (Josh 6–7) west of the Jordan, both reflect this understanding. The command not to *let anything that breathes remain alive* is interpreted inconsistently, sometimes understood absolutely as including people and animals (e.g., in the defeat of Jericho, Josh 6:21), sometimes as applying only to people, with the animals treated as the spoils of war (cf. 2:35; 3:7; Josh 8:2). This inconsistency reflects that the primary focus of these passages is not detailed procedures but the absolute priority of the first commandment in the face of temptation from other peoples. It is not coincidental that the term ḥerem is also used in Deuteronomy 13, which deals with temptations from within Israel to worship other gods (13:15, 17).

The present passage has numerous echoes from the opening and closing verses of chapter 7. The concern is that Israel not be tempted to adopt the practices of the nations as they worship their gods (20:18; cf. 7:4), which are *abhorrent* (20:18; cf. 7:25-26), with the list of nations identified virtually identical (only the Girgashites are missing from the list in 20:17; cf. 7:1). *Ḥerem* is the expected action (20:17; cf. 7:2, 26). The central issue here is not war, especially not its strategy or conduct, but the consistent Deuteronomic emphasis on the life-and-death nature of the obedience to the first commandment (cf. "Deuteronomy and the Scandal of Violence" in the introduction; comments on 7:1-5).

Consideration for Trees 20:19-20

Given the generally all-or-nothing nature of war, these verses impose an unusual and even illogical restraint. In the context of siege, trees might be cut down for at least two reasons. First, the wood is needed in the battle. The passage mentions building *siegeworks*, probably referring to a "siege wall, a series of fortifications built by an attacking army around a besieged city to blockade it so that it cannot be resupplied with food, weapons, and manpower, and to protect itself from raids by the city's defenders or its allies." It may also include "equipment used in assaulting the city; ladders, battering rams, and the ramps on which the rams were rolled up to the city wall" (Tigay: 190). Second, trees could be destroyed as a way of terrorizing the people of the city by reducing their future food supply.

The passage does allow the use of trees for siegeworks, but only trees not producing food are to be used, and by implication even these are not to be cut down "as an act of vandalism or psychological warfare" (Nelson 2002: 252). Although protecting food-producing trees may be considered a way of preserving possible future benefits that Israel might experience from a victory (the food that those trees could produce), the argument given by the text is different: *Are trees in the field human beings that they should come under siege from you?* This question does not imply that trees are more valuable than human beings but it does suggest some sympathy or consideration of the trees. God has created the trees also, so they should not be destroyed needlessly. The passage does reflect an ecological restraint, a concern for God's creation. This concern is so significant that the normal tendency of war to become unconditional is placed under an external limitation.

THE TEXT IN BIBLICAL CONTEXT
War in the Old Testament and "Pacifism" in the New Testament

There are at least two sides to war in the Old Testament. On the one side is the reality of Israel's experience. Although it is impossible to reconstruct exactly how Israel enters the Promised Land, it is likely that at least some conflict is involved. And yet the Old Testament is clear that Israel does not overrun the whole land in one quick campaign, as a first reading of the early chapters of Joshua might lead one to think (cf. Deut 7:22; Judg 1:27-36), but the proposal sometimes made that Israel evolves peacefully upon the land also is inadequate.

Once Israel is in the land, war continues to be a reality. The book of Judges depicts Israel as a threatened people, constantly on the defensive against neighboring peoples like the Midianites and especially the Philistines. Israel adopts kingship in response to such threats. The stories of Israel's kings show that they quickly establish armies and lead them into battle, sometimes defensively but other times offensively, in an effort to increase land or gain wealth. The one side of the Old Testament introduces us to a people who fights in wars very much like a typical small ancient Near Eastern state. It should not be surprising that war stories are common in the Old Testament.

But there is another side to the Old Testament passages about war. These passages are far from pacifist, but they challenge or undermine the typical ways of war. In these passages the model for war is the exodus, and most particularly the crossing of the Red Sea. In this "military" confrontation, the role of Israel is largely that of spectator as God defeats Pharaoh, a god of Egypt, and his technologically advanced army. In Judges, Israel defeats the peoples menacing it, but victory again depends not upon military strategy or superior forces but upon obedience to God, who then gives victory.

The story of Gideon and the Midianites represents this alternative perspective. The Midianites' oppression of Israel is due not to Israel's weakness or Midian's strength, but to the fact that Israel *did what was evil in the sight of the* LORD (Judg 6:1). Gideon's first action after being called to deliver Israel on behalf of God is to tear down the altar to Baal and to offer a sacrifice on a new altar to the true God (6:24-32). After Gideon gathers the militia, we have the bizarre narrative of how this group of volunteer soldiers is reduced from thirty-two thousand to three hundred (a 99 percent reduction) in order that no one might mistake the fact that victory comes from God and not the army (Judg 7:1-24).

This other side is also reflected in numerous other passages and ways. The one in Deuteronomy preventing the king from making a priority out of establishing a standing army (17:14-20) and our present passages stand in this tradition. Prophets indict kings for trusting in their armies, as in Isaiah's word: "Alas for those who go down to Egypt for help and who rely on horses, who trust in chariots because they are many, . . . but who do not look to the Holy One of Israel" (31:1). God is the one who defends Jerusalem, not the armies (e.g., 2 Kings 18:17–19:37). Neither war nor its heroes are glorified. David is prevented from building the temple with this explanation: "You have shed much blood and have waged great wars; you shall not build a house to my name, because you have shed so much blood before me upon the earth" (1 Chron 22:8). In the ideal future "the wolf shall live with the lamb" (Isa 11:6), nations "shall beat their swords into plowshares, and their spears into pruning hooks; nation shall not lift up sword against nation, neither shall they learn war any more" (Isa 2:4; cf. Mic 4:3). This is a future within which Israel is already invited to live (Isa 2:5; Mic 4:5).

War was part of Israel's experience. But the Old Testament systematically undermines commonsense assumptions about war. Deuteronomy 20, if obeyed, makes it virtually impossible to use war as an element of foreign policy. It assumes that the people's role in assuring victory is faithfulness to God and God's instructions, not superior numbers or technology or strategy. These passages do not result in what today is called pacifism—the Old Testament tends not to present systematic theories—but they do undermine war thinking.

On one level it may be legitimate to say that the New Testament does not address the question of war. War is normally fought by nations or states. By New Testament times the political nation of Israel has become a people without a state, a people living in the region of Judea and Galilee and beyond, under Roman occupation. The Christian church arose within this larger Roman Empire, also as a people without national boundaries or political structures. War as experienced by Israel thus is not directly addressed.

Yet on a more profound level, the logic of war is addressed very directly in a number of ways. On an interpersonal level, the New Testament repeatedly calls on the followers of Jesus to live lives characterized by love and nonviolence. Christians are to love each other (1 John 3:10, etc.) and their neighbor (Matt 19:19), and even their enemy (5:44). They are to turn the other cheek (5:39) and "live peaceably with all" (Rom 12:18). They are called to live the peace that the Old Testament presents as the ideal.

But this peaceable lifestyle has implications beyond interpersonal relations. During the time of Christ, an intense debate within Judaism concerned how Jews should or could respond to the oppressive Roman occupation. Some promoted violent rebellion against the Roman occupiers and understood this to be in the tradition of Old Testament wars and the Maccabean rebellion, in which God gave the victory. Jesus, however, gave no support to such rebellion. Instead, he called for living respectfully within the empire even as he invited people to be shaped by the ethic and ethos of the kingdom of God rather than the kingdom of Rome. His preaching represented a direct challenge to the ways of the Roman kingdom as well as to the ways that called for the violent overthrow of the empire. In his preaching, war is rejected.

Most significantly, the central logic of the New Testament represents a view of violence that makes war quite illogical. At the heart of the New Testament is the conviction that Jesus defeats evil by taking upon himself that evil. Jesus could have chosen to rule the world (the temptation in Luke 4:5-8) or to have angels protect him from the soldiers (Matt 26:53), but instead he chooses to allow himself to be crucified since this is the only way evil truly is defeated. As in the Old Testament, God gives the victory, but now there is the recognition that victory does not come through violence, or at least from committing violence. The final book of the New Testament expresses this most clearly: "The Lion of the tribe of Judah, the Root of David, has conquered" (Rev 5:5); but when this "Lion" appears, we discover that it is in fact "a Lamb" that has been "slain" (RSV: Rev 5:6, 12; 13:8). Victory and salvation come through "the blood of the Lamb" (12:11). God has created a world in which violence only causes more violence, and peace only comes through living peaceably.

Even within the Old Testament, stories of war are "thoroughly subordinated into the larger project that will, hopefully, reconcile all things into God's redemptive purpose, a purposeful and peaceful future that God himself has embodied and inaugurated in the life, death, and resurrection of Jesus Christ (Col 1:19-20)" (Matties: 461). The New Testament picks up the side of the Old Testament that undermines the logic of war and drives it to its logical conclusion. Here is true New Testament fulfillment of the Old.

TEXT IN THE LIFE OF THE CHURCH
Making Use of Deuteronomic War Passages

Deuteronomy 20 is not a favorite chapter for most Christian interpreters. Menno Simons, despite his hundreds of scriptural quotations, never once makes a reference to Deuteronomy 20 or one of the related passages. *Martyrs Mirror,* again filled with Scripture, entirely avoids these passages. That tendency is not unique to Anabaptists. John Calvin, typical of his day, regularly referenced Scripture in his *Institutes,* but never cites Deuteronomy 20.

That is not to say that biblical passages on war have not been used, even in support of going to war. As noted in the introduction ("Deuteronomy and the Scandal of Violence"), Deuteronomy has been used to validate what might be called ethnic cleansing. Early settlers in the United States, Afrikaner leaders in South Africa, Jewish radicals in Israel—all have used Deuteronomy to justify acts of extreme violence against earlier inhabitants of the land, comparing them with Ammon and Amalek. But this is a minority. Regardless of how these difficult passages are interpreted, the vast majority of Christians do not see support for Christian warfare in these passages.

In some ways Deuteronomy 20 may be like the just war tradition. The just war tradition does not reject war in principle, and in fact formally allows for war. It then sets a number of conditions that, if met, permit a nation to go to war. It requires that, in order to wage war, there is a just cause, that war is the last resort, that the principle of proportionality is applied in the conflict, and so forth. Although the just war tradition is often defended, it has the practical implication, or consequence, that if applied consistently and thoroughly, hardly any war would ever be feasible or justified, especially in a world with weapons of mass destruction.

In his commentary writing Martin Luther could not avoid these passages. After a discussion of the directives in Deuteronomy 20 (e.g., it warns Israel against trusting in "arms and powers, lest they think that they are the ones who win victories and triumphs"), he moves to an allegorical treatment. Here he explains, "The wars of this people signify spiritual wars waged in the cause of faith," and "This is not a material sword striking down bodies; it is the word of God smiting consciences" (202-6). This is not the same as Moberly's metaphorical treatment (see Introduction) yet it is not inconsistent with it. Deuteronomy is about the exclusive worship of God (e.g., Shema and the first commandment) and about what that means practically: *justice, and only justice you shall pursue* (16:20). Even common war traditions are tailored to that end.

Deuteronomy 21:1–25:19
Part 2D, Unit 6
Miscellaneous

PREVIEW
There is no clear structure for chapters 12–26 (see introduction to these chapters). That is especially evident in chapters 21–25. These thus are treated simply consecutively, in some cases in relationship to themes introduced earlier.

OUTLINE
Purging the Guilt of an Unsolved Murder, 21:1-9
Consideration for War Brides, 21:10-14
Difficulty in the Home, 21:15-21
    21:15-17   A Man with Two Wives
    21:18-21   Parents of a Rebellious Son
Handling the Body of One Executed, 21:22-23
Helping the Neighbor, 22:1-3
Consideration for Animals: The Fallen Donkey or Ox, 22:4
Abhorrent Mixtures, 22:5, 9-11
Consideration for Animals: Preserving the Mother Bird, 22:6-7
Avoiding Criminal Negligence, 22:8
Four Tassels on a Cloak, 22:12
A Man Slanders His Wife, 22:13-21
    22:13-14   The Crime
    22:15-17   The Indictment
    22:18-19   A Guilty Verdict

22:20-21 Epilogue: The Seriousness of the Original Allegation
Illicit Sexual Affairs, 22:22-30
Admission to the Assembly of the Lord, 23:1-8
    23:1-6   Exclusions from the Assembly of the Lord
    23:7-8   Policies for Edomites and Egyptians
Maintaining Purity in the Camp, 23:9-14
Escaped Slaves, 23:15-16
Abhorrent Cultic Practices, 23:17-18
Charitable Loans: Prohibition of Interest, 23:19-20
Making and Fulfilling Vows, 23:21-23
Gleaning: For the Gleaner, 23:24-25
A Twice-Divorced Woman, 24:1-4
Conscription and a Recently Married Man, 24:5
Charitable Loans: A Limitation on Pledges, 24:6
Stealing a Person, 24:7
Instructions in Cases of Skin Diseases, 24:8-9
Charitable Loans: Further Limitation on Pledges, 24:10-13
Payment of Wages, 24:14-15
Individual Legal Responsibility, 24:16
Justice for the Resident Alien, the Orphan, and the Widow, 24:17-18
Gleaning: For the Farmer, 24:19-22
Controlling Flogging, 25:1-3
Consideration for Animals: Muzzling the Ox, 25:4
A Widow without a Son, 25:5-10
A Woman and a Fight, 25:11-12
Honest Weights, 25:13-16
Remember Amalek, 25:17-19

EXPLANATORY NOTES

Purging the Guilt of an Unsolved Murder 21:1-9

As a holy people, Israel is expected to remain pure, to follow certain standards. Clean and unclean animals receive most concerted attention, yet the Moab covenant touches on a variety of other topics from all spheres of life, including domestic matters such as dress and agriculture and all the way to issues of murder and execution. In some cases the regulations clearly arise from (what for contemporary readers is) a foreign world of purity and holiness (e.g., 14:1-21), in some cases the logic for the directive is lost, and in other cases the standard required may make immediate sense (e.g., 22:12; 23:21-23). The broad range of topics in these regulations, combined with the relatively small number of these instructions, highlights the fact that these passages are representative and not comprehensive. These are examples of what it means for the people to live in a consistent manner as a holy people. They give a small glimpse into a much larger world.

Chapter 21 opens and closes with the virtually identical, *the land that the LORD your God is giving you to possess/for possession* (vv. 1, 23). This frame not only points to the larger context but also to the focus of the instruction, the gifted land. Deuteronomy never speaks of the land of Israel as holy (on one occasion it speaks of the war camp as holy; 23:14), but it retains the conviction that if the land is polluted or becomes unclean, Israel will suffer as result. Unclean land will not produce as it should, and the blessing Israel can expect to receive from the land will be impaired. It thus is important that Israel not pollute the land, or if something happens that otherwise might have this effect, that it perform the necessary ritual to deflect its negative consequences.

The killing of another human being, whether intentional or accidental, is a human transgression into God's authority. At creation, God breathed into the human "the breath of life" (Gen 2:7), and God continues to have sole authority over that life. When humans take this authority from God, they defile and pollute the land in which they live. To take care of this pollution, to cancel the murder's destructive effect upon those in its vicinity, action is required. Numbers 35:33 thus instructs, "You shall not pollute the land in which you live; for blood pollutes the land, and no expiation can be made for the land, for the blood that is shed in it, except by the blood of the one who shed it."

Deuteronomy 19:1-13 thus gives instructions to Israel on how to *purge the guilt of innocent blood* (19:13; cf. 21:9; the only two times this phrase appears in the OT) when someone has committed premeditated murder and the perpetrator is known. The death of the murderer then plays a ritual role, and the guilt is purged. But what can Israel do when a murder is unsolved, when Israel does not know who the perpetrator is? Deuteronomy 21:1-9 provides directions for such a situation so that the destructive effect of the pollution is avoided.

The discovery of a *body* murdered (lit., *one who has been pierced*) in the *open country* presents a challenge: in the absence of eyewitnesses, identifying the guilty person becomes difficult. As the passages on the judicial system shows, (eye)witnesses were the primary means of confirming guilt. The first task thus is to determine which town must take responsibility for removing the potentially fatal consequences of the murder. Although Deuteronomy 16:18

speaks of judges and officials *throughout your tribes*, the *elders and judges* of 21:2 may be from the central sanctuary (cf. 17:9), with authority over the land as a whole and over the towns in it.

Once responsibility is assigned, the *elders of the town nearest* to the crime take over. Despite the extended introduction of the priests in verse 5 (*priests, the sons of Levi, . . . for the* LORD *your God has chosen them to minister to him and to pronounce blessings in the name of the* LORD, *and by their decision all cases of dispute and assault shall be settled*), they have no formal role in the service. The priests and judge at the central sanctuary have responsibility for difficult cases (17:8-9), but in this situation there is no decision to be made so their presence may simply be to represent the people as a whole. Although the local elders are in charge of the ceremony, the consequences of not following through on it would impact the land as a whole (note the language of 21:8).

The *heifer that has never been worked, one that has not pulled in the yoke*; and a *wadi with running water, which is neither plowed nor sown*—both have an unspoiled quality to them and thus are appropriate for a sacred ceremony (v. 4). The text identifies three elements of the ceremony, all performed by the elders: they break the neck of the cow (v. 4), they wash their hands (v. 6), and they say a prayer (vv. 7-8).

Deuteronomy gives directions for the ritual but no interpretation of its logic. How does the death of the cow take care of the pollution that the unsolved murder has caused? David Wright suggests some possible explanations:

> to consider it a (1) sacrifice, (2) a symbolic or vicarious execution of the murderer, (3) the representation of the penalty that the elders will suffer if their confession of innocence is not true, (4) the means of preventing the animal laden with guilt from returning to the community, or (5) a reenactment of the murder that removes blood pollution from the inhabited to an uninhabited area. (388-89, numbering added)

Given the prominence of sacrifice in the Old Testament, we may be drawn to the first option, but a number of factors make it unlikely: the cow is killed by having its neck broken rather than its throat cut, there is no altar, the priests only enter the text after the cow is killed and even then remain largely bystanders, the event takes place away from the central sanctuary.

Wright's second, third, and fourth possible explanations also have their difficulties. The unusual location of the ceremony is not required by either the second or third proposal; unlike the ritual of the scapegoat (Lev 16:20-22) that informs the fourth proposal, the confession of sin over the animal only takes place after it has been killed. Wright and others contend that the ceremony in Deuteronomy 21 is an elimination rite in which the killing of the cow is a "reenactment of the murder that transfers bloodguilt from the inhabited land and the people to an innocuous locale" (393-94). The uncultivated wadi is removed from where the people live and cultivate the fields, and the *wadi with running water* flushes away the guilt even further.

This ritual may sound strange to contemporary ears, but Christopher Wright compares it to a ritual sometimes used today where "Christians are invited to write down their sins or besetting failures of the past, and then burn the paper or nail it to a symbolic cross," thereby symbolically removing sin. Those participating in this symbolic action understand that the "benefit of such action lies, of course, not in the ritual itself or any kind of sympathetic magic, but in the objective basis of God's atoning grace" (1996: 233).

Similarly, the climax of the event in the passage is not the killing of the cow, nor even the ritualistic act as the elders *wash their hands* over the dead heifer (a public statement of innocence still used today, in this case facilitated by the running water of the wadi; cf. Pss 26:6; 73:13; Isa 1:15-16; Matt 27:24), but the prayer offered to God. In fact, the grammar of its petition—*Absolve, O LORD, your people Israel*—exposes that Israel did not understand the ritual itself to take care of the guilt of the murder in some magical way (v. 8). The real removal of the guilt is God's action in response to the prayers of his people—*Then they will be absolved of bloodguilt*—and not a consequence of the mechanics of the ritual (v. 8).

Although it is the local elders who take responsibility for the ceremony, they do this on behalf of the people of Israel as a whole. It is *your people Israel* (twice in v. 8) whom God is asked to absolve of the guilt, where the guilt could remain. It is understood that the sin (in this case, murder) of one individual brings bloodguilt upon the whole people and pollutes the whole land. Through this ceremony, both the ritual (killing cow, washing hands) and the prayer, the purity of the land is restored, and God's blessing remains with them.

Consideration for War Brides 21:10-14

This regulation begins with the identical phrase as chapter 20, *When you go out to war against your enemies* . . . (cf. 20:10, 19). Like chapter 20, the background for this passage is the general ancient Near Eastern practice of war. As allowed in 20:10-18, on the conduct of war, this paragraph expects that war will likely result in the capture of women; the assumption is that the men have been killed (cf. 20:13-14). The question this passage addresses is how Israel is to treat women who have been taken captive in war, or more specifically, how an Israelite man is to treat a woman whom he wishes to take as wife.

The text regulates such a situation with three provisions:

1. The text does allow an Israelite man to marry a woman taken captive in war. The language of the passage, with its reference to *a beautiful woman whom you desire* opens the possibility that he might simply use her as a concubine or as a sex slave. Although the text may not explicitly prohibit this, the permission to marry makes this the preferred option. If he wants her, he should marry her and make her a full wife.

2. Before he marries her, he must allow her a monthlong period of transition so as to mourn the family she has lost. Even if her family may not have been killed in the battle, they clearly are no longer part of the picture. She is now part of a new life. The rituals in the passage (*shave her head, pare her nails, discard her captive's garb*) probably are not mourning rituals but rather ones that mark the transition from war captive to full member of the household. They allow the woman time to adjust to the new reality.

3. Perhaps most important, once the man has married her, he must never again treat her as a captive or prize of war. Once she has become his wife, she must not be treated as a slave and sold but must be treated exactly as an Israelite wife.

This passage is obviously rooted in the culture of its day and not in a contemporary understanding of male-female relations. Not only is capturing a woman in war possible; the passage also is entirely silent on whether or not the woman consents to the marriage arrangement. And although the law gives her some protection in the case of divorce, even this is only partial since she has no family within Israel to return to after any divorce.

Most remarkable, at least for Deuteronomy, is that the passage allows an Israelite man to marry a woman who clearly is foreign since she has been captured in war, an allowance in direct tension with the absolute rejection of all intermarriage with former inhabitants of the land (cf. 7:3). But perhaps this very tension points in a helpful direction. The point of this passage is not that capturing women in war is acceptable: such practice is simply part of their world. Rather, its point is that when this happens, and when an Israelite man finds such a woman attractive, he is allowed to make her a full wife rather than treat her as a slave; and once he has done this, he is to treat her with dignity and respect. Neither war nor the patriarchal culture are directly challenged, but both are weakened and undermined at least slightly.

Difficulty in the Home 21:15-21

Deuteronomy 16:20 reads, *Justice, and only justice, you shall pursue.* In the vision of Deuteronomy, that standard impacts not only the community as a whole, but also interactions within a household. The immense difference between our culture and the world of Deuteronomy, however, can overwhelm and conceal the concern of a passage. In some instances the gap may be so large that we can no longer be sure what Deuteronomy's concern may have been.

The home should be a happy place (e.g., *He shall be free at home one year, to be happy with the wife he has married,* 24:5). Yet there is the recognition that a variety of circumstances can undermine that. This chapter includes two examples: a man with two wives, and parents of a rebellious son (on family issues, see also 22:22-30; 24:1-4, 5-10). These passages give samples of how to apply *Justice, and only justice* to the home.

21:15-17 A Man with Two Wives

These verses assume two practices. First, although the stories of Israel's ancestors in Genesis may give the impression that polygamy is the norm, that is doubtful. More likely it was unusual, a sign of wealth and prestige or even royalty (e.g., David and Solomon). Abraham, Isaac, and Jacob were the heads of substantial households and not typical peasants. But even if uncommon, polygamy was permissible.

Second, the passage assumes that giving the eldest son a double inheritance is the norm. In neither case does the passage advocate for these practices but simply recognizes that they exist and have the potential to produce particular kinds of problems or temptation. In fact, perhaps by drawing attention to their potential problems, it is implicitly questioning them, although one should be careful not to impute contemporary sensitivities about monogamy and equality to the passage.

The complexity of the first case is not hard to understand. A man has taken a second wife, perhaps a younger and more attractive one, and has come to prefer her over the first. Not surprisingly, he then wishes to make the son of the favored wife his principal or "first" heir. Although hypothetical, the regulation echoes the story of

Jacob. He had two wives, Leah and Rachel, of whom the second was the more loved and attractive (cf. Gen 29:16-18; NRSV says Leah has "lovely eyes," but RSV suggests that her "eyes were weak"). It was the sons of Rachel, Joseph and Benjamin, whom Jacob loved. In the end Reuben, the eldest, loses his special place, and the sons of Joseph, Manasseh and Ephraim, are made equal to Joseph's brothers, thus giving Joseph a *double portion* (as in Deut 21:17). Since Manasseh and Ephraim each receive tribal territory in the Promised Land, Israel has a visible reminder of such special treatment.

But it is exactly such favoritism that our present passage prohibits. A father is not allowed to disregard the normal custom of giving the first son a double share even though he might prefer to do so. The point of this passage is not to support the traditional custom but rather to limit the arbitrary exercise of power by the father. As in some of the other regulations regarding justice in the home, Deuteronomy is concerned that the head of the house might become a law unto himself, and so its regulations govern and limit the behavior of the father.

21:18-21 *Parents of a Rebellious Son*

A contemporary reader is justifiably offended by the harshness of the punishment and the apparent life-and-death power that parents have over their offspring. But again, it is helpful if one tries to enter the world of the passage in order to uncover what its concern is. Order and stability are important in the world of Israel. The command to *honor your father and mother* (5:16) may have implied a respect for the larger social structure represented by the parents. The alternative to order is everyone doing what was right in their own eyes, a state of affairs that leads to chaos, rebellion, and disaster (Judg 17:6; 21:25).

Deuteronomy 21:18-21 lives in that world. Its conclusion speaks of the death penalty for someone who undermines this order, thereby purging *the evil from your midst* (v. 21; Jewish rabbis sometimes argued that this punishment was never actually applied and was included for educational purposes only; Tigay: 195). But before it arrives at this conclusion, it imposes another kind of order upon the people. Before the son can be punished, the regulation puts forward a series of requirements.

First, the son must have been *stubborn and rebellious* (stated twice, in vv. 18, 20), a repeat offender who *does not heed them when they discipline him* (v. 18). *He is a glutton and a drunkard* is typical Old Testament language for destructive behavior (v. 20; cf. Prov 23:20-21; 28:7). The denounced son is not one who has committed an isolated act of insolence but one who has demonstrated ongoing behavior that undermines the integrity of the home and stability of the community.

Second, the disobedience is against both mother and father, and both mother and father must agree to present the case to the elders of the town. This may have in mind a situation like the one of the previous regulation, in which a man has two wives, one less loved than the other. In such a context, the father cannot unilaterally accuse the son of the less loved wife. But more generally it reflects Deuteronomy's concern that both husband and wife are given protection (cf. the fifth commandment) and voice in the proceedings, a fairly radical point of view.

Third, the parents must defend their accusation before the *elders of his town at the gate*, where the case is considered, and where, if the verdict is guilty, *all the men of the town shall stone him to death* (vv. 19, 21). Previously in Deuteronomy the one(s) responsible for the initial indictment implement the death penalty themselves (e.g., 13:9), or are required to take the lead in its execution (e.g., 17:7). Here the parents are given no role at all. The conflict between parents and son becomes a public issue, debated before the elders at the gate, with the community as a whole exercising control over the situation.

Each of these requirements has the effect of limiting or controlling the arbitrary use of power by the father. The story of Judah and Tamar takes for granted that Judah has the authority to have his daughter-in-law executed for having "played the whore" (Gen 38:24). In the world of ancient Israel, parents do not require special regulations allowing them to exercise severe discipline over their children. In a time when cursing mother and father was understood to deserve death (Lev 20:9; cf. Deut 27:16), and when the larger household was the primary context for judicial decisions, parents had all the power they needed. This regulation controls the potential abuse of that power: a strong case of repeated rebellion is required, both mother and father must agree, and the community determines the verdict.

The central thrust of the passage may be limiting the unilateral authority of the father, but the reference to the *rebellious son* hints at another level of meaning. Previously Deuteronomy has spoken of Israel as a *child* whom God has carried through the harsh wilderness (1:31, lit., *son*), as a *child* whom God disciplines (8:5, again lit., *son*), as a people who has repeatedly rebelled against their God (1:26, 43; 9:7, 23). Is Israel the son about whom this passage is speaking?

Handling the Body of One Executed 21:22-23

Again, the concern is for *the land the LORD your God is giving you for possession* (cf. 21:1). The Hebrew root of the term translated *defile* in verse 23 is translated *unclean* four times in the dietary regulations (14:7, 8, 10, 19). It thus could be translated *to make unclean*. As in the opening passage of this chapter, we are in the realm of holiness and purity (21:1-9). Murder and a dead body defile the land, making it unclean.

Its location here may be due to the immediately preceding passage, which ends with the rebellious son being executed by stoning. As in that passage, the manner of execution assumed here is probably stoning. The *tree* of verse 22 thus is not an indication of crucifixion (although the early church makes use of this language in speaking of Jesus' death on the cross: cf. Acts 5:30; 10:39; 1 Pet 2:24; Gal 3:13), but rather where the executed body is hung. This practice was a statement of public shame and humiliation, serving to warn others (Gen 40:19; Num 25:4; Josh 8:29; 10:26-27; 1 Sam 31:10; 2 Sam 4:12; 21:5-9). As reflected by the Genesis passage, exposing a body in such a way opens the possibility of birds eating its flesh, thereby resulting in even further dishonor.

The phrase translated *is under God's curse* is somewhat ambiguous in the Hebrew; it may also signify that the body on the tree offends God, that it is a curse unto God. Here the NRSV remains the more likely, however. The reason for the curse is not the public exposure, or even the death itself, although both of these have defiling power, but the crime committed that led to the execution. Although Israel allows this manner of humiliation, it has its limits. Prolonged exposure, Deuteronomy suggests, "defiles the land and sets up a spreading contagion that threatens the land's fertility and endangers the population's well-being" (Cairns: 193). Although concern to protect the family of the executed person may play a factor, it is the danger of ritual impurity and its consequences that are stressed. Twice Joshua follows this directive (Josh 8:29; 10:26-27).

Helping the Neighbor 22:1-3

Within a community of brothers and sisters, helping each other should be the norm. This is the primary concern of these few verses as reflected by the last phrase, *You may not withhold your help* (v. 3). After an opening statement in apodictic form giving the basic directive (*Do not watch your neighbor's ox or sheep straying*, v. 1.), the text addresses possible questions, or perhaps potential loopholes: What do I do if the owner is not home or lives a distance away? Does this apply to an ox or also to a sheep? What if I find someone's garment?

In each case the answer to the hypothetical question broadens the meaning of the initial statement. The directive regarding the neighbor's ox or sheep is not a narrow or legalistic directive but represents an ethical direction.

But what is that direction? Is it care for animals in distress? Or is it the need to help the neighbor? Or does one need to decide between these two? Exodus includes a similar passage, but there the animal in difficulty belongs to an enemy (23:4-5). Deuteronomy shifts the focus to the *neighbor* or *fellow Israelite* (NIV; lit., *brother*; NRSV normally translates this as *member of the community*). As is clear from following verses (22:4, 6-7; 25:4), Deuteronomy does include animals in the justice that Israel is to establish in the land, but the issue here appears to be the way the Israelite treats a fellow community member. The expansion to *a neighbor's garment; and you shall do the same with anything else that your neighbor loses* confirms that concern right here is more for the neighbor than for the animal. The last phrase of the passage, *You may not withhold your help*, is especially striking. Walter Brueggemann notes, "The verb is 'conceal, hide,' stated in reflexive form. You may not hide yourself. You may not withdraw from neighborliness" (2001: 219).

As societies become more urban, more impersonal, as apparently happened in Israel in the ninth century BCE, the natural tendency is to narrow one's field of concern. The brother or sister or neighbor can become strangers and no longer part of "us." One is reminded of Jesus' parable of the good Samaritan (Luke 10:30-37). For Deuteronomy, Israel is a close body of brother and sisters, neighbors who help each without asking whether it is required or legislated.

Consideration for Animals: The Fallen Donkey or Ox 22:4

For Deuteronomy, the call for justice even touches on the animal world (note also 22:4, 6-7; 25:4). Informing these directives stands the order of creation as reflected in Genesis 1, an order in which animals stand between humans on the one side and plant life on the other. Like humans, animals are blessed and directed to "be fruitful and multiply" (Gen 1:22). Both humans and animals are given plants and trees for food (1:29-30), and both have the "breath of life" (1:30).

But only humans are in the "image of God" (Gen 1:27), and humans have "dominion over the fish of the sea and over the birds of the air and over every living thing that moves upon the earth" (1:28). Justice for animals is not the same as that for humans, nor does it receive equal attention. But the inclusion of even some passages that reflect concern for animals is noteworthy. The prohibitions against boiling a kid in its mother's milk (Deut 14:21) or plowing with an ox and donkey yoked together (22:10) may reflect similar consideration for animals.

This verse continues the short passage on helping the neighbor (note also their mutual relationship to Exod 23:4-5), but here the attention appears to be on the animal itself. The Exodus version helps explain the situation: a donkey or ox has collapsed under a heavy load and is unable to rise up on its own. This verse invites the one who notices this to help it up even if the animal belongs to someone else. Here is an act of kindness to an animal trapped by its burden. Kindness and consideration are not limited to the neighbor but are extended even to animals, fellow living members of God's creation.

Abhorrent Mixtures 22:5, 9-11

Four verses in chapter 22 deal with abhorrent mixtures (vv. 5, 9, 10, 11). Each is a directive that disallows some combination or mixture. Not only do they make little sense to us, scholars also struggle with their original intent. Leviticus includes the second and fourth and adds a further one, the breeding of two different kinds of animal (Lev 19:19). It is possible that originally these prohibitions may have been motivated by different concerns, but in their present context they appear to be tied together, with the last three occurring in consecutive verses somewhat similar in structure. An explanation that would cover all four thus would be the most persuasive, at least in terms of Deuteronomy's interests.

Interpreters have proposed a variety of explanations, often trying to find some parallel in foreign religions that might explain these prohibitions. The most plausible explanation, although not conclusive, relates them to the ancient need for order (Houtman; Douglas). A central concern of the story of creation is creation of order out of chaos. The seven days of creation give it a systematic format. An important theme is creation by separation, as light is separated from darkness in order to make day and night, and earth is separated from water to make seas and land. Vegetation and animal life are made "according to its kind" (Gen 1:11, 12, 21, 25 RSV). When God rests on the seventh day, the chaos of the *formless void* has been replaced by an ordered creation with a diversity of life, each with its own place in the created order.

But the threat of chaos returning always remains. Israel must be constantly vigilant not to endanger this order. The intermingling of the *sons of God* with the *daughters* born to humans (Gen 6:1-4) is an obvious transgression against this order. Sodomy violates the distinction between animal and human (e.g., Lev 18:23). Similarly, there is an order to the way we are to live that must be protected. As Houtman says, "Blurring separation and variety may induce a reversion of cosmos to chaos and must therefore be prevented" (227-28). Disregarding this order of creation is dangerous and causes ritual impurity. This overarching concern for order has probably influenced the set of prohibitions here, although individual factors impact their detail. Following these prohibitions also will contribute to distinguishing between Israel and other peoples, with the need for clear boundaries potentially also reflecting this concern for order.

The different terms used for the clothes (*garment, apparel*), as well as the lack of parallel construction (*wear, put on*), suggest that the first abhorrent mixture (v. 4) is more than a simple matter of cross-dressing. The term *apparel* can also include tools or weapons. The phrase *abhorrent to the LORD your God* is more commonly used in Deuteronomy of cultic practices associated with other gods. Canaanite religion was a fertility religion, one in which cultic prostitution flourished as a form of sympathetic magic, intended to ensure the fertility of herds and fields. There is archaeological evidence that sometimes this practice could include male-female exchange of clothing (Cairns: 194). We also know that at times cultic prostitution did enter Israel's worship life (e.g., 1 Kings 14:24; 2 Kings 23:7; cf. Deut. 23:17-18). Against such a background, this prohibition is consistent with many other Deuteronomic warnings against having anything to do with foreign religions.

But it is an oversimplification to understand this verse as simply another warning against the religion of the Canaanites. Along with Leviticus 19:19 and the other prohibitions in this chapter, this is another example of concern for order.

> Positively stated, the theological thrust of v. 5 is that Yahweh has created male and female with specific and complementary characteristics so that in their relationship the two constitute the full expression of humanity. To blur the intersexual distinction that Yahweh has established strikes at the natural order and harmony willed by the Creator. (Cairns 194-95)

A comparison of modern dress with ancient dress suggests fairly quickly that defining gender-specific clothing is problematic, but a sense of an appropriate order cannot be that easily dismissed.

The prohibition against adding *a second kind of seed* to a vineyard (v. 9) includes the striking phrase *or the whole yield will have to be forfeited*. The RSV (and NIV mg., *forfeited to the sanctuary*) draws attention to a term present in the Hebrew perhaps most literally translated *shall become holy.* This may mean that the crop then must be "transferred out of the normal profane state and thus become unavailable for common use" (Nelson 2002: 269). Israel's understanding of order does distinguish between what is allowed for the priests and what is allowed for other Israelites. This prohibition may also be a warning against greed by pushing the land too hard (Cairns: 196).

The phrase *plow with an ox and a donkey yoked together* (v. 10) may imply more than merely having them work together: it may also be a veiled reference to mating the two together (cf. Lev 19:19). But even if this is not the case, using the two together in work could be understood as an inappropriate crossing of boundaries. Not only are the two animals of different species, according to the dietary regulations (Deut 14:1-21), but also one is clean and the other unclean. In addition, there may be a concern here for the animals since the two are of unequal strength. Yoking them together thus could be an abuse of the donkey (see comments on 22:1-7).

Jeffrey Tigay reports that even older Jewish rabbis, who normally can be very resourceful in developing explanations, were unable to give an explanation for the prohibition of verse 11 (203). The verse prohibits wearing clothes made with wool and linen woven together, not the mere mixing of these fabrics. According to Exodus 28:6-14 priests were required to wear clothes that included mixed materials. Perhaps here is an example where a practice that is required in the realm of the holy then becomes excluded from the profane.

Consideration for Animals: Preserving the Mother Bird 22:6-7

This directive itself may be clear but not its rationale. An Israelite is free to take eggs or even a fledgling from a nest, but the mother bird is to be preserved. Future life, both for the birds as well as for Israel, depends on the fertility of mother animals. If both mother and eggs or fledglings are taken, there will be no more birds, and a future food source is threatened. The directive thus may be a way of protecting a future source of food for the people (cf. 20:19-20), yet it probably is more than that. The concluding promise, *in order that it may go well with you and you may live long*, appears to be an intended echo of the command to honor father and mother, with its promise *so that your days may be long and that it may go well with you* (5:16). Even a mother bird deserves a certain level of honor or respect for having brought new life into the world. Both of these considerations are consistent with contemporary ecological concerns.

Avoiding Criminal Negligence 22:8

Houses in the ancient world normally had a flat roof, which was used extensively in a variety of ways, including socializing, storage of grain and other items, and sleeping in warm weather. Understandably, the danger of falling off while walking or working or even rolling off while sleeping on the roof was a reality unless some restraint was constructed at the edge. A *parapet* was a low wall, approximately thirty inches high, according to Jewish tradition (Tigay: 201), erected to prevent exactly such an accident. It might be compared with the railings required at the edge of a deck by modern building codes, or the guardrails installed at the edge of a road at a particularly dangerous curve. The text warns that whoever does not take such a precaution is in danger of having *bloodguilt* on one's hand if someone falls off that roof. Bloodguilt results when an innocent person is killed (cf. 19:10; 21:8).

Criminal negligence is the phrase we use today for an action or nonaction that harms someone, even though not so intended, if this danger could have been reasonably anticipated. The reason for neglecting to build a restraining wall on a roof might be laziness or the desire to save resources, but certainly not an intention to hurt someone walking about on the roof. And yet, bloodguilt can result. Exodus presents a similar situation where a person digging a pit is warned to cover it lest an ox or donkey fall into it (Exod 21:33-34). As with the regulation requiring the Israelite farmer to muzzle an ox treading grain (Deut 25:4), this one reflects a general approach. We are not only liable for the consequences of actions intended to hurt or defraud others, but also for actions or nonactions that otherwise may be quite innocent, yet where we should have known that they might be dangerous. Deuteronomy warns the Israelite community to be aware of the potential consequences of all they do lest they become guilty of criminal negligence.

Four Tassels on a Cloak 22:12

The requirement to *make tassels on the four corners of the cloak* is possibly placed here because, like the immediately preceding verse, it deals with clothing. Its interest, however, appears to be different. Deuteronomy gives no explanation for the requirement, but the parallel passage in Numbers is more helpful. Not only does Numbers 15:37-41 add a blue cord on the fringe of each corner; it also adds that Israel is to do this so that "when you see it, you will remember all the commandments of the LORD and do them" (Num 15:39). The

A Man Slanders His Wife 22:13-21

The logic and central concern of this unusual passage are not entirely transparent. Marriage not only involves a man and a woman but also implicates their families. Although the passage opens with *Suppose a man marries a woman*, the marriage probably was arranged by the parents. Presumably the family of the groom agreed to make a payment for the bride, perhaps in the range of fifty shekels (cf. vv. 28-29; Exod 22:16-17), with the condition that the bride was a virgin. Since divorced women could marry, the issue is not necessarily the sexual purity of the bride, although that also may be a factor, but the integrity of the arrangement and the character of the bride. If the negotiations incorrectly attested that the bride was a virgin, then the marriage had been arranged under false pretenses, either on the part of the bride or her parents.

In addition to customs about marriage, the passage reflects the ancient significance of shame and honor. Honor and the reputation of a good name are extremely valued possessions of a person or family. A family can be destroyed if its integrity is shamed or its honor spoiled. This background begins to explain the passage, but some ambiguities or odd features remain.

There are two quite alternative ways of reading the passage. One possibility is to read the whole as a legal exchange, with the primary question being whether or not the bride was a virgin.

- 22:13-14 The formal indictment of the bride by the husband

- 22:15-17 The defense of the bride by the bride's family

- 22:18-19 The punishment if the verdict on the bride is "not guilty"

- 22:20-21 The punishment if the verdict on the bride is "guilty"

But there are hints that suggest an alternative reading is more true to the text. The legal exchange is limited to verses 15-21, with verses 13-14 providing the background information. The person under indictment in the legal portion then is the husband, not the bride, and the crime is the slander committed by the husband. Its logic then looks as follows:

- 22:13-14 Slander by the husband
- 22:15-17 The legal case against the husband
- 22:18-19 A guilty verdict and punishment
- 22:20-21 Epilogue: Punishing a woman who has entered a marriage unfaithfully

22:13-14 *The Crime*

That the latter (above) is the preferred reading is suggested very quickly by the text. This is not a neutral presentation of an accusation before the court, but a report of a man who without justification is slandering his wife: *he dislikes her [, he] makes up charges against her, slandering* [lit., *sends out a bad name against*] *her by saying . . .* The man is not bringing a formal charge against his wife before the court but rather is participating in malicious gossip within the community. The motivation for the husband's actions is not given. Perhaps the false charges are intended to provide grounds for granting a difficult divorce. Or perhaps the husband is trying to blackmail the bride's family into returning the original bride-price. In either case, the introductory wording signals that the husband's allegation is false and intentionally harmful, with the effect of dishonoring the bride and her family.

22:15-17 *The Indictment*

The family of the bride then takes legal action in an effort to protect their honor and clear their name (Pressler: 24). Both parents come to the *elders of the city at the gate* and present their case. The *evidence of the young woman's virginity* is a *cloth*, apparently with the woman's blood on it from the first instance of intercourse. McConville suggests that "the preservation of the sheet was presumably a matter of wedding ritual, the initial placing of it, its preservation and entrustment to the parents all being part of the festivities, certifying that the parents had fulfilled their part of the bargain; their daughter indeed was marriageable" (2002: 339). Jeffrey Tigay reports, "This custom is well-known in the Middle East and has been practiced among various Jewish and Arabic communities until recent times; in some places the cloth is displayed by the proud parents" (205). The passage assumes that the material evidence of the cloth is adequate to find the husband guilty.

Although on one level the logic of the indictment is clear, the larger situation itself is less so. In fact, on a practical level the law appears quite unworkable. If retaining a bloodstained cloth from the wedding night is general practice, then surely the man is aware of it and would be hesitant to make the false accusation. And given the nature of the evidence, the possibility of fabricating such evidence by the parents seems not out of the question (cf. Nelson 2002: 270). These observations suggest that the passage is not really a "regulation" but intended more as instruction.

22:18-19 A Guilty Verdict

The evidence is persuasive, the verdict is guilty, and the sentence is pronounced. It consists both of punishment, probably a public flogging, and a heavy fine. The beating would shame the man and represent a public statement that the woman has been innocent of the smear campaign against her. The fine may represent double the normal bride-price, or perhaps reflect that the man has maligned both the woman and her family. Additionally, the man is prohibited from ever divorcing the woman he has libeled. This may feel like a restriction on the freedom of the wife, but for that world it provides her protection. The language *He has slandered a virgin of Israel* suggests that the crime is understood as not only against the woman, or even just her family, but also all of Israel (Nelson 2002: 270).

It may be asked whether the punishment is severe enough: after all, if the man's initial allegation has been accurate, the woman could have been executed. The fact that the punishment for the man is not death by stoning supports the interpretation that the husband has not laid a legal charge against his wife in court, thereby risking the death penalty for himself on the basis of the Deuteronomic law of false witness (19:16-21). On the other side, if the goal of the slandering has been to recoup the original bride-price, the punishment can be understood as doubling the principle of lex talionis. Since the parents are able to defend their daughter's virtue simply by supplying a bloodstained cloth, the threatened punishment serves as a significant disincentive against carelessly or maliciously slandering one's wife.

22:20-21 Epilogue: The Seriousness of the Original Allegation

Stimulated by this case (*if, however, this charge is true*), verse 20 begins a new case. The previous case starts with an indication that the charge against the woman is false, so a just verdict could only be guilty for the man. These two verses (20-21) do not raise an alternative verdict for the previous case, a case of slander, but rather draw attention to the seriousness of the man's slander: it has the potential to kill the woman, both figuratively through the resulting shame, and possibly literally through execution. The harsh punishment meted out in verses 20-21 makes the slander of the previous verses so much more serious.

The punishment itself is described with typical Deuteronomic phrases and procedures. *If . . . the charge is true*, the citizens of the community are to *bring the young woman out* (cf. 21:19, where parents take their rebellious son and *bring him out*), and the *men of her town shall stone her to death* (cf. 13:10; 17:5; 21:21; 22:24), This is done in order to *purge the evil from your midst* (13:5; 17:7, 12; 19:13, 19; 21:21; 22:21, 24; 24:7). Each of these also occur in the story of the rebellious son (21:18-21). In both stories the actions of an individual have the potential to bring great shame on a particular family and threaten the social integrity of the community. The location of the execution in this case, at *the entrance of the father's house*, highlights this dimension.

Illicit Sexual Affairs 22:22-30

Again the radically different customs and culture of that day are obvious. As a patriarchal society, men dominated the family and home and controlled public life (although it is likely that in rural areas, where both spouses were involved in food production, relationships were more egalitarian than in urban, more upper-class families; Meyers). Deuteronomy may at times address men and women as equal members of the community (e.g., the Sabbath command, 5:14), and some of its regulations treat men and women in a relatively parallel manner (e.g., 5:14, 16; 12:12, 18; 15:17; 16:11, 14; 21:19; 22:15), but this direction should not be exaggerated. Deuteronomy is a book from ancient Israel, written from within and to the culture of its day.

The patriarchal nature of Israel's culture is especially obvious and offensive in regulations regarding marriage and sexual relationships. But it is not helpful to speak of the men in Israel as "owning" their wives as property. The passages that give women legal rights and voice make such language inappropriate and inaccurate. Nevertheless, men are the ones with the power. Until a woman is engaged or married, she is the responsibility of her father. The mother may play a significant role as well, but the father is the legal guardian. The father is responsible for negotiating his daughter's wedding and is the one to receive the bride-price. At the point of engagement, this responsibility shifts to the husband. Carolyn Pressler speaks of "the rights of the father to exclusive disposal of his daughter's sexuality and especially the rights of the husband to exclusive possession of his wife's sexuality" (42). Although one might speak of "responsibility for," rather than "rights," the emphasis holds. As a result, prior to engagement, an offense against a woman is an offense against her father, as well as the community as a whole, and after the engagement an offense against a woman is also against her husband.

Unfortunately, the foreign nature of this world makes it difficult for us to identify with confidence the central concern of each of these regulations. Given the well-established patriarchal system, it is doubtful that the regulations are intended to protect that system. But are these regulations protecting the rights of men within that system? Or are they protecting vulnerable women from the patriarchal system?

Carolyn Pressler speaks of these regulations largely in terms of how they protect the rights of the men, their claims to their daughters' and wives' sexuality, and the authority of the male head of the household. Yet at the same time she recognizes that there is another side to them: "The laws also protect the wife from false accusations, and provide for the socially vulnerable girl (22:28-29). It is not possible to distinguish completely in these cases the extent to which the laws protect the woman, and the extent to which they protect her father" (43).

The passage opens with two cases of adultery (vv. 22-24), followed by one of rape (vv. 25-27) and one in which a man violates an unengaged woman (vv. 28-29). In each a man acts inappropriately, in each a woman is in relationship with that man, in the first as *the wife of another man*, in the second as *engaged* as well as *his neighbor's wife*, in the third simply as *engaged,* and in the fourth as a *virgin* but yet as the daughter of her father. The patriarchal culture is most evident in the second case, which speaks of the man's crime as the violation of *his neighbor's wife*, and in the fourth case, which has the guilty man pay a fine to the *young woman's father*.

These four paragraphs exemplify how the judicial system might work at making fine distinctions. The three cases involve two variables: (1) the woman's status as married or engaged and (2) the woman's consent or lack of it (Pressler: 33). The first two assume that there is no question of guilt: the couple has been *caught*. They thus address the question of whether it makes a difference if the woman involved in the sexual relationship is married or only engaged. The answer of the passage is no. Even though the woman is still living with her father, for all practical purposes the engagement, at least as far as the possibility of having sex with another man is concerned, has made her like a married woman. The crime in the first two paragraphs thus is equally adultery, with the punishment death. Both paragraphs thus close with the statement, *so you shall purge the evil from your midst* (vv. 22, 24). Adultery may be a crime against the man whose wife is involved, but it certainly is also a crime against Israel as a whole, and against God, thus requiring severe punishment to cleanse the land and people.

The variable between the second and third case is the woman's consent to the sexual encounter. In the first of these two, the affair takes place *in the town*, where the woman can cry out for help if she does not want to participate in the sexual intercourse. Since she did not call for help, the verdict is that she voluntarily participated in the deed and thus is equally guilty with the man. Both are executed (v. 24, as in 22).

As in the second, the woman of the third paragraph is *engaged*, but now the meeting takes place in the *open country* (v. 25). The text hints that the man has forced himself upon the woman (suggested by the phrase *seizes her*), although this is not absolutely clear. Perhaps it is a case of seduction. This ambiguity may be intentional. If the woman participates in the affair voluntarily, she would deserve to die (as in previous case), but the account gives the woman the benefit of the doubt. Since the event takes place where a woman's cries would not be heard, and presumably since there are no witnesses, it is treated as rape, and only the man is executed. Here we see again Deuteronomy's concern that innocent blood not be shed (cf. 19:10), even if this means allowing someone who may be guilty go free. With these sample cases, Deuteronomy is suggesting logic that might be applied in actual judgments rather than be exhaustive. The text does not specify, for example, what Israel is to do if a married man has intercourse in the country with a woman married to another man, or many other possibilities. These sample cases, however, set the direction, both in terms of content and process.

The new variable presented in the fourth case is that of intercourse between a man and a young woman who is not yet engaged (v. 28). Although not a capital crime, it is a crime, not only against the young woman's father, although he receives the fine, but also against the woman (*he violated her*). Unlike the parallel passage in Exodus—where the text speaks of the man seducing the young woman, thereby implying that she may have consented (22:16-17)—our passage is less clear on that question. The phrase *He seizes her* may imply rape (as in v. 25), but ambiguously so. In this particular passage the question of the woman's consent is probably not legally significant (Pressler: 37). Whether voluntary or not, the effect is the same: the woman and her family have been shamed, with the result that her marriage prospects have been seriously damaged, making a negative financial impact upon her father. The punishment thus compensates the young woman's father (thereby protecting his rights), yet also requires that the man who committed the deed marry her without any possibility of divorce (thereby protecting the young woman who has become vulnerable through the action). With this second requirement, Deuteronomy goes beyond the regulation in Exodus, possibly reflecting greater sensitivity to the impact of the event upon the young woman.

The last regulation in the series (v. 30) imagines a situation in which a man has had more than one wife. It is not stated whether the man has died or whether he has divorced the woman in question; in either case, the man is no longer part of the scene (i.e., this is not a case of adultery). The woman whom the son is not to marry is not his mother (i.e., this is not a case of incest, at least not biologically, but a marriage regulation; cf. Lev 18:7-8; 20:11), but a former wife of his father. Since men could marry women over a considerable period of time, it is not impossible that the woman may have been close to the son's age, possibly even younger. And yet, the passage prohibits such a marriage. The logic of the prohibition is not entirely clear. The NRSV and NIV give interpretations (NRSV, *thereby violating his father's rights*; NIV, *he must not dishonor his father's bed*; lit., *uncovering his father's skirt*). The prohibition may be related to ancient perceptions of the father's honor and how it might be shamed through such a marriage. But it is also possible that the prohibition has to do with inheritance and the son's manipulative efforts to interfere with normal custom. In either case, the marriage would damage the stability and order of the extended family.

Admission to the Assembly of the Lord 23:1-8

Deuteronomy envisions Israel as a close community of brothers and sisters, together worshiping the one true God, together walking in the way of that God. The flip side of a close community and strong identity tends to be exclusion. The logic of the exclusions named here may appear ambiguous or even problematic, and it also was thus to some other biblical writers. Isaiah directly confronts the sentiment expressed here in Deuteronomy: "Do not let the foreigner joined to the LORD say, 'The LORD will surely separate me from his people'; and do not let the eunuch say, 'I am just a dry tree'" (Isa 56:3).

The passage explicitly excludes three groups of people (men whose genitals have been mutilated, children of an unacceptable marriage, Ammonites and Moabites), but then continues by identifying two other ethnic groups (Edomites and Egyptians) that are not to be despised and whose descendants are allowed into the assembly of God. The passage thus moves from harsh exclusion to greater openness to the outsider.

A key phrase, *the assembly of the LORD*, occurs six times, serving as a uniting theme for the passage (once each in the opening and closing verses, four times in between). The prominence of the phrase, combined with its total absence in the remainder of the book of Deuteronomy, is noteworthy. Normally the term *assembly* simply means a gathering of people. Deuteronomy uses the term for Israel gathered at Mount Horeb (5:22; 9:10; 10:4; 18:16), and of the whole community addressed by Moses on the plains of Moab, at the border of the Promised Land (31:30). The phrase *assembly of the LORD* probably refers to the community gathered specifically for worship, including sacrificing to God, and thus has a more focused meaning. Perhaps Deuteronomy is distinguishing between Israel as a political nation that includes Canaanites and the worshiping community from which they are excluded.

Yet it is striking that this is the only place Deuteronomy uses this phrase. In the remainder of the book, Deuteronomy highlights the inclusion of all in the faithful people, those without normal household heads (widow and orphan) and those without legal standing (resident alien, slave). Have some priestly regulations from elsewhere simply been inserted into the book? Normally Deuteronomy has limited if any interest in such detailed cultic policies.

The passage has two distinct parts. The first consists of three exclusions, each one beginning with the identical Hebrew phrase lost in most English translations (roughly *One shall not enter*), followed by an identification of the person or group who shall not enter *into the assembly of the LORD*. The first exclusion simply identifies those excluded, the second expands the exclusion somewhat with a statement making the exclusion virtually permanent, and the third expands the second by giving a rationale for the exclusion.

The second part of the passage employs a similar structure, now with two parallel phrases calling on Israel not to abhor a particular group of people (Edomites and Egyptians), with the first giving the rationale for the charge, and the second expanding upon the first by including a rationale and then expanding further. Both parts thus build toward a climax, the first negative, the second positive.

23:1-6 Exclusions from the Assembly of the Lord

The first group disqualified are men whose genitals have been mutilated (23:1). The verse does not indicate whether this applies regardless of whether the mutilation was intentional or accidental, nor does it give a rationale for the exclusion. Is it because the act of coming before God with a blemish profanes the sanctuary and thus is wrong (cf. rejection of animals with a blemish, 17:1)? Leviticus gives this rationale for why anyone with a blemish is prohibited from becoming a priest, including one who has crushed testicles (21:16-23). If so, then this verse may be calling for wholeness and holiness within the worship assembly.

Or is the concern to exclude those who have become eunuchs in order to participate in foreign religious practices? Although probably not practiced in Israel, castration for lifelong dedication to cultic or public service did take place in the ancient Near East. This verse then excludes those who have made lifelong commitments to other religions and thus would be consistent with Deuteronomy's consistent rejection of practices associated the worship of other gods.

Or is the logic that castration has made fathering future children impossible? Important in Israel's theology is the gift of the land and the passing on of this gift from generation to generation. The inability to contribute to this ongoing receipt of God's blessing may exclude those who cannot father children from full participation in the assembly of God. Unfortunately, the reason for this particular exclusion remains hidden.

The second group disqualified are those *born of an illicit union* (Deut 23:2). The Hebrew term translated *illicit union* occurs only one other time in the Old Testament (Zech 9:6) and probably refers to any forbidden or unacceptable marriage. The last verse of the previous chapter gives one such example, as it forbids marriage between a man and his father's wife (22:30). Leviticus (18:6-20; 20:10-20) gives a lengthy list of prohibited sexual relationships. Potentially this could include children born through incest, adultery, unmarried parents, and perhaps even mixed marriages between an Israelite and a foreigner. The time frame for the exclusion, *to the tenth generation*, is probably a colloquial way of saying "forever" (cf. vv. 3b and 6), since a literal reading results in roughly 250 years.

According to Genesis 19:30-38 the Moabites and the Ammonites are the descendants of Lot through his forbidden sexual relationship with his two daughters. Although Lot was the nephew of Abraham and thus the Moabites and Ammonites qualified as distant family, in this passage their exclusion may be a natural follow-up on the previous verse with its disqualification of children born of an *illicit union* (Deut 23:3-6).

Deuteronomy, however, bases it in two particular historical memories. First, Ammonites and Moabites are indicted for not providing food and water to the Israelites as they passed through their territory. This indictment is surprising since the earlier description of these encounters makes no reference to such refusal (2:9-23). That earlier account simply states that God has also given them—as the descendants of Lot, the nephew of Abraham—their land (2:9, 19). Indeed, a later request to buy food and water from King Sihon is supported by the claim that Edom and Moab had supplied these to them (2:28-29). Second, Deuteronomy 23:5 refers to the story of Moab commissioning the prophet Balaam to curse the Israelites (Num 22-24). The power and lasting effect of national embarrassment and offense is reflected in the closing call never to *promote their welfare* [*shalom*] *or their prosperity*. Such an offense can have permanent destructive effects.

23:7-8 Policies for Edomites and Egyptians

Although these two verses imply an exclusion from the assembly of the Lord, at least for two generations (v. 8), the command portion moves in the opposite direction: Israel is *not to abhor* either the Edomites or the Egyptians. The Edomites receive special status because they are *kin*, the descendants of Abraham through Esau, the brother of Jacob.

Including the Egyptians in this category is more surprising. Both inside and outside of Deuteronomy, Egypt is the land of slavery and oppression (e.g., 5:6). Here, however, Egypt is spoken of as the land in which Israel was a *resident alien* (AT). Shaping this memory is the story of Jacob and his family, first receiving food from Egypt, and then finding in Egypt a place of welcome and safety from famine in the time of Joseph. This positive experience overcomes or suppresses the longer history of oppression. By allowing the descendants of Edomites and Egyptians into the *assembly of the* LORD, this passage demonstrates that for Deuteronomy the community of Israel is not defined simply by ethnicity.

Maintaining Purity in the Camp 23:9-14

Although hidden in the NRSV, this passage opens with *When you go out* (AT), marking it as another in the series dealing with war (cf. 20:1-20; 21:10-14). The opening verse literally prohibits an *evil thing* (NRSV, *impropriety*; NIV, *impure*). The following verses place the evil thing within the category of something *unclean* (see comments on 14:1-20). Matters of clean and unclean are not central for Deuteronomy, but they also are not entirely absent.

In Deuteronomy all war falls under the foundational principles of 20:1-9. The war process begins with the representative of God, the priest, assuring the people that it is God who gives the victory. Now we learn that *God travels with your camp, to save you and to hand over your enemies to you* (23:14). Here is a reminder of how God has traveled with the people during their time in the wilderness from Egypt to the Promised Land ("And the LORD went before them in a pillar of cloud by day, to lead them along the way, and in a pillar of fire by night, to give them light"; Exod 13:21). This requires that the camp be kept *holy* and ritually clean. Uncleanness is incompatible with the presence of God.

The nature of the first case of uncleanness is not entirely clear (Deut 23:10-11). The Hebrew speaks of an uncleanness that *chanceth him by night* (KJV). It is not given any context here other than that it happens at night and probably involuntarily. The translation *nocturnal emission* is based on analogy with Leviticus 15:16-18, which speaks of an *emission of semen*, through intercourse or otherwise. Since it is a bodily fluid, semen is unclean. As here, the purification that Leviticus requires is bathing, with the person remaining unclean until the evening. The general nature of the phrase may suggest that it includes other types of bodily discharge, such as urination in the camp (Craigie 1976: 299).

The second case (Deut 23:12-14) again involves a bodily substance, excrement. Again the concern is to keep the camp ritually clean, this time by requiring that defecation take place outside the camp and that the excrement be covered with dirt. With these two cases, Deuteronomy is not giving an exhaustive list but rather identifying two samples of what might make the camp unclean. War, even when waged in a distant locale, is an activity under God, requiring God's people to conduct themselves in a particular way.

Escaped Slaves 23:15-16

Regardless of how the *slaves* of this passage are defined, this is an extraordinary order (whereas the Hebrew speaks of *a slave*, sg.,

NRSV puts it into the plural to avoid the use of masculine pronouns). The ambiguity is whether the *slaves* of this passage refers to all slaves, both Israelite and external, or only to foreign slaves who have fled to Israel, seeking asylum from their owners and their homeland. The strongest argument for reading the passage as speaking of foreign slaves is that it is hard to imagine such a protection for Israelite slaves. A regulation that allows any and all escaped slaves to be recognized as free would "spell the end of slavery in a short time," and so "obviously . . . not every case of slavery is intended here" (Cairns: 206). The language of verse 16, which allows slaves to *reside with you, . . . in any one of your towns*, may support understanding these escaped slaves as coming from elsewhere.

This interpretation may be correct (over against C. Wright 1996: 249-50). However, in that case the absence of any corresponding regulation governing how to treat an escaped Israelite slave becomes remarkable (Tigay: 215). But even if addressing only foreigners, the passage represents an extraordinary challenge of the way things are normally done. By its very nature, the institution of slavery requires that the ownership of slaves is enforced by law or societal compliance. That was true in the U.S. before the Civil War, and it was true in ancient societies. An escaped slave receives severe punishment when captured, and if anyone gives refuge to such a runaway slave, that person may also be punished. The Code of Hammurabi, for example, calls for the death penalty on someone who shelters an escaped slave (*ANET* 166-67). Ancient treaties required that slaves seeking asylum be extradited so they could be returned to their original owners (e.g., *ANET* 200-201, 203-4; cf. Tigay: 215).

In contrast, the Deuteronomic provision allows these escaped slaves to *reside in any place they choose in any one of your towns, wherever they please*. Not only is this a piling up of phrases emphasizing the freedom of the slave to live where the slave chooses; for Deuteronomy it also is highly theological language, a clear echo of the language of God choosing a place anywhere among their tribes where God's name will dwell (e.g., 12:5). Although the passage does not make the connection, the exodus narrative, so frequently referenced in Deuteronomy, colors it as well. Israel had been slaves in Egypt. God redeemed them from their slavery and is giving them the Promised Land. In parallel fashion this passage calls on Israel to treat other escaped slaves on this model. Slavery is not explicitly rejected, here or in the sabbatical release provisions, but the treatment it mandates for slaves undermines its very foundation (cf. Philemon).

The passage says little about the status of the former slave who has settled in Israel. If the slave has been an Israelite debt slave, then the absence of any further explanation is not significant. After all, this person has been a Hebrew kinsman and simply can settle into the community. If, however, as many commentators argue, this passage is dealing with escaped foreign slaves, then this omission becomes more interesting. Does the freed slave then become a resident alien (Tigay: 215), a category of non-Israelite people living in the land who are vulnerable to oppression but who receive special protection in Deuteronomy (e.g., 24:17)? The highly theological language of this passage, against the background of Israel's story, raises the possibility that this passage envisions a former slave becoming part of Israel, a "brother" living in their communities, *where they please*. If so, then this astonishing passage not only challenges all cultural norms of slavery but also puts into question any narrow reading of Deuteronomy that sees it as interested only in an ethnic Israel. Deuteronomy is a book that highlights Israel as a community of "brothers," of kinfolk, but this provision raises the possibility that foreigners may become those kinfolk.

Abhorrent Cultic Practices 23:17-18

That the practices named here are rejected is clear: the passage concludes with the denunciation that they *are abhorrent to the* LORD *your God* (cf. 7:25; 17:1; etc.). But the nature of the practices rejected is less than clear. The NRSV and NIV take verse 17 as prohibiting the sons and daughters of Israel from becoming a *temple* or *shrine prostitute* (cf. 1 Kings 14:24; 15:12; Hos 4:14). This commonly leads interpreters to speak of cult prostitution, often observing that it was common in Baalistic religion. Cult prostitution, it is suggested, was a kind of fertility rite intended via sympathetic magic to ensure the fertilities of fields and herds *[Cult, p. 546]*.

Cultic prostitution may have been practiced in the world of Israel, although the evidence is not conclusive, and this verse may be referring to such practice. However, the Hebrew of the verse does not require such a reading. A more literal rendering would be something like *None from the daughters of Israel shall be consecrated, neither shall any from the sons of Israel be consecrated* (AT). Each of the words in Hebrew is clear, but what they mean together is not. The key term is the one translated *consecrated*, a variation of the simple word for "holy." The verse itself does not speak explicitly of prostitution or sexual activity but simply of being *consecrated*, presumably implying some cultic role. Consecrated women and men did play a part in the religious practice of the ancient Near East, but their actual responsibilities are unclear (Nelson 2002: 280). The rejection here may be more because of association with Canaanite cultic practices and procedures than because of the actual activity itself.

The first part of verse 18 is relatively clear: the *fee of a prostitute* is not to be brought to the *house of the LORD your God*. Here the common term for prostitute is used. Proverbs 7:10-20 may provide some background since it appears to describe a woman who pays her vows with money earned through prostitution. Presumably influenced by the first part of the verse, the NRSV translates the second item rejected as *the wages of a male prostitute*. As the NRSV's marginal note admits, however, the underlying Hebrew does not speak of a male prostitute, but of the wages (or "price of") of *a dog* (cf. NIV mg., RSV, KJV). Interpreters propose various interpretations. Nelson suggests that "the payment forbidden here might even involve a real dog or an attempt to substitute monetary equivalent or another animal to satisfy a vow promising a dog to the temple, since a canine could not itself be sacrificed." The dog in the ancient world was a "pariah animal" and "urban carnivore," thus making it quite unfit for use in Israelite ritual. Any use of it thus would have been *abhorrent* to God (2002: 281).

In the end we must admit that we cannot be sure what Deuteronomy is speaking about in these two verses. The references to consecration (v. 17) and to the *house of the LORD* (v. 18, the only such reference in all of Deuteronomy) point to cultic practices, but the details are lost.

Charitable Loans: Prohibition of Interest 23:19-20

Deuteronomic regulations address the economic realities and practices of Israel, exhorting the people how to treat needy neighbors. Money was used in ancient Israel, but its economy was not based on money. Commercial activity tended to be the exchange of labor and products. In this simple subsistence economy, borrowing was an act of desperation in the face of great need. Those in desperation would borrow food or seed for the field (see Preview for 15:1-18). It is unclear exactly how pledges worked, whether they were part of the arrangement from the beginning or only used in cases of repayment default. But at some point the lender could request or demand a pledge, some piece of property belonging to the person who had borrowed. Given that those borrowing tended to be the very poor, with little property, this pledge commonly had little commercial value. The taking of the pledge thus was a way of pressuring the person to pay rather than a substitute way of paying off the loan (Tigay: 223).

Elsewhere Deuteronomy challenges the prosperous in the direction-setting sabbatical release provisions: *Do not be hard-hearted or tight-fisted toward your needy neighbor. You should rather open your hand, willingly lending enough to meet the need, whatever it may be* (15:7-8). Even though a loan will be forgiven in the seventh year, an Israelite is encouraged to help out a fellow member of the covenant community. This is not a business decision but a way of helping those in need. This passage assumes that such a charitable loan has been made, and then it provides direction for how such loans are to be handled.

Not only is the Israelite to lend when a neighbor is in need, but also is to charge no interest when doing so. The financial circumstances of the one borrowing are not addressed in this passage, but the parallel directives of Exodus and Leviticus both identify the lender as one in need: "the poor among you" (Exod 22:25); "If any of your kin fall into difficulty and become dependent on you" (Lev 25:35). The Leviticus reference to the kinship of the lender is consistent with Deuteronomy's repeated emphasis on Israel as a covenant community, in which people are to support each other.

Deuteronomy expands the earlier versions of this requirement by including *provisions . . . or anything that is lent* in the regulation (23:19). In the case of the *foreigner* (cf. 14:21; 15:3), a loan is more probably a commercial transaction with a business person or traveling merchant, an example of international trade rather than a desperation loan, and so interest may be charged. The reward for obedience, in typical Deuteronomic manner, is blessing within the Promised Land. Israel's fate will be determined by how those with means treat those without since it is God who gives them their blessing and wealth.

Making and Fulfilling Vows 23:21-23

A vow is a voluntary promise or commitment made by a person or people to God, frequently to praise God in public for what God has done. It is distinguished from oaths in that oaths normally are commitments made between people supported by a formula of self-cursing (although in Deuteronomy, God is regularly described as having sworn an oath to Israel, translated in the NRSV as *kept the oath he swore*, 7:8; or *promised on oath*, 6:23). Most frequently a vow is made in a time of crisis or need when an individual promises to give God something in exchange for deliverance from the crisis. The kinds of predicaments that can precipitate a vow are wide ranging, from sickness to physical danger, from barrenness to familial alienation. A natural setting for making vows is worship. A psalm of petition can include a vow to praise God if God delivers the person from the particular situation of need (e.g., Pss 22:25; 56:12; 61:8), with a psalm of thanksgiving declaring that the praise being offered is in fulfillment of a vow (e.g., Pss 66:13-15; 116:14, 18).

The voluntary nature of the vow is highlighted in these verses. They begin with the conditional *if*; they contain the statement that *if you refrain from vowing, you will not incur guilt*; and they include the adjective *freely* in the last sentence (v. 23). If despite this an Israelite chooses to make a vow to God, then it is critical for the person to fulfill the commitment made. No punishment is pronounced for failing to fulfill the vow, but it is stated that this failure will *incur guilt.* The Hebrew term translated *guilt* in verses 21 and 22 is frequently translated *sin*. This passage thus warns the Israelite of the seriousness of such a voluntary self-commitment.

Gleaning: For the Gleaner 23:24-25

Gleaning is an ancient custom that allows those in need to gather grain or fruit for their personal use from a field or orchard. Normally gleaning is practiced only after the harvest is completed, but these passages allow it even before that point. The Deuteronomic provision designating the third-year tithe for the needy (14:28-29) has a similar objective, as do the regulations allowing the poor to harvest what grows by itself during the sabbatical year, when fields are not seeded (Exod 23:10-11; Lev 25:2-7). Ruth and Naomi, upon their move from Moab to Judah, become an example of widows who are forced to glean in order to meet their basic needs (Ruth 2).

Deuteronomy includes two sets of guidelines that speak to the tradition of gleaning, one directed at the gleaners or those in need, the other at the farmer in whose field or orchard the gleaning takes place. Although most of Deuteronomy appears to be directed at those with means, those in a position to do something about the situation of the needy, this passage reminds us that the full audience of the book is broader than that.

The instructions directed to the gleaner give permission to glean, stated twice (*You may eat your fill.... You may pluck the ears*), but they also impose a limitation (cf. Mark 2:23, par.). The gleaner is not to carry away *grapes... in a container, nor put a sickle to your neighbor's standing grain.* To take from someone's field for eating is acceptable as a form of mutual support, but to take grapes away from the field or to begin the harvest process presumably in order to take away from the field is unacceptable, and thus a form of theft.

Deuteronomy's emphasis that all of Israel is to participate in receiving the blessings of the land does not lead to a simplistic "Everything belongs to everyone." The farmer has developed the vineyard and seeded the field. The farmer has a certain right to the produce even if elsewhere the farmer is challenged to remember always that the produce is a gift from God and not the result of human effort (8:11-20). This the gleaner recognizes by not taking produce away from the field. The tradition of gleaning in order to meet the need of hunger, however, is an appropriate way in which the community helps those in need. The poor are given some freedom (i.e., they can glean), but at the same time the text places a clear limitation on them, protecting the farmer.

A Twice-Divorced Woman 24:1-4

Although the KJV of this passage makes it appear to be a regulation permitting divorce, it is generally agreed, both by other translations (cf. RSV, NRSV, NIV, NABRE, NJPS) and interpreters (e.g., Nelson 2002: 286; Tigay: 220; McConville 2002: 358), that the passage takes the practice of divorce for granted and is attempting to regulate a particular variation of it. Divorce was a reality, in Israel and elsewhere. How common it was is unclear, but enough passages in the Old Testament refer to it that we must conclude it was not uncommon. The Old Testament does not provide general procedures for divorce. Presumably they were sufficiently well known among the people that they did not need to be spelled out. Within the patriarchal society of the day, no doubt men have considerable rights in the divorce process and in most cases are the initiators of proceedings; yet based on Exodus 21:1-11, Tigay suggests that women also could initiate a divorce on the grounds of nonsupport (221). The two other references to divorce within Deuteronomy both prohibit a man from divorcing his wife (i.e., they assume the initiative comes from the man), and both appear to be efforts to protect the woman from the consequences of divorce (22:19, 29).

Our passage can be divided into two parts: verses 1-3 describe the particular situation, and verse 4 gives the regulation. The background to the prohibition may be divided into four stages. First, a man marries a woman. Second, the man divorces his wife. The clause *She does not please him* may give the impression that the reasons for the divorce are emotional and not substantial, but the clause *He finds something objectionable about her* may allow for some legitimate grounds for the divorce. The term translated *objectionable* is the same term used in 23:10 for that which a soldier does in the camp that makes him unclean, there frequently translated *nocturnal emission*. What might make a wife offensive or objectionable in a similar way is unclear. It may hint at sexually indecent behavior, but probably not adultery, since then the punishment would be stoning. Beyond this it becomes dangerous to speculate. Some interpreters take this vagueness to imply that a man could divorce his wife for any reason at all, but in the absence of any general regulations on divorce, it is risky to speculate. The verse seems to take care to emphasize that the divorce itself has been handled properly: *He writes her a certificate of divorce, puts it in her hand, and sends her out*. This is not simply an oral announcement or crude eviction, but the description of divorce proceedings considered to be quite proper within that context (cf. Matt 5:31; 19:7; Mark 10:4).

Third, after the divorce the woman marries another man. And fourth, the woman's second husband now also divorces her. Again the text is silent on the grounds for the divorce and again takes care to describe the divorce itself as proper. That the divorce itself is not the issue is evident from the phrase put in parentheses in the NRSV: *or the second man who married her dies*. The key element here is that she has been married a second time, now no longer is married, and is quite properly free.

The regulation then states that the first man is prohibited from marrying her a second time. The prohibition is defended with typical Deuteronomic warnings: such a remarriage would be *abhorrent to the LORD* (cf. 7:25; 12:31; 17:1; 18:9, 12; 20:18; 22:5; 23:18; 25:16) and would *bring guilt on the land*. Further, 24:4 describes the woman herself as having *been defiled*, or *made unclean* (NJB), but does not state whether this is because she has remarried, been divorced, or some other reason. Again, the text is silent on the rationale for the prohibition.

Some explanations can be imagined. Perhaps the prohibition developed in order to prevent what might be called "wife-swapping," or even legalized adultery, in which the second marriage never was real but merely a legal fiction for the purpose of extramarital activity. Perhaps such a remarriage would violate Israel's standards of purity and holiness. Perhaps the prohibition was intended to discourage the first husband from divorcing too quickly: later he might wish her back. Perhaps the regulation was intended to prevent the financial exploitation of the woman: through the original divorce the man may have recovered the bride-price, and the second marriage might have been "free." None of these guesses is fully persuasive. The text does not give a clear rationale, and our present understanding of Israel's marriage customs and laws are inadequate to give a definite answer. It is striking, however, that a regulation as unusual and particular as this one is referred to as often as it is in the later biblical tradition (see TBC below).

Conscription and a Recently Married Man 24:5

The regulations on war exempt an engaged but unmarried man from serving in the militia (20:7). This verse exempts a recently married man from such service. As we noticed in the passages on adultery, however, limited if any distinction is made between someone engaged or married (22:22-24). The difference between the two passages (20:7; 24:5) is not the man's state but rather the perspective from which the subject is treated. Whereas chapter 20 focused on the dynamics of war, the primary interest here is life in the home and community. A newly married man is exempt from military service so that he can *be happy with the wife whom he has married*. The logic of the exemption may relate to the ancient concern that an action once started should be allowed to be completed: the time frame of a year would allow the marriage to be made complete through the joy of a child (cf. Jer 29:6). But the focus of the text is on the joy and happiness that the couple should have during this time, whether the correct translation is that of the NRSV, *to be happy with the wife* (cf. RSV), or of the NIV, *bring happiness to the wife* (cf. KJV, NABRE, NJB). Certainly included in this happiness is the joy of sexual activity (Nelson 2002: 289, cf. Prov 5:19).

Charitable Loans: A Limitation on Pledges 24:6

A home mill consisted of two pieces, a larger bottom stone on which the grain is placed, weighing up to ninety pounds, and a much smaller upper stone that is rubbed back and forth across the grain in order to grind it. The heavy wear on these stones required that they be very hard. Commonly this was basalt, an imported rock that was not easily replaced. These millstones were used on a daily basis to make the flour needed in a staple bread diet.

A lender could quite easily carry away the lighter upper stone as a pledge. But with that stone missing, the mill becomes useless, threatening accessible food and life itself, thus negating the purpose of the loan, to support life. The passage does not deny the lender's right to ensure that the loan is repaid and yet places a limitation on it. As in the prohibition of interest, the loan is viewed as a form of mutual support and not as a commercial investment. The value of the poor person's life is unquestionably greater than that which had been lent.

Stealing a Person 24:7

As in the similar regulation in Exodus (21:16), the punishment for kidnapping is death. Unlike the Exodus version, Deuteronomy speaks of the victim as *another Israelite*, but this need not imply that Deuteronomy considers the kidnapping of a non-Israelite a very different offense. Rather, it reflects Deuteronomy's consistent focus on the Israelite community. The text uses especially dramatic language to speak of the crime, literally, *stealing a life from his brothers* (cf. KJV). The person stolen may not have been murdered, but it is a "social murder." Although theft is treated elsewhere in Deuteronomy (e.g., 19:14), only in two places does it use the word "steal," here and in the eighth commandment of the Decalogue, and it is the only case of theft that results in the death penalty. Perhaps the motive given for the crime, financial profit, explains the harsh punishment. Some renderings highlight this element: the kidnapper tries to "barter or sell him" (McConville 2002: 355); the kidnapper "treats him as merchandise and he sells him" (Christensen 2002: 569). By stealing another person and selling that person for financial gain, the offender has placed a higher value on property than on humans. Israel's greater emphasis on people than on property at points distinguishes its law from that of others in the ancient Near East. (For the command *Purge the evil from your midst*, see on 13:5.)

This passage indicts contemporary technological society where it places a higher value on things than people, with the result that those who are considered unproductive, whether due to age, unemployment or disability, are not valued. Even God then becomes merely an object (Leddy: 70). Any actions based on this inversion of biblical values are comparable to the kidnapping of this passage. This is true whether such actions are clearly criminal (e.g., a drug trade insensitive to the human cost) or not (e.g., economic decisions that do not take into consideration impact upon other people, whether made by businesspeople or consumers).

Instructions in Cases of Skin Diseases 24:8-9

As generally recognized, the term translated *leprous skin* in this passage does not refer narrowly to the disease now called "leprosy," or Hansen's disease, but to a larger category of skin problems, especially those with a communicable nature. This particular word of warning, really not a law in any sense, is striking since it assumes instructions given elsewhere, which it then encourages the people to follow. The nature of the passage is also reflected in its language, with phrases like *Guard against . . ., by being very careful; you shall carefully observe*.

Leviticus 13–14 supplies the detailed instructions assumed here. Although the primary concern of the procedures appears to be health factors, with their emphasis on quarantining the individual with the infectious condition and washing or even burning their clothes, the judgment that someone with the condition is *unclean* (a term used twenty-four times in Lev 13–14 as it defines the procedures) indicates that it is more than that. Again we are in the realm of purity and ritual.

Deuteronomy, however, does not use the term *unclean* here. Moreover, the opening phrase, to *guard against an outbreak of a leprous skin disease*, suggests Deuteronomy's primary concern is the health of the community. Yet the concluding warning cautions against distinguishing too sharply between health and theological concern. Once again making use of history to teach (cf. 4:3), Deuteronomy reminds Israel of an event when rebellion was punished (story of Miriam receiving leprosy, described in Num 12:1–15).

Charitable Loans: Further Limitation on Pledges 24:10-13

For a second time Deuteronomy accepts the practice of taking a pledge as a way of encouraging repayment of a loan, but again places such a severe limitation on it that the whole procedure is put into question. This time the question is how far a lender can go to get a pledge from the debtor. The text allows the lender to request the pledge but prevents the lender from entering the home of the debtor to claim the pledge. For the lender to enter the home would be humiliating for the debtor and could suggest that the lender is now in charge of the home. The honor and dignity of the debtor, who remains a *neighbor*, is to be respected. This process also allows the debtor to determine what the pledge is rather than having the lender barge in and choose it.

The directive to return the garment taken as a pledge by sunset highlights the extreme poverty of the debtor. If a garment is the best option for a pledge, then obviously the debtor has very little to spare and very possibly will be unable to repay the loan. Additionally, the directive again makes the point that the loan process should not undermine the debtor's potential to live, not comfortably perhaps, yet with some essentials protected (cf. last phrase of 24:6, against *taking a life in pledge*). The reward for handling loans in this manner is that the *neighbor may . . . bless you*. Deuteronomy repeatedly speaks of blessing, most frequently of God blessing the people, occasionally of people blessing God, later of Moses blessing the people (33:1), but this is the only time it speaks of one Israelite blessing another. If a lender treats the person who borrows with such consideration and care that the debtor sleeps well and blesses the lender, then true community exists, and Deuteronomy assures the lender, *It will be to your credit* [lit., *righteousness*] *before the LORD your God*.

Payment of Wages 24:14-15

In most cases *poor and needy laborers* are those who have lost their land and thus are no longer in a position to produce their own food. Their situation is precarious indeed since they are forced to find work here and there to survive. Deuteronomy requires that the wages of such laborers be paid daily because *their livelihood depends on them* (cf. Lev 19:13; Matt 20:8). The call to pay *their wages before sunset* (cf. 24:13) insinuates day-to-day existence. Survival is the issue, not long-term financial planning. Deuteronomy here makes no distinction between the fellow Israelite or the resident alien: both are to be treated in a way that allows them to live.

The motivation for this directive is the warning that if the employer does not do this, *they might cry to the LORD against you, and you would incur guilt*. The same warning is used in the sabbatical release provision (15:9). The passage does not assume a civil legal system that will enforce this kind of regulation, but rather portrays a world in which God hears the cry of the weak and oppressed and responds to that cry. The cry of Israel in Egypt is the archetypical cry to God (Exod 2:23-25). God has responded to then, and God will respond again. The employer who disregards this becomes like the Egyptian oppressor.

Individual Legal Responsibility 24:16

Ancient society placed great weight on the corporate identity of family, village, and clan. Yet here Deuteronomy appears to recognize individual responsibility. The legal background of the passage is suggested by its threefold use of *put to death* (a single term in Hebrew), a verb generally used only within the legal system, not of divine punishment. This background distinguishes the verse from the Decalogue's recognition that sin can impact children and grandchildren and great-grandchildren (*punishing children for the iniquity of parents, to the third and fourth generation,* 5:9). But this is not to be the way of the court system or human justice.

With this emphasis on individual legal responsibility, Deuteronomy sets a path different from ancient Near Eastern law codes that tended to treat a man's family as a corporate unit, with the potential of punishing a whole family for the crime of one of its members (cf. Josh 7). Although this call for individual legal responsibility is consistent with other biblical passages, both prescriptive (e.g., Exod 21:31; Ezek 18; Jer 31:29-30) and descriptive (e.g., 2 Kings 14:6), some accounts show that this did not always happen (e.g., stories of Judg 17-21). The call challenged ancient traditions within Israel and beyond, just as it challenges contemporary practices by which families and communities are treated as one, sometimes legally but more often informally through prejudice and bigotry.

Justice for the Resident Alien, the Orphan, and the Widow 24:17-18

In 1961 Charles Fensham surveyed the ancient literature of Mesopotamia, Egypt, and Ugarit and argued that all of these civilizations espoused the conviction that "the protection of the weak is the will of the god" (137), that the king as the representative of the god on earth had a special responsibility to ensure that these weak were protected, and that this protection was to be normal for ordinary people. That conviction is shared by law codes, special edicts, and wisdom literature. At least officially there was a widespread recognition that the widow, the orphan, and the poor require special protection.

The widow and the orphan well represent the disadvantaged of the day. In a time when disease, famine, accident, and war combine to greatly shorten the average life span of the people, widows and orphans are common. The death of the male head of the household brings serious consequences, immediately threatening economic viability. Survival becomes a challenge. Many of those forced into debt slavery are from families without a male head. When Ruth becomes a widow, she moves with Naomi to her mother-in-law's home country, where she is forced to survive through gleaning in the field of a rich distant kinsman of her deceased husband (Ruth 1-2). A further consequence of becoming a widow or orphan is potential loss of identification. Despite the statement in Genesis 2:24, in Israel a woman normally joins the family of her husband. But the death of the husband weakens his wife's place in that family. Widows and orphans are also vulnerable to exploitation and abuse by less scrupulous members of society. Not only are they on the fringe of the community and thus naturally vulnerable, they also have no legal standing. Although obviously not the only poor or weak members in society, the widow and the orphan serve as prime representatives of this larger category.

Concern for the poor in the Old Testament, as represented by the widow and orphan, fit well into the larger ancient Near East. Psalm 72, likely used at the coronation of a new king, commits the king to "defend the cause of the poor of the people, give deliverance to the needy" (v. 4), to deliver "the needy when they call, the poor and those who have no helper" (v. 12). Exodus pronounces harsh judgment on those who abuse the widow and orphan (22:21-24). The prophets indict Israel for not fulfilling this responsibility and for oppressing the poor (note esp. Amos 2:7; 4:1; 5:11; 8:4, 6).

Deuteronomy may be the Old Testament's strongest advocate of this concern for the disadvantaged. The first half of the second speech sets the foundation (chs. 5-11), with the second half (chs. 12-26) repeatedly returning to this theme. The tithe and sabbatical release provisions set the direction, with the present passage providing a suitable closing summary of it (yet compare the work of Bennett: 173; see "Deuteronomy and a Hermeneutics of Suspicion" in the introduction).

With its opening, *You shall not deprive a resident alien or an orphan of justice*, the present passage may have the legal system in mind, but it clearly addresses the larger reality as well (24:17-18). A distinctive characteristic of Deuteronomy's concern for the poor is its inclusion of the *resident alien* in the category along with the widow and the orphan (cf. Exod 22:21). As a person without normal family networks and support systems, and probably without land, a *resident alien* is especially vulnerable. Furthermore, it is possible that the *resident alien* does not have access to the legal system of the day (cf. an illegal resident today?). Deuteronomy's inclusion of the *resident alien*, or *stranger*, at multiple points, as in this overall summary, in the Sabbath day requirement, and so forth (e.g., 5:14; 10:18-19; 16:11; 24:19-22; 26:13; 29:10), challenges a narrowly nationalistic reading of the book of Deuteronomy. The *resident alien* may not have been a full member of Deuteronomy's covenant community (e.g., 14:21), but the *resident alien* is not to be treated as an absolute outsider. Clearly the *resident alien* is vulnerable, and so Deuteronomy emphasizes that Israel's justice must include the *resident alien* as well (cf. 1:16).

Characteristically and importantly, the second verse of this summary passage grounds the call for justice in the story of God's special action on behalf of Israel (24:18). Israel has been poor, without power, unable to do anything but to cry to God for help. God's response was to redeem this people and give them the Promised Land, a land of milk and honey (e.g., 6:3; 11:9), a land of blessing. At regular intervals Deuteronomy reminds its audience of this story. The key to obedience, says Deuteronomy, is to remember and not forget (cf. 5:15; 7:18; 8:2, 18; 9:7; 15:15; 16:3, 12; 24:22).

Gleaning: For the Farmer 24:19-22

The farmer also is given instructions on gleaning. Not only do the instructions assume that gleaning is appropriate; they also encourage the farmer not to be too diligent in the harvesting process lest no produce is left behind for those gleaning. The intent is similar to the directions of Leviticus, where the farmer is asked to refrain from harvesting at the very edges or stripping the vineyard bare (19:9-10; 23:22). Care for the disadvantaged and needy again is translated into concrete action. The particular action may not relate easily to contemporary times, but the larger concern applies. For consideration of the triad *resident alien, orphan,* and *widow* in relationship to the story of Israel as slaves in Egypt, see on 24:17-18.

Controlling Flogging 25:1-3

The concern of this regulation is not how the court functions or determines guilt (cf. 16:18-20; 17:2-13; 19:15-21) but the protection of the one found guilty. The passage assumes a dispute between two people, leading to one laying a charge against the other. Whereas Western law formally treats crime as an offense against the state, in the ancient world transgressions were understood as crimes against each other. The case has been tried, and one of the two has been deemed guilty, whether the accused or the accuser is not important. The punishment is flogging. Flogging was not unusual in the ancient world and could be imposed on those guilty of offenses like vandalism, nonpayment of debt, fraud, theft, and so forth (Tigay: 230). Paying restitution may also be part of the settlement. Enforced confinement or jail, the most common form of punishment in the Western world today, is absent from Israel's system of justice.

This regulation then controls the punishment the guilty party receives by (1) having it take place in the *presence* (lit., *unto his face*) of the judge, (2) having the number of lashes *proportionate to the offense*, and (3) placing an upper limit on the number of lashes permitted: *forty*. These restrictions sharply limit the punishment someone could receive in a non-Israelite culture, where some crimes could be assigned up to one hundred strokes (Tigay: 230).

The concluding phrase may be the most significant of the whole passage, with its clarification of the intent of the regulation: so that *your neighbor* [lit., *your brother*] *will not be degraded in your sight*. Even after the punishment, the guilty party should not be degraded since he remains *a member of the community* (the usual NRSV translation of *your brother*, as in 15:12). In a society stressing honor and shame, this regulation limits punishment so that the guilty person does not lose all honor and standing in the community. The goals of punishment are restitution and reestablishing community. It does this within the customs of the day (i.e., including flogging), but the objective remains. Might contemporary practices, such as "enhanced interrogation techniques," even learn from Old Testament regulations on flogging?

Consideration for Animals: Muzzling the Ox 25:4

In premechanized societies, threshing is mostly done by animals as they walk over grain stalks on a threshing floor or pull some heavy object over the grain, perhaps a wooden sledge with pieces of stone or metal attached on the underside. This directive prohibits the muzzling of the ox while it works at the threshing process, thereby preventing the animal from eating from the grain. Just as a farmer is to leave some grain and fruit for the poor to glean, so the farmer is to allow the ox to glean (cf. 23:24-25; 24:19-22). Twice in the New Testament this law is mentioned in relationship to proper payment of Christian workers (1 Cor 9:8-12; 1 Tim 5:17-18). If oxen working the threshing floor are to receive fair payment, then those working for the church also should receive this consideration.

The relatively insignificant nature of this particular provision is a further example of how Old Testament regulations (including Deuteronomic) are samplings. Regulations demonstrating consideration for animals are representative or selected examples of what this means. Thus, one may not assume that the intent is being met by following only the specific commands given. That something this apparently insignificant should be included makes the additional point that following torah includes even little matters.

A Widow without a Son 25:5-10

Levirate (from *levir,* Latin for "brother-in-law") marriage was a common practice in the ancient Near East and in Israel (cf. Gen 38). If a man dies before having a child, his brother is expected to marry his widow and generate a child, who then is considered the child of the deceased. The child then carries forward the deceased man's name and is able to inherit his property. The custom has three purposes: (1) The widow is served: she is provided a place in her husband's home, receiving financial security and the prospect of having children with her husband's brother. (2) The family is served, although exactly what the widow's inheritance rights are is not clear: her marriage to someone in the same family assures them that the husband's land remains with the larger family. (3) The deceased man is served: through his brother his own name and posterity are preserved. Presumably the prohibitions in Leviticus against having a relationship with a brother's wife assume that brother is still alive (18:16; 20:21).

As the biblical accounts demonstrate, however, the brother expected to marry the widow may not always willingly participate in the practice. The child he sires with his brother's widow is not considered his (cf. Gen 38:9), and it is possible that by not marrying the widow and thereby depriving her of offspring, he might hope to inherit both his and his brother's share of the inheritance.

The opening two verses present the basic normal expectation: two brothers have lived together, one has died without a son, the surviving brother is expected to marry the widow, *performing the duty of a husband's brother to her.* This passage reflects two variations of the tradition. First, the brothers are living together. If this is to be taken literally (not the only option—it may simply refer to living in the same larger community; cf. Gen 13:6; 36:7), then the case may be one where the brothers have not divided the inheritance but are working it cooperatively. Such a situation complicates the dynamics if one brother dies. Second, the passage speaks of the one who has died as without a *son*. Despite the patriarchal nature of Israelite society, Tigay suggests that since daughters are allowed to inherit and carry on their father's name (note Num 27:1-11), normally levirate marriage would only be needed if the man had no offspring of either gender (231).

Although the practice of levirate marriage served multiple purposes in ancient society, this passage identifies only one, that *his name may not be blotted out of Israel* (Deut 25:6). Israel may not have had a fully developed understanding of life after death, but death was not considered the absolute end to existence. After death the person's spirit continued a shadowy existence in Sheol. Keeping a person's name alive was a way of keeping the person among the living. The primary way this happened was by carrying on the person's name in his offspring, although alternatives were possible. When Absalom was about to die, "he said, 'I have no son to keep my name in remembrance'; [so] he called the pillar by his own name, . . . Absalom's Monument" (2 Sam 18:18).

The last four verses then outline what to do if the brother does not wish to follow the practice expected of him. Presumably the practice is not legally enforced but is strongly encouraged through persuasion and the threat of shame or loss of reputation. The widow employs two techniques to persuade her brother-in-law to marry her. First, she reports his hesitance to the *elders of his town*, who then try to persuade him; second, she confronts him in a public forum. If the brother continues to refuse to *build up his brother's house*, a public ritual takes place. The spitting in the face is a way of shaming the brother for not doing his duty (cf. Num 12:14; Isa 50:6; Mark 10:34; 14:65). The exact significance of pulling the *sandal off his foot* is less clear. It may represent a legal transaction releasing the widow from her husband's family and formally transferring the deceased brother's property to the widow (cf. Ruth 4:7-8). Through it she now is "untied" from her former husband's house. The concluding statement that the family of the brother will become known as *the house of him whose sandal was pulled off* suggests, however, that the ritual has more than legal significance and constitutes a further act of disgrace, perhaps related to an ancient perception that going barefoot was humiliating (2 Sam 15:30; Isa 20:2).

A Woman and a Fight 25:11-12

This highly unusual and even perplexing passage raises several questions. The passage envisions a fight between two brothers (lit., *a man with his brother*). It is not clear whether these are biological brothers or simply both members of the Israelite community. During the fight, the wife of one of the two men, in an effort to assist her husband and free him *from the grip* [lit., *his hand*] *of his opponent, reaches out* [lit.] *her hand* and grabs her husband's opponent's genitals. The highly unusual and very specific nature of the offense immediately raises questions.

It is possible that what is at stake here is similar to that of the immediately preceding passage (25:5-10), namely, carrying on a family name through offspring. That the passages are connected is also suggested by the fact that both deal with brothers. But this interpretation requires that the seizing of his genitals is violent enough to cause serious and permanent injury so as to affect the ability to have children, a severity not really intimated by the text. Alternatively, the central issue may be the "immodest" woman whose assault causes immeasurable humiliation and shame for the one she has attacked.

However the crime is understood, the harshness of the sentence is shocking, especially when considered against other Old Testament passages. Although mutilation was not an uncommon punishment in the ancient world, this is the only case where it is prescribed for a particular crime in the whole Old Testament. The Old Testament lex talionis (*eye for an eye*) may be cited as another such example, but it is more a statement of principle than a prescriptive regulation (see comments on 19:21; cf. Exod 21:24; Lev 24:20). The severity here thus begs for explanation. Perhaps the punishment is an application of the lex talionis principle, with the woman's hand thought to be most comparable to the male organ. But this assumes a serious injury, something not stated by the text. Some Jewish exegesis suggests that to *cut off her hand* means that the woman be fined an equivalent to the monetary value of her hand (Tigay 234), but this explanation seems forced. The concluding phrase, *show no pity*, suggests that even in ancient times the verdict seemed extreme. Perhaps we simply need to admit that in this case we are unsure what the regulation is about. The detailed uniqueness of the case—along with the harshness of the penalty, especially when compared with the usual Deuteronomic tendencies—undercut any clear explanation.

Honest Weights 25:13-16

Deuteronomy's instruction for life in the community concludes with a relatively generic call for honesty in business practice. The temptation to be dishonest for personal gain is universal and timeless. It is an equal temptation for the businessperson and the consumer. This particular call for integrity in commerce envisions the ancient practice of using balance scales in buying and selling. Standardized weights placed on one tray of the scales then measure the weight of produce or merchandise that has been placed on the other tray of the scales. It is easy to imagine an unscrupulous merchant trying to defraud a customer with dishonest weights. A too-heavy weight could be used when buying and a too-light weight when selling (i.e., *large and small*). The reference to *measure* probably refers to pottery for measuring grain and possibly liquids. Again, it is easy to imagine how these could be manipulated for unjust gain. Four times this passage denounces such behavior (vv. 13, 14, 15a, 15b).

The crime of this passage is commonly named and condemned in ancient law codes. "In Egyptian religion the use of false weights and measures was thought to endanger one's passage to heaven, and a Babylonian magical text indicates that their use exposes one to a supernatural curse" (Tigay: 234). A healthy society requires honest social and economic dealings. Leviticus includes a similar law (19:35-37), Proverbs condemns false weights and measures (16:11; 20:10, 23), and the prophets indict Israel for transgressing this standard of honesty (e.g., Amos 8:4-5; Mic 6:10-11).

The concern thus is far from unique, within Israel or the ancient Near East, but the double motivation given for obedience is typically Deuteronomic. First, Deuteronomy speaks of the reward of obedience: *so that your days may be long in the land that the* LORD *your God is giving you*. The regulations of chapters 12–26 are the way for a life of blessing in the land. Integrity in commerce is a key factor in ensuring this long and good life in the land. Second, the directive is reinforced with a more theological incentive: to act dishonestly is *abhorrent to the* LORD *your God*. Dishonesty in business dealings tends to hurt the poor and therefore disregards God's care for the poor. Whoever ignores this is acting in a way *abhorrent* to God—language frequently depicting actions related to foreign religions (e.g., 7:26), but here applied to the sphere of justice within the community.

Remember Amalek 25:17-19

The chapter concludes with a notoriously difficult passage even if it includes a number of stereotypical Deuteronomic phrases and themes. It opens with the command *Remember*; refers to the *journey out of Egypt*; speaks of God giving Israel *rest from all your enemies on every hand, in the land that the* LORD *your God is giving you as an inheritance to possess*; and concludes with a further call not to *forget*. Yet what Israel is to remember is not the deliverance itself but the offense of a particular people, the Amalekites, along the way (Exod 17:8-16). In response to this memory, Israel is to *blot out the remembrance of Amalek from under heaven*. The irony of this command—to remember to blot out a memory, and never to forget this—is surely not lost on the original audience.

The earlier account of the confrontation between Amalek and Israel concludes with Moses announcing, "The LORD will have war with Amalek from generation to generation" (Exod 17:16; cf. Num

24:20). Deuteronomy here justifies its verdict with two phrases. First, Amalek's attack occurred when Israel was *faint and weary*. The regulations of the last few chapters have emphasized how God cares for the poor and weak and how Israel is to do likewise. Amalek is characterized as having ignored this basic element of Israel's justice. And second, Amalek *did not fear God*, a key Deuteronomic expectation for the relationship God expected of Israel, an attitude here also expected of others. Amalek has not feared God, and thus it will suffer the fate guaranteed Israel for its failure (10:12; 29:20; 32:26).

This raises the question: is this passage really an instruction to Israel on how to treat Amalek? Or do these chapters of Deuteronomy conclude with veiled warning to Israel of what will happen to it if it treats the weak poorly and does not fear God?

THE TEXT IN BIBLICAL CONTEXT
Does God Remarry a Previously Divorced Bride?

The regulation prohibiting a man from remarrying a woman whom he has previously divorced, and who in the intervening period has been married to someone else, is somewhat odd and unusually particular (24:1-4). After all, how often might such a situation arise? Is this regulation a "commentary" on the story of Abraham and Sarah? After Abraham told Pharaoh that Sarah was his sister, Pharaoh took Sarah into his home; when Pharaoh discovered that he had been lied to, he gave Sarah back to Abraham. Both the reason for the regulation and its rationale remain clouded.

It thus is striking how this particular regulation is used in Scripture to highlight God's unusual love for Israel. Jeremiah refers directly to this regulation as he raises the question, "If a man divorces his wife and she goes from him and becomes another man's wife, will he return to her?" The obvious answer is no, for this would greatly pollute the land (Jer 3:1). And yet, Jeremiah continues, despite Israel's having forsaken God after entering a covenant with God, God is open to accepting Israel back. God's love is not bound by this regulation. Similarly, Hosea takes back his former wife, Gomer, after she has forsaken him for other lovers. This then becomes a metaphor for how God will "allure" Israel back even after it has gone after Baals, and God will "take you for my wife forever" (Hos 2:14, 19). In these two passages God is willing to break this regulation because of his all-powerful, consuming love for Israel.

Isaiah also makes use of this regulation in his preaching but appears to search for a loophole. Again God is the husband whose wife has left him for others. But, Isaiah asks, perhaps the divorce is not official since a certificate of divorce has not been granted, therefore allowing restoration within the framework of the Deuteronomic regulation (Isa 50:1-3; contrast with Jer 3:8, which speaks of God having granted Israel a *decree of divorce*). The regulation may not have played that significant a role in Israel's daily life, but it provides imagery for prophetic declarations of God's remarkable love for Israel. God's love is so powerful that God is willing to go around this expectation in order to take Israel back after Israel has forsaken the true God for other gods.

Divorce in Scripture

Perhaps to our surprise, divorce receives limited attention in the Old Testament. Divorced women are mentioned a number of times (Lev 21:7, 14; 22:13; Num 30:9; Ezek 44:22), divorce is used metaphorically of God's relationship to Israel (Isa 50:1; Jer 3:1, 8; and perhaps Mal 2:16), and it is detested by God (Mal 2:16). But only Deuteronomy speaks of it in any detail. First, twice it states that in particular situations where women are especially vulnerable, men are not allowed to divorce them (22:19, 29). And second, there is the unusual regulation prohibiting a man from marrying a woman whom he has previously divorced, and who in the intervening period has married someone else (24:1-4). But in the Old Testament only this latter passage gets into the details of divorce, and even here essentially takes the practice for granted and regulates one particular and exceptional case of it. The Old Testament does not explicitly permit it but presupposes it as a reality in Israel. Other details about the practice remain unknown, such as how common it is, how difficult it is to obtain a divorce, and what kind of negative connotations, if any, are attached to the divorce.

The New Testament reveals that divorce was disputed among Jewish groups of the day. Some Pharisees ask Jesus, "Is it lawful for a man to divorce his wife for any cause?" In his response Jesus does not refer to Old Testament passages about divorce, either in affirmation or in critique, but to the story of creation and the intended arrangement for humanity: "Have you not read that the one who made them at the beginning 'made them male and female'?" After the Pharisees mention the Mosaic regulation that appears to allow divorce, Jesus speaks of divorce as a concession due to the hardness of their hearts: this was not the way men and women were intended to relate to each other (Matt 19:3-12; cf. Mark 10:2-12; Luke 16:18; Matt 5:31-32). Paul's words to the Corinthians fit well with this: "The wife should not separate from her husband, . . . and the husband should not divorce his wife" (1 Cor 7:10-11). That Paul here is not addressing all cases is reflected by his allowing divorce in certain circumstances (1 Cor 7:15).

But what was Jesus' concern in his statement on divorce? Was he taking a harsher stance than those Old Testament regulations speaking to divorce, or was he addressing a different issue? Lisa Sowle Cahill suggests that Jesus may have been challenging the way men were using divorce as a way of demonstrating their control of their spouses. If so, then "prohibiting divorce had the practical effect of limiting arbitrary male control over women and of protecting women from the social consequences of the fact that they were valued primarily as sexual prizes, son producers, economic bargaining chips, and tokens of family political status" (32). If so, then Jesus' words are far more consistent with our passages from Deuteronomy than often thought.

God Shows No Partiality

With the words "There is neither Jew nor Greek" (Gal 3:28 RSV), Paul symbolizes the New Testament vision of a body of Christ not limited by ethnicity. Jesus may speak of himself as "sent only to the lost sheep of Israel" (Matt 15:24) and direct his disciples not to preach to the Gentiles or Samaritans (10:5). Yet he already points to a much larger mission when he heals the servant of a centurion and then adds, "Truly I tell you, in no one in Israel have I found such faith" (8:10). This is consistent with his commission to his disciples at the end of his ministry to "make disciples of all nations" (28:19), "to the ends of the earth" (Acts 1:8). Peter's vision of the clean and unclean animals then leads him to conclude, "I truly understand that God shows no partiality, but in every nation anyone who fears him and does what is right is acceptable to him. . . . He is Lord of all" (Acts 10:34-36).

This was a challenge for the Jewish people of the day, whose leaders had erected defensive barriers between themselves and the Gentiles with circumcision, Sabbath observance, and dietary regulations as the primary gatekeepers. The Old Testament itself speaks less clearly about who can be part of the people of God. It does include passages like the ones excluding the Ammonite and Moabite from the *assembly of God*, and it does report how Nehemiah, making use of this passage, "separated from Israel all those of foreign descent" (Neh 13:3). But it also includes the wonderful story of Ruth, the Moabite woman, who confesses to her mother-in-law, of the tribe of Judah, "Your people shall be my people, and your God my God" (Ruth 1:16), and then she becomes the ancestor of King David. It does include the amazing story of Jonah preaching to Nineveh of the Assyrians, the enemies of Israel who subjugated Israel in the eighth and seventh centuries BCE, and the inhabitants repented and "believed God" (Jon 3:4). And it includes God saying (through Isaiah) that he will give eunuchs "an everlasting name" and make foreigners "joyful in my house of prayer, . . . for my house shall be called a house of prayer for all peoples" (Isa 56:3-7).

The Old Testament reflects intense debate over how to treat those outside of the ethnic community into which Israel develops. Deuteronomy emphasizes Israel as a close community of brothers and sisters, leading to a clear line between it and outsiders. Yet even Deuteronomy confirms that this is not absolute, as Edomites and even the oppressor Egypt are not permanently excluded, with the resident alien allowed to enter the covenant. That minority voice of Deuteronomy becomes more forceful later in the Old Testament, then becomes the norm for the New Testament church.

TEXT IN THE LIFE OF THE CHURCH
The Church and Divorce

Seldom are Deuteronomic passages dealing with justice in the home used by the church to develop a contemporary ethic. They tend to be ignored, or if referenced, it is as problems or vestiges of an "old" ethic that Jesus overcame. The only one of these passages referenced at all by Menno Simons occurs in a lament about the sinful practices of his day:

> It is manifest that the world is full of harlots, adulterers, fornicators, sexual perverts, bastards, and illegitimate children, and alas, it has come to such a pass that they live in freedom and liberty, notwithstanding that God has commanded through Moses that both adulterer and the adulteress should die (Deut 22:22). (378)

More common, especially with regard to divorce, is the tendency to view these passages as Old Testament laws that Jesus replaced with a new law: whereas in the Old Testament divorce was allowed, it is suggested, in the New Testament Jesus prohibits all divorce except in cases of "unchastity" (Matt 5:31-32; NIV, "sexual immorality"). A book on Jesus and divorce describes an "evangelical consensus" that assumes this. Wenham and Heth note that John Calvin even interpreted the Deuteronomy 24 passage in line with the

Matthew passage as allowing divorce only in cases of adultery (13-17, 81). But this treats Jesus as giving a law that replaces a former law, a problematic reading of both testaments *[Law, p. 555]*. Both testaments recognize the reality of divorce even as they consider it a failure, a departure from the ideal of creation (e.g., a priest is not allowed to marry a divorced woman; Lev 21:7, 14); both testaments then advocate practices that work against it and undermine the arbitrary use of power by the husband.

Syncretism

It is impossible for any religion, including Christianity, not to borrow symbols and thought patterns from the culture within which it is home. Stuart Murray speaks of an Anabaptism stripped down to its bare essentials, leading to the provocative title for his book: *The Naked Anabaptist*. But ultimately there is no such thing as a naked, or cultureless, Christianity: it is always clothed in some culture. It is increasingly recognized that the Christianity missionaries brought to Africa and India a century ago was clothed in the thought world and culture of the West. When Scripture and dogma are truly translated into a new setting and culture, borrowing from that culture not only is inevitable, it is necessary and appropriate.

Israel adopted numerous features into its life and religious practice from the world and culture of the day. One of the more prominent practices is the sacrificial system. Israel's sacrificial system was very much like, even if not identical to, that of its neighbors. One can speak of it as having been "baptized" into the worship of Yahweh, the only God, the God of the exodus. Agricultural festivals are another example.

But at other points Israel's prophets and leaders strongly denounce practices that some Israelites incorporated into their worship of God but that the leaders understood to be inappropriate borrowing and thus examples of syncretism. Setting up *a sacred pole* or *a stone pillar* (Deut 16:21-22) are two such examples. The *consecrated daughters and sons* (23:17-18 AT), even if we are not clear what they were, probably are another. We use the term "syncretism" for instances where this borrowing results in irreconcilable tension, or where that which is borrowed undermines central elements of the faith.

The challenge, of course, is in distinguishing what can be borrowed and adapted from a culture and what must be rejected. Whoever pretends that the church is not borrowing is simply blind. It may be obvious when moving from culture to culture, but it is no less the case within one's own culture. Unfortunately there are no simple criteria for distinguishing what can be faithfully borrowed and incorporated and what leads astray. Deuteronomy repeatedly calls on Israel to destroy the cultic objects of the previous inhabitants of the land and to reject their cultic practices. In a similar way we are called to be careful when we live in a culture (and there surely is no alternative to living in a culture), so that as we speak and think and act within that culture, we are not adopting elements in tension with our faith in the God of Jesus Christ. Deuteronomy calls us, the Christian church, to constantly review and test what we are doing to discern whether we are being faithful or whether we are guilty of modern syncretism (cf. Acts 15:28; 1 Cor 14:29; 1 Thess 5:21).

Deuteronomy 26:1-19

Part 2D, Unit 7
Theology through Worship

PREVIEW

The central portion of the book of Deuteronomy now moves to a close. A long time ago, it seems, Moses has announced to the people, *These are the statutes and ordinances that you must diligently observe in the land that the* LORD, *the God of your ancestors, has given you* (12:1). Deuteronomy may not be finished, but its presentation of *statutes and ordinances* is. The vision for Israel in chapters 12–26 begins with the call to worship only at *the place that the* LORD *your God will choose* (12:5) and ends in glorious celebration at The Place. Here is worship framed in sparse yet theologically packed narrative, filled with symbolic action, and highlighted by liturgical declarations, all together proclaiming central Deuteronomic themes. Chapters 12 and 26 serve as a frame for chapters 12–26.

At first chapter 26 may seem to be another regulation consistent with the central core of the book. It does request a particular response, but it really is not a regulation. Regulations regarding firstfruits and tithes have been presented previously (firstfruits, 18:4; third-year tithes, 14:28-29), so they need not be given again. The point of the chapter is not spelling out further directions for the cult but a dramatic presentation of Israel's faith and ethics through worship of *the* LORD *your* God, incorporating symbolic action and liturgical declaration. God has taken *a wandering Aramean*, made his descendants into a *great nation* even as they were oppressed by the Egyptians, brought them out of Egypt, and given them the Promised Land. In response the Israelite presents his firstfruits to God and shares the bounty of a land flowing with milk and honey, celebrating and sharing with the less fortunate.

Deuteronomy 26 consists of three distinct parts, the first developed around the presentation of firstfruits at The Place (vv. 1-11), the second largely a speech regarding the third-year tithes (vv. 12-15), and the third a narrative climax not only to the chapter but also to all of chapters 12-26. The first two parts are bound together by numerous common features. Both these parts are framed by brief narrative comments, they include ceremonial offerings and action, at their center is a longer formal speech by an individual Israelite that is to be recited *before the LORD your God*, and they characterize the land given to Israel as *flowing with milk and honey*. God's actions are foundational to both, but in the first the Israelite responds by presenting to God a gift from the firstfruits of the land, and in the second the Israelite shares some produce of the land with the disadvantaged. One might speak of the two responses together as balancing the vertical relationship (God-human) with the horizontal (human-human). God's gifts are for all. The Israelite's response is directed both to God and to neighbor.

The chapter and core of the second speech then conclude with a return to the *today* of Moab, formalizing the particular relationship between God and the people of God.

OUTLINE

Firstfruits, 26:1-11
Third-Year Tithes, 26:12-15
A Mutual Agreement, 26:16-19

EXPLANATORY NOTES

Firstfruits 26:1-11

The narrative opens by looking forward to the time when Israel not only will have *come into the land* promised and given by God, but also has possessed it and is settled in it (v. 1). The literary context for the passage remains the speech of Moses in Moab (cf. vv. 16-19), but the next stage is now anticipated. It is ambiguous whether the passage assumes a singular event taking place upon entrance, or whether it is calling for an annual ceremony: perhaps both are intended. One can well imagine a celebration after the initial harvest in the Promised Land that is unique and on one level unrepeatable. This is because it is the first and yet also an annual celebration of the harvest that each year returns to that inaugural event via themes and motifs.

The stereotypical language of the first verse alerts us that we are entering a chapter filled with Deuteronomic theology. The central actor of the whole is *the LORD your God*, whose name Yahweh (translated LORD) is used fourteen times within the space of only eleven verses. God's key action is giving the land to Israel, with some form of the verb "to give" used seven times in these verses. Six times the passage refers to Israel as "coming" into the land. The first speech combines these in a liturgical declaration: *Today I declare to the LORD your God that I have come into the land that the LORD swore to our ancestors to give us* (v. 3). With these words the worshiper personally recognizes that God's promises have been fulfilled and the land has been given. Now the people can enjoy its fruits.

The individual Israelite is to *take some of the first of all the fruit of the ground, which you harvest from the land that the LORD your God is giving you; . . . put it in a basket; . . . go to the place that the LORD your God will choose as a dwelling for his name; . . . and go to the priest who is in office at that time* (vv. 2-3). At first glance this appears to be a fairly straightforward instruction, but as soon as one examines it more carefully, a number of questions arise. Who sets down the basket, the priest (v. 4) or the worshiper (v. 10)? Is there one festival at which this happens, or does each Israelite do this whenever the harvest is ready? Does each Israelite do this every time a new crop is harvested? Given that harvest lasts several months as the various field and orchard crops mature, this would require a whole series of pilgrimages to the central sanctuary each year. Or does the Israelite put aside the firstfruits of each crop and then later bring them to the central sanctuary? But if so, would they really fit into a basket? How does this instruction regarding firstfruits relate to the one in 18:4, where the firstfruits belong to the priest, yet here they are consumed communally (26:11)? Again we see that Deuteronomy is not giving detailed instruction to the priests on how to administer Israel's cult, or even to the people on how to participate. Rather, Deuteronomy appears to use well-known ceremonial occasions—there is no reason to doubt that Israel did not regularly worship at its central sanctuary in this manner—as the vehicle to present its distinctive theology and vision. Each harvest becomes an opportunity to remember that God has given the land and its blessings; each is an opportunity to acknowledge that through symbolic action.

The declaration the worshiper makes after presenting the firstfruits is often called a "historical credo" (vv. 5-10). The two terms reflect its nature (historical summary) and function (credo, based on the Latin for "I believe," suggesting a brief summary of the faith; cf. 6:20-25). The Deuteronomic language makes it unlikely that it is an older Israelite confession inserted at this point. Its economy of words and poetic style, however, result in a short faith summary that would have been truly memorable and possibly frequently recited. The phrase *a wandering Aramean was my father* (RSV; NRSV, *ancestor*) has a ring to it in English. In Hebrew it begins in alliteration, *'arammi 'obed 'abi* (each beginning with the first letter of the Hebrew alphabet, *aleph*). The reference probably is to Jacob, renamed Israel, the traditional father of the twelve tribes. After his alienation from his brother, he flees to Paddan-aram, where he spends time with the extended family of his father, people called Arameans in the Old Testament (Gen 28:5). But it may also be a more general reference, perhaps to Jacob's family or the whole group of ancestors.

The particular identification is not as important as the situation. The term translated *wandering* has the connotations of homelessness and rootlessness, an unsettled and migratory existence. This is true to the story of Jacob. But it may also be translated as in the KJV, *ready to perish* (cf. Job 4:11; 29:13 RSV), with possible reference to the severe famine Jacob's family experienced. Or it may mean *fugitive*, with possible reference to Jacob's flight from his family in fear of his life (Tigay: 240). Altogether they reflect a family and origin easily characterized by despair. Initially Egypt was a land of life-giving food, but it became a land of struggle, with the family *as an alien*, a people without a true home. In Egypt they did become a large people, but this proved to be their undoing as Pharaoh became afraid of them (Exod 1:9-10). Three phrases summarize Egyptian treatment of Israel: they *treated us harshly*, they *afflicted us*, they imposed *hard labor* on us (Deut 26:6). Such a people has no future.

This sets the stage for God's action. But it all begins with a cry (v. 7). As typical of psalms of lament, at its center is a cry to God from the midst of suffering and in pain: *We cried to the LORD, the God of our ancestors*. God's response to their cry is expressed with three verbs, matching in number the three terms describing their situation: *The LORD heard our voice, and saw our affliction, our toil, and our oppression. The*

LORD <u>brought</u> us out . . . Exodus speaks of God's responding to Israel's cry similarly: "God <u>heard</u> their groaning, and God <u>remembered</u> his covenant. . . . God <u>saw</u> the people of Israel and <u>knew</u> their condition" (2:24-25 RSV). Majestically, with *power* and *signs* and *wonders*, references to the plagues and crossing of the sea, God brought them to *this place and gave us this land, a land flowing with milk and honey* (Deut 26:9). Whereas in verse 2 the reference to The Place clearly is to the central sanctuary chosen by God (cf. 12:5, 11, 14, 18, 21, 26; 14:23, 24, 25; 15:20; 16:2, 6, 7, 11, 15, 16; 17:8, 10; 18:6), in verse 9 it refers first of all to the larger land (cf. 1:31; 9:7; 11:5). The double meaning of the term allows the central sanctuary to stand for the land as a whole.

By the end of the declaration, the contrast with the *wandering Aramean* is complete. No longer are they wandering, about to perish, but they can say, *I have come into the land* (26:3, 9). It is the story of Israel, but even more it is the story of what God has done in response to the cry of aliens oppressed in a foreign land and about to die. After reciting the credo before the priest at the central sanctuary, the people symbolically and literally celebrate the bounty God has given them. Although the concluding invitation only identifies the Levites and aliens (v. 11), surely the celebration includes the widow and orphan and other poor of the land, consistent with Deuteronomy's regular inclusion of these. The presence of the alien in the celebration serves as a continuing visible reminder that they once also were aliens.

The radical nature of this event is easily missed. Recent arrivals in a new land may demonstrate their appreciation and attachment to the new land by kissing the soil, or they may plant a flag as a claim of ownership. But this ceremony is very different. It does not take place as soon as they have entered the land but only after the land has produced firstfruits. More important, the Israelite does not make a claim of ownership but acknowledges the gifted nature of the land and God's ownership of it. The special relationship is not between the Israelite and the land, important as that is, but between the Israelite and God (P. Miller 1990: 179). Further, although the celebration is associated with the harvest, it is not a fertility celebration as would have been all too common in the ancient world. The focus of the credo is not the cycle of nature nor the generative power of the soil when combined with the sun and the rain, but the historical actions of God in taking wandering aliens and giving them the land. For Israel, the category of history, with focus on God's actions in that history, takes precedence over the category of nature and its generative force.

"You" and "You"; "I," "We," "Us," and "Our"

The way we use personal pronouns says much about how we understand ourselves and our identity. Scholars have been baffled by the way hundreds of second-person pronouns in Deuteronomy jump back and forth between singular and plural, a phenomenon lost in English translation since standard English does not distinguish between singular *you* and plural *you* (KJV, *ye*; cf. "you-all" in some regions). Long ago some interpreters proposed that this reflects different editorial layers, with one editor or author preferring the singular and another preferring the plural. But even if this explanation might fit some cases, it certainly does not satisfy all. Whatever the origin of the phenomenon, and it is possible there will never be a satisfactory explanation, one impact of it is that it binds together the individual and the community in a distinctive and powerful manner. Deuteronomy simultaneously addresses each individual Israelite and the people as a whole.

Our present passage wonderfully reflects the dynamic of this relationship, but in a way largely lost in English translation. In Deuteronomy 26, verses 5-10 alone include twenty-five uses of a personal pronoun in reference to Israel or an Israelite (excluding pronouns for God or the Egyptians). The chart on the next page details this, with the pronouns present in Hebrew but omitted in the NRSV placed in parentheses (AT).

This survey is fascinating and instructive. First, notice that the passage as a whole is framed by pronouns in the singular person. This is true in a double way. Not only do the words of the narrative before and after the declaration speak of the worshiper with the second-person singular pronoun *you* but more significantly, the declaration begins and concludes with the worshiper using the first-person singular pronouns *I* and *me*. The passage envisions an individual Israelite presenting firstfruits to the priest before God. Conceivably this Israelite might not be doing this as part of a larger group, but nevertheless the instruction is to each individual Israelite, and each individual Israelite responds as an individual.

The confession of faith, however, is dominated by the first-person plural pronouns *us*, *we*, and *our*. It is true that the first three pronouns speak of an individual ancestor and thus use the third-person singular, but quickly this shifts to the first-person plural. Once the individual worshiper begins to confess the faith, it becomes *our* faith, and the individual is incorporated or even lost in the larger people. With this use of pronouns, this short passage brings out a key element of worship. Worship and liturgy involve

26:	Phrase with Pronoun	Person and Number
5	you shall answer	2nd, masc., sg.
5	and (you) shall say [= make response]	2nd, masc., sg.
5	the Lord your God	2nd, masc., sg.
5	my father/ancestor	1st, common, sg.
5	he went down	3rd, masc., sg.
5	(he) sojourned there (= was an alien)	3rd, masc., sg.
5	there he became a great nation	3rd, masc., sg.
6	the Egyptians treated us harshly	1st, common, pl.
6	they afflicted us	1st, common, pl.
6	they gave us hard labor	1st, common, pl.
7	we cried out to God	1st, common, pl.
7	the God of our fathers/ancestors	1st, common, pl.
7	the Lord heard our call	1st, common, pl.
7	and saw our affliction	1st, common, pl.
7	our toil	1st, common, pl.
7	our oppression	1st, common, pl.
8	the Lord brought us out of Egypt	1st, common, pl.
9	he brought us to this place	1st, common, pl.
9	and gave us this land	1st, common, pl.
10	so now I bring the first of the fruits	1st, common, sg.
10	that you, O Lord, have given to me	1st, common, sg.
10	you shall set it down	2nd, masc., sg.
10	before the Lord your God	2nd, masc., sg.
10	(you) shall bow down	2nd, masc., sg.
10	before the Lord your God	2nd, masc., sg.

every individual as an individual, but worship has as its goal the incorporation of every individual into the people of God as a whole. Each individual must respond as an individual, but in responding the individual becomes part of a body.

The core of the confession of faith (vv. 6-9) uses twelve first-person plural pronouns for the people of Israel. These divide into four natural groups of three each. First, the Egyptians are the main actors, with the people of Israel as the recipients of the Egyptians' action, thus the pronouns are all *us* (objective). The only use of the pronoun *we* (subjective) in the passage opens the second group: *We cried to the LORD*. The only action of Israel in the whole credo is the cry to God. Now the story changes. Israel did not win the land: its only involvement is a cry for help. The third set of three speaks of God seeing Israel's situation: *our affliction, our toil, and our oppression*. God now enters the picture; God is not mentioned in the first part and is first mentioned when Israel cries to God. The last group of three matches the first group, with Israel again the recipient of the action, again represented by the pronoun *us*. But the Egyptians of the first group have been replaced by God, who now is the one who acts. In a striking way the pronouns of the passage reflect the central theological emphases of Deuteronomy (cf. the Shema, 6:4-9, which similarly begins in the plural and then moves to the singular).

Third-Year Tithes 26:12-15

The communal celebration of firstfruits has a natural quality to it. It quite understandably marks the beginning of harvest as well as God's gift of the land. In this climactic chapter the contribution of the third-year tithe is less immediately obvious. The tithe system as such was addressed earlier (14:22-29), with its division between the annual tithe and the third-year tithe. Here only the third-year tithe is named.

Perhaps the omission of any reference to the annual tithe points us in a helpful direction. Although the annual tithe involves communal celebration (comparable to the firstfruits festival of vv. 1-11?), its background is the general ancient notion that part of the harvest is to be returned to God in thanksgiving for God's blessings. The third-year tithe is different. As a tithe it still reflects the conviction that all belongs to God, but now the actual produce is redirected to the needy. The third-year tithe represents a uniquely Israelite way of ensuring that the blessings of land, gifted by God, shall benefit all. The bounty of the land is so great that the disadvantaged will be able *eat their fill within your towns*, and not merely stave off starvation (26:12; cf. 14:29).

In this climactic chapter the third-year tithe reminds the people of the urgency of allowing the poor to share in the abundance of God's blessing, even as it gives Deuteronomy one more opportunity to include a liturgical expression. As in the first section, here also action is followed by declaration. Although the third-year tithes remain in the local community, the phrase *before the* LORD *your God* may suggest that the individual Israelite is to come to the central sanctuary, The Place God has chosen, to make this declaration, a series of assertions of innocence (vv. 13-14, adapted):

> *I have removed the sacred portion from the house.*
> *I have given it to the Levites, the resident aliens, the orphans, and the widows.*
> *I have not transgressed ... any of your commandments.*
> *I have not forgotten any of your commandments.*
> *I have not eaten of it while in mourning.*
> *I have not removed any of it while I was unclean.*
> *I have not offered any of it to the dead.*
> *I have obeyed the* LORD *my God, doing just as you have commanded me.*

The opening and closing are positive affirmations—the worshiper has given the tithe as commanded and obeyed the whole law—with the middle five protestations of innocence in the face of possible violations. Interestingly, it is the tithe given to the poor that is called *the sacred portion* (lit., *the holy*).

The last three negative statements (v. 14) speak to possible mishandling of the tithe that would result in its defilement. Their background may be opposition to Canaanite worship patterns (offerings to the dead were part of Baalistic worship), but they may simply be another example of Deuteronomy incorporating elements of Israel's concern for purity and holiness. Altogether these assertions make the claim that the worshiper has responded faithfully to God's commands, both in terms of cultic expectations and in terms of the requirement to share with the needy.

The ritual of innocence then turns into a prayer for continuing blessing (v. 15). Again one notices the way in which the individual is incorporated into the community. In the statements of innocence, the first-person singular pronoun *I* occurs eight times, yet the request for blessing is not for "me" but for *your people Israel*. The logic of Deuteronomy is consistent. Obedience to God's commands, especially as represented in concern for the weak and needy, is the precondition for further blessing. Even then obedience does not result in the blessings being deserved since the starting point for the relationship is always undeserved election, gift, and blessing (cf. 7:7-11). But in obedience the worshiper prays to God for continuing blessing of the people and the land given to the people.

A Mutual Agreement 26:16-19

After two passages set within the Promised Land, the concluding verses of the chapter return to Moab and the words of Moses. Verse 16 employs a number of terms that Deuteronomy uses at key junctures:

> 26:16, *today* [NRSV, *this very day*], *statutes and ordinances, observe, diligently*
> 5:1, *statutes and ordinances, today, observe, diligently*
> 6:1, *statutes and ordinances, observe*
> 12:1, *statutes and ordinances, diligently observe*

The outline shows that these verses open the three main parts of the second speech: "The Horeb Covenant" (ch. 5), "Preaching the Foundational Commandment" (chs. 6–11), and "Preaching the Moab Covenant" (chs. 12–26). A further echo of earlier preaching is provided by the phrase *with all your heart and with all your soul*, a reminder of the Shema (26:16; 6:4-9), the foundational commandment of chapters 6–11. These terms and verses thus identify the key sections of this core. The concluding chapters of the book (chs. 29–34) will give further exhortation and challenge, and speak of covenant and the death of Moses, but the preaching based on the regulations for life is coming to an end.

These verses outline a mutual understanding or *agreement* between God and Israel. The term "covenant" is not used, but its essence is here. Deuteronomy will describe the making of the Moab covenant in chapter 29, but it is already summarized here. The use of *today* (vv. 17, 18) points to a ritual context and, consistent with Deuteronomic emphasis, highlights the permanent up-to-dateness of the covenant.

The structure of these verses reflects the profound mutuality of the covenant even if the parties to it are far from equal.

> Each party has made a solemn declaration of the covenant relationship. At the heart of this mutual declaration is the relationship between Yahweh as Israel's "God," and Israel as Yahweh's "people." The basic formula has been filled out into a double declaration that is both poetic and intricately reciprocal. (Nelson 2002: 311)

From Israel's side, God is committing to be its God, Israel is committing *to walk in his ways, to keep his statutes, his commandments, and his ordinances, and to <u>obey him</u>* [lit., *to listen to his voice*]. From God's side, Israel is committing *to keep his commandments,* God is committing to making Israel *his treasured people,* to set Israel *high above all nations,* and to make it *a people holy to the LORD your God, as he promised.* As in chapter 14, Israel becomes holy through special action of God, not through its own doing (note 14:2, 21). "Taking the two declarations together, Yahweh commits to bring about and maintain the relationship of God and people ('treasured,' 'promised,' 'set high,' 'holy') and Israel commits itself to obey the law ('walk,' 'keep,' 'obey')" (Nelson 2002: 312). The unequal nature of the relationship is clear from the final term in Hebrew and in most English translations: *promised.* It is God's word that can be trusted, that initiates election, and that is foundational to the agreement of these verses.

THE TEXT IN BIBLICAL CONTEXT
The Two Greatest Commandments

When the lawyer asks Jesus, "Teacher, which commandment in the law is the greatest?" Jesus responds, "'You shall love the Lord your God with all your heart, and with all your soul, and with all your mind.' This is the greatest and the first commandment. And a second is like it: 'You shall love your neighbor as yourself.' On these two commandments hang all the law and the prophets" (Matt 22:36-40). It is common to understand Jesus' answer as a combining of words from the Shema of Deuteronomy (6:4-9) with a commandment from Leviticus (19:18).

This is probably correct. But the two commandments together also reflect the emphasis of Deuteronomy 26. The term "love" is not used in the passage about the firstfruits, but the focus is unquestionably on the God who loves Israel, heard its cry, and then has acted. By returning firstfruits to God and reciting the confession, the Israelite acknowledges this and affirms total commitment to God. The second passage then turns to the neighbor, the one who needs help. When Jesus is asked who the neighbor is, he responds with the story of the good Samaritan (Luke 10:29-37). Only when the Israelite has responded to the poor in the land by sharing with them the third-year tithe can the Israelite say, *I have obeyed the LORD my God, doing just as you commanded me* (26:14). The two commandments become inseparable both in Deuteronomy and in the teaching of Jesus. (For consideration of biblical confessionals in historical style, see comments on 6:20-25.)

THE TEXT IN THE LIFE OF THE CHURCH

Thanksgiving as a Remembrance Day

Thanksgiving, although celebrated at different times of the year in Canada and the United States, is a long-standing tradition in both countries, in society at large and in the church. Thanksgiving services in the church can include large displays of produce from the garden or field or, perhaps in nonagricultural communities, other objects symbolizing gifts from God. Such services have many elements comparable to the Israelite presentation of firstfruits.

Two observations: First, although firstfruits are the product of the soil, the focus of the declaration is not on how God sends rain and sunshine on the fields and orchards, making it possible for fields to produce corn and the vineyards grapes. Rather, the focus is on God's actions in the story of Israel, on how God has made a people out of a wandering Aramean, how God has heard the cry of the people in slavery and responded by delivering them and giving them a land. It is not wrong to thank God for sun and rain, for fertile soil and what it grows. The Bible consistently sees these as blessings from God. But perhaps contemporary thanksgiving services could also become remembrance days, when a community consciously remembers who it is as part of the larger body of Christ, what its particular story is, and what God has done for the church as a whole through Jesus Christ, and for that particular congregation or denomination.

Second, the presentation of firstfruits leads immediately to an account of the third-year tithe. To thank God for what God has given and for what God has done is a crucial first step, but only a first step. This recognition, and the consequent thanksgiving, must lead to treating the neighbor on the model of the way God has treated us. Sharing with the disadvantaged thus is not an option: it is an obligation.

Participation

The believers church tradition has tended to emphasize the preached word, supplemented with music, as the heart of worship. As noted earlier (TBC after 16:17), dramatic action combined with liturgical declaration has played a lesser role. The obvious exceptions to this are the celebrations of communion, baptism, and perhaps child dedication. But most people remain observers, at least for the latter two. Participation in most services thus is limited to hearing, saying, or singing words.

This chapter suggests that Israelite worship was highly participatory, with an integration of words and dramatic action. The worshiper brought the firstfruits and gave them to the priest. The worshiper recited the credo, very probably individually, beginning with *A wandering Aramean was my ancestor*, thereby including oneself directly in the story. It is likely that participation included huge dramatic actions (see ch. 27). In this manner children and adults would experience what was happening much beyond simply hearing what was said.

Contemporary family celebrations at religious occasions may include ritual elements (e.g., Christmas tree, Easter eggs, turkey at Thanksgiving), but all too often words giving these rituals meaning are absent. Jewish custom continues to emphasize the home as the place where Sabbath and festival are celebrated. Ritual action combined with responsive involvement reminds participants, including children, of the key events and then incorporates the "I" into the larger community and story.

Deuteronomy 27:1–28:68

Part 2E
Covenant Renewal, Blessings and Curses

PREVIEW

Chapter 27 reflects a complex literary history and appears to be an interruption in the present context. The last three verses of chapter 26 prepare for the formal ratification of the covenant on the plains of Moab, a topic picked up again at 28:1; but here chapter 27 looks forward to when Israel has entered the land and has a covenant-renewal ceremony at Shechem. Chapters 26 and 28 both have Moses speaking in the first person; but chapter 27 three times refers to Moses in the third person. Block suggests that the chapter was drafted to "clarify the context of the covenantal renewal ceremony on Mount Ebal," then later inserted between chapters 26 and 28 (2012: 43).

Despite features suggesting a longer literary history (e.g., v. 1 has *Moses and the elders of Israel* speaking; v. 9, *Moses and the levitical priests*; and then v. 11, simply *Moses*; the somewhat disjointed nature of vv. 1-8; the relationship of vv. 9-10 to the rest of the chapter—these are awkward), in its present form chapter 27 calls for a future covenant-renewal ceremony at Shechem, between Mount Ebal and Mount Gerizim. Three verses in which a narrator identifies the different speakers (vv. 1, 9, 11) divide the chapter into three parts.

Although the term "covenant" is not used, the similarity between the ceremony described here and the description of covenant making in Exodus 24, combined with the public proclamation of blessings and curses, shows that is intended (Tigay: 247).

With the introduction of this covenant-renewal ceremony, Deuteronomy's schema of covenants is complete. In addition to God's covenant with the ancestors (4:31; 7:12-13; 8:18), Deuteronomy speaks of three distinct covenant events. First, God made a covenant with Israel at Horeb when God proclaimed the Decalogue to the people (4:13, 23; 5:2-3; 9:9, 11, 15). Second, Moses mediates a new covenant with the people in Moab, with the preaching of Deuteronomy its core (29:1, 9, 12, 14). The mutual agreement of 26:16-19, and the blessings and curses of chapter 28, all look forward to this. Third, Deuteronomy calls for a covenant-renewal/reaffirmation ceremony after entrance into the land at Shechem (27:1-26; cf. 11:29-30), making use of Mounts Ebal and Gerizim. Joshua fulfills this last directive (Josh 8:30-35), with the event likely becoming a repeated or perhaps even annual observance. Horeb, Moab, and Shechem thus stand for these three covenant events.

Chapter 28 does not open with an introduction but moves directly into a long list of blessings and curses. Thus its relationship to the surrounding material is disputed. The absence of any narrative introduction (cf. 27:1) allows it to be read as a continuation of the previous chapter. Blessings and curses are exactly what Moses instructs in 27:11-14. Chapter 28 thus could be a continuation of the covenant-renewal ceremony in Shechem (ch. 27).

But the blessings and curses of chapter 28 also fit well as a continuation of chapter 26 on the one side, and as preparation for the covenant-making ceremony in Moab (ch. 29) on the other. Most interpreters follow the second option and see chapter 28 as a return to Moab after the interruption of chapter 27 (e.g., McConville: "It is best to suppose that the perspective reverts in 28:1 to Moab"; 2002: 400; cf. Nelson 2002: 329).

But perhaps one does not need to choose sharply between these two options, at least not with regard to the present role of chapter 28. Although the book does speak of three different covenant events associated with three different locations (Horeb, Moab, and Shechem), all three "make" Israel the people of God *today*. The *today* of Deuteronomy never fades into the past but is always present. The Moab covenant is built upon the Horeb covenant (made a generation earlier but also *with us . . . here alive today*, 5:3), with the Shechem ceremony renewing (i.e., making new) the covenant between God and Israel. The ambiguity about whether chapter 28 is connected to the Moab covenant or the Shechem covenant-renewal ceremony thus serves well to bind together Shechem with Moab. In both contexts God becomes (or is affirmed) as the God of Israel, and Israel becomes (or is affirmed) as the people of God (cf. 26:16-19; 27:9-10). And in both cases, blessings and curses are integral to Deuteronomy's depiction of covenant.

That this is the case (i.e., that blessings and curses are integral to Deuteronomy's depiction of covenant) may strike a contemporary reader as odd or even offensive. These blessings and curses all too easily support a theology that simplistically and mechanically correlates obedience with reward and disobedience with punishment. But an ancient audience likely would have anticipated a list of blessings and curses. Blessings and curses were a standard feature of ancient Near Eastern treaties and were employed to motivate response to their central stipulations (a carrot-and-stick method). Deuteronomy's characterization of Israel's covenant with God is influenced by these treaties. The terms "covenant" and "treaty" both refer to an agreement between two sides, with English versions using both to translate the same Hebrew term [*Deuteronomy, Covenant, and Political Treaties*, p. 547].

Not only does the influence of ancient political treaties account for the inclusion of blessings and curses, it also helps explain the preponderance of curses over blessings, as well as the sequence and content of a number of the curses. Presumably curses highlighting the negative consequences of disobedience were considered more effective (cf. political attack ads?) and thus predominated in the ancient treaties, in some cases eliminating blessings entirely (McConville 2002: 402). The disproportion of curses to blessings in Deuteronomy is not evidence that Deuteronomy has a negative focus but likely is a reflection of this literary form. Some interpreters even suggest that significant portions of chapter 28 were taken directly from an ancient political treaty (e.g., Steymans; cf. Weinfeld 1972: 116-29). Even if one does not go this far, a comparison with ancient treaties and law codes suggests that a general stock of curses was commonly known and used in a variety of contexts, from which Deuteronomy here borrows.

OUTLINE

Covenant Renewal at Shechem, 27:1-26
    27:1-8   A Commemorative Monument and an Altar
    27:9-10   Exhortation to Obey

27:11-26   Prohibitions in Curse Form
Covenant Blessings and Curses, 28:1-68
  28:1-14   Blessings
  28:15-68   Curses

EXPLANATORY NOTES

Covenant Renewal at Shechem 27:1-26

27:1-8 A Commemorative Monument and an Altar

The chapter opens with a stereotypical Deuteronomic call to *keep the entire commandment that I am commanding you today* (cf. 7:11; 8:1; 11:8, 13; 15:5; 19:9—all these refer to the commandments, call Israel to keep them, and specify *today*), yet now for the first time Moses is not alone in giving the call but accompanied by *the elders of Israel*. Deuteronomy is largely the words of Moses to Israel in Moab prior to entering the Promised Land. But Moses will die before Israel enters the land. As we approach the end of the book and the account of the death of Moses, Deuteronomy begins to prepare for that time, with others beginning to play a more significant role (cf. vv. 9 and 14, where the *levitical priests* first join Moses and then speak on their own). The message and covenant mediated by Moses as a result of the people's cry (cf. 5:22-33) will be carried on as others mediate between God and Israel.

The need to remember the covenant and its requirements also explains the logic of the chapter. Once the people have entered the Promised Land, Israel is to have a public ceremony commemorating or renewing its covenant with God (cf. 11:29-30; Josh 8:30-35). The phrase *on the day that you cross over the Jordan* (v. 2) is not intended literally, since Israel could not trek from the Jordan to Shechem in one day. Tigay thus translates it *as soon as you have crossed the Jordan* (249; cf. v. 4). The passage may very well already anticipate an annual ceremony even though it speaks of it as a onetime event (cf. the instructions regarding the presentation of firstfruits; 26:1-11). The requirement to set up permanent monuments as well as the liturgical style (esp. 27:11-26) point to a regular covenant-renewal service in Shechem.

The chapter highlights three elements of the covenant-renewal ceremony. First, Israel is to take large stones, cover them in plaster, write on them *all the words of this law* (vv. 3, 8; the *stones* of vv. 2-4 and v. 8 are the same, different from the stones in vv. 5-7), and place them on Mount Ebal, the highest mountain in the region. As in the earlier phrase, *this entire commandment* (cf. 6:25; etc.), the reference is to the whole teaching incorporated in the book of Deuteronomy. The practice of setting up monuments on which are recorded important events or public decrees was common in the ancient Near East. In Mesopotamia the tendency was to carve the words into a rock, and the practice of using plaster with some kind of ink or paint was common in Egypt. These stones will serve both as commemoration of the gift of land and as a continuing reminder of God's instruction to Israel. The call to write this law *very clearly* presumably means that the words are to be written clearly so that people can understand them, but probably includes with it the sense that God's law is clear and understandable (27:8; cf. 30:11-14).

Second, consistent with general ancient practice, the covenant-renewal ceremony is to be accompanied by *burnt offerings* and *sacrifices* offered on an altar constructed with *stones on which you have not used an iron tool*, of *unhewn stones [Sacrifices and Offerings, p. 565]*. The rationale for using only uncut stone is lost, but it is an old tradition within the Old Testament (27:5-6; cf. the altar law of Exod 20:24-25), and may have emphasized a contrast with the elaborate altars for Baal worship. Not surprisingly, Deuteronomy adds *rejoicing before the LORD* to the sacrifice (Deut 27:7).

The call to build an altar for sacrifice at Shechem raises the question of how this fits with the Deuteronomic requirement to worship God only at the one place chosen by God for his name (cf. 12:5; etc.). Is this a further sign that this chapter has not been fully integrated into Deuteronomy? Or does it suggest that Deuteronomy understands the centralization expectation to come into effect only after God has settled Israel in the land and given Israel *rest from your enemies all around you so that you live in safety* (12:10; Nelson 2002: 317)? If the latter, then this passage challenges any notion that Jerusalem is The Place because of some inherent sacred quality. God's choice remains God's choice.

Third, the passage calls for liturgical declarations (27:11-26).

27:9-10 Exhortation to Obey

The second section in the chapter opens with the narrator again having Moses speak together with others, this time the *levitical priests*, and opening with a call reminiscent of the foundational commandment, the Shema (6:4-9, using the imperative *Hear, O Israel*, v. 4). The relationship of these two verses to the rest of the chapter is ambiguous. They may be a "rhetorical bridge between 26:16-19 and 28:1," suggested by how they pick up terms and phrases from 26:16-19 on the one side and 28:1 on the other (*this very day* and *people of* the LORD point backward; *obey the LORD your God* and *commandments ... that I am commanding you today* point forward (Nelson 2002: 318). McConville suggests that they refer back to the Moab covenant introduced in 26:16-19 (2002: 390).

These connections may be reflecting an earlier literary connection, but now in chapter 27 they refer to the covenant-renewal ceremony at Shechem. Deuteronomy will shortly speak of the Moab covenant in similar terms (*in order that he may establish you today as his people*, 29:13), but even that is not the original event, which took place at Mount Horeb. Central to Deuteronomic theology is that the past is brought into *today—The LORD our God made a covenant with us at Horeb. Not with our ancestors did the LORD make this covenant, but with us, who are all of us here alive today* (5:2-3)—and today moves into the future. Although Deuteronomy speaks of the Moab covenant as *in addition to the covenant that he had made with them at Horeb* (29:1), in a sense it is a renewing of that covenant. Similarly, the Shechem event is a renewing of the covenant through which the people on *this very day* once again become *the people of the LORD your God*. "It should not be taken to mean that Israel had not already been Yahweh's people before the Moab covenant. Rather, the rhetoric illustrates that it must always enter the covenant afresh. That, indeed, is the essence of the idea enshrined in the Moab covenant itself" (McConville 2002: 390).

27:11-26 Prohibitions in Curse Form

Once again Moses speaks alone, giving a charge to the people for the time after they have *crossed the Jordan*. The location of the projected event between Mounts Gerizim and Ebal connect it with the first part of the chapter. Since Moses will not accompany the people into the Promised Land, the Levites take leadership in the ceremony. This does not refer to the tribe as a whole—after all, the previous verse has placed the tribe of Levi on Mount Gerizim—but to those within the tribe with specialized responsibility. This is consistent with the Levites' responsibility for maintaining and teaching the law. Again there is preparation for, and a gradual move to, a time when Moses will be absent, when the people will need to demonstrate their faithfulness to the torah with new leaders.

The ceremony described in the following verses was projected earlier (11:29-30) and is fulfilled in Joshua 8:30-35. Although the language of this text suggests that the tribes are expected to climb the two mountains, or at least stand at the foot of them facing each other, the Joshua account gives the impression of the tribes standing in the valley "on opposite sides of the ark of the covenant," with their backs to each other, facing the two mountains (8:33). Perhaps varying traditions are reflected here. But both have Mount Gerizim representing blessings and Mount Ebal signifying curses, the common ancient Near Eastern way of supporting obedience to a covenant or treaty (see discussion of Deut 28). Through this annually repeated event, the two mountains themselves, and not only the altar and stones with the law written on them, become monuments and reminders of the covenant.

The logic of the division between the two sets of tribes is not clear, although there are some hints that the text is giving preferential treatment to blessing over curse. Whereas the text speaks of *the blessing of the people*, the reference to the *curse* has no object (cf. 27:11, 13). Further, the tribes representing blessing are the two descended from Rachel, the favored wife of Jacob, and four of the sons of Leah, whereas the tribes representing curse are descended from Jacob's maids and the two remaining sons of Leah, the oldest, who had been deposed in rank (*Reuben*, Gen 49:3-4), and the youngest (*Zebulun*). It probably also is not coincidental that Judah, the ancestor of the Southern Kingdom, and Joseph and Benjamin, the favorite sons of Jacob, are all three associated with blessing. Thus despite the exclusive focus of Deuteronomy 27:15-26 upon curses, the verses setting the stage give priority to blessing.

At least three aspects of verses 14-26 do not follow naturally from verses 11-13. First, the introduction appears to suggest that the people themselves will shout out blessings and curses, but verse 14 has the Levites alone declaring them in *a loud voice*. Second, the introduction speaks of both blessing and curse, but only curses follow. And perhaps most significantly, although each verse begins with the word *cursed* (in both English and Hebrew), they really are not curses as normally used in a treaty. Their focus is not on the curse itself (i.e., the negative consequences that may follow) but on the action that is prohibited. Both in its overall structure (i.e., with both blessings and curses, with curses predominating), and in the form of the blessings and curses, chapter 28 would fit better after verse 13.

With their stylized form and their symbolic number (12, matching the tribes of Israel), the curses of chapter 27 are more like another law code, comparable to the Decalogue in the first part of the book, prohibiting and denouncing a set of actions. The responsive *Amen* at the end of each statement may suggest their use in some regular worship setting. One characteristic that ties all the actions together is that they can be done in secret (explicitly stated in vv. 15 and 24). The curses thus announce divine retribution in situations where it is likely that the deed may not become public knowledge, with consequent prosecution. Through its affirmation of these curses, the community both separates itself from such behavior and "protects itself from the consequences of transgressions it cannot control or even discover" (cf. 21:1-9; Nelson 2002: 319-20). They also proclaim that God is present everywhere, even when people might think of themselves as hidden from the view of God.

As the chart below shows (adapted from Brueggemann 2001: 253), there is very little new in the prohibitions formulated as curses. Most of the specific deeds denounced have been touched upon earlier, some directly, others indirectly. The prohibition against idols and images surely implies the rejection of the worship of other gods. This list, like the Decalogue, thus opens with the foundational commandment.

1st, idols and images	5:8-10; 4:15-20
2nd, dishonoring mother and father	5:16; 21:18-21
3rd, moving a boundary marker	19:14
4th, misleading the blind	new
5th, concern for alien, orphan, widow	14:29; 16:11, 14; 24:19-21; 26:12-13; etc.
6th, lying with father's wife	22:30
7th, lying with any animal	new
8th, lying with one's sister	new
9th, lying with one's mother-in-law	new
10th, striking a neighbor	cf. 5:17, 20
11th, taking a bribe	10:17; 16:19
12th, not upholding words of the law	general exhortation often repeated

Regarding the fourth prohibition: this is the first reference to caring for the *blind* in Deuteronomy, although blindness is identified as a defect earlier (15:21). Leviticus warns against putting "a stumbling block before the blind" (19:14). Within ancient societies, the blind are vulnerable and thus need special protection. Hence this warning is a natural extension of Deuteronomy's concern and care for the weak, reflected here in both the fourth and the fifth prohibitions.

Regarding the sixth, seventh, eighth, and ninth prohibitions: only the first of these four has been addressed previously. Incest and bestiality, like adultery, is a temptation in a rural, multigenerational, and possibly polygamous context (cf. Exod 22:19; Lev 18:6-23; 20:10-20). Each takes place in secret, and each transgresses the order of the family and creation. As such they threaten the social integrity of the society and are condemned.

Covenant Blessings and Curses 28:1-68

28:1-14 Blessings

The blessings are in two distinct paragraphs (vv. 3-6, 7-12), framed by statements making the blessings conditional upon obedience to God (vv. 1-2, 13-14). The language of the frame is stereotypically Deuteronomic, with its reference to *diligently observing all the commandments that I am commanding you today*, and with its warning against *following other gods to serve them*. The reference to setting Israel *high above all the nations* (said directly in the opening frame, v. 2; again with different wording in the closing frame, v. 13) is not as common but was introduced earlier (15:6; 26:19).

To speak of the blessings as conditional upon obedience must be distinguished from speaking of the blessings as a reward for obedience. To reflect this, the opening *if* in verses 1 and 14 might be translated *as long as* (McConville 2002: 404). That the land of milk and honey is an undeserved gift from God has been stated repeatedly in Deuteronomy, beginning with the book's first reference to the land (1:8). The passage on the presentation of the firstfruits, with its seven references to the land having been given to the Israelite worshiper, connects the gift of the land with the produce Israel receives from it (26:1-11). The land and its blessings thus always remain an undeserved gift. They must never be treated as if deserved or obtained through *my power and the might of my own hand* (8:17). The relationship between obedience and blessing thus is only one way: obedience makes continuing blessing possible, but blessing remains a gift and never becomes the deserved reward for obedience. The relationship between obedience and blessing thus is very different from the relationship between disobedience and curse (C. Wright 1996: 280).

The first set of blessings (28:3-6) are comprehensive and general. There is no reference to God as the source of these blessings, with the term "blessed" used as a passive participle six times. The opening and closing verses highlight the exhaustive nature of the blessing: Israel shall be blessed everywhere (*in the city, ... in the field*, v. 3) and all the time (*when you come in, ... when you go out*, v. 6). The technique here is similar to that of the Shema, which calls on the

Israelite to remember its words *when you are at home and when you are away, when you lie down and when you rise* (6:7). The middle two blessings speak of fertility of *womb, ground,* and *livestock* (perhaps no term is a closer synonym to "blessing" than "fertility"; v. 4), and its consequences for sufficient food (*basket, kneading bowl,* v. 5). This poetic expression of what blessing means for the people in the land may have had larger use in Israel.

The second set of blessings has a different style. Here God is the active subject of the verbs, with the proper name of God occurring nine times in verses 7-12. In these verses the more general blessings of the opening set are translated into particular promises for Israel (Nelson 2002: 329). Not surprisingly, in a time when the struggle to survive in the face of famine and enemies is a constant challenge, prosperity—understood as blessing on *barns* (v. 8) and fertility of field, flock, and *womb* (vv. 11-12), combined with protection from enemies (v. 7)—receives most attention.

But at the center is the promise that God *will establish you as his holy people,* with the consequence that *all the peoples of the earth shall see that you are called by the name of the* LORD (vv. 9-10; cf. 7:6; 14:1, 21). The unique relationship between God and Israel implied by this promise is not only for the sake of Israel but also has implications beyond Israel (cf. 4:5-8). When God called Abraham and Sarah, God promised to bless them, to make their name great, and that through them "all the families of the earth shall be blessed" (Gen 12:2-3). The blessings of Deuteronomy 28:1-14 speak to this original election promise: Israel will be blessed; its name will become great, as will that of its God; and through this election, blessing will flow to all. The last element is only hinted at (*You will lend to many nations,* v. 12; cf. 15:6) but becomes more explicit later in the Old Testament. Isaiah speaks of "the mountain of the LORD's house" being "established as the highest of the mountains," with the nations coming to the mountain so "that he may teach us his ways" (2:2; cf. Deut 28:1); and of God's servant as becoming "a light to the nations" (Isa 42:6; 49:6). But Deuteronomy's blessing for Israel begins the move in a direction that expands the blessing beyond Israel.

28:15-68 Curses

Verses 15-44. If Israel does not obey, well-deserved punishment will follow (v. 15). The short opening set of curses (vv. 16-19) are the negative counterpart to the opening blessings (vv. 3-6) and thus introduce curses as the withdrawal of blessing. As with the list of blessings, after a short general set in the passive voice, stating that

Israel will be cursed everywhere and all the time, the text continues with further curses in which God is the active agent against Israel. Only these curses expand much beyond the blessings.

In this expansion Deuteronomy borrows extensively from the larger ancient Near Eastern repertoire of curses used in ancient political treaties and legal codes, yet probably also commonplace elsewhere. Everything Israel attempts will be doomed (v. 20), disease and pestilence will come upon it (vv. 21-22, 27-29, 35), the sky will not rain nor will the earth produce (vv. 22-24, 42), its enemies will defeat and abuse Israel (vv. 25-29, 32-33, 36, 43-44), initiatives started will not bear fruit (futility curses, vv. 30-31, 33, 38-41). The formulaic nature of these curses is reflected when at a number of points they mirror the earlier blessings. For example, whereas verse 1 speaks of God setting Israel *high above all the nations of the earth*, verse 43 warns that *aliens residing among you shall ascend above you higher and higher, while you shall descend lower and lower*. Again, whereas verses 12-13 say, *You will lend to many nations, but you will not borrow. The LORD will make you the head, and not the tail*, verse 44 reverses both of these.

Verses 45-57. Verses 45-46 appear to conclude the presentation of curses and with verse 15 form a frame for the curses in a manner comparable to the way verses 1-2 and 13-14 frame the blessings. The reference to the curses being *a sign and a portent forever* has an ironic ring to it; previously Deuteronomy has used the combination *sign-portent* of God's actions in the exodus (usually translated *signs and wonders*; cf. 4:34; 6:22; 7:19; 26:8).

But instead of concluding the curses, 28:45-46 begins a new section, one in which the conditional nature of the curses fades into the background. Now the curses will fall upon Israel *because you did not obey* (v. 45), *because you did not serve the LORD your God joyfully and with gladness* (v. 47). In this larger block of curses, the focus is narrowed to portray the catastrophe resulting from siege and defeat at the hand of the enemy. Because Israel did not serve God, it will serve the enemy (vv. 47-48). Conventional images and language are employed with gruesome effect to describe what happens to a people when an enemy comes and besieges a city, causing starvation, cannibalism, and the loss of all dignity. In the process the land and the children God has given will be lost.

Verses 58-68. The concluding section of curses is once more conditional (v. 58 begins with *If you do not diligently observe all the words of this law*) and is more closely tied to the story of Israel and the book of Deuteronomy. The curses will rescind what Israel has received from God. The plagues of Egypt will come upon them (vv. 59-60).

Whereas God has fulfilled his promise to Abraham and Sarah to make their descendants as numerous as the stars, they will become *few in number* (v. 62; cf. Gen 15:5; 22:17; 26:4). Whereas God has given the people rest in the Promised Land, God will *scatter you among all peoples, where you shall find . . . no resting place for the sole of your foot* (Deut 28:63-65; cf. 3:20; 12:10; 25:19). In this context the reference to Israel worshiping *other gods, of wood and stone, which neither you nor your ancestors have known* is part of the curse (28:64; cf. 13:2, 6, 13). This theme reaches its climax with the warning that the God who has redeemed them from Egypt *will bring you back in ships to Egypt, where you shall offer yourselves for sale to your enemy as male and female slaves* (v. 68). The people whom God has freed will once more enter into bondage. The great acts of God, the signs and wonders, will be overturned because the people have ignored the words of torah.

With the reference to *this book* (v. 58; cf. v. 61), Deuteronomy moves to its conclusion. Previously there has been only one reference to a *book*, that in the law of the king (17:18 RSV). In the next few chapters these references increase as the text more consciously speaks of the content of Deuteronomy as a completed product (29:20, 21, 27; 30:10; 31:24, 26).

THE TEXT IN BIBLICAL CONTEXT

Blessing and Curse, Reward and Punishment

In the gospel of John, Jesus is walking with his disciples when they come upon a man blind from birth. "Who sinned, this man or his parents, that he was born blind?" his disciples ask him (9:2). With that question the disciples raise one of the difficult issues in Scripture.

On the one hand, many Scripture passages draw a strong association between our behavior and the consequences. Proverbs repeatedly mentions the positive results of wise action and the negative results of foolish behavior (e.g., "The wise will inherit honor, but stubborn fools, disgrace," 3:35; "The wage of the righteous leads to life, the gain of the wicked to sin," 10:16). Psalmists anticipate that the wicked will perish (e.g., 37:20). In a somewhat simplistic manner, Deuteronomy is sometimes characterized as reflecting this "rewards theology," with the chapters on blessings and curses a prime example of that: those who obey will be blessed, those who disobey will be cursed.

Yet on the other hand, such a simple way of expressing the book's position is not true to Deuteronomy nor to other parts of

Scripture. The book of Job tackles this question at length. Job's friends, using what is sometimes considered to be Deuteronomic theology, conclude from Job's suffering that he has sinned: why else would he be suffering as he is? (e.g., Job 8). Job heatedly denies this, and the introduction to the book speaks of Job as "blameless and upright" (1:1). His suffering is not due to his sin.

Perhaps in good Job tradition, Jesus responds to his disciples, "Neither this man nor his parents sinned; he was born blind so that God's works might be revealed in him" (John 9:3). Similarly, in Luke, Jesus challenges the notion that certain Galileans who suffered at the hand of Pilate were worse sinners than those who did not (13:1-5). Gerard Sloyan attempts to remove the tension between these two trajectories by suggesting that one can conclude from sin that suffering will follow, but one cannot conclude from suffering that sin has preceded (115). But Scripture challenges even this if understood mechanically (e.g., Job 8:16, "The wicked thrive before the sun, and their shoots spread over the garden"; Ps 73:3-4, "I saw the prosperity of the wicked. For they have no pain; their bodies are sound and sleek"). Life undermines a simple obedience-blessing correlation: Job, Jesus, and contemporary followers of Jesus can attest to this.

Despite Deuteronomy's long list of blessings and curses, Deuteronomy also does not commit to such a theology in a simple way. Blessings and curses do contain truth and are used by Deuteronomy to motivate faithful response to God and covenant, but they are not the first word or the last word. God's relationship with Israel begins with grace, with unmerited election and deliverance. Then, in chapters 4 and 30, Deuteronomy suggests that God's love and promise in the end will overwhelm Israel's disobedience, leading to Israel returning from punishment (4:31; 30:5). And yet, the curses remain part of the story.

THE TEXT IN THE LIFE OF THE CHURCH

Secret Sins

The church often uses slogans, or sayings, to teach theology. Even when such mottos have a biblical basis, they may simultaneously point to a truth and yet be deceptive. Consider the warning "Be sure your sin will find you out" (Num 32:23). On the one hand, experience confirms the truth of the claim: countless people have been surprised when their underhanded actions they expected never to become public do become public. "Watch out!" the saying shouts.

Yet on the other hand, we also know that countless others succeed in keeping their nefarious deeds hidden from their communities. The curses of Deuteronomy 27, not really curses but prohibitions in curse format, all deal with actions that can happen in secret, deeds that might never be caught. They identify some sins of sexual immorality but also those of greed and disregard of the weak. The curses thus call on God to exact judgment on such actions. The curses of chapter 28 imply that this judgment from God will have serious impact on the people: wherever they go, whatever they do, they will be frustrated as their efforts come to naught and doom overwhelms them. But what if this does not happen?

One response of the New Testament is to speak of all secrets being revealed eventually, perhaps after death (e.g., Luke 12:2) when the injustices of life on earth will be rectified. Jesus thus concludes the beatitudes with the promise, "Rejoice and be glad, for your reward is great in heaven" (Matt 5:12). The references to the Son of Man coming in glory to judge the nations, separating them into sheep and goats, fits in here as well (Matt 25:31-46).

In some times and communities the church emphasizes the heavenly righting of earthly wrongs so much that the truth of a passage like this is largely overwhelmed. The way we live does impact our future and that of those around us. Selfishness, alcohol, lust, violence, drugs, greed, gluttony—all can undermine a fulfilled and productive life. The curses and blessings of Deuteronomy 27 and 28 may motivate and reflect truth even if they are not a formula that inevitably produces the desired results. God is God, and with that affirmation comes mystery and uncertainty.

Part 3

Third Speech: The Covenant in Moab

Deuteronomy 29:1–30:20
Making a Covenant

PREVIEW

In the first two speeches, Moses expounds and preaches torah (1:1, 5; 4:44), God's instruction for Israel. The third speech (chs. 29–30), although still sermonic in style, now places this preaching within a particular understanding of the relationship between God and Israel.

The key term in Deuteronomy for this relationship is "covenant." Put most simply, a covenant is an agreement or understanding between two parties. There is good evidence that ancient political treaties influenced Deuteronomy's approach to covenant, serving as a useful metaphor for God's relationship with Israel [*Deuteronomy, Covenant, and Political Treaties, p. 547*]. This influence was evident in the blessings and curses of chapters 27–28 but is even more noticeable in chapters 29–30.

Ancient Political Treaty Elements	Deuteronomy
Identification of treaty parties	29:10-15
Historical review	29:2-8; cf. chs. 1–3; 5:6
Exclusive loyalty requirement	29:17-18, 26; cf. 5:7-10; 6:4-5
Specific stipulations	chs. 12–26
Blessings and curses	29:19–30:10; cf. 11:29-30; 27:15–28:68
Listing of witnesses	30:19; cf. 31:26, 28
Required reading of treaty	31:9-13; cf. 27:1-10
Reference to storing of treaty document	31:25-26; cf. 27:4-8; cf. 10:1-5

Through this covenant, Israel becomes the people of God, and the LORD becomes the God of Israel (29:12-13; cf. 26:16-19). God's actions in leading Israel out of Egypt and giving it the Promised Land serve as the foundation of the covenant (29:2-8). Israel's responsibility in the relationship is to give the God of the exodus exclusive loyalty (29:18; cf. 5:7-10; 6:4-5; etc.), and to live in a manner modeled after the way of that God (chs. 12-26; cf. 10:17-19). If Israel ignores its side of the covenant relationship, its fate is doom (29:19-29; cf. 27:15-26; 28:15-68); but if Israel is obedient, the blessings it has already received through the gift of the land will continue (cf. 28:1-14). The covenant renewal of these chapters thus gives a home to Moses' preaching.

OUTLINE FOR PART 3

Introduction, 29:1
A Historical Basis, 29:2-9
Entering the Covenant, 29:10-15
Words of Doom, 29:16-29
    29:16-21   For the Individual
    29:22-29   For the Community
A Word of Salvation, 30:1-10
The Near Word, 30:11-14
A Final Appeal, 30:15-20

EXPLANATORY NOTES

Introduction 29:1

The opening verse of chapter 29 serves equally as a fitting conclusion to the material that preceded it (in Hebrew it is the last verse of ch. 28), and as an introduction to chapters 29-30. The phrase *the words of the covenant* point back to all that has preceded it in the book of Deuteronomy: the historical retrospect and prospect of the opening chapters (chs. 1-4), the focus on the Decalogue and the Horeb covenant (ch. 5), the preaching on the foundational commandment (chs. 6-11), the preaching of the Moab covenant (chs. 12-26), and the concluding blessings and curses (chs. 27-28). This verse together with the introductory verses of the book (1:1-5) form a frame for the preaching in between.

Yet it also looks forward as one of a series of verses in Deuteronomy that open the three major speeches of the book (cf. 1:1-5; 4:44-48). Here it introduces the part of Deuteronomy most strongly influenced by the ancient political treaty structure. The term *covenant* occurs twice in the opening verse, replacing the focus on torah of the previous two speech introductions (1:5; 4:44), and then five more times in the remainder of the chapter (vv. 9, 12, 14, 21, 25), highlighting the emphasis of this third speech.

Perhaps most striking is the way it identifies the Horeb and Moab covenants. Previously Deuteronomy has used the term "covenant" for God's promises to the ancestors (4:31; 7:12; 8:18) and the Horeb theophany (4:13, 23; 5:2, 3; 9:9, 11, 15). Although the reference to the mutual agreement at the end of chapter 26 has clear covenantal implications (26:16-19), and the listing of blessings and curses show treaty influence (27:15-28:68), this is the first time *covenant* is used for the event taking place in Moab, on the border of the Promised Land. The Horeb covenant remains foundational, but Deuteronomy envisions another covenant associated with Moab, one that includes the Horeb covenant but expands it significantly since in Deuteronomy only the Decalogue is associated with Horeb. Moses' expounding on the law is all part of this Moab covenant.

A Historical Basis 29:2-9

As in the second speech, the introductory *These are the words . . .* is followed by a narrative notice that Moses *summoned all Israel, and said to them* (cf. 5:1, *Moses convened all Israel, and said to them*). The words that follow, then, are a brief historical survey of what God has done for Israel. Israel's covenant does not begin with law or stipulations but with God's acts of deliverance. This order is also reflected in the historical review of the opening chapters (chs. 1-3), in the presentation of the Decalogue with its opening *I am the LORD your God, who brought you out of the land of Egypt, out of the house of bondage* (5:6), and in the preaching itself, with its numerous references back to God's mighty acts. This same sequence is now represented in the account of the covenant.

The survey focuses on three main events: (1) the escape from Egypt (29:2b-3); (2) the period of wandering in the wilderness (vv. 5-6); and (3) the defeat of Kings Sihon and Og in the Transjordan, a foretaste of the gift of the Promised Land (vv. 7-8). Each of these are well-known themes in Deuteronomy. References to God's deliverance of Israel from Egypt, the most important of the three, pervade the whole book, consistently providing background to the preaching and motivation for obedience (1:27, 30; 4:20, 34, 37, 45, 46; 5:6, 15; 6:12, 21, 22; 7:8, 18-19; 8:14; 9:7, 12, 26, 29; 11:3, 10; 13:5, 10; 15:15; 16:1, 3, 6, 12; 20:1; 23:4; 24:9, 18, 22; 25:17; 26:8; 29:25; 34:11). The period in the wilderness is treated both as a time of miraculous care, with God providing manna and water for Israel (the probable meaning of the clauses *You have not eaten bread, and you have not drunk strong drink*; 29:6; cf. 8:3) and even taking care of their clothes (29:5; cf. 8:4), and as a time of testing and discipline (29:6; cf. 8:2-5). The defeat of Kings Sihon and Og is described in detail earlier in the book (2:24–3:17), and then mentioned again in the important chapter 4 (4:46-47). The survey is brief, but it makes the point: covenant stipulations are not the beginning of the story but a framework for response to God *after* God has delivered them from slavery, provided for them in the wilderness, and started to give them the Promised Land.

Two key phrases in the survey are *You have seen all that the LORD did before your eyes* (29:2; cf. 1:30; 3:21; 4:9, 34; 6:22; 7:19; 10:21; 11:7), and *so that you may know that I am the LORD your God* (19:6). The term "remember" is not used here, but the Deuteronomic concern that only as Israel remembers what God has done will Israel be able to know and respond (cf. 4:9, 23; 5:15; 6:12; 7:18; 8:2, 11, 14, 18, 19; 9:7; 15:15; 16:12; 24:9, 18, 22; 25:17; 32:7), to *diligently observe the words of this covenant* (29:9). The invitation is reminiscent of the opening to the second speech (5:1-5), as well as repeated later (4:6; 6:3, 25; 7:11; 11:22, 32; 12:1, 32; 16:12; 19:9; 31:12; 32:46), including the important short passage summarizing the covenant as a mutual agreement (26:16-19). Seeing and remembering are keys to knowing and obeying.

With this persistent Deuteronomic reasoning in the background, the statement of 29:4 becomes ambiguous or puzzling. The verse recognizes that not all seeing is really seeing or understanding. More than that, it suggests that in order to really see and understand, to hear and obey, requires an action of God. But how does this pronouncement fit into the larger rationale of the passage? Is the verse suggesting that even now, on the plains of Moab, Israel still does not understand? This appears to be the meaning implied by the NRSV and NIV, and certainly is the meaning of the NABRE: *But the LORD has not given you a heart to understand, or eyes to see, or ears to hear until this day* (29:3). If so, then this verse may be setting the stage for the time when God will *circumcise* their *heart* so that they truly will *love the LORD your God with all your heart and all your soul* (30:6). Or is the verse suggesting that previously Israel has not understood, as reflected in its fearful response to the report of the spies when it has arrived at the land the first time (1:22-45), but now it does, or at least can understand? Tigay suggests that the verse should be translated: *But the LORD did not give you a mind to understand . . . until today* (275). Similarly, Nelson proposes that the larger logic of Deuteronomy, and of this passage, demands that we interpret these verses to mean that now Israel is indeed able to understand. Now that Moses has promulgated the law and encouraged obedience to it, the implications of older memories can finally be grasped. Israel's past inadequacies are behind it; now it can obey the covenant. (2002: 340)

The interpretation of Tigay and Nelson does appear to better fit the paragraph within which the statement is made. And yet taking the verse as simply saying that although previously God has not given Israel a *mind to understand*, now through the teaching of Moses, God *has* given such ability—that understanding also is inadequate and makes the promise that God will circumcise their hearts unnecessary. As theologians and interpreters have recognized, the relationship between the human decision to obey and the divine gift of obedience is complex and difficult to describe. To place too much emphasis on the human ability to obey does not sufficiently recognize the nature of the human spirit, or that obedience is ultimately a gift. To place too much emphasis on obedience as a gift of God can lead to exonerating rebellion: after all, it is not the people's fault but God's fault for not giving the *mind to understand, or eyes to see, or ears to hear*, we might say.

Tigay quotes a rabbinic saying: "When a person seeks to purify himself, he receives help in doing so" (276, citing Babylonian Talmud, *Shabbat* 104a). In a similar vein, Hall adds, "The solution to this problem is that God grants insight in conjunction with the seeking heart but he withholds it from the nonseeking heart" (433). This may be true, but it is doubtful that even this language sufficiently recognizes the inherent tension between:

- the unrelenting invitation of Deuteronomy to obey, with the apparent implication that the people are able to respond positively to the challenge (cf. 30:11-14), and

- the significance of a verse like this one combined with the later promise to circumcise the people's hearts.

The paradox is one that Scripture consistently affirms (cf. Matt 25:29 par.; John 7:17).

Entering the Covenant 29:10-15

The structure and language of the passage suggests a formal ceremony. The people have been *summoned* (29:2) and now *stand assembled today . . . before the* LORD *your God* (v. 10). Only here does

Deuteronomy speak of the people listening to Moses preach as standing before God, both at the beginning and at the end of the passage framing the central core (vv. 10, 14; cf. the people standing before God at Horeb, 4:10). At the center of the passage is the covenant formula. Through the Moab covenant, God will establish Israel as *his people*, and God will become *your God* (29:13). The promises made to the ancestors will be fulfilled (v. 13; cf. Gen 17:7; Exod 6:7; Ezek 36:28), and the mutual agreement of Deuteronomy 26:16-19 is formalized.

The language here, however, is not as symmetrical as that of the earlier formulation (cf. 26:17-18). On one side, Israel will *enter into the covenant* (29:12). Deuteronomy commonly uses the term translated *enter* of Israel crossing over the Jordan to enter into the Promised Land (e.g., *When you cross over the Jordan and live in the land that the* LORD *your God is allotting to you,* 12:10; cf. 3:25, 28; 4:14, 21, 22, 26; 6:1; 9:1; 11:8, 11, 31; 27:2, 3, 4). Parallel to entering the land, Israel is entering the covenant.

The covenant that Israel enters, however, is one *which the* LORD *your God is making* (v. 12): God is the primary actor. Both in this verse and in verse 14, the Hebrew term translated *making* is the simple verb commonly translated "to cut." Both verbs, "to cross over" and "to cut," possibly reflect an ancient covenant ritual in which the covenant partners walk between parts of slaughtered animals with the implication that if they do not keep their side of the covenant, a similar fate will await them. See Jeremiah 34:18: *Those who transgressed my covenant and did not keep the terms of the covenant that they made with me, I will make like the calf when they cut it in two and passed between its parts* (cf. Gen 15:9-10, 17). The two references to the covenant *sworn by an oath* may very well refer to such an understanding (Deut 29:12, 14).

The Moab covenant includes everyone present, and is perennially contemporary, both important themes in Deuteronomy. Twelve different phrases, matching the tribes of Israel and representing completeness, are used to incorporate everyone into the covenant (cf. P. Miller 1990: 209):

- *all of you* (v. 10)

- *the leaders of your tribes* (v. 10)

- *your elders* (v. 10)

- *your officials* (v. 10)

- *all the men of Israel* (v. 10)
- *your children* (v. 11)
- *your women* (v. 11)
- *the aliens who are in your camp* (v. 11)
- *those who cut wood* (v. 11)
- *those who draw water* (v. 11)
- *you who stand here with us today before the* LORD *your God* (v. 14)
- *those who not here with us today* (v. 15)

The piling up of these phrases has a powerful effect, emphasizing that all are invited to enter the covenant and all fall under its sanctions.

Most striking is the inclusion of the alien. If, as is likely, the references to those who *cut wood* and *draw water* has in mind the Gibeonites, who were forced to become "hewers of wood and drawers of water" (Josh 9:21), then three of the twelve references are to outsiders. Previously Deuteronomy includes the alien in worship (5:14; 26:11), requires that the alien be given equal treatment under the law (1:16; 24:17), and provides generously for the alien as one of the disadvantaged groups within Israel (14:29; 24:14, 19, 20, 21; 26:12-13), but this now is a significant step further. Since it is by the covenant that the people become the people of God (v. 13), the alien here ceases to be an outsider and now becomes an insider. Through the symbolism of the number twelve, the alien becomes part of the tribes.

Not only does the covenant include everyone *assembled today* (29:10), but *also those who are not here with us today* (v. 15). This may be a reference to people who are not able to gather in the assembly and as such is one of the phrases that emphasize the inclusiveness of the covenant, but it certainly is more than that as well. Just as earlier Deuteronomy speaks of the Horeb covenant as one made not only with the previous generation (*Not with our ancestors did the* LORD *make this covenant, but with us, who are all of us here alive today,* 5:3) but also with those gathered there on that day, so the Moab covenant is always contemporary, always made with the people alive *today,* a term occurring five times within these few verses (vv. 10, 12, 13, 14, 15).

Words of Doom 29:16-29

Entering the covenant not only makes Israel the people of God, and Yahweh the God of Israel (v. 13; cf. 26:16-19), but also places upon Israel the obligation of obedience to the stipulations of the covenant, with serious consequences if it fails to follow through on this commitment. The commitment is stated explicitly in the mutual-agreement passage at the end of chapter 26 (Israel has agreed *to walk in his ways, to keep his statutes, his commandments, and his ordinances, and to obey him*, 26:17); it is implied by the listing of blessings and curses (27:15–28:68), as well as by the *oath*, or "curse," of the covenant (29:12, 14); and it may be reflected in the covenant ritual itself by having the people walk between the severed parts of an animal. Entering a covenant must not be taken lightly: curses enforce its obedience. The curses that follow (29:16-29) as well as the blessings (30:1-10) presume this obligation. Their form is more that of announcement than the traditional conditional format of blessings and curses (if you obey, . . . blessings will come—as in 28:1, 13; if you disobey, . . . curses will come—as in 28:15, 58).

29:16-21 For the Individual

Israel enters the covenant as a whole community, but each individual is implicated by this corporate action. The first word of doom focuses on the individual and the individual's responsibility for obedience (cf. 24:16). Unfortunately, this focus is largely lost in the NRSV, as it changes so many of the pronouns from the singular to the plural in order to be inclusive.

The passage begins by speaking to the people as a whole: *You* [pl.] *know . . .* (29:16). The background to the warning is the land of slavery, Egypt, where the people have experienced the worship of idols and other gods. Previously Deuteronomy associates idols and the worship of other gods exclusively with the worship of the gods of the Canaanites and the other former inhabitants of the land, but now idolatry is traced to the land of Egypt. The terms translated *detestable things* and *filthy idols* (29:17; Christensen suggests translating as "idol turds" to emphasize the repugnant nature of what they experienced [2002: 719]) are not used anywhere else in Deuteronomy (both are common in Ezekiel, the prophet of the exile, who presents thirty-nine of the forty-eight occurrences of "filthy idols" in the whole OT). The primary sin continues to be transgression against the first and foundational commandment by *turning away from the* LORD *our God to serve the gods of those nations* (v. 18).

After stating that the people as a whole have been confronted by the possibility of worshiping other gods, the text turns to the individual: *It may be that there is among you a man or a woman . . .* (v. 18). The phrase continues by including a *family or tribe*, but then concentrates on the individual person. This is more apparent in versions that retain the singular pronouns (e.g., NIV, *When such a person hears the words of this oath and they invoke a blessing on themselves, thinking, "I will be safe, even though I persist in going my own way,"* v. 19; similarly in RSV, NABRE, etc.)

The passage appears to envision a situation in which a person publicly participates in the covenant ceremony, but under false pretenses, with the assumption that he or she will escape: verse 18 specifies *man or woman*. On what grounds the person expects to escape is not given, perhaps simply by participating in the larger community worship of God even while practicing a private and secret worship of other gods. But this will not work. Such participation in the covenant ceremony is a fraud, already a *root sprouting poisonous and bitter growth*. God will *single* that faker *out* for punishment, *in accordance with the curses of the covenant written in this book of the law* (v. 21).

Twice the passage refers to the curses and speaks about them as written in a book (vv. 20, 21). Deuteronomy is now treated as a book with an authoritative and powerful word (cf. 2 Kings 22:16-17). The meaning of the phrase translated *thus bringing disaster on moist and dry alike* is unclear, perhaps having the connotation that the person's actions will have disastrous effect on all (Deut 29:19). But the end result is unchanged: the covenant curses will fall upon that rebellious person. Some suggest that the reference to God's unwillingness to *pardon* is an indication that the person does not repent of his or her actions (v. 20; e.g., C. Wright 1996: 288). The punishment of blotting out a people's or person's name is previously used of non-Israelites (7:24; 12:3; 25:19), and on one occasion for the people as a whole after their sin of building a golden calf at Mount Horeb (9:14).

29:22-29 For the Community

The second word of doom begins abruptly, moving into the distant future, when a future generation has experienced *the devastation of that land, and the affliction with which the* LORD *has afflicted it*. This is not a curse or a warning but an assessment that that the curse of 28:58-68 has come about (29:27; cf. 2 Kings 22:16-17): God has devastated the land (Deut 29:22), *uprooted* the people *from their land*, and *cast them into another land,* <u>as is now the case</u> (v. 28, emph. added). The word of doom to the individual views the pretender from the standpoint of Moses addressing the people in Moab, anticipating apostasy of individuals within Israel; but the word of doom to the community has the perspective of someone in exile, looking back at what has happened.

Although the paragraph assumes a very different situation from the previous one, its logic is identical. The people have *abandoned the covenant of their ancestors*, here referring not to Abraham, Isaac, and Jacob but to those who have entered the covenant at Horeb and Moab (v. 25). The representative or paradigmatic sin is idolatry, transgression against the foundational commandment: they have *turned and served other gods* (v. 26; cf. v. 18). As result, the *anger of the LORD was kindled against that land*, bringing upon it *every curse written in this book* (v. 27; cf. vv. 20-21). The anger of God receives greater attention in these two paragraphs than anywhere else in Deuteronomy. After declaring that God's *wrath and zeal will burn against them* (v. 20 NIV) in the first paragraph, the second expands this with four further references to God's *anger* (vv. 23, 24, 27, 28; here in vv. 16-19 are five of Deuteronomy's thirteen uses of this term) and warns of God's *fury and great wrath* (v. 28). It is the "fundamental breach of covenant," the betrayal of the mutual agreement (26:16-19) that Israel has solemnly sworn to accept that precipitates this heightened sense of passion (McConville 2002: 418). God's anger in Deuteronomy thus is directed at Israel, the same people God has loved and chosen as *his treasured possession* (e.g., 7:6).

Yet the passage speaks more of the land than of the people (*land* is mentioned six times in these eight verses). Although the paragraph concludes by stating that the people have been *uprooted* and exiled, it is the land that is devastated and afflicted (29:22), with its *soil burned out by sulphur and salt*. The land, *unable to support vegetation*, much less be a source of blessing for its inhabitants, is compared to *Sodom and Gomorrah* (v. 23). It is the land against which God's anger is kindled and against which the curses are brought (v. 27). In Deuteronomy the gift of a land of milk and honey is both evidence of God's election love and the source of blessing for the people. By transgressing the covenant, the people have forfeited that land and put their relationship with God and their very future in question.

This anger even causes the *foreigner who comes from a distant country* (v. 22), and *indeed all the nations* (v. 24) who witness this devastation, to ask, *Why has the LORD done this to this land?* (again, notice that the question is about the land). But the question is rhetorical because the answer is clear: Israel broke the covenant through idolatry and sparked God's anger. The technique of observing Israel through the eyes of the nations is reminiscent of chapter 4, where Israel's obedience of the *statutes and ordinances* would demonstrate to the nations its *wisdom and discernment,* causing them to remark, *Surely this great nation is a wise and discerning people!* (4:5-6). Again the nations learn about God through Israel, but now it is Israel's lack of obedience to the covenant, with its consequences for the land, that becomes the teaching moment. The devastation of the land, the exile of the people, set against the backdrop of the nations—all hint at the unspoken question whether this is the end for Israel, whether God's act of choosing Israel *out of all the peoples on earth* has been a mistake and whether God now will make a make a people for himself from someone else (7:6; 14:2; cf. 9:14).

The maxim or proverb that closes the chapter is enigmatic (29:29). It may be distinguishing between hidden sins known only to God and more public ones over which the community has responsibility. God is responsible for punishing the secret sins, as implied by verses 16-21 as well as by the curses of 27:15-26, and will not destroy the larger people because of private actions of individuals. The rabbinic saying "All Israelites are sureties for one another" means that "the entire community is held accountable for the conduct of its individual members unless it restrains or punishes the sinners" (Tigay: 283, citing Babylonian Talmud, *Shevuʿot* 39a). Or it may be distinguishing between what God has revealed to Israel—in the context of Deuteronomy, especially God's instructions for life—and what God has chosen not to reveal, perhaps the course of the future. The immediately preceding verse, with its locating of Israel in *another land* due to the *anger, fury, and great wrath* of God, *as is now the case,* inevitably raises questions about Israel's future. In light of this, the second option may fit better. It then sets the stage for the next chapter that, on the one hand, emphasizes the clarity of God's direction for Israel (30:11-14) and, on the other, addresses the implicit questions of this chapter (30:1-10).

A Word of Salvation 30:1-10

As in the previous paragraph, the people are in exile, having experienced both the blessings that life in the Promised Land has provided and the curses that have resulted in their expulsion from the land: they are living *among the nations where the* LORD *your God has driven you* (v. 1; cf. 29:28). But here the tone is dramatically different. Whereas the previous paragraph looked backward from exile and highlighted the passionate anger of God in response to Israel having *abandoned the covenant* (29:25), with the result that the land was devastated and the people cast out, this paragraph changes direction and looks into the future. The implicit question of 29:28—does Israel indeed have a future now that the curses have been implemented and Israel is *in another land?*—is answered with a resounding yes!

That future has two sides to it. One side is Israel taking the *blessings and curses* to heart (*call them to mind*, 30:1), returning to God by obeying God with *heart* and *soul* (v. 2; cf. the Shema, Deut 6:4-5). The phrase *blessings and curses* does not have a narrow meaning but refers to the covenant as a whole, and indeed the whole story of God and Israel (30:1). Responding to this story as summarized in Israel's faith statements (e.g., 6:20-25; 26:5-10) means doing what God has commanded. The other side is God's action: God will *restore your fortunes, have compassion on you, gather you*, and *bring you into the land that your ancestors possessed* (30:3-5). Just as the curses threatened the reversal of the gift of the land, this announcement now promises a new action of God that will reverse the curses. This is not simply blessing but a new *salvation* (cf. 32:15).

What is less clear is the relationship between these two sides. The NRSV opens the passage with *when*, but then places an *if* preceding the second clause, referring to Israel calling these things to mind (30:1); it puts an *and* preceding the third and fourth clauses (v. 2), which speak of Israel returning to the Lord and obeying what God has commanded. All of these clauses thus become governed by the first *if*, thereby making God's actions of verses 3-5 conditional upon Israel first having returned to God. With this reading, the passage then serves as a call to Israel in exile to turn to God and obey once more. As Walter Brueggemann puts it, "The future is a gift from YHWH, but it is a gift given only when Israel is in an obedient posture. YHWH's gift of the future will not be wasted on the unreceptive" (2001: 267; cf. vv. 1-3 NJB, *when, if, if, if, then*). Supporting such a reading is the unrelenting Deuteronomic challenge to obey God's directions given in the book, instruction that *is not too hard for you, nor is it too far away* (30:11).

But this is not the only possible reading. The NIV opens the passage with a *when*, just as the NRSV does, but then uses *and* before the second, third, and fourth clauses, thereby placing all of them within the temporal framework of the opening term. God's actions remain inseparably bound up with Israel's—when Israel does this, God will do thus—but the relationship between the two sets of actions is not a simple conditional one. So the text is not saying that *if* Israel returns God will act, but rather *when* Israel returns—the unstated implication is that Israel will return—*then* God will act. "The whole passage is building up a picture of a balanced set of conditions in which Israel returns to God, *and* God delivers them once more" (McConville 2002: 426). Again, various translations and interpreters support this reading (e.g., KJV, RSV; Tigay: 284). Grammatical analysis is not able to solve this question since both options are possible. The very ambiguity may be intended. Placing too much emphasis on the conditional nature of God's action makes the relationship one driven by human response, thus producing a human-centered relationship. Placing too much emphasis on God's initiative minimizes the need to respond and obey, which Deuteronomy consistently emphasizes.

Although the relationship between Israel's actions and God's may not be clear, the text highlights that both represent a "turning," with a form of this verb used seven times in the passage, producing a chiastic structure (adapted from Nelson 2002: 347):

A¹ **Israel** calls to mind, and repents
  call to mind (lit., *return to mind or heart*) (v. 1)
  and *return* to the LORD your God (v. 2)
   B¹ **God** restores fortunes and gathers together
     LORD your God will *restore* your fortunes (v. 3a)
     gathering you *again* (lit., *turn and gather*) (v. 3b)
       C **Israel** shall return to obey
         you shall *again* obey (lit., *you shall turn and obey*) (v. 8)
   B² **God** prospers Israel
     LORD your God will *again* take delight in prospering you (lit., *turn to take delight*) (v. 9)
A² **Israel** will return to God
  you *turn* to the LORD your God (v. 10)

In the passage Deuteronomy announces a turning, a turning that includes both covenant partners. Exile is not the end; God continues to act, will restore Israel's fortunes, and will bring it back to the land. But simultaneously Israel has the obligation to return to God. Both sides reflect dramatic reversals. The word includes both challenge and promise.

At the center of the passage is a dramatic promise: *The LORD your God will circumcise your heart and the heart of your descendants, so that you will love the LORD your God with all your heart and with all your soul, in order that you may live* (v. 6). This is the second time Deuteronomy uses the image of circumcising the heart. Earlier Deuteronomy has called on Israel to *circumcise, then, the foreskin of your heart, and do not be stubborn any longer* (10:16). The content of the image remains the same: circumcising the heart signifies an inner change that makes obedience natural or second nature. But the way the image is used is changed dramatically. Now Deuteronomy announces that *God* will act in changing Israel's innermost being so that Israel will respond to God in total love, in a manner like that required by the Shema (cf. 6:4-5).

Again it is risky to read from 30:1-10 a clear sequence, or to state in a simple way which is to come first, God's circumcision of the people's hearts or their turning to God. Richard Nelson, for example, sees five stages in the passage (2002: 348):

1. Israel will call to mind the blessings and the curses.

2. Israel initiates a return to God through renewed obedience.

3. God restores Israel's fortunes and returns it to the land.

4. God circumcises Israel's heart so that obedience becomes second nature.

5. The curses are transferred to Israel's enemies.

The text speaks of these actions in this order, but to conclude that this is the chronological order required is going too far. Clearly Israel needs to respond to its situation by returning to God and obeying with its total being (vv. 2, 8, 10). At the same time, the text promises that God will change the center of the people's being, their very heart, so that Israel will love God as required (three times in these verses the response to God is characterized as coming from *with all your heart and with all your soul*, including the final verse; vv. 2, 6, 10). Here Deuteronomy is addressing the same question the prophets of the exile face as they struggle with how to speak after the covenant has been broken.

The passage concludes by emphasizing the reversal of Israel's fortunes (vv. 7-10). The reference to God placing the *curses on your enemies* (v. 7) does not receive much attention but completes this reversal of fortunes. The peoples who have been used by God to punish Israel have taken advantage of Israel and thus also deserve the curses. The prosperity Israel will experience is reminiscent of the covenant blessings pronounced earlier (v. 9; cf. 28:4, *Blessed shall be the fruit of your womb, the fruit of your ground, and the fruit of your livestock*). Israel's obedience to the *commandments and the decrees* (30:10; cf. v. 8) is also part of this reversal, perhaps the most important part.

The Near Word 30:11-14

After two passages that envision Israel in exile (29:22-29; 30:1-10), we return to the plains of Moab and Moses speaking. With dramatic flourish, the paragraph emphasizes that the *commandment* (in the singular, but referring to the total teaching of Deuteronomy) *is not too hard for you, nor is it too far away* (30:11). The style, with the rhetorical questions and the creation-wide stage, is reminiscent of 4:5-8, where the nations marveled at Israel's discerning nature and the nearness of its God. Now the focus is the accessibility of Israel's law as preached in Deuteronomy, and as affirmed in the covenant ceremony (*in your mouth*, 30:14).

"The argument is that the law is not beyond human capacity to understand nor is it undisclosed and remote. This is a user-friendly law, easy to grasp and freely available. The essential point is simply to 'do it' (the last words of vv. 12, 13, 14)" (Nelson 2002: 349). The law is neither too complex or complicated for people to understand nor too demanding or ideal that obedience is not possible. Obedience is realistic (30:1-10), and choosing life is not some unachievable pipedream (30:15-20). Here is a word of encouragement.

A Final Appeal 30:15-20

The third speech concludes by presenting the choice before Israel in the starkest manner possible: *life and prosperity* on the one side, *death and adversity* on the other. These opposite alternatives dominate the passage, both in language and structure. This short passage includes eight references to *life* or *living* (the noun *life* occurs four times, in vv. 15, 19 [two times], 20; the verb *live* two times, vv. 16, 19; and twice there is the phrase translated *live long*, vv. 18, 20), and three references to *death* and or *perishing* (15, 18, 19). Three times it presents the options of life and death. Two brief statements of the choice (vv. 15, 19) frame the longer form, expanded both in terms of what it means to choose to obey or not to obey, and in terms of the consequences of the choice (vv. 16-18). The Israel faced with this choice is the Israel of *today*, whenever that today may be (v. 15).

The appeal to *heaven and earth to witness against* Israel is an unusual adaptation of the ancient political treaty format. Normally ancient treaties include as witnesses the gods of the treaty partners. This, of course, is impossible for Deuteronomy, given its strident rejection of all other gods. Heaven and earth thus substitute for the gods, allowing Deuteronomy to have witnesses for the covenant without recognizing the existence of the other gods (cf. 31:19, 26; 32:46).

Deuteronomy may present Israel with two options, but they definitely are not equal options. After presenting them for the third time, Deuteronomy pleads with Israel: *Choose life so that you and your descendants may live!* After the plea the appeal comes to a close with rhetorical flourish, employing stereotypical Deuteronomic phrases and themes. A positive response implies *loving the* LORD *your God* (cf. 6:5; 10:12; 11:1, 13, 22), *obeying him* (cf. 4:1, 6, 30; 5:1; 7:12; 11:13, 27, 28; 13:4, 18; 15:5; 26:14, 17; 28:2, 13, 15, 45; 30:2, 10), and *holding fast to him* (cf. 4:4; 10:20; 11:22; 13:4). A positive response will result in *life, . . . length of days, . . . in the land that the* LORD *swore to give to your ancestors* (30:20). The passage and speech thus closes with a final reference to the gift of land and the promises to the ancestors. Despite the emphases on curses in these final chapters, and despite the fact that the choice before Israel is between life and death, the closing words speak of life and promise. The promises made to the ancestors may have been fulfilled when Israel entered the land under Joshua, but that does not exhaust their life-giving force. They continue to hold promise for those much-later descendants of the Israel gathered in Moab, the descendants who have experienced the blessings and the curses, the destruction of the land and exile (29:22-29; 30:1). It is a promise to which those descendants need to respond *today*, but the power of God's promise remains.

Chapters 29–30 as Part of a Frame

Chapters 29–30 have numerous points of contact with chapter 4. Both consider Israel's relation to God from the perspective of exile (4:25-31; 29:22–30:10). Both refer to future children. Both include reference to worshiping other gods and thereby provoking God's anger, with the result that God scatters Israel among the peoples (4:27) or casts *them into another land, as is now the case* (29:28). In both passages, this is followed by the people returning to God, with God reassuring the people that he will not abandon them (4:31). Additionally, there is significant overlap in language and motifs. For example, both include a reference to the covenant with the ancestors (4:31; 30:20); both speak of the nearness of the God who gave the law, or the law itself (4:7; 30:11-14); and both emphasize Israel having seen God's actions with its own eyes (4:9, 34; 29:2-3).

Chapters 4 and 29-30 thus bracket the second speech of Deuteronomy (chs. 5-28), placing the teaching of Deuteronomy within a framework of exile, yet with hope for the future. In exile the people will turn to God, who will respond and will both restore Israel and change its very heart so that it will obey what God has commanded.

Chapters 29-30 also includes numerous echoes of 10:12-11:32, the summary-like challenge immediately before the regulations of chapters 12-26. Perhaps most striking, both present the choice facing Israel as polar opposites: *See, I am setting before you today a blessing and a curse* (11:26; cf. 11:29). *See, I have set before you today life and prosperity, death and adversity* (30:15; cf. 30:19). Yet there are other connections: both use the image of the circumcision of the heart (10:16; 30:6); both call on Israel to obey so that its descendants may live long in the land (11:8-9; 30:20); and both use similar vocabulary for what is required of Israel, to respond to God with *heart and soul* (10:12; 11:13; 30:2, 6, 10), to *love* God (10:12; 11:1, 13, 22; 30:6, 16, 20), to *obey* God (11:13, 27; 30:2, 8, 10, 16), and to *hold fast* to him (10:20; 11:22; 30:20). Along with chapters 10-11, chapters 29-30 thus also frame the central legal-like material of Deuteronomy.

THE TEXT IN BIBLICAL CONTEXT

Seeing and Seeing, Hearing and Hearing

Luke tells the story of two disciples walking from Jerusalem to Emmaus shortly after the crucifixion, expressing their disappointment to a stranger that the Jesus they had followed had not redeemed Israel. The unrecognized Jesus responds, "Oh, how foolish you are, and how slow of heart to believe all that the prophets have declared" (Luke 24:25). He then goes on to interpret "Moses and all the prophets," their Scripture, as all fulfilled in his story. They have heard and asked questions and observed, and still they have not understood.

That the God of Israel and Jesus is difficult to grasp is a theme common in Scripture. Deuteronomy projects that surrounding nations will see in Israel *a wise and discerning people,* a people with *a god so near, ... whenever we call to him* (4:6-7), but still admits that *to this day the* LORD *has not given you a mind to understand, or eyes to see, or ears to hear* (29:4). This, despite the frequent reminders that they have seen God at work in their deliverance from Egypt, in the theophany of Horeb, and in the capture of the Transjordan region. The call of Isaiah returns to this theme as it directs him to preach to the people,

"Keep listening, but do not comprehend; keep looking, but do not understand" (Isa 6:9).

This theme remains prominent in the preaching of Jesus. The Gospels depict Jesus as regularly using parables, stories that both reveal truth but also hide meaning. When Jesus' disciples ask him why he uses them, he responds that through them they receive the "secrets of the kingdom of heaven," but that for others it is a case of "seeing they do not perceive, and hearing they do not listen, nor do they understand," and then he goes on to quote the words from Isaiah (Matt 13:10-17, par.; cf. Mark 4:21-29). Private instruction may help the disciples understand ("But blessed are your eyes, for they see, and your ears, for they hear," Matt 13:16), but Mark notices that even the disciples are slow to grasp the truly alternative nature of Jesus message: "Then do you also fail to understand?" (Mark 7:18). When Jesus asks his disciples who they think he is, only Peter appears to understand; but after his Spirit-inspired confession, when Jesus begins to speak about how he must suffer and die, Peter reveals that even he has not comprehended, leading to Jesus' denunciation, "Get behind me, Satan! For you are setting your mind not on divine things but on human things" (Mark 8:33). The foolishness of the disciples on the road to Emmaus is nothing new; it is consistent with a pattern of misunderstanding.

Even the death, resurrection, and ascension of Jesus does not fully clarify issues. Intense debates in the early church about Jewish customs (e.g., circumcision, dietary regulations), reaching out to the Gentiles, and relationships within the new community reflect an ongoing challenge in understanding. The Ethiopian eunuch asks, "How can I [understand] unless someone guides me?" (Acts 8:31), but often people may think they understand (e.g., Peter) when they do not. Deuteronomy consistently warns against confusing the unique claims of the God of the exodus with the ways of the nations. Peter and the disciples were so much part of the world of their day that they had a hard time grasping the notion of a nonviolent Messiah. Whenever we think we understand, this reoccurring theme of Scripture warns us not to be too sure.

THE TEXT IN THE LIFE OF THE CHURCH

The Doable Law

Full understanding may be elusive, yet Deuteronomy assures us that obedience is doable: *This commandment ... is not too hard, nor is it too far away* (30:11). When we love God with all our heart, soul, and might (6:5); when we remember God's actions; when we assimilate God's torah through reading and practice—then obedience is not only doable, it can become second nature. Two stories reflect this reality.

Walter Brueggemann tells the story of a Christian community in France that protected Jews from the Nazis during the Second World War (2001: 270, drawing from a book by Philip Hallie, *Lest Innocent Blood Be Shed*):

> Among the remarkable features of that brave and faithful community was an inquiry after the war by a Jewish adult who was kept alive there as a child. When he interviewed his protectors about their reason for taking such risky actions on his behalf, they only shrugged their shoulders and indicated that it seemed obvious from their faith. They had no dramatic explanations or theological interpretations to offer him. It was rather a "habit" of neighborliness that was at the center of their embrace of the gospel; and it was enough!

The second story is more recent and perhaps even more astonishing. The world was stunned on October 2, 2006, when it learned of the bloodbath that had happened in a small Amish school not far from Lancaster, Pennsylvania: an intruder had shot ten young girls, killing five of them, and then committed suicide. And yet what amazed and dumbfounded those who followed the story even more was the Amish response to the tragedy.

"In the midst of their grief over the shocking loss, the Amish community didn't cast blame, they didn't point fingers, they didn't hold a press conference with attorneys at their sides. Instead, they reached out with grace and compassion toward their killer's family" (Lancaster County Information Center). They visited the killer's family in an effort to comfort them in their own sorrow and pain, and they expressed their forgiveness of the killer. At the killer's funeral, Amish mourners outnumbered others. In a world where justice is understood to include paying back what is deserved, where a desire for revenge is thought to be normal, the actions of these Amish were incomprehensible, if not naïve and irresponsible.

How could they forgive such a terrible, unprovoked act of violence? To this question the Amish tended to give an intuitive reaction: that's what it means to follow Christ, to love one's enemy. Daily recitation of the Lord's Prayer, with the words "Forgive us our debts, as we forgive our debtors" (Matt 6:12 KJV), is a way of absorbing God's torah, of helping make obedience doable, even when it seems impossible or illogical within the ethos of society.

Deuteronomy as Altar Call

See, I have set before you today life and prosperity, death and adversity. If you obey, . . . then you shall live. . . . But if your heart turns away, . . . you shall perish (30:15-18). Does that not sound a lot like the altar call of traditional evangelists, who threaten hell for all those who do not walk the sawdust trail? The contemporary church often struggles with this approach. Stuart Murray observes, "A key discovery of the Decade of Evangelism in the 1990s was that many people journey to faith gradually" (11). We live in a time of "process evangelism," where we debate the relationship of believing, belonging, and behaving.

This is an appropriate conversation. How does the call of Deuteronomy 30 enter the conversation? The Moses of Deuteronomy addresses the Israel of his *today*, and all future "todays," with the demand to make a decision. Similarly, Joshua challenges the Israel gathered at Shechem, "Choose this day whom you will serve" (Josh 24:15). Jesus speaks about the impossibility of serving two masters (Matt 6:24), he highlights the consequences of our choice of whom to serve with the parables of sheep and goats (25:31-46) and wheat and weeds (13:24-43), and he reminds us that the gate and road that leads to life is narrow (7:13-14).

For both Deuteronomy and Jesus, the response that leads to life is not merely words or belief but also service and obedience. For Deuteronomy, loving God means *walking in his ways, and observing his commandments* (Deut 30:16). Joshua speaks of serving God, and in Jesus' parable the sheep are separated from the goats on the basis of whether they fed the hungry, or gave water to the thirsty, or welcomed the stranger, or clothed the naked, or visited the sick or those in prison. But both for aliens entering the community (cf. Isa 56:3-8), and for those with long roots in the community, the response is a life-and-death choice.

Part 4

Transition: Toward a Moses-less People

Deuteronomy 31:1–34:12

OVERVIEW

Moses' exposition of torah consists of three major speeches (chs. 1–4, 5–28, 29–30). After formalizing the Moab covenant and giving a life-and-death charge (30:15-20), Deuteronomy begins the transition into the future. The opening chapters have already introduced that Moses will not accompany Israel into the Promised Land (1:34-40; 3:23-29; 4:21-22). Now Deuteronomy focuses on this reality as it prepares Israel for such a future without Moses, a Moses-less future. At the same time, these chapters serve as a transition from Deuteronomy to Joshua, from the Pentateuch to the rest of the Old Testament.

The plains of Moab remain the literary setting for these final chapters, with Moses still making speeches (at least in chs. 31–33), but the voice of the narrator gradually takes over as all is put into a narrative framework that speaks of Moses in the third person (31:1, 7, 9, etc.; cf. 1:1-5).

Preparation for a Moses-less future takes two forms. First, Joshua, a spy who did not lose faith in God when Israel arrived at the land the first time (Num 14:1-38), succeeds Moses as overall leader of the people. He is the one who will lead Israel into the Promised Land. Although introduced earlier (Deut 1:38; 3:28), now he is publicly proclaimed and commissioned for the task (31:7-8), with the commissioning confirmed by God (31:14-15, 23). He begins to function alongside Moses as a coleader as they together recite the Song of Moses to the people (32:44). When Moses dies, Joshua, *full of wisdom because Moses had laid his hands on him*, immediately steps into his role and the *Israelites obeyed him* (34:9). Even an unparalleled leader like Moses—*Never since has there arisen a prophet in Israel like Moses, whom the* LORD *knew face to face* (34:10)—does not remain with the people forever.

Second, the text deals with Moses' role as the one whom God has used to convey the torah to Israel. This role of Moses is not transferred to Joshua. The passing on of this role is less tidy and more diffuse, perhaps consistent with Moses' unparalleled prominence in preaching torah. God's commandments and regulations are recorded in a book that is stored next to the ark of the covenant, under the responsibility of the priests (31:9, 24-27), to be read regularly to all people, every seven years, at the Festival of Booths (31:10-13). Additionally, Moses prepares a song that is to be memorized and recited as a *witness against you today, . . . so that* [*your children*] *may diligently observe all the words of this law.* (32:1-43, 46). The book, including the Song, serves as a reminder and instrument of encouragement to the people to remain faithful to the torah God has taught through Moses. Moses thus leaves behind the torah of God, his song, and a blessing for the people (33:1-29). Life will never be the same once Moses is gone (e.g., 31:16-22), but these chapters highlight the measures God and Moses take to prepare the people for a Moses-less life in the land. And there is hope for the future: *The Israelites obeyed him* [*Joshua*], *doing as the* LORD *had commanded Moses* (34:9).

OUTLINE FOR PART 4

Preparation for Transition, 31:1-30
The Song of Moses, 32:1-52
The Blessing of Moses, 33:1-29
The Death of Moses, 34:1-12

Deuteronomy 31:1-30

Preparation for Transition

PREVIEW

The loss of a great leader inevitably leads to anxiety and doubt among the people. This is true when a longtime pastor leaves a congregation, when a respected institutional president passes away while in office, or when a strong business leader transitions out of the role. How much more is that the case when the leader is incomparable, without peer (as in 34:10-12). In the face of such doubts, chapter 31 affirms that on the macrolevel nothing will change: God will still lead the way and give Israel the land as promised, just as he has begun to do in the Transjordan. Israel need not fear since *it is the LORD your God who goes with you; he will not fail you or forsake you* (v. 6).

General words of assurance may be fine, but they require concrete content to persuade. This chapter introduces three ways in which God's ongoing presence will remain with them. First, Joshua will succeed Moses and have the specific assignment to *bring the Israelites into the land that I promised them* (v. 23). Second, the torah God has given Israel through Moses is to be recorded (vv. 9, 24), permanently safeguarded (vv. 25-26), and regularly read to the people (vv. 10-13). Third, Moses is to write a song (see ch. 32) that the people are to learn, memorize, and pass on to their children as a witness and reminder of their tendency to forsake God (vv. 16-22, 30). Through a series of intermingled speeches, the chapter unites these three into one whole, assuring Israel that God's presence will still be experienced after Moses is gone.

Both in style and in content, chapter 31 picks up where chapter 3 left off. Chapters 1-3 look backward from the plains of Moab and survey the period between Mount Horeb and Israel's second arrival at the Promised Land; now chapters 31-34 look forward from the plains of Moab to the time when Israel will be in the Promised Land, albeit without their matchless leader, Moses. Connecting these two sections is not only the continuous story (one can move directly from ch. 3 to ch. 31 without noticing that the large block between has been missed), but also the impending death of Moses and the commissioning of Joshua as his successor (1:34-40; 3:23-29; 31:7-8, 14-15; cf. 32:44-45; 34:9). Chapters 1-3 and 31-34 thus provide an outer frame for the main block of Deuteronomy.

OUTLINE

Moses to Israel: God Will Cross Over before You, 31:1-6
Moses to Joshua (before Israel): God Will Be with You, 31:7-8
Moses to Priests and Elders: Read the Law to Israel, 31:9-13
God to Moses: Prepare for Joshua's Commissioning, 31:14-15
God to Moses: Write This Song for Israel, 31:16-22
God to Joshua: I Will Be with You, 31:23
Moses to Levites: Place the Law, Assemble the People, 31:24-30

EXPLANATORY NOTES

Chapter 31 consists of seven short speeches, each introduced by a brief editorial comment identifying the speaker and audience, giving an initial impression of a carefully constructed whole. A closer examination, however, suggests a more complex origin. The speeches cover only three or so themes, which at points appear to interrupt each other (e.g., vv. 24-29 follow nicely after vv. 9-13; similarly, v. 23 would be a natural continuation of vv. 14-15), and there appears to be some tension between passages that are essentially pessimistic about the future (e.g., vv. 16-22) and others that have more hope (e.g., vv. 1-6, 14-15, 23). Yet despite the composite background, these speeches have been woven into a whole, with the central portion a chiastic structure, as argued by Norbert Lohfink (1990).

> A^1 Recording and reading *the law*, vv. 9-13
> B^1 Preparation for the *commissioning of Joshua*, vv. 14-15
>   C A rationale for the *Song of Moses*, vv. 16-22

B² The *commissioning of Joshua*, v. 23
A² Placing *this law* as a witness, vv. 24-27

Through this structure the law becomes "the framework for the appointment of Joshua and associates the Song with the law" (Nelson 2002: 357). The intermingled speeches of this chapter bind the commissioning of Joshua to the role of the law and the Song of Moses.

Moses to Israel: God Will Cross Over before You 31:1-6

The opening verse connects the chapters on transition with what has preceded, with the phrase *all these words* referring back to the appeal of chapters 29–30, as well as the rest of the Deuteronomic torah. Moses' age and imminent death become the stimulus for looking into the future. Although earlier it is suggested that Moses is prevented from entering the Promised Land because of the actions of the people (1:37; 3:26; 4:21), or even his own sin (32:50-51), here the only reason suggested is his age: he is *no longer able to get about* (31:2). Moses has achieved the maximum age allotted humans (cf. Gen 6:3), equivalent to three spans of forty, the number commonly used in the Bible for a generation (cf. 2:7) or an appropriate time of leadership (e.g., Eli, 1 Sam 4:18; David, 1 Kings 2:11).

Moses now prepares Israel for his death and the people's entrance into the Promised Land. The repeated use of *cross over* highlights the emphasis of the passage. Given the monumental role Moses has played, that he will *not cross over this Jordan* can only cause anxiety and alarm (Deut 31:3). But Moses encourages the people that they should not fear or be in dread (v. 6) because *the* LORD *God will cross over before you* (v. 3). Additionally, Joshua *also will cross over before you*. The leadership of Moses has been unparalleled (34:10-12), but God's presence with Israel will not cease when Moses dies. The opening paragraph sets the stage for the remainder of the chapter, especially the commissioning of Joshua. Although Joshua is mentioned, the focus does not yet move from Moses to Joshua, but first shifts from Moses to God. God has worked through Moses, and God will continue to work through people, but it is God who remains at the center as the principal actor.

This assurance is supported in typical Deuteronomic style with reference to God's previous actions on behalf of Israel. God's earlier defeat of the two Amorite kings (cf. 2:16–3:17) is a model for what will happen when Israel crosses the Jordan, with God in the lead. Notice that God is the subject of all the sentences and phrases in verses 3-5 except the last one. Israel's role is to mop up after God has given the enemy over to Israel (v. 5). The occupation of the land, repeatedly projected earlier, now will take place (cf. 7:1-5; 12:2-3; 20:16-17). Even in the face of a stronger enemy—remember the report of the spies (1:28)—Israel can be *strong and bold* and does not need to have *fear or dread,* for God *will not fail you or forsake you* (31:6). In this opening paragraph, these words of assurance are given to the people as a whole (cf. 1:21, 29; 20:1).

Moses to Joshua (before Israel): God Will Be with You 31:7-8

After assuring the people as a whole that God is with them, Moses turns his attention to Joshua, with the people continuing to listen in. The assurance Moses gives Joshua is essentially the same as that given to the people: verse 8 largely repeats the phrases of verse 6. With these words Moses publicly commissions Joshua for the new task, fulfilling the instructions God gave him earlier (3:28). The task for Joshua is twofold: he will lead Israel into the Promised Land, and he will *put them in possession of it,* a reference to his role in dividing the land among the tribes (cf. Josh 14–19). The elements of the commissioning are similar to other Old Testament commissioning accounts (see TBC). Later God will confirm this commissioning (v. 23).

Moses to Priests and Elders: Read the Law to Israel 31:9-13

The death of Moses results in an important shift in authority. Until now God has taught Israel by speaking to Moses directly (4:5; 5:22-33; cf. 34:10). Although Joshua will succeed Moses as the one whom God uses to lead Israel into the Promised Land, he will not succeed Moses as the one through whom God gives Israel his instruction. With the death of Moses, inspired face-to-face communication of torah (God to Moses) is replaced by a written document. The passage thus speaks of Moses as recording *this law* (i.e., the contents of the book of Deuteronomy) and giving it to *the priests, the sons of Levi* and to *all the elders of Israel* (31:9). The priests are responsible for both *the ark of the covenant* (the container of the Decalogue, the symbols of the Horeb covenant) and the teaching and preservation of the law, so they are the natural recipients. The addition of the elders may signify the support of the community leaders for God's teaching and its administration. Here is an important step in the movement toward Scripture, the recognition of a written text as the authoritative word of God (see TBC).

Not only is the law recorded and preserved; it also is to be read publicly and ceremonially *before the LORD your God at the place he will choose*, every seven years at the *festival of booths*, when *all Israel comes to appear* (v. 11). Tigay suggests that this

> was the most propitious occasion for the reading because it attracted the largest number of pilgrims and was the lengthiest of festivals, lasting seven days. Since it came after the harvest was processed and stored, the people could feel secure about their food for the coming year and could absorb the lessons of the reading with minds free of concern. (291)

The correlation of this reading with the *year of remission* (v. 10; cf. 15:1) highlights that Israel's God expects his people to care for each other. Again Deuteronomy emphasizes the inclusive nature of the community: *men, women, and children, as well as the alien residing in your towns* (31:12). All are to hear the proclamation of the law since all are responsible for their own response to it. By scheduling this reading every seven years, the text ensures that all will hear these words at least twice before they become adults.

Ancient political treaties may have influenced this periodic reading of the law since they commonly required that the text of the treaties be read periodically to the people. Yet its purpose in this context is also clear. A public proclamation of the law keeps the law alive and vital for future generations. "Written law can bridge the physical distance between Moab and the new land and the temporal gap between those who first hear it and their descendants" (Nelson 2002: 359). The text thus refers not only to *all Israel* assembling for the reading, but also to *their children*, the generation of the future (v. 13). Moses may be leaving the scene, but the directions God has given to Israel through Moses will remain with them, in written form and in public liturgy, always reminding the people who God is, what God has done, and what God expects of his people. The purpose for this practice is stated explicitly, both for the generation hearing the reading and their children: *so that they may hear and learn to fear the LORD your God* (vv. 12-13). Only such a response will result in long life in the land they are preparing to enter.

God to Moses: Prepare for Joshua's Commissioning 31:14-15

Previously God has instructed Moses to prepare Joshua to lead Israel (3:28), and Moses has commissioned Joshua before the people (31:7-8). Now God confirms this commissioning with two short speeches, the first calling upon Moses to set up the meeting and the second directed at Joshua. The first speech opens with a further reference to Moses' impending death, the dominant theme of these last chapters.

The introduction of the *tent of meeting* and the *pillar of cloud* is quite unexpected. Both of these play a prominent role in earlier books of the Pentateuch; for example, the *tent of meeting* is mentioned thirty-four times in Exodus, forty-three times in Leviticus, and fifty-six times in Numbers. Yet only the pillar of cloud has been mentioned previously in Deuteronomy (once, in 1:33; though cf. 5:22). This unexpected language may reflect later editorial activity, but within its present context both contribute to emphasizing the presence of God at this critical juncture in the story. The *tent of meeting* is the home for the ark of the covenant (Exod 40:3), the place where God communicates with Moses (e.g., Lev 1:1), whether it is understood as identical with the tabernacle and located in the middle of the camp, as most passages appear to imply, or whether it is understood as a "separate oracular tent *outside* the camp" (e.g., Exod 33:7-11; Tigay: 293). The *pillar of cloud* represented God's presence with Israel during the wilderness period (e.g., Exod 13:21-22). Commissioning Joshua at the *tent of meeting*, with God appearing in a *pillar of cloud*, reminds the audience of God's protective presence during the threats of the wilderness, when God carried Israel as a parent carries a child (Deut 1:31), when God fed them with manna (8:16), when neither clothes nor sandals wore out (8:4; 29:5). It confirms the words of assurance given Israel in the opening speech of the chapter (31:1-6) and Joshua in his commissioning by Moses (vv. 7-8). Just as God has gone with Israel and protected it in the past, God will go with Joshua and Israel into the Promised Land even though Moses remains behind.

God to Moses: Write This Song for Israel 31:16-22

God's commissioning of Joshua (vv. 1-15, 23) brackets a pessimistic look into the future, a projection providing the grounds for Moses writing a song. Once Moses has passed from the scene (v. 16; cf. Jacob in Gen 47:30), it is announced, Israel will break its covenant with God and turn to other gods. One is reminded of Israel building the golden calf when Moses ascended Mount Horeb (Deut 9:8-21), or the stories in the book of Judges where, as soon as a judge dies, Israel is described as *following other gods* (e.g., 2:19). The language of beginning *to prostitute themselves to foreign gods* (Deut 31:16) is unique for Deuteronomy but is consistent with Deuteronomy's central emphasis on the first commandment (cf. Hosea, who employs the image of prostitution for forsaking God, as in 4:10-15). The phrase "foreign gods" becomes more common in the following Deuteronomistic History (e.g., Josh 24:20, 23; Judg 10:16; 1 Sam 7:3; 1 Kings 11:3-4). The warnings expressed earlier in Deuteronomy now take on more concrete form (cf. 4:25; 8:19; 29:22).

The result is that God's *anger will be kindled against them in that day,* leading God to *hide my face from them* (31:17). And when God hides his face, *many terrible troubles will come upon them* (v. 21). Ironic expression highlights this separation. Whereas the covenant made Israel to be God's people, now they are called *this people* (v. 16), even though the individual Israelite still says *our God* (v. 17; lit., *my God*). Whereas Israel consistently is called to worship before God (lit., *to the face of God,* e.g., 12:7, 12, 18; 16:11; 26:5), now God will *hide* his *face* from Israel (31:17-18), language used in the Psalms for times when God appears to be absent (cf. 13:1; 44:24; 88:14). "A poetic justice is declared to be operative in God's scheme of things (vv. 16-17); those who abandon the Lord shall be abandoned by the Lord" (P. Miller 1990: 224; cf. 26:17-19). The primary consequence of breaking covenant is separation from God rather than projections of exile and scattering (cf. 28:64-65; 29:22-29).

At the center of the paragraph is the command to Moses to *write this song* so that it can serve as *a witness for me against the Israelites* (31:19; cf. v. 21). Just as Moses has been instructed to teach God's torah to Israel (cf. 4:5, 14; 5:31; 6:1), now he is directed to teach them the Song, even to the point of memorization, signified by the charge to *put it in their mouths* (31:19; Tigay: 295). Previously the heavens and the earth have been called to witness the covenant between God and Israel (30:19; cf. 4:26). In a time when Israel has forsaken God, when God is absent, a song known by the people is to remind them of their transgression and the justness of their situation. It becomes a supplement to the commandments and regulations, but part of the larger torah Moses has taught.

The projection of this paragraph is entirely negative, but it is not the only word. First, the Song for which the speech provides the rationale ends on a much more positive note (see on ch. 32). Second, the paragraph opens by associating the falling away of the people with the death of Moses. Yet the paragraph has been framed by the account of God commissioning Joshua as the successor of Moses, a commissioning that ends with God's promise to Joshua: *I will be with you* (31:14-15, 23). Although Moses will die, God is not leaving his people without a leader. And third, the chapter opens with Moses assuring Israel, *It is the* LORD *your God who goes with you; he will not fail you or forsake you* (v. 6). The people may be *inclined* to go after other gods when they *have eaten their full and grown fat* (v. 20), yet the paragraph at least hints that perhaps the negative future outlined may be avoided through the witness of the Song and the work of a leader commissioned by God.

God to Joshua: I Will Be with You 31:23

God's formal commissioning of Joshua returns to themes present in the opening paragraph of the chapter and again highlighted in Moses' words of commissioning: *Be strong and bold, for you shall bring the Israelites into the land that I promised them; I will be with you.* The term translated *bold* three times in this chapter by the NRSV is also translated *good courage* (KJV, RSV) or *courageous* (NIV)—yet unexpectedly the NRSV shifts to *courageous* when the same formula is used in the commissioning of Joshua in Joshua 1 (vv. 6, 7, 9, 18). A subtle shift in language has taken place. Earlier Moses has simply spoken of Joshua crossing over into the land *before Israel* (Deut 31:3), or entering the land *with this people* (v. 7). Once God has commissioned him, Joshua is qualified to <u>bring</u> the Israelites into the land (v. 23). It is God's presence and promise that qualifies him for this leadership responsibility (see TLC).

Moses to Levites: Place the Law, Assemble the People 31:24-30

The concluding paragraph of the chapter contributes further to the disjointed impression of the chapter, with its return to the theme of Moses *writing down* the law *in a book*. One can easily envision this paragraph as a continuation of verses 9-13, interrupted by God's commissioning of Joshua (vv. 14-15, 23), which in turn has been interrupted by God's speech to Moses to write the Song (vv. 16-22). But at the same time, the passage ties together a number of themes in the chapter: the pessimistic outlook into the future, the role of the torah, and the teaching of the Song.

Now Moses gives the *Levites* responsibility for safeguarding the completed law. Nelson suggests that although the priests and elders have been given responsibility for teaching the law (v. 10-11), now the concern is only "archival storage," and thus the task is given to the Levites (2002: 361). But such a reading is not required. Both passages give responsibility to those who *carried the ark of the covenant* (vv. 9, 25). The role of the elders may have been limited to the public reading of the law, but the priests or Levites (it is doubtful that this passage is distinguishing between these two) were integrally involved both in public instruction and in the preservation of the law (cf. 17:18). This passage may be dealing with preservation, but for a particular purpose, so that the document of the Moab covenant can serve as a constant and ongoing witness to Israel of the covenant it has entered with God. We must remember that the ark of the covenant contains the two tablets of the Decalogue, representing the Horeb covenant (10:1-5). Just as ancient political treaties required that the treaty text be maintained in a sacred place as a tangible reminder of an agreement, so Israel is to keep its covenant documents with its most important symbol, the ark of the covenant.

The reference to the law as a witness adds a third piece to Deuteronomy's witness language. Three times Deuteronomy calls upon *heaven and earth* to witness a speech of God or Moses (4:26; 30:19; 31:28). The Song of Moses is to be a witness *against* Israel in the future (31:19, 21). Now similar language is used of the law. These last two usages contribute to connecting the Song and the law. Both are to be safeguarded into a future beyond Moses, when Israel is settled in the land, the Song through memorization by the people, and the law through storage in a sacred place and periodic public readings. Together they remind the people of the covenant they have entered and warn the people of their tendency to abandon God.

The ambiguity of verses 16-22 is reflected in this paragraph as well. Again the primary tone is one of gloom. Israel is by nature *rebellious* (v. 27), as it has demonstrated from the beginning (9:24), and in the incident with the golden calf the previous time Moses left them (9:7). Once Moses is gone, it is projected, the people *will do what is evil in the sight of the* LORD, *provoking him to anger* (31:29; cf. 4:25; 9:18). Yet Joshua has been commissioned as the one who will lead Israel into the Promised Land. The priests and elders will lead Israel in periodic readings of the law, a document that will be maintained as a witness next to the ark. And Moses has written a song of warning that, nevertheless, concludes in praise and promise. There may be reason to be pessimistic (see TBC), but not unequivocally.

THE TEXT IN BIBLICAL CONTEXT

When God Gives an Assignment

The Bible includes multiple stories of God calling or commissioning people for particular assignments. A number of these commissioning accounts include three elements (McCarthy), each also present in both Moses' and God's commissioning of Joshua: (1) words of encouragement: *Be strong and of good courage* (Deut 31:7, 23 RSV); (2) the assignment of a particular task: *Bring the Israelites into the land* (v. 23; cf. v. 7); (3) assurance of God's presence: *He/I will be with you* (vv. 8, 23). The background to the words of assurance may be God's promise of his presence to all of Israel (cf. 31:3, 6), but they take on a distinctive quality when they are part of a charge to someone in preparation for a specific assignment on behalf of God.

When God confronts Moses at the burning bush and gives him the task of bringing Israel out of Egypt, Moses protests, "Who am I . . . ?" God's simple response is, "I will be with you" (Exod 3:7-12). When God calls Gideon to "deliver Israel from the hand of Midian," Gideon protests, "But sir, how can I deliver Israel?" God's response is the same, "But I will be with you" (Judg 6:14-16). Jeremiah protests his call as a prophet, and again God responds, "I am with you" (1:8). Abraham (Gen 26:3, 24), Jacob (31:3), God's servant in Isaiah (Isa 41:10), and Paul the apostle (Acts 18:10)—all also received this same promise. In each of these, the key characteristic qualifying the person for the assigned role is God's presence.

The gospel of Matthew closes with the same structure. At the end of his ministry on earth, Jesus gives his disciples the great commission (i.e., a particular assignment), and then concludes with the promise, "I am with you always, to the end of the age" (Matt 28:19-20). When the assignment is repeated, albeit in a slightly different style, as Jesus prepares to leave this earth, it again comes with words promising God's presence, now associated with the Holy Spirit: "But you shall receive power when the Holy Spirit has come upon you" (Acts 1:8). God's assignment always comes with God's promise that God will be with the person.

Inclined to Forsake, but . . .

Deuteronomy is filled with warnings that once Israel experiences the blessings of the land, the people will forget their God, begin to think they have produced their own wealth (e.g., 8:11-17), and/or worship other gods (e.g., 31:16). Here Deuteronomy reflects a consistent biblical view of humanity. Man and woman may be created in the image of God, but as the story of Adam and Eve already demonstrates, the inevitable and natural tendency of the human is to forget that each is a creature created by God and to begin to think that one can make independent decisions (Gen 3). The story of the flood begins with a bleak assessment: "The LORD saw that the wickedness of humankind was great in the earth, and that every inclination of the thoughts of their hearts was only evil continually" (Gen 6:5); it concludes with little if any change: "For the inclination of the human heart is evil from youth" (8:21). The language may change in the New Testament, but the essential appraisal is the same: "All have sinned and fall short of the glory of God" (Rom 3:23; cf. 7:13-25). It is this conviction, supported by experience, that resurfaces repeatedly in Deuteronomy as Moses warns the people about what will inevitably happen.

Despite this fatalistic foreboding about the future, however, Scripture consistently returns to notes of encouragement and hope. In Deuteronomy, God's words of encouragement and assurance to Israel and Joshua surround the pessimistic projections in chapter 31 and lead to praise in the Song of Moses; the warnings of disaster turn into predictions of deliverance (4:24-31; 29:16–30:10). Similarly, in the New Testament, God's love and grace in Jesus Christ overpower the human inclination to rebel (e.g., Phil 2:10-11).

From Direct Speech to Written Word

As Moses prepares to die, he carefully records *the words of this law*, has them placed beside the ark of the covenant, and commands Israel to read them publicly every seven years (31:9-13, 24-26). In this transition, God's dynamic word through Moses becomes a written document. Here is one of the first signs in Scripture of a written document replacing the word of God through living messengers. This reality is recognized by King Josiah when his workers discover "the book of the law" in the temple as they are renovating it, most likely a version of Deuteronomy (2 Kings 22:8-10). And it is recognized by Huldah, the prophetess who authenticates the discovered book (22:14-20). After the exiles have returned from Babylon, Ezra recognizes this as he reads "the book of the law" to the people in Jerusalem (Neh 8). By now this book of the law may have grown into the Pentateuch. At each stage the written document is recognized as God's continuing dynamic and authoritative word to the people. After Moses, there was no prophet *whom the* LORD *knew face to face* (34:10), through whom God spoke to the people directly. Instead, God gave the people a written word, traditionally understood as written by Moses (31:9), that was the guide and the norm for the people and by which prophets were measured.

THE TEXT IN THE LIFE OF THE CHURCH

Discerning Gifts and Calling

There was a time in the Mennonite tradition when ministers were called by lot, a custom still followed by the Amish and Old Order Mennonites today. The lot did not qualify the person but rather identified the person God was calling. Today we more commonly speak of discernment of gifts or charisms. Two different biblical themes appear to inform this language and its use. First, there is Paul's emphasis on the church as one body with many members, each with their own function and gift (Rom 12:3-8; 1 Cor 12:1-31). Second, there is Jesus' parable of the master who gave three servants varying *talents* (an ancient measure of weight with a particular monetary value), which concludes with Jesus praising the servants who invest their talents while chastising the one who does not (Matt 25:14-30). Discernment of gifts then can easily become a process of discerning "talents" understood as abilities and strengths of individuals in the church. For the individual this means a personal assessment and then using "gifts" for the building up of the kingdom.

This may not be inappropriate, but it is different from the biblical tradition of calling for a particular task in which that which qualifies the individual for the task is God's presence (see "When God Gives an Assignment" in TBC above). It is doubtful that God will call someone for a task for which a person does not have the necessary abilities (although the call of Moses challenges a too-simplistic way of understanding this), but a discernment of God's calling is more than a discernment of abilities. How God calls remains a mystery despite our best intentions to systematize this. Even if one may question whether the lot is the best way of determining God's call, that approach focuses on *call* rather than *gifts*. Once God has called someone, that person can be *strong and of good courage*, for both that person and that person's community are assured that God is with that person and will not forsake that person.

Deuteronomy 32:1-52
The Song of Moses

PREVIEW

Music and hymnody are integral elements of worship. It thus should not surprise us that Deuteronomy also includes a song.

After reading that God instructs Moses to *write this song ... in order that this song may be a witness for me against the Israelites* (31:19), the content of the Song may surprise us. After all, the instruction occurs in a paragraph where God announces that because of Israel's apostasy, *I will forsake them and hide my face from them* (31:17). The Song does witness for God as instructed, indict Israel for abandoning God and going after other gods (32:15-18), speak of God hiding his face from Israel (v. 20) and of disasters coming upon Israel (v. 23), and say God thought to *blot out the memory of them from humankind* (v. 26). But this is not the last word, nor in the context of the Song, even the first word. The Song opens with a fervent call to *ascribe greatness to our God! The Rock, his work is perfect* (vv. 3-4). It concludes with a moving declaration that God will *vindicate his people, have compassion on his servants* (v. 36), and *cleanse the land for his people* (v. 43). This is not an announcement of doom and gloom for the people of God as we might have anticipated based on the Song's introduction in chapter 31. Rather, it is a hymn of praise to a God who, despite the corruption of his people, remains the fully sovereign God who cares for his people.

OUTLINE

The Song, 32:1-43
    32:1-3   The Summons

32:4-18   A Survey of the Relationship
32:19-25 God Responds: I Will Hide My Face
32:26-35 God Relents
32:36-43 The One God Vindicates His People
Remember the Song, 32:44-47
Preparation for the Death of Moses, 32:48-52

EXPLANATORY NOTES

The Song 32:1-43

The Song of Moses includes a number of elements found in ancient lawsuits, whether that of an accusation by a suzerain that a vassal has broken a political treaty, or that of a prophetic lawsuit by God against Israel (cf. Hos 4:1-6; Mic 6:1-5; Jer 2:4-13). Like these indictments, the Song includes "the call of witnesses, an accusation, an account of the overlord's benevolence, an affirmation that the covenant has been broken, and an announcement of punishment" (McConville 2002: 451). But to categorize the Song of Moses as a prophetic lawsuit inadequately recognizes the concluding praise portion and does not do justice to the overall unity and message of the Song. The historical review, including the portion surveying Israel's apostasy, serves to highlight how great a God Israel has. The prophetic lawsuit may have influenced the composition of the Song, but in the end it is a hymn of praise that witnesses to God's greatness and compassion.

The Song is written as ancient Hebrew poetry and thus represents a significant shift from the narrative and legal format of Deuteronomy thus far. Most versions reflect this shift in the way they format the text on the page. Fortunately the essence of Hebrew poetry is not lost in translation. The key characteristic of Hebrew poetry is parallelism, a style in which a second, or sometimes third, clause repeats what has been said in the first clause. This repetition may take place by expressing the same thought through different wording (synonymous parallelism), through saying something similar in the opposite way (antithetic parallelism), or through expansion of an idea (complementary parallelism). That style is common in the book of Psalms.

32:1-3 *The Summons*

The role of the heavens and the earth may be that of formal witnesses to a lawsuit (cf. Isa 1:2-3; Jer 2:12-13), but the term "witness" is not used anywhere in the Song, and according to the words of the summons, that which the heavens and earth are to hear is not an indictment but the proclamation of the greatness of Israel's God (v. 3). One is reminded of psalms that regularly call on others to hear or join in the praise. Similar to the *peoples* of 4:5-8, and the *nations* of 29:24, the *heavens* and *the earth* will marvel and wonder at the greatness of the God of Israel and the obstinacy of the people of Israel. After suggesting that its words should be as appreciated and anticipated as gentle rain that allows new growth (v. 2), the summons concludes by announcing the central theme of the Song: the *greatness of our God* (v. 3).

32:4-18 A Survey of the Relationship

The opening statement contrasts the faithfulness and justice of God with the perverseness and foolishness of Israel through the use of two images, both of which play important roles in the Song. First, it introduces God as *the Rock* (v. 4), a picture used four more times in the Song (cf. vv. 15, 18, 30, 31). For an animal in the wilderness, a rock provides shade, refuge, and protection. But the symbol also represents God's strength and trustworthiness. On the one side of the relationship is a God who is *perfect, just, faithful, without deceit, just* (translating a different Hebrew term from the previous *just*), and *upright*—six different terms pointing to the greatness of God.

And then there is Israel. The second key image of the Song is that of parent-child. The Song speaks of Israel as *children* (vv. 5, 20; cf. v. 43), *sons and daughters* (v. 19) created by their father (v. 6), birthed by God (v. 18). Despite what should have been an intimate relationship, however, the children are *degenerate children,* they have *dealt falsely,* they are *perverse, crooked, foolish, senseless* (vv. 5-6). The phrase translated *degenerate children* literally means *to him they are not children,* and it echoes the symbolic naming of Hosea's son Lo-ammi, meaning "Not my people" (Hos 1:9 and mg.). God may treat Israel as his child, but they *have dealt falsely with him* (Deut 32:5; cf. 1:31; 8:5; Exod 4:22). The contrast is extreme.

Typical of Deuteronomy, the Song calls on Israel to *Remember* (32:7; cf. 5:15; 8:18; 9:7; 15:15; 16:3; 24:9, 18, 22). In the brief survey of *the days of old,* the Song gives attention to two themes: the election of Israel (32:7-9), and God's care for Israel in the wilderness and in the Promised Land (vv. 10-14). The election of Israel is placed at the beginning of time, when, within a divine council, peoples and lands were allocated. Although the text appears to envision a divine council with multiple gods, it is not a council of equals (manuscripts vary: taking the last phrase of v. 8 as *gods,* NRSV; *divine beings,* Nelson 2002:

363; or *sons of God,* McConville 2002: 445—rather than as *sons of Israel,* NASB; *children of Israel,* KJV; or *Israel's numbers,* NJPS). It has one God, who clearly is *the Most High* (cf. 1 Kings 22:19). In that divine council, the one supreme God has chosen Israel as *the LORD's own portion.* The language is different, but it reflects the same election theology as earlier Deuteronomic statements (cf. 7:6-8; 14:2).

Uncharacteristically, the Song makes no reference to the exodus as the text moves directly to Israel's experience in the wilderness. While in the *howling wilderness,* a place normally associated with death (cf. 1:19), God takes care of Israel (32:10). The language is different from earlier passages that highlight God's providential care in the wilderness (cf. 8:3-4, 16; 29:5), but it makes the same point with a series of terms: *sustained, shielded, cared, guarded, guided* (32:10-12). Consistent with the parent-child imagery, like a mighty eagle God pushes a young bird out of its nest in an effort to teach it to fly, and then spreads its wings and catches it. God protects as well as disciplines his children (cf. 8:5; Exod 19:4). The transition to the Promised Land takes place in Deuteronomy 32:13. Now God no longer sends manna from heaven but provides for the people with *produce of the field,* and *curds, milk,* and *fat* from the herds and flocks. The text accentuates the productivity and fertility of the land God is giving. The region of Bashan is known for its fertility and the strength and size of its herds. The phrase translated *choicest wheat* more literally means *the fat of kidneys of wheat* (v. 14 KJV). In every way possible, the Song emphasizes how God cared and provided for Israel, in the wilderness and in the land.

But instead of simply eating their fill and receiving their blessing from God (8:10), Israel *gorged* in its blessings and *grew fat* (v. 15). This theme, introduced in the summary statement of the Song (vv. 5-6), is now expanded. Ironically the Song calls Israel *Jeshurun* (v. 15), meaning "the upright one" (cf. its use in 33:5, 26; Isa 44:2). But as the text makes so clear, although the term may sound something like Israel, Israel has not lived up to this name. Israel *kicked* like an unruly animal does at its owner, Israel *abandoned God* and went after *strange gods,* a transgression of Deuteronomy's most fundamental commandment. The text emphasizes Israel's depravity when it speaks of Israel as even willing to sacrifice to *demons,* or *no-gods* (NABRE), to *new ones recently arrived,* gods whom they had *never known* (32:17; cf. 13:2, 6, 13; 28:64; 29:26). The concluding verse combines the image of God as the protecting dependable Rock with that of a parent giving birth (32:8). The language of the latter image is striking because it combines masculine pronouns with verbs normally associated with mothers. The first verb, *bore*, refers to giving birth, and the second literally speaks of a mother's labor pains (Tigay: 307). Israel's abandoning God is as reprehensible as someone forgetting both mother and father in a culture where children are responsible to take care of their parents.

32:19-25 God Responds: I Will Hide My Face

God's response to Israel's apostasy begins in cries of pain and passion arising out of broken personal relationship (vv. 19-22), and moves to an application of the covenant curses (vv. 23-25). The emotional language of these verses is moving. Whereas the small historical credo highlighted that God *heard our voice and saw our affliction and brought us out of Egypt* (26:7-8), now we read that God *saw it, and was jealous* (32:19; cf. v. 16). Although these are covenant curses, the tone is that of a family with *sons and daughters* (v. 19) and *children* (v. 20). But these children are *perverse* and have no *faithfulness*, leading to God spurning them and hiding his face from them (vv. 19-20; cf. 31:17). They have worshiped what are *no-gods* (32:17 NABRE): as a result God will punish them with *no people, with a foolish nation*. Not only is this a wordplay; it may also suggest that the instrument of God's punishment will be barbarians (i.e., not a real nation), and certainly not a people of God. The anger of God is so great that it will affect the whole earth (v. 22; cf. 29:22-28). Paul uses this verse in highlighting Israel's disobedience (Rom 10:18-21). God's profound and intense love for Israel, as reflected in the election, is one side of the coin (7:6-8; 32:8-9). But the other side is the deep pain and jealousy and anger when this love is rejected.

Anger turns to action against Israel. Language and imagery now shift to more typical covenant curses. Disaster will come upon the people (32:23; cf. 28:20; 29:19) in the form of *hunger, pestilence*, and war, resulting in wild animals overrunning the land (32:24-25), a common combination of threats in ancient curses (cf. 28:21-25; Jer 21:7; Ezek 14:21). The *chambers* should be a haven from attack, but even they will become a place of terror (Deut 32:25; cf. 1 Kings 22:25; Isa 26:20). Israel will face the devastating consequences of abandoning God.

32:26-35 God Relents

All has gone as one might expect, with God responding to Israel's rejection in pain and anger, leading to the implementation of the curses accepted by both parties of the covenant. But then comes the surprise—God has a change of heart: *I thought to scatter them and blot out the memory of them from humankind; but* . . . (vv. 26-27). The reference to exile and erasing all memory of Israel is taken from earlier threats and curses (exile, 4:27; 28:64; 29:28; erasing memory, 9:14; 29:20), and that would have been well deserved in light of Israel's provocation. But it is not to be; God determines not to carry through what God has thought to do (32:19-25). A more radical repenting of projected action is hardly imaginable. Everything changes with *but*.

The key factor in this unprecedented change of plans is not Israel's repentance or return to God but rather God's reputation among the nations (cf. arguments of Moses when God threatens to destroy Israel after the golden calf incident; 9:25-29). If God punishes Israel as deserved and planned, then the nations used by God as instruments of this punishment will misunderstand and say, *Our hand is triumphant* (32:27). This language is reminiscent of God's warnings to Israel earlier in the book (8:17). The human tendency to forget about God's role and misinterpret reality as created by *my own hand* is one that Israel shares with other nations. Although the text has shifted focus to the *enemy* and *adversaries* of Israel (these terms simultaneously reflect God's dramatic shift to the side of Israel), an undercurrent of indictment of Israel remains. Even as the passage explicitly speaks of these other nations as *void of sense*, lacking *understanding* and wisdom (32:28-29), the unspoken but implicit word is that the same could be said of Israel. These nations should have recognized that their surprising victory against God's people could only have happened if God had determined it and given Israel over to them (vv. 29-30).

The speaker shifts in verse 31. Whereas till now God is speaking, sharing his thoughts, in verse 31 Israel becomes the speaker, but the focus remains the same. After remaining silent until now, Israel joins God's side in denouncing the foolishness and corruption of the nations. The ways of the other nations are *vineyards* of *Sodom* and *Gomorrah*, and as a result they will produce fruit of *poison* (v. 32-33).

God again speaks in the concluding two verses (vv. 34-35), affirming the statements of Israel. God has stored and *sealed* the wine of *poison* that these nations will experience. God alone is in control of the future of both Israel and the nations and will *recompense* as God determines. God retains his freedom, with the nations expected to recognize God's role in reality. God's integrity and honor require that God not allow people to consider themselves as independent and able to determine their own fate apart from God. It is striking that here again in the process of focusing on Israel, the people of

God, Deuteronomy does so against a backdrop of the nations (cf. 4:5-8; 29:22-28). Even though God the *Most High* has chosen Israel as a treasured possession, God remains God over all nations and will protect that reputation among those nations (cf. 32:8).

32:36-43 The One God Vindicates His People

The implication of God's second thoughts for Israel now becomes explicit: God *will vindicate his people* (v. 36) and will *cleanse the land for his people* (v. 43). These two affirmations frame this final portion of the Song and dominate the overall picture. The people are once again *his people*, *his servants*, *his children* (v. 43). God's jealousy and anger has been replaced by *compassion* (v. 36). Once more God has a people with whom God is in relationship, a people for whom God prepares the land. The Hebrew term translated *cleanse* (lit., *cover*) is not a common word in Deuteronomy, occurring in only one other verse (v. 43; cf. 21:8). In Leviticus and Numbers it is an important term for cultic cleansing or making atonement (e.g., Lev 1:4). The Day of Atonement became important in later Israel (Lev 23:27-28; 25:9) as a day when the sins of the people were "covered," the literal meaning of the word, through cultic act. The connotations of the term thus provide further meaning for the closing verse of the Song. God will *make atonement for his land and people* (Deut 32:43 NIV), thereby allowing Israel to reenter the land afresh once more, as it did originally.

But if the frame emphasizes the resumption of God's relationship with his people, the central portion of this final block retains a vivid warning, even if only implicit. Israel's apostasy is again recognized through God's sarcastic questions: *Where are their gods*, those *who ate the fat of their sacrifices and drank the wine of their libations?* (vv. 37-38). When Israel has truly needed help, these *no-gods* (NABRE) to whom Israel has sacrificed (v. 17) were missing and could not provide *protection*. This part of the story also must be remembered as a warning for the future.

The God of the Song is utterly unique, all-powerful, and supreme, the sole deity. The declarations *I kill and I make alive; I wound and I heal* represent this total and exclusive power over life (v. 39; cf. Exod 4:11; 1 Sam 2:6-8). The order of these terms may very well reflect the movement of the Song, from intended retribution to redemption. Although earlier the Song has appeared to speak of a divine council (vv. 8-9), this verse makes it clear that God has no equals. The thought reflected here echoes the meaning of the Shema (6:4-9) and is similar to the assertions of Isaiah in the context of the Babylonian exile: "I, I am the LORD, and besides me there is no savior" (43:11). "I am God, and there is no other" (45:22; cf. 41:4; 43:10, 13; 44:6; 45:6-7; 48:12). As the sole power, God is quite able to unilaterally punish his *adversaries* and *those who hate me* (Deut 32:40-42). This claim may come across as words of assurance to *his people*, and that is their first significance within the Song, but at the same time they speak a warning to God's people, a people so inclined to abandon this one God for the *no-gods*.

The Song concludes on a high note of praise, matching the tone and theme of the opening verses (vv. 1-3). This is clear even if the Hebrew is not clear. Whether it is a call to the nations to praise *his people* (i.e., Israel) or whether it is a call to the heavens and divine beings to together praise God (as suggested by the Septuagint and Dead Sea Scrolls)—that is the question. In either case the Song ends on a note of praise, echoing its opening. The prophetic lawsuit format may have influenced its structure, but in the end it is a hymn of praise that witnesses to God's unparalleled supremacy, power that God uses on behalf of his people. The Deuteronomic movement from jealousy to mercy, or from punishment to redemption (even if at points in the Song punishment appears to be more intended than actual), once more is evident (cf. 4:24-31; 29:16–30:10).

Remember the Song 32:44-47

God called upon Moses to write the Song (31:19), and according to the introduction it is recited by Moses (v. 30), but now Joshua joins Moses in its presentation (32:44), reflecting the beginnings of the transition of leadership. Israel is to *take to heart all the words*, in other words, to remember the Song into the future (cf. v. 7) and teach it to the next generation. Israel's very life in the land depends upon it. One may speak of the Song as having a double role. First, it has an educational function as it encourages Israel to obey, reminding it of the nature of God on the one side, and of the tendency of human nature on the other. Second, when Israel sins, the Song serves as a *witness*, as a formal indictment of the people. Although a hymn of praise witnessing to God's greatness and compassion, it simultaneously becomes an indictment in a time of sin. Both roles of the Song (v. 46a) have as their goal obedience to the sermon of the larger book, *the words of this law* (v. 46b), and long life in the land.

Preparation for the Death of Moses 32:48-52

The theme of Moses' death receives increasing attention as the book nears its end. Although Moses cannot enter the Promised Land, he is able to view it from a distance, from the top of Mount Nebo, where he will die. The unusual element of this address is that whereas previously Moses' exclusion from the Promised Land was spoken of as *on your account* (1:37; 3:26), with the apparent implication that it was not because of his own wrongdoing, or possibly due to old age (31:2), here it is explained as a consequence of his own actions: both he and Aaron *broke faith with me* (God) at Meribath-kadesh (32:51). The narrative account of the incident speaks of Moses and Aaron not trusting God "to show my holiness before the eyes of the Israelites" (Num 20:7-12; cf. 27:12-14; Exod 17:1-7). The exact nature of the sin is not clear, but it is striking that a passage immediately following the Song of Moses draws attention even to his fallibility. Despite Moses' greatness, his special role in teaching God's instructions, and the uniqueness of his leadership (cf. 34:10), even he did not trust God fully. Perhaps it is intimating that if blessing and reward require full obedience, no one would ever receive them. God remains with his people, but this is due solely to his compassion and honor, not the people's obedience. And so Moses must die away from the land, along with all the other Israelites of his generation—the only exceptions are Caleb and Joshua, the one who now will lead the people into the land.

THE TEXT IN BIBLICAL CONTEXT
Punishing the Nations

The Song of Moses suggests a series of stages through which the relationship among God, Israel, and the nations progresses, an order also found in other places in the Old Testament. In each God is portrayed as a divine warrior who, together with his heavenly host, plays an active role among the nations of the world:

1. God delivers his chosen people from slavery and gives it the Promised Land, in both cases by fighting on behalf of Israel, first against the Egyptians through the plagues and at the Red Sea, and then by giving the former inhabitants of the land into Israel's hand.

2. When Israel sins and breaks its covenant with God, God uses other nations to punish Israel, either by fighting with them against Israel, or by withholding his protection from Israel.

3. The other nations used as an instruments of God's plan are deemed arrogant (i.e., they understand themselves to be masters rather than God's tools). God's honor and reputation thus require that these other nations now also be punished for their sin. God thus once more turns against these nations.

The first stage is foundational for the relationship between God and Israel. The second and third stages appear to go through cycles. The book of Judges repeatedly recounts how Israel sins, resulting in oppression by other peoples. When the Philistines defeat Israel, they even capture the ark of the covenant. Yet God is not defeated. When the Philistines place the ark in the house of Dagon, their god, the statute of Dagon falls onto its face before the ark, symbolizing the supremacy of the God of Israel and the impending defeat of the Philistines (1 Sam 4–7). Isaiah announces that God will use Assyria as the "rod of my anger" to punish the Israelites who "turn aside the needy from justice." But when Assyria begins to think that its victory has come "by the strength of my hand," then God "will punish the arrogant boasting of the king of Assyria" (Isa 10:1-13). Despite God's unique relationship with Israel, God is the God of all nations. All nations thus are subservient to God, and all nations fall under God's judgment when they ignore the ways of God (cf. Amos 1:3–2:3; Hab 2:6-20).

The New Testament does not place these relationships in the same cycle but, using different language, it ends up at a very similar point. Through the cross, God defeats the powers of evil. The book of Revelation proclaims this in richly symbolic and hymnic language. Salvation comes through the Lamb that was slain (5:1-14), for the Lamb has conquered and defeated "Babylon," the symbol of all evil (e.g., 18:2). God may use these powers for God's purposes, but in the end God's justice and judgment prevail over all peoples and nations.

The Vindication of God

The Song of Moses concludes with forceful yet enigmatic proclamations about God's sovereignty and unchallenged power to exact vengeance (Deut 32:35, 43), to kill and make alive (v. 39), and to vindicate his people (v. 36). This imagery and language powerfully reflect the Song's conviction of God's sovereignty. The claim is clear even if the detail is not, remaining painfully hidden.

This same faith moves the psalmists to cry to God in crisis, confident that God can and will respond as he did in the past, even when there is no present evidence of it (e.g., Pss 17; 22; 35; 54). There is faith that God will vindicate his people in the face of those "who devise evil against me" (e.g., Ps 35:1-4). Paul picks up this theme in his warning: "Beloved, never avenge yourselves, but leave room for the wrath of God, for it is written, 'Vengeance is mine, I will repay says the Lord'" (Rom 12:19; cf. Deut 32:35). God's sovereignty and justice give confidence that we do not need to "make things turn out right." God will vindicate his cause even if it is not clear to us exactly how. Perhaps this is one of the *secret things* that *belong to the* LORD (Deut 29:29). The final end is revealed to us, but along the way we must acknowledge "the hiddenness of the divine purpose, the possibility of mystery and plan in the mind of God that is not discernible or not yet revealed" (P. Miller 1990: 232).

THE TEXT IN THE LIFE OF THE CHURCH
The Power of the Song

Theologians have an inclination to focus on narrative and law and proposition. But often laypeople are deeply influenced by music and song. The power of song is reflected at many points. It is not coincidental that worship wars are fought largely over what type of music is played and sung in worship services. When early Anabaptists fled and moved, they commonly carried with them the Bible, stories of martyrs, and a hymnal. In times of deep crisis and illness, it is common for people to turn to the hymnal or the biblical book of Psalms. Preachers may teach theology from the Bible, but people often learn theology from the hymns they sing. The most prominent tone of song tends to be praise. The Song of Deuteronomy 32 thus provides a powerful and dramatic climax to the book. The pessimism and warnings of the narrative are not forgotten but they now are encased in words of praise to the Rock who bore Israel, who provided for them, and who in the end will vindicate himself and his people.

Deuteronomy 33:1-29

The Blessing of Moses

PREVIEW
When hearing of someone's passing, it is not uncommon to ask, "What were her/his last words?" In a sense all of Deuteronomy is Moses' last testament. But the words of chapter 33 represent these final words most particularly.

As Moses prepares to die, he gives a final blessing to all of the tribes, both as their "father" and as a prophet with a view into the future. An opening and closing frame enclose blessings for eleven tribes (Simeon is missing; vv. 1-5, 26-29) that emphasize "the ideal unity of the tribes as a single people and places their security and prosperity in the broader context of God's benefactions to Israel" (Tigay: 318). Prosperity and security also are the central themes of the blessings for the individual tribes. A unique God (v. 26) will protect and provide generously for a united, unique people (v. 29). That is a formula for a *happy* or *blessed* (NIV) people.

OUTLINE
Situating the Blessing, 33:1
Opening Hymn, 33:2-5
Blessing the Tribes, 33:6-25
    33:6   Reuben
    33:7   Judah
    33:8-11 Levi
    33:12   Benjamin
    33:13-17 Joseph

    33:18-19   Zebulun and Issachar
    33:20-21   Gad
    33:22   Dan
    33:23   Naphtali
    33:24-25   Asher
Concluding Hymn, 33:26-29

EXPLANATORY NOTES

Situating the Blessing 33:1

The custom of a father blessing his children before death may have been common in Israel, but within the Old Testament this blessing connects Moses directly to Isaac and his final words to Jacob and Esau (Gen 27:1-40), yet even more to Jacob in blessing his twelve sons (Gen 49). As the one who has led Israel out of Egypt and mediated the covenant at Horeb, Moses may be considered the father to Israel; here he speaks as one of the patriarchs of Israel. The phrase *man of God* is frequently applied to prophets in the Old Testament, such as Samuel, in 1 Samuel 9:6-10; Shemaiah, 1 Kings 12:22; Elijah, 1 Kings 17:18; Elisha, 2 Kings 1:9. Sometimes it serves as a formal title for someone whose name is not given but who is recognized as a spokesperson of God with regard to the future (Judg 13:6, 8; 1 Sam 2:27; 1 Kings 13:1-31; 20:28; cf. 1 Sam 9:6-10). The identification fits with the closing passage of the book (Deut 34:10) and serves to give special authority to the blessing.

As with the Song of Moses, the Blessing is written in poetic style, with parallelism a dominant element. The verbal and thematic points of contact with the book of Deuteronomy, however, are not nearly as obvious as with the Song. The blessings of the tribes (vv. 6-25) appear to have been inserted into a hymn that originally may have been a separate unified piece but that now provides an opening and closing frame for the blessings (vv. 2-5, 26-29). Joined together, the Blessing gives a distinct tone of praise and benediction to the work of Moses and the book of Deuteronomy before Moses ascends Mount Nebo to have a distant view of the Promised Land and to die (34:1-12).

Opening Hymn 33:2-5

The frame of the Blessing (vv. 2-5, 26-29) is united by the theme of praise to the incomparable God who delivers Israel, an incomparable people, and by an arrangement of proper names, each occurring in both parts in chiastic order (*the LORD*, vv. 2, 29; *Jacob*, vv. 4, 28; and *Jeshurun*, vv. 5, 26). Unfortunately, the detailed meaning of some of the verses is unclear, as any comparison of versions quickly shows. Whereas Deuteronomy generally uses fairly straightforward grammar and common vocabulary (it is often one of the first books read in Hebrew by those new to the language), the Blessing of Moses "is one of the most difficult texts in all of ancient literature. It is full of rare words, syntactic difficulties, grammatical inconsistencies, and opaque allusions" (Tigay: 318). This is especially true in the opening part of the frame (note variations in the translation of the last half of v. 2 and first part of v. 3).

The overall direction, however, is intelligible. God is depicted as coming from the region south of the Promised Land to deliver and lead *the united tribes of Israel* (vv. 2-3, 5). *Sinai* (the only reference to Sinai in the book of Deuteronomy), *Seir*, and *Mount Paran* are in desert regions of the Sinai Peninsula and Edom, southwest of the Dead Sea. It is disputed whether this is a reference to God giving the Decalogue at Mount Horeb (5:1-27) or whether it reflects the tradition that the worship of Yahweh originated from that general region (cf. Judg 5:4-5); yet the terminology (*came*, *dawned*, and *shone forth*; cf. Ps 50:2) does suggest a theophany, a divine encounter between God and human. Accompanying God are *myriads of holy ones*, a *host*, and *all his holy ones* (accepting NRSV here), probably a reference to the heavenly forces at God's disposal (cf. 1 Kings 22:19; 2 Kings 6:17; 19:35). The nature of the theophany is one in which God with his heavenly army wondrously delivers and protects his people.

The opening line of verse 3 has widely divergent translations but may be an affirmation of God's love for Israel (the Septuagint reads, *O lover of his people*). This heavenly God from Sinai then becomes king of the *united tribes of Israel* (v. 5); it is doubtful that this verse refers to the rise of kingship within Israel. Unlike in the Song of Moses (32:15), here *Jeshurun* is not used ironically but as a favorite name that reflects the tenor of the hymn, in which Israel is incomparable (cf. 33:26), the *upright one* (the literal meaning of *Jeshurun*).

The reference to Moses charging Israel with the law does not relate in a simple way to the rest of the opening hymn, but it does connect the Blessing more directly to Deuteronomy (33:4). Within the poem this assertion highlights that the God who delivers and provides security in wonderful ways is the same God who instructs his people through human agents. Its summary-like quality—that the law "was commanded by Moses, that it is a heritage, and that it belongs to the entire people, not just to an elite group"—led rabbis to select it along with the Shema (6:4-9) as the first verses taught young children when they learn to speak (Tigay: 322).

Blessing the Tribes 33:6-25

The core of the poem consists of compiled poetic statements of differing length about the tribes of Israel, now joined together by a common opening phrase, *of X he said* (the first two words of v. 2 serve as the opening for Reuben; cf. vv. 8, 12, etc.), all together placed under the heading *the blessing with which Moses, the man of God, blessed the Israelites* (v. 1). The statements are of three types: general undirected statements of blessing or wishes for a tribe (Reuben, Gad, and Joseph), prayers directed to God (Judah, Levi), and descriptions of a tribe's situation or way of life (remainder). Unlike the blessing of Jacob upon his twelve sons (Gen 49), all statements are positive, with no accusations of wrongdoing included.

The blessing identifies eleven sons of Jacob, now all representing the tribes named after them. The absence of Simeon from the list probably reflects the tribe's fairly early disappearance from Israel's history as it was absorbed into Judah. The Blessing thus

> takes the changing history of Israel seriously. The blessings, indeed, accommodate this changing history, via passing over Simeon, giving scant regard to Reuben and Dan, sketching dynamic portraits of Naphtali and Gad as still expanding, envisioning Judah in some unnamed crisis, and most important, foregrounding Joseph at the expense of Judah. This is a picture of history unfolding, with shifting centers of gravity. (McConville 2002: 475)

A provenance for the Blessing in the Northern Kingdom some time before its defeat by Assyria (in 722 BCE) appears likely; Judah receives scant attention, with no hint of Jerusalem or the Davidic kingship, whereas the northern tribes of Joseph (Ephraim and Manasseh), Naphtali, and Gad appear to be favored. The order of the blessings begins with Reuben, the oldest, and the location where the Israel of Deuteronomy is camped, and then appears to follow a somewhat geographic progression from south to north.

33:6 Reuben

Although Reuben was the oldest and thus the one who normally should have received a double share (21:15-17), his blessing promises nothing but is merely a wish that he survive. This may be intended as a retribution for his earlier misdeeds (cf. Gen 35:22; 49:3-4), but more likely simply reflects the struggle the tribe of Reuben had to survive.

33:7 Judah

Given the tribe of Judah's prominence in the story of Israel and the significant blessing it receives from Jacob (Gen 49:8-12), the blessing here is unexpectedly short. It is prayer to God to help Judah in a situation where it appears to be separated from the other tribes, perhaps reflecting the time of the divided kingdom. There is no sign of messianic expectation (cf. Gen 49:10).

33:8-11 Levi

The lengthy prayer on behalf of Levi reflects that tribe's significant priestly role. Three responsibilities of the priests are highlighted: (1) their role in determining the will of God through the deployment of the Urim and Thummim (v. 8a, the normal order in which these are given, as in Exod 28:30; Lev 8:8; etc), (2) their role in preserving and teaching the law (Deut 33:10a), and (3) their role in the sacrificial system (v. 10b). The reference to testing at Massah and Meribah may have in mind the incident earlier interpreted as Moses and Aaron breaking faith with God, thereby preventing Moses from entering the Promised Land (v. 8; 32:51; cf. Exod 17:1-7; Num 20:2-13), but no special role of the Levites in this incident is cited elsewhere. The role of the Levites in punishing Israel after Moses returned from Mount Horeb only to discover Israel had made a golden calf may lie behind the statement that Levi regards family less highly than God's word and covenant (Exod 32:25-29). It may, however, also be an indication that the Levites take seriously the priorities stipulated in Deuteronomy 13:6-11. The call of the concluding verse (33:11) may reflect battles within Israel over the priesthood.

33:12 Benjamin

Benjamin, the youngest and a favorite son of Jacob, now is called *beloved of the* LORD. The blessing speaks of the security the tribe experiences as it *rests between his* (i.e., God's) *shoulders*.

33:13-17 Joseph

The blessing of Joseph focuses on the fertility and bounty of the land inhabited by Ephraim and Manasseh, the two sons of Joseph, who each received tribal status (vv. 13-16a), and on their political stature among the tribes (vv. 16b-17). Both elements are present in Jacob's blessing of Joseph (Gen 49:22-26), even with some similar vocabulary: for example, both speak of Joseph as *nazir* (*prince* in Deut 33:16

NIV/NRSV, but *set apart* NRSV, *prince* NIV in Gen 49:26). Ephraim and part of Manasseh were in the central part of the land, with the other part of Manasseh in the Transjordan, both regions known for their fertility. This location translates into economic and political strength, although the phrase *prince among his brothers* also is reminiscent of Joseph's dreams of his brothers bowing down to him (Gen 37:5-11) or the events of the brothers coming to Joseph in Egypt for food (Gen 42:6). The Hebrew translated as *the one who dwells on Sinai* is rendered more literally by other versions as *the one who lives in a bush* (Deut 33:16; cf. KJV, NIV, RSV, ESV, NJPS, NRSV mg.; etc.). The *horns of a wild ox* may be a reference to the two sons of Joseph, Ephraim and Manasseh.

33:18-19 Zebulun and Issachar

Zebulun and Issachar were consecutive sons of Jacob by his wife Leah. Their tribes settled in bordering territories in southern Galilee, resulting in their being treated next to each other more than once in the story (blessing of Jacob, Gen 49:13-14; Song of Deborah, Judg 5:14-15). Their territories extended to the Mediterranean Sea, allowing these tribes to participate in fishing and other marine activities. The reference to inviting *peoples to the mountain* to *offer the right sacrifices* presumably is to either Mount Tabor or Mount Carmel, perhaps reflecting a time before Jerusalem gained its preeminent status.

33:20-21 Gad

The tribe of Gad is characterized as aggressive and expansive, with a political and possibly even judicial role in relationship to other tribes. The blessing of Jacob states that Gad "shall raid at their heels" (Gen 49:19). The historical background is not clear, although Gad was one of the tribes, along with Reuben and half of Manasseh, who requested Moses' permission to settle in the Transjordan. There also are hints that Gad at some point absorbed the tribe of Reuben (the Moabite Stone of the ninth century BCE speaks of Gad and not Reuben; McConville 2002: 472).

33:22 Dan

Dan may have been small, forced to relocate in the north when its original location on the coast proved unsuccessful (Josh 19:40-48), but as a *lion's whelp* (i.e., cub), it is characterized as surprisingly strong. Bashan was not part of Dan, but its reputation for fertile land

and strong herds may support the image of a vigorous and aggressive lion.

33:23 Naphtali
Naphtali's growth is attributed to God. The blessing may include a play on words, with the Hebrew term translatable as *west, sea,* or *lake* (RSV, *possess the lake and the south*; NIV, *southward to the lake*). Naphtali was located near the Sea of Galilee.

33:24-25 Asher
The blessing includes a play on words with the name *Asher* similar to the words for "blessed" and "foot." The tribe of Asher was located in the fertile northern region of Galilee. Both its fertile land and border location placed it in danger from the outside, thus requiring a strong defense (v. 25).

Closing Hymn 33:26-29
The closing hymn continues the theme, introduced in the opening, of God's extraordinary protection of his people from enemies (vv. 26-28), but now it includes God providing blessings from a fertile land (v. 28b), a central theme in the core of the poem. The closing hymn opens by highlighting the uniqueness of Israel's God—*There is none like God. . . . He subdues the ancient gods* (cf. discussion of 32:39)— and climaxes with reference to a joyful, triumphant, incomparable *people saved by the* LORD (v. 29). There is no hint of the curses that play such a prominent role in the chapters on covenant, at some points even overwhelming the blessings (cf. 27:15-26; 28:15-68), or of the punishment with which Israel is threatened if it does not obey God's directions (29:16-28; 30:15-20). Moses' last words to the people before ascending Mount Nebo to glimpse the Promised Land and die have an exuberant tone: *Blessed are you, Israel! Who is like you, a people saved by the* LORD? *He is your shield and helper and your glorious sword. Your enemies will cower before you, and you will tread on their heights* (NIV).

THE TEXT IN BIBLICAL CONTEXT
The Last Words of a Leader
The last words of an individual have special weight or significance. The Old Testament contains a number of "last words." When Jacob is about to die, he gathers his sons around him and pronounces last

words upon them (Gen 49). When David's death approaches, he charges his son Solomon, "Be strong, be courageous, and keep the charge of the LORD your God" (1 Kings 2:2-3). These two speeches reflect concern for succession in leadership (David) and blessing and continuation in the next generation (Jacob). Similarly, Jesus gives his disciples a final mandate and encouragement prior to leaving them (Matt 28:16-20; John 13–16; Acts 1:7-11).

Although all of Deuteronomy may be considered the final testament of Moses, the speeches of chapter 31 together with the Song of Moses are set against the background of his imminent death (31:2, 16), and the Blessing of Moses preserves the last words attributed to him before he dies. This gives these speeches special weight. Moses' concern continues to be the future. In these speeches Moses provides the future generations of Israel three instruments: (1) Joshua is commissioned to succeed him so that there will be faithful leadership. (2) The law is highlighted as God's guidance and directions for how to live in the future. (3) The Song is introduced as a warning to Israel. Significantly, they conclude in words of blessing, not unlike the words of blessing that Moses instructed Aaron and his sons to give Israel (Num 6:22-26).

THE TEXT IN THE LIFE OF THE CHURCH

Security and Prosperity

The Blessing of Moses has a decidedly materialistic tone to it as it prays for or projects security and prosperity for the tribes within the Promised Land. God will protect his people and will bless them with *choice gifts of heaven above* (v. 13) and with *choice gifts of the earth and its fullness* (v. 16). The two are combined in the summary of verse 28: *Untroubled is Jacob's abode in a land of grain and wine, where the heavens drop down dew*. The text appears to be unabashedly convinced that God wishes us to be safe and have what we need. Both aspects provide nuance to the way the Christian faith is understood in some circles.

First, those who emphasize God's invitation to his people to be peacemakers and to turn the other cheek sometimes forget that the desire for security and safety is natural and appropriate. This longing for security does not override God's other commands, but it is part of the equation and is God's will. As the church reflects on how it can be God's peaceable people in a world of violence, it must take this longing for security and prosperity on the part of God and humans into consideration.

Second, it questions a one-dimensional emphasis on a call for simple living. It does not advocate an unsustainable lifestyle, or sanction the huge disparity between nations and peoples in their use of the earth's resources, or endorse consumerism: Deuteronomy consistently calls for sharing the resources of the land with each other and with the resident alien. But these resources are to be shared since all are to experience the blessings and abundant prosperity of the land. Even this sharing assumes God's desire that we enjoy the blessings God provides.

Deuteronomy 34:1-12

The Death of Moses

PREVIEW

Not uncommonly, movies and biographies of heroic figures conclude with a moving account of the death of the hero with whom we have come to identify. After Moses says his last words, Deuteronomy shares Moses' death with us (vv. 5-8). A reference to the succession of Joshua (v. 9), and a eulogy for the incomparable Moses complete the book (vv. 10-12).

But before Moses dies, God shows him the land he is prevented from entering, the goal toward which he has been leading the people, and for which he has given Israel the torah (vv. 1-4). This may be a concession on the part of God, but it also becomes a symbolic taking possession of the land. Not only does this complete the life of Moses and the book of Deuteronomy, but also the Pentateuch as a whole, Judaism's foundational Scripture. The stage is now set for the story of Joshua and indeed the whole story of Israel. The rest of the Old Testament tells that part, a story of gaining land and losing land. But it is a story for which Deuteronomy provides the road map. The incomparable Moses may be gone, but he has left behind *the words of this law* and the Song: together they point in the direction Israel must take for long life in the land.

OUTLINE

Moses Views the Promised Land, 34:1-4
Moses Dies, 34:5-8
Joshua Succeeds Moses, 34:9
A Eulogy for the Incomparable Prophet, 34:10-12

EXPLANATORY NOTES

Moses Views the Promised Land 34:1-4

Deuteronomy opens with Israel and Moses *on the plain* (1:1), *in the land of Moab* (1:5). The whole book of Deuteronomy—the explication of the law, the making of the covenant, and the warnings and promises—all take place here. Moses now leaves Israel on the plain and ascends *Mount Nebo, to the top of Pisgah* (34:1). The text locates Pisgah in the Transjordan, just to the north of the Dead Sea, across the Jordan from Jericho. Pisgah may be an alternate name for Nebo, or the name of a particular peak of a larger mountain chain (cf. 3:27; 32:49).

From there God *showed him the whole land* in a panoramic survey. First Moses looks to the north and sees Gilead in the Transjordan and Dan in the far north of Galilee. The phrase "from Dan to Beer-sheba" becomes for Israel a colloquial way of describing the extent of the Promised Land, with Dan the northernmost extreme (Judg 20:1; 1 Sam 3:20; 2 Sam 3:10; etc.). Next Moses looks west across the central hill country all the way to the Mediterranean Sea. And last Moses looks down and westward just across the Jordan to Jericho, known as *the city of palm trees*, and southwest over the Dead Sea to the Negeb, where Beer-Sheba is located. Earlier, Deuteronomy has communicated the extent of the land via geographical features (*the Arabah, the hill country, the Shephelah, the Negeb, and seacoast,* 1:7; cf. 11:24), but now Moses sees into the future with Israelite tribal names already ascribed to regions. From Pisgah, the human eye cannot see the whole extent of the land as outlined here because of intervening mountains, but this is far more than human seeing: God is showing Moses a future for which he has prepared Israel but in which he will not be able to participate.

On a literal level, Deuteronomy and the Pentateuch end with Israel on the border of the Promised Land, yet outside of it. Although Israel has already conquered the Transjordan, it remains only a foretaste of what really counts. Later Joshua describes the actual entrance into the land, with the process only completed under David (2 Sam 7:1). But the systematic viewing of the land is more than Moses having the privilege of seeing what he cannot experience. It also is a symbolic taking possession of the land, possibly even an act of laying a legal claim to the land (Daube: 34-39). The reference to God's oath to the ancestors binds together the whole Pentateuch (note Gen 12:7) as well as the book of Deuteronomy (1:8).

Moses Dies 34:5-8

After seven advance notices (1:37; 3:23-29; 31:2, 14, 16, 29; 32:48-52), Moses finally dies in the land of Moab. At his death he receives the exalted designation *the servant of the* LORD (34:5), a phrase used repeatedly for him in the book of Joshua and beyond (Josh 1:1, 13, 15; 8:31, 33; etc.), but used only of a few other people in Scripture (Joshua, in Josh 24:29; Judg 2:8; David, in the superscriptions of Pss 18 and 36; of "the servant" in Isa 42:19; and Mary, the mother of Jesus, in Luke 1:38). The phrase *at the* LORD's *command* may refer either to the death itself or the specific location. Jewish tradition has interpreted it as the former, with the connotation that Moses did not die of old age or illness but from "a kiss from God" (Tigay: 338). Consistent with this, the text emphasizes that he remained strong until the end despite having reached the appropriate maximum age of 120 (see 31:2). Since the location of his grave is not known, establishing a shrine to Moses, or developing a cult around Moses attached to the grave, becomes highly speculative. The memorial he leaves behind is not some grave marker but *the words of this law* (31:24), the instructions on how to live a life that leads to blessing in the land. At his death Israel mourns the appropriate length of time (cf. 21:13).

Joshua Succeeds Moses 34:9

The other side of the death of Moses is the succession of Joshua. Deuteronomy carefully prepares for this change in leadership. Joshua is introduced as the one who will enter the land with Israel (1:38); Moses has encouraged him (3:21, 28) and commissioned him (31:7-8; cf. Num 27:18-23), and God has confirmed this commissioning (31:14-15, 23). The *spirit of wisdom* that fills Joshua may very well have royal connotations, with Joshua taking on a role not greatly unlike that of a king. When Solomon is granted a wish, he asks for "an understanding mind to govern your people," and God gives him "a wise and discerning mind" (1 Kings 3:3-14; cf. Isa 11:2). Surprisingly, we also read that *the Israelites obeyed him* [Joshua], *doing as the* LORD *had commanded Moses,* a statement in apparent tension with passages announcing that as soon as Moses leaves the scene, the people will *begin to prostrate themselves to the foreign gods in their midst* (Deut 31:16; cf. 31:27). But here Deuteronomy is reassuring Israel that the death of Moses is not the end of the story. Deuteronomy moves within a tension between, on the one hand, regularly warning the people against their inclination to rebel against God and, on the other hand, the assurance that the law can be obeyed and that if Israel has faithful leaders, they can choose life (cf. Josh 24; the stories of the judges). The death of Moses marks the end of one part of the story, but the accession of Joshua to leadership is the start of another, one filled not only with danger and threat but also of promise.

A Eulogy for the Incomparable Prophet 34:10-12

Moses, Deuteronomy concludes, was an incomparable prophet, in his communication with God (*whom the* LORD *knew face to face*) and in what he did (*for all the signs and wonders that the* LORD *sent him to perform*), combining the two central themes of law and exodus. At Mount Horeb, God also spoke to Israel *face to face* (5:4), but the people were afraid, and asked Moses to approach God and hear his words (5:22-27). Moses then becomes the mediator of the remainder of the law, teaching it to Israel. Israel is fortunate to have a God *so near to it as the* LORD *our God*, as reflected in the just ordinances and statutes it has received (4:5-8), and Moses is the one through whom this close God has revealed his ways (cf. Exod 33:11; the NRSV/NIV of Num 12:8 also has *face to face*, but a more literal rendering is *mouth to mouth*). The second grounds are perhaps more surprising since previously these *sign and wonders* and *mighty deeds* associated with the deliverance from Egypt have all been attributed to God (Deut 34:11-12; cf. 4:34; 6:22; 7:19; 26:8; 29:3). This shift in language reflects the uniquely intimate relationship Moses has had with God.

As McConville observes, the "incomparability clause has something conventional about it"; somewhat similar statements are made of Hezekiah and Josiah, suggesting that they cannot be applied literally (2 Kings 18:5; 23:25; 2002: 477). The statement on Moses' uniqueness, however, presents a powerful conclusion to the book, providing validation of Moses and the book from the narrator and from God. It is a word of "support for Deuteronomy's unparalleled and permanent authority" (Nelson 2002: 397). Although Moses is the model for future prophets (*God will raise up for you a prophet like me*, 18:15), none will really compare to Moses. Perhaps most significantly, the word of future prophets will now be judged by whether it coheres with the words of God through Moses in Deuteronomy. Whereas the Blessing of Moses connected the incomparability of Yahweh, the God of Israel, with that of the people Israel (33:26-29), now the incomparability of Moses is presented with an unstated but implicit message: this incomparable prophet with whom God spoke face-to-face has given his incomparable word to the people, and this is the book of Deuteronomy.

THE TEXT IN BIBLICAL CONTEXT
Moses after the Pentateuch

Moses is the dominant figure in the Pentateuch, the scrolls traditionally known as the books of Moses. The story of his birth is told early in Exodus, after which he is at the center of the narrative until his death in Deuteronomy 34. It is to him that God reveals his name; he is God's mouthpiece in negotiations with Pharaoh; he is the one who leads Israel out of Egypt, mediates the covenant at Horeb, and then teaches torah on the plains of Moab. The exodus from Egypt and then the torah of Horeb and Moab become central themes in Jewish theology, Moses is central to each. It is not surprising that Old Testament religion is sometimes considered to be founded by Moses.

It thus is surprising how little a role Moses plays in the Prophets or Writings of the Old Testament. Isaiah refers to him at one point in a reference to the exodus (63:11-12); Jeremiah makes one passing reference to Moses, associating him with Samuel (15:1); Ezekiel never mentions him; Micah has one reference to Moses and the exodus (6:4). Six psalms mention him (Pss 77:20; 90:1; 99:6; 103:7; 105:26; 106:16, 23, 32), five of which concern the exodus narratives, with Psalm 90 simply named a Prayer of Moses. His image begins to change slightly in two late Old Testament books. Malachi connects Moses with statutes and ordinances (4:4), and Daniel speaks of the law of Moses (9:11, 13). In other words, only late Old Testament writings associate Moses with law, with prophetic books giving him minimal attention, usually in relationship to the exodus.

By New Testament times, however, Moses has become the defining figure for Judaism. Judaism had become a religion and tradition defined by law, with Moses the one used by God to give the law. Moses' humanity and fallibility were recognized, but Judaism understood itself as "based on the laws of Moses as interpreted and amplified by the rabbis. At its center lies a belief in the revelation at Sinai and Moses' all-important part in it" (Daiches: 237). Consistent with this, Jesus regularly refers to the law of Moses, or Moses' teachings (e.g., Matt 4:4; Mark 10:1-12; Luke 2:22; John 1:17).

The centrality of Moses for Judaism is reflected in the story of Stephen's martyrdom. The charge against him is that spoke "blasphemous words against Moses and God": here Moses and God are paired. Stephen and the Jesus he worshiped were accused of changing the customs handed down from Moses (Acts 6:11, 13). When Stephen defends himself, he places himself in the larger story of

Israel, in the process mentioning Moses ten times (Acts 7). Though diverse in various ways, the Judaism of Jesus' day was Mosaic.

It thus is not surprising that, for the early church, Moses was seen as prefiguring Jesus, so that Jesus was like Moses, only greater. On more than one occasion Jesus refers to the law of Moses, but then expands it or reinterprets (e.g., Jesus' teaching on the Sabbath). Hebrews compares them as follows:

> Therefore, brothers and sisters, holy partners in a heavenly calling, consider that Jesus, the apostle and high priest of our confession, was faithful to the one who appointed him, just as Moses also "was faithful in all God's house." Yet Jesus is worthy of more glory than Moses, just as the builder of a house has more honor than the house itself. (For every house is built by someone, but the builder of all things is God.) Now Moses was faithful in all God's house as a servant, to testify to the things that would be spoken later. Christ, however, was faithful over God's house as a son, and we are his house if we hold firm the confidence and the pride that belong to hope. (Heb 3:1-6)

Jesus is the new Moses, the clearest mediator between God and people. Interestingly, Judaism after Jesus became more cautious, careful so as "not to make claims for Moses that could be compared to claims made by Christians for Jesus" (Daiches: 240).

THE TEXT IN THE LIFE OF THE CHURCH
Moses Made Public

Cecil B. DeMille's movie *The Ten Commandments* is arguably the most watched and influential movie version of a biblical story. In the year of its release, it took in $34 million, and that was in 1956 dollars. Since then it has been viewed by countless more, and is still seen on television and home video. Who can forget the closing scene where, just before his death, Moses hands over five scrolls (five books of Moses), which we are told he wrote at God's direction. For a generation of North Americans, Moses looks and acts like Charlton Heston (M. Wright: 89-90).

Although the movie was very much a Hollywood production, shaped and tweaked for entertainment and profit, DeMille himself was a dedicated Christian "who saw himself in a missionary role, making the Scriptures attractive and fascinating to the masses in an age of increasing materialism" (Charles Higham, as quoted by M. Wright: 92). He announced to clergy and educators that he would use the profits from the film to create a charitable trust, and he urged them to "use this picture, as I hope and pray that God himself will use it, for the good of the world." (M. Wright: 92). There is no reason to question DeMille's intention and integrity in conveying the essence and truth of a biblical story to the public via the medium of film.

Yet a more careful viewing of the movie reveals that it is not so simple. Critics have long drawn attention to how the movie subtly interacts with critical issues of the day. Although released in the year after the Montgomery bus boycott, the movie is very cautious in the way it handles race and ethnicity. For example, there is no hint in the movie that Moses may have had a black wife (Num 12:1), something that would have greatly offended many in that day. Conversely, the movie is more vocal in support of the Cold War between the West and the Soviet Union, at its peak during this time. In language reminiscent of the way communism was denounced, DeMille introduces the movie with the question, "Are men the property of the state, or are they free souls under God?" The repressive pharaoh, with his foreign accent (Yul Brynner), sounds like the Soviets, with the brave Hebrews struggling for freedom representing Americans. The Jubilee command to Israel (Lev 25:10) is altered slightly but with significant impact: DeMille's Moses proclaims, "Go! Proclaim liberty throughout all the lands." The change to the plural, "lands," converts the call to one for spreading American-style freedom and democracy around the world.

More significantly, as a way of increasing the movie's appeal, the story becomes generic and general, lifting it out of the larger biblical narrative. Israel is not some *peculiar people* (KJV: Deut 14:2; 26:18; NRSV, *treasured possession*), but one that has been "de-ethnicized and departicularized" (M. Wright: 100). Not only does this happen to the people but also to their particular traditions (e.g., the tabernacle and the Aaronic priesthood disappear) and law. Only the Ten Commandments survive, and they are not associated with the particular story. DeMille tells a universalized story with an "emphasis on ethical and abstract notions like freedom and divine mercy," reflecting the longing for shared principles characteristic of the 1950s, rather than "detailed specifics of a particular religion" (M. Wright: 101).

Moses is a huge biblical character. Moving him into the public realm, although having attraction and potential, risks creating a universalized Moses who becomes a tool in the battles of the day.

Martin Luther King Jr. Speaks in Memphis

On April 3, 1968, merely hours before he was assassinated, Martin Luther King Jr. addressed a rally in a church in Memphis, Tennessee.

After referring to the escape of Israel from the bondage of Pharaoh, and to Jesus announcing that he has been anointed to bring good news to the poor, King concludes his speech by putting himself in the shoes of Moses in Deuteronomy 34: "I've been to the mountaintop. . . . I just want to do God's will. And he's allowed me to go up to the mountain. And I've looked over. And I've seen the Promised Land. I may not get there with you. But I want you to know that we, as a people, will get to the promised land." His final public words were "Mine eyes have seen the glory of the coming of the Lord!"

His famous "I Have a Dream" speech, delivered in front of the Lincoln Memorial in Washington, made use of Amos ("We will not be satisfied until justice rolls down like waters and righteousness like a mighty stream"; cf. Amos 5:24) and Isaiah ("I have a dream that one day every valley shall be exalted, every hill and mountain made low"; cf. Isa 40:4-5). Whether it is appropriate to use the category of prophet for King may be debated, but he was someone who consciously tried to live and think within the biblical story.

Outline of Deuteronomy

PART 1, FIRST SPEECH: RETROSPECT AND PROSPECT	**1:1–4:43**
Introduction	**1:1-5**
Retrospect	**1:6–3:29**
Retrospect: Dividing the Load	1:6-18
Instructions to Leave Mount Horeb	1:6-8
The Appointment of Judges	1:9-18
Selection of Judges	1:9-15
Charge to the Judges	1:16-17
Conclusion	1:18
Retrospect: Rebellion at the Border	1:19–2:1
Arrival at the Given Land	1:19-21
Spies Sent to Explore the Land	1:22-25
Rebellion: Refusal to Enter the Land	1:26-33
Refusal to Enter	1:26-28
Moses' Entreaty	1:29-31
Continuing Refusal to Trust	1:32-33
Yahweh's Verdict	1:34-40
Adult Generation Denied Entrance	1:34-36
Moses Shares the Fate of the People	1:37-38
The Little Ones Reprieved	1:39-40
Rebellion: Presumptuous Attempt to Enter Land	1:41-45

Decision to Enter	1:41
Yahweh's Entreaty	1:42
Disastrous Effort to Enter Land	1:43-44
The Closing of Yahweh's Ears	1:45
Outcome: Aimless Wandering	1:46–2:1
Retrospect: Peaceful Encounters	2:2-23
Crossing the Land of Esau	2:2-8
God's Instructions	2:2-6
Review of Wilderness Period	2:7
Travel Report	2:8
Crossing the Land of Moab	2:9-15
God's Instructions	2:9
Historical Interruption	2:10-12
God's Instructions Continued	2:13a
Travel Report	2:13b
Review of Wilderness Period	2:14-15
Bypassing the Land of Ammon	2:16-23
The End of the Wilderness Period	2:16
God's Instructions	2:17-19
Historical Interruption	2:20-23
Retrospect: Hostile Confrontations	2:24–3:11
Begin to Take Possession	2:24-25
The Defeat of Sihon, King of Heshbon	2:26-37
Unsuccessful Peace Negotiations	2:26-30
Yahweh Announces Victory	2:31
The Victory Report	2:32-36
Ammon Obediently Bypassed	2:37
The Defeat of Og, King of Bashan	3:1-7
Og Confronts Israel	3:1
Yahweh Announces Victory	3:2
The Victory Report	3:3-7
Concluding Summary	3:8-11
Retrospect: Final Arrangements for Crossing the Jordan	3:12-29
Allocation of the Land beyond the Jordan	3:12-17
Allocation of Land to Reuben, Gad, and Half of Manasseh	3:12-13a
Historical Interruption	3:13b
More Detailed Description of Allotments	3:14-17
Solidarity for the Crossing	3:18-20
Charge to Joshua: *Fear Not!*	3:21-22
Moses Denied Permission to Cross the Jordan	3:23-28
Moses' Request: *Let Me Cross*	3:23-25

Yahweh's Response: *No*	3:26-28
Geographical Location: Valley opposite Beth-peor	3:29

Prospect	**4:1-43**
Opening Challenge	4:1-4
The Uniqueness of Israel	4:5-8
Preaching against Graven Images	4:9-31
Basis of the Command	4:9-14
Expounding the Command	4:15-22
Consequences of Disobeying the Command	4:23-31
The Uniqueness of the God of Israel	4:32-39
Concluding Challenge	4:40
Appendix: Designating Cities of Refuge	4:41-43

PART 2, SECOND SPEECH: PREACHING TORAH	**4:44–28:68**
Introduction	**4:44-49**
The Horeb Covenant	**5:1-33**
A Covenant for *Today*	5:1-5
The Content of the Horeb Covenant	5:6-22
Prologue	5:6
The Commandments	5:7-21
The First: Other Gods	5:7
The Second: Idols	5:8-10
The Third: Name of Yahweh	5:11
The Fourth: Sabbath	5:12-15
The Fifth: Father and Mother	5:16
The Sixth: Murder	5:17
The Seventh: Adultery	5:18
The Eighth: Stealing	5:19
The Ninth: False Witness	5:20
The Tenth: Coveting	5:21
Conclusion	5:22
Moses Appointed Mediator	5:23-33
Israel Asks Moses to Serve as Mediator	5:23-27
God Confirms Moses as Mediator	5:28-31
Concluding Exhortation	5:32-33

Preaching the Foundational Commandment	**6:1–11:32**
Yahweh Is One—Yahweh Alone	6:1-9
Introduction	6:1-3

The Foundational Commandment	6:4-9
Remembering Yahweh in the Land	6:10-25
Two Warnings for the Land	6:10-19
The Gifted Nature of the Land	6:10-15
The Danger of Testing God	6:16-19
The Story Provides the Meaning	6:20-25
Chosen to Be a Holy Possession	7:1-26
Election Requires Separation	7:1-5
Election and Its Basis	7:6-11
Israel's Election	7:6
Rejection of Erroneous Explanation	7:7
Election Grounded in God's Love	7:8
Therefore Yahweh Your God Is God	7:9-11
Faithfulness to Election Leads to Blessing	7:12-26
Outline of Blessing	7:12-16
Blessing and the Awesome God	7:17-26
Remember! Do Not Forget!	8:1-20
Introductory Entreaty	8:1
Remember!	8:2-10
Do Not Forget!	8:11-17
Concluding Warning: Remember! Do Not Forget!	8:18-20
Israel: Stubborn, Not Righteous	9:1–10:11
Explaining God, Characterizing Israel	9:1-6
God, the Devouring Fire, Crosses Over before Israel	9:1-3
Justification: Not Because of Righteousness, for Israel Is Stubborn	9:4-6
Israel's Stubbornness Epitomized at Horeb	9:7–10:11
Introduction	9:7-8
Moses on Horeb	9:9-14
Moses Intercedes on Behalf of the People	9:15-29
The Covenant Renewed	10:1-5
Interruption: Death of Aaron, Designation of Levites	10:6-9
Return to the Journey	10:10-11
A Midcourse Review	10:12–11:32
God's Requirement	10:12–11:1
God's Requirement Pronounced	10:12-13
The Wonder of Election	10:14-15
The Justice of God	10:16-19
God's Requirement Repeated	10:20–11:1
Lessons from the Past	11:2-7
Enjoying the Land of Milk and Honey	11:8-17
Call to Obey	11:8

Outline of Deuteronomy

A Land Cared for by God	11:9-12
The Fruit of Obedience	11:13-15
The Consequence of Apostasy	11:16-17
A Reminder of the Great Commandment	11:18-25
The Alternatives: Blessing and Curse	11:26-32

Preaching the Moab Covenant — 12:1–26:19

Exclusive Worship of the One God	12:1–14:21
Worship at The Place	12:1-32
Introductory Exhortation: *Diligently Observe*	12:1
Demolish the Places of the Nations	12:2-3
Seek The Place	12:4-28
Presentation of the Directive	12:4-7
Expansion of the Directive	12:8-28
Centralization	12:8-12
Secular Slaughter	12:13-16
Centralization	12:17-19
Secular Slaughter	12:20-25
Centralization	12:26-28
Do Not Imitate the Worship of the Nations	12:29-31
Concluding Exhortation: *Diligently Observe*	12:32
Purging Apostasy	13:1-18
If a Prophet Leads You Astray	13:1-5
If Anyone Close to You Leads You Astray	13:6-11
If a Town Goes Astray	13:12-18
Cleanliness and Purity for a Holy People	14:1-21
Introduction	14:1-2
Do Not Eat Any Abhorrent Thing	14:3-20
Summary Prohibition	14:3
Clean and Unclean Life of the Land	14:4-8
Clean and Unclean Life in the Sea	14:9-10
Clean and Unclean Life in the Sky	14:11-20
Conclusion	14:21
Justice in Israel: The Community	14:22–15:18
The Annual Tithe	14:22-29
The Annual Tithe Command	14:22
The Annual Tithe of Celebration	14:23-27
The Third-Year Tithe of Assistance	14:28-29
A Sabbatical Release	15:1-18
The Sabbatical Debt Release	15:1-11
The Debt Release Command	15:1
The Manner of Release	15:2-3

Consequences of Obedience	15:4-6
Exhortation: Give Generously to Those in Need	15:7-11
The Sabbatical Slave Release	15:12-18
The Slave Release Command	15:12
The Manner of Release	15:13-14
Exhortation: Remember	15:15
An Escape Clause	15:16-17
Concluding Exhortation	15:18
Festivals and the Cult	15:19–16:17
Consecrating the Firstborn	15:19-23
A Festival Calendar for The Place	16:1-17
Passover and Unleavened Bread	16:1-8
Festival of Weeks	16:9-12
Festival of Booths	16:13-15
Concluding Summary	16:16-17
Leadership and Judicial Procedures	16:18–19:21
Judges and Judicial Procedures	16:18–17:13
Appointment of Judges and Officials	16:18-20
Two Instructions for the Cult	16:21–17:1
Judicial Procedures	17:2-13
Local Courts	17:2-7
The Court at The Place	17:8-13
The King	17:14-20
Permission to Have a King	17:14-15
Directives for the King	17:16-20a
Restrictions on Royal Policies	17:16-17
A Torah Scholar	17:18-19
An Obedient *Brother*	17:20a
The Outcome: A Dynasty	17:20b
Levitical Priests	18:1-8
Basic Principles	18:1-2
The Dues Owed the Priests	18:3-5
Levites at The Place	18:6-8
Prophets	18:9-22
Rejection of False Prophetic Practices	18:9-14
A Prophet Raised by God	18:15-22
Further Judicial Procedures	19:1-21
Cities of Refuge	19:1-13
The Neighbor's Boundary Marker	19:14
Regulations Governing Witnesses	19:15-21
A Single Witness Is Insufficient to Convict	19:15
Punishment for a Malicious Witness	19:16-21

Outline of Deuteronomy

War	20:1-20
Foundational Principles of War	20:1-9
Trusting God for Victory	20:1-4
Reducing the Militia	20:5-9
The Conduct of War	20:10-18
Distant Cities	20:10-14
Cities of the Land	20:15-18
Consideration for Trees	20:19-20
Miscellaneous	21:1–25:19
Purging the Guilt of an Unsolved Murder	21:1-9
Consideration for War Brides	21:10-14
Difficulty in the Home	21:15-21
A Man with Two Wives	21:15-17
Parents of a Rebellious Son	21:18-21
Handling the Body of One Executed	21:22-23
Helping the Neighbor	22:1-3
Consideration for Animals: The Fallen Donkey or Ox	22:4
Abhorrent Mixtures	22:5, 9-11
Consideration for Animals: Preserving the Mother Bird	22:6-7
Avoiding Criminal Negligence	22:8
Four Tassels on a Cloak	22:12
A Man Slanders His Wife	22:13-21
The Crime	22:13-14
The Indictment	22:15-17
A Guilty Verdict	22:18-19
Epilogue: The Seriousness of the Original Allegation	22:20-21
Illicit Sexual Affairs	22:22-30
Admission to the Assembly of the Lord	23:1-8
Exclusions from the Assembly of the Lord	23:1-6
Policies for Edomites and Egyptians	23:7-8
Maintaining Purity in the Camp	23:9-14
Escaped Slaves	23:15-16
Abhorrent Cultic Practices	23:17-18
Charitable Loans: Prohibition of Interest	23:19-20
Making and Fulfilling Vows	23:21-23
Gleaning: For the Gleaner	23:24-25
A Twice-Divorced Woman	24:1-4
Conscription and a Recently Married Man	24:5
Charitable Loans: A Limitation on Pledges	24:6
Stealing a Person	24:7
Instructions in Cases of Skin Diseases	24:8-9
Charitable Loans: Further Limitation on Pledges	24:10-13

Payment of Wages	24:14-15
Individual Legal Responsibility	24:16
Justice for the Resident Alien, the Orphan, and the Widow	24:17-18
Gleaning: For the Farmer	24:19-22
Controlling Flogging	25:1-3
Consideration for Animals: Muzzling the Ox	25:4
A Widow without a Son	25:5-10
A Woman and a Fight	25:11-12
Honest Weights	25:13-16
Remember Amalek	25:17-19
Theology through Worship	26:1-19
Firstfruits	26:1-11
Third-Year Tithes	26:12-15
A Mutual Agreement	26:16-19

Covenant Renewal, Blessings and Curses — 27:1–28:68

Covenant Renewal at Shechem	27:1-26
A Commemorative Monument and an Altar	27:1-8
Exhortation to Obey	27:9-10
Prohibitions in Curse Form	27:11-26
Covenant Blessings and Curses	28:1-68
Blessings	28:1-14
Curses	28:15-68

PART 3, THIRD SPEECH: THE COVENANT IN MOAB — 29:1–30:20

Introduction	29:1
A Historical Basis	29:2-9
Entering the Covenant	29:10-15
Words of Doom	29:16-29
For the Individual	29:16-21
For the Community	29:22-29
A Word of Salvation	30:1-10
The Near Word	30:11-14
A Final Appeal	30:15-20

PART 4, TRANSITION: TOWARD A MOSES-LESS PEOPLE — 31:1–34:12

Preparation for Transition	31:1-30
Moses to Israel: God Will Cross Over before You	31:1-6

Moses to Joshua (before Israel): God Will Be with You	31:7-8
Moses to Priests and Elders: Read the Law to Israel	31:9-13
God to Moses: Prepare for Joshua's Commissioning	31:14-15
God to Moses: Write This Song for Israel	31:16-22
God to Joshua: I Will Be with You	31:23
Moses to Levites: Place the Law, Assemble the People	31:24-30
The Song of Moses	32:1-52
The Song	32:1-43
The Summons	32:1-3
A Survey of the Relationship	32:4-18
God Responds: I Will Hide My Face	32:19-25
God Relents	32:26-35
The One God Vindicates His People	32:36-43
Remember the Song	32:44-47
Preparation for the Death of Moses	32:48-52
The Blessing of Moses	33:1-29
Situating the Blessing	33:1
Opening Hymn	33:2-5
Blessing the Tribes	33:6-25
Reuben	33:6
Judah	33:7
Levi	33:8-11
Benjamin	33:12
Joseph	33:13-17
Zebulun and Issachar	33:18-19
Gad	33:20-21
Dan	33:22
Naphtali	33:23
Asher	33:24-25
Concluding Hymn	33:26-29
The Death of Moses	34:1-12
Moses Views the Promised Land	34:1-4
Moses Dies	34:5-8
Joshua Succeeds Moses	34:9
A Eulogy for the Incomparable Prophet	34:10-12

Essays

BIBLICAL MONOTHEISM For most contemporary Westerners, the definition of monotheism is fairly simple: the belief that only one God exists. Its opposite is polytheism, the belief that more than one God exists. We then consider Christians, Jews, and Muslims to be monotheistic faiths, with many "pagan religions" considered polytheistic. But is it that simple?

There is much evidence in the Old Testament that the people of Israel were not consistently monotheistic. The story of Elijah and the prophets of Baal and Asherah may be the most blatant example (1 Kings 18), but countless other stories, psalms, and pronouncements make it clear that throughout its history, people in Israel recognized or worshiped other gods in addition to Yahweh, the God of Moses and the exodus.

The contemporary definition does not quite fit the Old Testament either. For one thing, the Old Testament lacks the contemporary interest in philosophical statements about reality. Far more significant are observations or directives about relationships and practice. Further, numerous passages appear to reflect an acknowledgment of other gods or at least divine powers. In the Song of Miriam we read, "Who is like you, O LORD, among the gods?" (Exod 15:11). Deuteronomy speaks of *myriads of holy ones at his* [God's] *right* (33:2) and of God having fixed the boundaries of peoples *according to the number of the gods* (32:8). Psalm 29 addresses "sons of gods" (v. 1 NRSV mg., lit.), and Micaiah speaks of God "sitting on his throne, with all the host of heaven standing beside him to the right and to the left of him" (1 Kings 22:19). Even the first commandment references *other gods* without challenging their existence. Israel lived in a world of heavenly and divine beings (Deut 5:7).

And yet it has integrity to speak of biblical monotheism, and not only as a conviction that developed late in Israel's story. Describing the religion of Israel's ancestors before the time of Moses is fraught with difficulty, but from Moses' time at least a practical or effective monotheism is present, one that understands Yahweh as the particular God who has redeemed

Israel from slavery, entering into an exclusive relationship with it at Mount Sinai/Horeb. Through these events Israel came to know God (e.g., Exod 6:7; 14:30-31), to *know that the* LORD *is God; there is no other besides him* (Deut 4:35 RSV, emph. added; cf. 4:39), and to speak of Yahweh as *God of gods and Lord of lords, the great God, mighty and awesome* (Deut 10:17). This may not be contemporary theoretical monotheism, but as Richard Bauckham puts it, "The element that makes it a kind of monotheism, is not the denial or existence of other 'gods,' but an understanding of the uniqueness of YHWH that puts him in a class of his own, a wholly different class from any other heavenly or supernatural being, even if these are called 'gods'" (210).

This God demands undivided loyalty and worship and is understood as the supreme power of the universe. This covenantal Yahwism "was likely only one religious perspective among many in ancient Israel," and may even have been a minority position (Cook 2004: 11; cf. Halpern 1987). But it is the position strongly advocated by prophets like Hosea and Micah and the Deuteronomic movement, eventually becoming the normative position of the Old Testament.

CHIASM This is also called inclusio, envelope, or concentric construction. Chiasm is a literary technique in which words, statements, events, or themes in a passage or longer unit repeat, so that the beginning corresponds with the end, the next item with the item next to the end, and so on. The term comes from the Greek letter *chi* (shaped like an X) because the elements of a chiasm can be arranged to resemble an X.

Biblical writers frequently use chiasm, though often it is not recognized by contemporary readers. Chiasm has the effect of drawing focus on its central elements (which may be part of the chiasm) or element (the one point not repeated), usually the most important part of the passage. Consider an example from Matthew 6:24 RSV:

A¹ No one can serve two masters;
   B¹ for either he will hate the one
      C¹ and love the other,
      C² or he will be devoted to the one
   B² and despise the other.
A² You cannot serve God and mammon.

Deuteronomy makes considerable use of chiasm, with the structure of the book as a whole having a chiastic element (see "The Structure and Logic of Deuteronomy" in the introduction). A good example from within the book is 1:1-5. Unlike Matthew 6:24, here the central point stands by itself, although it expands upon A¹ and A² (emph. added):

A¹ *These are the words that Moses spoke* . . ., (1:1a)
   B¹ Place: *beyond the Jordan* . . ., (1:1b)
      C¹ Time: *eleven days* . . ., (1:2)
         D *Moses spoke* . . . *just as the* LORD *had commanded*, (1:3)

    C² Time: *after he had defeated* . . ., (1:4)
    B² Place: *Beyond the Jordan* . . ., (1:5a)
    A² Moses undertook to <u>expound</u> this law . . . , (1:5b)

CHRISTIANS AND OLD TESTAMENT (AS) LAW In one of his disputes with the Pharisees, Jesus says, "The law and the prophets were in effect until John came; since then the good news of the kingdom of God is proclaimed" (Luke 16:16). With this verse in mind, many Christians consider the Old Testament to be a book of law superseded by the gospel preached and personified by Jesus Christ and the New Testament. The use of the term *law* as a kind of shorthand for the Old Testament, sometimes in conjunction with the term *prophets*, only supports this perception (e.g., Matt 5:18; 7:12; 22:40; Luke 5:17; John 10:34; 12:34; 15:25; Rom 3:19; 1 Cor 14:21).

Although perhaps not stating it explicitly, for many this designation connotes not only that the Old Testament contains many laws or regulations, but also that the God of the Old Testament responds to people legalistically, on the basis of their obedience to law. Jesus, in contrast, delivers a message of grace and forgiveness. Stories like Jesus rescuing the woman caught in adultery (John 8:1-11), or Jesus forgiving the sinful woman who washed his feet with her hair (Luke 7:37-50), in this line of thinking, exemplify the New Testament gospel; in contrast, the story of God sending a plague upon Israel for worshiping the golden calf (Exod 32:1-35) is considered more typical of the Old Testament. The Old and New Testaments then are easily contrasted as law and grace.

This misrepresents both testaments. Like the New Testament, the Old Testament consistently gives God's grace preeminence over law. It does this with regard to the order of salvation; God's act of salvation, election, and exodus, based entirely on unmerited love, precedes any call for response or law. And it does this in its vision for the future; in the end, God's grace will overcome the law/punishment dynamic as God circumcises Israel's heart and causes it to return to God (see comments on Deut 4:23-31; 30:1-10). On the other side, punishment also is very much part of the New Testament, as Jesus' parable of sheep and goats makes abundantly clear (Matt 25:31-46). In both testaments, grace is the prior and ultimately more powerful force, even as the consequences of disobediences are not disregarded.

Despite this image, however, Christians continue to use the Old Testament as a resource for ethical discernment. The most common way of doing this, by scholars and laypeople alike, is to focus on Old Testament commandments or lawlike materials. The practice of early rabbinic Judaism to identify ethics with obedience to the commands of the Old Testament has been influential for this approach. Jesus' disputes with the Pharisees, as found in the Gospels, seem to reflect it as well. Consistent with this, a recent book on Old Testament ethics states, "The heart of Old Testament ethics is to be placed squarely on the explicit commands found mainly in the Pentateuch" (Kaiser: 42).

Of course, not all Old Testament "laws" are considered equally applicable. One way of distinguishing among laws is to categorize them as cultic/ritual, moral, or civil regulations (e.g., Kaiser; cf. Block 2012: 128). Since the church is not a state, Old Testament civil regulations fall by the way, at least for the church. Cultic or ritual regulations are dismissed as obsolete because of Christ's teaching and death on the cross (e.g., directions for sacrifice; Block 2012: 134), or as inconsistent with the freedom of the gospel (e.g., OT dietary regulations). This limits ethical direction largely to selected sets of commandments (e.g., the Decalogue) and other regulations categorized as moral.

But this approach is unsound and unworkable. There is no evidence for such categorization within the Old Testament itself. The categories represent an external imposition on Old Testament material that forces it into a mold quite foreign to it, a mold that distorts rather than enlightens (Martens). Such an approach also continues to treat Old Testament torah as contemporary law, intended to be followed and implemented in a manner similar to laws drafted by legislation *[Law, p. 555]*.

More helpful, although still incomplete, is the effort to find timeless principles reflected by the material, both the legal-like material and the narratives. Block thus encourages Christians to "seize the underlying principles of those that are culturally and contextually specific and apply these principles to the contexts in which we live" (2012: 136–37). It is true that one can deduce principles like loving God and neighbor from various passages, but these general principles often are quite lifeless and so non-particular that meaning tends to be fairly shallow. Such a "search for principles ignores the storied setting and is in danger of ending up with abstractions detached from the person of God" (Martens: 203).

Remembering that the Old Testament is rooted within a larger narrative context points in a more helpful direction. The Bible is the story of a people of God experiencing God, entering into a covenant with God, with torah providing a vision for what it means to be a holy community faithful to that God. Within that larger account, the Old Testament plays a direction-setting role. For Christians, the New Testament affixes to it the story of Jesus fulfilling that direction, establishing the new covenant. This story as a whole, with Jesus at the center, then becomes the vision for what faithful community life entails, with practices that are life-giving to those in the community while also bringing blessing to those surrounding it. Old Testament legal-like material contributes to the fullness of this vision, but also important are the stories, the prophetic announcements, and the proverbs. All take part in that narrative, painting a picture of faithfulness (see W. Janzen 1994, with his "paradigmatic approach"; C. Wright 1983; 1990; 1995; 2004; Birch 1985; 1991).

Such an approach is not as tidy or simple as applying some laws and ignoring others, or perhaps even as workable as ethical guidance based on principles. Yet it is an approach more faithful to the nature and style of the Old Testament material. In this way the Old Testament, with both its narrative and its legal-like material, contributes to revealing a paradigm of faithfulness to God for the twenty-first-century church.

COMPOSITION OF DEUTERONOMY The basic story line of Deuteronomy is fairly straightforward. After arriving at the border of the Promised Land for the second time, there is a pause in the action. There, in the plains of Moab near the Jordan, Moses gives a final address to the people, providing direction, or torah, for how to live toward blessing in the Promised Land. Deuteronomy, then, is a record of that speech.

Already centuries ago, Jewish and Christian sages questioned whether Moses could have written about his own death (ch. 34). They also noticed that a number of passages speak of Moses in third person (e.g., 1:1-5; 4:41-46; 5:1; ch. 31). As scholars studied the text more carefully, other questions arose. For example, although Deuteronomy calls for the centralization of all sacrifice at *the place* God will choose (ch. 12), until the time of Josiah there is no hint that such a prohibition was observed or even known. Further, some passages in Deuteronomy appear to have as their background the time of exile, 587–539 BCE (e.g., 4:24-31; 30:1-5).

The simple literary schema of the book conceals a long and complex composition process. Traditions and memories of Moses and Horeb were told and passed on from generation to generation, around the campfire, in worship, and in festival. Von Rad, for example, suggests that Levitical preaching at an ancient sanctuary, such as Bethel or Shechem, may have carried on the tradition (1966: 26). Deuteronomy then makes use of these memories of early history along with legal-like material. Moses proclaiming his last words to the people as they prepare to enter the Promised Land, giving them the key for a life of blessing within that land, becomes a powerful symbol and vision for historic tradition. Moses as the voice through which God spoke in a foundational way to Israel thus retains authentic memory.

Detailing how that voice became central to a later book is a risky proposition, but hints suggest that something like the following is possible. The crucial period for shaping the book is likely Israel and Judah in the eighth and seventh centuries BCE. These were challenging times politically, economically, and religiously. After some years in decline, Assyria reasserted itself as a major power; Tiglath-pileser III grew the Assyrian Empire in a systematic manner, extending its domination over the region. In 722 Assyrian armies captured Samaria, the capital of Israel, marking the end of the Northern Kingdom. Judah did survive but only as a small rump state, with many of its outlying towns and cities captured. Judah's more fortunate fate was probably due to its remote location in the highlands as well as its willingness to pay tribute to Assyria.

These centuries also were a time of significant social upheaval and economic change. Land that had been treated as an inheritance from God gradually became a commodity that could be bought and sold, leading to corruption and indebtedness. The power of the central state grew, taxation increased, and a well-to-do middle class developed, with the classical eighth-century prophets challenging this breakdown of traditional society.

Whether due to Assyrian pressure or natural developments, Assyrian gods and ritual began to enter both Israel and Judah even as older regional gods and practices remained a temptation for the people. The confrontation between Elijah and the prophets of Baal in the ninth century BCE reflects the intensity of the conflict. Kings in both Israel and Judah promoted or at least allowed these intrusions. Influenced by his wife Jezebel of Tyre, King Ahab of Israel himself worshiped Baal and built an altar for him (1 Kings 16:30-34). Later King Ahaz of Judah "even made his son pass through fire" and instructed his priest to construct an altar in Jerusalem based on one he had seen in Damascus (2 Kings 16:3, 10-18; cf. Deut 18:10). Historic Israelite faith and tradition were under siege.

In these turbulent times and in the face of intense opposition, proponents of a monotheistic Yahwism (Yahweh is the one true God) stood up for the historic faith of Moses. The eighth-century prophet Hosea represents this dedication. Israel has played the harlot, he preaches, chasing after gods other than the God of the exodus. People are oppressing each other. For all of these transgressions, he announces, the people will be punished, with a return to Egypt threatened. And yet, Hosea proclaims, the love of God will prevail, leading him to take back his adulterous partner.

At some point the theology of this reform movement eventually became a written document. This was possibly after 722 BCE and the fall of Samaria, an event that led to a flight of refugees from the Northern Kingdom to Judah in the South. This reform effort likely had significant influence from those in the North; the preaching of Hosea was probably associated with it in some way. But it was not limited to the North. An early draft of Deuteronomy thus was an impassioned rallying cry in the midst of an intense battle over historic Mosaic Yahwism. It is common to see this initial draft as the core of our Deuteronomy, largely chapters 5–28 or 5–30 (e.g., P. Miller 1990: 3; Nelson 2002: 4-5; Weinfeld 1991: 10; C. Wright 1996: 6).

Correlation between the content of Deuteronomy and the reform of Josiah suggests that this initial draft is the lawbook Josiah's workmen discovered when renovating the temple in 622 BCE, which then influenced his reform (2 Kings 22–23). The same commitments and convictions that fueled this reform movement appear to have previously influenced Hezekiah's actions nearly a century earlier. Through his efforts, Josiah functionally canonized Deuteronomy, giving it constitution-like status for the nation.

Josiah's reform may have impacted the people of Israel, transforming their understanding of God and their cultic practices, but on the political level it was a failure. Judah did not become powerful; Josiah was killed at Megiddo in a battle with Egypt shortly after initiating the reform. A few years later, Babylon, the new superpower of the day, took control of the region. In 587 BCE Nebuchadnezzar captured and sacked Jerusalem, burning the temple of Solomon to the ground. Many were killed, with the leading citizens, including the last king, taken to Babylon in exile. The period of Israel, and then Israel and Judah as political nations, had come to an end. The book of Lamentations contains dirges likely inspired by this situation, the most traumatic event in the story of Old Testament Israel.

But the destruction of Jerusalem not only ended an era; it also inaugurated a new era. The trauma of 587 BCE raised serious questions about Israel's future and its relationship to the God who delivered it from Egypt and had given it the Promised Land. Probably making use of an earlier version, an epic history of Israel was produced (Joshua to 2 Kings) with the core theology of Deuteronomy serving as the lens through which that story is told. With the addition of its opening chapters (Deut 1–4), as well as editorial additions throughout, Deuteronomy becomes the introduction to this history.

Canonical Deuteronomy thus is a post-587 published sermon—whether exilic or postexilic may be debated—calling each new generation to a vigorous faithfulness to Yahweh, the God of the exodus. Over the centuries it evolved from a rallying cry in the midst of intense debate over monotheism, to what became a *normative summation of Jewish orthodoxy*, to be read aloud to the people every seven years (31:10-11).

Who within Israel was responsible for the development of the book is another debated question. Each specific proposal, however, runs into difficulties. The book's exhortatory style, its strong advocacy of social justice, as well as thematic connections with the book of Hosea—all may suggest a prophetic origin, but prophets themselves play a fairly minor role in the book. Priests are another option. Toward the end of Deuteronomy, Moses gives the priests responsibility for the book of torah, but at the same time, its regulations are costly for the priests, since they lose some of their tithes. More significantly, Deuteronomy reflects little interest in sacrifice and the kind of ritual over which priests are responsible. Given Josiah's use of the book, one might think of the royal court as a possible home, but the role of the king is so minimal for Deuteronomy that this is unlikely. Affinities with wisdom literature, including a tendency toward secularization, have suggested sages and scribes as the possible originators (Weinfeld 1972), but this is too narrow as well.

Frank Crüsemann has proposed that a reform movement representing a coalition across the usual social and vocational boundaries may have been responsible for the book. Among these will have been "people of the land," agricultural landowners who championed loyalty to Yahweh, the God of Israel, rather than to Assyria or its god (201–75). This proposal may also be too narrow, but it locates the origin firmly within the period of Assyrian domination, probably beginning in the Northern Kingdom in the eighth century. Initially the royal court of Judah may not have been sympathetic to this demand for loyalty to Yahweh since the court allied itself with Assyria and would not have wanted to risk that relationship; but with the capture of Samaria in 722, and then the rise of Hezekiah to the throne of Jerusalem, it fell on more receptive ears. Such a background also fits the rhetoric of Deuteronomy, with its all-Israel emphasis aimed at the heads of all households. What bound these people together was their common commitment to historical monotheistic Yahwism, with a vision for an Israel in which justice and impartiality shaped their life together.

The Deuteronomy we have, this suggests, may not have been penned directly by Moses, yet one can affirm it as Mosaic.

According to a Talmudic tale, when Moses was on Sinai receiving the Torah, he was shown the classroom of Rabbi Akiba, the great legal scholar of many centuries later. Moses grieved when he could not understand the discussion, until he heard a student ask Akiba for the source of what he was saying, and Akiba answered, "This is a law given to Moses at Sinai." The great structure of Jewish law that eventuated from Moses' original teachings is ultimately his, even if he would not recognize the forms it would eventually take. In that sense, the writers of Deuteronomy, too, have given us the teachings of Moses, that is, a statement of his fundamental monotheistic teaching, designed to resist the assimilatory temptations of the writers' age and to preserve monotheism for the future. (Tigay: xxxi)

Over the years scholars have devoted inordinate energy and research on historical and literary critical questions. Beyond conjecturing here how traditions going back to Moses might have developed into an exilic or postexilic book, this commentary forgoes those issues. Rather, it will treat the book as a whole as a post-587 document addressed to a Moses-less people, challenging them to faithfulness in their day, whether in hope of returning to the land (if placed during the exile), or remaining in the land (if placed in postexilic Judah). At the same time the older, traditional setting in the plains of Moab, and the battles over monotheism in the eighth and seventh centuries, will remain in view. Whatever the setting, Deuteronomy calls for faithfulness *today*.

CULT Religion, social scientists sometimes suggest, can be viewed as a composite of belief, ritual, and ethics. *Belief* is the abstract aspect, the way people think about God, the world, humans, and how they interact. Today some might call this *worldview*. *Ritual*, or *cult* as it is often termed, is the liturgical practices of the religion, or worship, especially corporate but also individual. When used technically like this, cult is not a pejorative term referring to flawed religious groups but simply one aspect of religion, whether Jewish, Christian, or anything else. *Ethics* is the morality of the religion, how people interact with each other and what is considered right or wrong. These three may provide a simplistic description, with the lines between them far from clean. But they can serve as a helpful grid for looking at different religious bodies.

Different religious traditions tend to give more weight to one of these than the other. This grid can be helpful, for example, in getting at a significant difference between the way Christianity and Judaism have developed. Although one can debate whether this is faithful to Scripture, Christianity for many has become a religion in which the belief or faith element is most important, as reflected in the term *believer* that some use as a synonym for *Christian*. Creeds or confessions, in that case, are central for the *faith*. Jewish groups, in contrast, tend to put comparatively less weight on correct belief and greater weight on a combination of ethics and ritual, or practice. As a result Christian-Jewish dialogue has sometimes faltered as Christians have wanted to debate theology (how we understand God, how we understand evil, etc.) with Jews who have comparatively less interest in those issues *[Sacrifices and Offerings, p. 565]*.

DEUTERONOMISTIC HISTORY Deuteronomistic History is a name for the Old Testament books of Deuteronomy to Kings (excluding Ruth). It tells the story of Israel from the time it reached the borders of the Promised Land until the destruction of Jerusalem and the beginning of the Babylonian exile in 587 BCE.

In 1943 Martin Noth proposed that these were not individual books but rather a unified history written during the time of the exile, providing a theological explanation for the traumatic events of 722 (the defeat of Samaria and end of the Northern Kingdom) and 587. These national disasters did not happen because God was unfaithful, nor because the gods of the enemy had defeated the God of Israel, but because Israel had broken its covenant with God and worshiped other gods. Deuteronomy (at least its core) served as the theological lens through which this history was told, pointing to this explanation. King Josiah's workers had found this "book of the law" in the temple, and he had given it prominence in his reform (2 Kings 22–23). Regular evaluations of the kings, each of whom is judged on the basis of whether or not he had centralized worship in Jerusalem as required by Deuteronomy 12, provides a key connection between Deuteronomy and the history. Noth also suggested that an exilic historian had drafted the opening chapters of Deuteronomy (chs. 1–4) as an introduction to the history as a whole, and then placed the book at the beginning of the history.

Noth's proposal has generated significant discussion. Some American scholars suggest that there already was a preexilic version of this history, written prior to or around the time of King Josiah (e.g., Cross). This history then received further editing and additional material during the exile, bringing it up to date. Some more radical scholars argue that the whole history was written much later, perhaps even during the Persian period (e.g., Lemche; Thompson). Yet the basic thesis that these books represent a unified story of Israel, with Deuteronomy providing the theological lens through which this story is viewed, remains a common position.

DEUTERONOMY, COVENANT, AND POLITICAL TREATIES That covenant (or treaty) is important in the Old Testament, especially in Deuteronomy, is indisputable. What is debated is whether the term *covenant* (Hebrew *berit*) has a single core meaning, at what point in Israel's history covenant became an important word for the relationship between God and Israel, and whether Israel's understanding of covenant was influenced by ancient political treaties, and if so, how.

With regard to the first question, this commentary takes the position that regardless of whether or not the term *covenant* originally emphasized obligation in a unilateral manner (either a self-obligation or one externally imposed), within the Old Testament it is used more generally as an agreement or formally acknowledged understanding between two parties. This is consistent with Deuteronomy's use of it for both the promise of God to the ancestors as well as the more conditional relationship associated with Mount Horeb.

The question of when covenant became an important term for the relationship between God and Israel is more difficult. The biblical text does use it in Genesis for the promises God makes to Noah (6:18; 9:9) and later to Israel's ancestors (15:18; 17:2; etc.), as well as in Exodus for the relationship confirmed between God and Israel at Mount Sinai (19:5; 24:8, etc.). Ever since the work of Julius Wellhausen, however, it is common to argue that this reflects later theological reflection on early traditions, with the covenant emphasis originating in the late preexilic period, with the preaching of prophets and the Deuteronomic movement. Scholars challenged this in the 1950s and 1960s, arguing that not only was covenant—as a theological concept for God's relationship to Israel—old, but that it quite early had a sociopolitical expression reflected in the twelve tribes bound together in a confederation (cf. work of Martin Noth). But the critique of Lothar Perlitt had a significant impact: once again it is common to contend that covenant is "a relative latecomer in the history of Israelite religion" (Nicholson 1986: 65).

Debate about the relationship between covenant and treaty was instigated by George Mendenhall's 1954 article, reprinted (and now online) as a 1955 booklet. Consistent with the near consensus of the time, he considered covenant to be integral to the relationship between the tribes already before the time of the monarchy. More significantly, he argued that second-millennium (BCE) Hittite suzerainty treaties had shaped this use of covenant. These treaties bound a weaker vassal to a more powerful king, requiring the vassal's absolute loyalty in exchange for the king's generosity and protection. Old Testament historical passages were considered parallel to the historical prologue of these treaties, with the legal material serving as the stipulations imposed on the vassal.

This proposal sparked major excitement and much writing. For a time scholars saw treaty evidence everywhere, with key Old Testament terms like *love* and *know* explained in terms of their treaty background. Some argued that Deuteronomy as a book was modeled after an ancient treaty (e.g., Kline). Whereas Mendenhall focused on second-millennium Hittite treaties, many who came after him saw a closer relationship to later Assyrian treaties, especially in the similarity of curses.

Although little of the detailed connections suggested by the covenant-treaty research instigated by Mendenhall has stood the test of time, it has highlighted how Israel's theological reflection took place against a backdrop of international politics and agreements, with the language and metaphors used by biblical writers influenced by that world. Deuteronomy especially emphasizes *covenant* as a term for the relationship between God and Israel, with the connotations of the term colored by the way it was used in that day. For Deuteronomy, the term *covenant* underlined that Israel's relationship with God was not a nature-based relationship but one initiated through God's choice in election (Nicholson 1986).

DEUTERONOMY AND THE REFORM OF JOSIAH According to 2 Kings 22, in the eighteenth year of King Josiah, in the midst of temple renovations, the high priest informed Josiah, "I have found the book of the law in the house of the LORD" (22:8). Ever since the work of W. M. L. de Wette in 1805, it is common to identify this "book of the law" with an early form of Deuteronomy.

The arguments for this identification are numerous. The 2 Kings account speaks of the discovered book as "the book of the law" (22:8, 11), and as "the book of the covenant" (23:2-3, 21), both phrases consistent with how Deuteronomy speaks of itself (cf. 28:58, 61; 29:1, 9, 12, 14, 21; 30:10; 31:24, 26). Josiah's immediate response to reading the book (22:11-13), along with the prophetess Huldah's words of authentication (22:14-20), fit the message of Deuteronomy: Israel has sinned by worshiping other gods, with the consequence that the curses of Deuteronomy will fall upon the people. Josiah then leads the people in a covenant-renewal ceremony (2 Kings 23:1-4; cf. Deut 27–28). The reform then moves on to purge the Yahwistic cult of Canaanite and foreign elements (2 Kings 23:5-14) as repeatedly demanded in Deuteronomy *[Cult, p. 546]*. Josiah defiled and destroyed the high places and even the altar erected by Jeroboam in Bethel (23:8-10, 13, 15-16), consistent with the Deuteronomic demand for centralization of worship (Deut 12). The reform concludes with a national Passover in Jerusalem (i.e., centralized) as "prescribed in this book of the covenant," an event that had not happened "since the days of the judges who judged Israel" (2 Kings 23:21-22; cf. Deut 16:1-8).

Indeed, since the correlation between Josiah's reform as recorded in Kings and the call of Deuteronomy is so great, some propose that the discovery of Deuteronomy in the temple was a hoax, with the book having been written in Josiah's court as a blueprint for the reform, or even as a consequence of the reform. But this is unlikely. Hezekiah's reform a century earlier had already attempted similar measures, suggesting that the book of Deuteronomy, or at least some of its key ideas, were in circulation. Further, not all aspects of Deuteronomy were implemented. Although Deuteronomy requires that rural priests be allowed to move to Jerusalem when their source of living is eliminated by the centralization of the cult (Deut 18:6), the Kings account acknowledges that this did not happen (2 Kings 23:9).

Even if one concludes that Josiah's workers found an early draft of Deuteronomy in the temple that influenced the direction of Josiah's reform, much remains unsettled and probably always will be. For example, it is likely that the Deuteronomy found by Josiah was only its nucleus (chs. 5–26?). That raises the obvious question of how much this core was edited after Josiah, or how much may have been added to the core.

It is also important to acknowledge that Josiah's reform did not take place in a vacuum, motivated solely by religions concerns. Ever since the middle of the eighth century BCE, Assyria had been the dominant power in the Near East. In 722 Assyria conquered Samaria and soon sharply reduced Judah under Hezekiah: even though Jerusalem was besieged yet left standing (ca. 701 BCE), Judah was largely a vassal state under its next king, Manasseh. But by the time of Josiah (640–609 BCE), Assyrian power was in decline. Josiah's reform represents not only a return to monotheistic Yahwism as understood by Deuteronomy, but also a political statement of independence. The destruction of Assyrian religious practices within the land thus served both goals.

A final word about the "people of the land." The reform movement that resulted in Deuteronomy cannot be tied tightly to any group such as priests, prophets, or scribes. Rather, it is possible that the "people of the land"—independent, rural landowners—may have played a role in bringing these groups together (Crüsemann). In this light it is striking that Josiah became king through the power of these "people of the land" (2 Kings 21:24). One thus can imagine this body as representing a lengthy history of faithful worship of God, a people who supported Hezekiah's reform, generated Deuteronomy, and after Manasseh's reign set Josiah on the throne, with the hope that he could return the people to God.

DIETARY REGULATIONS Over the centuries scholars have tested a variety of proposals to explain the rationale behind Israel's dietary regulations, with none generating a consensus.

1. One of the oldest proposals, going back at least to the eleventh century, is that some animals were considered unclean for health or hygienic reasons. God in his wisdom, or Israel through its astute observation, recognized that some animals were more likely to carry disease, whether because these animals were themselves meat eaters and thus more likely to transmit disease from other animals or because they tended to carry parasites. Although at one time this was perhaps the most commonly accepted solution, it no longer is persuasive to most interpreters. True, when pork is inadequately prepared, it can be dangerous, but within the biblical text there is no hint that this is the concern, and some of the animals excluded present no greater health hazard than the ones included.

2. A second long-standing proposal is that the unclean animals were associated with foreign religions and thus were rejected for cultic reasons. Rejecting these animals was another way of rejecting the religious practices of the previous inhabitants of the land or of other nations. The strength of this proposal is that it fits with the biblical and Deuteronomic hostility to other religions, but it falters before the fact that the clean bull, sheep, and goat also happened to be the primary sacrificial animals of neighboring religions. This explanation thus is not adequate for explaining Israel's dietary regulations.

3. Meat-eating animals were rejected because they had eaten blood and thus eating them would be a violation of the biblical command not to eat blood. This may explain some of the unclean animals (see esp. the discussion of unclean birds), but it does not appear to play a significant role for either land or sea animals and thus is not a comprehensive solution.

4. Some give a symbolic interpretation to the categories of clean and unclean animals, with each unclean animal representing some particular sin. The dietary regulations thus represent a symbolic way of teaching

ethics. One can well imagine the dietary rules developing into this role, but there is no evidence in the text that this was the original rationale.

5. Some animals, it is suggested, were rejected simply because of a long-standing revulsion of them, without any clearly understood logic, a form of cultural taboo. It is possible that this played a role in one or two cases, but it is doubtful that it was more significant than that.

6. A proposal by Mary Douglas based on anthropological study of ancient societies has received considerable attention and support from biblical interpreters. She rejects a piecemeal approach to these dietary rules and argues that a comprehensive approach to the ritual and symbols of Israel is needed, one that accepts at face value the text's claim that these regulations relate to Israel's holiness. Holiness, she contends, "is exemplified by completeness. Holiness requires that individuals shall conform to the class to which they belong. And holiness requires that different classes of things shall not be confused. Holiness means keeping distinct categories of creation" (53). Israel's system of clean and unclean animals, then, arises from and supports this understanding. Each category of animal has a standard pure or normal type of animal, especially with regard to how it moves about. Animals that conformed to this standard thus were considered clean; animals that deviated from it were considered unclean.

7. Jacob Milgrom argues that the system of clean and unclean animals has an ethical foundation, with the limitation reflecting a constant warning against doing violence to animals.

8. Another scholar, Edwin Firmage, argues for what might be called a sacrificial paradigm. The starting point for the distinction between clean and unclean animals is Israel's sacrificial system. The land animals that resemble animals used in the sacrificial system were considered clean. Fish (e.g., eels) without scales and fins resemble snakes, an unclean land animal, and thus were rejected. Firmage recognizes that this logic breaks down when considering birds, where he suggests that the key criterion was whether or not the bird was a meat eater.

Today most scholars recognize that although some of these proposals may have played factors in some cases, none is a fully satisfactory explanation for the list as a whole. The proposal by Mary Douglas attempts to be comprehensive, and it probably has received more support than any other, and yet more recent reviews of it raise some serious questions, especially as it attempts to explain the dietary regulations (e.g., Firmage).

Perhaps over time various animals came to be considered unclean for differing reasons, some of which may be included in the list above. At the same time, criteria developed over time that tried to explain why some animals were included and others were not, criteria that may have been applied to animals not previously categorized but that did not play an absolute role (e.g., the exclusion of the pig). The biblical writers (or their predecessors) then tried to systematize these practices and criteria. This then shaped Israel's traditions and customs, which then were used by the biblical writers. Walter Houston's reminder is important: "The text is not concerned to impose a system on the populace in defiance of current custom, but rather to integrate custom into its system" (1993: 236).

HEREM Modern readers and interpreters tend to assume that the call for *ḥerem*, to *utterly destroy* the original inhabitants of the Promised Land (Deut 7:2; etc.), was originally intended and understood historically and literally, and then they have struggled with what to do with it (cf. the essay "*Ḥerem*, 'Devoted to Destruction'" in Matties: 433–34). One approach—perhaps especially attractive in the Reformed tradition, with its emphasis on the sovereignty of God—is to accept the text at face value and then place it all in the mystery of God. God has the right to act the way God determines, with it being inappropriate for humans to judge God.

An alternative, common approach again takes the text at face value, but then moves from there to conclude that Israel misunderstood God at that point. This may be done unconsciously or intuitively, on the basis that it simply is unreasonable to believe that God would command genocide. Or it may be done more systematically, as Seibert does in his contributions, by arguing that the "textual God" is different from the "actual God," and that by careful reading, especially of the teachings of Jesus, one can determine that the "actual God" could not have commanded such mass slaughter, so clearly the Israelites misunderstood or misrepresented God at that point.

But are these the only options? As a number of recent scholars observe, earlier interpreters tended to take a different approach. Origen, for example, began his treatment of Scripture with the conviction that all Scripture has a contribution to make to the Christian life, and that Scripture is a unity and thus speaks with one voice. In light of "stumbling blocks" in passages that call for *ḥerem*, he urges "us to move away from seeing the value and purpose of these stories in terms of their 'historicity'" (Earl 2010: 9). He then argues that "the order to place under ban all residents of the land is not an injunction to kill other human beings. Rather it is a figurative way of saying that the Christian must purge the self of all that would hinder pure devotion to God" (Creach: 102).

By the eighth century it had become common among Christians to identify the seven nations of Deuteronomy 7:1 allegorically as the seven chief vices. This reading continued in the medieval period as the faithful were called to be spiritual warriors who, with God's grace, would overcome these "seven nations." Martin Luther develops this approach further, although in a somewhat different direction, by linking the idolatry of this chapter to "works without faith" (Earl 2009: 50–52).

Some recent scholars are suggesting that this earlier approach may have more integrity than usually granted it, even if they do not follow it exactly. Consistent with this traditional approach, R. W. L. Moberly proposes that Deuteronomy here is using the ritual of *ḥerem* as a metaphor for God's demand for absolute loyalty or fidelity, as stated in the Shema (6:4-9). Deuteronomy 7 thus is an interpretation of and follow-up to the first commandment and the Shema, with "two primary practical expectations, neither of which involve the taking of life" (1999: 135). These two are the prohibition of intermarriage, which would lead to religious unfaithfulness; and the removal of all religious objects belonging to the cult of other religions. "What we have is a retention of the (in all likelihood) traditional language of *ḥerem*, but a shift in the direction of acquiring significance as a metaphor.... The practice of *ḥerem* as a metaphor for religious fidelity, is that which demonstrates and enables Israel's unreserved love for YHWH" (1999: 136). One might compare this with Jesus' direction that "if your right hand causes you to sin, cut it off and throw it away; it is better for you to lose one of your members than for your whole body to go into hell" (Matt 5:30; cf. 18:8; Mark 9:43). Absolute devotion to God requires absolute separation.

Douglas Earl goes in a similar direction, suggesting that *ḥerem* in Deuteronomy 7 was from the beginning intended symbolically and not literally. The prohibition against making marriages and treaties assumes that annihilation has not taken place. Rather, "it seems possible at least that *ḥerem* in Deuteronomy 7:1-5 has a rhetorical function, i.e., to urge the separation of Israel from non-Israel." The death and destruction implied by *ḥerem* "*are the ultimate symbolic expressions of separation*" (Earl 2010: 60, his emph.).

Perhaps the Ephesian passage on spiritual warfare continues the trajectory of Deuteronomy 7 (Eph 6:10-17), a direction already hinted at by Origen as he developed "the significance of Joshua in terms of spiritual combat" (Earl 2009: 52). Such an approach also speaks to the apparent tension between the *ḥerem* directive on the one hand, and Deuteronomy's regular references to aliens or foreigners in the midst of Israel on the other hand. If the *ḥerem* references were originally intended metaphorically, this contradiction fades into the background.

HOLY, HOLINESS For most people today the term *holy*, or the realms of purity and clean/unclean, have little practical meaning. They may think of God as holy, although what this means other than some exalted way of speaking of God may be quite ambiguous. Or it may remind them of an earlier time when the church sanctuary (cf. Latin *sanctus*, "holy"), or at least the platform, were considered holy and thus treated with a special respect and reverence.

A recent hymn reflects the contemporary approach, "What is this place where we are meeting? Only a house, the earth its floor..." (*HWB* 1). The hymn helpfully draws attention to the people who gather, and to the significance of what happens when the people celebrate the Lord's Supper; yet in the process it contributes to a modern, rational approach that has little room for the notion of holiness. Space and objects are merely physical and functional.

Israel's understanding of holiness was simultaneously derived from the culture and religions of its day, yet distinct from it. Jacob Milgrom, a Jewish scholar, describes the ancient perception as follows:

> An examination of Semitic polytheism (and indeed of any primitive religion) shows that the realm of the gods was never wholly separate from and transcendent to the world of people. Natural objects, such as specific trees, rivers, or stones was [*sic*] invested with supernatural force. This

earthbound power was independent of the gods and can be an unpredictable danger to the latter as well as to humans. "Holy" is thus aptly defined, in any context, as "that which is unapproachable except through divinely imposed restrictions," or "that which is withdrawn from common use." (1990: 187)

The Hebrew term translated *holy* literally means that which is "separated," or "set apart." "Holiness demands separation. Just as God at creation separated the day from the night, the waters above the firmament from the waters below, the seas from the dry land, and the days of labor from the day of rest, so God blessed the seventh day and 'set it apart'" (Gammie: 9). Certain objects, people, or places had unique powers or forces that distinguished or separated them from the profane or common. In ancient societies these powers were inherent in the object. To disregard them could be life threatening.

In Israel's world, objects, people, and places could be holy, with powerful consequences. It was dangerous to come into contact with something or someone ritually unclean. When Uzzah inappropriately puts out his hand and takes hold of the ark, he dies on the spot (2 Sam 6:6-8). As in other cultures, holiness in Israel was nothing to be trifled with. But in Israel, all holiness was derived. Only God was truly holy. All other objects, places, and people derived their holiness from God. Nothing other than the one God was inherently holy. The God who designated something holy could also recall this quality, thereby once again making it profane or everyday.

Within the Old Testament it is the priestly literature that places the greatest emphasis on holiness, with the most developed understanding. According to Leviticus, a primary responsibility of the priests is to distinguish between the holy and the common (Lev 10:10; cf. Ezek 22:26; 44:23). Patrick Miller speaks of gradations or a hierarchy of holiness (2000: 144–48). Among people the high priest was most holy. Next came the priestly class as a whole, then the Levites, then the people of Israel, and finally the other nations. A similar continuum can be imagined for space, with the ark in the holy of holies at the one extreme, followed by the land of Israel, and finally the whole earth.

In contrast to the priestly approach, and consistent with its tendency to move away from cultic detail, Deuteronomy presents a somewhat simpler conception. Some form of the word *holy* is used fifteen times in Deuteronomy (compared with nearly one hundred times in Leviticus), with the most common referent the people of Israel (seven times: 7:6; 14:2, 21; 15:19; 26:19; 28:9; 33:3). Neither the priests nor the land of Israel are ever spoken of as holy in Deuteronomy. The tabernacle is never mentioned once, compared with fifty-five references in Exodus and thirty-two in Numbers. For Deuteronomy, it is the people of Israel who are holy. And they are holy through their election. As a holy people, Israel is special, God's *treasured possession*, different and distinct from other nations. Its life is to reflect this difference (see "Election, Separation, and Mission" in TBC at the end of ch. 7).

LAW

For additional discussion, see the essay "Christians and Old Testament (as) Law," p. 541.

Contemporary Law, Ancient Law Old Testament lawlike material is not contemporary law. As Dale Patrick states, "Law is necessary for civilized living. Through law, community is established and maintained; without it people could not live together" (1). Conflict, the abuse of relationships, and violence is an ever-present reality in all cultures and societies. Efforts at minimizing these and establishing order and justice follow.

But when the term *law* appears in the Old Testament to describe these efforts at maintaining order and security, it is being used in a manner very different from contemporary law. When we think of law, we intuitively have in mind features like the following:

- Law is set or *established* by an *authorized, legitimate entity*. This may happen at multiple levels (e.g., a national or regional legislature, a city council), but in each case there is a formal action by a recognized body, establishing a particular policy or prohibition as law.

- Law is *comprehensive*: it covers all of life, with the understanding that if something is not covered at some level, it is outside the law.

- Law is *inclusive*: it applies equally to all covered by the jurisdiction.

- In order for a law to be useful or complete, it identifies *sanctions* or consequences for not following the law.

- Law is *enforced*: agents of the state are engaged (e.g., police) to maintain the law.

- Law is *administered*: further agents of the state are engaged (e.g., judges) to interpret and apply the law.

- Law is *clear, self-contained, and self-interpreting*, thereby making it possible for judges of different backgrounds and perspectives to administer it in a consistent manner.

These connotations simply do not fit earlier societies' response to conflict, crime, and justice. Douglas Knight observes, "Laws, particularly in traditional folk societies, tend to emerge not through formalized legislative action but through a gradual process rooted either in customs or conflicts between parties" (1). In other words, traditional societies are more likely to deal with issues of conflict through *custom and informal efforts* at justice and order than does contemporary law. Over time this may evolve into a more formal legal system, with written laws and procedures, but that requires an extensive scribal system and central administration. It thus may continue for generations and even centuries without such formalization.

One major difference between contemporary law and traditional efforts at achieving justice relates to the administration of law. Contemporary society assigns the task of administering law to the judicial system. The judicial system then begins with the laws and precedents of the day and applies them to particular cases.

Two stories from the Old Testament reflect a different, more traditional approach to handling disputes. The first is set in the time of Moses. Zelophehad, the head of the family, has passed away, leaving only daughters behind. Israelite custom (law?) dictates that his name and property rights pass on to his larger family. His daughters count this custom as unjust. They therefore present their case to "Moses, Eleazar the priest, the leaders, and all the congregation, at the entrance of the tent of meeting" (Num 27:2). After consulting with God, Moses announces the verdict: "The daughters of Zelophehad are right" (27:7). Furthermore, Moses declares this verdict as setting a precedent.

The Zelophehad story demonstrates that previous custom (or law) is not simply determinative for how a particular case is handled. The argument of the daughters of Zelophehad is considered sufficiently persuasive to overturn existing practice. But once settled, the outcome of the dispute is deemed to be direction setting. Does that mean that future administrators of justice are obliged to now apply this verdict? Perhaps, but not necessarily. Just as Moses does in this story, the task of future judges is to administer justice, not simply to apply existing law or precedent. The story of Ruth and Boaz provides a further example of how traditional Israelite society handled what we would consider to be legal matters (Ruth 4).

The second story takes place during the time of the monarchy, with the king now formally responsible for justice and legal matters. Two women present Solomon with a dilemma. Both claim to be the mother of a surviving child. Rather than applying some law or custom to the situation, wise Solomon uses a ruse to determine who in fact is the mother of the child. The story concludes with the summation, "All Israel heard of the judgment that the king had rendered; and they stood in awe of the king, because they perceived that the wisdom of God was with him, to execute justice" (1 Kings 3:28).

Additional factors impacted the way law and justice worked in Israel. Reading and writing, although known, were not common, with a very small portion of the people having this skill. The vast majority of people (estimated at more than 80 percent for most of this period) lived in villages and communities removed from the control of the larger cities. Kings, although symbols and advocates of justice, probably did not exercise this role through establishing regulations as much as through individual actions. For the average Israelite, justice was not a product of laws arising in Jerusalem or Samaria but instead dependent upon the wisdom and fairness of village and clan leaders and others with judicial responsibilities.

And yet, as in the Old Testament, there were law codes in the ancient world. One of the earliest is the Laws of Ur-Nammu, a king in Mesopotamia around the twenty-first century BCE, well before the time of Israel, perhaps one thousand years before the time of Moses. The best-known example is the Code of Hammurabi, from the eighteenth century BCE. It consists of nearly three hundred paragraphs outlining duties and regulations. Its lengthy poetic prologue praises Hammurabi, and its epilogue proclaims how he has established justice and curses anyone who would alter his law (Patrick: 27–30). But it is doubtful that these royal law codes were ever intended to be applied in local settings. Their more likely function was to enhance the image of the just king, as intimated by the poetic prologue of Hammurabi's Code.

Significant similarities in style and content make it clear there were points of contact between Israelite understandings of justice and that of the ancient world. Most of the Old Testament directives have some parallel in other ancient writings. For example, in the Egyptian "Instruction of Amenemopet" we read, "Do not carry off the landmark at the boundaries of arable land" (7.12–15; in *ANET* 416 [tenth–sixth centuries BCE]; cf. Deut 19:14; Prov 22:28; Malchow: 3). Israel certainly was part of its world.

But such comparison also highlights differences. It is often recognized that Israel's legal material places a higher value on human life than property and is generally classless. Perhaps more significantly, although the king in Israel also is the one ultimately responsible for justice, the king is not the source of law: in Israel, God is the source of all law and morality. Law and justice belong to the people as a whole, with its content generally not in written form but circulating "quite naturally as social norms or directives during their respective periods of validity" (Knight: 11; see esp. ch. 2, "The Power of Law," 30–57). Although Old Testament blocks like the Covenant Code (Exod 20:23–23:19) are often treated as legal codes, there is no evidence they ever circulated separately as independent codes.

Apodictic and Casuistic Lawlike Materials Years ago the German scholar Albrecht Alt observed that Old Testament lawlike materials have two styles. *Apodictic law* is absolute or unconditional in style, directly addressing the reader or listener with a prohibition or command. The Decalogue, with prohibitions like *You shall not kill* or *You shall not steal*, represents this category most simply (Deut 5:17 mg., 19; Exod 20:13 mg., 15). A slight variation are prohibitions in which the perpetrator is cursed (e.g., *Cursed is he who slays his neighbor in secret*, Deut 27:24, cf. RSV), or where death is identified as the consequence (e.g., "Whoever strikes a man so that he dies shall be put to death," Exod 21:12 RSV). The second formulation is called *casuistic law*. These are impersonal in nature and describe a particular crime or misdeed, followed by a description of legal consequences. Frequently they begin with "if" or "when" that describes the action, with "then" introducing the consequences.

Although these are helpful formal categories, they do not clarify where these statements come from or how they may have functioned within Israel. Alt suggested that the apodictic laws were unique to Israel and had as their setting Israel's religious life, where God addressed the people in the imperative tone with absolute commands. Further research has found that this form is not unique to Israel, and scholars like Gerstenberger have argued that a more likely setting for them may be the everyday life of the family and clan, where parents quite naturally give absolute directives to their children. Regardless of their original setting, these prohibitions or commands are quite different from contemporary law. With their absolute nonnuanced nature, and the absence of specific sanctions (the reference to being put to death may very well be another way of speaking of the person being cursed), they clearly are not intended for application to specific cases, nor do they have a judicial setting in mind.

The situation may be somewhat less clear for the casuistic laws. Their literary style appears to point to actual cases, with the implication that they are eventually regarded as setting precedents. But even they are not law in any contemporary sense. The absence of modern court reporters, combined with the reality that there will have been significant differences across the land as to how justice was implemented—such considerations warn against seeing them as a comprehensive survey of legal precedents. At most they are one way of illustrating what the moral life would look like, rather than the measure of the moral life.

All of this supports that, although Old Testament lawlike material has, in common with our contemporary law, an interest in justice and the moral life, *it is not law in any contemporary sense*. These regulations are not "clear, self-contained, and self-interpreting," and they are filled with motive clauses that are "pleading, preaching, persuading" (W. Janzen 1994: 61).

What we have in Scripture is literature with lawlike material incorporated into a larger narrative of God and the people of God. The role of the lawlike material in the Old Testament is not so much to provide directions to a judicial system, or to be implemented or applied, as much as to paint a picture of what justice and faithfulness to God look like. It is God's torah for God's people. As such, it is preached, with a variety of rhetorical techniques employed, all to help persuade the listener or reader to respond in a manner consistent with the picture presented. It is part of a larger body of sermonic literature, written to persuade a community to take on the character shaped by the story of God and the people of God. That story recounts how God first liberated slaves from oppression and then entered into a covenant with them, forming the people as his special *treasured possession* (Deut 7:6). That narrative of liberation is foundational to this torah and substantially colors its content.

PEOPLES AND PLACES IN DEUTERONOMY

(Biblical references, based on the NRSV, are exhaustive unless otherwise indicated)

Abarim, mountain of (32:49) A mountain range northeast of the Dead Sea, with Mount Nebo one of its peaks.

Ammonites (2:19-21, 37; 3:11, 16) The people of a political state that developed in the Transjordan some time before Israel appeared on the scene. Deuteronomy speaks of Ammon as located north of the Wadi Arnon, and east of that part of the Wadi Jabbok that runs north–south. According to the Bible, the Ammonites were descendants of Lot through his son Ben-ammi (Gen 19:38).

Essays

Amorite(s) (1: 4, 7, 19-20, 27, 44; 2:24; 3:2, 8-9; 4:46-47; 7:1; 20:17; 31:4) A people who dominated much of the Fertile Crescent during the second millennium BCE. After approximately 1200 BCE, however, there does not appear to have been any definable group known as Amorites. Within Deuteronomy the term is used fairly generally of the pre-Israelite inhabitants of the Promised Land, at points suggesting that the Amorites had special connections with the central highlands and the Transjordan (thus Sihon and Og are called Amorite), and the Canaanites with the seacoast (cf. 1:7).

Anakim (1:28; 2:10-11, 21; 9:2) The name of an ancient people with the reputation for being giants (cf. Emim, Rephaim, Zamzummim), already mentioned in Egyptian texts of the early second millennium BCE. The Anakim tend to be associated with the southern part of the land, in the vicinity of Hebron.

Ar (2:9, 18, 29) The meaning or location of Ar is unclear. In 2:9, 29 it appears to be another name for the land of Moab, but in 2:18 it appears to refer to a specific location or city on the Wadi Arnon, possibly to be identified with Aroer.

Arabah (1:7; 2:8; 3:17; 4:49; 11:30) The Arabah is the geological depression, or rift valley, running north from the Gulf of Aqaba, including the Dead Sea, the Jordan River, and the Sea of Chinnereth (Galilee). At times the name is used almost as a proper name for that part of the rift between the Dead Sea and the Gulf (e.g., 2:8); at other times it is used more generally of the whole valley. Deuteronomy 1:1 (NIV, RSV, etc.) as well as 3:17 use it in this more general sense, and refer to the Jordan Valley.

Argob (3:4, 13-14) Although possibly originally referring to a district within Bashan, Deuteronomy uses the term synonymously with the whole region of Bashan.

Arnon, Wadi (2:24, 36; 3:8, 12, 16; 4:48) A dry river valley (wadi) entering the Dead Sea from the east, about 40 kilometers (25 miles) south of its northern shore. In Deuteronomy it marks the northern boundary of Moab and the southern boundary of the kingdom of Sihon of Heshbon. After the defeat of Sihon, it set the southern boundary of the region allocated to the tribes of Reuben and Gad.

Aroer (2:36; 3:12; 4:48) A city or village located on the northern edge of the Wadi Arnon, east of the Dead Sea.

Asher (27:13; 33:24) A son of Jacob with Zilpah, the maid of Leah; a tribal region in the far north along the Mediterranean.

Ashtaroth (1:4) Located in Bashan, it along with Edrei are named as the home of Og, king of Bashan.

Avvim (2:23) Early inhabitants of the southwestern portion of Palestine who were, according to Deuteronomy 2:23, displaced by the Caphtorim.

Baal of Peor (4:3-4) Possibly another name for Beth-peor (see below).

Bashan (1:4; 3:1, 3-4, 10-11, 13-14; 4:43, 47; 29:7; 32:14; 33:22) The region located east of the Sea of Chinnereth and largely north of the Wadi Yarmuk, in the Transjordan. It had a reputation for fertile land, oak forests, rich pasture, and fat animals (cf. Deut 32:14; Amos 4:1; Ps 22:12). According to Deuteronomy, before Israel's arrival, it was ruled by King Og. After Og's defeat, it was allocated to Jair, part of the tribe of Manasseh.

Beeroth-bene-jaakan (10:6) Probably Bene-Jaakan, near the southern border of Edom, a campsite during the time of wilderness wandering.

Benjamin (27:12; 33:12) The last son of Jacob, his second with his favorite wife, Rachel; a small tribal region immediately north of Judah in the central highlands.

Beth-peor (3:29; 4:46; 34:6) The exact location is unknown, but it appears to have been situated near the Jordan River, just north of the Dead Sea, and opposite Jericho (cf. 1:1). It is the setting given the book of Deuteronomy. It very well may be the same place called Baal of Peor in Deuteronomy 4:3-4 (cf. Num 25:3, 5).

Bezer (4:43) A city to the east of the Jordan, in the area allocated to the tribe of Reuben. Deuteronomy designates it as one of three cities of refuge in the Transjordan.

Canaan, Canaanites (1:7; 7:1; 11:30; 20:17; 32:49) General terms for the Promised Land, the region currently occupied by Lebanon, Israel, Jordan, and part of Syria, with its inhabitants as Israel arrives.

Caphtor, Caphtorim (2:23) Caphtor is traditionally identified as Crete, although Cyprus is also suggested. According to Deuteronomy 2:23, the Caphtorim displaced the Avvim in the southwestern region of Palestine. Their geographical location as well as a number of other biblical passages (Gen 10:14; Jer 47:4; Amos 9:7) associate the Caphtorim with the Philistines.

Chinnereth (3:17) The lake through which the Jordan River flows southward to the Dead Sea, better known as the Sea of Galilee (or Tiberias). A fortified town by the name of Chinnereth (= Gennesaret in Mark 6:53) was located on the northwest shore of the lake (cf. Josh 19:35).

Dan (27:13; 33:22; 34:1) A son of Jacob with Bilhah, the maid of Rachel; a city representing the northern extreme of the Promised Land; a tribal region perhaps originally to the west of Judah and Benjamin, but after their migration (Judg 18) limited largely to the city of Dan, at the southern foot of Mount Hermon.

Di-zahab (1:1) The exact location is unknown. Israel camped here after leaving Horeb, so it likely was just west of the Gulf of Aqaba.

Edomites (23:7) The inhabitants of Edom, one of the nation-states in the Transjordan area, southeast of the Dead Sea. Deuteronomy regularly uses *sons of Esau* as a substitute for Edomites (cf. Gen 25:30; ch. 36).

Edrei (1:4; 3:1, 10) A city on the southern border of Bashan, approximately 50 kilometers (31 miles) east of the Sea of Chinnereth.

Elath (2:8) Elath and Ezion-geber were two ports (or possibly two names for the same port) on the northern end of the Gulf of Aqaba.

Emim (2:10-11) According to Deuteronomy 2:10, the Moabites called the people who preceded them in their land *the Emim*. The name itself suggests that they cause terror or fear. As is suggested by 2:11, it appears to be one of a number of names used for legendary giants of earlier times (cf. Anakim, Rephaim, Zamzummim).

Ephraim (33:17; 34:2) Ephraim and Manasseh were the two sons of Joseph. Since Levi received no tribal allocation, Joseph received two, one for each of his sons, with Ephraim located north of Benjamin, in the central highlands.

Esau, descendants of (2:4-5, 8, 12, 22, 29) In Genesis (32:3; 36:1, 9) the descendants of Esau constitute Edom, living in the region of Seir, southwest of the Dead Sea. Deuteronomy often uses *descendants of Esau* as a substitute for the name Edom.

Ezion-geber (2:8) Ezion-geber and Elath were two ports (or possibly two names for the same port) on the northern end of the Gulf of Aqaba.

Gad, Gadites (3:12, 16; 4:43; 27:13; 29:8; 33:20) A son of Jacob with Zilpah, the maid of Leah. The Gadites are his descendants, settled in a tribal region in the central Transjordan, and at Dibon, east of the Dead Sea.

Gaza (2:23) A city near the Mediterranean coast in the southern part of Palestine. During most of Israel's history, it was a Philistine city.

Geshurites (3:14) A state or people on the eastern shore of the Sea of Chinnereth, south of Mount Hermon, north and west of Bashan. It was not considered part of the area that Israel captured in the conquest and thus was not allocated.

Gilead (2:36; 3:10, 12-13, 15-16; 4:43; 34:1) The central Transjordan region. Deuteronomy divides the Transjordan area north of the Wadi Arnon into three regions: the plateau or tableland, Gilead, and Bashan. Gilead extends from approximately Heshbon in the south to the Wadi Yarmuk in the north, with the Wadi Jabbok dividing it in half. Deuteronomy appears to consider all of Gilead to be part of the kingdom of Sihon at the time of Israel's arrival (in contrast to Num 21). After Sihon's defeat, the southern half of Gilead, together with the plateau extending south to the Wadi Arnon, was allotted to the tribes of Reuben and Gad, and the northern half of Gilead was allotted to Machir, part of the tribe of Manasseh.

Gilgal (11:30) Located near Jericho, it is where Israel established its first camp after crossing the Jordan. It became a significant cultic center during the time of Samuel (e.g., 1 Sam 7:16).

Golan in Bashan (4:43) A city in Bashan, in the later territory of Manasseh, and thus east of the Sea of Chinnereth.

Gudgodah (10:7) The location is unknown. Israel camped here after leaving Horeb (cf. Num 33:31-33).

Havvoth-jair (3:14) According to Deuteronomy, the name given by Jair (or his descendants) to the area settled by Jair. The term itself means villages of Jair.

Hazeroth (1:1) The location is unknown. After leaving Horeb, Israel passed through Hazeroth, where Aaron and Miriam then spoke out against Moses (Num 12).

Hermon, Mount (3:8-9; 4:48) A mountain range north of the Transjordan, sourcing the Jordan River. Its peak reaches a height of 2,814 meters (9,232 feet) and is covered with snow year-round. It represented the northern boundary of Bashan.

Heshbon (1:4; 2:24, 26, 30; 3:2, 6; 4:46; 29:7) Heshbon, the capital of Sihon's kingdom, was located some 20 kilometers (12.5 miles) east of the Jordan River, just north of the northern end of the Dead Sea.

Hor, Mount (32:50) A mountain perhaps in Edom but more likely in the Negeb near Kadesh (cf. Num 20:22–21:4). Deuteronomy speaks of Aaron as having died on Mount Hor, yet also names Moserah (perhaps near Mount Hor) as the place of his death (10:6; cf. Num 33:30, 37-38).

Horeb, Mount (1:2, 6, 19; 4:10, 15; 5:2; 9:8; 18:16; 29:1) The mountain where God entered into a covenant with Israel (Exod 19–20), likely located somewhere in the Sinai Peninsula: its exact location is unknown. Elsewhere in the Old Testament it is generally known as Mount Sinai, although the term *Horeb* is also occasionally used (e.g., Exod 3:1, "Horeb, the mountain of God").

Horim (2:12, 22) The Horim (or Horites, as the same Hebrew term is translated in Gen 14:6; 36:20) were a group who originated in Mesopotamia in the third millennium BCE, eventually spreading into Syria and Palestine. According to Deuteronomy, they inhabited the region of Seir before the arrival of the Edomites, the descendants of Esau.

Issachar (27:12; 33:18) A son of Jacob with Leah; a tribal region north of Manasseh, southwest of Sea of Chinnereth.

Jabbok, Wadi (2:37; 3:16) A valley (becoming a stream or river after heavy rains) entering the Jordan River from the east about three-fifths of the way from the Sea of Chinnereth to the Dead Sea. It divides the region of Gilead into two parts. Gilead south of the Jabbok was allocated to Gad and Reuben, and Gilead north of the Jabbok was allocated to Machir, part of the tribe of Manasseh. Although it is flowing west when it enters to Jordan, there is a stretch where it runs north to south. According to Deuteronomy, it thus serves as the western boundary of Ammon.

Jahaz (2:32) The location is unknown, but narrative evidence suggests that it was a city in the southern plateau of the Transjordan, in the vicinity of Kedemoth (cf. Josh 13:18), about 30 kilometers (19 miles) east of the Dead Sea.

Jair (3:14) A descendant (a son, or possibly a great-grandson; cf. 1 Chron 2:21-22) of Manasseh. Deuteronomy allocates Bashan, or Argob, to the descendants of Jair. According to Numbers 32:41, the region (although in Numbers as well as Judg 10:4 the area appears to be located in Gilead, thus south of the Yarmuk) was given to the descendants of Jair since they captured its villages.

Jordan (1:1, 5; 2:29; 3:8, 17, plus twenty-one times) The river flowing south from Mount Hermon, through the Sea of Chinnereth, and eventually into the Dead Sea.

Joseph (27:12; 33:13, 16) A son of Jacob with his favorite wife, Rachel. Joseph received two portions of the land north of Judah and Benjamin, allocated to his sons Ephraim and Manasseh.

Jotbathah (10:7) The location is unknown: *a land with flowing streams*, along the route from Horeb to the Promised Land.

Judah (27:12; 33:7; 34:2) A son of Jacob with Leah; a tribal region west of the Dead Sea.

Kadesh-barnea (1:2, 19; 2:14; 9:23) A significant oasis on the northern edge of the Wilderness of Paran and the Wilderness of Zin, in the northern part of the Sinai Desert, not far south of Israel's later border.

According to Deuteronomy, Israel tried its first entrance into the Promised Land from this location (1:19–2:1).

Kedemoth, Wilderness of (2:26) Apparently a region in the southern part of the Transjordan, not far north of the Wadi Arnon and about 32 kilometers (20 miles) east of the Dead Sea.

Laban (1:1) Location is unknown, but along the route from Horeb to the Promised Land.

Lebanon (1:7; 3:25; 11:24) The land to the north of Palestine. It was known for its beauty and valuable trees. Although never part of Israel itself, it was included in the ideal boundaries of the land.

Levi, Levites (10:8-9; 12:12, 18; 14:27, 29; 16:11, 14; 18:1, 5; 21:5; 26:11-13; 27:12, 14; 31:9, 25; 33:8) A son of Jacob with Leah. The descendants of Levi, the Levites, did not receive a portion of the land since they were designated the priestly tribe.

Lot, descendants of (2:9, 19) According to Genesis 19:37-38, Lot had two sons. The first, Moab, became the ancestor of the Moabites, and the second, Ben-ammi, became the ancestor of the Ammonites.

Maacathites (3:14) A state or people located south of Mount Hermon, north of the Geshurites, west of Bashan, and east of the Jordan. It was not considered part of the area Israel captured in the conquest and thus was not allocated.

Machir (3:15) Deuteronomy speaks of Machir as that part of the tribe of Manasseh to whom was allocated the northern half of Gilead. Joshua 17:1 names Machir as the first son of Manasseh. In the Song of Deborah (Judg 5:14) Machir is treated as a separate tribe located on the western side of the Jordan.

Manasseh, Manassite (3:13-14; 29:8; 33:17; 34:2) Manasseh and Ephraim were the two sons of Joseph. Since Levi received no tribal allocation, Joseph received two, one for each of his sons. Half of Manasseh's allocation was in the Transjordan north of Gad, and half in the land on the west side of the Jordan and north of Ephraim.

Moab, Moabites (1:5; 2:8-9, 11, 18, 29; 29:1; 32:49; 34:1, 5-6, 8) A political state (and its inhabitants) that developed in the Transjordan region some time before Israel appeared on the scene. Deuteronomy speaks of it as located south of the Wadi Arnon, although there is evidence that at various times it also controlled land north of the wadi. According to the Bible, the Moabites were descendants of Lot through his son Moab (Gen 19:37).

Moserah (10:6) The location is unknown. Israel camps here after leaving Horeb. Deuteronomy speaks of Aaron as having died in Moserah yet also names Mount Hor as his place of death, so perhaps Moserah is near Mount Hor (32:50).

Naphtali (27:13; 33:23; 34:2) A son of Jacob with Bilhah, the maid of Rachel; a tribal region in the far north, east of Asher and northwest of the Sea of Chinnereth.

Nebo, Mount (32:49; 34:1) Deuteronomy speaks of Moses climbing Pisgah (3:27) as well as Mount Nebo. Perhaps Pisgah was the name of a range of mountains in the region a short distance east of the northern end of the Dead Sea, with Mount Nebo its highest peak; perhaps it was a headland in the range.

Og, King (1:4; 3:1, 3-4, 10-11, 13; 4:47; 29:7; 31:4) According to Deuteronomy, the king of Bashan, defeated by the Israelites.

Paran (1:1; 33:2) The wilderness area stretching from Mount Sinai to Kadesh-barnea, from which spies were sent to scout out the Promised Land.

Pethor (23:4) The home of Balaam, near the Euphrates River (cf. Num 22:5).

Pisgah (3:17, 27; 4:49; 34:1) Deuteronomy speaks of Moses climbing to the top of Pisgah, as well as Mount Nebo (34:1). Perhaps Pisgah was the name of a range of mountains in the region a short distance east of the northern end of the Dead Sea, with Mount Nebo its highest peak; perhaps it was a headland in the range.

Rabbah (3:11) The capital city of Ammon (modern-day Amman, capital of Jordan).

Ramoth in Gilead (4:43) A city in the Transjordan allocated to the tribe of Gad, about 48 kilometers (30 miles) east of the Jordan.

Rephaim (2:11, 20; 3:11, 13) Apparently one of several terms used for ancient, legendary giants (cf. Anakim, Emim, Zamzummim). In Deuteronomy they are especially associated with the land of Bashan. Non-Israelite writings seem to associate them with spirits of dead heroes or with gods.

Reuben, Reubenites (2:11; 3:12, 16; 4:43; 11:6; 27:13; 29:8; 33:6) The eldest son of Jacob, with Leah, and his descendants; a tribal region in the Transjordan, south of Gad.

Salecah (3:10) The location is unknown, but the text appears to identify it as a city on one of the borders of Bashan's kingdom, possibly the far southeastern side.

Seir (1:2, 44; 2:1, 4-5, 8, 12, 22, 29; 33:2) A mountain range (called Mount Seir in 2:1, 5) located southeast of the Dead Sea, thus on the eastern side of the Arabah. The biblical text consistently speaks of it as the land of Edom.

Senir (3:9) According to Deuteronomy 3:9, the name the Amorites used for Mount Hermon.

Sidonians (3:9) The citizens of Sidon, the Phoenician city located on the Mediterranean coast within Lebanon.

Sihon, King (1:4; 2:24, 26, 30-32; 3:2, 6; 4:46; 29:7; 31:4) According to Deuteronomy, the king of Heshbon, northeast of the Dead Sea about 24 kilometers (15 miles).

Simeon (27:12) A son of Jacob with Leah. The allotment for Simeon's tribe was absorbed into Judah, apparently fairly early; a tribal region in the far south, south of Judah, including Beer-sheba.

Sirion (3:9) According to Deuteronomy, the name the Sidonians used for Mount Hermon.

Tophel (1:1) The location is unknown, but is identified with the area from where Moses proclaimed Deuteronomy, on the plain of Moab, just east of the Jordan.

Transjordan (*beyond the Jordan* in NRSV, RSV; *east of the Jordan* in NIV, at 1:1, 5, etc.) Territories east of the Jordan River, referred to as "beyond the Jordan" in Deuteronomy and elsewhere. This term is sometimes used of all the highland area east of the Jordan rift valley, from the Yarmuq River in the north to the head of the Gulf of Aqabah in the south. In Deuteronomy, the focus is upon the regions north of the Wadi Arnon, thus Ammon, the land of the Amorites, Gilead, and Bashan, but excluding Moab and Edom. Unlike for most other sections of the Old Testament, the Promised Land in Deuteronomy includes portions of the Transjordan.
Valley of Eshcol (1:24) A fertile valley in the vicinity of Hebron from which the spies brought back large clusters of grapes.
Zamzummim (2:20) The name of an ancient people with the reputation for being giants (cf. Anakim, Emim, Rephaim). According to Deuteronomy, the Ammonites called the previous inhabitants of their land Zamzummim.
Zebulun (27:3; 33:18) A son of Jacob with Leah; a tribal region in the north, between Issachar and Naphtali, east of Mount Carmel.
Zered, Wadi (2:13-14) A dry river valley entering the southern end of the Dead Sea from the east, serving as the boundary between Moab and Edom (with Moab to the north, and Edom to the south).
Zoar (34:3) A city just south of the Dead Sea, near the Wadi Zered.

SACRIFICES AND OFFERINGS Sacrifices and offerings, both public and private, were an important element of the religious practice of Israel from earliest times until the destruction of the temple in 70 CE. When Abraham and Sarah arrived in the land to which God sent them, they built altars at Shechem and Bethel (Gen 12:6, 8). Other than the relatively brief interruption between the destruction of the first temple by Babylon in the early sixth century BCE until the construction of the second temple late in 515 BCE, sacrifices and offerings remained central to the way the people of Israel related to God. In this Israel reflected the general religious practices of the day.

Despite the prominence of sacrifices in the religion of Israel as well as in other ancient religions, their meaning remains largely shrouded in mystery. Scholars have proposed various explanations, trying to provide an all-encompassing motivation for sacrifice (e.g., sacrifices are gifts to God), but generally this has been unsuccessful. Complicating the task are the many different terms used for sacrifice in the Old Testament, the variation and diversity of the sacrifices and offerings themselves, along with the absence of any systematic reflection on how sacrifice was understood or what it meant.

In addition, the history of Israel's sacrificial practices is a factor: no doubt the understanding of it changed over the years, though most Old Testament description of sacrifice is quite late. For a modern Christian, the Old Testament sacrificial system represents a foreign world, not only to our own experience but also to our sense of how faith in God should be expressed.

All offerings, whether sacrifices or not, were presentations made to or before God. Animal sacrifices could be fully burned to God, or partially burned and then eaten by the people. Offerings of grain (e.g., firstfruits) could be presented as rough grain, as flour, or in cakes that again could be burned or eaten. Motivation for these offerings could cover a broad range: gifts and tributes to God, thanksgiving or food for God, communion with God, community celebration, peace offerings, establishing purity, forgiveness of sin. The last, the forgiveness of sin, became a key element of the Day of Atonement, when the sin of the people was ritually placed on two goats: one that was sacrificed and the other that was turned loose into the wilderness (Lev 16). Although probably only a postexilic development, the Day of Atonement ritual has played a major role in shaping the way Jews and Christians have viewed Old Testament sacrifice.

Typical of the Old Testament, Deuteronomy uses multiple words for offerings: in chapter 12 alone it speaks of the following: *burnt offerings* (vv. 6, 11, 14, 26), *sacrifices* (vv. 6, 11), *tithes* (vv. 6, 11), *donations* (vv. 6, 11, 17, 26), *votive gifts* (vv. 6, 11, 17, 26), *freewill offerings* (v. 6, 17), *firstlings of your herds and flocks* (vv. 6, 17), *tithe of your grain, your wine, and your oil* (v. 17). Unlike Old Testament priestly literature, Deuteronomy has little interest in the details of these offerings, either with regard to how they are offered or how they might purify. Its focus is largely on where the sacrifice takes place (at The Place) and how these offerings support important Deuteronomic themes like remembering the story of God's deliverance, inclusive celebration, and providing for the disadvantaged *[Cult, p. 546]*.

YAHWEH WAR Israel knew the realities of war firsthand. As a small, relatively weak nation located on the eastern shore of the Mediterranean, it regularly suffered under the militaristic might of Egypt, Assyria, and Babylon, and it repeatedly had clashes with other small nations in its area. War was part of life.

Israel, as did other peoples and nations of the ancient Near East, made no sharp distinction between the sacred and secular. The divine permeated all of life, including war. Victories were attributed to deities, defeats were understood either as the defeat of one national god by another or as punishment by one's own national god. The spoils of war were offered to the national deity as a sacrifice. In many ways, Israel acted and thought like the nations of the time.

Some Old Testament stories speak of war with an almost liturgical framework, with its own technical language. Ever since the work of Friedrich Schwally (1901) and of Gerhard von Rad (1991 [German, 1958]), it is common to speak of "holy war" in the Old Testament. More recent scholarship tends to prefer the name "Yahweh war," but continues to distinguish a particular Old Testament tradition.

Yahweh, the God of Israel, makes the decision whether or not to go to war, with this decision communicated by a prophet or priest, perhaps accompanied by a ritual sacrifice (cf. 1 Sam 7:10). God is a divine warrior who fights on behalf of Israel. Israel's responsibility is to observe or to crush an already-defeated enemy. The spoils of the war belong to God. Not all components are equally present in every account, but this is the basic outline of Yahweh war.

The crossing of the Red Sea serves as the model and prime example of such an account (Exod 14–15). Miriam summarizes the confrontation in her song: "Sing to the LORD, for he has triumphed gloriously; horse and rider he has thrown into the sea" (Exod 15:21). Israel is delivered as it watches: God receives the praise (Lind: 46–64). Other stories follow a similar format. The battle of Jericho begins with God announcing, "See, I have handed Jericho over to you" (Josh 6:2), and it concludes with the walls amazingly collapsed. Deborah calls on Barak, "Up! For this is the day on which the LORD has given Sisera into your hand" (Judg 4:14), and then celebrates the victory by singing, "The stars fought from heaven, from their courses they fought against Sisera" (Judg 5:20). The story of Gideon makes much of the fact that Gideon's army must be small, otherwise Israel will "take the credit away from me [God], saying 'My own hand has delivered me'" (Judg 7:2). Later Gideon rouses his three hundred men by proclaiming "Get up; for the LORD has given the army of Midian into your hand" (7:15); in the battle itself, "the LORD set every [Midianite] man's sword against his fellow and against all the army" (7:22). In one of the last accounts of military action before the rise of kingship in Israel, Samuel leads the people against the Philistines in a battle that is summarized with "the Philistines drew near to attack Israel; but the LORD thundered with a mighty voice that day against the Philistines and threw them into confusion; and they were routed before Israel" (1 Sam 7:10).

Integral to this Yahweh war tradition is that Yahweh as warrior can never be controlled by Israel: God is sovereign, and independently so. The story in 1 Samuel 4–6 underscores this point. Israel has lost a skirmish with the Philistines and determines to take the ark of the covenant, the symbol of the presence of God, into the next confrontation. Surely God then will fight for Israel. Even the Philistines become afraid when they hear of Israel's plans. But in the subsequent battle, the Philistines again emerge as victors, even capturing the ark of the covenant. Yet any hint that the God of Israel has been captured by Dagon, the god of the Philistines, is directly rejected by the story. When the ark of the covenant is placed into the house of Dagon, Dagon falls down before the ark (1 Sam 5:3).

That Yahweh as warrior can never be controlled by Israel is also reflected by the stories in which Yahweh fights against and not for Israel. It is striking that in Deuteronomy, Yahweh war language is first used against Israel (in the story of the spies, 1:19–2:1) well before God fights on behalf of Israel in the story of Sihon and Og. Later prophets warn the people that unless they change their ways, God will become their enemy rather than their deliverer (e.g., Isa 63:10). The defeat of Samaria and the Northern Kingdom in 722 BCE and of Jerusalem and the Southern Kingdom in 587 BCE are interpreted in this way: "Therefore the LORD was very angry with Israel and removed them out of his sight" (2 Kings 17:18). Not only can God as warrior not be controlled by Israel; God as warrior can also come out against Israel.

Related to this Yahweh war theology is the idea of *ḥerem* (noun, with its related verb *[Ḥerem, p. 552]*). The term probably has a cultic background referring to objects separated out or set aside to be devoted to God. The Old Testament uses it in this cultic sense (e.g., Lev 27:21), yet also in the context of war stories, where it implies the total destruction or even sacrifice of the enemy to God, although primarily when speaking of the conquest. For example, in Deuteronomy 7:26 it is translated *set apart for destruction*, and in 2:34 and 3:6 it is translated *utterly destroyed*. Earl argues that the term is used differently in different books and so should not be treated as a unified concept (2013).

Israel was not unique in understanding its war as divinely directed, with all spoils devoted to God. A victory stele set up by Mesha, the king of Moab, reports that Chemosh, the god of Moab, had commanded him, "Go seize Nebo from Israel." The king complied, killing everyone, thus devoting them to the god of Moab. It then goes on to say that Israel has "utterly perished forever" (Niditch: 31). The continued existence of Israel reveals that the claim included an element of exaggeration and likely was a typical example of using religious rhetoric and framework to speak of a military confrontation, where rhetoric and reality did not quite match.

Scholars are still debating whether Yahweh war was ever practiced by Israel, or whether it was an ideology into which stories were placed. Peter Craigie, for example, suggests, "While war was religious by association, it was no more a cultic and holy act than was sheep shearing" (1978: 49). War was war, with the theological component added later.

It is striking that the vast majority of the war stories told within the Yahweh war framework are of confrontations from the early history of Israel. They begin with the story of the exodus from Egypt and then cluster in the period between the exodus and the rise of kingship in Israel. Once kingship with its professional armies becomes an institution, these stories fade into the background. The stories of 1 Samuel exemplify this transition. Prior to the monarchy, Samuel presides as God defeats the Philistines (1 Sam 7). Similarly, prior to Saul becoming king, he functions as the charismatic leader in the defeat of the Ammonites (1 Sam 11). War stories are common during the time of David, but victory now comes through David's strategy and troops rather than through Yahweh war.

This may reflect a shift in practice, with war becoming a strategic enterprise of the state under the monarchy, whereas earlier Israel had trusted God the warrior to deliver them. But it may also suggest, as Weinfeld argues, that Yahweh war rhetoric was Deuteronomic "utopian theory" imposed on the traditions of Israel's formation in the land: "It was the book of Deuteronomy that conceived the *ḥerem* as a commandment applying automatically to all the inhabitants of the land, whether or not they fought. This *ḥerem* . . . belongs more to utopian theory than to practice" (1993: 89) *[Ḥerem, p. 552]*. It is striking that Yahweh war is especially prominent in the Deuteronomistic History, but only when it speaks of events many centuries earlier.

This raises the question of whether this "utopian theory" was considered an actual ideal or rather as a metaphor or symbol for something quite different. Deuteronomy itself includes hints that it was not understood literally. The generous treatment of the resident aliens, at least some of whom no doubt were descendants of the former inhabitants, demonstrates both that Israel was very aware that the original inhabitants had not been destroyed and that they now should be treated kindly. Further, the strong rejection of human sacrifice in Deuteronomy would caution against taking literally commands to sacrifice humans in war.

It is difficult for someone living in the twenty-first century to know at what points texts written millennia ago were intended literally or figuratively. Even today this becomes ambiguous when stories are translated from one culture to another. We should not dismiss these passages due to our modern liberal sense of what makes for a reasonable God, but at the same time we cannot simply assume they were intended to be followed literally by Israel. And they certainly do not provide divine sanction for contemporary war.

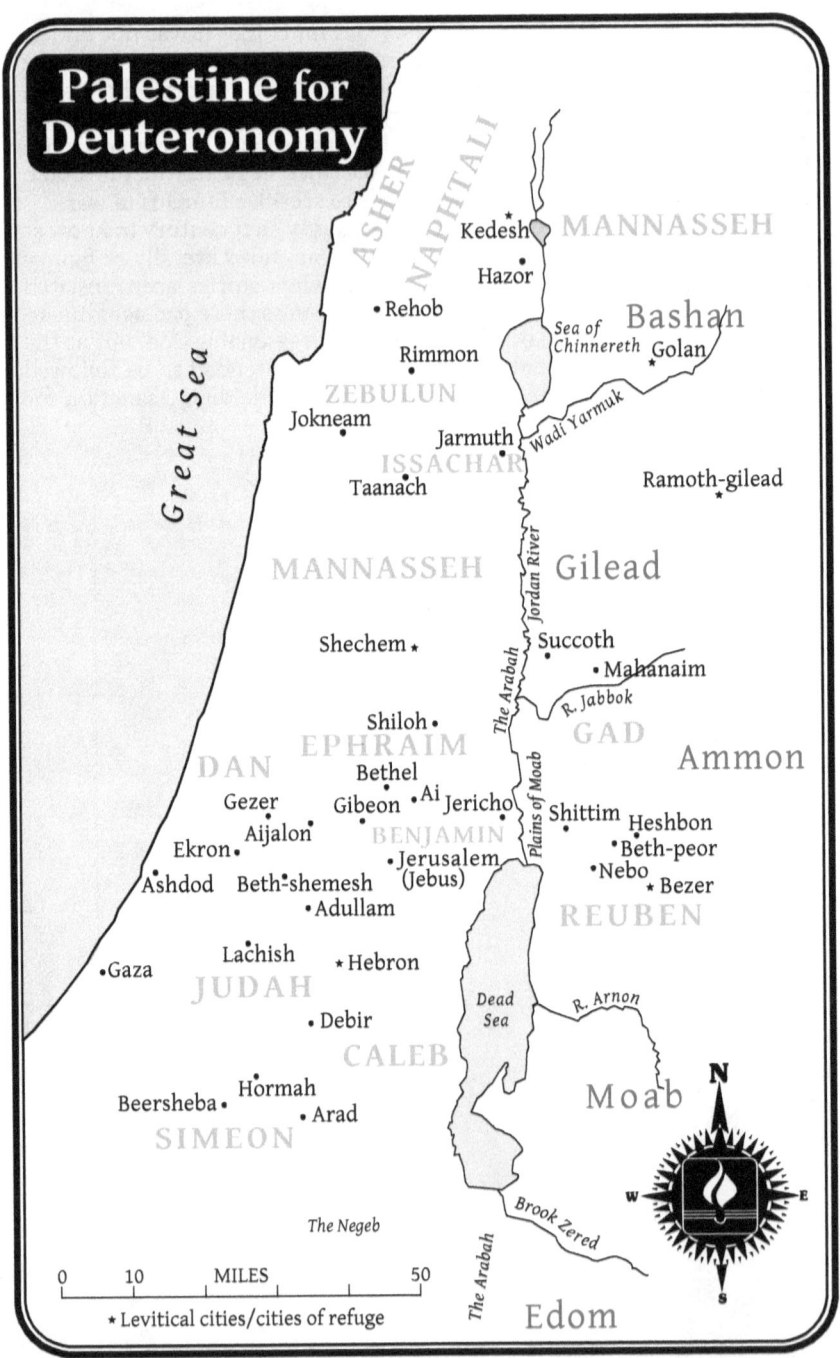

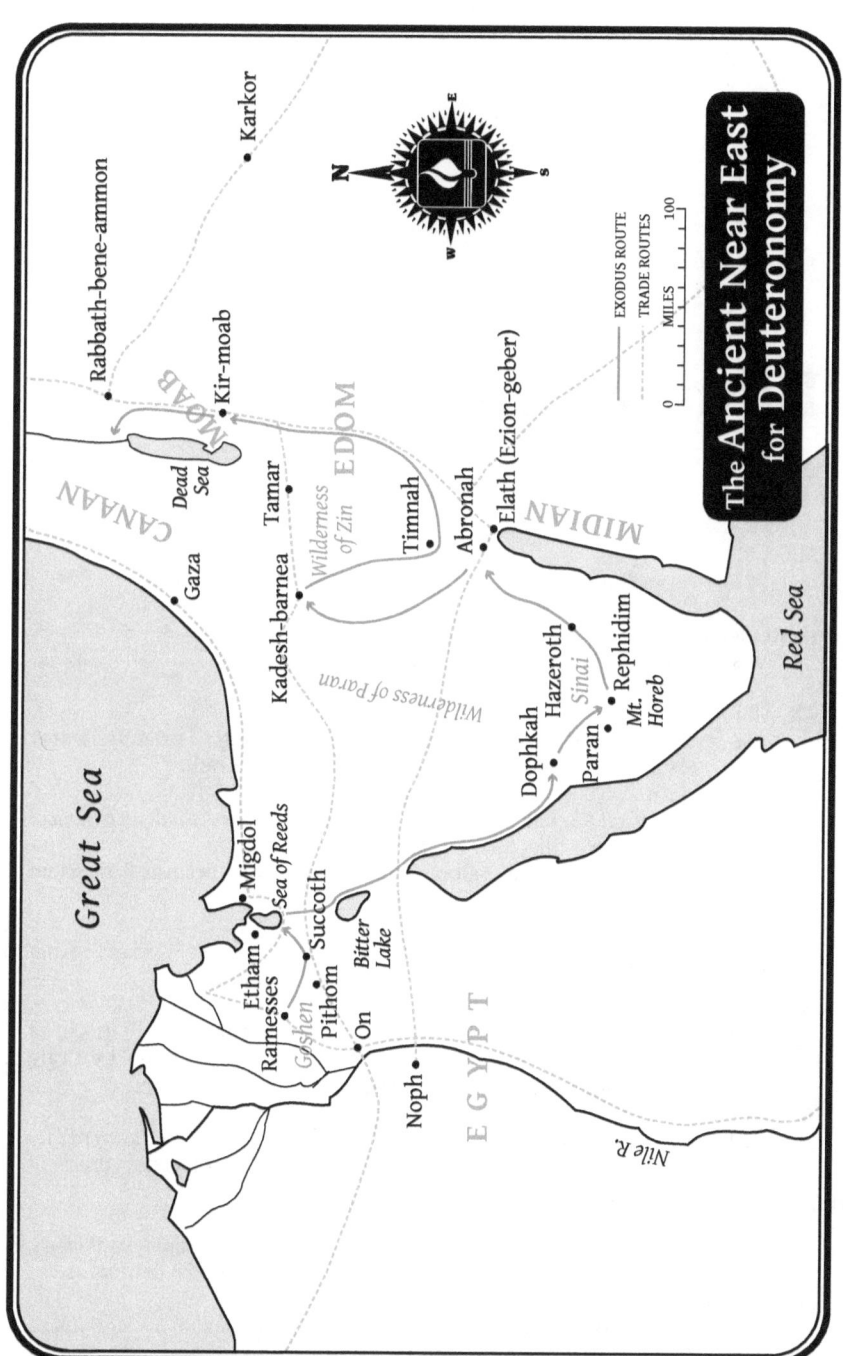

Bibliography

Abba, R.
    1977   "Priests and Levites in Deuteronomy." *Vetus Testamentum* 27:247–67.

Achtemeier, Elizabeth
    1978   *Deuteronomy, Jeremiah*. Proclamation Commentaries. Philadelphia: Fortress.

Alt, Albrecht
    1966   "The Origins of Old Testament Law." In *Essays in Old Testament History and Religion*, 79–132. Oxford: Basil Blackwell.

Bailey, Wilma Ann
    2005   *"You Shall Not Kill" or "You Shall Not Murder"? The Assault on a Biblical Text*. Collegeville, MN: Liturgical.
    2011   "Thoughts on Eric Seibert's *Disturbing Divine Behavior*." *Direction* 40/2:163–67.

Barth, Karl
    1957   "The Strange New World within the Bible." In *The Word of God and the Word of Man*, 28–50. New York: Harper & Row.

Bauckham, Richard
    2004   "Biblical Theology and the Problems of Monotheism." In *Out of Egypt: Biblical Theology and Biblical Interpretation*, edited by Craig Bartholomew et al., 187–232. Grand Rapids: Zondervan.

Benjamin, Don C.
    1983   *Deuteronomy and City Life: A Form Criticism of Texts with the Word City (ʿir) in Deuteronomy 4:41–26:19*. Lanham, MD: University Press of America.

Bennett, Harold
    2002   *Injustice Made Legal: Deuteronomic Law and the Plight of Widows, Strangers and Orphans in Ancient Israel*. Grand Rapids: Eerdmans.

Birch, Bruce C.
    1985   *What Does the Lord Require? The Old Testament Call to Social Witness*. Philadelphia: Westminster.

Bibliography

Birch, Bruce C.
    1991   *Let Justice Roll Down: The Old Testament, Ethics, and Christian Life*. Louisville, KY: Westminster/John Knox.

Birch, Bruce C., and Larry L. Rasmussen
    1976   *Bible and Ethics in the Christian Life*. Minneapolis: Augsburg.

Block, Daniel I.
    2011   *How I Love Your Torah, O Lord! Studies in the Book of Deuteronomy*. Eugene, OR: Cascade.
    2012   *The Gospel according to Moses: Theological and Ethical Reflections on the Book of Deuteronomy*. Eugene, OR: Cascade.

Bockmuehl, Marcus
    2005   "'Keeping It Holy': Old Testament Commandment and New Testament Faith." In *I Am the Lord Your God: Christian Reflections on the Ten Commandments*, edited by Carl E. Braaten and Christopher R. Seitz, 95–124. Grand Rapids: Eermans.

Boecker, Hans J.
    1980   *Law and the Administration of Justice in the Old Testament and Ancient East*. Minneapolis: Augsburg. First published by Neukirchener Verlag in 1976.

Braulik, Georg
    1991   *Die deuteronomischen Gesetze und der Dekalog: Studien zum Aufbau von Deuteronomium 12-26*. Stuttgarter Bibel-Studien 145. Stuttgart: Verlag Katholisches Bibelwerk.
    1994   *The Theology of Deuteronomy: Collected Essays of Georg Braulik, O.S.B.* N. Richland Hills, TX: BIBAL.

Bridges out of Poverty
    2001   Sponsored by Aha! Process Solutions. http://www.ahaprocess.com/solutions/community/. *See also* Payne, Ruby K. et al.

Brueggemann, Walter
    1977   *The Land: Place as Gift, Promise, and Challenge in Biblical Faith*. Philadelphia: Fortress. 2nd ed. Overtures to Biblical Theology 1. Minneapolis: Fortress, 2002.
    1982   *The Creative Word: Canon as a Model for Biblical Education*. Philadelphia: Fortress.
    1997   *Theology of the Old Testament: Testimony, Dispute, Advocacy*. Minneapolis: Fortress.
    1998   "'Exodus' in the Plural." In *Many Voices, One God: Being Faithful in a Pluralistic World*, edited by Walter Brueggemann and George W. Stroup, 15–34. Louisville, KY: Westminster John Knox.
    2001   *Deuteronomy*. Abingdon Old Testament Commentaries. Nashville: Abingdon.

Cahill, Lisa Sowle
    2000   *Family: A Christian Social Perspective*. Minneapolis: Fortress.

Cairns, Ian
    1992   *Deuteronomy: Word and Presence*. International Theological Commentary. Grand Rapids: Eerdmans.

Calvin, John
    1964   *Institutes of the Christian Religion*. Translated by Henry Beveridge. 2 vols. Grand Rapids, MI: Eerdmans.

Carmichael, Calum
    1974   *The Laws of Deuteronomy*. Ithaca, NY: Cornell University Press.
    1985   *Law and Narrative in the Bible: The Evidence of the Deuteronomic Laws and the Decalogue*. Ithaca, NY: Cornell University Press.

Catholic Encyclopedia, The
    1913   "Original Sin." In *The Catholic Encyclopedia*, edited by C. G. Herbermann et al., 11:312-15. New York: Encyclopedia Press. http://www.newadvent.org/cathen/11312a.htm.

Christensen, Duane L.
    2001   *Deuteronomy 1:1-21:9*. Rev. ed. Word Biblical Commentary 6A. Dallas: Word.
    2002   *Deuteronomy 21:10-34:12*. Word Biblical Commentary 6B. Dallas: Word.

Christian Reformed Church
    2010   "What Is the Cycle of Poverty?" www2.crcna.org/pages/sea_cycleofpoverty.cfm.

Circles USA
    1992   [founded] "About Us." http://www.circlesusa.org/index.php?page=about-us. https://www.linkedin.com/company/move-the-mountain-leadership-center.

Clements, Ronald
    1968   *God's Chosen People: A Theological Interpretation of the Book of Deuteronomy*. London: SCM.

Clifford, Richard
    1989   *Deuteronomy with an Excursus on Covenant and Law*. Old Testament Message. Wilmington, DE: Michael Glazier.

Cook, Stephen L.
    2004   *The Social Roots of Biblical Yahwism*. Studies in Biblical Literature. Atlanta: Society of Biblical Literature.
    2011   "Those Stubborn Levites: Overcoming Levitical Disenfranchisement." In *Levites and Priests in Biblical History and Tradition*, edited by Mark Leuchter and Jeremy M. Hutton, 155-70. Atlanta: Society of Biblical Literature.

Copan, Paul
    2011   *Is God a Moral Monster? Making Sense of the Old Testament God*. Grand Rapids: Baker.

Cowles, C. S., Eugene H. Merrill, Daniel L. Gard, and Tremper Longman III
    2003   *Show Them No Mercy: Four Views on God and Canaanite Genocide*. Grand Rapids: Zondervan.

Craigie, Peter
    1976   *The Book of Deuteronomy*. New International Commentary on the Old Testament. Grand Rapids: Eerdmans
    1978   *The Problem of War in the Old Testament*. Grand Rapids: Eerdmans.

Creach, Jerome F. D.
    2013   *Violence in Scripture*. Resources for the Use of Scripture in the Church. Louisville, KY: Westminster John Knox.

Cross, Frank Moore
    1973   *Canaanite Myth and Hebrew Epic: Essays in the History of the Religion of Israel*. Cambridge, MA: Harvard University Press.

Crüsemann, Frank
    1996   *The Torah: Theology and Social History of Old Testament Law*. Minneapolis: Fortress.

Daiches, David
    1975   *Moses: The Man and His Vision*. New York: Praeger.

Daube, David
    1969   *Studies in Biblical Law*. New York: Ktav.

Bibliography

Davies, Eryl W.
   2010   *The Immoral Bible: Approaches to Biblical Ethics*. London: T&T Clark.

Davis, Ellen
   2003   "Teaching the Bible Confessionally in the Church." In *The Art of Reading Scripture*, edited by Ellen F. Davis and Richard B. Hayes, 9–26. Grand Rapids: Eerdmans.

Deist, Ferdinand E.
   1994   "The Dangers of Deuteronomy. A Page from the Reception History of the Book." In *Studies in Deuteronomy: In Honour of C. J. Labuschagne on the Occasion of His 65th birthday*, edited by Florentino García Martínez et al., 13–29. Leiden: Brill.

Douglas, Mary
   1966   *Purity and Danger*. London: Routledge & Kegan Paul.

Driver, S. R
   1902   *A Critical and Exegetical Commentary on Deuteronomy*. 3rd ed. International Critical Commentary. Edinburgh: T&T Clark.

Earl, Douglas S.
   2009   "The Christian Significance of Deuteronomy 7." *Journal of Theological Interpretation* 3/1:41–62.
   2010   *The Joshua Delusion? Rethinking Genocide in the Bible*. Eugene, OR: Cascade.
   2013   "Holy War and ḤRM." In *Holy War in the Bible: Christian Morality and an Old Testament Problem*, edited by Heath A. Thomas, Jeremy Evans, and Paul Copan, 152–75. Downers Grove, IL: IVP Academic.

Elias, Jacob W.
   2004   "A New Testament Model for Ministry and Leadership." In *The Heart of the Matter: Pastoral Ministry in Anabaptist Perspective*, edited by Erick Sawatzky, 85–104. Scottdale, PA: Herald.

Emerton, J. A.
   1962   "Priests and Levites in Deuteronomy: An Examination of Dr. G. E. Wright's Theory." *Vetus Testamentum* 12/2:129–38.

Epp-Tiessen, Daniel
   2012   *Concerning the Prophets: True and False Prophecy in Jeremiah 23:9–29:32*. Eugene, OR: Pickwick Publications.

Fensham, Charles F.
   1961   "Widow, Orphan and the Poor in Ancient Near Eastern Legal and Wisdom Literature." *Journal of Near Eastern Studies* 21:129–39.

Firmage, Edwin B.
   1990   "The Biblical Dietary Laws and the Concept of Holiness." In *Studies in the Pentateuch*, edited by J. A. Emerton, 177–208. Vetus Testamentum Supplements 41. Leiden: Brill.

Fox, Matthew et al.
   2013   *Living the Questions 2.0*. A DVD and Internet-based curriculum. http://livingthequestionsonline.com/tag/matthew-fox.

Gammie, John G.
   1989   *Holiness in Israel*. Overtures to Biblical Theology 1. Minneapolis: Fortress.

García Martínez, Florentino et al., eds.
   1994   *Studies in Deuteronomy in Honour of C. J. Labschagne on the Occasion of His 65th Birthday*. Vetus Testamentum Supplements 53. Leiden: Brill.

Gerbrandt, Gerald E.
  1986   *Kingship according to the Deuteronomistic History.* SBL Dissertation Series 87. Atlanta: Scholars.
Gerstenberger, Erhard S.
  1965   *Wesen und Herkunft des "Apodiktischen Rechts."* Neukirchen-Vluyn: Neukirchener Verlag.
Ginzberg, Louis, Henrietta Szold, Paul Radin, and Boaz Cohen
  1909-38 *The Legends of the Jews.* 7 vols. Philadelphia: Jewish Publication Society.
Graybill, Lyn S.
  2002   *Truth and Reconciliation in South Africa: Miracle or Model?* London: Boulder.
Gutiérrez, Gustavo
  1973   *A Theology of Liberation.* Maryknoll, NY: Orbis. Spanish original, 1971.
Hagner, Donald
  1993-95 *Matthew.* 2 vols. Word Bible Commentaries. Dallas: Word.
Hall, Gary Harlan
  2000   *Deuteronomy.* College Press NIV Commentary. Joplin, MO: College.
Hallie, Philip
  1979   *Lest Innocent Blood Be Shed.* New York: Harper & Row.
Halpern, Baruch
  1981   *The Constitution of the Monarchy in Israel.* Harvard Semitic Monographs. Chico, CA: Scholars.
  1983   *The Emergence of Israel in Canaan.* Chico, CA: Scholars.
  1987   "'Brisker Pipes than Poetry': The Development of Israelite Monotheism." In *Judaic Perspectives on Ancient Israel,* edited by Jacob Neusner, Baruch A. Levine, and Ernest S. Frerichs, 77-115. Philadelphia: Fortress.
Hamilton, Jeffries M.
  1992   *Social Justice and Deuteronomy: The Case of Deuteronomy 15.* Atlanta: Scholars.
Harrelson, Walter J.
  1980   *The Ten Commandments and Human Rights.* Philadelphia: Fortress.
Hauerwas, Stanley, and William H. Willimon
  1989   *Resident Aliens: Life in the Christian Colony.* Nashville: Abingdon.
Herrmann, Siegfried
  1971   "Die konstructive Restauration: Das Deuteronomium als Mitte biblischer Theologie." In *Probleme biblischer Theologie,* edited by Hans W. Wolff, 155-70. Munich: Chr. Kaiser.
Hirsch, Alan
  2006   *The Forgotten Ways.* Grand Rapids: Brazos.
Hoffman, Sue A.
  2005   "The Real History of the Ten Commandments Project of the Fraternal Order of Eagles." Sponsored by Ontario Consultants of Religious Tolerance. http://www.religioustolerance.org/hoffman01.htm.
Houston, Walter
  1993   *Purity and Monotheism: Clean and Unclean Animals in Biblical Law.* Sheffield: Sheffield Academic.

2006   *Contending for Justice: Ideologies and Theologies of Social Justice in the Old Testament.* London: T&T Clark.

Houtman, C.
    1984   "Another Look at Forbidden Mixtures [re: Deut 22]." *Vetus Testamentum* 34:226–28.

Jacobs, Louis
    1995   *The Jewish Religion: A Companion.* Oxford: Oxford University Press.

Janzen, J. Gerald
    1987a   "On the Most Important Word in the Shema (Deuteronomy VI 4-5)." *Vetus Testamentum* 37:280–300.
    1987b   "The Yoke That Gives Rest." *Interpretation* 41:256–68.

Janzen, Waldemar
    1994   *Old Testament Ethics: A Paradigmatic Approach.* Louisville, KY: Westminster John Knox.
    1999   *Work and Rest in Biblical Perspective.* Winnipeg, MB: Conference of Mennonites in Canada.
    2000   *Exodus.* Believers Church Bible Commentary. Waterloo, ON: Herald.
    2011   "Teaching the Old Testament: The 'Problem' of the Old Testament Revisited." *Direction* 40/2:179–97.

Jenkins, Philip
    2011   *Laying Down the Sword: Why We Can't Ignore the Bible's Violent Verses.* New York: Harper Collins.

Jeschke, Marlin
    1988   *Discipling in the Church: Recovering a Ministry of the Gospel.* Scottdale, PA: Herald. Original edition, *Discipling the Brother*, 1972.

Kaiser, Walter C., Jr.
    1983   *Toward Old Testament Ethics.* Grand Rapids: Zondervan.

Kaufman, Stephen A.
    1979   "The Structure of the Deuteronomic Law." *Maarav* 1/2:105–58.

Kline, Meredith G.
    1963   *Treaty of the Great King: The Covenant Structure of Deuteronomy; Studies and Commentary.* Grand Rapids: Eerdmans.

Knight, Douglas A.
    2011   *Law, Power, and Justice in Ancient Israel.* Louisville: Westminster John Knox.

Koop, Karl
    2004   *Anabaptist-Mennonite Confessions of Faith: The Development of a Tradition.* Kitchener, ON: Pandora.

Kushner, Harold S.
    1981   *When Bad Things Happen to Good People.* New York: Schocken.

Lancaster County Information Center
    2013   "Amish Grace and Forgiveness." http://lancasterpa.com/amish-forgiveness/.

Lapsley, Jacqueline E.
    2003   "Feeling Our Way: Love for God in Deuteronomy." *Catholic Biblical Quarterly* 65:350–69.

Leddy, Mary Jo
    1990   *Reweaving Religious Life: Beyond the Liberal Model.* New London, CT: Twenty-Third Publications.

Lemche, Niels Peter
    1988   *Ancient Israel: A New History of Israelite Society.* Sheffield: JSOT Press.

Levinson, Bernard
    1996   "Recovering the Lost Original Meaning wlʾ tksh ʿlyw (Deuteronomy 13:9 [13:8 ET])." *Journal of Biblical Literature* 115/4:601–20.
    1997   *Deuteronomy and the Hermeneutics of Legal Innovation*. New York: Oxford University Press.

Lind, Millard C.
    1980   *Yahweh Is a Warrior: The Theology of Warfare in Ancient Israel*. Scottdale, PA: Herald.

Lindquist, Maria
    2011   "King Og's Iron Bed." *Catholic Biblical Quarterly* 73/3:477–92.

Lohfink, Norbert
    1963   *Das Hauptgebot: Eine Untersuchung literarischer Einleitungsfragen zu Dtn 5–11*. Analecta biblica 20. Rome: Pontifical Biblical Institute.
    1965   *Höre, Israel! Auslegung von Texten aus dem Buch Deuteronomium*. Düsseldorf: Patmos.
    1968   "The Great Commandment." In *The Christian Meaning of the Old Testament*, 87–102. Milwaukee: Bruce.
    1971   "Die Sicherung der Wirksamkeit des Gotteswortes durch das Prinzip der Schriftlichkeit der Tora und durch das Prinzip der Gewaltenteilung nach den Ämtergesetzen des Buches Deuteronomium (Dt 16,18–18:22)." In *Testimonium veritati*, edited by Hans Wolter, 143–55. Frankfurt: Knecht.
    1982   *Great Themes from the Old Testament*. Edinburgh: T&T Clark.
    1990   "Bundesschluss." In *Studien zum Deuteronomium und zur deuteronomistischen Literatur*, 1:48–51. Stuttgart: Katholisches Bibelwerk.
    1991   *Die Väter Israels im Deuteronomium: Mit einer Stellungnahme von Thomas Römer*. Orbis biblicus et orientalis 111. Göttingen: Vandenhoeck & Ruprecht.

Luther, Martin
    1960   *Lectures on Deuteronomy*. Edited by Jaroslav Pelikan. Vol. 9 of *Luther's Works*. Saint Louis: Concordia.

Malchow, Bruce V.
    1996   *Social Justice in the Hebrew Bible*. Collegeville, MN: Liturgical.

Manley, G. T.
    1957   *The Book of the Law: Studies in the Date of Deuteronomy*. Grand Rapids: Eerdmans.

Marsden, George
    1994   *The Soul of the American University: From Protestant Establishment to Established Nonbelief*. New York: Oxford University Press.

Martens, Elmer
    2002   "How Is the Christian to Construe Old Testament Law." *Bulletin for Biblical Research* 12/2:199–216.

Marty, Martin
    1970   *Righteous Empire: The Protestant Experience in America*. New York: Dial.

Matties, Gordon H.
    2012   *Joshua*. Believers Church Bible Commentary. Harrisonburg, VA: Herald.

Mayes, A. D. H.
    1979   *Deuteronomy*. New Century Bible Commentary. Grand Rapids: Eerdmans.

Bibliography

McBride, S. Dean
   1973   "The Yoke of the Kingdom: An Exposition of Deuteronomy 6:4-5." *Interpretation* 27:273–306.
   1987   "Polity of the Covenant People: The Book of Deuteronomy." *Interpretation* 41:229–44.

McCarthy, Dennis J.
   1972   *Old Testament Covenant: A Survey of Current Opinions*. Richmond, VA: John Knox.

McConville, J. G.
   1984   *Law and Theology in Deuteronomy*. Sheffield: JSOT Press.
   2002   *Deuteronomy*. Apollos Old Testament Commentary. Downers Grove, IL: InterVarsity.

McConville, J. G., and J. Gary Millar
   1994   *Time and Place in Deuteronomy*. Journal for the Study of the Old Testament: Supplement Series 179. Sheffield: Sheffield Academic.

McLaren, Brian
   2001   *A New Kind of Christian: A Tale of Two Friends on a Spiritual Journey*. San Francisco: Jossey-Bass.
   2010   *A New Kind of Christianity: Ten Questions That Are Transforming the Faith*. New York: HarperOne.

MEDA: Mennonite Economic Development Associates
   1953–   "Our Vision, Mission and Values." http://www.meda.org/about/who-we-are/our-vision-mission-and-values.

Mendenhall, George E.
   1954   "Law and Covenant in Israel and the Ancient Near East." *Biblical Archaeologist* 17/2:49–76. http://home.earthlink.net/~cadman777/Law_Cov_Mendenhall_TITLE.htm.
   1955   *Law and Covenant in Israel and the Ancient Near East*. Pittsburgh: Biblical Colloquium (Presbyterian Board of Colportage of Western Pennsylvania).
   1973   *The Tenth Generation: The Origins of the Biblical Tradition*. Baltimore: Johns Hopkins University Press.

Menno Simons
   1956   *The Complete Writings of Menno Simons, c. 1496–1561*. Translated by Leonard Verduin. Edited by J. C. Wenger. Scottdale, PA: Herald.

Merendino, Rosario Pius
   1968   *Das deuteronomische Gesetz: Eine literarkritische, gattungs- und überlieferungsgeschichtliche Untersuchung zu Dt 12–26*. Bonner biblische Beiträge 31. Bonn: Peter Hanstein.

Merrill, Eugene
   1994   *Deuteronomy*. New American Commentary. Nashville: Broadman & Holman.

Meyers, Carol
   1997   "The Family in Early Israel." In *Families in Ancient Israel*, edited by John J. Collins, Joseph Blenkinsopp, Leo Perdue, and Carol Meyers, 1–47. Louisville: Westminster John Knox.

Milgrom, Jacob
   1963   "The Biblical Diet Laws as an Ethical System: Food and Faith." *Interpretation* 17:288–301
   1976   "Profane Slaughter and a Formulaic Key to the Composition of Deuteronomy." *Hebrew Union College Annual* 47:1–17.

    1990   "Ethics and Ritual: The Foundations of Biblical Dietary Laws." In *Religion and Law: Biblical-Judaic and Islamic Perspectives*, edited by E. B. Firmage, J. W. Welch, and B. Weiss, 159–91. Winona Lake, IN: Eisenbrauns.

Millar, J. Gary
    1998   *Now Choose Life: Theology and Ethics in Deuteronomy*. New Studies in Biblical Theology. Grand Rapids: Eerdmans.

Miller Marlin
    1990   "Priesthood of All Believers," *The Mennonite Encyclopedia*. 5:721–22. Scottdale, PA: Herald.

Miller, Patrick D.
    1987   "The Way of Torah." *Princeton Theological Seminary Bulletin* 8:17–27.
    1990   *Deuteronomy*. Interpretation: A Bible Commentary for Teaching and Preaching. Louisville: John Knox.
    2000   *The Religion of Ancient Israel*. Library of Ancient Israel. Louisville, KY: Westminster John Knox.
    2009   *The Ten Commandments*. Interpretation: Resources for the Use of Scripture in the Church. Louisville: Westminster John Knox.

Mitchell, Christopher Wright
    1987   *The Meaning of BRK "to bless" in the Old Testament*. SBL Dissertation Series 95. Atlanta: Scholars.

Moberly, R. W. L.
    1999   "Toward an Interpretation of the Shema." In *Theological Exegesis: Essays in Honor of Brevard S. Childs*, edited by Christopher Seitz and Kathryn Greene-McCreight, 124–44. Grand Rapids: Eerdmans.
    2003   "Living Dangerously: Genesis 22 and the Quest for Good Biblical Interpretation." In *The Art of Reading Scripture*, edited by Ellen F. Davis and Richard B. Hays, 181–97. Grand Rapids: Eerdmans.
    2006   *Prophecy and Discernment*. Cambridge Studies in Christian Doctrine. Cambridge: Cambridge University Press.

Moore, Megan Bishop, and Brad E. Kelle
    2011   *Biblical History and Israel's Past: The Changing Study of the Bible and History*. Grand Rapids: Eerdmans.

Moran, William L.
    1963   "The Ancient Near Eastern Background of the Love of God in Deuteronomy." *Catholic Biblical Quarterly* 25:77–87.
    1969   "Deuteronomy." In *A New Catholic Commentary on Holy Scripture*, edited by R. C. Fuller et al. London: Thomas Nelson.

Murray, Stuart
    2004   *Church after Christendom*. Milton Keynes, UK: Paternoster.

Nelson, Richard
    1991   "The Role of the Priesthood in the Deuteronomistic History." In *Congress Volume, Leuven, 1989*, edited by John A. Emerton, 132–47. Leiden: Brill.
    1993   *Raising Up a Faithful Priest: Community and Priesthood in Biblical Theology*. Louisville: Westminster/John Knox.
    2002   *Deuteronomy*. Old Testament Library. Louisville: Westminster John Knox.

Nichols, Aidan, O.P.
    1999   *Christendom Awake: On Reenergizing the Church in Culture*. Grand Rapids: Eerdmans.

Bibliography

Nicholson, E. W.
- 1973   *Exodus and Sinai in History and Tradition.* Richmond, VA: John Knox.
- 1976   *Deuteronomy and Tradition.* Philadelphia: Fortress.
- 1986   "Covenant in a Century of Study since Wellhausen." In *Crises and Perspectives.* Oudtestamentische Studiën 24. Leiden: Brill.

Niditch, Susan
- 1993   *War in the Hebrew Bible: A Study in the Ethics of Violence.* New York: Oxford University Press.

Niebuhr, H. Richard
- 1951   *Christ and Culture.* New York: Harper & Row.

Nielsen, E.
- 1968   *The Ten Commandments in New Perspective.* London: SCM.

Noth, Martin
- 1930   *Das System der zwölf Stämme Israels.* Beiträge zur Wissenschaft vom Alten und Neuen Testament 52 (= 4/1). Stuttgart: Kohlhammer.
- 1981   *The Deuteronomistic History.* Sheffield: JSOT Press. Originally published in German in 1943.

Olson, Dennis T.
- 1994   *Deuteronomy and the Death of Moses: A Theological Reading.* Overtures to Biblical Theology. Minneapolis: Fortress.

Ontario, Ministry of Children and Youth Services
- 2009   "Breaking the Cycle of Poverty." http://news.ontario.ca/mcys/en/2009/12/breaking-the-cycle-of-poverty.html.

Patrick, Dale
- 1985   *Old Testament Law.* Atlanta: John Knox.

Payne, David F.
- 1985   *Deuteronomy.* Daily Study Bible Series. Philadelphia: Westminster.

Payne, Ruby K., Phil DeVol, and Terie Dreussi-Smith
- 2001   *Bridges out of Poverty: Strategies for Professionals and Communities.* Highlands, TX: Aha! Process, Inc. Rev. eds., 2006, 2009.

Perlitt, Lothar
- 1969   *Bundestheologie im Altentestament.* Wissenschaftliche Monographien zum Alten und Neuen Testament 36. Neukirchen-Vluyn: Neukirchener Verlag.
- 1980   "'Ein einzig Volk von Brüdern': Zur deuteronomischen Herkunft der biblischen Bezeichnung 'Bruder.'" In *Kirche: Festschrift für Günther Bornkamm zum 75. Geburtstag,* edited by Dieter Lührmann and George Strecker, 27–52. Tübingen: J. C. B. Mohr.

Philips, Dirk
- 1992   *The Writings of Dirk Philips, 1504–1568.* Translated and edited by Cornelius J. Dyck, William E. Keeney, and Alvin J. Beachy. Scottdale, PA: Herald.

Polzin, Robert
- 1980   *Deuteronomy, Joshua, Judges.* Part 1 of *Moses and the Deuteronomist: A Literary Study of the Deuteronomic History.* New York: Seabury.

Pressler, Carolyn
- 1993   *The View of Women in the Deuteronomic Family Laws.* Beihefte zur Zeitschrift für die alttestamentliche Wissenschaft 216. Berlin: Walter de Gruyter.

Rad, Gerhard von
- 1929   *Das Gottesvolk im Deuteronomium.* Beiträge zur Wissenschaft vom Alten und Neuen Testament 3. Stuttgart: Kohlhammer.

1933   "There Remains Still a Rest for the People of God: An Investigation of a Biblical Conception" (originally published in 1933). In *The Problem of the Hexateuch and Other Essays*, 94–102. New York: McGraw-Hill.
1953   *Studies in Deuteronomy*. Studies in Biblical Theology 9. London: SCM.
1966   *Deuteronomy*. Old Testament Library. Philadelphia: Westminster.
1991   *Holy War in Ancient Israel*. Marva Dawn's translation of the 1958 German edition. Introduced by Ben Ollenburger. Grand Rapids: Eerdmans.
1993   *The Promise of the Land. The Inheritance of the Land of Canaan by the Israelites*. Berkley: University of California Press.

Schlabach, Gerald W.
1999   "Deuteronomic or Constantinian: What Is the Most Basic Problem for Christian Ethics?" In *The Wisdom of the Cross: Essays in Honor of John Howard Yoder*, edited by Stanley Hauerwas, Chris K. Huebner, Harry Huebner, and Mark Thiessen Nation, 449–71. Grand Rapids: Eerdmans.

Schwally, Friedrich Zacharias
1901   *Der heilige Krieg im alten Israel*. Vol. 1 of *Semitische Kriegsaltertümer*. Leipzig: Dieterich.

Seibert, Eric A.
2009   *Disturbing Divine Behavior: Troubling Old Testament Images of God*. Minneapolis: Fortress.
2012   *The Violence of Scripture: Overcoming the Old Testament's Troubling Legacy*. Minneapolis: Fortress.

Sloyan, Gerard
1988   *John*. Interpretation: A Bible Commentary for Teaching and Preaching. Atlanta: John Knox.

Stamm, J. J., with Andrew, M. E.
1967   *The Ten Commandments in Recent Research*. London: SCM.

Stassen, Glen H., D. M. Yeager, and John Howard Yoder
1996   *Authentic Transformation: A New Vision of Christ and Culture*. Nashville: Abingdon.

Steuernagel, Carl
1896   *Die Enstehung des deuteronomischen Gesetzes kritisch und biblisch-theologisch untersucht*. Halle: J. Krause.

Steymans, Hans Ulrich
1995   *Deuteronomium 28 und die adê zur Thronfolgeregelung Asarhaddons: Segen un Fluch im alten Orient und in Israel*. Göttingen: Vandenhoeck & Ruprecht.

Swezey, Charles M.
1980   "Exodus 20:16—'Thou shalt not bear false witness against thy neighbor.'" *Interpretation* 34:405–10.

Thomas, Heath A., Jeremy Evans, and Paul Copan, eds.
2013   *Holy War in the Bible: Christian Morality and an Old Testament Problem*. Downers Grove, IL: IVP Academic.

Thompson, Thomas L.
1987   *The Literary Formation of Genesis and Exodus 1–23*. Vol. 1 of *The Origin Tradition of Ancient Israel*. Sheffield: JSOT Press.

Bibliography

Tickle, Phyllis
    2008   *The Great Emergence: How Christianity Is Changing and Why.* Grand Rapids: Baker.
    2012   *Emergence Christianity: What It Is, Where It Is Going, and Why It Matters.* Grand Rapids: Baker.

Tigay, Jeffrey H.
    1996   *Deuteronomy.* The JPS Torah Commentary. Philadelphia: Jewish Publication Society.

Toews, John E.
    2004   *Romans.* Believers Church Bible Commentary. Scottdale, PA: Herald.

Trible, Phyllis
    1984   *Texts of Terror: Literary-Feminist Readings of Biblical Narratives.* Overtures to Biblical Theology. Philadelphia: Fortress.

Truth and Reconciliation Commission of Canada
    2008–   http://www.trc.ca/.

Weinfeld, Moshe
    1972   *Deuteronomy and the Deuteronomistic School.* Oxford: Oxford University Press.
    1990   "The Uniqueness of the Decalogue and Its Place in Jewish Tradition." In *The Ten Commandments in History and Tradition,* edited by Ben-Zion Segal, 1–44. Jerusalem: Magnes.
    1991   *Deuteronomy 1-11.* Anchor Bible. New York: Doubleday.
    1993   *The Promise of the Land: The Inheritance of the Land of Canaan by the Israelites.* Berkeley: University of California Press.
    1995   *Social Justice in Ancient Israel and in the Ancient Near East.* Minneapolis: Fortress.

Welch, A. C.
    1924   *The Code of Deuteronomy.* London: J. Clarke.

Wellhausen, Julius
    1957   *Prolegomena to the History of Ancient Israel.* Cleveland: Meridian. Originally published in German in 1878.

Wenham, Gordon J., and Heth, William E.
    1997   *Jesus and Divorce.* Updated ed. Carlisle, UK: Paternoster.

Westermann, Claus
    1962   *A Thousand Years and a Day: Our Time in the Old Testament.* Philadelphia: Fortress.
    1978   *Blessing in the Bible and the Life of the Church.* Overtures to Biblical Theology. Philadelphia: Fortress.

Wette, W. M. L. de
    1805   *Dissertatio critica qua Deuteronomium a prioribus Pentateuchi libris diversum alius cuiusdam recentioris auctoris opus esse monstratur.* Jena.

White, R. Fowler
    2007   "Does God Speak Today Apart from the Bible?" In *Reformed Perspective Magazine* 9/15. http://www.the-highway.com/God_Speak.html.

Whitelam, K. W.
    1989   "Israelite Kingship: The Royal Ideology and Its Opponents." In *The World of Ancient Israel: Sociological, Anthropological, and Political Perspectives,* edited by R. E. Clements, 119–39. Cambridge: Cambridge University Press.

Wiesel, Elie
    2013   *Living the Questions 2.0*. A quotation by Matthew Fox in a DVD and Internet-based curriculum.

Wilson, Ian
    1995   *Out of the Midst of the Fire*. Society of Biblical Literature Dissertation Series 151. Atlanta: Scholars.

Woods, Edward J.
    2011   *Deuteronomy*. Tyndale Old Testament Commentaries. Downers Grove, IL: InterVarsity.

Wright, Christopher J. H.
    1983   *An Eye for An Eye: The Place of Old Testament Ethics Today*. Downers Grove, IL: InterVarsity.
    1990   *God's People in God's Land: Family, Land, and Property in the Old Testament*. Grand Rapids: Eerdmans.
    1995   *Walking in the Ways of the Lord: The Ethical Authority of the Old Testament*. Downers Grove, IL: InterVarsity.
    1996   *Deuteronomy*. New International Bible Commentary. Peabody, MA: Hendrickson.
    2004   *Old Testament Ethics for the People of God*. Downers Grove, IL: IVP Academic.

Wright, David
    1987   "Deuteronomy 21:1-9 as a Rite of Elimination." *Catholic Biblical Quarterly* 49/3:387–403.

Wright, Melanie J.
    2003   *Moses in America: The Cultural Use of Biblical Narrative*. Oxford: Oxford University Press.

Yoder, John H.
    1980   "Exodus 20:13—'Thou shalt not kill.'" *Interpretation* 34:394–99.

Yoder Neufeld, Thomas R.
    2011   *Killing Enmity: Violence and the New Testament*. Grand Rapids: Baker Academic.

Selected Resources

Block, Daniel. 2012. *The Gospel according to Moses*. Eugene, OR: Cascade. A volume of theological and ethical essays on Deuteronomy by an important contemporary evangelical scholar.

Brenneman, James E. 2004. *On Jordan's Stormy Banks: Lessons from the Book of Deuteronomy*. Scottdale, PA: Herald. An excellent, brief window into the theological emphases of Deuteronomy.

Brueggemann, Walter. 2001. *Deuteronomy*. Abingdon Old Testament Commentaries. Nashville: Abingdon. A provocative commentary on Deuteronomy, connecting scholarly analysis with contemporary relevance.

———. 2002. *The Land: Place as Gift, Promise, and Challenge in Biblical Faith*. 2nd ed. Overtures to Biblical Theology. Minneapolis: Fortress. An examination of the biblical theme of land, with significant attention to the book of Deuteronomy. Deuteronomy, he suggests, presents land as gift, temptation, task, and threat.

Cook, Stephen L. 2004. *The Social Roots of Biblical Yahwism*. Studies in Biblical Literature. Atlanta: Scholars. A scholarly study of biblical Yahwism in Israel.

Creach, Jerome F. D. 2013. *Violence in Scripture*. Resources for the Use of Scripture in the Church. Louisville, KY: Westminster John Knox. A study of violence in Scripture, including some attention to Deuteronomy.

Houston, Walter J. 2006. *Contending for Justice: Ideologies and Theologies of Social Justice in the Old Testament*. London: T&T Clark. An exploration of social justice in the Old Testament, oriented toward uncovering resources for shaping a Christian theological approach to social and global injustice.

McConville, J. G. 1984. *Law and Theology in Deuteronomy*. JSOT Supplement Series. Sheffield: JSOT Press. A detailed study exploring how Deuteronomy's distinctive theology is reflected in its presentation of its laws.

———. 2002. *Deuteronomy*. Apollos Old Testament Commentary. Downers Grove, IL: InterVarsity. A significant evangelical commentary on Deuteronomy.

Miller, Patrick D. 1990. *Deuteronomy*. Interpretation: A Bible Commentary for Teaching and Preaching. Louisville, KY: John Knox. A solid commentary on Deuteronomy, oriented to preaching and teaching.

———. 2000. *The Religion of Ancient Israel*. Library of Ancient Israel. Louisville, KY: Westminster John Knox. An excellent guide to the religion of Israel as practiced during Old Testament times.

———. 2009. *The Ten Commandments*. Interpretation: Resources for the Use of Scripture in the Church. Louisville, KY: Westminster John Knox. A recent, expansive (432 pages) study of the Decalogue that considers the meaning of each commandment, and then follows the trajectory of the commandment through both testaments.

Nelson, Richard D. 2002. *Deuteronomy*. Old Testament Library. Louisville, KY: Westminster John Knox. A scholarly and theologically middle-of-the-road commentary on Deuteronomy.

Nicholson, Ernest W. 1986. *God and People: Covenant and Theology in the Old Testament*. Oxford: Clarendon. A historical examination of covenant in Israel and the Old Testament.

Olson, Dennis T. 1994. *Deuteronomy and the Death of Moses*. Overtures to Biblical Theology. Minneapolis: Fortress. An insightful monograph proposing that the death of Moses provides a key for the structure and message of Deuteronomy.

Tigay, Jeffrey H. 1996. *Deuteronomy*. The JPS Torah Commentary. Philadelphia: Jewish Publication Society. An excellent commentary by a Jewish scholar that regularly introduces how Deuteronomy was read in the Jewish tradition.

Index of Ancient Sources

OLD TESTAMENT

Pentateuch
........................43, 89, 179

Genesis
........................20, 41, 43
1 ....257, 265, 394
1–11 ....75, 181, 205
1:11-12......................395
1:16 113
1:20-25......................112
1:21 395
1:22 179
1:25 395
1:26-27......................112
1:28 179
1:29 270
2:7 386
2:24 ....213, 421
3 325
3:6 149
4 ....72, 145
4:23 368
4:23-24......................361
6:1-4...........................395
6:3 491
6:18 548
9:3-4..................242, 271
9:4 262
9:9 548
9:41 262
10:14 560
12 ....45, 49, 75, 89
12–50 179
12:2 ....47, 116–17, 201
12:2-3 457
12:3 ..75, 105, 178, 182–83
12:6-7.........................242
12:6-8.........................565
12:7 ....45, 522
12:8 242
12:10-20..............66, 216
13 99
13:6 425
13:10 216
13:14-15......................99
13:18 242
14:6 562
14:20 275
15:5 ....26, 117, 459
15:9-10.......................470
15:16 197
15:17 470
15:18 ....49, 548
17 212
17:1 161
17:2 548
17:5 137
17:7 470
17:15 137
18 205
18:14 324
18:16-33......................98
19:30-38....................408
19:37 563
19:37-38....................563
19:38 558
20 146
20:3-7........................249
22:1-19......................242
22:12 219
22:17 ....26, 51, 459
22:18 75–76
23:1-16.........................45
24:7 45
25:7-11.........................45
25:30 560
26:3 ....45, 498
26:4 ....26, 51, 459
26:11 250
26:23-25....................242
26:24 498
27:1-40......................513
28:13-15......................45
28:22 275
29:16-18....................391
31:3 498
31:33-35....................112
32:3 561
34:3 213
34:25 361
35:1 45
35:22 515
36 560
36:1 561

36:1-8 72	7–14 83	16:4-36 190
36:7 425	7:3-4 83	17:1-7 169
36:9 561	7:11 352	17:3 169
36:20 562	7:13 .... 83, 162	17:1-6 190
37:5-11 .... 249, 517	7:13-14 83	17:1-7 .... 202, 509, 516
38 425	7:16 162	17:8-16 428
38:9 425	7:22 83	18:13-27 .... 50, 317
38:24 392	8:1 162	18:15 325
39 .... 146, 148	8:15 83	18:17-18 50
39:7-9 146	8:19 83	18:21 .... 52, 56
40:19 393	8:20 162	18:25 52
41–47 216	8:32 83	19–20 562
42:6 517	9:1 162	19–40 223
44:5 352	9:7 83	19:1 308
44:15 352	9:12 83	19:4 504
46:3 116	9:13 162	19:4-6 171
46:27 213	9:17 333	19:5 .... 155, 548
47:30 494	9:34-35 83	19:6 .... 27, 133, 177, 348
48 391	10:1 83	19:11 140
49 .... 28, 513, 515, 519	10:3 162	19:12 250
49:3-4 .... 454, 515	10:20 83	20 .... 31, 242
49:8-12 516	10:27 83	20:1-17 105
49:10 516	11:10 83	20:2 132
49:13-14 517	12–13 303–5	20:1–17 130–31
49:19 517	12:5 353	20:2-17 128
49:22-26 516–17	12:6 306	20:11 139
	12:35-36 292	20:13-15 557
Exodus	13:2 301	20:18-21 128
.... 20, 43, 236, 494, 525	13:4 306	20:23–23:19 .... 223, 557
1–15 132	13:10-16 301	20:24 .... 228, 237, 364
1:5 213	13:21 409	20:24-25 452
1:7 .... 51, 117	13:21-22 .... 62, 494	21:1-11 .... 415, 294–95
1:8 45	14 32	21:2-11 291
1:9-10 438	14–15 .... 214, 312, 567	21:6 293
2:23 290	14:4 83	21:12 557
2:23-25 420	14:5-9 374	21:13-14 362
2:24 45	14:6 330	21:16 .... 147, 418
2:24-25 439	14:8 83	21:23-25 367
3 .... 45, 238	14:9 330	21:24 427
3:1 562	14:13-14 .... 330, 358, 374	21:31 421
3:7-12 498	14:30-31 540	21:33-34 398
3:13-15 160	14:31 .... 170, 214, 330	22:7-8 323
3:13-16 137	15:11 539	22:11 323
3:14 137	15:21 567	22:16-17 399
4:11 507	15:22-26 60	22:18 351–52
4:22 503	15:24 66	22:19 456
4:22-23 259–60	16:1-3 60	22:21-24 422
6:2-3 .... 137, 161	16:2 66	22:25 413
6:7 ...... 170, 214, 470, 540	16:3 190–91	22:29-30 301–2
6:12 212	16:12 132	23 .... 303, 307
6:30 212	16:1-36 189	23:1-3 148

Index of Ancient Sources

23:4-5 395	3 343	20:26 263
23:6-8 318	3:1 353	20:27 351
23:10-11 .... 284, 294, 414	7:11 257	21:7 .... 430, 433
23:12-17 304	7:28-34 344	21:14 .... 430, 433
23:16 308–9	8:8 516	22:13 430
23:19 .... 262, 301	10:10 554	23:3-44 304
23:20-33 176	10:11 342	23:4-44 303
23:24 136	11 .... 257–58, 267–68	23:15-21 308
24 .... 336, 449	11:44 132	23:22 423
24:7 150	11:44-45 263	23:27-28 507
24:8 548	11:45 265	23:43 309–10
24:15-18 139	13–14 .... 257, 419	24:19-20 367
26–31 257	15:16-18 410	24:20 427
28:6-14 397	16 566	25–27 297
28:30 .... 324, 516	16:20-22 388	25:2-7 414
29:16-18 344	17–26 223	25:8-55 294–95
29:26-28 344	17:10-13 242	25:9 507
30:20 344	18:2 132	25:10 527
31:18 128	18:4 132	25:35 413
32–34 200	18:6-20 407	25:39-46 .... 291, 293
32 .... 136, 195, 254	18:6-23 456	27:21 568
32:1-5 201	18:7-8 405	27:26-27 301
32:1-35 .... 189, 541	18:16 425	27:30-33 .... 275, 279, 281
32:4 200	18:20 146	
32:9 198	18:23 396	**Numbers**
32:11-14 98	18:30 132	.... 20, 70, 276, 280, 300,
32:13 51	19 .... 128, 152	494, 525, 554
32:14 207	19:2 .... 152, 263	1–10 223
32:15 132	19:3-4 132	1:50 344
32:20 202	19:9-10 423	3:31 344
32:25-29 .... 204, 516	19:10 132	6:22-26 519
33:3 198	19:12 .... 138, 213	10:10 132
33:5 198	19:13 420	10:35 203
33:7-11 494	19:14 455	11:1 66
33:11 524	19:15 318	11:1-3 .... 202, 205
33:20 150	19:18 .. 143, 152, 368, 445	11:4-34 202
34 .... 128, 203	19:19 395–97	11:11-15 50
34:6-7 137	19:20 250	11:11-17 50
34:18-24 303–4	19:28 260	12 561
34:22 308–9	19:31 351	12:1 527
34:26 262	19:34 143	12:1-15 419
34:28 .... 128, 151	19:35-37 428	12:6 249
40:3 494	20:6 351	12:8 524
40:38 62	20:9 392	12:9-16 205
	20:10 146	12:14 426
Leviticus	20:10-20 .... 407, 456	13–14 .... 57, 202
..... 20, 223, 264, 276, 280,	20:11 405	13:1-2 59
300, 494, 525, 554	20:21 425	13:27-33 60
1:1 494	20:22-26 267	13:30 62
1:3 353	20:23-24 197	14:1-25 205
1:4 507	20:25-26 265	14:1-38 487

14:2 66	33:30 562	6:25 78
14:13-25 98	33:30-33 204	7 ....183, 251, 421
14:14 62	33:31-33 561	7:2-3 59
14:18 137	33:37-38 ....204, 562	8:1 59
14:42-44 203	34 81	8:2 378
15:37-41 398	34:5 48	8:29 393
15:39 398	35 ....343, 365–66	8:30 243
15:41 132	35:6 362	8:30-35..183, 449, 451, 453
16 214–15	35:9-34 362–63	8:31-33 523
16:12-14 215	35:22-28 145	9 .... 176, 183
18:9-24 344	35:25 364	9:3-15 377
18:15 267	35:28 364	9:10 88
18:20 343	35:30 145	9:21 471
18:21 ....276, 278	35:33 386	10:25 59
18:21-32 ......275, 279, 281		10:26-27 393
18:26 ....276, 278	**Deuteronomy–Kings**	12:2 88
20 72	.... 7, 18, 20, 66, 88, 242,	12:4 88
20–24 70	244, 315, 336–38,	12:5 88
20:2-13 516	494, 545, 547, 568,	13:10 88
20:7-12 509	589	13:12 88
20:12 63		13:16-19 243
20:22–21:4 562	**Deuteronomy**	13:18 562
21 561	(not indexed)	13:21 88
21:4-9 205		13:27 88
21:21-32 86	**Joshua**	13:30-31 88
21:32-35 86	.................20–21, 183, 499	14–19 492
22–24 408	1–5 94	14:6-15 63
22:5 564	1:1 523	17:1 563
24:20 428	1:4 49	19:35 560
25:1-5 100	1:6-9 496	19:40-48 517
25:3-5 560	1:7 333	20:7 362
25:4 393	1:12-16 96	20:8 116
27:1-11 ....55, 425	1:13-15 523	21 343
27:2 556	1:18 496	21:2-4 243
27:7 556	2:1-7 59	21:44 100
27:12-14 ....63, 509	2:10 88	22 .... 95, 244
27:18-23 523	2:11 60	22:5 213
27:19 97	3–4 81	22:19 94
27:21 97	3–6 203	23:7 136
27:23 97	3:6 203	23:8 213
28–29 303–4	3:8 203	23:16 136
28:26 308	4 312	24 524
28:26-31 308	4:7 203	24:15 .....28, 211, 247, 484
30:9 430	4:18 203	24:20 495
32 94	5:1 60	24:23 495
32:16 96	6–7 378	24:29 523
32:16-27 96	6:2 567	
32:23 460	6:17 175	**Judges**
32:33 88	6:21 ....175, 378	........................20, 380, 510
32:38 232	6:22-25 183	1:27-36 380
32:41 562	6:24 243	1:28 377

1:33-35 377	**1 Samuel**	3:10 522
2:8 523	 20–21	3:26-30 361
3:6 182	1–4 237	4:12 393
3:12 336	1:9 .... 243, 310	5:10 337
4:1 336	1:13 310	6 237
4:14 567	1:21 310	6:6-8 554
5:4-5 514	2:12-17 344	7:1 .... 96, 100
5:14 .... 95, 563	2:27 513	7:16 .... 338, 522
5:14-15 517	3:3 243	10:1 328
5:17-21 95	3:20 522	11 149
5:20 567	4–6 567	11–12 338
6:1 .... 336, 380	4–7 510	11:1 374
6:10 132	4:1-9 203	12 .... 147, 332
6:14-16 498	4:18 491	12:28 238
6:24-32 380	5:3 567	15:1-6 324
7:1-24 381	7 568	15:30 426
7:2 567	7:3 495	16:13 328
7:2-7 376	7:10 566–67	18:18 426
7:9-23 89	7:16 561	21:5-9 393
7:15 567	7:17 243	
7:22 567	8 338	**1 Kings**
8:18-21 361	8–10 354	 20
10:4 562	8–12 ... 319, 327, 330, 337	2:2-3 519
10:6 336	8:3 319	2:11 491
10:16 495	8:7-9 337	2:26 347
11 72	8:10-18 331	3:2 232
12:3 163	8:11-18 .... 35, 280	3:3-14 .... 338, 523
13:1 336	8:12 52	3:4 243
13:4 268	8:15-17 275	3:5-9 249
13:6-8 513	8:20 .... 330, 374	3:9 54
13:7 268	9:1-10:16 337	3:12 .... 54, 162
13:14 268	9:6-10 513	3:16-22 324
17–21 421	9:9 325	3:28 556
17:6 .... 235, 391	10:1 337	4:1-9 203
18 560	10:17-24 328	4:19 88
18:1-6 59	11 568	5:13-18 338
19–21 368	11–12 146	8:9 203
19:1 337	12 28	8:11-18 274
20:1 522	14:35 243	8:15-17 275–76
21:19 310	16–26 328	8:27 211
21:19-21 310	16:1-13 337	8:27-53 107
21:25 .... 235, 337, 391	16:13 337	8:56 100
	17:18 52	9:20-21 377
Ruth	22:7 52	10:9 .... 55, 164
.... 76, 142, 547	25:3 137	11 .... 182, 337
1–2 421	28:3-25 .... 351, 353	11:1-8 .... 331, 338
1:16 431–32	31:10 393	11:1-13 176
2 414		11:2 213
4 .... 147, 556	**2 Samuel**	11:3-4 495
4:1-12 318	 20	11:26-40 328
4:7-8 426	2:6-8 507	11:33 338

12:22 513	17:18 567	34:2 333
12:25-31 243	17:35 136	
12:26-29 200	18:3-4 338	**Ezra**
12:28 .... 136, 200	18:4 244	.... 90, 254
12:31 232	18:5 524	1:6-11 292
13:1-31 513	18:6 213	6:19-22 311
14:24 .... 396, 411	18:17–19:37 381	9:2 182
15:12 411	19:35 514	10 77
15:13 202	21:3 320	10:2-5 182
15:15-26 244	21:6 352–53	10:10-11 182
16:30-34 544	21:16 66	10:18-19 182
16:31 .... 176, 182	21:24 550	
16:31-33 331	22–23 .. 333, 338, 544, 547	**Nehemiah**
16:33 320	22:2 333	.... 90, 254
17:1 217	22:8 549	8 499
17:18 513	22:8-10 499	9:6-7 211
18 .... 134, 217, 539	22:11 549	9:9-25 88
18:17-40 243	22:11-20 549	9:18 200
18:21 .. 135, 164, 218, 247	22:14-20 499	9:22 88
18:28 261	22:16-17 473	10:30 182
18:39 164	23:1-16 549	10:35-38 280
20:28 513	23:2 111	12:44 280
21 148–49	23:2-3 549	13 77
21:3 365	23:4 345	13:3 431
21:7 328	23:7 396	13:4-5 280
21:9-13 366	23:8-9 345	13:23-27 182
21:10 254	23:8-10 345	
22 358	23:12 202	**Job**
22:19 .... 504, 514, 539	23:21 .... 244, 311, 549	.... 181, 250
22:25 505	23:21-22 .... 306, 549	1:1 460
23 346	23:25 524	4:11 438
	23:26 336	8 460
2 Kings	23:26-27 .... 66, 245, 253	8:16 460
.... 20, 90	24:3 338	24 128
1:9 .... 52, 513		24:2 365
1:11 52	**1 Chronicles**	29:13 438
1:13 52	.... 90, 244	42:1-6 211–12
4:1 282	2:21-22 562	42:3 324
6:17 514	22:8 381	
8 237	24:27 291	**Psalms**
8:14-61 239		.... 19, 105
12:3 232	**2 Chronicles**	6:4 163
14:6 421	.... 90, 244	8 113
16:3 544	2:11 164	14:1 134
16:10-18 544	9:8 164	15 128
17 .... 244, 320	14:3 232	17 510
17:7-9 253	19:4-11 54	18 523
17:7-18 .... 66, 336	30 244	18:23 353
17:8 197	30:1-27 306	18:50 338
17:9-11 233	30:6 311	19 136
17:17 352–53	33:17 232	19:1 113

Index of Ancient Sources

22 510	135:8-12 88	11:6 381
22:12 559	135:11 88	15:2 260
22:25 414	135:13-14 88	20:2 426
26:6 388	136 88	22:12 260
27:12 148	136:2 212	26:20 505
29:1 539	136:19-20 88	31:1 381
35 510	148:4 211	37:6-7 358
35:1-4 510		40:3 101
36 523	**Proverbs**	40:4-5 528
37:20 459	3:11-12 192	40:18-20 114
50 127	3:35 459	41:4 508
50:2 514	5:19 417	41:10 498
54 510	7:10-20 412	42 55
56:12 414	8:12-16 52	42:6 .... 182, 457
58:5 352	8:15-16 54–55	42:19 523
61:8 414	10:16 459	43:3 132
63:11 213	16:11 428	43:4 164
66:13-15 414	20:10 428	43:6 260
72 .... 212, 422	20:23 428	43:10 508
72:1 336	22:13 144	43:10-13 108
72:1-2 .... 54, 334	22:28 .... 365, 557	43:11 507–8
72:2 317	23:10 365	43:13 508
73:3-4 460	23:20-21 391	44:2 504
73:13 388	28:7 391	44:6 .... 108, 508
77:20 525	29:4 55	44:18 114
78:56 169	30:6 105	45:6-7 .... 108, 508
78:59 98	30:18 324	45:11 260
78:62 98		45:12-13 211
81 127	**Ecclesiastes**	45:20-21 114
81:9-10 134	3:14 105	45:20-23 108
84:2 228	7:20 66	45:22 508
89:3-4 338		45:23 213
89:14 317	**Isaiah**	46:5-7 114
90:1 525	 19	47:9 352
99:4 55	1:2-3 502	47:12 352
99:6 525	1:10 337	48:1 213
103:7 525	1:15-16 388	48:12 508
105:26 525	2:1-4 183	49 76
106:16 525	2:1-5 117	49:6 .... 76–77, 178,
106:19-20 200	2:2-3 117	182–83, 457
106:23 525	2:4–5 381	50:1 430
106:24-27 66–67	2:6 352	50:1-3 429–30
106:32 525	2:7 330	50:6 426
116:14 414	3:3 52	53 63
116:18 414	3:24 260	53:12 206
119:1-3 210	5:8 365	56:3 405–6
119:27 210	6 354	56:3-7 432
119:59 210	6:1-13 249	56:3-8 484
119:105 210	6:9 482	58:6 368
131:1 324	10:1-13 510	61 55
135–136 172	11:2 523	61:1-2 368

63:10 567
63:11-12 525

Jeremiah
1:1 27
1:1-13 354
1:8 498
2:4-13 502
2:8 337
2:12-13 502
3:1 430
3:1-4:4 429
3:6-14 146
3:8 430
4:2 213
4:4 212
5:2 213
6:10 212
7:9 .... 138, 152
7:11-15 237
7:12 237
7:23 218
7:26 198
10:11-16 244
13:27 146
15:1 525
16:6 260
17:23 198
19:5 232
21:7 505
23:5 55
26:2 105
27:5-6 211
27:9 .... 351–52, 357
27:14 357
28 357–58
29:5-6 375
29:6 417
29:12-14 118
31:3 164
31:9 260
31:29-30 421
32:18 137
32:39-40 151
34:9 291
34:17 295
34:18 470
41:5 260
47:4 .... 164, 560
47:5 260
49:7-22 72

51 148

Lamentations
.... 118, 544

Ezekiel
.... 472, 525
1:1 249
6:3 232
7:18 260
8:1-18 244
14:21 505
16 146
16:21 260
18 421
18:5-9 128
20:5 132
22:26 554
23 146
26:7-14 358
29:17-20 358
36:28 470
44:22 430
44:23 554

Daniel
1:8 267–68
9:11-13 525

Hosea
.... 218, 253, 540, 545
1–3 .... 146, 164
1:9 503
1:10 259
2:14 429
2:14-15 192
2:14-23 146
2:19 429
3:1 164
4:1-6 502
4:2 .... 148, 152
4:6 192
4:10-15 494
4:14 411
5:3 248
5:10 365
8:5-6 200
9:3 267
9:15 164
10:5 200
10:8 232

10:15 243
11:1 .... 164, 191–92, 259
11:3-4 191–92
13:2 200
14:4 164

Joel
2:28 359

Amos
1–2 75
1:1 27
1:3-2:3 510
2:7 422
4:1 .... 422, 559
4:4 .... 275, 280
5 269
5:7 316
5:10 316
5:11 422
5:15 318
5:21 311
5:21-24 .... 269, 280
5:24 .... 318, 528
6:4 192
7:1-9 249
7:2 .... 116, 205
7:3 206
7:5 .... 116, 205
7:14-15 354
8:4-5 428
8:4-6 422
8:5 141
8:10 260
9:7 .... 75, 560

Obadiah
8-21 72

Jonah
.... 76
1:2 358
1:9 291
3:4 .... 358, 432
3:10 358

Micah
.... 540
1:3 232
1:16 260
2:1-2 .... 149, 365

Index of Ancient Sources

2:2 .... 192, 369
3:1 337
3:7 351
4:1-5 117
4:3 381
4:5 381
5:10 330
5:12 352
6:1-5 502
6:4 525
6:8 209
6:10-11 428
6:12 148

Nahum
1:2-3 137

Habakkuk
2:6-20 510

Zechariah
9:6 407

Malachi
1:2 164
1:6-8 320
2:16 430
3:8-12 280
3:10 281
4:4 525

NEW TESTAMENT

Matthew
1:1-2:4 108
1:26 136
1:28 141
1:31 141
2:3 139
2:15 141
3:2 45
3:3 101
4:1-4 189
4:1-11 .... 19, 192
4:4 525
4:10 134
5-7 27
5:5 90
5:9 260
5:12 461
5:18 541
5:21-22 145
5:21-37 .... 149, 153
5:27-28 146
5:29 .... 369, 370
5:29-30 254–55
5:30 553
5:31 416
5:31-32 .... 430, 432
5:32 146
5:33-37 148
5:38-42 369
5:39 382
5:44 382
5:48 353
6:5 498
6:10 101
6:12 483
6:24 ... 135, 218, 253, 484,
540
7:12 541
7:13 218
7:13-14 .... 254, 484
7:15 359
7:15-20 359
7:17 .... 218, 469
8:10 431
8:21 498
9:10-13 77
10:5 431
10:34 426
10:35-37 257
11:28-30 101
12:1-14 77
12:2-5 526
12:42 337
13:10-17 482
13:16 482
13:24-43 484
13:29-30 256
14:65 426
15:24 .... 269, 431
16:16-17 338–39
16:21-23 339
18 255–56
18:8 553
18:15-20 16
19:3-12 430
19:7 416
19:9 146
19:14 64
19:18-19 152
19:19 382
19:21 153
20:8 420
21:9 339
22:34-40 .... 19, 158, 165
22:36-40 445
22:37-38 134
22:39-40 143
22:40 .... 165, 541
23:23 .... 280, 319
23:23-28 269
24:11 359
24:24 359
25:14-30 500
25:29 469
25:31-45 219
25:31-46 ..... 254, 461, 484,
541
25:33 218
26:53 382
26:60-11 366
26:61 245
27:24 388
28:5 438
28:16-20 519
28:18-19 77
28:19 .... 183, 431
28:19-20 498

Mark
1:15 45
2:23 414
2:27 222
2:27-28 140
4:21-29 482
6:53 560
7:9-13 143
7:18 482
7:18-19 .... 258, 269
7:24-30 269
8:33 482
9:43 553
10:1-12 525
10:2-12 430
10:4 416
10:11-12 146
10:19 152–53
10:21 153
12:28 158
12:28-34 .... 19, 164
12:29-30 134

12:32 165
14 306

Luke
1:8 347
1:23 347
1:38 523
1:39-40 347
2:22 525
4:1-13 192
4:5-8 382
4:8 134
4:14-30 76
4:16-21 55
4:16-30 358
4:18 .... 55, 140, 147, 368
4:25-30 183
4:28 76
5:17 541
7:37-50 541
10:25 368–69
10:25-28 19
10:25-37 .... 183, 369
10:29-37 445
10:30-37 394
11:47 66
12:2 461
12:6-7 216
13:1-5 460
13:16 140
14:26-27 143
15:11-32 118
16:16 541
16:18 .... 146, 430
17:3 256
18:9-14 280
18:16 64
18:20 152-53
18:22 .... 153, 369
19:1-9 256
19:10 205
19:18 164
23:34 206
24:25 481
24:27 .... 55, 172

John
1:14 205
1:16 205
1:17 525
1:21 .... 354, 359

1:25 .... 354, 359
4:21-23 245
4:24 246
6:14 .... 354, 359
7:40 .... 354, 359
8:1-11 .... 254–55, 541
8:11 146
8:12 307
9:2 459
9:3 460
10:34 541
12:34 541
13–16 519
13–17 28
13:21-30 256
13:34-35 281
14:6 .... 210, 253
14:12 219
15:25 541
17:15-16 183

Acts
1:7-11 519
1:8 ... 76–77, 183, 431, 498
2:15-21 359
2:43-47 369
2:44-45 280
3:17-26 337
3:22 .... 354, 359
4:32-37 369
4:34 .... 280, 369
5:1-11 .... 66, 280–81
5:30 393
6:1 .... 66, 369
6:1-6 .... 280–81, 297
6:11-13 525
7 .... 172, 526
7:35-41 66
7:60 206
8:26-40 269
8:31 .... 210, 482
10:10-16 270
10:34-36 431
10:39 393
11:1-18 270
11:27 359
13:1 359
13:16 210
13:26 210
15 .... 258, 270, 272
15:20 270

15:28 434
15:29 242
15:32 359
17:7 337
17:23 166
18:10 498

Romans
3:19 541
3:23 .... 66, 499
3:23-24 205
3:29-30a 166
4:1-5 219
5:12 206
7:7-13 149
7:13-25 499
8:14-21 260
9:8 260
9:26 260
10:18-21 505
12:3-8 .... 349, 500
12:18 382
12:19 510
13:9 152
15:25-28 280
15:26 369

1 Corinthians
3:11 295–96
5:1-13 256
5:6-13 254
5:7 311
6:19-20 261
7:10-11 430–31
7:12-14 183
7:15 431
8:1-13 183
8:6 134
9:8-12 424
10:1-5 66
10:25-30 272
12:1-31 500
12:4-31 349
14:21 541
12:28-29 359
14:29 434
16:1-3 280

2 Corinthians
5:11 210
6:14-18 183

Index of Ancient Sources

7:1 210
9:7 280

Galatians
2:16 219
3:13 393
3:26 260
3:28 431

Ephesians
2:8-9 168
2:11-22 43
3:5 359
4:25 148
4:28 280
4:11-12 359
4:11-13 349
6:2 .... 142, 152
6:10-17 553

Philippians
2 173
2:10-11 499
2:12 .... 210, 254
2:15 260

Colossians
1:19-20 382

1 Thessalonians
5:21 434

1 Timothy
5:17-18 424
5:19 366

2 Timothy
4:1 337
4:8 337

Philemon
.... 410

Hebrews
2:17 .... 337, 347
3:1 .... 337, 347
3:1-6 526
4 101
7–10 347
11:31 183

James
1:22 219
2:24 219
2:25 183
4:1-2 149–50

1 Peter
2:9 .... 183, 272, 348
2:16 133
2:24 393

2 Peter
2:1 359

1 John
3:10 382
4:1 359
4:19 210

Revelation
1:6 348
5:1-14 510
5:5–6 382
5:10 348
5:12 382
12:11 382
13:8 382
15:3 337
18:2 510
22:18-19 105

APOCRYPHA

2 Maccabees
6 268
6:18-31 268–69
7:1-41 268

Sirach
3:10-13 142
3:16 142

Susanna
50-62 367

JUDAISM
Akiba 546
b. Shabbat 104a 469
b. Shevuʿot 39a 475
tradition 89

CHRISTIANITY
Constantine 67
Augustine 67
Origen 553

OTHER SOURCES
ANE law codes 421
ANE writings 421
Assyrian treaties 548
Buddhist tradition 133
Code of Hammurabi 410, 556–57
"Enuma Elish" 34
Greek tradition 133
Hittite treaties 548
"Instruction of Amenemopet" 557
Laws of Ur-Nammu 556
Mesha Stele 568
Neo-Assyrian tradition 87
Thutmose III 53
Treaties 410

The Author

Gerald E. Gerbrandt was born in Mexico, where his parents were doing mission work among the Tarahumara people, and grew up in Altona, Manitoba. During a summer pastoral internship in Reedley, California, Gerbrandt experienced a call to ministry and higher education that led him to Canadian Mennonite Bible College/Canadian Mennonite University, where he taught Bible and served as academic dean (1982–97) and as president (1997–2012). He also served one year as interim president of Associated Mennonite Biblical Seminary (1995–96). In addition to various congregational and denominational involvements, he continues to teach part time at CMU.

Gerbrandt completed his doctoral work in Bible at Union Theological Seminary in Virginia in 1980. He received an MDiv from Mennonite Biblical Seminary in 1973. He did his undergraduate work at Canadian Mennonite Bible College and Bethel College. He has also served as a fellow at Tyndale House in Cambridge, England, at the Institute for Ecumenical and Cultural Research in Collegeville, and as a visiting scholar at Acadia Divinity College in Wolfville, Nova Scotia.

Gerbrandt's doctoral dissertation was published by Scholars Press as *Kingship according to the Deuteronomistic History*. In addition to a variety of articles and book reviews, he has also written a Sunday school curriculum for high schoolers called *Clues for Gracious Living (Deuteronomy)* and a Bible study on Micah, *Better than Rivers of Oil*.

Gerbrandt and his wife, Esther, are active members of Bethel Mennonite Church, Winnipeg, Manitoba. They have three married children and four grandchildren.

Deuteronomy

"Gerbrandt does a masterful job of explaining Deuteronomy, both in terms of its original meaning and how that ancient word to Israel can still be heard as a living Word of God to the church. This volume will serve pastors, seminarians, and laity as a valuable companion when studying Deuteronomy." —*Phillip C. Camp, associate professor of Bible, Hazelip School of Theology, Lipscomb University*

"Gerbrandt tells us that he has lived with Deuteronomy for over a decade, and it was worth it. He has read long and deeply in the book, thought widely about it, read systematically in the scholarship about it, and now written a thoughtful, sure-footed, illuminating, and judicious commentary." —*John Goldingay, professor of Old Testament, Fuller Theological Seminary*

"Engaging the diverse wealth of Deuteronomy, Gerbrandt invites readers to consider how ancient covenant law code comes alive today as preaching that shapes community identity while addressing such tough issues as war, injustice, and exclusivism." —*Lynn Jost, professor of Old Testament and preaching, Fresno Pacific Biblical Seminary*

"Gerbrandt is a first-class guide into and through this sermonic book of Deuteronomy. He is thorough in exegesis, sensitive to literary niceties, irenic in style, and often forceful in applying the text to the here and now. He deftly handles the sticky problem of divinely ordered wars and violence. The style is that of a teacher with clear exposition, helpful charts, and language often in a conversational mode." —*Elmer A. Martens, president emeritus and professor emeritus of Old Testament, Fresno Pacific Biblical Seminary*

"Gerbrandt reveals the theological treasures of Deuteronomy but also faces honestly the challenging issues of violence, a warrior God, and exclusion of the 'other' that have been part of Deuteronomy's legacy over centuries of interpretation. A reliable and informed commentary." —*Dennis Olson, professor of Old Testament theology, Princeton Theological Seminary*

www.ingramcontent.com/pod-product-compliance
Lightning Source LLC
Chambersburg PA
CBHW021413300426
44114CB00010B/475